Published by The Disinformation Company Ltd.
163 Third Avenue, Suite 108
New York, NY 10003
Tel.: +1.212.529.2330
Fax: +1.212.387.8152
www.disinfo.com

Editor: Russ Kick
Publisher: Gary Baddeley

Designer: Leen Al-Bassam

First Printing May 2002

Library of Congress Card Number: 2001099925

ISBN 0-9713942-0-2

Printed in USA

Distributed by Consortium Book Sales and Distribution
1045 Westgate Drive, Suite 90
St Paul, MN 55114
Toll Free: +1.800.283.3572
Local: +1.651.221.9035
Fax: +1.651.221.0124
www.cbsd.com

EVERYTHING YOU KNOW IS WRONG

THE DISINFORMATION GUIDE TO SECRETS AND LIES

EDITED BY RUSS KICK

To my grandmother, Aurora Kick, who nurtured my love of language, helping to turn it into the skills of writing and editing.

— Russ Kick

ACKNOWLEDGMENTS

Thanks of a personal nature are due to Anne, Ruthanne, Jennifer, and (as always) my parents, who give me support in many ways. The same goes for that unholy trinity of Billy, Darrell, and Terry, who let me vent and make me laugh.

I'd like to thank Richard Metzger and Gary Baddeley for letting me edit the book line and taking a *laissez-faire* approach. Also, many thanks go to Leen Al-Bassam, who turned a bunch of computer files into the beautiful object you now hold in your hands. And thanks also head out to the many other people involved in the creation and distribution of this book, including everyone at Disinformation, Consortium, Green Galactic, the printers, the retailers, and elsewhere. It takes a lot of people to make a book!

Last but definitely not least, I express my gratitude toward all the contributors, without whom there would be no *Everything You Know Is Wrong*. None of you will be able to retire early because of appearing in these pages, so I know you contributed because you believe so strongly in what you're doing. And you believed in me, which I deeply appreciate.

— R.K.

Major thanks are due to everyone at The Disinformation Company, especially Alex Burns, Nimrod Erez, Lee Hoffman and Nick Hodulik, everyone at Consortium—Julie Schaper, Peter Heege, Jim Nichols, Michael Cashin, Katherine Bright-Holmes and the complete team, Brian Pang, Adam Parfrey, Mike Backes, Brian Butler, Peter Giblin, A.J. Peralta, Steven Daly, Howard Bloom, Douglas Rushkoff, Grant Morrison, Joe Coleman, Genesis P-Orridge, Sean Fernald, Adam Peters, Robert Sterling, Preston Peet, Nick Mamatas, Alexandra Bruce, Matt Webster, Jose Caballer, Lisa Shimamura, Stevan Keane, Susan Mainzer and the Green Galactic crew, Ben Silverman, Howard Owens, Mark Koops and the gang at William Morris Agency NY, Gail Silverman and the team at R.R. Donnelley, Brandon Geist, Diego Hernandez and our friends at Bookspan, Naomi Nelson, Sumayah Jamal, and all those who have helped us along the way—especially the reviewers, buyers, and everyone working in bookstores, who have shown us so much love and support—and YOU for buying this book!

— Gary Baddeley and Richard Metzger

ABOUT DISINFORMATION®

Disinformation® is more than it seems. Literally. From its beginnings almost a decade ago as an idea for an alternative *Sixty Minutes*-type TV news show to the book that you are now holding, Richard Metzger and Gary Baddeley have taken a dictionary term and given it secondary meaning to a wide audience of hipsters, thinkers, anti-establishmentarians and the merely curious.

The Disinformation® Website went live on September 13, 1996, to immediate applause from the very same news media that it was criticizing as being under the influence of both government and big business. The honeymoon was short—some three weeks after launch the CEO of the large US media company funding the site discovered it and immediately ordered it closed down. Needless to say, Metzger and a few loyal members of his team managed to keep the site going and today it is the largest and most popular alternative news and underground culture destination on the Web, having won just about every award that's ever been dreamed up.

Disinformation® is also a TV series, initially broadcast on the UK's Channel 4 and since licensed to various broadcasters around the world, a music imprint in the US in a joint venture with Sony Music's Loud Records, and a huge counterculture conference, the first of which was held shortly after the turn of the Millennium in 2000. By the time this book rests in your hands, Disinformation® will probably have manifested itself in other media, too. Based in New York City, The Disinformation Company Ltd. is a vibrant media company that Baddeley and Metzger continue to helm. They continue to look for the strangest, freakiest, and most disturbing news and phenomena in order to balance the homogenized, sanitized, and policed fare that is found in the traditional media.

Coming in 2002 - Disinformation TV on DVD. Original, uncut version of the TV series that was too hot for USA Networks (banned) and the UK's Channel 4 Television (heavily censored). Richard Metzger hosts the most mind-warping, bizarre, and subversive TV show ever. Also contains highlights from the legendary Disinfo.Con 2000 conference.

Features Robert Anton Wilson, Douglas Rushkoff, Grant Morrison, Genesis P-Orridge, Joe Coleman, Paul Laffoley, Kembra Pfahler, Peter Russell, Duncan Laurie, Norbert Kox, Frank Bruno, Mark Pesce, Adam Parfrey, The Montauk Project, Extreme Pornography, Satanism and much, much more.

You Are Being Lied To: The Disinformation Guide to Media Distortion, Historical Whitewashes and Cultural Myths
edited by Russ Kick   ISBN 0966410076

Editor Russ Kick, a Village Voice columnist, has collected essays from writers across the political spectrum offering an interpretation of recent events that is often counter to that of the mainstream media. Taken as a whole, this anthology represents an instruction manual in how to "read" the news. – Publishers Weekly

You Are Being Lied To acts as a battering ram against the distortions, myths, and outright lies that have been shoved down our throats by the government, the media, corporations, organized religion, the scientific establishment, and others who want to keep the truth from us.

Includes contributions from Noam Chomsky, Howard Zinn, Howard Bloom, Michael Parenti, Norman Solomon, Douglas Rushkoff, James Ridgeway, Jim Marrs, Judith Rich Harris, Tristan Taormino, Jim Hogshire, Riane Eisler, Peter Russell, and dozens of others. Over 60 articles in all!

CONTENTS

PREFACE: EVERYTHING YOU KNOW IS WRONG

RICHARD METZGER

In his introduction to the first book in this series of Disinformation Guides, editor Russ Kick mulled over how nervy it felt to title a book *You Are Being Lied To*. Obviously, a book with a name like that had better deliver. Judging from the response to *YABLT* (as we call it around the office) from the reading public, the book did indeed come up with the goods. For our second Disinformation Guide, again helmed by Russ, we decided to up the ante considerably and title the damned thing *Everything You Know is Wrong*.[1]

Everything?

We're nothing if not provocative, here at Disinformation! Nonetheless, daily interaction with the readers of our Website <www.disinfo.com> has helped us tune into a widespread angst that something **is** very wrong with the barrage of information and advertising that we are bombarded with, not just daily, but during virtually every moment of our waking days. (I suspect that the assault is so hegemonic that "they" may well aim to colonize our dreams, as well.)

While the credibility of government sponsored "news" and information has long been considered suspect by both right (Waco, Ruby Ridge, etc.) and left (Chomsky, Herman, F.A.I.R., etc.), we've recently sensed a burgeoning perception by middle-of-the-road, mainstream Americans that "disinformation" is everywhere—medicine, science, finance, commerce, media—often sponsored by very complex webs of power and influence. Bestselling books like *No Logo*, *Silent Takeover*, *Fast Food Nation*, and *Trust Us! We're Experts* are creating widespread interest in how corporations don't play fair by manipulating the information found in magazines, newspapers, and television.

Indeed, a growing sensibility amongst the up and coming Gen Y is the sneaking suspicion that we are all being sold a bill of goods that we never asked for in the first place. If we weren't all left wondering if there isn't *something* that they aren't telling us, then a film like *The Matrix* wouldn't have struck such a notable chord with the public.

_CONSPIRACY?

I am often asked if I think that there is a "conspiracy" to shut alternative journalists or thinkers out of the mainstream, but I don't think so. I'd argue that just the opposite is going on.

This book is just one small example of that trend. Many of you reading this right now will have purchased (or stolen!) this tome from one of the large book chains like Barnes and Noble, Borders, Virgin, or perhaps online from Amazon. In order for this book now to be nestled in your hands, it had to go through the very same channels that many other—and decidedly more mainstream—titles had to go through to reach the shelves of the store where you picked it up.

I can assure you that there was no attempt to "shut out" this book by anyone along the way. Quite the contrary, we had lots of help! (Not least, incidentally and by way of thanks, the many bookstore employees who took it upon themselves to promote the book.) Moreover, the popularity of the book's predecessor, *You Are Being Lied To*, has not gone unnoticed by the "mainstream" media; we've had numerous calls from Hollywood and from major publishers wishing to acquire our "secret" formula.

_FUCK CONSENSUS REALITY!

Which brings me to my next point: There used to be no mass-market outlets for this kind of information to get out there and have any real penetration and influence in the culture. Too few TV channels—anyone remember when Fox was called the "fourth network" and cable consisted of just ten channels?—and too few national magazines that published investigative journalism, etc. "News" in America has always been crowded out by "entertainment." If it's a truism in any media-saturated culture that "whoever controls what you see, controls what you think," it was relatively easy for the powers that be to corral public opinion into a collective "groupthink" until fairly recently in human history.

The "desktop publishing revolution" that ushered in "zine" culture during the mid-1980s is when the cracks first started to occur, but consensus reality finally died—just keeled over and died—somewhere around 1996, by the time a critical mass of early adopters was connected to the Internet. All of a sudden there were places—*hundreds of them*—where you could find high quality "alt" reporting on a variety of topics—foreign news, investigative journalism, health, and yes, even conspiracy theories, UFOs, fundamentalist Christian doomsday prophecy, and niche sexual perversions. Whatever it was that you were looking for, you could now find it, sitting in the comfort of your own home and with very, very little effort on your part. What's more, it was probably *free!*

And still the pace of mass illumination goes on and even accelerates, aided further by broadband Internet connections and all of the new digital cable channels getting pumped into our homes. With this many new channels *needing all of that airtime filled in order to have something to hang their commercials on*, there has never been a time when it has been **easier** to obtain airtime for views or stories that were heretofore outside of the mainstream media's concerns. And these programs attract large enough audiences for it to be financially viable, even attractive, for media conglomerates to devote airtime to such things. Examples of this range from Christopher Hitchens being given network talking head status to Douglas Rushkoff's *Merchants of Cool* documentary to the two years' worth of TV shows that The Disinformation Company made for British network Channel 4.

Now would be (and could be and should be) a terrific time for what's left of the left, progressives, and everyone willing to fly their freak flag high to stop complaining about the media and **become the media** (and actually, it's not just the left who fly freak flags, so yes, the right and anyone else wanting to make themselves heard can do and *are* doing so). A very good example of this increased media access is Free Speech TV <www.freespeech.org>. Originally a Web destination for alternative video that could *not* find a media outlet, FSTV now reaches over nine million US homes via direct broadcast satellite on EchoStar's DISH Network. It also airs part-time on a network of 35 community access cable stations across the United States, including some of the largest markets, such as New York and Los Angeles.

The public wants and *needs* contrarian thinkers—and the megamedia corporations are happy to give it to them. They figured out a long time ago that the public wants to see what it hasn't seen before. A new counterculture is infiltrating mainstream culture aided and abetted by the very hand it intends to bite.

This is a very interesting time to be alive, kids. It really is.

_THE TRUTH IS OUT THERE, BUT *WHERE?*

The answer: It's in a lot of different places.

But if the media is open to alternative expressions and Gen Y consumers of media are hungry, educated, postmodern hipsters, then what's the problem? Doesn't this mean that the counterculture actually *won?* Well for one thing, there's *so much* out there now that just

sorting the wheat from the chaff is a full-time occupation (mine!). Secondly, every reporter, producer, editor, broadcaster has his or her own bias that will affect the presentation and organization of news and information. It may seem as though there is no discernible difference between ABC, CBS, NBC, etc., but open yourself to a wider range of voices (merely adding the comically self-described "unbiased" Fox News to your media diet will do), and you'll start to realize that the end product has been massaged such that the same basic information has taken on different hues and nuances. Thus, it's important to be able to sense biases (and lies!) even if they are coming from a source that is ostensibly in your camp (whether that be left, right, red, yellow, or purple).

If consensus reality is dead, then this leaves a much trickier info-jungle to traverse. If you should "trust no one," then whom *can* you trust?

When we launched our Website in 1996, our mission was to reveal not just two sides to every story, but many, many more. In this book, as with all Disinformation Guides, we try to bring you views that may help you realize the complicated goal of decoding the information barrage. Our agenda is—of course—biased in *its* own way, but what we have tried to do is offer a selection of alternative—and sometimes conflicting—views, thoughts, and "facts" intended to help you learn how to question the motives and agendas of the purveyors of news and information. Is Everything You Know Wrong? We're confident that after reading this book you'll begin to wonder whenever you read a newspaper, watch television, see a billboard, surf the Web, listen to the radio, or otherwise bathe in the multimedia megaplexed info-flood.

"And you can believe me, because I never lie, and I'm always right."[2]

Richard Metzger
Los Angeles, January 2002

Endnotes

1. This is a classic line from the Firesign Theatre, a comedy troupe started in the 1960s and still going strong <www.firesigntheatre.com>. **2.** This is another Firesign Theatre line.

INTRODUCTION

Like so many other things, *Everything You Know Is Wrong* was affected by the terrorist attacks on September 11, 2001. The clouds of toxic dust and smoke over Manhattan hadn't even dissipated when the attitude toward dissent suddenly changed. Questioning the authorities was equated with handing over a nuclear bomb to Osama bin Laden. (A very convenient atmosphere for those in power, no?) President Bush intoned, "You are either with us or against us in the fight on terror."[1] Attorney General Ashcroft declared that people who questioned his destructive police-state tactics "only aid terrorists."[2] Local news stories relayed incidents of citizens being harassed by the FBI and the police for besmirching the motives behind Operation Enduring Freedom or asking for stamps not bearing the US flag at the corner post office.[3] The snitch-line set up by the feds had received almost half a million tips by the beginning of 2002.[4]

Railing against the status quo is never a risk-free proposition, but post-911 it felt almost suicidal. Would people even *want* to read investigative and contrarian material, I wondered? Nonetheless, I plowed ahead, as did colleagues. As I write these words at the start of 2002, the situation has calmed down a tad. The hysteria has lessened, although the US is still saddled with the most unfortunate byproducts of that hyperdefensiveness, the USA Patriot Act and similar legislation and executive orders, which set up secret military tribunals, destroy the attorney-client privilege, expand the country's DNA database, allow the CIA to engage in domestic operations, and let the FBI infiltrate and destroy groups it considers subversive, among many other nightmarish powers. (In the original draft of the Patriot Act, Ashcroft called for the suspension of *habeas corpus*, allowing the authorities to arrest people without cause and detain them indefinitely without charges or a trial.[5] Thankfully, this provision didn't make it into the final version.)

But I believe that dissent is never more needed than when conformity is at an all-time high. When the fewest questions are being asked is when they're most needed. In his preface to this book, Disinformation's cofounder and Creative Director Richard Metzger says that the mainstream is hungry for alternative viewpoints. While I agree with that statement in general, it still doesn't mean that all opinions and facts are welcome. For every industry exposé like *Fast Food Nation* that is put out by a corporate publisher, five are published by independent presses, and an untold number are never published at all. Another example: The media are still loath to report on the huge number of violent crimes that are prevented or cut short by citizens with guns. And look what happened when Fox News broadcast a series breaking the story of an Israeli spy ring in the US: nothing. The other media outlets stayed away in droves. So, while mainstream media are more open than they've ever been to alternative voices, the truth still faces a hard, uphill battle.

_SOME NOTES TO READERS

Nonfiction collections typically are either academic or alternative, leftist or rightist, atheistic or religious, or otherwise unified in some similar way. *Everything You Know Is Wrong* rejects this intellectual balkanization, and, in doing so, brings together contributors who ordinarily wouldn't be appearing together in the same book. Some of the contributors were aware of only a handful of others who would be appearing, while most of them didn't know who else would be sharing pages with them. All this means is that you shouldn't make the assumption—which is quite easy to unknowingly make with most nonfiction anthologies—that every contributor agrees with or thinks favorably of every other contributor. Hey, maybe they all just love each other to death. I don't know one way or the other, but the point is that I alone am responsible for the group that appears here. So, if you just can't believe that Person A would *ever* appear in a book with Person B, don't blame either of them. All responsibility lies with Person K (for Kick). Put another way: *No contributor necessarily endorses the message of any other contributor.*

Since most countries write dates with the day first (e.g., 11 September 2001), everyone outside the United States may not be familiar with the abbreviations 911, 9-11, and 9/11, all of which have become shorthand for referring to the terrorist attacks of September 11, 2001 (aka, 9/11/2001). I have chosen to use 911 for this purpose.

Because of constraints of time and page count, *Everything You Know Is Wrong* and *You Are Being Lied To* don't contain indexes. These indexes are available at the Website for Disinformation Books <books.disinfo.com>.

Endnotes

1. Unsigned. "You Are Either With Us or Against Us." CNN, 6 Nov 2001. **2.** Unsigned. "Ashcroft: Critics of New Terror Measures Undermine Effort." CNN, 7 Dec 2001. **3.** Guillermo, Emil. "The FBI's House Calls." SF Gate/*San Francisco Chronicle* 18 Dec 2001. Rothschild, Matthew. "If You Don't Want American Flag Stamps, Watch Out!" *The Progressive* 8 Dec 2001. **4.** Axtman, Kris. "Political Dissent Can Bring Federal Agents to Door." *Christian Science Monitor* 8 Jan 2002. **5.** Watson, Roland. "Bush Law Chief Tried to Suspend Habeas Corpus." *Times* (London) 3 Dec 2001.

BURN THE OLIVE TREE, SELL THE LEXUS

GREG PALAST AND OLIVER SHYKLES

Globalization is really neat. Just ask Thomas Friedman. He has a column in the *New York Times*, and he wrote a big, fat, bestselling book, *The Lexus and the Olive Tree*, which explains it all to us—the marvels of the *New Globalization Order*.

Now, right here in my *Lexus* book it says that in this brave new world we will all have Internet-enabled cell phones which will allow us to trade Amazon.com stock and, at the very same time, we can talk to Eskimos. The really exciting part is we will all be able to do this from our bedrooms in our pajamas.

When he's not in his pajamas, Friedman is in fact one of a gaggle of happy-go-lucky globalizers running around chirruping the virtues of globalization in its current form. In *The Lexus and the Olive Tree* Friedman lays out, on a level of detail never seen before, the ability of globalization to democratize three key areas: technology, finance, and information. He argues that everyone in this global New World Order will have access to all the technology, finance, and information they need to live healthy and happy lives.

And so when I finished reading his book, I thought to myself, "Wow! This is a future I want to be a part of." Just imagine, every village from the Andes to Shaker Heights will be connected, empowered, and enabled, and that's one heck of a future. I want this, and I want it now.

But hold on a minute.... I just picked up the paper, and it says that 100,000 people massed in Genoa to protest against the G8 (that is, the eight largest industrial nations driving forward globalization). And ten months before that, 20,000 people had gathered in Prague to demonstrate against the World Bank and the International Monetary Fund—two of the key international agencies driving free trade expansion, a guiding force behind globalization.

So what the heck is wrong with these protestors; don't they understand? Haven't they heard about the Eskimos? Don't they understand economics? As the Prime Minister of Britain, Tony Blair, explains, "The protests and people who indulge in the protests are completely misguided. World Trade is good for peoples' jobs and peoples' living standards.... These protests are a complete outrage."

But you have to forgive youth its lack of sophistication. They obviously haven't read the Gospel of Globalization according to

Thomas, nor the daily scripture, the *New York Times*. The answers became widely known as "Thatcherism" in Britain and "Reaganomics" in the US; then later as the "Washington Consensus." As Friedman puts it, "The Golden Straightjacket first began to be stitched together...by British Prime Minister Margaret Thatcher.... That Thatcherite coat was soon reinforced by Ronald Reagan."

In fact, it's a very lucky thing that global capitalism happens to be such a good system, because as far as Friedman is concerned it's now the only one left. Socialism, communism, and fascism have all gone kaput. "The Cold War had the Mao suit, the Nehru jackets, the Russian fur. Globalization has only the Golden Straightjacket." And so all that's left in our closet is Friedman's golden straightjacket, but that's okay because, as Friedman puts it, "The tighter you wear it the more gold it produces." So strap yourselves in! Everyone still breathing okay? Then I'll continue.

So there are no dissenters now, we all agree; we're all wearing the same straightjacket. As Friedman explains on page 106 of his book, it was all democratic; we all got to take part in the debate. I thought about this, and Friedman was right—I remembered that we did have a choice. We had our choice of George W. Thatcher, Reagan Clinton Bush, or Al Thatcher Reagan Gore. You see, there's no room in the golden straightjacket for anyone who doesn't agree. And as Friedman himself admits, "It is increasingly difficult these days to find any real difference between ruling and opposition parties in those countries that have put on the Golden Straightjacket[,]...be they led by Democrats or Republicans, Conservatives or Labourites, Christian Democrats or Social Democrats."

So just when I was getting sized up for my own straightjacket—and, boy, was I excited—I read that there were riots in Ecuador. And I remember thinking to myself, "Oh my, why are they in the streets?" There are people in the streets, and there are tanks, too. And I thought to myself, "Perhaps the Internet is down. Perhaps they're trying to unload their Amazon.com stock, which is dropping like crazy. They can't log on. It's all jammed up. I mean, the future's on hold here. Will someone please call AOL?"

But it turned out that these people were in the streets, facing down the tanks because the price of cooking gas had just been raised by 60 percent. This is odd because at the time the world was in a glut of fuel, and oil prices were way down. Ecuador had been a member of OPEC; it has more gas than it knows what to do with. It's drowning in oil.

That was one of the reasons Ecuador was in financial trouble. So who would be bonkers enough as to raise the price of cooking gas and create all that needless suffering? The people on the streets claimed that this was a requirement placed upon Ecuador by the World Bank. Now, I didn't believe this for a second; Reagan and Thatcher gave us the answers 20 years ago, and there was nothing about cooking gas.

But then I showed up at my office, and while I was quietly sipping my coffee and leafing through the paper, a pile of documents flew in through the window.

Right on the front of one of them it said, "restricted distribution," and, "it may not otherwise be disclosed without World Bank authorization." It was a "confidential," for-eyes-only document. I couldn't resist the temptation, so pretend you never saw what I'm about to reveal to you—when you've finished, rip out this chapter and eat it right up.

I opened up the document. It was called "The Ecuador Interim Country Assistance Strategy." I read this strategy, and it included a schedule for raising the price of cooking gas. They used to call these things "Structural Assistance Plans," but, oops, those got a bad name, so like all the best PR firms, they did the right thing and changed the name. Now they're known as "Poverty Reduction Strategies." Nothing like a little whitewash to keep people quiet. But the people of Ecuador weren't keeping quiet, so I read on....

Along with the forced hike in cooking gas prices, the World Bank required the elimination of 26,000 government jobs. Other poverty reduction strategies included a cut in pensions and a cut in real wages nationwide, by half, no less; all this through World Bank-directed macroeconomic manipulation. Part of the plan included the handing over of a license for a trans-Andes pipeline controlled by British Petroleum. I wasn't sure, perhaps I had become confused. Maybe they meant that the poverty reduction program was a poverty reduction program for British Petroleum.

In all, the World Bank and IMF helpfully "suggested" 167 strategies as part of its loan package. Ecuador was broke; that's why it had asked for the World Bank's help in the first place. It desperately needed the wampum, so desperately, in fact, that it had no choice but to accept these strategies. I shall, therefore, refer to these "strategies" as conditions, which is what they are—loan conditions. No ifs, no buts, sign on the line, thank you very much.

Oddly, I didn't read about Structural Assistance Plans or the 167 conditionalities for Ecuador in my copy of *Lexus* nor in the *Times*.

But just hold on a moment—what happened to *democratic finance*? Thomas Friedman, our new apostle, said that now anyone can obtain finance capital; it's all democratic. Hey, he said, even David Bowie can issue bonds (to the tune of $55 million, no less). Maybe Ecuador's problem was that it didn't have a rock star to co-sign with them.

But there's a bigger problem here: These conditions weren't put together especially for Ecuador. Any country in crisis receiving a loan package from the World Bank gets a neat little set of conditions—111 on average—along with their loans.

You'd think that if they were doing all these wonderful things to reduce poverty, they'd want to shout it from the rooftops. Hey, perhaps they're just modest. In fact, talk about modesty, did you know they even found a cure for AIDS? Yes indeed, I kid you not.

But before I tell you how they did it, you first have to understand all the conditions, all the little nuggets that can be found in the pockets of our golden straightjackets. So let's enumerate them, just as Thomas Friedman does on page 105 of his book.

ANY COUNTRY IN CRISIS RECEIVING A LOAN PACKAGE FROM THE WORLD BANK GETS A NEAT LITTLE SET OF CONDITIONS—111 ON AVERAGE—ALONG WITH THEIR LOANS.

Okay, *privatization* is number one. Second is *deregulation*—you've got to get rid of all those dull bureaucrats and their thick rule books. You know they just get in the way of things. Next is *free trade*—drop the borders between people and all the nice things they want. Fourth, *free up the capital markets*—let capital flow in order to generate business and jobs worldwide. Fifth, support those *international agencies* which enforce our new international order—the International Monetary Fund, the World Bank, and let's not forget the good ol' World Trade Organization. In other words, don't dye your hair green and go into the streets of Seattle and break the windows of a Starbucks. And finally you must look for a *market-based solution*. Remember, that's the one that gives you the "win-win" situation.

Now, I can tell you that it's with the market-based solution that they found a cure for AIDS in Tanzania. In Tanzania the silly things used to give away health care. Can you believe it? So the World Bank said, "You've got to stop being so scatterbrained and start charging for medical care. You've got a health care crisis, and you've got to cure it with our market-based solution."

A nation with 1.4 million people with HIV/AIDS means a lot of visits to the hospital. So when you start charging those people to visit the hospital, they stop coming. In Dar Es Salaam the number of hospital visits dropped by 53 percent. That's quite a cure, and I don't think anyone could beat that.

Globalization has many other "success" stories. In Britain, Margaret Thatcher took the electricity system, and she privatized and deregulated it. Electricity used to be cheaper in Britain than in the US, but now consumers pay 70 percent more per unit than their American counterparts. The same process was applied to the gas system, and the charges shot up to a level some 60 percent higher than in the US where some type of regulation still exists. Water in the US is still mostly a publicly-owned system, but the British, still not satisfied with the privatization and deregulation of the gas and electricity industries, went about the same process with the water industry. Now the happily straightjacketed folks there pay 250 percent more than we do in the US.

So tickled were they with their clever programs of privatization and deregulation that they decided to share the good news. The system spread, via a World Bank loan condition, to Brazil. There the electricity industry was targeted, and the Rio Light Company of Rio de Janeiro was taken out of public hands. The new British, French, and American owners came along, and they said, "Just look, look at this bloated and inefficient company and its huge payroll." So they immediately set to work making it lean and mean. And mean it was—they knocked off 40 percent of the workforce. But there was a problem—the workers knew where the transformers were. The lights in Rio de Janeiro started flickering, and Rio Light is now known as Rio Dark. But that wasn't all: For a flickering light system, the people of Rio de Janeiro got to pay double what they had paid prior to privatization. But don't panic, it's not all doom and gloom. There was a huge increase in profits.

So after the failed attempt at privatization in Brazil, they said, "Well, let's try it again; we'll do it right this time. We'll go to India." And that failed, so they went to Pakistan. The attempt there became one of the reasons why they had a military coup. So they went to Chile, and it didn't work there, either. So they said, "Let's try one more desperate time. We'll go to a place that understands the future. We'll go to California and they'll get it; they'll be able to deal with deregulation. They'll get the wonderful effects of reductions due to the miracles of the markets. There'll be competition, and prices in California, which are too high, will plummet." In fact, when the Californian legislature voted to deregulate the price of electricity, they even changed the law to the effect that prices would *fall* 20 percent. Yet, year after year prices rose in the wholesale market in California. In one year they rose 380 percent. So, faced with a terrible problem in California, they went to Cleveland instead.

While I was in Cleveland to debate Thomas Friedman, I got a letter from my friendly-faced hotelier. It read: "Dear Guest, due to the current energy issue, a surcharge is being applied nightly to all guest accounts." Well, I'll tell you it's not an "energy issue." It's a crisis. And it's not a crisis of energy; it's a crisis of globalization. It's a crisis of a plan that never seems to work.

I used to work as an advisor with the utility commission of Ohio, amongst others, and we were thinking about what to do about the billions spent on nuclear plants and other wasteful projects that went nowhere. That was in the 1980s, in the bad old days before deregulation, so the answer we came up with was simple: You put a cap on the price. You just put a cap on it. You regulate in the public's interest. But little did I know that we should have looked for the market-based solution. I am now reading Paul Krugman. He's the guy who appears in the *New York Times* with Thomas Friedman. So there it was—Friedman the globalizer and Krugman the globalizer, and they agree with each other. Krugman says, "I know the solution to bring down the prices of supplies; what we should do is remove all caps and allow electricity prices to rise." And I said, "Wow!" I didn't think of it. That's really deep. If you want the prices to go *down*, you *raise* them. And I thought about that. It's like a one hand clapping thing.

I have to confess I didn't understand it at all. I said, "This is beyond me. I had better go to one of the gurus of globalization. I mean one of the inventors of market-based solutions. You know, the top banana." So I went to Cambridge University with my camera crew from the BBC. And I sat down, for several hours, with the man himself—*the* voice of globalization—Professor Joseph Stiglitz, who has since co-won the Nobel Prize in Economics. You see, Stiglitz was the Chief Economist of the World Bank. The guy who wrote some of these plans and conditions. The guy who came up with these market-based solutions. And so I said, "You've gotta answer this for me. I'm really losing it, Professor Stiglitz. To cut electricity prices, you raise the prices. To cure AIDS, you raise the price of medicine. To stop the hemorrhage of capital in Ecuador, you remove capital controls on the export of capital. I don't get it."

And so he explained it to me sort of like this: "You see, in the Middle Ages, they used to put leeches on people's bodies when they were ill, and they would get sicker and sicker. And you know what they would say? They would say, 'You know what's wrong? There's still blood.' So they would apply more leeches. And so that's how the globalization program works. You just keep applying leeches, and if a little deregulation seems to be making the system sick, what you need is more deregulation to try to cure the system."

And I said, "You know what? You don't sound like you're wearing your straightjacket." And he replied, "Well, I'm not; not anymore." Despite the fact that there's supposedly no dissent, *he was dissenting*, and this is the guy who *conceived* the system.

So I asked him, "What happened here then?" And he said, "You know, economics is a science—it's a dismal science, but it's a science. And you know what the problem with globalization and the

ELECTRICITY USED TO BE CHEAPER IN BRITAIN THAN IN THE US, BUT NOW CONSUMERS PAY 70 PERCENT MORE PER UNIT THAN THEIR AMERICAN COUNTERPARTS.

program of privatizations, deregulation, liberalization of capital markets is? They don't work." And he told me to take a look at Latin America in the period 1960 to 1980. In the dark ages in which it had all kinds of government regulations, controls, quasi-socialist economies, and government intervention, Latin America's per capita income grew by 73 percent. The same went for Africa; its per capita income grew by 34 percent. But it was "inefficient," and we thought we could do better with free-market solutions.

And so it began in 1980, with the International Monetary Fund and then the World Bank sending out structural assistance programs with loan conditions. They said, "If we're going to give you money, you've got to change your economy." Then came the economic miracle. Latin America, in the next 20 years in its straightjacket, went from 73 percent growth per capita income to just about nothing: 6 percent. Africa, which had grown at a pokey 34 percent during those 20 years, has since *dropped* by 23 percent. The privatization program became what Professor Stiglitz calls the "briberization" program. What happened was that privatization became the means to sell off the country to bandits who then had no reason to operate businesses, so instead they just sold off the assets. And that's what happened in Russia, and there it resulted in a depression.

I said to him, "You sound like a bitter man. Did it work for anyone; is it all doom and gloom?" He said, "Oh no, you look at the numbers for Asia; the World Bank always talks about how well Asia did. That's because of China and the tremendous growth it experienced." I asked him what China's trick was, and he replied, "They didn't listen to us!" China said, "We're not privatizing; we're not liberalizing. Sorry. Keep your straightjacket."

I asked him if there were any other good stories. He said, "Yeah, Botswana." "So what did they do?" I asked. He said—no points for guessing—Botswana also told them, "Forget it." Botswana was the one nation in Africa that refused the International Monetary Fund's and the World Bank's help.

So it had all gone bad. The protesters were going to be out in the streets this week, and there were protests going on in Ecuador. In fact, when we talk about protests we think about Seattle and Genoa and the claims that all these white college kids are just out there because they don't know what to do with themselves and because they just don't understand economics. But what you didn't hear about were the *400* protests that took place in the Third World in 1999 alone. There they understand exactly what's going on.

But how come we never hear about these demonstrations on our televisions or in our newspapers? Well, it's because Thomas Friedman the globalizer, on the political left, writing in the *New York Times*, agrees with Milton Friedman the globalizer, on the political right. And the opinion in the *Times* matches the opinion in the *Washington Post*, which matches the *Financial Times*, which matches ABC, NBC, BBC, CBC, and any other mainstream media outlet you care to mention. So it would seem that everyone agrees now. That is, everyone who is doing quite well, thank you very much, from globalization and from the suffering of billions of people. They are not going to tell you about suffering on the streets in the First World and the Third World caused by the undemocratic international agencies and our supposedly democratically elected governments (the idea of democracy is based on a choice—a real choice, not a choice between globalistas and globalistas). They won't tell you that this system is a mess because it is not in *their* best interests to do so.

Currently the wealth of the world's 475 billionaires is greater than the combined income of the poorest half of humanity. But Friedman still wants to assure us that, "The answer is free-market capitalism. Other systems may be able to distribute and divide income more efficiently and equitably, but none can generate income to distribute as efficiently as free-market capitalism." I'm sure that the poorest half of humanity feels much better now, Mr. Friedman. Thank you.

But there was nothing wrong with the international control of trade when the World Bank—that is, the World Bank that John Maynard Keynes devised—came along and rebuilt the nations that had been flattened by World War II. The International Monetary Fund also helped by correcting the imbalance of trade that resulted from changes in commodity prices. But things changed in 1980 when we all climbed into our golden straightjackets with Thatcher, Reagan, and Milton Friedman. The agencies were taken over by the Free-Market Believers who had plans for structural adjustment, globalizing, and economies free of government.

"So where did we go wrong?" I asked myself. In my pile of confidential papers I found a "General Agreement on Trade and Services" (GATS) from the Secretariat of the World Trade Organization. You're not supposed to see this either, but what the heck. This document contains a discussion of something called the "necessity test," and it tells you the real plan behind the several "democracies" Friedman says are the gift of globalization.

The "necessity test" appears within GATS article 6.4. I realize this has nothing to do with trading stock in your pajamas, but this is what globalization is really about. This is the plan for the establishment of a panel which will vet national laws and regulations. What this innocuous-looking article means is that only those regulations of a nation which are "least burdensome" to business for "legitimate policy purposes" are allowed. Legitimate policy purposes? But I thought that's why nations had congresses and parliaments; it is for legislatures to decide what is legitimate and what is not.

A "necessity test" already exists in the North American Free Trade Agreement (NAFTA), and it will be expanded in the Free Trade Area of the Americas (FTAA), an even bigger version of NAFTA that will cover the entire Western hemisphere. *This* is why there were people in the streets in Quebec in April 2001.

So what happened under NAFTA with this "necessity test"? Well, there's an interesting story here. It's the case of Metalclad, a US-based company that wanted to build a toxic dump in Mexico. It was one of the new breed of globalizers following the advice of Larry Summers, who said that the Third World is underpolluted from an economic point of view. Summers is the guy who was US Secretary of the Treasury and Stiglitz's predecessor at the World Bank, so he must know what he's talking about. He was also the guy who demanded that Stiglitz be fired for dissent. (So now there cannot be any dissenting, because we all agree, right? There is no dissent now, because if you dissent your head is cut off and put on a spike on L Street, Washington. But I digress.)

Metalclad wanted to put a toxic dump into a central Mexican state, on top of an aquifer, no less. Mexico said, "You know, we have our rules. You can't put a toxic dump above our water supply." And Metalclad said, "Have you read NAFTA?" And so Metalclad took Mexico to court under the NAFTA "necessity test" rules.

But the NAFTA disputes panel is not like the courts as you know them, where things are open. The NAFTA disputes panel is secret, closed to the public. So Metalclad made their case, and it turned out that Mexico was being "trade restrictive." So not only did Mexico get a toxic waste dump right on top of their aquifer, but they also received a bill for millions of dollars for delaying the toxic dumping.

THEY RAISED THE PRICE OF WATER. THAT'S WHY THERE WERE PEOPLE IN THE STREETS.

It's not just Mexico that has experienced the full force of NAFTA. California now faces a bill for $976 million as punishment for not changing its anti-pollution laws. The trade-restrictive hooligans there wanted to stop a Canadian company from selling them their toxic gasoline additive.

But I just couldn't get Ecuador off my mind, so I went back to Stiglitz and asked him about how those pesky folks got into financial trouble in the first place. He told me the International Monetary Fund and World Bank years ago forced Ecuador to liberalize its capital markets, to remove all restrictions on ownership of bonds or the movement of money across borders. This way, capital can easily flow in and flow out. But the capital flowed out and it flowed out. So the IMF said, "My god, you gotta get that money back—start raising interest rates!" So Ecuador raised their rates 10 ... 20 ... 30 ... 40 ... 50 ... 60 ... 70 ... 80 ... 90 percent. But that caused the economy to go into the tank. Then the World Bank said, "Well you can't raise interest rates anymore, so start selling everything that isn't nailed down." And when that money was used up to pay creditors, the Bank ordered a price hike in items like cooking gas.

Yet despite the World Bank's success, some people didn't want to put on their golden straightjackets. In 2000 there was a protest in Cochabamba, Bolivia. It was a protest against the privatization and deregulation of the local water company, and it was led by the local archbishop and a union leader named Oscar Olivera. The privatization and deregulation were part of the World Bank's cure because Cochabamba had problems: Only 35 percent of the people there had good drinking water. Of course, the World Bank said, "We have an idea—let's privatize the water company." And so they passed Cochbamba's problems to Bechtel, an American company, and International Water of London, because they will know what to do; they'll apply a market-based solution. And they did: They raised the price of water. That's why there were people in the streets.

Hugo Banzar, who used to be Bolivia's dictator but who had now become president, sent in the tanks. And then I got this note which told me that two days later a 17-year-old, Hugo Daza, had been killed, shot through the face. A friend of mine, who knows his family, told me that he was just in town to run an errand for his mother. In the protests that ensued, four more people were shot dead. Jim Wolfensohn, president of the World Bank, was asked about the incident a couple of days later. He said, "The riots in Bolivia, I am pleased to say, are quieting down." He then went on to warn the Bolivians that they had better start paying their water bills.

A year later the protesters won, and the price of water dropped. But it started creeping up again. Then I got another note telling me that Oscar Olivera and the archbishop, head of the human rights committee, had led another peaceful protest. The authorities had responded by sending in close to 1,000 heavily-armed members of the Bolivian security forces to disperse the peaceful marchers with tear gas, beating them and confiscating their personal possessions. Oscar Olivera went missing.

It turned out that he had been detained by the authorities, an action which contravened Bolivian law: Article 7 of the Bolivian constitution guarantees citizens the right to protest and the freedom to meet and associate for legal ends. I understand now why Thomas Friedman, despite talking at length about the democratization of technology, of finance, and of information, only once mentions the democratization of democracy, and it's right there on page 167 where he proudly explains democracy IMF-style: "It's one dollar, one vote."

I've gotta go now. I gotta get my cell phone, get in my pajamas, and tell those Eskimos what's really goin' on.

This essay grew out of Palast's remarks in a debate with Thomas Friedman before a World Economic Forum meeting in Cleveland in April 2001.

DRUG COMPANIES
SELL HARD, SELL FAST ... AND COUNT THE BODIES LATER
ARIANNA HUFFINGTON

For over three years, the big pharmaceutical companies had been spit-shining their image as mankind's saviors while simultaneously waging a legal battle to keep low-cost versions of life-saving drugs from the millions of people dying of AIDS in Africa.

On April 19, 2001, the 39 drug companies suing the South African government dropped their lawsuit. Typically, they tried to spin the decision as a humanitarian gesture, but it really was the only way to extricate themselves from the public relations nightmare their cold-blooded effort had become. You can see why they've never tried to develop a truth pill.

From AIDS activists who started protesting two years ago to Nelson Mandela, who called the lawsuit a "gross error...that is completely wrong and must be condemned," the public outcry had reached a crescendo the industry could no longer afford to ignore.

This, after all, is the same industry that in 2000 spent $1.7 billion on TV ads promoting its products and painting itself as a paragon of virtue and compassion.

Ironically, it was not long after I had seen for the umpteenth time Pfizer's heartstring-tugging TV spot proclaiming, "Life is our life's work," that I heard the drug companies—including Warner-Lambert, which merged with Pfizer in the summer of 2000—had waved the blood-stained white flag in Pretoria.

That it took the world turning on them—and three long years of thousands of people dying—to get them to drop their suit proves that the industry's collective slogan should be, "Profit is our life's work."

And lucrative work it is. In 2000, according to *Fortune* magazine, the pharmaceutical industry was the most profitable in America—by far. This profitability, however, came with a human price tag.

In a series of investigative reports that earned him a Pulitzer Prize, the *Los Angeles Times'* David Willman exposed the risks taken with the public's health by drug companies in their frenetic drive for ever-higher profits. He uncovered documents that reveal how Warner-Lambert, which produced the now-banned diabetes drug Rezulin, willfully ignored evidence of the drug's life-threatening liver toxicity, and even managed to get senior Food and Drug Administration officials to disregard the warnings of their own medical experts.

This collusion between the pharmaceutical industry, the FDA, and the Congressional Oversight Committee—which more often resembles the Congressional Turn-a-blind-eye Committee—is becoming deadly. Literally. Ten drugs have been pulled off the market for safety reasons since 1997 after causing more than a thousand deaths and countless serious injuries.

And, according to drug safety expert Thomas Moore, these numbers only scratch the surface of the suffering. "I believe the number of people injured by these drugs," he told me, "is grossly underestimated because only a small fraction of cases are reported. We have a flawed system that gives drug companies the benefit of the doubt, and as a result, thousands of people are dying."

> THIS COLLUSION BETWEEN THE PHARMACEUTICAL INDUSTRY, THE FDA, AND THE CONGRESSIONAL OVERSIGHT COMMITTEE—WHICH MORE OFTEN RESEMBLES THE CONGRESSIONAL TURN-A-BLIND-EYE COMMITTEE—IS BECOMING DEADLY.

This lack of real government oversight is compounded by the industry's aggressive marketing tactics—which make it seem like these powerful drugs are just like any other consumer product.

It's a misperception with lethal side effects. Just as Hollywood knows how to make a blockbuster movie "open big," the pharmaceutical companies have learned how to build interest in their latest blockbuster drug. As a result, new, relatively untested drugs are being sampled by millions of people soon after they're approved, so when something goes wrong, the fallout is widespread.

A particularly loathsome example of this involves Duract, a painkiller that research proved could damage the liver. But under pressure from Wyeth-Ayerst, Duract's manufacturer, the FDA approved the drug anyway, with a warning to physicians about its toxicity. The drug company wasn't about to let a little thing like fatal liver damage get in its way.

It pushed the flawed drug so effectively that more than 2.5 million prescriptions were written in the ten months before Duract started racking up liver-related deaths and was yanked off pharmacy shelves. As they say in that other kind of drug ad: "Speed Kills."

But bamboozling the American public on the way to massive profits only earns you a slap on the wrist. Glaxo Wellcome (now GlaxoSmithKline) was reprimanded a remarkable fourteen times for misleading consumers about its asthma drugs Flovent and Flonase. You'd think they'd have gotten the message after rebuke number four. Or nine. Or twelve. And the FDA recently wagged its finger—for the third time in fourteen months—at Pfizer and Pharmacia for running deceptive TV spots touting Celebrex, their jointly marketed arthritis drug.

GLAXO WELLCOME WAS REPRIMANDED A REMARKABLE FOURTEEN TIMES FOR MISLEADING CONSUMERS ABOUT ITS ASTHMA DRUGS FLOVENT AND FLONASE.

Hoping to explore this less-than-stellar track record further, I put in a call to Pfizer and was transferred to the company's department of Corporate Reputation. I kid you not, that's what it's called. When I asked about obtaining a copy of some of their ads, I was told this wouldn't be possible due to my "tight deadline."

I guess 36 hours wasn't enough time for them to fax me the script of a 30-second ad that seems to air every 60 seconds. I understand—I'd also be embarrassed if my ads overstated product effectiveness or contained the hyper-defensive tag line: "We have fathers, sisters and best friends, too." Some of those best friends are apparently employed at the FDA.

And why not—it's easy to bond with government officials who are ignoring warnings from their own medical specialists and issuing toothless scoldings to the industry.

It's now abundantly clear that the decision to allow drug companies to inundate consumers with ads for prescription drugs was a serious mistake. It should be reversed, but that's easier said than done. The industry has covered its legislative flank by making extremely generous contributions to elected officials on both sides of the aisle— more than $18.6 million during the 2000 election cycle alone.

But the industry's surrender in South Africa shows that public pressure and grassroots protests really work. So let's build on this victory and rid our airwaves of the plague of prescription drug ads.

THE VATICAN BANK

JONATHAN LEVY

Many believe the Vatican Bank to be a myth; after all, what would Vatican City—home to palaces, museums, and cathedrals—need with a bank? But the Vatican Bank does exist in the heart of Vatican City (near the Santa Anna Gate) in a tower that is closed to outsiders. Officially the Vatican Bank is known as the Institute for Religious Works (Instituto per le Opere di Religione), or IOR. However, religion has very little to do with the bank, unless one is referring to the moneychangers in the temple.

And Jesus went into the temple of God, and cast out all them that sold and bought in the temple, and overthrew the tables of the moneychangers, and the seats of them that sold doves.[1]

And while the moneychangers were simply providing a service so that temple fees could be paid, the Vatican Bank has been involved in tax evasion, financial scams, and money laundering of Nazi gold. The Pope, as the sole shareholder of the Vatican Bank, is one of the richest men in the world and, by association, one of the least moral.

The Vatican Bank has the distinction of being one of the most notorious and secretive financial institutions in the world. Very little is actually known about the bank other than what limited information the Vatican releases. In my own capacity as co-counsel for plaintiffs in the case *Alperin v. Vatican Bank (IOR)*—an ongoing lawsuit by Holocaust survivors seeking an accounting and restitution of Nazi loot held at the Vatican Bank—I have learned just how tenuous and slippery the few public facts about the bank can be.

Ownership of the Vatican Bank is a thorny issue and apparently a great mystery, if the Vatican is to be believed. One of the most reliable authorities *was* Fr. Thomas J. Reese, SJ, who is the author of several books on the Catholic Church, including the bestsellers *Inside the Vatican* and *Archbishop*. Based on his interviews with Vatican insiders, Reese devoted an entire chapter of *Inside the Vatican* to Vatican finances. Reese was quite clear about who owns the Vatican Bank: "The IOR is the Pope's bank, in a sense, he is the one and only stockholder. He owns it, he controls it."[2]

When Reese's book was brought to the attention of the federal court in order to prove the private ownership of the bank, the Vatican's attorneys went into action. A lengthy declaration by Father Reese, so full of contradictions it was worthy of Bill Clinton, was quickly presented to the court. In the declaration the truly unfortunate Fr. Reese recanted his opinions, denigrated his own scholarship, quibbled about the meaning of the word "sense," denied any expertise on Vatican finances, and stated: "I do not know in what capacity the Pope acts, with respect to the IOR." Jesuitical hairsplitting aside, Reese had it right the first time: The IOR is the Pope's bank, His Holiness' personal piggy bank.

Additional information about the IOR can be gleaned from civil and criminal court cases. The Pope founded the precursor to the IOR in 1887 as the Commission for Pious Causes. In 1941, the Commission was transformed into the "for profit" Institute for Religious Works by the issuance of bylaws promulgated with the approval of Pius XII. The core fund upon which the IOR was founded consisted of Holy See moneys.[3] Surplus profits, if any, are turned over to the Holy See; in recent years the IOR has been both a source of Vatican operating funds and a current liability, as in the case of *Alperin v. Vatican Bank*.

> THE VATICAN BANK HAS THE DISTINCTION OF BEING ONE OF THE MOST NOTORIOUS AND SECRETIVE FINANCIAL INSTITUTIONS IN THE WORLD.

The public position of the bank is that it has always adhered to its charter and exists to serve the Church as set forth in the bank's bylaws, called chirographs.[4] The Holy See[5] is the official government of both the Roman Catholic Church and Vatican City State, a fully independent microstate located by the Tiber River in Rome. Vatican City is home to three financial institutions: the Apostolic Patrimony of the Holy See (APSA), which functions as the Vatican Central Bank, the Ministry of Economics, and the aforementioned Vatican Bank (IOR). While Vatican City State—with a population of only about 800 and a total territory of 109 acres—is the world's smallest nation and may not seem to need three major financial institutions, the Holy See is also the temporal government of the world's one billion Catholics and as such has requirements and goals that cannot be met by or entrusted to conventional banking institutions.

The Vatican Bank is answerable neither to the Vatican Central Bank nor the Economics Ministry; instead it functions independently with three boards of directors: one consisting of high-ranking cardinals, another consisting of international bankers, with Vatican bank officers and a directorate running the day-to-day affairs. Such obtuse organizational structures are the norm for the Holy See and serve well to mask bank operations.[6]

■ ■ ■ ■ ■ ■ ■ ■ ■ ■

The IOR functions as the Church's private banker, as is fitting a bank owned by the Pope. The Pope's ownership notwithstanding, the bank from its inception has been linked to the most unholy of scandals, scams, and plots. Auspiciously, the bank's inception in 1941 at the order of Pius XII, so-called Hitler's Pope, provided a convenient banking outlet for Italian Fascists, the aristocracy, and the Mafia. Unable to collect its Peter's pence[7] from North and South America, the Pope cast about for other sources of income, and acting as a banker for totalitarian elements in war-torn Europe proved to be too much of a temptation.

The Vatican Bank claims to have no records from the World War II period; indeed, according to the Vatican Bank's attorney, Franzo Grande Stevens,[8] the IOR destroys *all* of its records every ten

> THE POPE'S OWNERSHIP NOTWITHSTANDING, THE BANK FROM ITS INCEPTION HAS BEEN LINKED TO THE MOST UNHOLY OF SCANDALS, SCAMS, AND PLOTS.

years,[9] a claim to which no responsible banker would ever give credence. Nonetheless, other records do exist in German and American archives, and these show Nazi transfers of funds to the IOR from the Reichsbank and transfers of funds from the IOR to Nazi-controlled banks in Switzerland. A well-known attorney who specialized in Holocaust restitution has documented transfers of gold from SS accounts[10] to an unnamed bank in Rome in September 1943, just as the Allies were approaching the city. It is unlikely that these transfers were to the normal Italian gold clearinghouse banks, as they were under orders to transfer their funds to Milan to avoid imminent capture of their assets by the Allies.

Transfer of Nazi gold, known as "victim gold," from SS accounts enriched the coffers of the neutral Vatican Bank. And the story of Nazi gold and the Church does not end at the Vatican Bank but provides tantalizing clues as to how a large cache of Nazi gold ended up hidden at Catholicism's holiest shrine, Fatima, Portugal.[11] Insider sources at Fatima report the shrine is controlled by Masonic elements,[12] a connection with the IOR that will be explained more fully below.

The Vatican Bank, therefore, was born of a need for cash during WWII and its aftermath. The IOR was a major partner in the disappearance of the treasury of Independent Croatia (a German puppet

state), which was valued as high as $200 million in 1945. The Croatian Nazis, or Ustashe, were virulent nationalists whose brand of debased Catholicism was as fanatic as their hatred of Orthodox Christian Serbs, of which they slaughtered 500,000, along with tens of thousands of Jews and Gypsies. The Ustashe banked the proceeds of genocide[13] with the Vatican to fund their government-in-exile in Argentina and to send their members (along with select Nazis like Klaus Barbie and Adolph Eichman) to South America via the so-called "ratline."[14]

While the exact details of the Ustashe Treasury laundering are the subject of an ongoing lawsuit[15] filed by the few remaining survivors of Croatian atrocities, the US State Department, in its 1998 report "The Fate of the Ustasha Treasury," fingered the Vatican and its archives as likely places to look for answers. According to reports from the Office of Strategic Services (OSS, the CIA's precursor) and records from US Army Counterintelligence, in the last days of WWII a Croatian treasure convoy made its way to Austria, where it was intercepted by British officials. A deal was struck, money changed hands, and the remainder of the treasure proceeded to Rome unimpeded by the military authorities.[16] In Rome, the powerful treasurer of the Franciscan order, Dominic Mandic, made available the Franciscan accounts at the Vatican Bank. From there the treasure disappeared and was dispersed, as usually happens to funds parked at the IOR.

According to John Loftus,[17] author and former US Department of Justice prosecutor with the Nazi-hunting OSI unit, the Vatican Bank is never audited; hence, funds deposited there may simply vanish without a trace. In declarations filed with the *Alperin* court, Loftus concludes that large parts of the Ustasha Treasury ended up at the Vatican Bank and that a warm relationship between the Vatican and the Ustasha continued well into the 1950s. Loftus names not only Draganovic and the Franciscan Treasurer Mandic as prime movers of Nazi loot, but also Bishop Rozman of Slovenia, another Nazi quisling coddled at the postwar Vatican.

While the IOR was stonewalling on the Croatian treasury issue in US federal court, the Vatican Secretary of State[18] sent a diplomatic note to the US government asking it to pressure the court into dismissing the lawsuit. However, the State Department has declined to act, and the matter persists under submission to the court awaiting a ruling.

The Vatican's own hand-picked Jewish-Catholic Historical Commission unsuccessfully questioned the Vatican's relationship with the Ustashe during and after WWII, when the top Ustashe leadership was sheltered at the Vatican and Franciscan properties in Italy. The Vatican claims that all relevant records are sealed, so the historical commission indefinitely suspended its operations. When Jewish members of the commission persisted in their queries,

Vatican spokesman Rev. Gumpel accused them of slander.

Unlike that commission, few Jewish or Catholic organizations are willing to face the awful truth documented in US government records. Pope Pius XII and his Secretary of State Montini (who later became Pope Paul VI)—two leading candidates for sainthood—were moneychangers, travel agents, and landlords for Nazi war criminals. The Ustashe leader Pavelic and his bodyguard were sheltered at various monasteries and safe houses in Rome and met frequently with high Church officials, including Vatican Secretary of State Montini, according to Pavelic's file with US Army Counter Intelligence. The Vatican ratline sent tens of thousands of Nazis to South America, Australia, and elsewhere, including almost all of the big-name war criminals: Pavelic, Eichman, Stengel, Barbie "the Butcher of Lyons," and Artukovic, the Croatian Justice Minister.[19] US Army Counter Intelligence was well aware of the damaging consequences these facts could have for the Pope when its special agents wrote in 1947: "Pavelic's contacts are so high and present position is so compromising to the Vatican, that any extradition of the subject would deal a staggering blow to the Roman Catholic Church."

■ ■ ■ ■ ■ ■ ■ ■ ■ ■

During the 1950s and 1960s, the IOR prospered by laundering funds for wealthy Italian families who could not easily move money abroad due to Italian currency transfer restrictions. Vatican Bank accounts are nominally restricted to clerics and Roman Catholic organizations; however, this policy has been waived in certain instances throughout the bank's history. According to Nick Tosches—author of *Power on Earth*, the biography of Michele Sindona—the Vatican Bank's president, Bishop Paul Marcinkus, boasted that their system of exporting lire and evading Italian taxes was the "perfect crime."

One example of the Mafia's infiltration of the Vatican Bank was the IOR's attempt to pass off counterfeit US bonds with a face value of $14.5 million in 1973. David Guyatt—investigative journalist and author of *Deep Black Lies*—in a declaration to the *Alperin* court, stated that the $14.5 million was but the tip of the iceberg. Vatican Bank President Marcinkus and "financier" Michele Sindona had offered to purchase up to *$950 million* worth of the fraudulent bonds at a steep discount from the New York Mafia. The US Department of Justice intervened before the deal was consummated, but Marcinkus and Sindona went on to bigger and better scams, at one point controlling most of Italy's banking system.

By the late 1970s, the IOR had become a major player in the world's financial markets. Under the tutelage of the 6'3" American Bishop Paul "the Gorilla" Marcinkus,[20] Bishop Paolo Hnilica,[21] Licio Gelli,[22] Roberto Calvi,[23]

and Michele Sindona,[24] the Vatican Bank became integral to several Papal and Mafia money-laundering schemes, in which it was difficult to determine where the Vatican left off and the Mafia began. Calvi's Banco Ambrosiano[25] and several IOR-owned Panamanian and Luxemburg shell corporations (with the auspicious names of Manic, Bellatrix, Belarosa, Erin, Starfield, and United Trading Corporation) took over much of Italy's banking business and acted as a conduit for funds flowing to Eastern Europe to support the anti-communist trade union movement. Marcinkus, chairman of the IOR, was a Director of Banco Ambrosiano (Nassau, Bahamas), and there existed a close personal and banking relationship between Calvi and Marcinkus. Unfortunately, many of those involved were not only Mob-connected but also members of the notorious P2 Masonic lodge, with the net result being the disappearance of other people's money, including a single transaction involving $95 million (documented by the Irish Supreme Court).[26]

As the various schemes unraveled due to a miscalculation attributed to Calvi, heads literally began to roll. The Ambrosiano banking empire was destabilized by an internal power struggle involving the Vatican Bank, the Mafia, and the financial arm of the murky Catholic order Opus Dei. Calvi jetted around the world trying to shore up the damage, but he was too late. Guyatt's declaration to the court reveals one probable reason for Calvi's fate:

During a personal conversation with a very highly placed former merchant banker—who at one time held central banking authority and who personally knew Roberto Calvi—I was informed of the reason for Calvi's murder. The individual explained that Calvi's bank was on the verge of collapse due to the disappearance of hundreds of millions of dollars via IOR banking conduits that were connected to Mafia money laundering. In desperation, Calvi had traveled to London to seek a financial rescue package from a senior representative of Opus Dei—a right-wing, shadowy, wealthy and extremely powerful Catholic sect which is widely regarded to engage in highly dubious activities.[27]

Opus Dei, however, decided against bailing out Banco Ambrosiano, and Calvi was found "suicided"—hanging under Blackfriars Bridge in London with rocks stuffed in his pockets, a scene rife with Masonic symbolism. His son, Carlo, has tried all these years to disprove the suicide and has made a compelling case for a Mafia hit, but at whose instigation remains unknown. Opus Dei—which coveted the Vatican Bank and whose financial headquarters coincidentally are in

THE VATICAN RATLINE SENT TENS OF THOUSANDS OF NAZIS TO SOUTH AMERICA, AUSTRALIA, AND ELSEWHERE, INCLUDING ALMOST ALL OF THE BIG-NAME WAR CRIMINALS: PAVELIC, EICHMAN, STENGEL, BARBIE "THE BUTCHER OF LYONS," AND ARTUKOVIC, THE CROATIAN JUSTICE MINISTER.

London—remains a potential suspect.[28]

According to the *Sunday Times* of London,[29] the Calvi case remains open, with the Sicilian Mafia enforcer Frank "the Strangler" DiCarlo as the main suspect. Banco Ambrosiano's collapse resulted in losses of $1.5 billion, a portion of which (estimated at $250 million) was covered by the Vatican Bank, threatening the solvency of the Vatican itself. Calvi's personal secretary died twelve hours after Calvi, "jumping" out of her fourth floor office window at the Ambrosiano headquarters in Milan, another apparent suicide. Michele Sindona, Calvi's mentor, after staging his own kidnapping, was arrested for charges based on the looting of the Franklin National Bank. He expired in an Italian jail in 1986 after consuming a cup of coffee laced with arsenic. Sindona's FBI file, obtained under the Freedom of Information Act, runs an incredible 27 volumes. Although the documents were heavily sanitized by the FBI prior to release to attorneys in the *Alperin* case, Sindona is linked repeatedly to unnamed corrupt forces in the Vatican. In his "official" biography, *Power on Earth*, Sindona denigrates Licio Gelli and openly discusses his control of both Marcinkus and Calvi.

Bishop Paolo Hnilica was arrested after attempting to buy the contents of Calvi's missing suitcase—which had mysteriously disappeared upon Calvi's death—with money provided by the Roman Mafia via the IOR. Guyatt reports the suitcase's contents included a letter demanding the Vatican refund $1 billion that it had borrowed from Ambrosiano. Hnilica, as a fellow victim of communism and devoted Marianist,[30] had the Pope's ear, and despite prosecution in an Italian court, never served jail time. Nonetheless, the volumes of Italian police files (obtained from Carlo Calvi) on Hnilica and his Mafia associates make fascinating reading. Marcinkus, who likewise found himself on the wrong end of an Italian criminal court, successfully plead diplomatic immunity. Marcinkus' disdain for civil authorities was legendary, and he was once quoted as saying, "You can't run the Church on Hail Marys." As for the Vatican Bank, it never forgets a trick. Vatican lawyers have argued to the *Alperin* court that Marcinkus' narrow escape from justice is proof positive that no court, save the Pope's own rigged tribunals, may hold the Vatican Bank accountable for its actions at home or abroad.

The Hnilica prosecution offers a rare glimpse into how the IOR conducted business. Hnilica, according to the Vatican yearbook, was born in 1921 in the Archdiocese of Travni in Slovakia. Pope Paul VI appointed Hnilica titular Bishop of Rusado (an ancient city in the Roman province of Mauretania) on May 13, 1964, after he escaped from Czechoslovakia. In 1968, Hnilica founded the organization Pro Fratribus to aid the Church in Eastern Europe. Hnilica raised huge sums of money and became involved with the mobsters Lena and Carboni, as well the entire Vatican bank crowd. When an attempt was made to retrieve the suitcase of Roberto Calvi after his death, the task was delegated to Lena and Hnilica. Hnilica ended up being prosecuted by the Italian courts for money laundering but never served time in prison despite voluminous evidence of his wrongdoing.

A chart prepared by the Italian Guardia di Finanza (the police arm of the Italian Finance Ministry) reveals Hnilica and Pro Fratribus used IOR accounts, as well as accounts at the allied banks Banco Nazionale de Lavora and Banco di Napoli. The flowchart indicates Hnilica at the helm of a massive money-laundering scheme, with profits diverted to the IOR. Such wildly profitable operations were the norm during Marcinkus' reign as chief of the Vatican Bank. Credible sources indicate that the "boss" himself, Paul VI, made many major decisions at the IOR.

> MARCINKUS' DISDAIN FOR CIVIL AUTHORITIES WAS LEGENDARY, AND HE WAS ONCE QUOTED AS SAYING, "YOU CAN'T RUN THE CHURCH ON HAIL MARYS."

Marcinkus later became John Paul II's chief of security after the untimely death of John Paul I. Investigative author David Yallop has made a compelling argument that John Paul I was poisoned due in part to his commitment to closing or cleaning up the Vatican Bank.[31] The avid golfer Marcinkus is now retired to the Scottsdale, Arizona, area and has taken his secrets with him. Hnilica continues as a Vatican operative, pushing his new venture—touting the unapproved Marian shrine at Medjugorje, Bosnia, and a creation of his own called The Lady of All Nations.[32] Hnilica remains a Vatican money-man and does not shy away from asking for substantial donations from rich Catholics. Those who refuse, like Phillip Kronzer,[33] a wealthy Silicon Valley businessman, find themselves separated from their wealth in other ways. Kronzer's wife divorced him after she fell under Hnilica's sway; Kronzer's substantial California real estate holdings and investments were divided by court order and found their way into the coffers of Pro Fratribus' IOR account. Not to be outdone, Kronzer says that he showed up at Hnilica's opulent Rome apartment with a camera crew in tow; Hnilica, however, refused to grant admittance.

■ ■ ■ ■ ■ ■ ■ ■ ■ ■

Angelo Caloia, the present Vatican Bank chief, has unsuccessfully tried to clean up the IOR's scruffy image by stressing prudence and service to the Church. The IOR runs the ATM machines at the Vatican and maintains accounts for priests and religious organizations, but even these modest efforts have been abused. In 1993, the IOR admitted past involvement in filtering bribes to Italian politicians. More recently, as documented in a major investigative piece by *Fortune* magazine,[34] Martin Frankel, an American con artist, used IOR accounts to make disappear hundreds of millions of dollars looted from insurance funds. Frankel is now sitting in a Connecticut jail awaiting trial, but the cash that went to the IOR has become untraceable. This is due in part to banking secrecy but even more so to the complete lack of knowledge by law enforcement of the Vatican Bank and its global operations.

The IOR has denied involvement with Frankel, but Frankel's former attorney, Thomas Bolan (Roy Cohn's former law partner), used his influence with Church officials on Frankel's behalf to set up the St. Francis Foundation, through which up to $1.98 billion may have been laundered. Bolan, as well as his connections in the clergy, claims to have been duped by Frankel, but Bolan was once the counsel for Michele Sindona. Mere coincidence, perhaps? Investigative reporter Guyatt thinks not, and in his court declaration he implicates leading members of the Vatican Supreme Court and Secretariat in the opening of the IOR account for Frankel's operations. The arrest in September 2001 of Vatican legal advisor Monsignor Colagiovanni in Cleveland confirms Guyatt's suspicions of Frankel being part of a major Vatican Bank scandal:

Colagiovanni, who is president of the Monitor Ecclesiasticus Foundation, which publishes a journal of Roman Catholic canon law, is accused of scheming to defraud Capitol Life Insurance Co., Western United Life Insurance Co. and the Thunor Trust insurance companies and their policy holders. If convicted, he faces up to five years in prison for wire fraud and up to 20 years for conspiracy to launder money.[35]

As the Frankel case promises to go even higher in the Vatican hierarchy and banking structure, one would not be surprised to learn any day of Frankel's untimely death, joining the ranks of Calvi and Sindona, who also dared to harness the IOR for their own purposes.

Other fresh stories involve a Mafia plot, apparently foiled, to use the Internet and the IOR to embezzle funds[36] and the impending trial of the Archbishop of Naples on tax fraud and money-laundering charges involving his position as legal advisor to the Vatican Bank.[37]

■ ■ ■ ■ ■ ■ ■ ■ ■ ■

There is a method behind the IOR's madness. Banking and intelligence experts agree that one of the best ways to launder money is to emulate the Roman Catholic Church. The Vatican Bank from its inception has maintained gold accounts with the Federal Reserve and has correspondent banking relations with most of the world's major banks. Correspondent banking relationships enable relatively small banks to work through much larger, prestigious ones without maintaining a physical presence. The IOR, which claims to conduct no business in the United States, is thought to work through such banking giants as Republic Bank of New York, Bank of America, and J.P. Morgan Chase. Since correspondent accounts do not usually subject a bank to the host country's judicial jurisdiction, the IOR functions in the US with relative immunity from prosecution, doubly protected by its claim to sovereign immunity as part of the Holy See.

Few banking experts know much about the IOR, and those who do are often involved in black gold transaction and loathe talking. Thus the Vatican Bank, while oft mentioned in connection with scams and frauds, has yet to be held fully accountable due to the paucity of knowledge about its inner workings and its claims to sovereign immunity.

IN 1993, THE IOR ADMITTED PAST INVOLVEMENT IN FILTERING BRIBES TO ITALIAN POLITICIANS.

To sum up, the IOR is the Pope's bank, but it is also the bank of the Mafia, Masons, and Nazis. Since IOR transactions are far from transparent, we have only the holy word of its president and board as to its dealings. Paradoxically, the Pope owns the Vatican Bank, but when John Paul I tried to intervene in his own bank's affairs, he turned up dead. And while the Vatican Bank claims to have cleaned up its act, it pointedly refuses to address the more than 50-year-old issue of Nazi gold laundering. As John Paul II apologizes to Jews, Orthodox Christians, Ukrainians, and descendants of African slaves for past wrongs, his lawyers are busy defending the Vatican Bank in a US federal court in order to prevent recovery of Nazi gold or even the start of the process to officially determine if it exists. Nonetheless, as the IOR enters the twenty-first century, it continues to be haunted by ghosts from its past: Calvi, Nazis, and its reputation as a haven for swindlers' money. While the European Union and the United States pressure small offshore islands to clean up their banking acts, the Vatican Bank remains aloof. Dirty banking practices are one vice the Popes apparently will never abandon; it pays too damn well.

Endnotes

1. Matthew 21:12, King James Version **2.** Reese, Thomas J. *Inside the Vatican.* Cambridge, MA: Harvard University Press, 1996: 205. **3.** In 1929, the Lateran Treaty was signed between Benito Mussolini and Pietro Cardinale Gasparri, creating Vatican City as compensation for the loss of the Papal States to Italy in 1870. Fascist Italy agreed in the Financial Convention to provide the Holy See with a payment of approximately $40 million in cash and $60 million in bonds. This was the likely source of the initial funding of the IOR. **4.** The Vatican Bank chirographs are versions of handwritten instructions by the Pope. **5.** The Holy See is the government of both Vatican City State (the microstate composed of the Vatican grounds) and the Roman Catholic Church. By means of the former, the Holy See has obtained diplomatic recognition from most countries and by the latter wields power and influence over close to a billion Catholics worldwide, *far* beyond that of a typical microstate. **6.** The Vatican Bank's official position is that it is an agency of the Holy See that does business in the manner of the US Department of Agriculture, *but an absolute monarch never owned the Agriculture Department.* **7.** Peter's Pence is the money sent to Rome by local dioceses from church collections. During WWII there was no way to transfer these funds to the Vatican, which was surrounded by Fascist Italy. Indeed, US authorities suggested the Pope abandon Rome and go into exile. **8.** Franzo Grande Stevens is a senior Italian attorney with ties to Italy's largest banks and industrialists. **9.** Submitted under penalty of perjury by Stevens to Judge Maxine Chesney in the court case *Alperin v. Vatican Bank.* Stevens declared that literally *all* documents, not just some, were destroyed at ten-year intervals. This seemingly implausible statement is at odds with all established banking procedures; however, the IOR is far from a standard bank. Former Vatican Bank official Phillippe De Weck made a similar claim in a 1997 interview, using the ten-year figure, too. **10.** Nazi SS gold was from the Melmer account. This was victim gold from concentration camps, including eyeglasses, teeth, and wedding rings resmelted into bars bearing the German swastika. There is little doubt that the IOR knew about the origins of Nazi gold, the Vatican having agents throughout the Axis nations. They simply didn't care, as the Vatican, like Switzerland, was officially neutral and had no qualms about doing business with Hitler's Germany. Unlike the Vatican, Switzerland has admitted its wrongdoing in part and has paid over $1 billion in compensation to Nazi victims for its role in the Holocaust. **11.** "Pope to Pray at Nazi Gold Bank." *Irish Independent*

6 April 2000. **12.** While Freemasonry and Catholicism would at first glance appear to be incompatible, a curious overlap exists among certain high-ranking Church officials and European financiers, particularly in Italy, Spain, France, and Portugal. The connection of Italy's elite P2 Masonic lodge and the Vatican Bank is well documented. High-ranking cardinals have been Masons with Papal consent, including the famous French Cardinal Tisserant, who was a member of the Grand Orient Lodge after World War II (according to declassified Army files obtained under the Freedom of Information Act). Others—such as former Vatican Finance Minister Cardinal Castillo Lara—quoted in *Inside the Vatican* blame the "Masonic influence" for unjustly attacking the IOR. As for the Masons themselves, the official position is that P2 is a banned lodge, operating as a rogue secret society controlled from within the Vatican (Robinson, John J. *Born in Blood: The Lost Secrets of Freemasonry.* New York: M. Evans & Company, 1989). **13.** Although approximately 500,000 Serbs were murdered by the Ustashe bands and in Croatian-run concentration camps, Jewish organizations refuse to recognize this as part of the Holocaust. Curiously, several of the top Ustashe—including their leader, Pavelic, the original "butcher of the Balkans"—were of partial Jewish extraction or had Jewish spouses. However, this did not spare Jews or necessarily all relatives of Ustashe leadership from the concentration camps. **14.** The Vatican "ratline" escape route was financed by the Ustashe and was used by thousands of Germans, Croatians, and Balkan Nazis. The ratline was headquartered at San Girolamo Monastery in Rome and was directed by the Ustashe priest and Vatican agent Krunoslav Draganovic. (Draganovic, who was also employed by the CIA and US Army, had a reputation for being parsimonious. He wore old, frayed clothing and once boasted of dining on a single boiled egg for his usual dinner.) Draganovic was wanted for war crimes involving the ethnic cleansing of Serbs in Yugoslavia during WWII. The priest was a paid agent of United States intelligence as confirmed by the release of over 300 pages of declassified documents in the case *Levy v. CIA.* (See also Sloat, Bill. "Cold War Spy Was Nazi Henchman." *Cleveland Plain Dealer* 12 Aug 2001.) **15.** *Alperin v. Vatican Bank* class action filed in the United States District Court for the Northern District of California in November 1999. Plaintiffs include Serbs, Ukrainians, and Jews. The Vatican Bank, Swiss National Bank, Franciscan order, and Croatian Liberation Movement are the defendants. As a collateral result of this lawsuit, thousands of pages of US government documents have been declassified. **16.** The Ustashe were also ferocious anticommunists. British and American intelligence later made use of this during the Cold War, conveniently overlooking the fact that the Ustashe were war criminals, thugs, and murderers. **17.** Loftus, along with Mark Aarons, is author of *Unholy Trinity* (St. Martin's Press, 1991) and *The Secret War Against the Jews* (St. Martin's Press, 1994), and by himself, *The Belarus Secret* (Knopf, 1982). Loftus has spent over fifteen years researching the Vatican's role in World War II and is plaintiffs' expert witness in the lawsuit against the Vatican Bank. **18.** The Vatican Secretariat is headed by Cardinal Sodano, who has vehemently opposed release of Vatican archives from World War II. **19.** Of course, the Nazis themselves did not run the Vatican, and the ratlines may have been set up partly for financial rather than purely ideological reasons. **20.** Marcinkus is an American and hails from Al Capone's hometown, Cicero, Illinois. **21.** Hnilica is of Czech extraction and is a titular bishop without a diocese. His former organization Pro Fratribus has been used by Western intelligence agencies to move funds to Eastern Europe in the 1980s and, more recently, to promote apparitions of the Virgin Mary at Medjugorje, Bosnia. The main interest of Hnilica being money, moving funds to anticommunists in the 1980s pales in comparison to the annual multimillion-dollar gross from Western pilgrims at Medjugorje. He is also involved with The Family of the Mother Co-Redemptrix, whose members are young female and male missionaries who live in celibacy, and The Lady of All Nations cult based in Amsterdam. **22.** Gelli is head of a secret Masonic lodge in Italy called P2, or Propaganda 2, which has since been declared illegal because of its apparent widespread corrupt influence in Italian political and financial circuits. Gelli had strong links to Peronists in Argentina. **23.** President of Banco Ambrosiano, Calvi was the victim of an alleged Mafia hit in London. He partnered with the IOR but overextended his worldwide financial empire and became himself a victim of others' machinations. **24.** An international lawyer and banker, once one of the world's wealthiest men, Sindona was also a verified mobster. He looted the Franklin Savings and Loan, the biggest bank failure in the US at the time. Sindona's declassified FBI files discuss his connections with "corrupt Vatican officials" and numerous other illegal exploits. **25.** Up to 1982, Banco Ambrosiano was one of the largest and most influential banking institutions in Italy. In addition to its central offices in Milan, it had more than 100 branches throughout Italy and employed more than 4,000 persons. It was furthermore the head of a large group of companies—financial and otherwise—known, though not formally incorporated, as the Banco Ambrosiano Group. Offshore Ambrosiano companies were based in Nassau, Bahamas, Lima, Peru, and Luxembourg. **26.** *Banco Ambrosiano v. Ansbacher,* Irish Supreme Court, 1987. **27.** Declaration of David Guyatt in Support of Jurisdictional Discovery, December 5, 2000, *Alperin v. Vatican Bank.* **28.** For more on Opus Dei, see Hutchison, Robert. *Their Kingdom Come: Inside the Secret World of Opus Dei.* New York: St. Martin's Press, 1999. **29.** Follain, John. "Scientists Believe Roberto Calvi Was Murdered." *The Sunday Times* (London) 10 Dec 2000 **30.** A member of the Roman Catholic Society of Mary of Paris. **31.** Yallop, David. *In God's Name: An Investigation into the Murder of John Paul I.* New York: Bantam Books, 1984. **32.** Hnilica was previously associated with a Colorado visionary, Theresa Lopez, who had a history of bad check convictions in the US, and with former cultist Denis Nolan, now running Indiana-based Children of Medjugorje, which has been accused of selling phony Papal indulgences via the Internet. **33.** Phillip Kronzer is the most vocal opponent of Medjugorje within the Catholic Church and heads the Kronzer Foundation for Religious Research <www.kronzer.org>. **34.** Behar, Richard. "Washing Money in the Holy See." *Fortune* 16 Aug 1999 **35.** "Monsignor Arrested for Abetting Frankel." *The Review Appeal & Brentwood Journal* 1 Sept 2001. **36.** "Vatican Bank Involved in Mafia's On Line Money Washing." Xinhua (Chinese newswire) 3 Oct 2000. **37.** Phillips, John. "Archbishop Faces Trial for Fraud." *The Times* (London) 17 July 2001.

THE ANTITRUST AND MONOPOLY MYTH

DOMINICK T. ARMENTANO

Antitrust regulation is so righteously correct in the public conscious-ness (and at all fashionable law schools) that to question seriously its intent and performance amounts to near religious blasphemy. Antitrust has its own sacred texts (the laws and the many bewilder-ing court decisions), its own set of high priests (lawyers and judges and economists) who alone can fathom textual meanings, its own tortured theories of sinful behavior (price fixing, predatory pricing, price discrimination, tying agreements), and its own notions of redemption, retribution, and salvation (various fines, jail sentences, and even corporate divestiture if your sins have been mortal). Like all religions, antitrust is energized by a core belief that is faithfully accepted by the congregation: Satanic monopolists will plunder innocent consumers absent antitrust protection. Justice Department, save us, please save us!

Likewise, hard facts that might contradict the conventional antitrust wisdom are conveniently ignored, while serious critics are ridiculed as mean-spirited or incompetent. Every regulatory failure is written off as some one-time judgmental error never to be repeated. Never mind that the theories behind antitrust enforcement are not compelling. Never mind that the empirical evidence taken from the leading antitrust cases cannot support the case for "vigorous enforcement" of the laws; indeed, it explicitly contradicts it. And never mind that many of the cases are propelled forward by politically ambitious attorneys general at the state and federal level and that most antitrust litiga-tion (more than 90 percent) is initiated by the disgruntled business rivals of some would-be defendant. All of this is high heresy as far as the antitrust establishment is concerned, and heretics must be excommunicated and muzzled.

Well not here, at least.

_FREE MARKET MONOPOLY

One of the biggest raps against capitalism (at least since Karl Marx) is that competitive "free markets" will tend inevitably toward monop-oly with shoddy products, restricted outputs, and high prices. But this core belief about inevitable monopoly is logically flawed and lacks empirical support (as we shall see in our review of classic antitrust cases, below). While it's true that in a free market any firm could *attempt* to monopolize some raw material, product, or service, it is likewise true that any such attempt could also be prohibitively expensive (costly mergers, buying up available supplies of raw materials, etc.) and, therefore, uncertain and unprofitable.

More important, it is also true that any other entrepreneur would be perfectly free to compete with any would-be monopolist—free to innovate, free to improve product, free to increase output and lower prices—and that consumers would also be free to take advantage of this competition. Thus, any firm that attempted to monopolize and restrict output and raise prices would lose sales and profits to any other business organization that found it profitable to cater to con-sumers and compete. Any monopoly that attempted to "restrain trade" would create profitable opportunities for competitors and potential competitors, and these profitable opportunities would exist as long as markets were *legally* open to new suppliers and con-sumers *legally* free to support alternative suppliers.

> MOST ANTITRUST LITIGATION (MORE THAN 90 PERCENT) IS INITIATED BY THE DISGRUNTLED BUSINESS RIVALS OF SOME WOULD-BE DEFENDANT.

A free-market monopoly is not impossible. If a firm were substan-tially more efficient than all of its competitors and potential competi-tors—that is, if it were able to produce at the lowest cost and charge the lowest price to consumers—it could become (temporarily, per-haps) the only supplier in some market. (Efficiency is a central eco-nomic concern. Scarce labor, capital, natural resources, and time should be used economically so that economic welfare is maxi-mized.) Alternatively, consumers could "monopolize" all of their choices for a specific product on only one company, making that company a "monopoly."

But what's wrong with any of this? Clearly this is *not* the devilish monopoly "problem" envisioned by critics of free markets, since low costs, expanded outputs, lower prices, and free consumer choice are the beneficial fruits of an open market process, and they clearly enhance, not harm, consumer welfare. So a free market monopoly is theoretically possible but not necessarily harmful. (If buyers want to support less efficient suppliers just to have alternative sources of supply, they are perfectly free to do that, too.)

_CARTELS AND PREDATORY PRACTICES

But what about business cartels and so-called predatory practices? Can't competitors get together and restrict production and fix higher prices? Or, alternatively, can't a dominant firm drive its rivals from the market by slashing prices and then raise them when all of the competitors disappear?

Free market cartels are possible, but they would be inherently unstable for all of the reasons reviewed above concerning free market monopoly.[1] Indeed, they would be *more* unstable, since cartels, unlike a one-firm monopoly, would require inter-firm cooperation and coordination in order to achieve their objectives. How is market output for each cartel member to be reduced? How are the reductions to be monitored? Won't the firms attempt to "cheat," and won't the cheating lead to larger outputs and lower prices? Won't the higher cartel prices encourage new supply from outside the cartel, and won't that lead to lower prices? Free market cartels (absent governmental support) have been notoriously short-lived and unsuccessful. Moreover, the government prosecution of price-fixing under the antitrust laws does *not* demonstrate that voluntary cartels can fix prices above competitive levels.[2]

"Predatory practices" are another monopoly chimera. It is usually not rational for a dominant firm to attempt to eliminate all of its competition through severe price-cutting, since this "war" is inherently expensive and uncertain, especially if the market is easily open to new supply.[3] Even if a dominant firm were to succeed temporarily, competition would likely return if prices were increased above competitive levels. Where, then, are the victory profits from the "war"?

But what is all of this concern about lower prices to consumers? Lower prices, for whatever reason and for whatever length of time, are extremely pro-consumer; the jungle-like metaphor ("predatory") employed by critics is completely inappropriate. (Would critics rather have dominant firms fix prices and not ever reduce them, or not respond to lower costs or the lower prices of rivals?) Consumers, of course, can always decide whether they prefer the lower prices of the dominant firm or not. If they prefer them, they buy more from the dominant firm; if they don't, then they continue to support the rivals of the dominant firm. Either way, there is nothing whatever to be regretted about lower prices either initiated by (or matched by or undercut by) dominant firms. To attempt to restrict price competition by law would be anti-consumer in the extreme.[4]

_GOVERNMENT AND MONOPOLY POWER

If we drop the strict free-market assumption, however, a monopoly problem is fairly easy to visualize. For example, government could license only one supplier (i.e., a taxi cab company) in some city market and restrict entry to all other suppliers; the market would then be monopolized by law. Or government could establish legal monopoly in telecommunications, electricity generation, telephone service, first-class mail delivery, and in many other areas; indeed, government in the US *has* historically done precisely this.[5] Clearly this is a monopoly problem since consumers, regardless of their preferences, would then be legally tied to only one supplier. In addition, would-be entrepreneurs with new products or services would be legally prohibited from offering those products to willing buyers. And with competition prohibited, the monopoly supplier would have few (if any) incentives to innovate, to expand output, and to lower prices. But this monopoly problem ought *not* to be associated with "free markets" since its explicit source is the power of government to exclude competitors. Removing all legal barriers to entry and competition (deregulation, correctly understood) would end this monopoly problem.

Ironically, perhaps, state regulation and monopoly licensing has a general immunity from antitrust law.[6] Yet the real monopoly problem in the economy has always been government regulations that restrict entry and competition and that serve to raise prices to consumers. The milk cartel in several Northeastern states is a government-run monopoly that restricts production by law and keeps milk prices high for producers. The government Post Office has a first-class mail monopoly because postal statutes and various court decisions have legally prevented private rivals from delivering first-class mail along the "post" roads and into private postal mailboxes. Government tariffs and quotas on imported goods force domestic consumers to pay high prices for hundreds of protected foodstuffs and products. Historically, state governments protected local telephone companies from competition for decades while the Federal Communications Commission (FCC) prevented competition with AT&T's long-distance monopoly service. Deregulating telecommunications in the early 1970s, not "breaking up" the AT&T holding company, restored some semblance of competition and choice for consumers in this industry.[7] Thus, most of the pernicious monopoly in the system is State-created and generally immune from antitrust.

_THE ANTITRUST MYTH

The oldest and most important antitrust law, the Sherman Antitrust Act (1890), prohibits "every contract or combination in restraint of trade" and prohibits any person who "monopolizes" or "attempts to monopolize" trade or commerce within the US. Interestingly,

THUS, MOST OF THE PERNICIOUS MONOPOLY IN THE SYSTEM IS STATE-CREATED AND GENERALLY IMMUNE FROM ANTITRUST.

"monopoly" is not mentioned in the language of the law and, accordingly, is not illegal *per se*. What is illegal is behavior associated with "monopolization," and this can include price-fixing, price discrimination, tying agreements, and so-called predatory practices, such as charging prices below "costs" to eliminate competitors. But "monopoly" itself is not illegal under the Sherman Act since it is always possible (as noted above) that one efficient firm, absent any of these practices, could come to supply all of one market.

As an example, assume that three firms, A, B, and C, are competing in an open market. Firms B and C go out of business because their customers shun their products or because they are simply less efficient than firm A. The result is that A is alone in the market (perhaps temporarily) and supplies all of the product. In congressional debate about the meaning of the Sherman Act, it was argued that just such a situation as described ought not to be illegal. It should not be the purpose of antitrust law (to paraphrase Judge Caffey in the *Alcoa* case[8]) to seek to punish firm A for what firms B and C did, or failed to do, or for what their customers freely chose to do. That, he said, would be both bad economics and bad law.

Efficient firms can be hampered by antitrust regulation (as we will argue below), and their lost output and lost innovations are a cost that lowers societal welfare and makes everyone poorer. In addition, antitrust laws serve to "protect" inefficient business organizations with high cost structures. Most antitrust cases are filed by the business community, one firm suing another, usually over lower (not higher) prices or some innovation that threatens to reallocate substantial sales and profits from the plaintiff to the defendant. (This should dispel the wrongheaded notion that the business community generally supports free enterprise. Never has, never will. They support private enterprise—big difference.) Antitrust regulation is fundamentally "protectionist" of special business interests in exactly the same way as import tariffs (on foodstuffs and steel, for example) are protectionist of domestic suppliers and harmful to consumers.

ANTITRUST LAWS SERVE TO "PROTECT" INEFFICIENT BUSINESS ORGANIZATIONS WITH HIGH COST STRUCTURES.

To see how this works consider the following scenario: Firm A innovates a new product (or lowers the price of an old product), and this is warmly received by consumers; however, the shifting of consumer demand to product A inevitably hurts A's competitors, B and C. Firm A does more business because its product is now more desirable, and Firms B and C do less business because consumers at the margin buy more from Firm A and less from Firms B and C. The government, or Firm B or C, then brings an antitrust suit against Firm A claiming that A is engaging in predatory behavior and attempting to monopolize the market. The antitrust suit, or even the threat of it, now acts as a tariff or tax on efficiency and on overall consumer welfare.

Antitrust scholar Robert Bork has maintained that the laws were passed to maximize consumer welfare but this "immaculate conception" theory of the origin of antitrust law is not persuasive.[9] Legislators may well have talked about the interests of consumers, but there are solid reasons to believe that this would not have been their actual motivation. The most important reason for this skepticism is so-called "public choice theory" and the inherent nature of the legislative process itself.[10] Public choice theory holds that the benefits of legislation are usually concentrated on various special interest groups that, accordingly, have the most to gain in lobbying for and in achieving legislative success. On the other hand, the costs of legislation are usually spread thinly over the mass of consumers or taxpayers, creating incentives for them to remain "rationally ignorant" of the outcome of any legislative process.

This cost-benefit calculus ensures that public policy is rarely, if ever, designed to help consumers but is, instead, intended to provide benefits for special interests at the expense of consumers (or taxpayers). Since consumers were and remain a diverse, unorganized group, it is unlikely in the extreme that they (or their interests) played any role whatever in the passage of any antitrust legislation.

Who did? Most state antitrust laws were passed in the latter part of the nineteenth century at the insistence of small businesses and agricultural interests that faced increasing competition in their markets from larger rivals employing new organizational structures and more efficient transportation (railroads). Prices for most commodities and services were decreasing in the post-Civil war period, and frustrated local suppliers attempted to use the state legislative process to regulate their increasingly efficient competitors.[11] Of course, they could not call these rival suppliers "increasingly efficient competitors" because that would have given away the game. Instead, the talk was of preventing "ruinous" competition and saving small business and the American way of life.

The new forms of industrial organization (corporations, holding companies, and so-called "trusts") were all denounced in the most strident terms, even though as later antitrust cases would demonstrate, they were generally lowering prices in the marketplace. That small business interests lobbied for antitrust protectionism and for laws restricting the charging of lower prices is beyond historical dispute (see, especially, the Clayton Act of 1914 and the Robinson-Patman Act of 1936).

_THE MONOPOLY MYTH

If firms in free markets are really able to monopolize in restraint of trade, the empirical proof should reside in the many classic antitrust cases brought over the last 100 years. Yet an examination of those cases reveals that the firms indicted and (mostly) convicted were generally innovating new products or increasing market outputs and lowering market prices.[12] To attack firms that innovate or that lower prices to consumers is blatantly and explicitly anti-consumer, regardless of the rhetorical spin employed to rationalize such attacks. Let's summarize a few of the major cases below with the following disclaimer: There are many dozens of similar cases in the long, sad history of antitrust enforcement.

One of the most famous (and misunderstood) antitrust cases in history is *US v. Standard Oil of New Jersey* (1911).[13] The popular explanation of this case goes something like this: Standard Oil monopolized the oil industry, destroyed rivals through the use of predatory price-cutting, raised prices to consumers, and was punished by the Supreme Court for these proven transgressions. Nice story, but totally false. First, Standard never even monopolized petroleum refining, let alone the entire oil industry (production, transportation, refining, distribution), which would have been an impossibility. Even in domestic refining, Standard's share of the market *declined* for decades prior to the antitrust case (64 percent in 1907), and there were at least 137 competitors (firms like Shell, Gulf, Texaco) in oil refining in 1911.

> MOST STATE ANTITRUST LAWS WERE PASSED IN THE LATTER PART OF THE NINETEENTH CENTURY AT THE INSISTENCE OF SMALL BUSINESSES AND AGRICULTURAL INTERESTS THAT FACED INCREASING COMPETITION IN THEIR MARKETS.

Second, although predatory practices were alleged by the government at trial, Standard offered rebuttal on all counts. Neither the trial court nor the Supreme Court ever made any specific finding of guilt on the conflicting charges of predatory practices.

Third, petroleum market outputs *increased* and prices *declined* for decades during the alleged period of "monopolization" by Standard Oil. For example, prices for kerosene (the industry's major product) were 30 cents a gallon in 1869 and fell to about 6 cents a gallon at the time of the antitrust trial.

Finally, the Supreme Court broke up the Standard Oil holding company not because of any demonstrable harm to consumers (there was none) but because it discerned some vague "intent" to monopolize through Standard's many mergers, an "intent" that just as clearly never succeeded in producing any monopoly. Yet generations of economic and legal commentators have been misled about monopoly and the alleged efficacy of antitrust policy because of the "facts everybody knows" concerning the Standard Oil antitrust case.

The antitrust case against the American Tobacco Company (*US v. American Tobacco*, 1911[14]) is similar in many respects to *Standard Oil*. American Tobacco put together a large, diversified tobacco company through mergers with smaller specialty companies. Yet they were never able to monopolize the tobacco industry as the government alleged, nor were they able to raise prices of tobacco products. Outputs increased and prices fell for decades prior to the antitrust suit. Thousands of cigarette, smoking tobacco, snuff, and cigar com-

panies competed against the American companies, and ease of entry and availability of raw materials (leaf tobacco obtained at auction) made vigorous competition inevitable. The American Tobacco holding company was broken up by the Supreme Court because of some vague intent to monopolize (again, as evidenced through mergers), but, like Standard Oil, there was a total absence of demonstrable (economic) injury to consumers of tobacco products.

US v. Aluminum Company of America (1945)[15] is one of the most egregious anti-consumer antitrust cases on record. Modern trustbusters are forever offering apologies for *Alcoa*. And with good reason. The government pursued Alcoa in court for thirteen years (between 1937 and 1950). Yet after a long and laborious trial that ended in 1939, Judge Caffey dismissed almost 150 separate government charges against Alcoa, including allegations that they monopolized water-power sites (for producing electricity) and monopolized the raw material bauxite, from which aluminum ingot is made.[16] Caffey also determined that Alcoa innovated rapidly, expanded aluminum refining capacity and outputs continuously, and had lowered aluminum ingot prices for 50 years, while taking a very modest return on its investment.

Yet an appellate court in 1945 (acting in lieu of the Supreme Court) decided that expanding outputs and lowering prices illegally *excluded* rivals from the opportunity to compete(!) and thereby violated antitrust law. (Translation: If Alcoa had been less efficient in serving its customers, there would have been more "competition" (read: competitors), less exclusion, and no antitrust violation.) The *Alcoa* appellate decision confirmed that antitrust was charging full-speed in the totally wrong direction (i.e., that efficiency was illegally exclusionary and ultimately a violation of law).

This trend was confirmed in *US v. American Can* (1949)[17] and in *US v. United Shoe Machinery Corporation* (1953).[18] In *American Can*, the trial judge determined that American Can held its dominant market position because it "coerced" its customers into signing long-term leases. How, in a free market, did it do that? Why, by offering its customers attractive terms, such as generous price discounts for large orders of cans. Well, we can't have that! As a part of his final decision in the case, the judge ordered American Can to *raise prices* to its can customers so that there could be more competition with less efficient can producers and can-closing machinery makers. Thus, consumers of cans ultimately paid for this contrived increase in "competition"

In *United Shoe*, United had manufactured shoe machinery and leased its many machines to hundreds of domestic and international shoe makers. Its market share was always high (85 percent) because (as the trial court found) its machines were technologically superior to those of competitors, its leasing rates were reasonable, and it repaired machines promptly and at no extra charge to the customer. As a consequence of this superior economic performance, customers were extremely loyal and tended to renew leases when old ones expired; less efficient rivals had great difficulty convincing shoe companies to switch their business since the shoe companies were generally satisfied with United's terms. (Several shoe makers testified for the defendant United Shoe at the trial).

Yet the trial judge spied the evil illegality inherent in superior economic performance provided over many decades: Smaller rivals were thereby *excluded* from competing, and this fact violated the antitrust laws! The judge then saddled United with regulations that, he reasoned, would destroy its unique economic advantages and put it back in the same (less efficient) class as its competitors. But when the regulations failed to really hamper United Shoe's efficiency, the Department of Justice appealed the lower court decision to the US Supreme Court, which divested (and eventually wrecked) the company in 1968.[19] Thank you, antitrust.

The perverse theory being actualized in all of these cases is the notion that free consumer choice and business "efficiency" somehow restrain trade and violate the law, the exact opposite of the truth. Efficient firms such as Alcoa and United Shoe innovated new products and production techniques and lowered prices; they always did *more* business (while less efficient rivals did less) in order to keep and even expand their dominant market position. But this is precisely how free markets are supposed to work, such that scare resources tend to maximize consumer value. Yet consistently throughout business history, antitrust regulation has been employed as a legal weapon to bludgeon aggressively competitive firms that innovate and lower costs and prices.

Despite any so-called reforms, this pernicious trend in antitrust regulation has continued to the present. The best and most recent example is, of course, *US v. Microsoft*.[20] The heart of the antitrust case brought by the Department of Justice and nineteen state attorneys general in 1998 was that Microsoft's decision to integrate its Web browser, Explorer, into its Windows 98 operating software system illegally excluded competitive browsers, such as rival Netscape's Navigator, and evidenced an intent to "monopolize" in violation of the Sherman Act. Since Microsoft already held a "monopoly" in operating systems and employed its monopoly power to exclude competitors unfairly, trial court judge Thomas Penfield Jackson, having agreed with the bulk of the government's argument, found them guilty of illegal monopolization and ordered the firm regulated and divested.[21] Important parts of this decision, in particular the divestiture order, were overturned on appeal.[22]

The government charges were always baseless. The plaintiffs first argued that Microsoft held a "monopoly" in operating systems (a near 90 percent market share) and that they had leveraged that market power into the browser market to crush Netscape. But the government's market share numbers are grossly inaccurate.[23] To arrive at a so-called monopoly market share, the trial court accepted a definition of the relevant market ("single-user desktop PCs that use an Intel-compatible chip") that conveniently excluded all of the computers and networking software made by Microsoft's major rivals such as Apple, Sun, Novell, and a host of other companies.

In addition, counting only licensed systems allowed Judge Jackson to exclude arbitrarily all of the operating systems sold at retail, those downloaded from the Web, and all "naked" computers shipped without any operating system installed at all. These factual errors narrowed severely the actual competitive market and simply turned Microsoft into the "monopolist" the government required for its antitrust violation. If market share is meaningful at all in antitrust analysis (doubtful), Microsoft's actual share of any realistic market was less than 70 percent and not enough for any monopoly designation.

But if Microsoft had no actual monopoly, then its battle with Netscape over the browser market takes on a totally different perspective. When Microsoft first integrated its browser into its operating system software, it was Netscape that held the bulk of the browser sales. Netscape held the "dominant" market position in browsers, and it was Microsoft that was attempting to better compete by improving the terms of exchange for PC consumers. Microsoft proceeded to fully integrate its browser and reduce its price to zero, and consumers responded favorably; Microsoft's browser did more business and Netscape's browser did less.

Nor was the Netscape browser ever unfairly "foreclosed" or "excluded" from the market; PC users downloaded *millions* of copies of Netscape's browser during the period of alleged exclusion by Microsoft.[24] Thus, as usual, the government's entire case was an attempt to regulate innovation and consumer choice at the behest of ambitious attorneys and disgruntled competitors.

THE JUDGE ORDERED AMERICAN CAN TO RAISE PRICES TO ITS CAN CUSTOMERS SO THAT THERE COULD BE MORE COMPETITION WITH LESS EFFICIENT CAN PRODUCERS AND CAN-CLOSING MACHINERY MAKERS.

_CONCLUSIONS

Antitrust regulation is both a myth and a hoax. The laws were never intended to help consumers, and their long historical track record shows that, indeed, they have not helped consumers. They have, instead, punished innovative and efficient business organizations while protecting their less efficient competitors and every State-sanctioned monopoly.[25] They have tended to make consumers poorer and the overall economy less efficient, and they should all be repealed.[26] That the antitrust paradigm still can find support among a majority of economists, lawyers, and the public is a testament to intellectual laziness, to the power of special interest, and to decades of successful public myth-making.

Endnotes

1. On the inherent instability of collusion and cartels, see Stigler, George J. "A Theory of Oligopoly." *Journal of Political Economy* 72.11 (Feb 1964): 44-61. **2.** Asch, Peter and Joseph J. Seneca. "Is Collusion Profitable?" *Review of Economics and Statistics* 58 (Feb 1976): 1-12. On the failure of cartels to sustain "monopoly" prices, see Armentano, Dominick T. *Antitrust and Monopoly: Anatomy of Policy Failure.* Independent Institute, 1998, chapter 5. **3.** The classic article here is McGee, John S. "Predatory Price Cutting: The Standard Oil of New Jersey Case." *Journal of Law and Economics* 1 (Oct 1958): 137-69. See also Armentano, Dominick T. "Antitrust Reform: Predatory Practices and the Competitive Process." *Review of Austrian Economics* 3 (1989): 61-74. **4.** Yet this is precisely what the Robinson-Patman Act (1936) attempts to do. See Liebeler, Wesley J. "The Robinson-Patman Act: Let's Repeal It!" *Antitrust Law Journal* 44 (1975): 18. **5.** Brozen, Yale. "Is Government the Source of Monopoly?" *Intercollegiate Review* (Winter 1968-9): 34-54. **6.** *Parker v. Brown*, 317 U.S. 341 (1943) makes explicitly authorized state regulation, including state franchise monopoly, exempt from federal antitrust jurisdiction. But even as early as 1872 and 1873, in the *Slaughter House Cases* (83 U.S. 36), the Supreme Court upheld a Louisiana statute that had established a monopoly slaughterhouse in New Orleans. **7.** Noll, Roger and Bruce Owen. "The Anti-competitive Uses of Regulation: *United States v. AT&T*." *The Antitrust Revolution*. Eds. John Kwoka, Jr. and Lawrence White. Scott Foresman, 1990: 290-337. **8.** *United States v. Aluminum Company of America*, 44 F.Supp. at 154 **9.** Bork, Robert. *The Antitrust Paradox.* New

> AS USUAL, THE GOVERNMENT'S ENTIRE CASE WAS AN ATTEMPT TO REGULATE INNOVATION AND CONSUMER CHOICE AT THE BEHEST OF AMBITIOUS ATTORNEYS AND DISGRUNTLED COMPETITORS.

York: Basic Books, 1978. **10.** For a discussion of public choice theory and antitrust policy, see Tollison, Robert D. "Public Choice and Antitrust." *Cato Journal* 4.3 (Winter 1985): 905-16. **11.** DiLorenzo, Thomas J. "The Origins of Antitrust." *International Review of Law and Economics* 5 (1985): 73-90. See also Hazlett, Thomas. "The Legislative History of the Sherman Act Reexamined." *Economic Inquiry* 30 (1992): 263-76. **12.** Armentano, Dominick T. *Antitrust and Monopoly: Anatomy of a Policy Failure.* Independent Institute, 1998; Armentano, Dominick T. *Antitrust: The Case for Repeal.* Mises Institute, 1999. **13.** 221 U.S. 1. **14.** 221 U.S. 105. **15.** 148 F. 2d 416. **16.** 44 F Supp. 107. **17.** 87 F Supp. 18. **18.** 110 F Supp. 295. **19.** 391 U.S. 244. **20.** *United States v. Microsoft Corporation*, Civ. Action No.98-1232 (1998). **21.** *Ibid.*, Memorandum and Order, June 7, 2000. **22.** The United States Appeals Court (DC District) reversed in part and remanded in part, the trial court decision of Judge Jackson. See *Wall Street Journal* 29 June 2001: B1. **23.** Levy, Robert A. "Microsoft Redux: Anatomy of a Baseless Lawsuit." *Policy Analysis*, No. 352. Cato Institute, 30 Sept 1999: 1-21. See also Reynolds, Alan. "The Monopoly Myth." *Wall Street Journal* 9 April 1999: A12. **24.** More than 100 million copies of the Netscape browser were downloaded from the Web in 1998. Netscape was hardly "foreclosed" from any market. See *Wall Street Journal*, 6 Nov 1998: A3. **25.** Baumol, William J. and Janusz A. Ordover. "Use of Antitrust to Subvert Competition." *Journal of Law and Economics* 28 (May 1985): 247-65. **26.** One of the few courageous calls to abolish antitrust is Smith, Fred. "Why Not Abolish Antitrust?" *Regulation* (Jan/Feb 1983): 25-33. Instead of being repealed, however, antitrust regulation has been expanded to the international arena, where the European Commission has assumed jurisdiction over certain proposed mergers in the US. See *New York Times*, 19 June 2001.

DIRTY MONEY AND GLOBAL BANKING SECRECY
LUCY KOMISAR

For a long time, it's been the dirty little secret among rich people and corporations: Middle-class people pay taxes. The rich have secret offshore bank accounts.

In about 60 countries, known as offshore or tax havens, people and businesses can set up companies and open accounts without real names or identification. They often use phony banks which are really just letter-drops that funnel money to real banks through "correspondent accounts." The "shell banks" commonly bundle all the transfers and don't say who they're coming from. Real banks in the US routinely ask no questions when the money passes through.

For example, the Al-Shamal Islamic Bank, set up by Osama bin Laden in Khartoum, Sudan, had correspondent accounts at Citibank, Chase Manhattan, and American Express Bank.

At the February 2001 trial of men charged in the 1998 bombings of the US embassies in Kenya and Tanzania, Jamal Ahmed al-Fadl, who had handled financial transactions for bin Laden's al Qaeda, testified that al Qaeda had used a half-dozen accounts at the Shamal Bank. Essam al Ridi, who worked for bin Laden, testified that the Shamal Bank sent a $250,000 wire transfer to his bank in Texas, and he used the money to buy a plane for bin Laden. The transfer was sent through Shamal's correspondent account at American Express.

Citibank lobbied mightily but failed to derail legislation passed after September 11, 2001, to bar such shell banks from having correspondent accounts that let them move money into the US banking system.

But terrorists, drug traffickers, and other crooks can still go through "legitimate" banks in Liechtenstein or the Isle of Man or some other offshore haven. September 11 hijacker Mohamed Atta had an account at a Citibank branch in Dubai, with frequent transfers of $10,000 to $15,000. Before the attack, he received $100,000 from an unidentified account in Dubai.

And though US banks are now supposed to ask about the owners of wire transfers sent from abroad, foreign banks or branches of US banks can bundle cash from numerous customers and send the lump sum to their correspondent accounts in the US. Then they move the money wherever their clients order. And in spite of the new law, the financial industry is geared to fight adoption and enforcement of meaningful regulations on what it means to verify customer identity.

The Republicans have opposed piercing bank secrecy because they and their supporters use the system to hide money from taxes. The bin Laden events forced them to try to find the terrorists' money, which means piercing bank secrecy. But they are attempting to do this by fiat rather than by permanently changing the system and abolishing bank and corporate secrecy.

_AFTER DIRTY AIR, DIRTY MONEY

Before September 11, 2001, the Bush Administration was staunchly opposed to any challenge to offshore havens.

When Treasury Secretary Paul O'Neill said after the February 2001 meeting of the top industrialized countries, known as the G-7, that a European initiative to clamp down on money laundering "is not about dictating to any country what should be the appropriate level of tax rates," it was clear what US policy would be.

For about eighteen months, under Clinton, the United States had signaled that it was serious about joining the Europeans in modest efforts to deal with the tide of illicit money that washes around the world. Now Washington was backing off the US commitment to reform the offshore banking system. Instead, the "tough on crime" Republicans would stand shoulder to shoulder with the shady characters in Nauru, Aruba, Liechtenstein, and elsewhere who offer state-of-the-art financial services for crooks.

The immediate issue was an initiative by the Organization for Economic Cooperation and Development to stop tax evaders from hiding money in offshore havens. The OECD in July 2000 had named 35 jurisdictions that offered foreigners secrecy, low or no taxes, and protection from inquiries by home-country legal and tax authorities. It said it would take "defensive measures" against countries that didn't change those policies, and it began negotiating with such worried targets as the Cayman Islands.

In April 2001, O'Neill rebuffed pressure from France, Japan, and Italy to reiterate US support for the initiative. Then in May, without prior consultations or negotiations with allies (à la the Kyoto environmental treaty), he announced in a newspaper op-ed that the OECD demands were "too broad," and he withdrew US support. French Minister of Finance Laurent Fabius publicly expressed his concern, saying that "until now, the United States and France were at the forefront of this fight." *Le Monde* editorialized: "After dirty air, dirty money."

O'Neill may have some sympathy for tax evaders. He doesn't like taxes. He said he favors abolishing US taxes on businesses. He thinks the government should spend money on national defense and security, but that able-bodied adults should save for their own retirement and for their health and medical needs. And he might make good use of places that don't charge foreigners taxes. In 2000, before he became Treasury Secretary, he was chairman of Alcoa Inc., the world's biggest aluminum producer. His pay, benefits, and stock options? Over $56 million.

In the wake of O'Neill's comments, some tax havens pulled back from negotiating with the OECD, confident that the Americans would keep offshore banking safe for tax evaders and other crooks.

The Bush Administration's actions represented a continuation of policies—interrupted only by brief Clinton moves—that go back to the Reagan era, and that in the past have been defended as based on US opposition to impeding the free flow of capital or decreasing other countries' reliance on the dollar. "Treasury was looking to free up economies, not regulate them," says Jonathan Winer, a former high-level crime-policy official in the Clinton State Department.

Others take a darker view of US motives. Jack Blum, a Washington lawyer who cowrote a 1998 report for the United Nations on the offshore phenomenon, says US policy has been influenced by the facts that "the hot money from the rest of world [fueled] one of the greatest booms in the stock market" and that big brokerage firms "find it profitable to run private banking operations for rich people all over the world who don't want to pay taxes." He estimates that at least $70 billion in US taxes is evaded annually through offshore accounts. That's just above the $65 billion in the projected federal budget for education, training, employment, and social services. Elsewhere, Oxfam International calculates that money sucked out of developing countries to tax havens is $50 billion a year, nearly the size of the $57 billion annual global aid budget.

Nobel laureate Joseph Stiglitz was fired as chief economist of the World Bank two years ago because he criticized the disastrous Western policy pressing for fast privatization in Russia. He told me, "You ask why, if you believe there's an important role for a regulated banking system, do you allow a non-regulated banking system to continue? The answer is, it's in the interests of some of the moneyed interests to allow this to occur. It's not an accident; it could have been shut down at any time."

New York District Attorney Robert Morgenthau told me, "Years ago, when I was tracing black-market money coming out of Vietnam through Hong Kong to Manufacturers Hanover in New York and then the Union Bank in Switzerland, I subpoenaed the records of an account code-named 'Shotgun.' The next thing I knew, the account had been changed to an account in Dubai. I wrote a letter to Dubai asking for the records. They wrote back—they're sorry, the laws of Dubai prohibited that. I looked up to see who owned the bank; it was Citicorp."

Morgenthau continued, "The banks want deposits; they want the Middle Eastern people with the most cash to feel comfortable depositing money. We want to sell the countries making deposits tanks and planes and fertilizer plants. We don't want to offend them."

And there are US political concerns. Morgenthau said, "I saw a confidential State Department memo about money laundering listing countries where there is a problem. It's a problem in England, but we don't want to do anything about it, because we need the Brits to help us with their intelligence service."

_THE BIRTH OF SECRET BANKING

The offshore system started with the Swiss, who in the 1930s opened numbered bank accounts purportedly only to hide the money of victims of the Nazis. People who feared confiscation of their wealth would deposit it in accounts identified by number, not name, so the Germans could not trace and seize funds. The money could be claimed only by someone who knew the number.

From the beginning, reputable uses provided cover for disreputable ones. French elites put money in Switzerland to evade taxes, and in the 1950s, mobster Meyer Lansky, who got worried after US crooks were nabbed on tax evasion, bought a Swiss bank. His operatives would deposit cash in Miami banks as earnings from his Havana casinos, then wire-transfer it to Switzerland, safe from US investigation and seizure. Increasingly, rich people all over the world went offshore to evade taxes.

Big banks discovered that there was profit in helping such people, and they established "private banking" departments with offices in secrecy jurisdictions such as the Cayman Islands and Switzerland. Private banking profits are generally twice those of most other departments, but clients think they're getting a bargain. Some open offshore accounts with foreign brokers who handle investment funds free from income and capital gains tax. To access cash, clients get credit cards issued by offshore banks and stock brokerages so that records of accounts and charges are not on file at home.

Today, with 1.2 percent of the world's population, the 60 offshore zones hold 26 percent of the world's assets. According to Merrill Lynch & Gemini Consulting's "World Wealth Report," one-third of the wealth of the world's high net-worth individuals, or nearly $6 trillion, may be held offshore. Offshore havens also hold an estimated 31 percent of the profits of US multinationals. About a third of offshore accounts are in Switzerland, which ignores money-laundering (unless subject to embarrassing press reports or international pressure) and refuses to consider tax cheating by foreigners a crime that triggers money-laundering charges.

_THE USES OF OFFSHORE BANKING

Corporations use offshore banking to move profits to jurisdictions that tax them less or not at all. Using "transfer pricing," a US company that wants to buy widgets in Hong Kong makes the purchase through a trading company in Grand Cayman. The trading company, which it secretly owns, buys the items in Hong Kong, then resells them to the US parent firm at a falsely high price, reducing taxable US profits.

Between 1989 and 1995, nearly a third of large corporations operating in the United States with assets of at least $250 million or sales of at least $50 million paid no US income tax.

Criminals of all stripes depend on offshore banking. In May 1994, the UN embargoed arms to Rwanda, but arms traffickers based in Britain, France, and South Africa used offshore financial centers to carry out their transactions. In 1999, the German secret service reported that a Liechtenstein combine using secret foundations, companies, and bank accounts served the international drug cartels, particularly the mafias of Italy, Colombia, and Russia.

_RUSSIA'S OFFSHORNAYA ZONA

Thefts from other countries pale in relation to the looting of Russia, with the indispensable assistance of the "Offshornaya Zona." The 1995 "loans for shares" scheme transferred state ownership of privatized industries worth billions of dollars to companies whose offshore registrations hid true owners. More billions were stolen around the time of the August 1998 crash.

Insider banks knew about the coming devaluation and shipped billions in assets as "loans" to offshore companies. The banks' statements show that their loan portfolios grew after the date when they got loans from the Russian Central Bank, which were supposed to stave off default. After the crash, it was revealed that the top bor-

rowers in all the big bankrupt banks were offshore. For example, the five largest creditors of Rossiisky Credit were shell companies registered in Nauru and in the Caribbean. As the debtors' ownerships were secret, they could easily "disappear." Stuck with "uncollectable" loans and "no assets," the banks announced their own bankruptcies. Swiss officials are investigating leads that some of the $4.8 billion International Monetary Fund tranche (i.e., bonds) to Russia was moved by banks to offshore accounts before the 1998 crash.

The biggest current scam is being effected by a secretly owned Russian company called Itera, which is using offshore shells in Curaçao and elsewhere to gobble up the assets of Gazprom, the national gas company, which is 38-percent owned by the government. Itera's owners are widely believed to be Gazprom managers, their relatives, and Viktor Chernomyrdin, former chairman of Gazprom's board of directors and Prime Minister during much of the privatization. Gazprom, which projected nearly $16 billion in revenues for 2000, uses Itera as its marketing agent and has been selling it gas fields at cut-rate prices. Its 1999 annual report did not account for sales of 13 percent of production. As its taxes supply a quarter of government revenues, this is a devastating loss. Itera has a Florida office, which has been used to register other Florida companies, making it a vehicle for investment in the US economy.

_CITIBANK AND HANK

Citigroup proclaims that its "private bankers act as financial architects, designing and coordinating insightful solutions for individual client needs, with an emphasis on personalized, confidential service." That is so colorless. It might better boast, "We set up shell companies, secret trusts, and bank accounts, and we dispatch anonymous wire transfers so you can launder drug money, hide stolen assets, embezzle, defraud, cheat on your taxes, avoid court judgments, pay and receive bribes, and loot your country." It could solicit testimonials from former clients, including sons of late Nigerian dictator Sani Abacha; Asif Ali Zardari, husband of Benazir Bhutto, former Prime Minister of Pakistan; El Hadj Omar Bongo, the corrupt President of Gabon; deposed Paraguayan dictator Alfredo Stroessner; and Raul Salinas, jailed brother of the ex-President of Mexico. All stole and laundered millions using private accounts at Citibank (Citigroup's previous incarnation).

One lesser-known client, Carlos Hank Rhon of Mexico, was the object of a suit by the Federal Reserve to ban him from the US banking business. Hank belongs to a powerful Mexican clan whose holdings include banks, investment firms, transportation companies, and real estate. Hank bought an interest in Laredo National Bank in Texas in 1990. Six years later, when he wanted to merge Laredo

> INSIDER BANKS KNEW ABOUT THE COMING DEVALUATION AND SHIPPED BILLIONS IN ASSETS AS "LOANS" TO OFFSHORE COMPANIES.

with Brownsville's Mercantile Bank, the Fed found that Citibank had helped him use offshore shell companies in the British Virgin Islands to gain control of his bank by hiding secret partners and engaging in self-dealing, in violation of US law. One of the offshore companies was managed by shell companies that were subsidiaries of Cititrust, owned by Citibank.

The Fed says that in 1993, Hank's father, Carlos Hank González, met with his Citibank private banker, Amy Elliott, and said he wanted to buy a $20 million share of the bank with payment from Citibank accounts of his offshore companies, done in a way that hid his involvement. Citibank granted him $20 million in loans and sent the money to his son Hank Rhon's personal account at Citibank New York and to an investment account in Citibank London in the name of another offshore company.

Citigroup spokesman Richard Howe said, "We always cooperate fully with authorities in investigations, but we do not discuss the details of any individual's account." Hank settled with the Fed by agreeing to pay an astonishing $40-million fine and to get out of the US banking business.

_DEALING WITH IT

As offshore banking has grown, so has an awareness that it harms the public interest. In 1970, Congress voted to require taxpayers to report foreign bank accounts. In 1985, a Senate investigations subcommittee report said offshore banking thwarted the collection of "massive amounts" of taxes, guessing at up to $600 billion in unreported income.

Beginning in the early 1980s—the Reagan period, when the issue of offshore tax havens was taken up in US Congressional hearings—and except for a few years at the end of the Clinton Administration, the American government's prime interest has been to do nothing to impede the free flow of capital or decrease other countries' reliance on the dollar.

The big banks were making a lot of profit from hiding the assets of rich people who didn't want to pay taxes. The brokerage firms liked the fact that hot money from the rest of world was fueling the boom in the stock market. Because at the end, a lot of that money funnels back to Wall Street, into the market, and the Treasury Department responds to Wall Street.

The US government got interested in tracing offshore money when it related to a political objective.

It had the G-7 create the Financial Action Task Force (FATF) in 1989 to go after drug money, because Washington wanted to get Manuel Noriega, then in power in Panama. After Noriega was caught the next year, the FATF spent most of the 1990s writing recommendations rather than taking enforcement action.

Stiglitz, who served as head of President Clinton's Council of Economic Advisers before going to the World Bank, says the offshore issue "didn't come up much" in the United States until the 1997 Asia meltdown and subsequent problems.

One of the causes of the Japanese financial crisis was the collapse of Daiwa Bank and Yamaichi Securities, which used offshore accounts to hide losses. Then there was the Russian bank disaster of August 1998, caused by crooked managers lending massive amounts to offshore companies they secretly owned, and the failure a month later of Long-Term Capital Management, which routed its transactions through the Caymans, where they were invisible to regulators from the US and other countries.

So the G-7 worried about the offshore system's threat to financial markets. In 1999, it set up the Financial Stability Forum to develop proposals to reform the international financial system. The members include finance ministers, heads of central banks, representatives of bank supervisory authorities, and delegates from the OECD, the IMF, and the World Bank.

Stiglitz said, "Everybody said you need more transparency. But it has to be comprehensive. People said if you're going to be comprehensive, you have to include offshore countries and hedge funds. At that point, the United States and Britain began talking about the advantages of non-full disclosure—that if all the information were made public, you'd have incentives not to gather it. This argument was never used earlier, only when it came to offshore banks and hedge funds."

Stiglitz says that then-Deputy Treasury Secretary Lawrence Summers was the one who voiced the concerns but that "behind it were the hedge funds and offshore centers whose advantages lie in secrecy.... He was reflecting those interests." He added, "If you said the United States, Britain, and the major G-7 banks will not deal with offshore bank centers that don't comply with G-7 bank regulations, these banks could not exist. They exist because they can engage in transactions with standard banks."

By the time the G-7 met in Washington in April 1999, the Europeans were also raising concerns that the offshore system threatened their own countries' welfare because it facilitated tax evasion. French

Finance Minister Dominique Strauss-Kahn offered a proposal that offshore centers that failed to properly regulate accounts and cooperate with law enforcement be cut off by the world's financial powers.

He proposed that the G-7 require financial institutions to identify their customers; report suspicious transactions of high amounts involving individuals or legal entities with accounts at financial institutions in poorly regulated jurisdictions; and, as a last resort, ban financial transactions with countries or territories whose procedures were unacceptable.

During the April 1999 meeting of the G-7, the offshore issue was not at the top of the agenda for US Treasury Secretary Robert Rubin, who is now co-chairman of Citigroup, the holding company of Citibank. When I saw Strauss-Kahn after that meeting, he told me that Rubin and other G-7 leaders had turned down his proposals. He also got a negative response from banking leaders in Washington. He said, "They didn't want to hear about it. They all use the offshore centers."

Rubin denied this account when I questioned him later at a speech he gave in New York, but he declined repeated requests—sent through the Citibank public relations office—to clarify what he did say. I believe Strauss-Kahn.

After Rubin left Treasury, the United States began to show more interest in the subject. The new Treasury Secretary, Larry Summers, ordered an analysis of the connection between offshore banking and the East Asia financial crisis, and the administration worked with a Republican liberal then heading the House Banking Committee to write a law banning anonymous bank transfers into US banks from abroad.

That bill, and Democrat Carl Levin's bill in the Senate, were blocked by House majority leader Dick Armey of Texas and Senate Banking Committee chairman Phil Gramm, also of Texas. The Texas Bankers Association had lobbied against the bill, saying it would hurt the banks' business with Mexico. A Clinton official told me, "If Texas bankers know their customers, they know whom they're dealing with, and if they're dealing with Mexican banks, they know there's dirty money." He suggested that the Republicans blocked the bill so they could keep the drug money flowing to Texas banks. I expect that Texan George W. Bush has similar concerns about the welfare of Texas banks.

Some European countries also want to protect money-laundering in their favorite jurisdictions. In June 2000, after a decade of toothless pronouncements, the FATF issued a "blacklist" of fifteen countries that maintained banking secrecy even in the face of criminal investigations. FATF countries' banks were asked to exercise "reinforced vigilance" in dealings with those countries. But the list was highly political. Britain refused to allow Guernsey, Jersey, the Isle of Man, the British Virgin Islands, and Gibraltar to be included. France kept Monaco off the list.

Jean-François Thony—until 2000, a program manager of the UN Global Program Against Money Laundering and now a French judge—said, "Britain said to France, 'If you want to include the Channel Islands, we will ask Monaco to be put there as well.' Now the French government is very tough on Monaco, but France has something to do with the fact that the situation has lasted for so long." French banking authorities oversee Monaco. Antigua was excluded at the insistence of Canada, which represents it on the board of directors of the IMF. Thony added, "There's a lot of hypocrisy, pointing the finger at those countries which are supposed not to comply with international rules when the banks really operating them are the major banks of our countries. That is the heart of the problem."

_BANKS WANT BUSINESS AS USUAL

The biggest obstacle to ending money laundering or terrorists' use of the international financial system is the banks. Bill Clinton in 1995 ordered the Departments of Justice, State, and Treasury, the National Security Council, and the CIA and other intelligence agencies to increase and integrate their efforts against international money laundering by terrorists and criminals. The government agencies tried to penetrate the bin Laden network of businesses, charities, banks, and front companies. They failed. Even as it seeks to get at bank accounts connected to Osama bin Laden, Washington is carefully avoiding a challenge to the structure of the offshore system.

After September 11, there's been a lot of red, white, and blue flag-waving in America, but the flag the administration and the big banks wave is green.

Meanwhile, even among groups concerned about drug crime, the ills of globalization, and wealth disparities, there is little awareness in the US of the relationship of those issues to the offshore system. NGOs in Europe are pressing for reform, and European governments can be expected to continue their modest efforts, but not much will change unless the United States decides to participate. Until then, international banks will continue to make it easy for dictators to loot their countries, the rich to evade taxes, and terrorists to finance their operations, while ordinary citizens underwrite ever more of the cost of government.

GLOBALIZATION FOR THE GOOD OF ALL
EMBRACING THE NEW AGENDA
NOREENA HERTZ

We live increasingly in a world of haves and have-nots, of gated communities next to ghettos, of extreme poverty and unbelievable riches. Some enjoy rights that are completely denied to others. Vast numbers of people see almost no benefits from the advances of the past century. Relative inequalities are exploding, and the world's poorest, despite all the advances of globalization, may even be getting poorer.

Trickle-down, the main rationale of neoliberal globalization, has turned out to be an illusion. Special interests have gained in power. Some have a voice, but many remain voiceless.

It is a world of extremes, which can be characterized most clearly in terms of exclusion: political, social, and economic.

What do I mean by political exclusion? The rights of citizens marginalized by the interests of big business—whether this is George W.'s environmental policy, clearly formulated with the interests of American energy companies in mind, or the infamous World Trade Organization, which puts trade interests before the environment, labor standards, or human rights. Governments can no longer be counted on to safeguard the public interest or protect the public realm.

Economic exclusion? That is self-explanatory and can be seen everywhere in growing inequality and polarization of wealth, in countries in the South crippled by debt repayments and growing income gaps both within and between countries. In almost every developing country in the world, the number of people living on less than a dollar a day has increased rather than fallen in the 20 years since the "Washington consensus" became mainstream.

And social exclusion? In a world like this, few can gain redress for the injustices inflicted upon them. In the South we often see a race to the bottom: companies scouring the globe for the cheapest and easiest places to manufacture. Regulatory standards, health and safety standards fall, while rights are junked, communities displaced, unions outlawed. Tobacco workers in Brazil are poisoned by banned pesticides, but there is no hope of compensation, let alone improvement in working conditions. These are Southern workers and Southern communities, excluded from the access to justice that we in the First World take for granted.

What arises from these patterns of exclusion is a deep and growing chasm between the global economy and social justice. If it is not bridged, it will result not only in seething conflicts but, over time, in a growing movement of people that will make even our gated communities impossible to protect.

So, for our sakes, as well as those of the two million-plus children who die each year from diarrhea brought on by lack of clean water, the issue of exclusion must be addressed head-on. This is not just a long-term goal; it is something that has to be done at once, a project that can and must be part of a contemporary political process. We need to realize that what has prevented the pursuit of this objective has not been an absolute scarcity of resources; it has been an absence of moral imperative, responsibility, or will.

We must therefore embrace a new agenda based on inclusiveness, a commitment to reconnecting the social and the economic, a relinking of the latter to a plausible redistributive system, and a determination to ensure access to justice for all. All these things are within our reach.

In practical terms these should be the immediate first steps.

First, an inclusive political process must be set up to investigate and consider the impact of economic globalization. This should take the form of an international independent commission, transparent, open, and involving all major stakeholders: representatives of the South as well as the North, members of communities who are affected as well as those who are beneficiaries, the poor as well as the rich.

IN ALMOST EVERY DEVELOPING COUNTRY IN THE WORLD, THE NUMBER OF PEOPLE LIVING ON LESS THAN A DOLLAR A DAY HAS INCREASED RATHER THAN FALLEN IN THE 20 YEARS SINCE THE "WASHINGTON CONSENSUS" BECAME MAINSTREAM.

And the issues to address? What is the impact of trade liberalization on the poorest members of the global society? What is the cost of economic growth to the environment? What price are we paying for big business influencing the rules of the game on the quality of the air we breathe and the food we eat? What is the justification for allowing the North to continue to protect key industries, such as agriculture and textiles, while the South is told to open up all of its markets?

This is not a matter of simply looking at economic costs. We have to examine the impact of economic globalization on human development, on social capital, and in particular on the poor. What are the implications for society of rural communities collapsing overnight, or for farmers when their indigenous plants are patented by corporations?

We do not yet know the answers to all these questions. Much of the research on impact is confined to aggregate economic data that tell us little if anything at all about impact on particular groups; figures of rising GDP tell us nothing about who gains and who loses. And there is at present no forum in which these issues can be rigorously addressed and examined. But now more than ever there is a real need to confront the beliefs of the market fundamentalists away from the streets and in a public forum, to investigate the costs of economic globalization framed around the issue of exclusion.

WHAT ARE THE IMPLICATIONS FOR SOCIETY OF RURAL COMMUNITIES COLLAPSING OVERNIGHT, OR FOR FARMERS WHEN THEIR INDIGENOUS PLANTS ARE PATENTED BY CORPORATIONS?

Next we must commit to putting into motion the necessary steps to create a World Social Organization, which will seek to reframe market mechanisms in rules and regulations that ensure that the costs of side effects, such as pollution and human rights abuses, are factored into all aspects of economic activity. This organization will provide a real counterweight to the dominance of the WTO—with teeth as sharp and powers of enforcement as real.

For if the status quo, where trade interests have been given primacy, is maintained, if the economic is allowed to dominate, and if we never reconnect the social with the economic, we will exacerbate divides and perpetuate a system in which the rules of the game all too often serve the interests of big business before people, and profit before social or environmental justice.

Of course we must be careful that the North should not use this new organization as a form of protectionism. Assistance must be provided by the developed world to help its developing partners bear the costs associated with better global regulation, and different responsibilities should be attached to nations of the South in the short-term, at least. The South cannot be penalized for joining this organization from a singularly disadvantaged starting point.

But relinking the social to the economic, though necessary, is not sufficient. There still remains the problem of alleviating the positions of those who are most excluded and marginalized. At the least this means the cancellation of debt, reversing the outflows of capital from the South to the North. Overseas aid, which to the least developed countries has fallen 45 percent in real terms since 1990, must be significantly increased, while the ways in which it is delivered need to be rethought.

It will simply be impossible for countries to reach the goals agreed upon at the Millennium Summit if these steps are not taken. We shall not be able to halve the proportion of people living in extreme poverty by 2015, nor halve the proportion of people suffering from hunger, without an end to the financial drain and a real financial boost.

But more than this, *new* resources have to be created to empower people to gain access to better lives. And these resources can only be raised by new forms of taxation, global indirect taxes, raised by a new global tax authority, which are then redistributed. At the same time, these taxes must be used to protect our environment and our resources, so they would be taxes on the use of energy and resources, and on pollution.

Finally, mechanisms must be put into place to help people fight injustice as part of a wider political rebuilding of institutions. All people, wherever they are, must be extended the rights we take for granted. Workers and communities everywhere must be able to safeguard basic rights to minimum health and safety standards, to minimum wages, to not be dispossessed without adequate compensation.

In the long-term this is a matter of strengthening both local and international regulation of companies and making enforcement effective. In the short-term, there are clear steps that can be taken by governments of countries in which multinationals are domiciled.

Several test cases are underway in which companies are being sued in the North for actions carried out by their subsidiaries in the South. They include Unocal in the US in connection with its activities in Burma, and Cape in the UK in connection with its activities in South Africa. But this means of redress is usually blocked on two fronts. First, it is very seldom possible to lift the corporate veil and make parent companies accountable for the actions of their subsidiaries. Second, even when this is done, there are usually no funds available for workers or communities to take on multinationals with relatively unlimited resources.

A world in which people have no access to justice is one in which discontent will continue to fester. So my final recommendation is to ensure that the perpetrators of corporate crimes shall be taken to account, wherever they are, and that their victims will have redress, whomever they are. This means committing both to legislative reforms that will ensure that the corporate veil can be lifted and parent companies can be held responsible for the actions of their subsidiaries, and to the establishment of a global legal aid fund so that workers and communities everywhere can be allowed access to justice.

SEVERAL TEST CASES ARE UNDER WAY IN WHICH COMPANIES ARE BEING SUED IN THE NORTH FOR ACTIONS CARRIED OUT BY THEIR SUBSIDIARIES IN THE SOUTH.

A tall order, perhaps, my plan for the world—but not inconceivable. For now more than ever it is clear that this divided world, of injustice, inequity, and power asymmetries, is untenable. The events of September 11, 2001, have shown us all too clearly that we do not and cannot live in isolation. We are inexorably linked, standing as global citizens side by side. And to allow the exclusion of groups of people is to invite peril. It cannot be that the only issues upon which we as a world unite are terrorism and trade. We must commit to a global coalition to deal with the issue of exclusion, too.

Based on a speech given in Belgium, October 30, 2001.

THE SENATOR'S ASHES
BOB KERREY, CIA WAR CRIMES AND THE NEED FOR A WAR CRIMES TRIAL
DOUGLAS VALENTINE

As of late April 2001, everybody knows that former Senator Bob Kerrey led a seven-member team of Navy Seals into Vietnam's Thanh Phong village in February 1969, murdering in cold blood more than a dozen women and children. The revelation made front-page headlines around the world and fueled many hours of TV news shows.

What hardly anyone knows, and what no one in the press talked about (although many of them know), is that Kerrey was on a CIA mission, and its specific purpose was to kill those women and children. It was illegal, premeditated mass murder—and it was a war crime.

> **KERREY WAS ON A CIA MISSION, AND ITS SPECIFIC PURPOSE WAS TO KILL THOSE WOMEN AND CHILDREN.**

It's time to hold the CIA responsible. It's time for a war crimes tribunal to examine the CIA's illegal activities during and since the Vietnam War.

_WAR CRIMES AS POLICY

War crimes were a central part of a CIA strategy for fighting the Vietnam War. The strategy, known as Contre Coup, was the manifestation of a belief that the war was essentially political, not military, in nature. The CIA theorized that opposing ideological factions were fighting the war. It believed that each faction amounted to about 5 percent of the total population, and that the remaining 90 percent simply wanted the war to go away.

According to the CIA's mythology, on one side were the communist insurgents, supported by comrades in Hanoi, Moscow, and Peking. The communists fought for land reform, to rid Vietnam of foreign intervention, and to unite the north and south. The other faction was composed of free-wheeling capitalists, often Catholics relocated from North Vietnam in 1954 by the CIA. This freedom-loving faction was fighting, under the direction of quiet Americans, to keep South Vietnam a subsidiary of the United States.

Caught in the crossfire was the silent majority. The object shared by both factions was to win the uncommitted people over to its side.

Contre Coup was the CIA's response to the realization that the communists were winning the war for the hearts and minds of the people. It also was a response to the belief that the communists were winning through the use of psychological warfare; specifically, through selective terror—the murder and mutilation of specific government officials.

In December 1963, Peer DeSilva arrived in Saigon as the CIA's station chief. He claims to have been shocked by what he saw. In his autobiography, *Sub Rosa* (Times Books, 1978), DeSilva describes how the Vietcong had "impaled a young boy, a village chief, and his pregnant wife on sharp poles. To make sure this horrible sight would remain with the villagers, one of the terror squad allegedly used his machete to disembowel the woman, spilling the fetus onto the ground."

"The Vietcong," DeSilva said, "were monstrous in the application of torture and murder to achieve the political and psychological impact they wanted."

But the methodology was successful and had tremendous intelligence potential, so DeSilva authorized the creation of small "counter-terror teams" designed "to bring danger and death to the Vietcong functionaries themselves, especially in areas where they felt secure." Three years later, this plan—based on the Contre Coup concept—would become one of the foundation stones of the CIA's infamous Phoenix Program.

_HOW COUNTER-TERROR WORKED IN VIETNAM

Thanh Phong village was one of those areas where Vietcong functionaries felt secure. It was located near the coast in what the Government of Vietnam called Kien Hoa Province, about 50 miles south of Saigon in the Mekong Delta. Kien Hoa was one of

EVERYTHING YOU KNOW IS WRONG

Vietnam's most densely populated provinces. Criss-crossed with waterways and rice paddies, it was an important rice production area for the insurgents as well as the Government of Vietnam, and thus was one of the eight most heavily infiltrated provinces in South Vietnam. The estimated 4,700 VC functionaries in Kien Hoa Province accounted for more than 5 percent of the insurgency's total leadership.

WAR CRIMES WERE A CENTRAL PART OF A CIA STRATEGY FOR FIGHTING THE VIETNAM WAR.

As a result, the CIA and US Army concentrated much of their firepower in the region, most of which was designated a "free fire zone." Operation Speedy Express, a Ninth Infantry Division sweep through Kien Hoa in the first six months of 1969, killed an estimated 11,000 civilians—all supposedly VC sympathizers.

These so-called sympathizers formed what the CIA called the Vietcong Infrastructure (VCI). The VCI consisted of members of the People's Revolutionary Party, the National Liberation Front, and other communist outfits like the Women's and Student's Liberation Associations. Its members were politicians and administrators managing committees for business, communications, security, intelligence, and military affairs. Among the VCI's main functions were the collection of taxes and the recruitment of young men and women into the insurgency. But the main point is this: These people were civilians.

As the CIA was well aware, Ho Chi Minh boasted that with two cadre in every hamlet, he could win the war, no matter how many soldiers the Americans threw at him.

So the CIA adopted Ho's strategy—but on a grander and bloodier scale. The object of Contre Coup and the eventual Phoenix Program was to identify and terrorize each and every individual VCI and his/her family, friends, and fellow villagers. To this end the CIA in 1964 launched a massive intelligence operation called the Provincial Interrogation Center Program. The CIA (employing the US company Pacific Architects and Engineers) built an interrogation center in each of South Vietnam's 44 provinces. Staffed by members of the brutal Special Police, who ran extensive informant networks and were advised by CIA officers, the purpose of the PICs was to identify, through the systematic "interrogation" (read: torture) of VCI suspects, the membership of the VCI at every level of its organization—from its elusive headquarters somewhere along the Cambodian border, through the region, city, province, district, village, and hamlet committees.

The "indispensable link" in the VCI was the District Party Secretary—the same individual Bob Kerrey's Seal team was out to assassinate in its mission in Thanh Phong.

_FRANKENSTEIN'S MONSTER

Initially the CIA had trouble finding people who were willing to murder and mutilate, so the Agency's original "counter-terror teams" were composed of ex-convicts, VC defectors, Chinese Nungs, Cambodians, Montagnards, and mercenaries. In a February 1970 article written for *True Magazine*, titled "The CIA's Hired Killers," Georgie-Anne Geyer compared "our boys" to "their boys" with the qualification that, "Their boys did it for faith; our boys did it for money."

The other big problem was security. The VC had infiltrated every facet of the GVN—even the CIA's unilateral counter-terror program. So in an attempt to bring greater effectiveness to its secret war, the CIA started employing Navy Seals, US Army Special Forces, Force Recon Marines, and other highly trained Americans who, like Bob Kerrey, were "motivationally indoctrinated" by their masters and turned into killing machines with all the social inhibitions and moral compunctions of a Timmy McVeigh. Except they were secure in the knowledge that what they were doing was, if not legal or moral, fraught with Old Testament-style justice, because (as Contre Coup posited) the Vietcong did it first.

Eventually the irrepressible Americans added their own improvements. In his autobiography, *Soldier*, Anthony Herbert describes arriving in Saigon in 1965, reporting to the CIA's Special Operations Group, and being asked to join a top-secret psywar program. The CIA wanted Herbert "to take charge of execution teams that wiped out entire families."

By 1967, killing entire families had become an integral facet of the CIA's counter-terror program. Robert Slater was the chief of the CIA's Province Interrogation Center Program from June 1967 through 1969. In a March 1970 thesis for the Defense Intelligence School, titled "The History, Organization and Modus Operandi of the Viet Cong Infrastructure," Slater wrote that "the District Party Secretary usually does not sleep in the same house or even hamlet where his family lived, to preclude any injury to his family during assassination attempts."

But, Slater added, "[T]he Allies have frequently found out where the District Party Secretaries live and raided their homes: in an ensuing fire fight the secretary's wife and children have been killed and injured."

This is the intellectual context in which the Kerrey atrocity took place. This CIA strategy of committing war crimes for psychological reasons—to terrorize the enemy's supporters into submission—also is what differentiates Kerrey's atrocity, in legal terms, from other popular methods of mass-murdering civilians, such as bombs from the sky or economic sanctions.

Yes, the CIA has a global, illegal strategy of terrorizing people, although in typical CIA-speak it's called "anti-terrorism."

When you're waging illegal warfare, language is every bit as important as weaponry and the will to kill. As George Orwell or Noam Chomsky might explain, when you're deliberately killing innocent women and children, half the court-of-public-opinion battle is making it sound legal.

Making CIA terror sound legal, or just not reporting it, was the responsibility of the American press corps in Vietnam, and three old Vietnam hands in particular stand out as examples of the incestuous relationship between the CIA and the press. Neil Sheehan, CIA-nik and author of the aptly-titled *Bright Shining Lie*, recently confessed that in 1966 he saw US forces massacre as many as 600 Vietnamese civilians in five fishing villages. He'd been in Vietnam for three years by then, but it didn't occur to him that he had discovered a war crime. Now he realizes that the war crimes issue was always present, but still no mention of his friends in the CIA.

AT LEAST ONE CIA OFFICER WHO WAS DEEPLY INVOLVED IN THE PHOENIX PROGRAM IS NOW A US CONGRESSMAN FROM CONNECTICUT.

Former *New York Times* reporter and author of *The Best and The Brightest*, David Halberstam, defended Kerrey on behalf of the media establishment at the New School campus the week after the story broke. CIA flack Halberstam described the region around Thanh Phong as "the purest bandit country," adding that "by 1969 everyone who lived there would have been third-generation Vietcong." Which is CIA revisionism at its sickest.

Finally there's *New York Times* reporter James Lemoyne. Why did he never write any articles linking the CIA to war crimes in Vietnam? Because his brother Charles, a Navy officer, was in charge of the CIA's counter-terror teams in the Delta in 1968.

At least one CIA officer who was deeply involved in the Phoenix Program is now a US Congressman from Connecticut. From November 1970 until June 1972, Rob Simmons ran the Phu Yen Province Interrogation Center and mounted numerous paramilitary (read: assassination) and psychological warfare operations against the VCI. One wonders how many other Phoenix alumni are wandering the halls of Congress and sitting behind desks at the major networks.

_PHOENIX COMES TO THANH PHONG

The CIA launched its Phoenix Program in June 1967, after thirteen years of tinkering with several experimental counter-terror and psy-war programs, and building its network of secret interrogation centers. The stated policy was to replace the bludgeon of indiscriminate bombings and military search-and-destroy operations—which had alienated the people from the Government of Vietnam—with, ostensibly, the scalpel of assassinations of selected members of the Vietcong Infrastructure.

A typical Phoenix operation began in a Province Interrogation Center where a suspected member of the VCI was brought for questioning. After a few days or weeks or months undergoing various forms of torture, the VCI suspect would die or give the names and locations of his VCI comrades and superiors. That information would be sent from the Interrogation Center to the local Phoenix office, which was staffed by Special Branch and Vietnamese military officers under the supervision of CIA officers. Depending on the relative importance of the targeted VCI, the Phoenix staff would then dispatch one of the various action arms available to it, including Seal teams like the one Bob Kerrey led into Thanh Phong.

In February 1969, the Phoenix Program was still under CIA control. But because Kien Hoa Province was so important, and because the VCI's District Party Secretary was thought to be in Thanh Phong, the CIA decided to handle this particular assassination and mass murder mission without involving the local Vietnamese. So instead of dispensing the local counter-terror team, the CIA sent Kerrey's Raiders.

And that, very simply, is how it happened. Kerrey and crew admittedly went to Thanh Phong to kill the District Party Secretary, and anyone else who got in the way, including his family and all their friends.

_PHOENIX COMES HOME TO ROOST

By 1969, through Phoenix, the CIA was targeting individual VCI and their families all across Vietnam. Over 20,000 people were assassinated by the end of the year, and hundreds of thousands had been tortured in Province Interrogation Centers.

On June 20, 1969, the Lower House of the Vietnamese Congress held hearings about abuses in the Phoenix VCI elimination program. Eighty-six deputies signed a petition calling for its immediate termination. Among the charges: Special Police knowingly arrested innocent people for the purpose of extortion; people were detained for as long as eight months before being tried; torture was commonplace. Noting that it was illegal to do so, several deputies protested instances in which American troops detained or murdered suspects without Vietnamese authority. Others complained that village chiefs were not consulted before raids, such as the one on Thanh Phong.

After an investigation in 1970, four US Congresspersons concluded that the CIA's Phoenix Program violated international law. "The people of these United States," they jointly stated, "have deliberately imposed upon the Vietnamese people a system of justice which admittedly denies due process of law," and that in doing so, "we appear to have violated the 1949 Geneva Convention for the protection of civilian people."

During the hearings, US Representative Ogden Reid said, "If the Union had had a Phoenix program during the Civil War, its targets would have been civilians like Jefferson Davis or the mayor of Macon, Georgia."

But the American establishment and media denied it then and continue to deny it today, because Phoenix was a racist, genocidal program—and the CIA officials, members of the media who were complicit through their silence, and the red-blooded American boys who carried it out are all war criminals. As Michael Ratner, a lawyer at the Center for Constitutional Rights, told this writer: "Kerrey should be tried as a war criminal. His actions on the night of February 24-25, 1969, when the seven-man Navy Seal unit which he headed killed approximately 20 unarmed Vietnamese civilians, eighteen of whom were women and children, was a war crime. Like those who murdered at My Lai, he too should be brought into the dock and tried for his crimes."

> NOTING THAT IT WAS ILLEGAL TO DO SO, SEVERAL DEPUTIES PROTESTED INSTANCES IN WHICH AMERICAN TROOPS DETAINED OR MURDERED SUSPECTS WITHOUT VIETNAMESE AUTHORITY.

Phoenix, alas, also was fiendishly effective and became a template for future CIA operations. Developed in Vietnam and perfected with the death squads and media blackout of Afghanistan and El Salvador, it is now employed by the CIA around the world: in Colombia, in Kosovo, in Ireland with the British MI6, and in Israel with its other kindred spirit, the Mossad.

The paymasters at the Pentagon will keep cranking out billion-dollar

missile defense shields and other Bush-league boondoggles. But when it comes to making the world safe for international capitalism, the political trick is being more of a homicidal maniac, and more cost effective, than the terrorists.

Incredibly, Phoenix has become fashionable, acquiring a kind of political cachet. Governor Jesse Ventura claims to have been a Navy Seal and to have "hunted man." Fanatical right-wing US Representative Bob Barr, one of the Republican impeachment clique, has introduced legislation to "re-legalize" assassinations. David Hackworth, representing the military establishment, defended Kerrey by saying "there were thousands of such atrocities," and that in 1969 his own unit committed "at least a dozen such horrors." Jack Valenti, representing the business establishment and its financial stake in the issue, defended Kerrey in the *LA Times*, saying, "[A]ll the normalities [sic] of a social contract are abandoned" in war.

Bullshit.

A famous Phoenix operation, known as the My Lai massacre, was proceeding along smoothly, with a grand total of 504 Vietnamese women and children killed, when a soldier named Hugh Thompson in a helicopter gunship saw what was happening. Risking his life to preserve that "social contract," Thomson landed his helicopter between the mass murderers and their victims, turned his machine guns on his fellow Americans, and brought the carnage to a halt.

Same with screenwriter and journalist Bill Broyles, a Vietnam veteran and author of *Brothers In Arms*, an excellent book about the Vietnam War. Broyles turned in a bunch of his fellow Marines for killing civilians.

If Thompson and Broyles were capable of taking individual responsibility, everyone is. And many did.

_PHOENIX REBORN

There is no doubt that Bob Kerrey committed a war crime. As he admits, he went to Vietnam with a knife clenched between his teeth and did what he was trained to do—kidnap, assassinate, and mass-murder civilians. But there was no point to his atrocity, as he soon learned, no controlling legal authority. He became a conflicted individual. He remembers that they killed women and children. But he thinks they came under fire first, before they panicked and started shooting back. The fog of war clouds his memory.

But there isn't that much to forget. Thanh Phong was Kerrey's first mission, and on his second mission a grenade blew off his foot, abruptly ending his military career.

Plus, there are plenty of other people to remind Kerrey of what happened, if anyone will listen. There's Gerhard Klann, the Navy Seal who disputes Kerrey's account, and two Vietnamese survivors of the raid, Pham Tri Lanh and Bui Thi Luam, both of whom corroborate Klann's account, as does a veteran Vietcong soldier Tran Van Rung.

As CBS News was careful to point out, these Vietnamese were former VC and thus hostile witnesses, and because there were slight inconsistencies in their stories, they could not be believed. Klann became the target of Kerrey's PR machine, which dismissed him as an alcoholic with a chip on his shoulder.

HE SAYS HIS ACTIONS AT THAN PHONG WERE AN ATROCITY, BUT NOT A WAR CRIME. HE SAYS HE FEELS REMORSE, BUT NOT GUILT.

Then there is John DeCamp. An army captain in Vietnam, DeCamp worked under CIA executive William Colby for the organization that ostensibly managed Phoenix after the CIA let it go in June 1969. DeCamp was elected to the Nebraska State Senate while in Vietnam, serving until 1990. A Republican, he claims that Kerrey led an anti-war march on the Nebraska state capitol in May 1971. DeCamp claims that Kerrey put a medal, possibly the bronze star he received for the Thanh Phong mission, in a mock coffin, and said, "Vietcong or North Vietnamese troops are angelic compared with the ruthless Americans…."

Kerrey claims he was in Peru visiting his brother that day. But he definitely accepted his Medal of Honor from Richard Nixon on May 14, 1970, a mere ten days after the Ohio National guard killed four student protestors at Kent State. With that badge of honor pinned on his chest, Kerrey began walking the gilded road to success. Elected Governor of Nebraska in November 1982, he started dating Deborah Winger, became a celebrity war hero, was elected to the US Senate, became vice-chair of the Senate Committee on Intelligence, and in 1990 staged a run for president. One of the most highly regarded politicians in America, he showered self-righteous criticism on draft-dodger Bill Clinton for lying.

Bob Kerrey is a symbol of what it means to be an American, and the patriots have rallied to his defense. Yet Kerrey accepted a bronze star under false pretenses, and as John DeCamp suggests, he may have been fragged by his fellow Seals. For this, he received the Medal of Honor.

John DeCamp calls Bob Kerrey "emotionally disturbed" as a result of his Vietnam experience.

Kerrey's behavior has been pathetic. In order to protect himself and his CIA patrons from being tried as war criminals, Bob Kerrey has become a pathological liar. He says his actions at Than Phong were an atrocity, but not a war crime. He says he feels remorse, but not guilt. In fact, he has continually rehabbed his position on the war itself—moving from an opponent to an enthusiast. In a 1999 column in the *Washington Post*, for example, Kerrey said he had come to view Vietnam as a "just war." "Was the war worth the effort and sacrifice, or was it a mistake?" Kerrey wrote. "When I came home in 1969 and for many years afterward, I did not believe it was worth it. Today, with the passage of time and the experience of seeing both the benefits of freedom won by our sacrifice and the human destruction done by dictatorships, I believe the cause was just and the sacrifice not in vain."

At the 2000 Democratic Party Convention in Los Angeles, Kerrey lectured the delegates that they shouldn't be ashamed of the war and that they should treat Vietnam veterans as war heroes: "I believe I speak for Max Baucus and every person who has ever served when I say I never felt more free than when I wore the uniform of our country. This country—this party—must remember." Free? Free to murder women and children. Is this a consciousness of guilt or immunity?

CBS News also participates in constructing a curtain of lies, as does every other government or media outlet that knows about the CIA's Phoenix Program, which continues to exist and operate worldwide today, but fails to mention it.

Why?

Because if the name of one targeted Vietcong cadre can be obtained, then all the names can be obtained, and then a war crimes trial becomes imperative. And that's the last thing the Establishment will allow to happen.

Average Americans, however, consider themselves a nation ruled by laws and an ethic of fair play, and with the Kerry confession comes an opportunity for America to redefine itself in more realistic terms. The discrepancies in his story beg investigation. He says he was never briefed on the rules of engagement, but a "pocket card" with the Laws of Land Warfare was given to each member of the US Armed Forces in Vietnam.

Does it matter that Kerrey would lie about this? Yes. General Bruce Palmer, commander of the same Ninth Division that devastated Kien

Koa Province in 1969, objected to the "involuntary assignment" of American soldiers to Phoenix. He did not believe that "people in uniform, who are pledged to abide by the Geneva Conventions, should be put in the position of having to break those laws of warfare."

It was the CIA that forced soldiers like Kerrey into Phoenix operations, and the hidden hand of the CIA lingers over his war crime. Kerrey now even uses the same hypocritical rationale offered by CIA officer DeSilva. According to Kerrey, "The Viet Cong were a thousand per cent more ruthless than" the Seals or US Army.

But the Geneva Conventions, customary international law, and the Uniform Code of Military Justice all prohibit the killing of noncombatant civilians. The alleged brutality of others is no justification. By saying it is, Kerrey implicates the people who generated that rationale: the CIA. That is why there is a moral imperative to scrutinize the Phoenix Program and the CIA officers who created it, the people who participated in it, and the journalists who covered it up—to expose the dark side of our national psyche, the part that allows us to employ terror to assure our world dominance.

To accomplish this there must be a war crimes tribunal. This won't be easy. The US government has gone to great lengths to shield itself from such legal scrutiny, at the same time it selectively manipulates international institutions, such as the UN, to go after people like Slobodan Milosevic.

According to human rights lawyer Michael Ratner, the legal avenues for bringing Kerrey and his cohorts to justice are quite limited. Under the Alien Tort Claims Act, a civil suit could be lodged against Kerrey in the United States by the families of the victims. "These are the kinds of cases I did against Gramajo, Pangaitan (Timor)," Ratner said. "The main problem here is that it is doubtful the Vietnamese would sue a liberal when they are dying to have better relations with the US. I would do this case if could get plaintiffs—so far no luck." According to Ratner, there is no statute of limitations problem, as it is newly discovered evidence and there is a strong argument—particularly in the criminal context—that there is no statute of limitations for war crimes.

But criminal cases in the US present a difficult, if not impossible, prospect. Now that Kerrey is discharged from the Navy, the military courts, which went after Lt. Calley for the My Lai massacre, have no jurisdiction over him. "As to a criminal case in the US—my answer is no," says Ratner. "The US first passed a war crimes statute (18 USC sec. 2441 War Crimes) in 1996—that statute makes what Kerrey did a war crime punishable by death or life imprisonment—but it was passed after the crime, and criminal statutes are not retroactive."

In 1988, Congress enacted a statute against genocide, which might apply to Kerrey's actions, but it, too, can't be applied retroactively. Generally, at the time of Kerrey's acts in Vietnam, US criminal law did not extend to what US citizens did overseas unless they were military. (It should be noted that as a senator, Kerrey voted for the war crimes law, thus opening the opportunity for others to be prosecuted for crimes similar to those he committed but is shielded from.)

The United Nations is a possibility but a long shot. It could establish an ad hoc tribunal such as it did with the Rwanda ICTR and Yugoslavia ICTY. "This would require action by the UN Security Council. They could do it, but what are the chances?" says Ratner. "There is still the prospect for a US veto. And what that really points out is how those tribunals are bent toward what the US and West want."

| EXTRADITION TO AND PROSECUTION IN VIETNAM AND/OR ANOTHER COUNTRY IS ALSO A POSSIBILITY.

Extradition to and prosecution in Vietnam and/or another country is also a possibility. It can be argued that war crimes are crimes over which there is universal jurisdiction—in fact, it's the obligation of countries under the Geneva Convention of 1948 to seek out and prosecute war criminals. "Universal jurisdiction does not require the presence of the defendant—he can be indicted and tried in some countries in absentia—or his extradition can be requested," says Ratner. "Some countries may have statutes permitting this. Kerrey should check his travel plans and hire a good lawyer before he gets on a plane. He can use Kissinger's lawyer."

OLYMPIC INDUSTRY MYTHOLOGY
A CONSUMER'S GUIDE
HELEN JEFFERSON LENSKYJ

Here are the profiles of two "Olympians," that rare breed of men and women who, if one believes the rhetoric, are nobler than most mere mortals.

The first is David Fidler, who represented Australia in swimming in the 1968 Olympics in Mexico City and later became a TV news broadcaster in Darwin, Australia.

The second is Jan Borowy, who played on the Canadian women's field hockey squad that trained for the 1984 Olympics. Today Borowy is a union organizer and has been a community activist with Toronto's anti-Olympic group, the Bread Not Circuses (BNC) coalition, since 1989.

Which of these stories is true? Why does it matter? The Olympic mystique, which I have identified as "the myth of the pure athlete and pure sport,"[1] helps to lift the Olympics out of the realm of mundane hallmark events like world fairs, and ordinary urban megaprojects like entertainment centers and theme parks. Metaphors like "Olympic movement," "Olympic family," and "Olympic spirit" obscure the reality: The organization and hosting of the Olympic Games is an *industry*, not a lifestyle, an extended family, or a religious cult.

Following critical sport scholars in the 1970s who renamed the fitness movement the "fitness *industry*" when it became evident that profit-making was its major function, some critical sport scholars and community activists have adopted the equivalent term to apply to the Olympic machine. Of greater economic and global significance than a mere sporting event, the Olympics are systematically organized to maximize private sector investment, generate huge television revenues, and exploit competition between transnational corporations for exclusive Olympic sponsorship status.

And so, back to the question: Whose story is true? Jan Borowy does, in fact, fit the profile. Her participation in international sport changed her life, but not in the predictable way about which Olympians boast. The world travel and cultural exchanges that she experienced as a high-performance athlete radicalized her; she began to analyze Olympic ideologies and sporting practices, soon becoming an anti-Olympic activist. This outcome would not, of course, count as an Olympic success story in the eyes of most other retired athletes. For example, a few months before the Sydney

Olympics, former Olympic swimmer Nicole Stevenson was quoted in the *Sydney Morning Herald*: "Unfortunately, some of the younger athletes are so amazed by how big and how wonderful it [the Olympic Village] is, they lose sight that they are there for one reason—to compete."[2] Stevenson herself seems to have lost sight of the other staples of "Olympic spirit" rhetoric: the cultural celebrations, the contribution to international understanding, the festival of world youth, the camaraderie of the Olympic village, and so on. Indeed, many athletes refuse to live in the village, thereby shattering that particular illusion.

It is not difficult to understand why most Olympic athletes choose not to rock the boat. Their status brings with it considerable symbolic privilege and, for professional athletes, significant financial and material benefit. At the same time, it is difficult for young athletes to challenge coaches' and administrators' almost absolute power over their lives. Even after they retire, many athletes continue to have a heavy personal investment in the "Olympic movement" and never fail to identify themselves publicly as former "Olympians." It is hard to imagine a parallel example in the world of intellectual endeavor: Would an elderly man who had won a scholarship during his college years continue to cite this achievement and to cling to this identity throughout his entire life?

Unlike Borowy, David Fidler was a self-described "ratbag"—a schemer, a fraud (although admittedly Borowy and other Bread Not Circuses members have been called worse names!). Fidler simply invented his Olympic identity and for fifteen years traded on that myth to boost his media career, until the deception was exposed and he was forced to resign.[3]

Events over the last three years at the highest levels of the Olympic industry are relevant to both Fidler's and Borowy's experiences. From November 1998 to the present, extensive evidence of bribery and corruption in host-city bidding processes has come to light through several formal investigations in North America, Australia, and elsewhere. Those involved came up with two favorite explanations: that giving of gifts and services was simply a manifestation of friendship within the Olympic family, and that such practices were justified because "everybody does it." At least four new connotations of "friendship" emerged from these reports:

- Friendship as the special relationships among people in the Olympic industry that legitimate bid committees giving—and International Olympic Committee (IOC) members and their families receiving—money, presents, medical services, university tuition, immigration assistance, etc. in contravention of IOC guidelines. A recent example involved arrangements between Australian IOC member Kevin Gosper and the Greek Olympic Committee to permit Gosper's daughter to participate in the torch relay run.

- Friendship as the opportunistic cultivation of personal relationships with IOC members and their families in order to influence their votes. Dossiers prepared by Australian IOC member Phil Coles and "agents" employed by bid committees were used to facilitate these relationships as part of several recent bid processes.

- Friendship as the logical outcome of one's personal identity as a one-time Olympic competitor who has subsequently developed a circle of exclusively "Olympian" friends. Toronto's 1996 bid committee chair, Paul Henderson, has claimed that all of his friends are "Olympians," and Sydney's Olympic organizing committee even provided an "Olympian Reunion Center" for this elite group.

- Friendship as the mutually rewarding relationships typical in international trade and business circles, with gifts or services provided where necessary to satisfy local customs and oil the wheels of commerce.[4]

Liberal discourses of "cultural difference" were employed to support allegations and sanctions that were indisputably shaped by geography, culture, and race, despite IOC assertions to the contrary. Following disclosures about Salt Lake City's bid process, it was argued that people from developing countries had different cultural practices than those of the Western world. For example, it was alleged that they expected gifts or bribes as part of normal business transactions. It was also argued that African and South American IOC members, coming from hot climates, had limited knowledge of Olympic winter sports, and thus were easily swayed by luxury accommodations, gifts, and services offered by cities bidding for the 2002 Winter Games; in other words, they were less ethical than white Anglo-Saxon members. It soon became clear that charges of misconduct were more likely to stick to black or ethnic minority IOC members than to white members, and that sanctions were less likely to be applied to powerful IOC members, those from powerful countries, or those in the running for the IOC presidency. This was not a level playing field.

On the rare occasions when the mass media criticize any aspect of the Olympics, they're more likely to target individuals than to attack the *system* that normalizes dishonesty at all levels—from the IOC and national Olympic committees to sport administrators and coaches—and promotes the "values" of competitive sport, which might best be characterized as winning at all costs by whatever means necessary.

On the question of values, an Olympic promotional program for children sponsored by Westpac Bank, a Sydney 2000 Olympic sponsor, carried some disturbing messages. Called the "Values for Life" program, one Westpac advertisement displayed on Sydney's bus shelters early in 2000 showed a boy holding a soccer ball, with the caption: "I might never be an Olympic athlete but at least I can think like one." Which one? we might ask. Many of the men and women implicated in the IOC bribery scandal were retired Olympic athletes. They are obviously not an undifferentiated mass; some are ethical, intelligent, insightful, progressive, and some are not. Why would we expect otherwise? Yet the Olympic industry, like Fidler, trades extensively on Olympic mythology, particularly the myth of the pure Olympic athlete.

There are, of course, many more Olympic industry myths that need to be exposed.

_MYTH: THE BARCELONA AND ATLANTA OLYMPICS HAD POSITIVE SOCIAL LEGACIES

Reality of Barcelona, 1992:[5]

- There were police crackdowns on petty crime, street sweeps targeting sex trade workers and homeless people, and arrests of dissidents before and during the Games.

- About 400 homeless people were subjected to police "control and supervision" during the Games.

- In 1986, the city promised to include subsidized housing in the post-Games Olympic village; by 1992 most of the 6,000 units had been sold to upper-middle-class residents for over $350,000.

- From 1986 to 1992, new house prices rose by 250 percent, with accompanying increases in the numbers of renters and widespread rent increases.

- The pattern of out-migration of disadvantaged groups from the city was exacerbated by Olympic preparations, with an increase of over 50 percent in the number leaving in 1992 compared to 1986.

■ ■ ■ ■ ■ ■ ■ ■ ■ ■

Reality of Atlanta, 1996:[6]

- 9,500 units of affordable housing were lost during Olympic preparations, and only 30 percent of about 200 new houses and townhouses were affordable, in an area where the average annual income was only $7,800.

- Atlanta police took hundreds of homeless people to the outskirts of the city and threatened them with six months in jail if they returned.

- Police had the power to arrest anyone found "loitering," and over 9,000 homeless African-American men—who made up about 90 percent of homeless people in Atlanta—were arrested.

- In a typical Olympic "legacy," the stadium—now Turner Field, home of the Atlanta Braves professional baseball team—was built despite community opposition by Summerhill's mostly black residents who gained minimal benefits, most notably an 8.5 percent share of parking revenues for community development.

Meanwhile, as Salt Lake City prepared for the 2002 Winter Games, advocates for homeless people were concerned at police statements that they would "maintain the status quo" in February 2002—that is, continue to issue citations for minor infractions, and homeless people who can't pay the fines face arrest. When homeless shelters are full, people are usually accommodated at cheap hotels, but these, too, are full during the Olympics.[7]

ATLANTA POLICE TOOK HUNDREDS OF HOMELESS PEOPLE TO THE OUTSKIRTS OF THE CITY AND THREATENED THEM WITH SIX MONTHS IN JAIL IF THEY RETURNED.

_MYTH: SALT LAKE CITY WAS AN INNOCENT VICTIM OF THE "CULTURE OF BRIBERY" THAT PERMEATED THE IOC

Reality: In 1989, according to the Salt Lake Board of Ethics (SLBE) report, then-IOC president Juan Antonio Samaranch advised Salt Lake bid officials Tom Welch and Dave Johnson "to become personally acquainted with as many IOC members as possible and to become part of the 'Olympic Family.'"[8] They took his advice to heart.

- Salt Lake City's bid strategy: "Establish and maintain long-term, *vote influencing* relationships with IOC members,...with

other key people of the Olympic Family...[and] with USOC [US Olympic Committee]." Methods ranged from sending greeting cards to IOC families, to providing unlimited credit for their shopping excursions; one major department store made a $250,000 value-in-kind donation to the bid committee.[9]

- The SLBE reported that IOC member Alexandru Siperco and his son Andrei resisted Johnson's repeated attempts to press favors upon them: airline tickets, housing, and living expenses for Andrei while he studied at Brigham Young University. Johnson told Andrei that these "grants" were approved components of the organizing committee's "scholarship program."[10]

- In February 1989, KTVX reporter (and Olympic whistleblower) John Harrington was planning to give the US Olympic Committee's ethics panel a state auditor's report which implicated Welch and Johnson in unethical business practices, but his employers warned him of the consequences—that he would be fired.[11] (It was not until 1999 that the *Salt Lake Tribune* published the complete story.)

- In 1994, Harrington exposed environmental controversies at the proposed Olympic ski jump site in a *Salt Lake Weekly* article, which, he later claimed, irreparably damaged his independent sports video business. He also reported that other journalists who tried to cover Olympic news objectively jeopardized their careers, while many simply joined the Olympic gravy train.[12]

- At the end of the day, Samaranch claimed that, since only about $1 million was allegedly involved in the Salt Lake bribery scandal, it was less serious than the European Union scandal, which had involved about $1 billion.[13]

_MYTH: THE IOC HAS BEEN SUCCESSFULLY REFORMED

Reality:[14] Basically the same group of privileged, mostly male members are in power, with a few additions to make the organization appear more athlete-friendly. These include recently retired athletes who lack the power bases that are essential to influence future directions. The inclusion of international federation presidents, whose primary interest lies in promoting their own sport, is not conducive to so-called Olympic movement ideals.

- Another new member is Paul Henderson, the chair of the Toronto's was one of the few bid committees that avoided a formal investigation in 1999, despite evidence produced by other commissions of inquiry demonstrating the bid committee's role in assisting IOC members and their families (for example, Pirjo Haeggman, who was the first to resign).

• Australian IOC member Kevin Gosper had to withdraw from the IOC presidential race following a scandal in May 2000, when he let his daughter take the place of a Greek-Australian girl who had been selected to run the first leg of the torch relay in Greece. His rationale? He was an "Olympian," so it was only right that his daughter should have the honor of running first.

_MYTH: THE SYDNEY 2000 OLYMPICS CONSTITUTED A MAJOR STEP TOWARD RECONCILIATION BETWEEN BLACK AND WHITE AUSTRALIANS

Reality:[15] The notion that over 200 years of oppression experienced by Indigenous Australians at the hands of European colonizers could be wiped out by a sporting event was insulting, to say the least. Efforts towards reconciliation between black and white Australians, particularly on native land rights issues, suffered significant setbacks in the 1990s, and support for anti-immigration, anti-refugee, and anti-Aboriginal politicians and platforms steadily increased.

While television audiences around the world were fed a steady diet of "symbolic reconciliation"–including Kathy Freeman's lighting of the cauldron, Indigenous cultural content in the opening and closing ceremonies, and national euphoria over Freeman's gold medal—the real situation was very different. Here are some examples:

• In a 7-week period in mid-2000, eight Indigenous people died in police custody.

• A week before the Games, the Australian government attacked the UN for criticizing its treatment of Aborigines, then refused to cooperate with the UN monitoring team.

• Two days after the Games ended, both the Northern Territory and the Commonwealth governments renewed their efforts to dilute Indigenous land rights legislation.

• A national health study released in 2000 reported that the life expectancy of Aborigines was equivalent to that of non-Indigenous people born 100 years ago: that is, 20 years shorter.

_MYTH: THE HIGH LEVEL OF GOVERNMENT INVOLVEMENT IN SYDNEY'S OLYMPIC PREPARATIONS ENSURED THAT CITIZENS' RIGHTS WERE PROTECTED AND DEMOCRATIC PROCESSES WERE FOLLOWED

Reality:[16] It was certainly true that the New South Wales (NSW) government played a central role in staging the Sydney Olympics—as did NSW taxpayers, who footed over 50 percent of the bill. State politician Michael Knight wore two hats: 1) Minister for Sport and the Olympics and 2) president of the Sydney organizing committee, an arrangement that pleased the IOC and was rarely criticized locally despite the obvious conflict of interest. Indeed, both the IOC and the government warned politicians to suspend partisan politics for the duration.

The IOC Charter prohibits peaceful protests in or near Olympic sites; Sydney wanted to present a "clean" image to tourists; and multinational sponsors expected their exclusive rights to Olympic advertising to be protected. These factors, together with Sydney 2000's rigid timelines that demanded fast-tracking all Olympic-related legislation and development applications, meant that normal political debate and democratic decision-making processes were seriously compromised.

• The major political parties in the NSW government refused to enact any legislation to control greedy landlords or to protect homeless people.

• The number of homeless people in Sydney almost tripled between 1992 and 1999, and there were significant increases in inquiries to tenants' advice services about rent increases and "no-cause" evictions by landlords.

• Rents in some suburbs doubled in the period 1998 to 2000, and the number of households paying more than 30 percent of their income in rent increased significantly throughout the 1990s.

• A series of legislative acts relating to police power and public behavior, passed by a large majority in the NSW parliament, criminalized poverty and restricted peaceful public assembly, while federal legislation empowered the government to deploy armed troops to quash civil unrest.

• The homelessness protocol that social service and community groups eventually negotiated with Olympic authorities was only a code of practice for Sydney police and security, not a Parliamentary regulation, and not applicable to the region where most Olympic events were held.

_MYTH: THE SYDNEY OLYMPICS HAD UNANIMOUS SUPPORT AMONG AUSTRALIANS

Reality:[17] Indigenous people, environmentalists, advocates for homeless people, human rights groups, anti-globalization activists, and others mobilized in the early 1990s. Some called for boycotts, and others demanded thorough social impact assessments and a genuine commitment to environmentally sustainable development. In the years before the Games, representatives from social service organizations and community groups had extensive meetings—mostly unproductive—with police, politicians, the Olympic organizing committee, and the IOC to discuss housing and homelessness, the criminalization of poverty, Indigenous protest, environmental problems, and other key concerns.

> • Protests were organized on a regular basis from February 2000 on, as well as during the Games, to draw public attention to all of these social and environmental issues.
>
> • Undercover police infiltrated Aboriginal and other nonviolent anti-Olympic groups, successfully using divide-and-conquer tactics to undermine the protest efforts—allegedly in the interests of "national security."
>
> • The giant Murdoch newspaper chain purchased exclusive rights to major Olympic news stories, thereby jeopardizing the freedom of the press. Olympic protests were either trivialized or ignored in most mainstream media.

_MYTH: SYDNEY POLICE AND OLYMPIC SECURITY FORCES WERE POLITE AND FRIENDLY, AND DID NOT HARASS HOMELESS PEOPLE OR PROTESTERS

Reality:[18] Local and international media made much of Sydney's so-called "feel-good" atmosphere in September 2000, and a year later, Olympic boosters were still enthusing about the magic Olympic feeling and downplaying the negative social impacts. There was, in fact, clear evidence that the privilege of "sharing the spirit"—the official Olympic slogan—wasn't extended to all citizens.

> • Police and security guards broke up protests, removed homeless people from the streets, and prevented ambush marketing—even policing so-called "illegal" messages on T-shirts worn by spectators.
>
> • Environmentalists were evicted from the Sydney Media Centre when they tried to distribute flyers on Australia's greenhouse emissions and other environmental problems.

> • Members of the Anti-Olympic Alliance were threatened with arrest for distributing flyers in a downtown public thoroughfare designated as an Olympic live site.
>
> • In a suburb near Olympic Park, police arrested seven homeless men and charged them with petty offenses; this took place a few days before the Olympics ended, just after a temporary shelter for homeless people had closed down.

_MYTH: SYDNEY 2000 WAS AN UNQUALIFIED ENVIRONMENTAL SUCCESS STORY

Reality:[19]

> • Environmental watchdog organizations struggled for years to obtain full information about environmental impacts and remediation plans.
>
> • The cleanup of contaminated soil, sediment, and water in and near the Olympic site is still incomplete.
>
> • More than 12,000 residents signed a petition to Parliament, opposing the construction of a temporary beach volleyball stadium on the sands of Bondi Beach, a location demanded by NBC and the international federation regardless of negative environmental and social impacts.
>
> • Bondi Olympic Watch campaigned against the stadium for eighteen months; their efforts were dismissed in the international press during the Olympics.
>
> • Construction of the Bankstown velodrome and cycling track destroyed an endangered fragment of woodland and about $15,000 worth of native bush regeneration carried out by volunteers from local environmental groups.
>
> • A second area of endangered woodland was destroyed to construct a cycling warmup track; again, environmentalists' protests were ignored.
>
> • Sydney's major Olympic sponsors—Nike, Coca Cola, Westpac Bank, etc.—are among the worst national and transnational corporations in terms of environmental and/or human rights abuses.

_DECODING OLYMPICSPEAK: TORONTO'S 2008 BID

Everything the IOC says is code for something else. If,

for example, they describe the Atlanta Games as "exceptional," that's the equivalent of saying, "Hand me a twig, please, I'd like to scrape the Atlanta Olympics off the sole of my shoe."
—John Clarke, main character in the Australian Broadcasting Commission's satirical TV series *The Games*, 1998

Bread Not Circuses had firsthand experience with Olympicspeak during the Toronto 2008 bid process. In March 2000, the IOC Evaluation Commission, chaired by Hein Verbruggen, visited Toronto to assess the bid. Despite numerous obstacles put up by the Toronto bid committee (TOBid), some BNC members were finally granted an "audience" with this esteemed group. At the time, it appeared that they were listening politely and attentively, but they proceeded to trash BNC in subsequent newspaper coverage.

▌"ESTABLISH AND MAINTAIN LONG-TERM, *VOTE INFLUENCING* ▌ RELATIONSHIPS WITH IOC MEMBERS."

At the end of their visit, the IOC committee held a press conference to talk about Toronto's bid. Here's a guide to decoding Verbruggen's words of praise:

1. *The "impressive" level of athlete involvement*—Toronto promises "Games for Athletes." Olympic industry officials like to have different labels for different audiences and occasions. Sydney Olympic promoters started by calling Sydney 2000 the "Athletes' Games," then switched to "Green Games," then reverted to the "Athletes' Games" when Greenpeace criticized their environmental plans.

When Randy Starkman, Olympic columnist for Toronto newspaper *The Star*, asked if the most important consideration was to have the "best Games for the athletes," IOC veteran Verbruggen hedged, but novice member Sergei Bubka fell into the trap: "Oh yes," he said. The real answer is a little different: The only groups worth worrying about are the sponsors, NBC, and international sport federation presidents, all of whom can make or break the event. The one and only feature that would keep athletes away would be fool-proof drug-testing.

2. *Strong government support*. This meant that the IOC was satisfied that federal, provincial, and municipal taxpayers would be fully responsible for covering the costs—and the deficits. The IOC refuses to accept any financial liability and wants to make sure that taxpayers bear the entire risk, as required by Rule 42 of the International Olympic Charter.

3. *Excellent sport complex and "legacy."* Faint praise: The reference to "legacy" is irrelevant since the IOC repeatedly states that it's only interested in the 16-day sporting event. IOC rules forbid Olympic revenues, such as broadcast rights, corporate sponsorships, and ticket sales, from being used to cover costs, such as construction,

environmental remediation, and infrastructure. At the local level, bid committees focus on the sporting event and the related intangible benefits (civic pride, "world class city" status, "opportunity of a lifetime" for youth and Olympic volunteers, etc.) when it suits their interests to do so. At other times, they promote the long-term legacies, such as state-of-the-art sporting facilities, increased tourism, and economic growth—benefits that are enjoyed only by a minority of residents, if indeed they materialize at all. In the case of Sydney, many of the new facilities became white elephants a few short months after the Olympics left town.

Infrastructure costs, such as upgrades to roads, highways, public transport, and airports—as well as the hidden costs of police, immigration officials, and emergency services—are often invisible in Olympic budgets. An audit of the Sydney 2000 budget, for example, revealed that organizers had included indirect benefits while failing to list indirect costs on the other side of the ledger. TOBid's security plan called for 6,000 police for more than three *weeks* during the Olympics and Paralympics. It is interesting to compare this level of police deployment to the April 2001 Quebec Summit, where about 5,000 police were needed for just three *days*. But while the cost of policing anti-globalization protesters is routinely criticized by conservatives as a drain on the public purse (and by radicals for very different reasons), Olympic security budgets seem immune to such criticism.

_MYTH: THE TORONTO 2008 BID COMMITTEE WAS COMMITTED TO AN OPEN AND TRANSPARENT PROCESS

Reality: During the IOC's inspection visit, TOBid boosters pointed to Toronto's Air Canada Center (the city's major professional basketball and ice hockey venue) as a model for Olympic construction, claiming that the center was built "on budget and on time." In fact, its costs rose 50 percent over a four-year period, and construction was two years late, thereby incurring fines of about $640,000.

These developments had been thoroughly covered in *The Star* of Toronto.[20] Yet when a BNC representative sent letters to *The Star's* editor and its ombudsperson, pointing out that TOBid's reported claims were not only inaccurate but also were contradicted by *The Star's* own coverage, she received no reply and the letter was not published.

This lack of response came as no surprise. Several months earlier, it had become clear that this newspaper, which was an official TOBid sponsor, did not welcome BNC's letters. Shortly after I managed to get a critical letter published, a senior reporter, in conversation with another BNC member, alleged that I had misrepresented myself as a "citizen" when I really represented BNC—a fact that apparently rendered me *persona non grata* as a letter-writer. I had provided my residential address and phone number, in accordance with *The Star's* letters policy, as well as my university affiliation and contact details; however, my earlier experience had shown that *The Star* rarely publishes university affiliations unless it serves their interests to do so. One of my colleagues, for example, was identified as a University of Toronto professor in a letter on a non-Olympic issue, but I was not.

On related issues of financial openness and accountability, TOBid eventually agreed to give a BNC representative access to its complete budget—but the written conditions for such access included a ban on discussing any of the contents, under threat of injunction, and TOBid's right to preview all proposed articles for publication, thereby demonstrating again typical Olympic industry patterns of secrecy and media manipulation.

_OLYMPIC RESISTANCE

The problems of disadvantaged people—low income tenants, homeless people, immigrants, and ethnic minorities—have been made demonstrably worse in Olympic host cities since the 1980s.[21] While the mass media wallow in "Olympic dream" rhetoric, the dreams of poor people who long for adequate food and shelter are forgotten.

> **WHILE THE MASS MEDIA WALLOW IN "OLYMPIC DREAM" RHETORIC, THE DREAMS OF POOR PEOPLE WHO LONG FOR ADEQUATE FOOD AND SHELTER ARE FORGOTTEN.**

Community groups have been resisting the Olympic industry for over a decade.[22] In the United States, fledgling anti-Olympic groups are in several of the cities that are currently competing for the right to bid for the 2012 Olympics, while the BNC coalition, active for over a decade, no doubt helped to derail Toronto's two recent bids (for the 1996 and the 2008 Games). Community groups in Salt Lake City have been active for many years in an attempt to alleviate the worst Olympic-related problems, particularly in relation to the plight of homeless people and the threat to freedom of assembly during the Games. And in Sydney in 2000, anti-globalization activists made important links between the Olympic industry and global capitalism, while Indigenous groups and their allies used the opportunity to draw world attention to racist oppression.

Olympic critics have suggested a number of strategies, including refusing to watch television coverage or buy tickets to events, organizing protest events and mock-Olympics, boycotting sponsors' products, and creating alternative community-based sporting events—all actions designed to challenge the myth that the Olympics are the only game in town.

Endnotes

1. Lenskyj, H. *Inside the Olympic Industry: Power, Politics and Activism.* Albany NY: SUNY Press, 2000.   **2.** Bernoth, A. "Inside Sydney's New Global Village." *Sydney Morning Herald* 11 April 2000.   **3.** Temple, W. "Confessions of an Olympic 'Ratbag'." *Daily Telegraph* 28 March 2000.   **4.** See *op. cit.*, Lenskyj   **5.** Cox, G., M. Darcy, and M. Bounds. *The Olympics and Housing.* Sydney: Shelter NSW (Sept 1994); Montalban, M. *Barcelonas* (translated by Andy Robinson). London: Verso, 1992.   **6.** Beaty, A. (1998a). E-mail communication to Bread Not Circuses (4 June 1998); Beaty, A. (1998b). Extracts from August 10 speech to NSW Parliament. *Rent Report 2* (Dec 1998); Beaty, A. (1999a). "The Homeless Olympics?" *Homelessness: The Unfinished Agenda.* Ed. C. James, R. Plant, J. South, B. Beeston, and D. Long. Sydney: University of Sydney, 1999: 46-51; Beaty, A. (1999b). Personal communication (12 Nov 1999); Rutheiser, D. *Imagineering* Atlanta. New York: Verso, 1996.   **7.** Vosepka, R. "Advocates for Homeless Leery of Olympics." Associated Press (28 March 2001).   **8.** SLBE. *Report of the Salt Lake Olympic Committee Board of Ethics Inquiry* (9 Feb 1999): 5.   **9.** *Ibid.*: 7, 32 [emphasis added].   **10.** *Ibid.*: Conclusion, 2-3   **11.** Harrington, J. "Capitol of hypocrisy." *Salt Lake City Weekly* 7 Aug 1997; Harrington, J. *CBC Sportsworld* transcript (5 May 1999).   **12.** *Ibid.*   **13.** Vincent, D. (1999e). "Samaranch to Face Vote of Confidence." *The Star* (Toronto) 14 March 1999.   **14.** Booth, D. Review of *Inside the Olympic Industry. Olympika IX* (2000): 122-6; *op. cit.*, Lenskyj; MacAloon, J. (2001). "IOC Reform, Then and Now: An Insider's View." Presentation to faculty of Physical Education and Health, University of Toronto (5 Feb 2001); McKay, J, B. Hutchins, and J. Mikosza. "'Shame and Scandal in the Family': Australian Media Narratives of the IOC/SOCOG Scandal Matrix." Keynote address, "Bridging Three Centuries: Intellectual Crossroads and the Modern Olympic Movement," Sydney (8-10 Sept 2000).   **15.** Australian Institute of Health and Welfare. *Australia's Health 2000.* Canberra: AISW (2000); Lenskyj, H. *The Best Ever Olympics?: Social Impacts of Sydney 2000.* Albany NY: SUNY Press, 2002 (forthcoming); *op. cit.*, Boyle.   **16.** Blunden, H. *The Impact of the Olympics on Housing in Sydney.* Draft report, Redfern Legal Center and Rentwatchers (Oct 2000); Boon-Kuo, L. "Police Powers and Technology, and the Sydney 2000 Olympic Games." Research projects, Faculty of Law, UTS (Autumn 1998); Head, M. "Olympic Security." *Alternative Law Journal* 25:3 (June 2000): 75-80; Lye, J. "The Olympics: Where Have All the Boarding Houses Gone?" *Alternative Law Journal* 25:1 (2000). <www.austlii.edu.au/au/journals/AltLJ/2000/1.html>; Rentwatchers. "We Can't Share the Spirit if We Can't Pay the Rent: Rentwatchers Information Kit." Sydney: Rentwatchers, 2000.   **17.** Jackson, R. "SOCOG 3: and You're Out." *Djadi-Dugarang* 3:2 (April 2001): 1-6; *op. cit.*, Lenskyj 2000, 2002.   **18.** *Op cit.*, Blunden; *op cit.*, Lenskyj 2002; Vinson, T. *Counting the Street Homeless.* Sydney: Shelter NSW, 2000.   **19.** Greenpeace (2000a). "The Environmental Record of the OCA." Greenpeace Olympics campaign briefing (16 Feb 2000); Greenpeace (2000b). *Green Olympics, Dirty Sponsors.* Sydney: Greenpeace Australia, 20000; Latham, H. "Sport vs. Bushland." *Green Games Watch 2000* 11 (Spring 2000): 3-5.   **20.** For example: *The Star*, 27 Sept 1996, 22 Nov 1996, 9 Feb 1999.   **21.** *Op. cit.*, Lenskyj 2000.   **22.** *Ibid.*: chapter 6.

Further Sources

Calvin, M. "The Cycle of Cynicism." *Mail on Sunday* 4 Jul 1999; Grange, M. "Summer Olympic Red Alert." *Report on Business Magazine* (Sept 2000): 25-34; SpoilSport. "SpoilSport's Guidebook to Atlanta" (brochure). 1996.

THE EUROPEAN UNION UNMASKED
DICTATORSHIP REVEALED

LINDSAY JENKINS

In his address to the US Congress on September 21, 2001, President George W. Bush claimed, "America has no truer friend than Great Britain. Once again, we are joined together in a great cause. I'm so honored the British Prime Minister has crossed an ocean to show his unity with America. Thank you for coming, friend."

In the public gallery, Britain's Prime Minister, Tony Blair, stood at attention, tight-lipped and serious of face to acknowledge the warm applause from the Congressmen below.

Blair's support for America in the dark hours after the terrorist attacks on the World Trade Center and the Pentagon would have been worth little had his words not been backed by Britain's world-class armed forces, ready to support American military action. Britain's example helped to bring in rapid offers of military aid from other countries, such as France, that are not automatically on America's side in a fight. A military coalition stood against Osama bin Laden and his terrorists. America was not alone in the world.

It is therefore astonishing to review events of less than three years earlier, when in December 1998 the same British Prime Minister, Tony Blair, went to meet the President of France, Jacques Chirac, at St. Malo in France.

Blair and Chirac effectively agreed to end the independence of the British and French forces in favor of a European Union[1] (EU) defense force. Here is part of their joint statement after the talks ended:

> The EU needs to be [able] to play its full role on the international stage... [T]he Union must have the capacity for *autonomous* action, backed up by credible military forces, the means to decide to use them, and a readiness to do so in order to respond to international crises.... The EU will also need to have recourse to suitable military means...within NATO's European pillar or...means *outside the NATO framework.*

Since that turning point in military history, Tony Blair agreed to the EU's Rapid Reaction Force of 60,000 men, backed by 300 aircraft and a naval force by the year 2003. Roughly a quarter of Britain's armed forces were pledged to serve in the new force. With normal rotation, most British forces will be allocated to the EU army.

Many would argue that defense is the first duty of government. Yet here was the British Prime Minister prepared to give up his country's armed forces to the control of a foreign power.

Two British admirals warned: "It would probably mean that we would ultimately have to obtain [EU] approval if we wished to use [our forces] on a purely national basis."[2]

YET HERE WAS THE BRITISH PRIME MINISTER PREPARED TO GIVE UP HIS COUNTRY'S ARMED FORCES TO THE CONTROL OF A FOREIGN POWER.

Both British and European leaders have been engaging in doubles-peak with the Americans, assuring them that this is not the end of NATO while at the same time planning for exactly that—the end of NATO.

George Robertson, when British Defense Secretary, quickly reassured the Americans that "[there is] no question of a European single army; no [EU] Commission or European Parliament involvement in decision making; no transfer of decision making on military capability from individual Governments; and no undermining or duplication of NATO."

But the division between Britain and the US was laid bare on October 7, 1999, when the recently ennobled Lord Robertson, in his new job as NATO's Secretary General, backed the EU and not NATO: "We want to ensure that strong and effective military resources are also available to the EU, so that we can take action in support of the CFSP [the EU's foreign policy] when NATO...is not engaged militarily."[3]

The EU's President, Romano Prodi from Italy, was even franker: "When I was talking about the European army, I was not joking.... If you don't want to call it a European army, don't call it a European army.... You can call it 'Margaret,' you can call it 'Mary-Anne,' you can find any name, but it is a joint effort for peacekeeping missions—the first time you have a joint, not bilateral, effort at European level."[4]

A Military Committee of EU Chiefs of Defense Staff from all EU countries now meets regularly. It started work in early 2000 with a projected staff of 90 for its head-quarters. The first director was the German General Klaus Schuwirth. A Political and Security Committee of ambassadors controls the political and strategic direction of any crisis operation, sending guidelines to the Military Committee.

The terrorist attacks in the United States, and the resulting renewal of the "special relationship" with Britain, did nothing to stop or even slow the creation of the EU's army. They did the opposite. The lack of military force obviously limited the EU's world influence at a critical time, so the EU army project moved forward apace. It now included a committee of EU intelligence chiefs. That must give US intelligence agencies pause for thought before passing secret material to their British ally.

Winston Churchill had presciently written years before: "A European army would be a sludgy amalgam."[5] Today at the heart of that "amalgam" are the forces of three countries: Britain, France, and Germany. But for Germany, sending its forces abroad represents a *volte face* after 50 years of legal limits on the use of its armed forces entrenched in its post-WWII constitution and a strong peace movement within the country. The EU army is further complicated because the EU includes both non-NATO countries and neutrals like Ireland and Sweden; there is no common language; and, last but not least, European defense is seriously underfunded.

Where will this new army be used? Anywhere up to 2,500 miles from its base, which includes the Balkans, the Middle East, and half of Africa. As Senator John McCain shrewdly remarked: "It is not hard to envision our allies intervening militarily, under the auspices of their new defense organization and without our concurrence, in very difficult problems that they are unprepared to resolve, necessitating an eventual appeal to NATO to bail them out."[6]

■ ■ ■ ■ ■ ■ ■ ■ ■ ■

Though no politician would say so, creating a defense force had always been on the agenda for the new European state, but it was scheduled to be the last piece of the jigsaw to be slotted into place.

Jean Monnet, the so-called father of the EU, wrote of the outbreak of the Korean War in 1950: "The federation of Europe would have to become an immediate objective. The army...[would] have to be placed...under joint sovereignty. *We could no longer wait, as we had once planned*, for political Europe to be the culminating point of a gradual process, since its joint defense was inconceivable without a joint political authority...."[7]

MONNET'S "GRADUAL PROCESS" HAS ALREADY ACHIEVED THE SUPREMACY OF EU LAW OVER NATIONAL LAW, WITH THE EUROPEAN COURT OF JUSTICE IN LUXEMBOURG AS THE ULTIMATE COURT OF APPEAL.

For 50 years the federalists pretended that the EU (and its predecessors) was no more than a trading bloc and that the acquisition of more power was only to promote free trade. The existence of an EU army, depriving the constituent nations of their own defense and wrapping them in the foreign policy of the EU, powerfully demonstrates that trade was indeed a pretense.

The reality is a new country called "Europe."

Monnet's "gradual process" has already achieved the supremacy of EU law over national law, with the European Court of Justice in Luxembourg as the ultimate court of appeal. Trade farming and fishing are controlled from Brussels, Belgium; no individual country can sign a trade treaty, which means, for example, that only the EU can negotiate at the World Trade Organization (WTO); and foreign policy, taxation, and national finances are already heavily circumscribed. Both an EU-wide criminal justice system and an EU-wide police force, which will eventually run all national police forces, are well on the way.[8]

This long process of integration has been notable by the absence of any democratic choice. The origins of the EU can be traced directly to chance meetings at the 1919 peace conference at the end of the First World War. A small group of largely British and American elites kept in touch and developed ideas for a united Europe while waiting for any chance to start the process. The first attempt, the Franco-Anglo Union, took place in the dark days of 1940 when German armies were overrunning Europe. It failed. The second try was the Council of Europe, which Britain deliberately reduced to talking shop by 1950. Finally, the European Coal and Steel Community (ECSC) of six countries began in 1952, with the unelected Jean Monnet at its head. That, too, was nearly stillborn because of the Korean War. While the ECSC purported to be a trading alliance, it could levy taxes and was responsible to a supranational assembly and a

European Court of Justice. It was an embryonic state.

A further push with the Treaty of Rome in 1957 turned the ECSC into the European Economic Community (EEC), embracing all economic activity, not just coal and steel. Over 40 years later, the fifteen countries of the European Union (EU) may enlarge to 28 countries. Even Russia is waiting in the wings.[9]

There is still a hole at the center of the EU jigsaw. The EU does not have legal personality; therefore, it is not yet a state. An EU constitution is likely to be high on the agenda at the 2004 intergovernmental conference. These conferences always precede the next amendment to the fundamental EU document, the Treaty of Rome.

Progress toward one state has been made by a ratchet technique—small advances that only specialist watchers might appreciate for what they really are. Direct assaults on national independence are avoided. Some countries have held referendums on treaty changes. Most infamous were the two Danish referendums on the Maastricht Treaty. The Danes voted "no" in June 1992 and were promptly told they had to vote again. Less than a year later, and with substantial bribery and bullying—"You will lose your job if you vote no"—the Danes voted "yes."

In every treaty is the term "irrevocable." The idea that the movement toward a single European state is inevitable is a constant refrain. Legally speaking, no treaty is irrevocable, and in the words of the old tag, only death and taxes are inevitable. Yet this propaganda is constant.

As a former French Foreign Secretary admitted: "The Europe of Maastricht could only have been created in the absence of democracy."[10]

■ ■ ■ ■ ■ ■ ■ ■ ■ ■

Propaganda has been key to oil the wheels of integration. In 1984 (some might well remember George Orwell's *1984*), an inner group of EU countries agreed that there should be a greater "European consciousness" to overwhelm national feeling, and they set up the Committee for a People's Europe to do just that. The committee created a "pretend" country.

As a result, the EU flag of twelve yellow stars on a blue background flies over the EU's 132 "embassies"—diplomatically called "delegations"—around the world and over its capital city, Brussels; the EU anthem, *Ode to Joy* from Beethoven's Ninth Symphony, is frequently played in Brussels with EU Commissioners

standing to attention; every EU country has adopted the red EU passport; EU driver's licenses are being introduced; and in 2002, the EU's currency, the euro, replaced the individual currencies of all EU countries except Denmark, Sweden, and Britain. Even car license plates are now uniform, with the EU flag on every one.

Brussels is even using religion to promote its political agenda. Some estimates suggest the European Commission's program "A Soul for Europe" has given over $38 million to pro-EU projects throughout Europe. Applicants for grants must "promote the integration of Europe" and "publicly acknowledge that assistance has been received from the EU." Though supposedly set up to promote the religious and spiritual aspects of a unified Europe, "Soul for Europe" literature doesn't mention the scriptures; this is strictly political.

The Vatican sees advantages in backing the EU. To promote a Europe in which Catholicism might dominate, the Vatican has pursued EU integration from at least the early 1940s and mainly in secret.[11] The first six members of the EEC were largely Catholic countries.

The Vatican is now taking a more public stance. The Rome Synod of October 1999 declared that it is necessary to "pursue, with courage and urgency, the process of European integration." Two months later, the Vatican began the canonization process for the so-called "Founding Fathers of Europe" from Germany, Italy, and France: Konrad Adenauer, Alcide de Gasperi, and Robert Schuman.

■ ■ ■ ■ ■ ■ ■ ■ ■ ■

In the first 50 years of political integration, it was easy to disguise what was really happening beneath an economic cloak. As a British Conservative MP wrote in 1947 (while praising the good Adolph Hitler had done to make Europe one economic unit): "No government dependent upon a democratic vote could possibly agree in advance to the sacrifices which any adequate plan must involve. The people must be led slowly and unconsciously into the abandonment of their traditional economic defences, not asked, in advance of having received any of the benefits which will accrue to them from the plan to make changes of which they may not at first recognise the advantages to themselves..."[12]

But once the police and the armed forces were to be combined into multinational units, with one justice system, including local EU courts, disguising the true ends would be difficult. Local opposition

"NO GOVERNMENT DEPENDENT UPON A DEMOCRATIC VOTE COULD POSSIBLY AGREE IN ADVANCE TO THE SACRIFICES WHICH ANY ADEQUATE PLAN MUST INVOLVE."

THE EUROPEAN UNION UNMASKED
LINDSAY JENKINS

could even imperil the enterprise.

The EU is now poised at a critical stage. Its true nature is emerging from the shadows.

At this late stage, political union had to be achieved quickly before serious opposition—even rebellion—could appear, so an inner core of countries is essential. Rules were included in the Nice Treaty for five or more countries to accelerate to full union, leaving the others to catch up later. France and Germany, the two countries that have led the integration process since the beginning, say that full union can be achieved by 2010.

Democracy has been largely conspicuous by its absence in the creation of the EU, and the EU is not run as a democracy. The government of the EU, though not yet in name, is the unelected European Commission in Brussels. At its heart is the tension between the Commission and the only institution representing the nation-states against the centrifugal power of the EU—the Council of Ministers.

Steadily, the nations are losing their powers to the Commission, as the national veto decreases treaty by treaty. Two Germans politicians wrote in 1998: "It is therefore necessary and legitimate for participating countries to take part in each other's domestic debate...: it is not interference in their *internal affairs*, of which the number is in any case constantly diminishing."[13]

Once in Brussels, the 20 Commissioners are independent of their "home" government, or in the words of Lady Thatcher: "They go native." Each Commissioner swears "[t]o perform my duties in complete independence, in the general interest of the Communities; in carrying out my duties, neither to seek, nor to take, instruction from any government..."[14] About a third of them are former national ministers; governments usually send to Brussels those they regard as politically dispensable. Others may have been diplomats or international civil servants.

Nearly 30,000 civil servants (i.e., Eurocrats) back them, though this is still not enough to run such a huge empire. When plans were laid for the present EU in the late 1940s, the College of Bruges solved the problem of a massive and highly visible central bureaucracy. The College suggested a takeover of national civil services.

This clever scheme meant that national opposition would not be aroused; it was erosion from within. A passerby would see the same old government buildings, but inside civil servants would be shedding one master, the national government, in favor of Brussels. To facilitate the process, Brussels encouraged civil servants to sit on Brussels committees. This committee system has further subverted democracy. A British parliamentary Select Committee deplored: "In most cases the only scrutiny of the Commission's implementing measures is that undertaken by national civil servants in the [Brussels] committees. In practice there is little action in European or national parliaments...."[15]

■ ■ ■ ■ ■ ■ ■ ■ ■ ■

So today, unseen by the general population, over 250 EU committees influence the way every country is governed. Out of the public eye, national civil servants horse-trade their way to consensus positions on subjects of which their mastery may be limited or nonexistent. The result is thousands of directives a year, often poorly drafted and inappropriate, replacing national legislation.

A best guess is that about 80 percent of all legislation going through the British Houses of Parliament merely rubberstamps Brussels' directives. An additional 3,000 of Brussels' regulations are enacted every year by civil servants without any democratic scrutiny whatsoever. It is government by decree.

SO TODAY, UNSEEN BY THE GENERAL POPULATION, OVER 250 EU COMMITTEES INFLUENCE THE WAY EVERY COUNTRY IS GOVERNED.

If that were not a sufficient destroyer of democracy, the EU has set up a charade of a parliament with EU-wide parties, or as the Treaty of Rome has it: "Political parties at European level are important as a factor for integration within the Union. They contribute to forming a European awareness and to expressing the political will of the citizens of the Union."[16]

The European Parliament started in 1951 with nominated members until the first elections were held in 1979. Each Member of European Parliament (MEP) represents a very large number of people, few of whom can actually name their representative. Any EU citizen can vote wherever he happens to be, and nationality no longer counts. The 626 members of the Parliament are elected by proportional representation (PR) every five years.

PR voting is a clever way to divide and rule. Votes are not for an individual but for a party. The party chooses candidates, listing them in order of their importance to the party. The number of seats a party wins is proportional to the number of votes cast for that party.

The usual result of a PR election is a compromise. No one party has a majority, and government becomes merely a theater of bartering and horse-trading as coalitions form and reform.

The European Parliament has virtually no powers; it follows the Latin tradition of legitimizing the decisions of the unelected Commission. It has no similarity to parliaments based on the Westminster principle, such as the British and Commonwealth parliaments or the US Congress.

All major decisions are decided by deals between the leaders of the party groups, and MEPs cannot initiate or repeal legislation; they only amend or reject proposals submitted by the Commission.

The European Parliament is like a medieval court: MEPs and their offices are constantly on the move, carrying all their files with them. They sit in Strasbourg for one week and in Brussels for another week. The secretariat is divided between Brussels and Luxembourg. MEPs are often absent because of the peripatetic nature of the Parliament and the technical nature of most of the work as the EU extends its remit into the smallest nook and cranny of everyday life. But they (like the Eurocrats) are financially well rewarded with excellent pensions and other perks.

Free speech is rationed. The time an MEP may speak in debates is allocated among the party groups according to the numbers in each group. A member of a small party has only one and half minutes to make his point in a debate before his microphone is automatically cut off.

MEPs vote on Commission proposals by following numbers on a list and pressing a button 100 to 300 times in an hour, allowing perhaps ten seconds for each vote. They have trouble trying to follow the voting list, which will only have been available for a few hours and is published in French.

Mistakes are easily made. Some British MEPs, voting 300 times in a two-hour session, inadvertently agreed to *corpus juris* effectively abolishing the British criminal justice system, including trial by jury and *habeas corpus*.

Even worse, an absent MEP is taken to have voted for the motion.

> SOME BRITISH MEPS, VOTING 300 TIMES IN A TWO-HOUR SESSION, INADVERTENTLY AGREED TO *CORPUS JURIS* EFFECTIVELY ABOLISHING THE BRITISH CRIMINAL JUSTICE SYSTEM, INCLUDING TRIAL BY JURY AND *HABEAS CORPUS*.

European parties, without any country links, will become the norm. All "recognized" party groups are funded from the parliamentary budget according to the size of the group.[17] The corollary must be that parties which are not "recognized" will be closed down.

■ ■ ■ ■ ■ ■ ■ ■ ■ ■

With such a lack of democracy, it is important to watch for signs that the new state might crush any dissent. Every nation has a treason law holding individuals to account for offenses against the state. So far treason in the EU has not been explicitly mentioned, but the EU set up a European Monitoring Center on Racism and Xenophobia in Vienna in 1998.[18] According to the pan-EU Party of European Socialists, "Right-wing populism is one of the major dangers to the European experiment.... By attacking European integration and its alleged damage to nation states...right-wing populism can use a new face of nationalism.... This new populist nationalism is also displayed in anti-European rhetoric, blaming *Brussels* for all kinds of economic, political and social problems."[19]

The EU has already taken action against a country. The EU can cancel a country's voting and other undefined rights but leave it with all its obligations, including payments to Brussels and the enforcement of EU laws. Such a country would be reduced to a colony.

The first case was Austria. Following a free and democratic election in February 2000, Joerg Haider's Freedom Party formed a coalition government with the conservative People's Party. In a move which sent shock waves around the world, the other fourteen EU countries promptly sanctioned Austria, claiming the Freedom Party was fascist.

In retaliation the Austrian Chancellor, Wolfgang Schuessel, set a deadline for the EU to end sanctions against Austria; otherwise he would poll Austrians for their endorsement of using "all suitable means" against the EU, which would have derailed the Treaty of Nice. The EU immediately appointed three "wise men" to find a face-saving solution. Sanctions were duly lifted.

After the Austrian debacle one British MEP asked in the European Parliament if anti-EU parties should be banned.[20] Many MEPs shouted, "Yes."

The EU's attack on Austria may be just the beginning. The Nice Treaty strengthens the provisions of Article 7, under which Austria was sanctioned. Only two-thirds of the member states (i.e., ten) would be needed to ban a country, so even if the victim country had an ally or two, it would not be enough to save it from colony status. It will be even easier for the EU to gang up on one country, saying it is violating the principles of liberty, democracy, respect for human rights and fundamental freedoms and the rule of law. Those principles are open to any interpretation: whose law and whose freedoms?

Even worse, to attract a ban, a country may not have to violate the vague EU principles; it may merely pose "the threat of such a breach." Again, that is open to interpretation.

If countries and parties might be banned, what about newspapers, books, magazines, even television and radio stations? The only evidence to emerge so far that this could be in the cards is the case of Bernard Connolly, a former head of the EU Commission unit for "EMS, national and community monetary polices."

In the European Court of Justice on October 19, 2000, the EU's Advocate-General surprisingly argued that Connolly's book, *The Rotten Heart Of Europe*, an academic analysis of monetary union, was akin to the publication of a blasphemous work. Since blasphemy could be punished under the European Convention on Human Rights, then a punishment was permissible for "blaspheming" against Europe.

A further hint came at a conference in 2000 on "Media and Democracy" when the European Socialist Party (PES) proposed a European Communications Authority. Such an authority could "recognize" journalists, fund programs, and exert EU control over the media.

■ ■ ■ ■ ■ ■ ■ ■ ■ ■

The EU Commission is not only emasculating the power of each state, but it has divided the fifteen EU countries into 111 regions. All EU regions are described in the same way—for example, as "London in Europe"—thus abolishing the name of the country and making clear that it is not free or independent.

Each region is in the process of acquiring an elected assembly and a development agency with the same boundaries as the European parliamentary constituencies. Their remits include regional planning, transport, and increased regional ownership, economic development, agriculture, energy, and waste, all to fit in with EU planning and funding. All have offices in Brussels.

Each region sends two representatives to the EU's Committee of the Regions "representing" the people in Brussels. A second committee of 222 people, the Economic and Social Committee, entrenches lobby groups in the EU, such as employers' groups, trade unions, farmers, consumer associations, charities, and family groups.

Both committees are no more than Brussels' wallpaper, but they

have created a new political class in every EU country, an inner group to match the new political class in Brussels. Many local officials have reacted enthusiastically to more power and links with other regions in the EU. A few have benefited financially in a substantial manner. Not surprisingly, they are eager apostles for "more" EU. It may not occur to them that this destroys the nation-state

What will be the future role of the national parliaments when all the regional "governments" are fully operational? The EU is silent on this point, and the assumption must be that they will fade into obscurity, as decisions are made in Brussels and rubberstamped in the EU regions.

The Commission has invented even larger areas, Euro-Regions, linking places which have never in recorded history been united or which once belonged to a neighboring country, deliberately reopening old wounds. The EU funds television and radio to broadcast across these borders, to build a new identity, although many locals switch off their sets.

Part of the British southeast is "linked" across 70 miles of sea with the French area of Haute-Normandy and Picardy. Germany, abutting eight countries, has Euro-Regions enveloping neighboring lands once claimed by Germany. For example, Rhine-Maas, a German-speaking area of Belgium, is joined with part of Germany; and Southern Jutland in Denmark is linked with Schleswig and Holstein in Northern Germany, which the Germans conquered in the war of 1864.

The EU plans that by 2004 all "internal" border controls will be abolished and one outer EU border set up. Border policy then will be totally under Brussels' control. A huge border police force is being built up. From 2001, the German and Italian governments exchanged border troops as the vanguard of an EU force to secure the EU's outer frontiers after the next wave of enlargement to the east.

■ ■ ■ ■ ■ ■ ■ ■ ■ ■

While the EU is outlawing most national differences, from imperial weights and measures (anyone selling in pounds and ounces is now a criminal) to currencies and legal systems, it is promoting other local differences at great cost. This can only be part of its deliberate policy to divide and rule.

SINCE BLASPHEMY COULD BE PUNISHED UNDER THE EUROPEAN CONVENTION ON HUMAN RIGHTS, THEN A PUNISHMENT WAS PERMISSIBLE FOR "BLASPHEMING" AGAINST EUROPE.

EVERYTHING YOU KNOW IS WRONG

English, the world's leading language, is spoken by half of the EU, yet the signatory countries to the Charter of Minority Languages of 1992 agreed to promote regional or minority languages. Across Europe there are over 100 languages, usually around national borders, reflecting Europe's checkered past. Most of them had virtually died out by 1600. In a bizarre move to reverse this historical trend, within one generation and with EU money, much of local life may once again be carried out in these languages.

THE EU PLANS THAT BY 2004 ALL "INTERNAL" BORDER CONTROLS WILL BE ABOLISHED AND ONE OUTER EU BORDER SET UP.

Insistence on the use of minority languages, especially in educating children, will ensure that the locality is isolated and will limit the opportunities for people in the wider world. It will make them second-class citizens and easier to control. All regional assemblies will have multiple translation services, which will further reduce their effectiveness.

The EU, which describes itself as a Tower of Babel, already has eleven official languages, which causes confusion and vast expense with every document translated and every speech interpreted. On enlargement the number will shoot up again. Germany is already promoting German to become the EU's official language, reducing English to minority status.

■ ■ ■ ■ ■ ■ ■ ■ ■ ■

Why is it that so many countries have queued to join the EU? The answer, simply put, is money. Only a few countries are net contributors to the EU's funds (Germany is by far the largest), and most get more than their own money back but naturally only to fund EU-approved projects. And surprisingly few politicians across Europe understand the EU's undemocratic nature.

The EU's superstructure is already in place. Enlargement to include countries of Eastern Europe is on track for 2006. The divide and rule policy, actively pursued for years, is accelerating. Strong national governments are being replaced with weak regional assemblies speaking a multitude of languages and reporting directly to Brussels. The EU inner core, led by Germany and France, is gaining strength and may have the power to advance to one country by 2010.

If so, the United States of Europe will have arrived. It will not be a democracy but a dictatorship. The EU sees its place in the world as a counter and challenger to the power of the United States of America. Unless there is rebellion, the world may become an even more unstable place.

Endnotes

1. The European Union is currently comprised of Belgium, Germany, France, Italy, Luxembourg, the Netherlands, Denmark, Ireland, the United Kingdom, Greece, Spain, Portugal, Austria, Finland, and Sweden. **2.** Letter to the *Daily Telegraph* (London) 13 June 2001. **3.** Chatham House lecture in London. **4.** *Independent* (London) 4 Feb 2000. **5.** Quoted in Mayne, Richard, *et al. The Federal Union: The Pioneers.* London: Macmillan, 1990. **6.** From a Kansas State University lecture, 15 March 1999. **7.** Monnet, Jean. *Memoirs.* Trans. Richard Mayne. London: William Collins and Son Ltd., 1976. (Author's italics.) **8.** For a review of how far national governments have already been abolished, see Jenkins, Lindsay. *The Last Days of Britain: The Final Betrayal.* Orange State Press, 2001. **9.** For the history of who created the EU and why, see Jenkins, Lindsay. *Britain Held Hostage: The Coming Euro-Dictatorship.* 2nd ed. Orange State Press, 1998. **10.** Clause Cheysson. **11.** For the early history, see Cornwall, John. *Hitler's Pope: The Secret History of Pius XII.* New York: Viking Press, 1999. **12.** Booklet published in 1947 under the banner "Design for Freedom," whose 24 members were mainly Conservative MPs, led by Peter Thorneycroft. **13.** Dr. Schäuble and Karl Lamers in a CDU/CSU paper. **14.** Treaty of Rome, Article 157. **15.** Extracts from House of Lords Select Committee on European Communities Third Report, Delegation of Powers to the Commission: Reforming Comitology, 2 Feb 1999. **16.** Treaty of Rome, Article 191. **17.** Nice Treaty, Article 191. **18.** Amsterdam Treaty, Article 29, Title VI. **19.** A discussion paper produced for the Bern Round Table of the PES, July 2000. **20.** Jeffrey Titford, a UKIP MEP.

WATCHDOG NATION
CLETUS NELSON

_INTRODUCTION: HATING THOSE WHO HATE

Racial prejudice, like most social pathologies, is an irrational social force that has dogged our species since the origins of tribal society. While we can study it, observe it, and decry it, the dynamics which compel a man to despise his neighbor seemingly defy the cold logic of scientific inquiry. Yet, in a well-intentioned effort to solve this intractable problem, we now define racism as a political malevolence fomented by a far-reaching conspiracy of cultural terrorists. The chief adherents of this widely accepted theory are a select body of "experts" who earn their livings by interpreting the sinister permutations of the far right. We call them "watchdog groups," and this small minority of powerful anti-racist advocacy groups unwittingly shapes our collective perception of organized racism and anti-government dissent.

Typically, these organizations reside in the upper echelon of the nonprofit public policy milieu, which presents an onerous problem—as their financial existence is closely tethered to the rise and fall of ethnic intolerance, one cannot help but question the objectivity of these renowned political soothsayers. Moreover, the marked dislike these modern-day demagogues display toward the subjects of their research further erodes their façade of scholarly detachment. As political researcher Laird Wilcox remarks, "There is an anti-racism industry entrenched in the United States that has attracted bullying, moralizing fanatics, whose identity and livelihood depend upon growth and expansion of their particular kind of victimization."[1]

While their passionate defenders will certainly object to such a charge by citing the threats posed by America's expanding political fringe, such protests fail to address the questionable methodology and often politically motivated criteria used by these media-savvy experts to classify unconventional social and religious movements. As we shall soon see, one needn't stockpile weapons or espouse reactionary beliefs to fall under the watchful eye of these formidable private surveillance networks. Indeed, imputing racist motives to alleged enemies of the State has become a notorious tactic among prominent watchdog groups such as the Anti-Defamation League of B'nai B'rith (ADL), the Southern Poverty Law Center (SPLC), and other purveyors of fear. To our detriment, this unchallenged "information disease"[2] has unleashed an unprecedented expansion of State power. With this uncomfortable thought in mind, it is impera-

tive that conscientious civil libertarians rethink the real threat posed by the extremists in our midst and closely examine watchdog tactics.

_REASSESSING THE FAR RIGHT

Despite their similar agendas, each of these organizations has a different method of promoting its central message. Spokesmen for the Seattle-based Northwest Coalition for Human Dignity (NWCHD) consider themselves experts in youth-related topics and primarily focus on issues ranging from racist skinhead gangs to the controversial "Black Metal" subculture. The SPLC and the Atlanta-based Center for Democratic Renewal (CDR) adeptly play upon Northern stereotypes of the deep South with tabloid-style headlines decrying the allegedly fearsome motives lurking behind rural political movements. Mark Pitcavage, the chief researcher for the Militia Watchdog Website, adopts an intellectual tone and employs a rich academic argot to decry militia conspiracy theories and their supposedly racist subtext. Yet there is one unifying theme that permeates watchdog literature: Violent "hate groups" are metastasizing at unprecedented levels.

The motive behind this clever marketing strategy isn't difficult to fathom: Combating the dark forces of "hate" has become a perpetual money-making machine. By issuing teeth-chattering predictions of impending racial terror, the more visible anti-racist groups gain access to an endless supply of lucrative foundation grants and a stream of donations from terrified constituents. Struggling at the lower end of the watchdog spectrum is the NWCHD, which nevertheless boasts a yearly budget of some $600,000.[3] Further up the scale is the ADL, whose annual expenditures exceed $30 million.[4] However, for sheer wealth, few can match the SPLC, which enjoys combined assets of over $136 million, with a yearly take of nearly $40 million.[5]

These substantial sums beg an important question: How big a threat is the far right? When viewed objectively, the rising diversity of the nation's population coupled with public intolerance toward racist beliefs is greatly undermining the influence and popularity of organized racism. Even watchdog groups are coming to terms with this uncomfortable (yet reassuring) reality. "We are talking about a tiny number of Americans who are members of hate groups—I mean infinitesimal," SPLC spokesman Mark Potok conceded in a 1999 Associated Press article.[6]

> **"WE ARE TALKING ABOUT A TINY NUMBER OF AMERICANS WHO ARE MEMBERS OF HATE GROUPS–I MEAN INFINITESIMAL," SPLC SPOKESMAN MARK POTOK CONCEDED IN A 1999 ASSOCIATED PRESS ARTICLE.**

Potok's assertion is echoed by Wilcox, who edits the well-researched *Guide to the American Right* (now in its 24th edition) and *Guide to the American Left* (now in its 21st edition). Contradicting watchdog claims that hundreds of violent racist groups stalk the American political landscape, the Kansas academic asserts that "in terms of viable groups i.e., groups that are objectively significant, are actually functioning and have more than a handful of real members...the actual figure is about 50."[7] Out of a national population which now exceeds 280 million, Wilcox estimates that "the Ku Klux Klan are down to about 3,000 people," with an additional 1,500-2,000 members of organized fascist groups.[8]

By contrast, the SPLC (which is considered an irrefutable source by the mainstream press) lists over 600 "hate groups" on its Website. Yet when closely scrutinized, this authoritative directory is quite suspect. Little or no information is provided beyond the name of a purported racist group and the city in which it is located. With no contact information or mailing address, who can verify these individuals or groups even exist? Having closely examined this data, Wilcox asserts that "a large number" of organizations included on the SPLC's list "are either unconfirmed or consist of a single individual."[9]

In some instances, watchdog groups will even contradict previous data in order to promulgate a culturally constructed "rise" in white nationalism. One such example is a 1999 report issued by the NWCHD entitled "Hate by State." According to the widely publicized study, the state of Oregon is undergoing a "rise" in white nationalist activism substantiated by the presence of some thirteen hate groups.[10] Among the groups listed are "patriot" folk singer Carl Klang (who apparently constitutes a one-man white supremacist group), the avowedly anti-racist Southern Oregon Militia (SOM), a record label, and other questionable entries. However, this alleged proliferation of racist beliefs in a state best known for its bottle-throwing anarchists and tie-dyed hippie subculture is at odds with data from the organization's precursor, the Coalition for Human Dignity (CHD). The CHD issued a similar report in 1990 which documented some three-dozen well-organized "skinhead," "Christian Identity," "Christian Patriot," and "Nazi" groups in the same locale.[11] Based on these numbers—from 36 to thirteen—it would appear that Oregon is witnessing a marked *decline* in far-right political activism.

Due to the underlying ethical considerations, few reporters would dare cite a study commissioned by the Philip Morris Company for an article discussing the health risks of smoking. Yet when otherwise well-meaning reporters regurgitate this type of tendentious watch-dog research, their journalistic efforts are no less compromised. In some cases, the publication of unsubstantiated watchdog misinformation has enduring consequences. A 1996 media blitz conducted by the Center for Democratic Renewal (CDR) provides a cautionary tale as to the perils of publicizing watchdog allegations.

_ANATOMY OF A HOAX

It was a dramatic tale straight out of a John Grisham screenplay. In the spring of 1996, a team of investigators affiliated with the CDR crisscrossed the South in order to examine a troubling series of church fires. Despite the allegedly malevolent presence of hostile rednecks, corrupt small-town sheriffs, and indifferent townspeople, the dedicated researchers pressed on. By summer, the disturbing truth was revealed: Since 1990, scores of African-American churches had been set aflame as part of a racist conspiracy. JoAnn Watson, CDR's president, was unequivocal in denouncing the unspeakable attacks. "This is domestic terrorism," she announced to the press. "It is not an isolated phenomenon. It's an epidemic."[12] This "epidemic" would later appear some 2,200 times in the popular press and become an operative metaphor for America's growing racial disunity.[13]

With the poll-conscious Clinton White House demanding immediate action, a full-scale task force was mobilized to catch the craven perpetrators behind this "conspiracy." However, when the investigation was completed in 1997, it painted a far different picture than the sinister tableau depicted by the CDR. "We have not seen hard evidence to support the theory of a nationwide conspiracy," asserted Assistant Treasury Secretary James E. Johnson.[14] Indeed, it was found that the fires occurred against a "backdrop of widespread arson against houses of religion of all kinds, including white churches, mosques and synagogues."[15] As skeptical reporters began to delve deeper into the facts, it would soon be revealed that the only "conspiracy" in evidence was hatched by the CDR and its allies.

Michael Fumento, a former attorney with the US Commission on Civil Rights and a notorious debunker of media myths, closely scrutinized the initial CDR report and found the document fraught with selective omissions and factual errors. After discussions with fire officials in several Southern states, Fumento learned that the CDR had "regularly ignored fires set by blacks and those that occurred in the early part of the decade, and labeled fires as arsons that were not—all in an apparent effort to make black church torchings appear to be an escalating phenomenon."[16] Citing statistics from the National Fire Protection Association, Fumento noted that in actuality Americans were seeing a radical decline in the number of church arsons, from 1,420 in 1980 to just over 500 in 1994.

As the story unraveled, other publications began to question the

CDR's dubious claims. But the damage was done, and the profits were in: The anti-hate group and its affiliate, the National Council of Churches (NCC), secured a multimillion dollar windfall in donations. To this day, many still believe in this malicious urban myth which subsequently unleashed a series of copycat crimes by opportunistic racists. Therein lies the ultimate irony of this disturbing saga: By disseminating this ill-founded claim, the CDR spread terror among black churchgoers, fostered fear and resentment among varying racial groups, and actually contributed to an upsurge in racially-motivated violence toward African-American places of worship. "That which the Ku Klux Klan can no longer do, a group established to fight the Klan has done for them," Fumento observed.[17]

In the aftermath of this obvious hoax, the credibility of the press suffered little. Yet to discerning observers, this unsavory incident revealed the symbiotic relationship watchdog groups enjoy with sympathetic members of the media.

_WHEN TRAGEDY STRIKES

The aforementioned sham illustrates the tendency among watchdog groups to divine racist subcurrents behind highly publicized events. Thus, when the Alfred P. Murrah building exploded in Oklahoma City, Oklahoma, on April 19, 1995, these high-profile nonprofits unleashed a sustained offensive against the nascent citizen militia movement. "We warned Attorney General Janet Reno six months before the Oklahoma City bombing that private militia groups posed a serious threat," bragged SPLC founder Morris Dees in a self-aggrandizing fundraising letter.[18] "Our Militia Task Force," Dees continued, "has been able to provide critical information to federal and state agencies investigating the Oklahoma City Bombing."

Few bothered to question the accuracy of this "critical information," especially in light of the fact that militia groups have yet to be implicated in the 1995 blast. Indeed, following one of the most exhaustive investigations in FBI history, federal officials were unable to establish a direct link between citizen militias and the bombing plot. In fact, since 1999, FBI agents across the country have been involved in an innovative effort to build a trusting relationship with patriot and militia groups. "The idea we're pushing is that it's not a crime to be a member of the militia," FBI agent Bill Crowley remarked to the Associated Press.[19] Among the agents taking part in the outreach program is Danny Defenbaugh, the former head of the Oklahoma City investigation. Nevertheless, in the wake of the OKC attack, the SPLC, ADL, and other groups, in concert with the media, waged a heated information war against allegedly racist patriot groups and their sympathizers.

With no shortage of experts available to validate the most lurid claims, reporters were uninterested in anyone willing to depart from

their institutional bias against patriot groups. "The militias—whoever the fuck they are...are a ticking time bomb composed of paranoid lunatics," remarked a reporter from the *Washington Post* seeking an interview with writer and publisher Adam Parfrey after the OKC bombing.[20] When Parfrey offered a more balanced (and less hysterical) assessment of this evolving political phenomenon, his observations fell on deaf ears.

The ensuing anti-militia crusade would crescendo with the passage of the Anti-Terrorism and Effective Death Penalty Act of 1996, a repressive statute which relaxed laws governing the use of electronic surveillance, expanded the State's right to investigate politically suspect individuals or organizations, and implemented other Orwellian measures to ferret out alleged domestic terrorists.

In the years since this well-orchestrated campaign to demonize primarily law-abiding constitutional militias, watchdog groups have now come to embrace the federal government's highly dubious "lone wolf" theory, which ascribes responsibility for the mass murder to convicted bomber Timothy McVeigh and his confederate Terry Nichols. However, a substantial body of evidence has surfaced which ties an armed, well-organized hate group known as the Aryan Republican Army (ARA) to the blast. "It is now believed the ARA financed and helped to stage the bombing," reports Andrew Gumbel in a special investigation for the *Independent* of London.[21] The marked silence emanating from the watchdog camp in regards to this grave development would suggest that their initial preoccupation with uncovering a far-flung rightist conspiracy behind the blast was far from sincere.

> "THAT WHICH THE KU KLUX KLAN CAN NO LONGER DO, A GROUP ESTABLISHED TO FIGHT THE KLAN HAS DONE FOR THEM," FUMENTO OBSERVED.

Four years later, the Columbine High School mass-shooting provided yet another avenue for watchdog advocates to cynically exploit yet another inexplicable act of violence. Within weeks of the high-school shootings, the NWCHD began placing a racially-charged spin on the highly-publicized murders. Citing "evidence of Hitler worship as a component of their motives," Coalition Research Director Robert Crawford inveighed in an editorial appearing in the Portland *Oregonian* that both Dylan Klebold and Eric Harris "were known to hate African-Americans and Hispanics and speak adoringly of Hitler."[22] Crawford further alleged that the two teenage gunmen had been poisoned by "Neo-Nazi" music.

While the murder of African-American student Isaiah Sholes provides a thin veneer of justification for this sweeping (and sensationalistic) version of events, the argument falls apart under close scrutiny. If the Columbine killings were an act of racial terror, why were the vast majority of the victims white, suburban teens? Moreover, even if it is conceded that there was a modicum of racism lurking behind Harris and Klebold's deadly attack on the Colorado school, it would seem their alleged "hate" wasn't limited by the confines of racial identity.

A *Time* magazine analysis of a series of videotapes made by Klebold and Harris prior to their murderous spree depicts the two teens assailing every racial group on the face of the earth. This sustained verbal bombast displayed an "ecumenical" hatred that often bordered on the self-referential, as the two denigrated various minority groups, along with Christians, whites, and Jews.[23] There is also evidence which indicates that both Eric Harris and Dylan Klebold had little interest in racism. One might even argue that Harris possessed the virulent anti-racism notorious among watchdog groups.

"Don't let me catch you making fun of someone just becasue [sic] they are a different color because I will come and break your fucking legs," the deceased shooter wrote on his Webpage prior to the killings.[24] After investigating the adolescent killers, *Salon* reporter Dave Cullen asserted, "The biggest myths about the tragedy have to do with the question of who Harris and Klebold were really targeting in their rampage. Jocks, African-Americans and Christians have been widely described as their chief targets. Not a scrap of evidence supports that conclusion."[25] Further imperiling allegations of Nazi inclinations are Dylan Klebold's Jewish background, which would certainly undermine any purported affinity with National Socialism.

Although a prolonged sociological autopsy has severely undercut allegations of racist intent behind this disturbing incident of mass murder, the NWCHD (and later the SPLC) continued to propagate the misguided notion that the perpetrators were part of a highly organized crypto-fascist "Black-Metal" subculture. Yet there is utterly no evidence to prove the two youths were even remotely connected with the "extreme music" scene. In fact, Harris and Klebold enjoyed the German electronic group KMFDM, who consider their creative efforts a "statement against war, oppression, fascism and violence against others."[26] Unfortunately, these types of inconvenient facts have never proved an obstacle to watchdog propaganda efforts.

_DEFENDERS OF THE REGIME

While these vigilant defenders of "tolerance" will typically concede that racism permeates every stratum of society, rarely do these staunchly pro-law enforcement, pro-government groups ever address instances of State-sanctioned racism. If they are looking for examples of racial injustice, they need only review the tragic effects of the "War on Drugs," which has dealt a crippling blow to minority communities.

According to the Justice Policy Institute, the number of nonviolent offenders in American prisons has exploded due to the escalating

Drug War. A recent study reports that the incarceration rate for African Americans has skyrocketed due to "increases in drug sentencing over the past two decades."[27] At a bare minimum, 1.4 million African-America men—over 10 percent of the black male adult population—have lost the right to vote due to their brush with the criminal justice system.[28] To echo Fumento, even the most diabolical Klansman couldn't have dreamed of a more repressive policy to disproportionately punish minorities!

Obviously, taking on moribund Klan groups or cynically hyping another racist scare offers greater rewards than dealing with uncomfortable topics which threaten the legitimacy of the Beltway power elite. Indeed, in many instances watchdog groups have aided and abetted abuses of State power. The 1993 paramilitary siege of the Mt. Carmel religious complex in Waco, Texas, offers substantial evidence of watchdog complicity.

According to a report from the Committee for Waco Justice, the ADL worked in concert with federal officials by providing "precise documentation" on the Davidian "cult" and "how it operated in the past."[29] Although we can only speculate as to the nature of this intelligence, the inherent brutality of the initial raid conducted by the Bureau of Alcohol, Tobacco and Firearms (ATF) and the subsequent tank assault which led to the tragic death of over six-dozen members of a multiracial spiritual community suggest that this questionable information was of an inflammatory nature.

The role of quasi-governmental watchdog groups didn't cease once bloodthirsty ATF agents cravenly raised their flag above the smoldering Mt. Carmel complex. As Washington officials braced for Congressional hearings and the possibility of answering a number of difficult questions regarding the alleged "disappearance" of key pieces of evidence, watchdog groups stepped forward to wholeheartedly endorse the law enforcement debacle.

"I am more concerned with the victims of militia terrorists than with FBI or ATF excesses," SPLC figurehead Morris Dees remarked glibly, while failing to articulate a single instance of militia-sponsored terrorism.[30] Nevertheless, SPLC "experts" repeatedly attacked those willing to question the Justice Department's factually untenable (yet media-sanctified) "mass suicide" theory. Mark Pitcavage of Militia Watchdog similarly assailed the allegedly sinister agenda of determined Waco investigators. "These guys have ulterior motives," whined the pro-government activist to *Salon* magazine.[31] Tragically, few reporters bothered to question the "ulterior motives" of these well-connected Waco apologists who played a crucial role in the ensuing cover-up, which continues to shroud this unprecedented atrocity.

Five years later, the SPLC would wage a similar attack against those who attended the 1999 World Trade Organization demonstrations in Seattle, Washington. In its quarterly publication, *Intelligence Report*, the Alabama watchdog group made the stark allegation that the protests were thoroughly infiltrated by the "hard-edged soldiers of Neo-Fascism."[32] Providing utterly no credible evidence to substantiate this charge, the anonymous author asserted that the WTO protests represented a convergence of the far left and far right in America, made possible by the increasing willingness of avowed Nazi and racist groups to co-opt traditional leftist stances on issues such as economic inequality and global trade policy.

These well-calculated attacks display how watchdog groups have long departed from their once progressive beliefs in order to curry favor with the National Security State. The ADL has been at the forefront of this disquieting trend.

_COINTELPRO REDUX

It has long been believed that controversial government counterinsurgency operations such as the FBI's COINTELPRO program were disbanded during the brief era of reform which occurred in the wake of the Watergate scandals. While it is true that federal guidelines which curtailed government spying on political groups were adopted in the late 1970s, watchdog groups have allowed law enforcement to effectively sidestep these administrative prohibitions. Indeed, operatives for the ADL have played a key role in spying on suspected political dissidents from across the political spectrum.

"By the mid-1980s, the ADL was swapping files with hundreds of 'official friends,' the organization's euphemism for US law enforcement and intelligence sources," writes Robert I. Friedman in the *Village Voice*.[33] The organization doesn't limit itself to merely observing and identifying political dissidents—this human rights group frequently uses paid informants to infiltrate and gather information on various political factions.

In one instance during the 1980s, a Michigan ADL operative named James Mitchell Rosenberg penetrated the extreme right and became a leading member of the Ku Klux Klan and other white supremacist groups. This shadowy *agent provocateur* even gave racially inflammatory speeches at white nationalist rallies until another organization, People Against Racist Terror (PART), spoke out about his involvement, which "crossed the line from collecting information which is vital and necessary in dealing with violence-prone racists, to acting as an initiator of racist organizing and proponent of racist violence."[34]

Despite the progressive rhetoric which inundates ADL publications, the organization is no less dedicated to monitoring the other end of the political spectrum. The sheer scope of this counterintelligence effort was briefly brought to light in January 1993 when a San Francisco police investigation linked Roy Bullock, a self-admitted ADL spy, to Tom Gerard, an SFPD intelligence officer. Apparently Gerard had provided Bullock with access to confidential police files, and as the story unfolded, it was revealed that the seasoned ADL

operative had subsequently compiled files on nearly 10,000 individuals and more than 950 political organizations.[35] To the horror of the West Coast progressive community, it was learned that on behalf of the ADL, Bullock was covertly monitoring the National Association for the Advancement of Colored People (NAACP), the American Civil Liberties Union (ACLU), the Center for Investigative Reporting (CIR), and a surfeit of other left-leaning groups.[36]

Yet one needn't traffic in the political milieu to gain the attention of police-connected ADL officials. The organization's adversarial and confrontational tactics leave anyone open to charges of race hatred and the possibility of arrest. In the fall of 1994, a Colorado ADL affiliate transformed a seemingly innocent neighborhood dispute into a scorched-earth campaign to jail and ruin a middle-class couple.

The escalating feud, which began over an alleged dog attack, reached its apex when William Quigley drove his car recklessly (and illegally) in a threatening manner toward his neighbor Candice Aronson. In retaliation, Mrs. Aronson and her husband, Mitchell, began recording the Quigleys' cellular phone conversations by listening to a police scanner. In a highly emotional conversation in which Dorothy Quigley vented her frustrations over the dispute, she made a number of grossly insensitive remarks, such as her sadness that the Aronsons hadn't been on a bus "blown up by terrorists."[37]

Although Mrs. Quigley immediately regretted making these statements and, in the same conversation, admitted that her comments were "sick," the Aronsons grew alarmed and took steps to initiate legal proceedings against their neighbors.[38] After contacting the ADL that October, the couple was encouraged by League officials to continue taping the phone calls (which is illegal under federal law). In December, the Aronsons filed a federal lawsuit against the Quigleys, and within days, the local District Attorney charged them with several counts of ethnic intimidation. As the controversy spun out of control, an ADL spokesman accused them of "perpetrating the worst anti-Semitic incident in the area since the slaying of Jewish talk-show host Alan Berg."[39]

However, there was little evidence to back up this hyperbole. After closely examining the evidence, Jefferson County D.A. David Thomas sheepishly concluded that the entire episode was "a basic garden-variety neighborhood dispute" and "the ethnic part of it came as an outgrowth, not a cause of it."[40] Indeed, this was far from a one-sided affair. Reporter Eric Dexheimer notes that "both families volleyed verbal insults that would make a prison guard blush."[41] Nevertheless, the ill-conceived prosecution conducted "under pressure from the ADL" had dire results for the Quigleys, who were publicly accused of conducting a virulent anti-Semitic campaign against their neighbors.[42]

Facing an uncertain financial future with their reputations effectively ruined, the Quigleys launched their own legal offensive, which ironically charged the League with defamation and other offenses. In

April 2000, a jury agreed, declaring that ADL statements at a news conference and on talk radio were both defamatory and "not substantially true." They awarded the embattled husband and wife a judgement in excess of $10 million.[43]

Although the Quigleys enjoyed their proverbial day in court, how many average citizens could afford to retain counsel in order to defend themselves against such charges? Moreover, it is unlikely that this ephemeral moment of justice will curtail the extralegal surveillance efforts of dossier-compiling watchdog advocates. In fact, the SPLC still brags of its "unique computer database," which is considered the "largest in the United States"[44] and contains files on thousands of Americans accused *in absentia* of possessing political views deemed suspect. According to *US News and World Report*, on any given day "[f]ourteen researchers with the SPLC's 'Intelligence Project' spend long hours in front of computers, cross-filing data from press reports, hate-group literature, and web sites."[45]

In essence, the SPLC constitutes a "virtual arm of the state…acting as an informant, a chronicler, and a clearinghouse for information to be placed at the disposal of federal agencies," remarks anti-war activist Justin Raimondo.[46] While smaller organizations such as the NWCHD may lack the elaborate and sophisticated surveillance apparatus of their wealthier peers, coalition members are not above attending rightist functions in order to take down license plate numbers and "photo document" alleged thought criminals for possible use by law enforcement.[47]

> IN APRIL 2000, A JURY AGREED, DECLARING THAT ADL STATEMENTS AT A NEWS CONFERENCE AND ON TALK RADIO WERE BOTH DEFAMATORY AND "NOT SUBSTANTIALLY TRUE."

This disquieting nexus between watchdogs and the State has become so pervasive that spokesmen for other watchdog groups are beginning to register their dissent. "If you claim to be a broad-based human rights group you should not have a backdoor relationship with police," comments John Foster "Chip" Berlet of Political Research Associates (PRA), a Massachusetts think tank which studies right-wing extremism.[48]

_A THREAT TO FREEDOM?

You will find almost no reporting on these disturbing issues in the mainstream press. Why? Watchdog groups are extremely aggressive in pressuring members of the media to toe the official line. Indeed, those who dare deviate from scripted watchdog propaganda run the risk of offending this highly intolerant and politically powerful lobby. Nevertheless, remaining silent will only serve to embolden these determined enemies of freedom. While a vast segment of the population may find it difficult to find common cause with militias, gun owners, and even outright racists, history tells us that it is the opinions which many may find objectionable that most deserve pro-

tection under the US Constitution. However, so long as the public believes that we are besieged by church-burning "conspiracies," anthrax-wielding militia terrorists, and metastasizing "hate groups," Americans will remain under the iron heel of the watchdog nation.

Endnotes

1. Wilcox, Laird. *The Watchdogs: A Close Look at Anti-Racist "Watchdog" Groups.* Olathe, KS: Editorial Research Services, 1999: 3. **2.** The writer's use of this term is taken from Conway and Siegelman's *Snapping: America's Epidemic of Sudden Personality Change.* (Philadelphia & New York: JB Lippincot & Company, 1978: 154.) The condition is described as a "sustained altered state of awareness" resulting in "narrowed or reduced awareness." A major symptom of this intellectually myopic state is the severe impairment of an "individual's fundamental ability to question"—a cognitive lapse which has become prevalent among watchdog-friendly reporters! **3.** "Northwest Coalition for Human Dignity Cutting Staff," *Seattle Gay News On-Line* 23 Feb 2001. <www.sgn.org/2001/02/23/nw.htm>. **4.** *Op cit.*, Wilcox: 26. **5.** Better Business Bureau Philanthropic Advisory Service, Charity Reports, Dec 2000. <www.give.org/reports/splc.asp>. The SPLC was rebuked by the Bureau for expending a mere 35 percent of its yearly take on actual program expenses. **6.** Levinson, Arlene. "Hate Groups, Crimes Said Rare in the US." Associated Press 8 July 1999. **7.** *Op cit.*, Wilcox: 49 . **8.** McCain, Robert Stacy. "Researcher Says Hate 'Fringe' Isn't as Crowded as Claimed." *Washington Times* 9 May 2000. **9.** *Op cit.*, Wilcox: 49. **10.** Northwest Coalition for Human Dignity. "Hate by State." 1999: 5-6. **11.** Coalition for Human Dignity. "Organized White Supremacists in Oregon." 1990: 8. **12.** "Rash of Church Fires Part of Racial Violence." *Catholic World News* 29 March 1996. **13.** Fumento, Michael. "The Great Black Church Burning Hoax." consumeralert.org 9 July 1996. **14.** Savage, David. "Probe Finds No Conspiracy in Church Arsons." *Los Angeles Times* 9 June 1997. **15.** Booth, William. "In Church Fires, a Pattern but No Conspiracy." *Washington Post* 19 June 1996. **16.** *Op cit.*, Fumento. **17.** *Ibid.* **18.** SPLC fundraising letter dated 17 May 1995. **19.** Hull, C. Bryson. "FBI Meets with Militia Groups." Associated Press 12 July 1999. **20.** Parfrey, Adam. *Cult Rapture.* Los Angeles: Feral House, 1995: 346. **21.** Gumbel, Andrew. "McVeigh 'Did Not Act Alone in Oklahoma Bombing." *Independent* (London) 11 May 2001. **22.** Crawford, Robert. "Neo-Nazi Background Music to School Massacre." *Oregonian* (Portland) 13 May 1999. **23.** Gibbs, Nancy, and Timothy Roche. "Special Report/The Columbine Tapes." *Time* 20 Dec 1999. **24.** Eric Harris' Webpage ["HatePage"]. <http://www.webone.com.au/~khat/EricP.htm>. **25.** Cullen, Dave. "Inside the Columbine High Investigation." *Salon* 23 Sept 1999. **26.** Bryson, Wyatt. "Columbine High School Massacre—The Web Connection." *Rock Hill Herald* (South Carolina) *Online* 21 April 1999. **27.** Schiraldi, Vincent, Jason Ziedenberg, and John Irwin, PhD. "America's One Million Non Violent Prisoners." Justice Policy Institute 1999. <www.cjcj.org/jpi/onemillion.html>. **28.** "Poor Prescription: The Costs of Imprisoning Drug Offenders in the United States." Justice Policy Institute 2000. <www.cjcj.org/drug>. **29.** Moore, Carol, *et al.* "The Massacre of the Branch Davidians: A Study of Government Violations of Rights, Excessive Force and Cover-Up." Committee for Waco Justice 28 Jan 1994. <www.shadeslanding.com/firearms/waco.massacre.html> **30.** Grigg, William Norman. "SPLC's 'Extremist Cash Cow.'" *New American* 10 June 1996. **31.** Elder, Sean. "Great Balls of Fire." *Salon* 9 Sept 1999. **32.** "Neither Left Nor Right." *Intelligence Report* Winter 2000. **33.** Friedman, Robert I. "How the ADL Turned the Notion of Human Rights on Its Head, Spying on Progressives and Funneling Information to Law Enforcement." *Village Voice* 11 May 1993. **34.** Redden, Jim. *Snitch Culture.* Los Angeles: Feral House, 2001: 79. **35.** *Op cit.*, Friedman. **36.** *Op cit.*, Wilcox: 32. **37.** Lane, George. "Charges of Bigotry Backfire." *Denver Post* 29 April 2000. **38.** Janofsky, Michael. "Spat Leads to Huge a Award Against the Anti-Defamation League." *New York Times* 13 May 2000. **39.** *Op cit.*, Lane. **40.** Dexheimer, Eric. "War of the Words: How an Eager DA Transformed a Neighborhood Spat Into a Headline Grabbing Hate Crime." *Westword Online* 9 August 1995. <www.westword.com/issues/1995-08-09/feature2.html/page1.html>. **41.** *Op cit.*, Dexheimer. **42.** *Ibid.* **43.** *Op cit.*, Lane. **44.** SPLC mailing dated 7 Nov 1997. **45.** Shapiro, Joseph P. "Hitting Before Hate Strikes." *US News & World Report* 6 Sept 1999. **46.** Raimondo, Justin. "Behind the Headlines." Antiwar.com 3 Sept 1999. **47.** Redden, Jim. "Good Guy Spies." *Hustler* April 1994. **48.** *Op cit.*, Shapiro.

HENRY: FABRICATION OF A SERIAL KILLER

BRAD SHELLADY

In the mid-1980s a collective fear—initiated and fueled by law enforcement and the media—gripped the world, and the myth of the serial killer was born. If one were to believe all the hype, a monster was lurking at every turn, just waiting to destroy another life. The FBI even went so far as to state that their numbers showed 500 serial killers on the loose in the US at any given time (the actual number is probably much closer to 50[1]). Supposed experts and authors came out of the woodwork and have ridden this wave of hysteria in the way of badly researched (and in many cases, fabricated) quickie true-crime books and dubious hypotheses and theories. This was a cash cow that law enforcement and the academic society could really get behind.

The emphasis quickly became one of body count, the number of people killed. The few multiple killers already incarcerated (John Wayne Gacy, Ted Bundy, etc.) had their totals adjusted upward again and again by those with something to gain by these inflated figures. What was there to be gained? Well, through this atmosphere of foreboding, law enforcement attempted to justify their strong-arm tactics; academics, their positions; and politicians, their oppressive legislation. All that was needed to sell this bill of goods was a fresh face for the masses. They got this face in 46-year-old Henry Lee Lucas, their poster child for serial killing.

So far, roughly 30 to 40 books (including *Henry Lucas*, *The Confessions of Henry Lucas*, and *Human Monsters*) have been written either using Lucas as the lone subject or profiling him alongside notorious serial and mass murderers. His concocted story has been loosely adapted for at least two movies, *Henry: Portrait of a Serial Killer* being the more widely recognized.

I followed this case with fascination from the very onset. Having a keen interest in true crime and working at the time toward my degree in criminal justice, I found practically every aspect of this case to be a watershed in regard to serial killing. I wanted more detail. I wanted to get past what was being reported, dispense with the generalities and get down to specifics. My feeling was that to have committed hundreds of murders, Lucas must be the ultimate predator, a literal two-legged beast. But I was enough of a realist to see that getting any kind of access to Lucas during the initial media blitz was nothing short of impossible. True, there were numerous writers given an audience with him, but it appears their curiosity went no further than being able to say that they interviewed Lucas. Most of the articles and books were hackneyed regurgitations of the Texas Rangers' stance on the case. Few probing questions were ever put forth. It appears the only criterion needed to talk to Lucas was an assurance that one would toe the line. I decided to wait for a chance to approach Lucas on my terms.

That chance came in 1988, five years after Lucas' celebrity had reached its zenith. He was now residing in the Ellis One Unit of the Texas Department of Corrections, awaiting a death sentence. I first reached Lucas by letter and asked him a number of questions regarding his case. The response I received couldn't have been further from what I'd expected. My thought was that Lucas would either never respond or would send back a load of verbal bullshit. Instead, his letter was a short, courteous half a page directing me to people (attorneys, judges, law officers, etc.) who were more in a position to divulge the details I wanted. He ended with, "I am not a serial killer." This was to be the first of many revelations in a case fraught with contradiction.

Lucas and Texas Ranger Phil Ryan (left)

EVERYTHING YOU KNOW IS WRONG

■ ■ ■ ■ ■ ■ ■ ■ ■ ■

Lucas' early years were the stuff of nightmares. He was a literal whipping boy for his mother, Viola Lucas, who used every excuse to degrade him. He stated in later years, "She was strict on everything. If it didn't suit her, she just got whatever she could and started hitting. I still carry beatings and marks." His father, Anderson Lucas—a disabled railroad brakeman who lost both legs after getting run over by a train—was as abused by Viola as his son was, and he died drunk while sleeping in bed alongside young Henry. With the death of his father, Lucas became the sole recipient of his mother's rage; she once hit him so hard that he went into a coma. Only after three days did Viola decide to seek medical help for him.

Henry told me, "When I was young, I was given a Palomino pony by the people where dad worked as a mink skinner. I brought it home by leading it 25 miles from Christenburg [Virginia]. When I got home, mom went crazy, saying I could not keep it and if I didn't do my work she would shoot it. One day I was out riding it, and in just a few minutes here come mom. She went into the house, got her pistol, and shot it right in front of me. I cried so hard, and from that day I could not stand her." Incidents such as these—symptomatic of his overall treatment by his mother—were to define Lucas' lifelong personality traits of wanting to be accepted, being overly compliant, and being easily manipulated. But in later life, his abuse was to manifest in a burst of anger that culminated in the death of his mother.

After his father died, Lucas left home at the age of seventeen and went to Tecumseh, Michigan, staying with a half-sister, Opal. During the Christmas season of 1959, his sister brought Viola from Virginia for a visit. Lucas had become engaged, and his mother, upon learning of this, characteristically disapproved. "Mom demanded I not do it and go back home with her."

At the Tecumseh Tavern on the evening of January 11, 1960, after, by his own admission, having had too much to drink, the argument with his mother reignited. She was again ordering Henry to return home with her. "I told her no and that led to more argument, so I told Opal I was going, and I did around ten or eleven." Lucas went to bed but was violently awakened around 2:00 AM by his mother beating him across the head with a broom handle. In his January 16, 1960, statement to the Ohio State Police, he said, "She came up and started all over again. And I reached in my pocket, or had the knife in my hand. I don't know which. And I hit her with the knife and she fell on the floor and I ran."

He then stole a car at a local automotive garage and headed toward Virginia. "I got to thinking about what happened and started back to Michigan. I made it back to Ohio, where the trooper arrested me on a Michigan warrant." He was found guilty of second-degree murder and sent to the Michigan State Prison for a term of 20 to 40 years, serving fifteen years and being paroled on August 22, 1975. This conviction would later be one of the linchpins authorities would use to convince the public that Lucas was a bloodthirsty animal—an image needed to sell the hoax.

■ ■ ■ ■ ■ ■ ■ ■ ■ ■

Lucas' clichéd image as a savvy, streetwise psychopath who seduced the media is much at odds with the visage one saw when meeting him face-to-face. I first spoke to Lucas in person in the fall of 1988. Separated by glass in the visiting room of the infamous Texas death row, I was met by a man who was light years from the Lucas of legend. In comparison to his press photos, he appeared to have aged centuries. Instead of the swaggering confidence of yesteryear, Lucas' movements now appeared labored and difficult, since he had acquired a large potbelly and a myriad of health problems. Considering how he had been portrayed by law enforcement as forthcoming and gregarious, I was very surprised to find him soft-spoken and introverted. But Lucas was to surprise me many times over the years. When we discussed his confession spree, as we often did, he always expressed deep regret and sorrow that he had been instrumental in such a travesty of justice. "I do take responsibility for not being man enough to take the lies and treatment I was put into in Montague County [Texas]. I was not aware as to how crooked they were until it was too late."

Spending the years after his parole scrounging and working day jobs, Lucas was arrested in June 1983 in the town of Ringold, Montague County, Texas, for the murder of 82-year-old Kate Rich (Lucas was said to have burnt her remains in a small woodstove). While in open court pleading guilty to this crime, he stated, "And I killed about a hundred more women." Those in attendance were stunned by this revelation, and a media firestorm immediately ensued. When I asked him years later why he did this, Lucas said, "If they were going to make me confess to one I didn't do, then I was going to confess to everything."

IF ONE WERE TO BELIEVE ALL THE HYPE, A MONSTER WAS LURKING AT EVERY TURN, JUST WAITING TO DESTROY ANOTHER LIFE.

Also, Lucas was distraught because his traveling companion and—according to Lucas—lover,[2] 14-year-old Frieda Powell, had left with a truck driver. The authorities, however, thought Lucas had murdered her. "After I was charged that I killed Frieda I really didn't care what happened to me." Powell—the niece of Lucas' friend and supposed partner in crime, Ottis Toole—was an escapee from a Florida youth detention center. Having to quickly get out of Florida, they drove west with no particular destination in mind. During this time they both referred to Frieda as "Becky," partially to disguise her identity but also because Frieda liked that name much better than her own. They eventually took refuge at a religious commune called the House of Prayer in Stoneburg, Texas. Lucas found roofing work through the commune owner and minister, Ruben Moore. Moore and his wife, Faye, also gave Lucas and "Becky" a small apartment on the grounds. Referring to this time, Lucas stated, "I enjoyed being at the House of Prayer. I always thought I had a lifetime place to live and work." But Frieda was becoming restless, missing Florida and her family.

In August 1982, Lucas stated that he gave in to Powell's demands to return to Florida, and they left the House of Prayer. According to Lucas' account, they made their way to a truck stop in Bowie, Texas, where, when Lucas wasn't around, Powell accepted a ride from a truck driver, leaving Lucas by himself. "While I was at the truck stop, a Red Arrow truck came. She was getting into it when I ran out of the truck stop and hollered at her. I haven't seen her since." At trial, a waitress from the truck stop in question verified Lucas' story, and further investigation revealed logs showing a Red Arrow truck at this location at approximately the time Powell left. But these weren't the only troubling facts that were at odds with law enforcement's version.

The forensic findings in both the Powell and Rich cases were dubious, at best. No positive identification could be made in either case, and both autopsies state that "on the basis of circumstantial identification," they believe the remains to be those of Powell and Rich. In the Rich case, the medical examiners could infer anything they wanted because they had no remains to speak of (a piece of human bone measuring 1-1/4 x 3/4 x 1/4 inches was the only alleged remains of Rich recovered by law enforcement). But with Powell they had a practically complete skeleton, yet their findings do nothing to convince the impartial observer that the remains are those of Frieda Powell. In other words, they came to their conclusions because they were *told* the remains were those of Rich and Powell.

Even in these early cases (the first two Lucas ever confessed to), it appears that coercion, intimidation, and deprivation were the tactics employed by the officers in charge. Upon being arrested for a trumped-up felon-with-a-handgun charge (a charge Texas Ranger Phil Ryan described as "feather-legged"), Lucas was stripped of his clothes, cigarettes, and bedding, denied a phone call and a lawyer, and detained in a freezing cell. "They came and told me if I told them where Kate Rich was, they would give me whatever I wanted. I didn't know, so I couldn't tell them." After four days of this treatment, he began to confess. "I made up my mind to tell them anything I wanted so I could get an attorney and good treatment." Lucas' tactic worked. He was instantly given all he asked for—except, of course, an attorney.

Lucas wrote a jailhouse confession in which he stated that he had killed both Rich and Powell but that he couldn't take authorities to their remains. The last paragraph offers insight into the real reason for Lucas' sudden admission:

I am not aloud to contact any one I'm here in by myself

and still can't talk with a lawyer on this I have no rights so what can I do to convince you about all this

Lucas' lawyer—when he was finally given access to one—stated to the court that the treatment given Lucas was "inhumane" and "calculated solely to require the defendant to confess guilt, whether innocent or guilty." But Lucas had already learned a valuable lesson: Confession was the key to the kingdom.

■ ■ ■ ■ ■ ■ ■ ■ ■ ■

With Lucas' bogus admissions came a widespread infamy rivaled only by the Prohibition gangsters of the 1930s. Books and magazine articles were cranked out at an amazing pace. The race to make a buck off Lucas became so fevered that, at one point, his captors (Texas Ranger Bob Prince and Williamson County Sheriff Jim Boutwell) both jockeyed to be the first in line to sign a book deal. This, coupled with the accolades (awards, citations, etc.) that law enforcement was receiving because of the Lucas case, assured that Henry was treated to the best of everything—as long as he kept confessing.

"IF THEY WERE GOING TO MAKE ME CONFESS TO ONE I DIDN'T DO, THEN I WAS GOING TO CONFESS TO EVERYTHING."

(A good portion of the public has heard, over the years, that Lucas confessed to as many as 350 homicides, but the staggering truth is that he confessed to roughly *3,000*. The Lucas Task Force whittled the number down to a more workable and "believable" 350.)

Lucas was being flown around the country in the governor's plane, given the best of food, showered with privileges unknown to any convict, and, for the first time in his life, was the center of attention. When one sees a picture or video of Lucas and his handlers together, Lucas seems much more a partner than a prisoner. As a matter of fact, in Ranger Ryan's words, Lucas became "cocky" and started "dictating orders." Judge Brunson Moore of El Paso, Texas—who officiated over a 1985 Lucas pretrial hearing and threw out his confession as coerced—told me, "He [Lucas] came out here, and they took him to a Mexican restaurant. He had never eaten Mexican food. He sits down and says, 'I want a grilled cheese sandwich.' They say, 'Well, we don't serve grilled cheese sandwiches.' He says, 'Then I don't eat.' Guess what? They [the law officers] stood up, went out, and got him a grilled cheese sandwich. Now is that special treatment?"

While it appears that Lucas was overly indulged to the extreme, further circumstantial evidence illustrates that Lucas' jailors didn't think of this "prolific serial killer" as dangerous. He was rarely handcuffed and, according to a religious layperson who brought suppers to him in the Georgetown Jail, Lucas knew the security code to open the door separating the jail and the sheriff's office. According to longtime

Lucas investigator, Rick Perkins, Lucas was once left unattended in an airport by police and given the instructions, "Wait here—an officer will be along to pick you up." Lucas waited. When I asked him why he didn't run, he said, "Where was I going to go? They [law enforcement] were treating me great."

Regarding a Huntington, West Virginia, case that Lucas confessed to—changing the official cause of death from suicide to homicide and netting the widow a six-figure settlement—Perkins stated, "They [the Rangers] take him back to their room at the Holiday Inn and throw a $3,000 party with hookers and booze, and this serial killer is sitting there at the party. Do you think they thought he was a serial killer? Would you get drunk with a serial killer sitting in the same room?"

tiae), impartiality becomes a luxury. I don't claim to be impartial, but this is only because the evidence simply doesn't support the official view of Lucas. Because of my accumulated documentation and in-depth knowledge, Lucas' appellate attorneys had me federally appointed to the case in 1993.

While held in the Montague County Jail, Lucas was increasingly sought after by curious law enforcement agencies around the US; they wanted to know if Lucas had killed in their jurisdictions. Texas Ranger Phil Ryan advised these agencies that Lucas would be asked about their cases, and—if Lucas admitted complicity—that they should send a case packet with pertinent documents and photos so Lucas could be questioned at length.

It should be noted at this point that Lucas had previously given Ranger Ryan confessions to 75 murders, but Ryan was never able to substantiate *any* of these cases and dismissed them as fabrications. Regarding his interviewing of Lucas, Ryan said, "Every day I would invent one [murder], and I would say, 'All right, what about this one?' A high percentage of the time, 'Yeah, yeah, I did that.' I knew he was lying because there wasn't no such case, but what do you do?"

Well, if Lucas were determined to fabricate all of his confessions, then this massive influx of information being sent from outside agencies would give his lies the legs they needed to stand. Through familiarity with the interview process and inexperienced or dishonest officers, Lucas was able to use the information provided him to lend some credence to his statements. After repeatedly being questioned about the same cases, Lucas would parrot them back as if he were using his own words, thus making it appear that he had knowledge "only the killer would know." Ranger Ryan told me, "Henry had a good enough memory on a lot of this stuff to where if you asked him questions—and he later learned about the type of questions almost how to answer them because he had been exposed to a lot more of it than we was."

Lucas was transferred to the jail in Williamson County, Texas, in November 1983, and soon the Lucas Task Force (consisting of Ranger Bob Prince, Ranger Clayton Smith, and Williamson County Sheriff Jim Boutwell) was born. It became a veritable clearinghouse for modern murders, courtesy of the Texas Rangers.

Lucas' talent for fabrication was to be aided and abetted by the officers who were charged with overseeing his captivity and making him available to outside agencies. Truman Simons, former investigator for the Waco, Texas, District Attorney's Office, stated years later, "As far as the flood of different agencies from all over the United States that came down there, they were kind of led into a

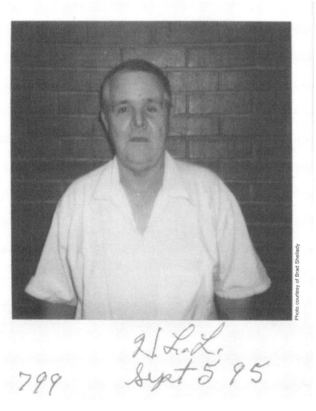

Lucas on September 5, 1995

If Lucas' overseers didn't believe him to be the aberration he was built up to be, neither did the many detractors of the case. Reams of information (which, in later years, amounted to hundreds of thousands of documents) were made available to me from a number of sources, solely, I believe, because I was an outsider not inclined to view the information with a jaundiced eye. I came to the case with impartiality, but after one gives the information even a cursory look (let alone spends over a decade, as I have, pouring over the minu-

trap. As far as my opinion, the culprits were the two that were running the task force [Ranger Prince and Ranger Smith], because they were giving Henry a lot of information before these guys ever got there, and a lot of these guys that came in were duped. Henry had read a lot of offense reports and seen a lot of pictures and everything before the guys actually working the cases ever got to see him."

Senior task force member Ranger Bob Prince said, "If you ask him about a homicide and he says he did it you better not believe him unless he gives you some information that only the killer would know." But, of course, Lucas knew these salient facts before the officers arrived because the reports had conveniently been shown to or discussed with him.

Ranger Prince continually repeated in the press that the only time an agency should believe a Lucas confession is "when you can confirm it," but what can been seen after reviewing Lucas' statements is that *none* of them can be confirmed. There is nothing in the way of independent evidence to bolster his claims. In response to criticism in the press, Ranger Prince's 1985 internal memo to Col. James Adams, Director of the Texas Department of Safety, states: "Several cases have corroborating, physical or eyewitness evidence. There are in excess of one-hundred cases where he physically led officers to sites where homicides occurred. Many others he had drawn maps of how to locate a scene or diagrams of the house, interior of the house, where furniture was located in the house, description of the furniture, and picking victims out of photo line-ups." This is simply untrue. While it is true that Lucas drew sketches of the above-mentioned objects, it would appear that all he was doing was crudely copying, from memory, diagrams he had already been shown. Most were incomprehensible and of no value. One must remember that all relevant information ever offered by Lucas was already known by law enforcement and was enclosed in the files sent to the task force for the purpose of questioning Lucas.

The Texas Attorney General at the time, Jim Maddox, observed: "Of all these people he theoretically killed, he never once ever led them to a body that had not been previously found. He never led them to a crime scene that hadn't already been found. They never tied him to a single gun. They never found a footprint. Never found a tire print to tie him in there. There was nothing that ever caused me to believe that he was the kind of guy that committed the crime."

In response to charges of case conflicts regarding "cleared cases" (murder cases that are considered solved and then closed), Prince's notes reflect, "[I]t should be stressed that the task force did not clear cases but had to rely on other agency information as to the sufficiency of evidence to clear such cases." But it would appear that the task force, by giving Lucas access to the information, did enable Lucas to "clear" the cases with other agencies. Still the nagging question was: If Lucas had done all these things, where was the physical evidence? To this day it is nonexistent, but there was a mountain of evidence being unearthed to illustrate that Lucas literally *couldn't* have committed the crimes he was claiming.

■ ■ ■ ■ ■ ■ ■ ■ ■

Lucas' claims had become more and more fantastical—besides the thousands of regular confessions, he also claimed responsibility for killing Jimmy Hoffa, delivering the poison to Jim Jones in Guyana, and stalking Jimmy Carter. Because of these and other troubling aspects, in April 1986, the Texas Attorney General's Office released their own investigation in the form of the aptly named "Lucas Report." Attorney General Jim Maddox's introduction was certainly to the point and damning in its candor: "Unfortunately, when Lucas was confessing to hundreds of murders, those with custody of Lucas did nothing to bring an end to his hoax." This statement in itself strongly implies that the task force perpetuated something they themselves knew to be factitious. The report went on to say: "We have found information that would lead us to believe that some officials 'cleared cases' just to get them off the books."

The body of the report was comprised of a timeline detailing cases Lucas confessed to, alongside his actual whereabouts at the times of the offenses. In most instances, records showed Lucas to be in another state when the crime was committed. The following few cases illustrate the norm regarding the confessions. These cases are culled from the Texas Ranger task force logs and are considered "cleared" on Lucas:

Murder: Curby Reeves shot in the top of the head with a .22-caliber pistol in Smith County, Texas, on August 10, 1975. Lucas was working at Kaolin Mushroom Company, Kaolin, Pennsylvania, on this date per payroll records on file.

Murder: Lindy Beicher stabbed nineteen times with a knife in Lancaster, Pennsylvania, on December 5, 1975. Lucas was married on this date in Maryland (per records) and spent the night with relatives.

Murder: Police officer Clemmie Curtis shot with .38-caliber pistol in Cabell County, West Virginia, on August 3, 1976. Lucas paid rent at Benjamin's Trailer Park, Port Deposit, Maryland, per rent records on file.

Murder: Paula Elaine Tollett shot in the head with a .32-caliber pistol in Tulsa, Oklahoma, on March 20, 1979. Per records, Lucas was in a community hospital in Bluefield, West Virginia.

Murder: Arley Belle Killian stabbed and mutilated in Oklahoma City, Oklahoma, on April 19, 1979. Lucas was working in Jacksonville, Florida, and was issued a LABOR, INC. check #3547 for $105.65.

Sadly, these cases are representative of the hundreds closed on Lucas. All are tainted with a plethora of problems. In summing up the "Lucas Report," Maddox wrote: "I hope through our efforts, the real murderers of innocent victims will be brought to justice by a careful reexamination of Lucas' contrived confessions." With this statement, the crux of the Lucas case is brought to the forefront: These bogus admissions have enabled hundreds of killers to escape justice, and the high probability is that many of these offenders have taken more innocent lives. Long after he had recanted his confessions, Lucas told me in 1992: "The [victims'] families need to find the truth. The killers who committed these crimes I am accused of and serving time for are still somewhere out there. Don't let the police con you anymore. Demand the truth."

A bigger travesty is the fact that even if an offender had already been tried and convicted, Lucas could still be his "get out of jail free" card. Certainly investigations were diverted and sidetracked (many stalled forever), but some empty confessions enabled the actual perpetrators a chance at a new trial. And in the most extreme cases, they were let out of prison altogether. This is what happened in the murder of gas station attendant Betty Thornton.

On November 6, 1981, Thornton was and shot and killed in a day-light robbery. Within hours of the murder, a 24-year-old by the name of Scotty Scott, the son of an Arkansas State Trooper, was apprehended. A witness' statement declared that he (the witness) had paid Scott $5 for the gas he had pumped. It appears that the witness, while stopping to get gas, had caught Scott right after killing Thornton. Scott had removed her body from the immediate area, and the witness assumed that this young man was the station attendant. Other witnesses also placed Scott at the scene, describing in detail his appearance (height, weight, age, and clothing) and his automobile.

LUCAS WAS BEING FLOWN AROUND THE COUNTRY IN THE GOVERNOR'S PLANE, GIVEN THE BEST OF FOOD, SHOWERED WITH PRIVILEGES UNKNOWN TO ANY CONVICT, AND, FOR THE FIRST TIME IN HIS LIFE, WAS THE CENTER OF ATTENTION.

In mid-1983 Scott was convicted of first-degree murder and received a 25-year sentence. In the fall of the same year—a few months after Scott had been remanded to the state prison—a representative of Scott's brought the case to the Lucas Task Force and eventually to Lucas himself. As usual, Lucas obliged with a confession.

Two Arkansas sheriff's deputies and an assistant prosecutor were dispatched to Texas to question Lucas at length. He offered few facts regarding the case, and he said that the ones he did offer were told to him "by some lawyer or detective" who spoke with him on the phone before the three investigators had arrived. Arkansas prosecutors admitted his other statements were inconsistent and vague. But in January 1984 and again in March, Scott's attorneys had a meeting with Lucas in which Lucas "remembered" more facts.

Scott's attorneys filed a motion with the courts claiming Lucas was the actual killer and that their client was innocent.

A petition hearing was held on July 30, 1984, and Lucas was brought to Little Rock to attend. Then-prosecutor Chris Piazza wrote in a post-hearing brief, "The testimony of Henry Lee Lucas that he committed this murder and robbery is dubious, to say the least.... [R]etrial on the basis of Lucas' testimony would be a farce." In closing he states:

Henry Lucas has made three (3) statements and has testified in this matter. The inaccuracies of Lucas' accounts of the convenience store murder show that he lacks first hand knowledge of Betty Thornton's murder. He is unaware of the type of weapon used, the location of the bullets, the type of store involved, the location of the store, the type of businesses located in the area or the time of day this murder was committed. He is inaccurate in almost every detail. The only facts that Lucas can give which are subject to corroboration show that Lucas is not telling the truth.

All of these statements, and more, were true of Lucas' erroneous confession and testimony, but even weightier evidence was available. Lucas stated that on the day of the murder he was driving a 1973 Pontiac station wagon, but the Texas Rangers had received information that he had sold this car six months previously in Del Rio, Texas. This overwhelming evidence would, in itself, seem enough to dismiss Lucas' words as meaningless ramblings, but there was one piece left that should have sewn it up. Records came to light proving that on the morning of November 6, 1981, the day of the murder, Lucas was in fact 800 miles away in Jacksonville, Florida, purchasing automobile insurance. This, one would think, would leave no doubt that Lucas had not committed the crime. But, as the Lucas case demonstrates time and time again, logic is not an issue.

Flying in the face of reason and common sense, the Arkansas court ordered another trial for Scotty Scott and set him free on bail. As of this writing, he has never been retried and is still a free man.

■ ■ ■ ■ ■ ■ ■ ■ ■ ■

When the smoke cleared, Lucas had been convicted of eleven homicides, one of which—the killing of an unidentified woman near Georgetown, Texas—netted him the death penalty. Because of the possibility of Lucas being put to death anytime, this was to be the case that occupied the lion's share of my investigation.

On October 31, 1979, the strangled body of a young woman was found lying in a culvert alongside I-35 in Williamson County, Texas.

The case came to be known as the "Orange Socks" case because the victim was found nude except for a pair of orange socks.

According to Sheriff Jim Boutwell, the case from the outset was at a standstill and never produced a suspect until Lucas came along, but former Williamson County investigator Cecil Kuykendall contends that this is not the case. In a sworn statement taken in 1990 he related that previous to Lucas becoming involved, he had had a strong suspect:

The Sheriff, Jim Boutwell, was at all times aware of my investigation of the suspect Elmer Gene Washington, and had full knowledge of the facts and the strong evidence in this case. In my estimation this case was not done by Henry Lee Lucas in any manner. The Sheriff was using him as a patsy to clear unsolved murder cases off the books.

Boutwell was made aware of Lucas by Sheriff Conway of Montague County, Texas—the county in which Lucas was originally arrested and was, at the time, incarcerated. Boutwell stated to me, "Conway called me and said, 'Jim, I've got an old boy up here you should talk to.'" And with this Boutwell initiated a series of interrogations with Lucas that produced a number of wildly diverging scenarios concerning the "Orange Socks" murder. The recorded interviews between Boutwell and Lucas very plainly show Boutwell guiding Lucas into a version of the facts which would correlate with the minimal evidence in the case. But even with this coaching, Lucas' story changed constantly. He stated more than once that the victim was stabbed and that she was killed in Oklahoma; he gave at least three different locations where her body was deposited. All of these statements were wrong, and with each fabrication Boutwell would correct Lucas, giving him the facts. Eventually Lucas parroted them back well enough that the Sheriff felt confident in charging him with the case.

Amazingly, when the taped confessions were entered into court, they very obviously had been edited. They consisted only of Lucas' regurgitation of the bare facts. All offending comments were muted. A video of Lucas giving a roadside confession at the I-35 location where the body was dropped has many spots where the audio goes silent, though one can still see Lucas speaking. When I viewed the unedited version, the previously censored remarks had Lucas stating, "After I dropped her [Orange Socks] off here, I went down into Austin and picked another up." At this point, which had also been muted, Sheriff Boutwell discourages Lucas from bringing up anything that is a deviation from the set story: "We don't need any of that." Lucas also stated that he had sex—"which was voluntary"—with her. This was muted because the prosecution wanted to estab-

lish that Lucas had both raped (despite the medical examiner's testimony that there was no evidence of rape) and murdered the victim, so he would be eligible for the death penalty.

In addition to the excised comments and the glaring inconsistencies in Lucas' statements, solid documentary evidence existed which established that Lucas had been in Jacksonville, Florida (over 1,000 miles away), on the date of the killing. Work records were uncovered that showed Lucas was present on a roofing job on the day in question and that he had cashed a paycheck at a local market. But, true to form, Lucas was always his own worst enemy—he proceeded to tell Sheriff Boutwell that the records and check were forged as a result of bribes from Lucas to the job foreman. It appeared Lucas was *trying* to get the death penalty. He stated to me in the early 1990s: "I was trying to commit legal suicide. I was tired and just didn't care anymore. I just wanted to die." The jury obliged Lucas by finding him guilty, therefore giving him his death sentence.

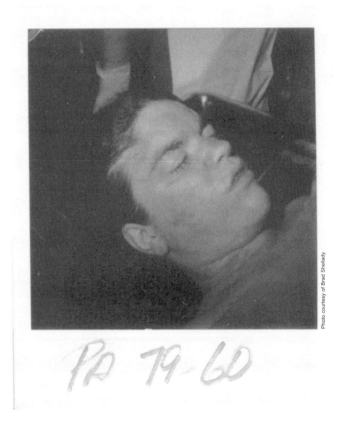

Photo courtesy of Brad Shellady

The victim known as Orange Socks

Only after years of exhaustive appeals and numerous public disclosures showing the Lucas cases to be untrustworthy and fabricated were we, the defense team, given the opportunity to present the case to then-Governor of Texas George W. Bush. After a series of meetings and a near-unanimous vote by the Texas Board of Pardons and Parole to commute Lucas' death sentence, on June 26, 1998 (three days before Lucas was to be executed), Governor Bush granted him clemency. As of this writing, the "Orange Socks" victim still has not been identified, and no other suspects have been unearthed.

■ ■ ■ ■ ■ ■ ■ ■ ■ ■

On March 12, 2001, while still in the custody of the Texas Department of Corrections, Henry Lee Lucas quietly passed away from heart failure. In doing so, he took with him almost all hope of these cases ever receiving the investigation they deserve. To this day, 214 homicides (half in Texas) remain closed on Lucas.

Judge Moore stated it best: "What I am saying to you is not my opinion or my version of what happened. What I am saying to you is what can be proven by just reading the transcripts. You first start off with the premise that here's a serial killer. Then as you look at all the evidence in each case that comes up, you begin to see a pattern of a state agency making a serial killer out of a person that may not have killed anybody."

THESE BOGUS ADMISSIONS HAVE ENABLED HUNDREDS OF KILLERS TO ESCAPE JUSTICE, AND THE HIGH PROBABILITY IS THAT MANY OF THESE OFFENDERS HAVE TAKEN MORE INNOCENT LIVES.

This case, in the worst possible terms, illustrates that the path of least resistance is the one most often traveled. When reputations and egos hang in the balance, it is easier to lay the blame at the feet of a dead man than bring into question the integrity of the living.

Endnotes

1. Jenkins, Philip. *Using Murder: The Social Construction of Serial Homicide*. New York: Aldine De Gruyter, 1994. **2.** For a period during his confession spree, Lucas claimed he had been having sex with Powell, but evidence was to come to light years later in an appellate investigation that once again spotlighted Lucas' tendency to fabricate. By Lucas' own account, backed up by prison records, he was stabbed in the lower abdomen in a prison attack in late 1958. According to him, he was told by the medical personnel who attended him that he would most likely be rendered impotent. We on the defense team, upon learning this information, had Lucas psychologically and medically tested. He had confessed to raping scores of victims, and this would certainly be a revelation if true. When testing was completed, Lucas had shown no stimulus response whatsoever, with the conclusion being that he was "functionally impotent." Gisli Gudjonson, a world-renowned psychologist specializing in false confessions who examined Lucas, stated: "He was living a vicarious sex life through his false statements."

THE MONSTER OF FLORENCE
SERIAL KILLINGS LEAD TO ITALY'S HIGH SOCIETY
RORY CARROLL

ROME (*Guardian* and *Observer*) — Police in Italy have reopened inquiries into the Monster of Florence case, the serial killings that inspired the creation of Hannibal Lecter. The people of Tuscany had thought the story was over—the last victims were killed sixteen years ago, while the "monster" alleged to have murdered them died in 1998. But on August 7, 2001, detectives in Florence said there were new suspects for the murder and mutilation of eight couples between 1968 and 1985.

Police now believe that a group of between ten and twelve wealthy, sophisticated Italians orchestrated ritualized murders over the course of three decades and got away with it, allowing their careers and reputations to blossom to this day.

Detectives who were tipped off by a series of anonymous letters are questioning a key witness and have sent magistrates a file which is believed to name some of the suspects, including a doctor and an artist.

The sect's requirements were precise: night-time executions of courting couples followed by mutilation with the help of a .22 Beretta revolver and a surgical knife.

Pietro Pacciani, an illiterate farm laborer, was convicted in 1994 of seven of the eight double-killings. The conviction was overturned, and he was awaiting a new trial when he died. Despite his denials, few doubted that the stocky Tuscan, who in his youth had murdered a traveling salesman by stabbing him and stamping on him, was indeed the Monster of Florence.

A month before his death, two friends—Mario Vanni and Giancarlo Lotti—were convicted and jailed for helping to kill the couples, and were sentenced to life and 26 years, respectively.

Case closed, it seemed.

But some investigators were uneasy. There were unexplained factors and leads that were not followed up. How, for instance, had Pacciani saved more than £50,000 [$72,500] and bought two houses? What did he do with his bloody trophies? Who was the mysterious doctor Lotti referred to in court as the man who ordered the jobs?

The novelist Thomas Harris, sitting in on the original hearings, seemed to share suspicions that a society figure had masterminded the gore and so made his fictional killer, Hannibal Lecter, a psychiatrist.

The head of Florence's detective force, Michele Giuttari, believed Pacciani was too sloppy to have planned the crimes. They started in August 1968 when Antonio Lo Bianco, 29, and Barbara Locci, 32, were shot in their car. A pattern was set: It was always a moonless night on a weekend in an isolated lane.

The Germans Horst Meyer and Uwe Rusch Sens were murdered in woods near Galluzo in September 1983. One had long hair and may have been thought to be a woman. The last couple, French, were slain in September 1985 as they camped in a vineyard near the village of Scopeti.

Detectives have found evidence of what they believe was an occult group which directed the three peasants—Pacciani, Vanni, and Lotti (who were known collectively as the peeping toms because of their nocturnal ramblings)—to commit the murders. The real monsters were allegedly the wealthy and respected members of Tuscan society—including a doctor, ambassador and an artist—who to this day have remained undetected.

Pacciani and Vanni were also alleged to have participated in black masses which used female body parts at the house of a supposed wizard in San Caciano, a popular tourist destination because of its Romanesque Pisan church. Nurses at a clinic which hired Pacciani as a gardener claimed that he told them a doctor presided at other satanic ceremonies.

A cover-up involving secret service agents and missing money is now said to be unraveling. In early September 2001, detectives from Florence raided the homes and offices of Aurelio Mattei, a psychologist with the secret service, Sisde, and of Francesco Bruno, Italy's leading criminal psychologist.

Computer disks, books, and notes about the killings were confiscated, and both men were questioned for up to nine hours.

Neither is a murder suspect and they have not been charged, but

EVERYTHING YOU KNOW IS WRONG

detectives believe they may have withheld evidence from the original investigation into Pacciani, for which they were retained as consultants.

In 1992 Mattei wrote a book, *Rabbit on Tuesday*, which anticipated evidence uncovered only since the investigation was reopened earlier in 2001.

Bruno, a regular guest on chat shows, outlined the theory of an occult sect in a report commissioned by the secret service in 1985—before the final killing. He sent it to Vincenzo Parisi, who has since risen to head the service, but the report was never forwarded to police.

The head of Florence's detective force, Michele Giuttari, discovered its existence only recently, after groping towards the same theory.

The report suggested the mutilations—the women's left breast and pubic area were removed—could have been used in occult ceremonies and even told of a remote villa where they could have taken place.

Pacciani worked as a gardener in Villa Verde, a former nursing home, which police belatedly searched in 1997.

Giuttari wants to know why the secret service buried the report during a parallel investigation, which spent hundreds of thousands of pounds from a "black fund," of which no records were kept.

Giuttari hopes that following the money trail could lead to a breakthrough by revealing suspects who were protected by Sisde. "We will clarify everything and in good time," he said. Two members of the secret service have been questioned.

A Swiss artist, now being questioned by police, was allegedly part of the group. After he left the area in 1997, police found drawings of mutilated women and newspaper cuttings of Pacciani's trial in the artist's farmhouse.

The investigating magistrate, Paolo Canessa, believed Pacciani's heart attack in February 1998 was triggered by drugs to silence him, lest he reveal the real monster, or monsters. The original verdict of a heart attack has been discredited and his death is now being treated as murder.

_FETISHISTS

Detectives made little progress until spring 2001, when a series of anonymous letters, containing details about the killings that had never been made public, revealed that a woman in Genoa had use-

ful information.

Although she was described in letters but not actually named, she was tracked down in August to an apartment shared with her sister. Italian media suggested she was one of the prostitutes that Pacciani visited during trips to Genoa's red-light district in the 1980s. Detectives are checking why the last letter was intercepted and opened by someone in the police station.

Massimo Introvigne, a religious historian who helped police in the original inquiry and advised the FBI, told the newspaper *La Repubblica* that Tuscany, which partly inspired the poet Dante to write his classic about the inferno, had a long tradition of sorcery. He said American anthropologists noted a phenomenon of medieval chants and invocation of the devil in the nineteenth century. "There are elements that make the [police] hypothesis possible. Experience teaches us that deviant groups do exist," said Professor Introvigne.

He stressed that occult sects were not necessarily satanists and that the ritual nature of the murders suggested fetishists were to blame.

Magistrates must now decide whether to seek prosecutions for those named in the police file.

POLICE NOW BELIEVE THAT A GROUP OF BETWEEN TEN AND TWELVE WEALTHY, SOPHISTICATED ITALIANS ORCHESTRATED RITUALIZED MURDERS OVER THE COURSE OF THREE DECADES AND GOT AWAY WITH IT.

_WHY HANNIBAL WENT TO THE TUSCAN CAPITAL

One of the visitors to the Florence court spellbound by the 1992 trial of Pietro Pacciani was the novelist Thomas Harris. The true tale of serial killers who shot and mutilated courting couples in Tuscany caught his imagination. Not just for its horror but because of the suspicion that Pacciani was not the real Monster of Florence but a pawn who acted on the orders of a powerful high-society figure, possibly a doctor or surgeon.

Harris was inspired to locate his third novel, *Hannibal*, in the Tuscan capital, and echoes of the real-life case reverberated during filming of the novel in Florence in 2000. In the fictional story, Lecter (played by Sir Anthony Hopkins) escapes from custody in the US and resurfaces as the custodian of the Capponi library, with all the refinement and homicidal impulses attributed to the suspected "real" monster.

Politicians and locals objected to the filming on the grounds that Florence's reputation had been sullied enough by the murders without being used as the setting for Hannibal's appetites.

THE MONSTER OF FLORENCE
RORY CARROLL

WITNESSES TO A MASSACRE
OTHER PARTICIPANTS IN THE COLUMBINE SHOOTING
RUSS KICK

The mass shooting at Columbine High School in Littleton, Colorado, still stands as the most bloody and most infamous school shooting in US history. In the end, a dozen students, one teacher, and two gunmen lay dead. Even if another incident surpasses it with regard to body count, Columbine will remain seared into the public psyche as the archetypal school shooting. Despite its unique status, despite the controversies it triggered (provoking arguments about guns, Marilyn Manson, bullying, and parental responsibility, among many other topics) and the subsequent incidents and near-incidents it inspired, many unanswered questions swirl around the events of April 20, 1999.

Though many pieces of the puzzle remain hidden, many others are buried in the voluminous public record regarding the case. As revealed in "Anatomy of a School Shooting" in *You Are Being Lied To*, press reports and official statements made on and immediately after the tragic day don't jibe with the Official Version of Events. We know, for example, that a *Denver Post* article reported shots still being fired in the school three and a half hours after the two gunmen supposedly died. We know that Sheriff John Stone indicated that there were others involved, a charge he has now backed away from, at least in public. Similarly, contemporaneous reports declared that numerous students saw more than two gunmen.

Another treasure trove of information is found in the thousands of official documents that have been released. In November 2000, Jefferson County, Colorado, unleashed a blizzard of 11,000 pages of raw documents. This has been followed by thousands more pages, plus police dispatches, some autopsy reports and autopsy summaries, videotape of the cafeteria, and yet more material. A small group of individuals combing this material in a quest to find the truth has gathered at the Website for the Columbine Research Task Force. There they post their findings, while debating what they mean. By sifting through the material myself and with pointers from the Task Force, I've assembled some eyewitness statements that don't jibe with the official report of the incident. Of course, recollections of witnesses can be inaccurate, but I found an amazing amount of congruity among the statements of people who saw other participants in the massacre. These are important pieces of the puzzle, and when fitted with other pieces (early media reports, statements from officials, etc.), a form takes shape that stands in distinct relief to the orthodox account of these events.

Unfortunately, the limits of time and page count mean that a full examination of the realities of Columbine will have to wait even longer. In the meantime, though, feast your eyes on the following eyewitness reports taken from the original 11,000-page release. As you do, keep in mind the particulars of the Official Version of Events. We've been told:

> • Students Eric Harris and Dylan Klebold planned and executed this attack completely by themselves. Some other people bought guns for them (since they were minors), but these buyers had no idea what Harris and Klebold were about to perpetrate.
>
> • The two gunmen were dressed in black trenchcoats and pants.
>
> • The shooting started at approximately 11:19 AM. By 12:08 PM—at the latest—Harris and Klebold were dead, having killed themselves.

_THE BOMB-THROWER IN THE WHITE T-SHIRT

Outside the school, numerous witnesses saw a young man dressed in a white T-shirt and blue jeans taking part in the attack. Remember, Harris and Klebold were dressed in black pants. Harris was wearing a white T-shirt under his trenchcoat, but he wasn't wearing jeans. While Harris and Klebold both had guns, the guy in the white T-shirt contented himself with giving the signal to start the rampage, then throwing explosives. Many witnesses simultaneously saw all three of them, eliminating the possibility that the white T-shirt bomber was one of the two known gunmen. As *USA Today* reported on the day after the shooting: "Beyond the two dead gunmen, students

MANY UNANSWERED QUESTIONS SWIRL AROUND THE EVENTS OF APRIL 20, 1999.

described seeing another youth dressed in a white shirt throwing bombs that looked like soda cans. A youth matching that description later was seen being led away by police."[1]

Chris Wisher, student (written statement made 1:30 PM on April 20, 1999): "Me and my friends were about 100 yards away from the people. There were 3 of them[:] 2 wearing trench coats and one wearing a white shirt. We heard what we thought was a gun & started running. Then we figured that they were fireworks & went back. We saw one of them aim a gun at us and started shooting at us. We heard the gun shots going by our heads so we fell to the ground. We got up & saw the kid in the white throw what looked like grenades on the roof. That is when we got back up and started running."[2]

"THERE WERE 3 OF THEM[:] 2 WEARING TRENCH COATS AND ONE WEARING A WHITE SHIRT."

Jake Apodaca, student (written statement made 1:30 PM on April 20, 1999): "Me and my friend were at the soccer field and we heard what sounded like fire crackers and we looked over and saw 3 men by the school and they were shooting guns[.] One of them threw a couple of bombs on roof of school. And then they shot what looked like a shot gun at us."[3]

Jake Apodaca (interviewed April 20, 1999, by Detective Brian Lynch): "at soccer field with friend and heard what sounded like firecrackers; saw 3 subjects near school, shooting; one threw bombs onto roof of school; subjects shot shotgun toward him and his friend; he and his friend ran to a house and called 911; he saw a gunman ducked down with a shotgun in Weaver Park; subjects were W/M [white male], 2 wearing black trenchcoats, black berets, black pants, black Army boots, black T-shirts, carrying shotguns; he has seen them at school before, but did not find them in the yearbook he was shown; the third subject had light brown hair, wearing a white T-shirt and jeans, throwing bombs onto the roof; saw one explode; Apodaca has not seen him at school before (SEE WRITTEN STATEMENT)."[4]

William Arapkiles, freshman (interviewed May 5, 1999, by Agent Timothy Steffes[5]): While on the soccer field, Arapkiles heard sounds like firecrackers coming from the area around the cafeteria. "He said that he looked toward the school and observed three people near the west entrance to the north main hall. Billy stated that two [of] the subjects were wearing trench coats, and the third was wearing a white shirt. According to Billy the two subjects wearing trench coats had guns. He did not see the subject with the white shirt with a fire arm. Billy related that the subject wearing the white shirt was pacing back and forth and was about five feet away from the two in trench coats. Billy did not think the subject wearing the white shirt was a victim but was with the other two. Billy reported that he was too far away to recognize the subjects."[6]

Donald Arnold, Jr., sophomore (interviewed May 11, 1999, by Special Agent Michael W. Howell): Arnold was on the soccer field. "Arnold looked towards the school and saw a short, pudgy male, wearing a white T-shirt, and throwing something onto the roof of the school near the electrical transformers. Arnold heard [an] explosion and saw dust on the roof soon after. Arnold could provide no further description of this person and did not see this person with a gun.

"Arnold then saw another male, whom he could not describe, shooting a shotgun towards the senior parking lot. This individual was standing on the upper level, north of the parking lot and near the school building, approximately 30 yards Southwest of the first male."[7]

Patrick Neville, student (interviewed May 6, 1999, by McFadden): Another student on the soccer field. "Neville described the first gunmen [sic] as tall with a black trench coat, dressed all in black, carrying a gun, described as a long gun. Neville stated that the second gunmen [sic] was a white male, with a white shirt, blue jeans, who he observed throwing something on the roof which exploded."[8]

Mike Kenny, sophomore (interviewed May 1, 1999, by Denver Police Detective Terry Kemmel): Kenny and his companions on the soccer field heard what they thought were firecrackers near the library. "They observed a party in a black trench coat with black pants; Mike stated that he was approximately 100 yards away. Mike reported that the guy had a TEC 9 in his hand, a person wearing a white T-shirt and blue jeans was about 10 feet behind the guy in the trench coat and they both appeared to be together." The guy in the trenchcoat shot at them, so they ran. When Kenny looked back, he saw an explosion and smoke on the roof in the area of the two suspects.[9]

Jonathan Cole, student (interviewed June 1, 1999, by Agents Linda R. Holloway and Jerry Means, Colorado Bureau of Investigation): "COLE finished his fourth period class and walked out of the school via the doors located on the upper level just north of the library of the west side. He met up with Jack ABODACA and CHRIS WISHER when he noticed two males in trench coats. One was wearing a ski make [sic] with one large hole in it. Both were tall and [he] believes that they had just come through the same doors he had exited from. He did not recall them wearing hats, however, it was his perception that one had a white shirt on under his trench coat and one was wearing a black shirt and black or dark pants or jeans. He recalled that one had brown 'puffy' hair. The two males walked to the corner of the building and stood off of the sidewalk looking down the steps that lead to the cafeteria and senior parking lot. He recalled seeing a third male who was wearing a white tee-shirt that had either short sleeves or no sleeves, blue jeans exit the building behind the two trenched males. He next remembered that the male in the white shirt yelled at the other two males in trench coats to 'GO!! GO!!'

"He then observed the two males with trench coats draw weapons.

One pulled a shotgun and one pulled a large semi-automatic gun. They began shooting at students below. He recalled hearing kids scream and one student fall to the ground. He began to run in a westerly direction. He recalled looking back and seeing the male in the white shirt throw what he believes are bombs on the roof area of the library. He thought that he threw four or five bombs and that some exploded....

"JONATHAN COLE related that when he went to pick up his backpack and other belongings that he had left at the school with his mother today, that he saw a male that reminded him of the male in the white shirt who was throwing the bombs. His [sic] male was described as 5'10", wearing black glasses and having collar length blondish brown hair. He did not know that student's name."[10]

Jessica Guertz, student (interviewed May 18, 1999, by Denver Police Detective Mark Allen): Guertz was in the cafeteria with friends. "Jessica said someone yelled that there was a fight and they all got up to look out the windows. Jessica said she saw two guys dressed in Trench Coats, and a guy in white T-shirt possibly with them standing near the cement stairs." After hearing shots, she ran out of the cafeteria, then out of the school.

Jessica Guertz (reinterviewed August 10, 1999, by unknown person from the Jefferson County Sheriff's Office): "She said she saw two tall, about 6 feet, adult males standing close to the cement stairs out side of the cafeteria, (West side). She said they appeared to be very calm, she said they were dressed in black. She could not be for sure the exact clothing. She just said it was all black.

"She also said another male in a white shirt was standing close to the cement stairs and appeared to be very calm also. She told me that she thought it was strange that the three were standing so calmly when everyone else was so paniced [sic].

"The adult in the white shirt was also tall, thin and estimated his height to be 6'."[11]

Stefanie Haney, student (interviewed May 25, 1999, by Jefferson County Sheriff Investigator C. Schoshke): Around 11:15 AM, Haney was walking out of the cafeteria doors and noticed three people walking into the school through nearby doors. "Haney further told me that she did see and greet Harris and Klebold who were entering those doors at that time. Both Harris and Klebold were wearing their 'trenchcoats' with their hands in their pockets. She knows both Harris and Klebold from school and described Harris as having shorter hair than Klebold who's [sic] hair is fairly long over the ears and collar length. She could not say what type of pants or footwear they had on. At that time neither had anything on their heads. Haney also described a third male walking with Harris and Klebold. The white male looked older than a high school student and she did not recognize him from any of the four years she had attended CHS.

The unknown male was about the same height as Harris, his hair was dark in a kind of bowl cut and shaved on the sides. He was wearing a white 'T' or 'V'necked shirt (like a man's undershirt) with its sleeves rolled up once or twice."[12]

Ann Marie Kelly, sophomore (written statement made May 5, 1999): "Pat Newel said he was out side [sic] at the time of the attack. He saw 3 guy's [sic] walk up the hill. 2 had trench coats. 1 had a white shirt. The guy with the shirt threw something onto the roof which exploded."[13] (Unfortunately, no interview with Pat Newel is contained in the 11,000 pages of documents.)

Nathan Vanderau, student (interviewed April 30, 1999, by Special Agents Jeffery C. Diehl and John M. Elvig): While eating lunch in the cafeteria, Vanderau heard an explosion and looked out a window. "Van saw two individuals outside of the school. One individual he saw only from the waist up was dressed in a white shirt and blue jeans. This person was throwing something in a side arm motion up towards the school roof. Van saw him throw one or two items. The second individual Van got a glimpse of was dressed in black and was taller than the other person."[14]

_THE ACNE SHOOTER

Several students report seeing a fellow student, not Harris or Klebold, taking part in the shooting. He is identified by his acute acne, bad teeth, long face, great height, fairly long hair, and a pigeon-toed manner of walking—in other words, a distinctive character not likely to be confused with someone else. (Although Klebold was tall, he didn't have an acne-riddled face, bad teeth, or an unusual manner of walking.) As with any time a suspect other than Harris or Klebold is mentioned, this student's name is redacted (i.e., blacked out) in the documents, although the censors occasionally slipped up and let his name sneak through unmarred.

> **"SHE STATED SHE KNEW IT WAS [REDACTED] IN THE TRENCH COAT, STANDING OVER THE TWO KIDS, BECAUSE SHE RECOGNIZED HIM."**

Bijen Monte, junior (interviewed April 30, 1999, by Agent Jerry W. Means and Agent Ricky S. Mundine, Colorado Bureau of Investigation): "MONTE stated she was near the cafeteria when the shooting started and she saw one of the gunmen. She stated the gunman she saw was not one of the guys identified on television [i.e., Harris and Klebold]."

Monte was sitting outside on the south side of the building at the time. "She thought she saw fireworks sparkling on the sidewalk, and then saw a guy in a trench coat coming down the hill. Three kids went 'down' to the ground, and the guy in the trench coat was standing over two of the downed kids. She stated she knew it was [redacted] in the trench coat, standing over the two kids, because she recognized him...."

"She stated [redacted] had a gun hanging from his neck on some type of strap. The gun was all black and approximately 15-18 inches long. She stated it looked like a machine gun, and there was no Duct Tape on it. She stated that was the only gun she saw him with, and it was in his right hand.

"The following is a physical description of the man she saw with a gun:

"He had on a black trench coat that extended to between his knees and his ankles. He had on a black baseball cap in the backward position. His face was long and his neck was long. He had a narrow chin. His teeth were crooked and he had an obvious overbite. He had no glasses or facial hair. His complexion had lots of acne, there were indentations like pieces were cut out, and his face was white in color with some redness..."

Bijen Monte (scene walk-through on May 1, 1999, with agents Mundine, Means, and Mark Wilson): "Bijen MONTE stated she wanted the Agents present at the interview to know that she assumed the gunmen got their weapons from [redacted] house because she knew through her friends they had a lot of guns. She stated she had been to the [redacted] house one time and she did see weapons mounted on the wall as a display...."

"MONTE stated she was positive that the man with the gun standing over the two kids was [redacted]. She stated she could recognize [redacted] and that is whom she saw. She stated she could see his complexion was rough with acne, and she could see his messed up teeth and overbite from where she was standing. MONTE was asked if there was any doubt in her mind about who she saw. MONTE stated there was no doubt, it was [redacted]."[15]

Crystal Archuleta, junior (interviewed April 27, 1999, by Detective Terry Demmel): Archuleta and some friends ran into the parking lot to check on an injured girl (Anne Marie Hochhalter, who is now paralyzed from being shot). "Crystal observed a male party wearing a trench coat, a black ball cap turned around backwards, very tall; that Crystal believed to be a student she knew as a [redacted]. Crystal observed the party in the trench coat throw one pipe bomb on the hill above the cafeteria. She did not see the party carrying a gun. The party was alone and had no one with him as he then walked up the stairs and into the entrance door next to the library. When asked by det. Demmel how she knew it was [redacted] she said that [student's name] was pigeon toe'd and that the person was walking that way and went up the stairs in a very distinct pigeon toe'd manner."[16]

Crystal Archuleta (reinterviewed May 3, 1999, by Mike Heylin): "When asked about other trench coat students, she said that she knows a [redacted] to be one of them. She said it was [redacted] she saw walking up the hill by the stairs outside the cafeteria when the shooting began. She did not know [redacted] name prior to the shooting. She said that she looked in her 1997 yearbook and iden-

tified him as the trench coat student she has seen around school and as the one she saw walking up the hill.

"She described [redacted] from seeing him in school at times. She said he is a white male, very tall 'almost 7 feet,' very thin, with very curly dirty blond or brown hair down to the neck, always had a black ball cap turned backwards, bad acne, no facial hair, hair would stick out from under cap, further described as having a 'weird walk' as in being pigeon-toed with long strides. (She was then shown the color class photograph with Dylan Klebold and Eric Harris. She said she did not recognize anyone from that photo. When asked specifically if the photograph of Dylan Klebold could be the student she saw in school at time with the trench coat she said it was not.)"[17]

Lacey Smith, student (interviewed May 4, 1999, by detectives Kreutzer and Watson): "Smith seemed to be expecting that she would be contacted by investigators. She immediately opened her yearbook, and pointed out [redacted] picture. She said that his appearance has changed from that picture; that now he has long hair, and his face is 'really broken out'....

"SMITH described [redacted] as always dressing the same every day, with a black 'trench coat', and black baseball cap turned backwards. The hat had a circular logo on it - possibly 'the world', and white letters 'NO SHIT!'. SMITH said [redacted] wore his trench coat religiously.

"SMITH did not see [redacted] with a gun, but she believes he had a gun concealed under his long coat. She states that when he stopped, facing toward the main area of the cafeteria, she heard what she described as 'rapid fire' shooting coming from [redacted], and observed him 'turning'. She described his as 'shooting from the hip'. SMITH said, 'The noise was coming from him'. She described the noise as 'piercing' and 'loud'. It made her ears ring. She also heard glass breaking, but did not see where this was occurring. SMITH could not tell how many shots she heard, but believed it was less than 15....

"When she got home, SMITH told her mother there were three shooters, and told her what she had seen....

"SMITH told investigators that during the prior school year (97-98) [redacted] was frequently seen with a group of individuals dressed in similar 'trench coats'; one of whom was a neighbor of the SMITH's, Bobby CRAIG. CRAIG is the subject who killed his father, then committed suicide...."[18]

Brian Frye, student (reinterviewed May 11, 1999, by Lauck): During his May 7 interview, Frye thought that he had seen Eric Harris with a pistol outside the cafeteria as the shooting started. However, he is reinterviewed after changing his mind. "He advised that while at school, he heard a rumor that [redacted] has turned himself in as having been involved in the shootings at Columbine. He went on to say that when he received his year book, he began looking at the pictures of both Dylan Klebold and Eric Harris. He said that he then looked at the picture of [redacted] and became convinced in his mind that the person he saw outside the student entrance holding and then shooting the Tec-9 was [redacted], not Eric Harris. He said that he had assumed the shooter was Eric Harris because he did not recognize him as Dylan Klebold that day and knew that the media had announced the shooters as Eric and Dylan. He advised that the shooter took very long strides and was close enough to him - he estimates about fifteen feet, that he saw the acne on his face."[19]

Katelyn Sue Place, freshman (interviewed May 14, 1999, by P.J. Doyle, "a commissioned peace officer"): Place was in the cafeteria when she saw a bunch of kids duck under the table. She did, too, then got up on her knees. "She saw a person coming down the stairs on the outside. She could see through the windows[.] He was shooting a rifle. He was tall and she described his height as 'lengthy'[.] He had a long shaped face[.] He was wearing a trench coat[.] He was not wearing a mask[.] She doesn't remember if he was wearing a hat or not, but said that he had short hair[.] She couldn't see below his knees[.]

"He was holding the rifle in his right hand[.] He was just pointing and shooting at people at the outside commons area[.] She couldn't see his left hand. She said that she didn't notice if he had anything on or about his trench coat.

"Kate said, 'It was [redacted][.] I'm almost positive of it[.] I remember looking him dead in the eye[.] He was in my debate class for a little bit either the end of last semester or the beginning of this one[.]'

"She then stated she recognized him as [redacted][.]...

"Kate said that, 'Dyland [*sic*] kind of looks like [redacted], but Dyland doesn't have the long face[.] [Redacted] teeth are messed up and he was smiling and I saw his teeth then[.]' Kate said that she has since seen pictures of Dyland Klebold and Eric Harris, and she said, 'It's not one of them[.]'

"Kate said she looked at [redacted] for about 30 seconds until he looked at her and he smiled[.] She ducked back down[.] She remembers him shooting Anne Marie[.] She said that Tony Samorrow (spelling?), Jason Unreath (spelling?) and Jason's girlfriend were out with Anne Marie[.] They were sitting by the tree where they sit every day[.] [Redacted] was randomly shooting[.] Kate looked in the direction of Anne Marie[.] [Redacted] was still shooting. Kate saw Anne Marie drop[.] Kate didn't remember which direction Anne Marie dropped[.] Kate went back under the table[.] Kate said that [redacted] shot Anne Marie before he smiled at Kate[.]"[20]

"SHE THEN STATED SHE RECOGNIZED HIM AS [REDACTED][.]"

_THE SUSPECT OUTSIDE THE SCIENCE ROOM

Several witnesses who were holed up in a science room describe seeing Dylan Klebold with an older male, who was at least in his mid-20s. His short, spiked hair—either blonde or else dark with blonde streaks or tips—is unlike that of either of the two known gunmen. He carried a tan sawed-off shotgun and detonated an explosive device.

Jennifer Smull, student (undated written statement): "I saw a senior standing outside our classroom door. I knew he was the shooter. Then I saw an adult (blond, short spiky hair[;] thought he was in 30s). I thought he was a cop until he held up a sawed off shot gun. Then he and the senior tried to break into the room where a shot teacher went. When they couldn't get in they ran away shooting down the hall once or twice."[21]

Jennifer Smull (interviewed April 28, 1999, by Investigator Jill Reuteler, Colorado State Patrol): "She said that between 11 45am and noon, she looked into the hallway and saw Dylan in the hallway, and another white male. She said that had he looked past the other person he would have seen her easily[.] Ms. Smull was asked to describe Dylan and she said he was wearing a black T shirt with writing on it, (she didn't know what it said) and a black hat on backwards with writing on it and that he had long curly hair.

"She said that the person with Dylan appeared to be older, had short blonde hair, like a buzz cut, and was wearing a white T shirt, tight fit with no pocket, and was carrying a tan-colored sawed off shotgun[.] She said that they tried to break down the door where Mr Sanders was and when they couldn't break the door down, they threw a bomb and ran down the hall."[22]

During this interview, Smull was shown a photo line-up and was easily able to pick out Harris and Klebold.

Jennifer Smull (reinterviewed on October 12, 1999, by Larry Erzen): "I asked Jennifer about the statement that she made that between 11:45 a.m. and noon she observed two armed gunmen in the hallway, just outside her science class. Jennifer identified Dylan Klebold as being one of the armed gunmen and describes him as wearing a black t-shirt with writing on it, had a black hat on, turned backwards with writing on it, and she saw his long curly hair extend below his baseball cap. Jennifer stated that she was positive that person was Dylan Klebold. In her statement, she then describes a second armed gunman, who is unknown to her.

"Jennifer described the second gunman as being older, had short blond hair, like a buzz cut, was wearing a white t-shirt, tight fit with no pockets and was carrying a tan colored sawed off shotgun. Jennifer said that that description was accurate, at which time she provided me with a composite drawing she had done in reference to the suspect she saw at the high school and provided a complete description of the subject. Jennifer described the subject as having natural strawberry blond hair, it was buzz cut, stating that his face was well defined, high cheekbones, chiseled. The party had a wide forehead and muscular neck. He was about 5'11" to 6'0", oval face, small upper lip, narrow nose and small eyebrows. I took the two items as evidence and later placed them into the Jefferson County Sheriff's Office Evidence Vault for safekeeping. I asked Jennifer if she could provide the identification of that second armed gunman. She told me that she did not recognize the individual and that she did not believe the party was Eric Harris. I explained to Jennifer that throughout this investigator [sic], that we relied not only on Forensic evidence that was recovered at the scene, but with the assistance of witness identification that the two gunmen that were in Columbine High School have been identified as Eric Harris and Dylan Klebold. I also told Jennifer that a videotape did exist which showed two armed gunmen in the cafeteria at the school and I asked her if I could show her still photos of that videotape and have her determine if these were the two individuals that she saw at the high school on the incident date. Jennifer and her mom were shown still photos, #44, #47, #52 and #53[.] The still photos clearly depict Dylan Klebold and Eric Harris as being the two armed gunmen in the school. One of the photos has the time of 11:46 a.m. This is one minute after Jennifer claims she saw them in the upper level of the school. Eric Harris is shown in the photo wearing a white colored t-shirt. He has a short haircut, dark pants, and is carrying a sawed off shotgun. Jennifer looked at the photos and again I asked her are these the two individuals she saw at the high school. Jennifer posi-

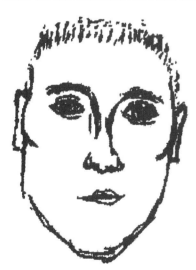

Sketch by witness Jennifer Smull of the unknown gunman outside the science room.

tively identified Dylan Klebold, but stated the other suspect she saw was not Eric Harris. She told me that the party she saw was about 25 to 30 years old, had a thick muscular neck and muscular build and that Eric Harris was too scrawny to be the party she observed. I again reiterated with Jennifer that the still photos are of Eric Harris and is the same description she is giving us. Jennifer again told me that she could not positively identify the second gunman as being Eric Harris and believed that the second gunman she saw was somebody other than Eric Harris."[23]

Erin Walton, student (written statement made at 3:40 PM on April 20, 1999): "We saw two guys standing in the doorway, backs to us — heard them fire 2 - 3 shots — don't know where (poss towards the science teacher's room) then they left. One of the guys was tall, long blk. hair wearing all black. The other one had short bln hair (like he was going bald). He looked like he was in his late 30's."[24]

Jonathan Vandemark, student (interviewed May 4, 1999, by Greg McComas, Colorado State Patrol): Through the window in a door, Vandemark saw two suspects in the hallway taping a foot-long explosive device to the wall. "He described the first one as being tall and skinny with long dark hair, wearing a black shirt, black pants and a black hat, which was on backwards. He also saw that the individual had a small black 'two handled' gun strapped around his neck. He stated he did not personally know the individual but had seen him around school before. He stated he had seen the photographs shown by the media and could positively identify the individual as Dylan Klebold.

"He described 'the other kid' as being about one foot shorter than Dylan, with dark hair that was spiked on top with blonde tips. That individual was wearing a white T-shirt and had on what appeared to be a dark green backpack. He was unable to see what type of pants were worn but stated he also had a gun strapped around his neck, that appeared to be similar as the one carried by Dylan."[25]

David Eagle, student (interviewed April 27, 1999, by P.J. Doyle): "David was sitting behind the turned over desks. He could see out the window in the door. Through it he saw 'the killers.' He said that one was holding a sawed off shotgun. The killer was holding it with the barrel pointing up. There was smoke in the hall. David described this person holding the gun as someone with black shaved hair with blonde streaks. The hair was longer on the top than it was on the bottom. He couldn't see any facial features because of the smoke and the shadows. He has since seen pictures of Eric Harris and Dylan Klebold on television. He did not know these students from school. David said that the person he saw did not look like the people he'd seen on television. David said that he saw the person with the gun from the chest up. He could see a black shirt; the sleeves stopping on the arms, like a tee shirt would fit.

"David said that there was another person standing next to the killer, but he couldn't see that person at all."[26]

_THE CAMOUFLAGE-PANTS SUSPECT

As with the demolition man in the white T-shirt and jeans, we also have reports of a gunman decked out in clothing which neither

Harris or Klebold was wearing—camouflage pants.

Adam Foss, student (interviewed May 14, 1999, by Burkhalter): While running from class, Foss saw teacher David Sanders get shot. He caught a glimpse of the gunman's lower body: "Adam stated he could only see camouflage pants and high black boots."[27]

Jennifer Smull, student (interviewed April 28, 1999, by Investigator Jill Reuteler, Colorado State Patrol): "Ms Smull said that between 11 10am and 11 15am she saw a person, who she thought was [redacted], someone who hung out with Dylan, near the main doors and it appeared that he had just come in[.] (She later identified this person as [redacted]. She said that he was wearing a black trench coat, black shirt, black and white camouflage pants (he normally tucks his pants into his boots, but she didn't remember if they were tucked in or not), and he was carrying a black colored duffel bag with one or two yellow stripes, or maybe just some yellow color on it, and the bag appeared to be heavy by the way it was being carried upon his shoulder. Ms Smull said that [redacted] is about 2 to 3 inches shorter than Dylan[.]..."[28]

It seems likely this student was carrying a duffel bag filled with explosives and weapons. After all, it is beyond belief that Harris and Klebold could've transported and planted 95 explosive devices at the school by themselves (which is exactly what authorities now claim they somehow managed). As Colorado Governor Bill Owens said after touring the school on April 23: "There are backpacks with bombs in there everywhere. The officers in there are convinced there had to be more people involved. There's just too much stuff in there."[29]

Patrick Robert Vassar, freshman (interviewed April 30, 1999, by FBI Agent Ricky V. Wright): "At approximately 11:15 am, immediately after Vassar sat down with his lunch, he saw four or five individuals in black walking away from the school. Everyone in the group was wearing trench coats, except one, who was wearing camouflage pants."[30]

_THE ROOFTOP SHOOTER

According to the official story, no gunman was ever on the roof. However, early media reports and police radio communications mention a sniper on the roof. Many eyewitnesses mention this rooftop suspect in their statements.

Candice Cushman, student (written statement made May 6, 1999): "When we got outside I saw someone on the roof with what I thought was a black trenchcoat. He was aiming a gun so Erica, Nick & I ran toward the smoker's pit."[31]

Nathan Vanderau, student (written statement made April 21, 1999): "I sprinted to Clement's [Park] where a cop told me to keep going because there was a gunman on the roof."[32]

Penny Zerr, teacher (interviewed July 15, 1999, by Ester): "She indicated that police had approached her and continued to tell her and other individuals to keep moving away from the building as there may be a person with a gun on the school roof."[33]

Jessica Lucero, sophomore (interviewed May 4, 1999, by Erzen): "She stated that as she was running out the east doors of the high school that she believes she saw an individual dressed in black holding a gun up on the roof of the school. I asked if she could provide a description of the individual. She stated she couldn't. I asked if she could provide a description of the gun this person was carrying. She said it wasn't a pistol, it appeared to be some long gun."[34]

Michelle Fox, student (interviewed May 14, 1999, by Brooks): Fox ran out of the school and was headed away from the gymnasium when "she looked back towards the gymnasium and noticed an individual 'wearing white' standing on the roof of the gymnasium, along its north side, approximately fifteen yards from its west side.... Michelle said that this person on the roof was holding something that was 'long,' and appeared to be pointing it northward. At the same time she heard about four 'pops,' which she assumed were gunshots coming from this individual on the roof, but acknowledged could have been coming from the west side of the school."[35]

Lindsay Conwell, junior (interviewed May 4, 1999, by P.J. Doyle): "She ran out the doors. So many people were trying to get out the doors. She hit a set of steps and tripped. When she looked back, there was someone on the roof. It was just a glance. She couldn't tell what the person was wearing or holding, or what the person looked like. She kept running after that."[36]

Stephen "Austin" Eubanks, student (interviewed at 12:40 PM on April 20, 1999, by Agent Greenwell): "Once outside, Austin said they were met by officers and told to get behind a police car as there was someone on the roof. Austin said he heard someone say there were three of them and he thought he heard the name [redacted]."[37]

Nicole Nowlen, student (interviewed May 6, 1999, by Arvada Police Detective Boatright): After running out of the school, Nowlen hit the ground beside other students behind a "patrol vehicle." "Nicole Nowlen stated during that time frame, she believed she observed someone on the roof of the school, but she could not provide a description of that individual. Nicole Nowlen stated her observation was later confirmed when she heard others near where she was located, making similar comments."[38]

> "I SPRINTED TO CLEMENT'S [PARK] WHERE A COP TOLD ME TO KEEP GOING BECAUSE THERE WAS A GUNMAN ON THE ROOF."

George Sneddon, substitute teacher (interviewed August 9, 1999, by Ester): "He indicated that he began moving northward towards the tennis courts when he heard someone say, 'They're still shooting.' He did not know who had said this, and he indicated that he was also told shortly after this time by other teachers to escort the kids into the Clement Park area as to their possibly being a person with a gun up on the roof."[39]

Andrew T. Lowry, coach (interviewed May 27, 1999, by Glenn More, Golden Police Department): Lowry ran out of the school by the faculty parking lot next to the gym. "At this point Deputy Gardner and 'Andy' the Campus Supervisor yelled at him to 'get down,' and 'get out of there!' LOWRY said Gardner and 'Andy' was behind a car in the senior's parking lot, and out of his peripheral vision saw someone ducking down on the roof, above the library area wearing what he recalled as a red shirt. 'Andy' then yelled that there was gunfire, and thinking that the person he had seen ducking down on the roof was a shooter he ran the opposite direction, westward."[40]

_GUNMEN TALK TO ANOTHER ACCOMPLICE, JOE

Dorrain Salazar, student (written statement made 4:10 PM on April 20, 1999): Salazar was hiding in a storage room. "We heard the people shooting and talking[;] one said the school is on fire[;] another said[,] Hey [redacted] where are you? And another said 'I want to die today!'"[41] (Because of sloppy redacting, the statement below reveals the name that Salazar heard.)

Denver Police Officer *Robert A. Craft*, in a report dated April 20, 1999, at 5:00 PM, wrote: "At 1610 hours, Dorrain Salazar was interviewed, written statement was obtained. Salazar could not describe suspects. He did hear one suspect call the other one 'Joe'."[42]

Courtney Herivel, sophomore (interviewed by phone May 7, 1999, by FBI Special Agent John Elvig): "At one point, she heard who she thought was a gunman say, "[redacted] I have three of them in here.' She's very positive she heard the word [redacted] and not the word 'yo'."[43] Obviously, she also had heard the name "Joe."

Katelyn Sue Place, freshman (interviewed May 14, 1999, by P.J. Doyle, "a commissioned peace officer"): "Kate said that her cousin, Courtney Herivel [phone number], heard someone say, '[Redacted] stop—put it down.' Courtney was up in Miss Williams' science room."[44]

Elisha Encinias, student (interviewed at 2:00 PM on April 20, 1999, during the SWAT evacuation of the school, by Agent Jerry Means, Colorado Bureau of Investigation): "Ms. ENCINIAS stated as the gunmen were walking around the cafeteria and the stairway she heard one of them say, '[Redacted], Where Are You? I got three of them'. She stated they were very calm."[45]

■ "HE DID HEAR ONE SUSPECT CALL THE OTHER ONE 'JOE'."

_OTHER SHOOTERS

Witnesses identified more gunmen who apparently don't correspond to the above suspects. (Although it is certainly possible that any of them could've moved to a different area of the school building or grounds, and thus have been sighted twice.) Keep in mind that whenever a name is redacted, the witness is identifying someone other than Harris or Klebold.

Ashley Egeland, freshman (interviewed April 27, 1999, by Agent Timothy Steffes): Egeland was in gym for P.E. when the class heard shooting from the library. From the gym hallway, Egeland went into the North hallway, where she saw a girl she knew as Lacey. At that time, two gunmen walked around the corner of the North hallway and started shooting at Egeland and Lacey, who ran back into the gym. "ASHLEY IDENTIFIED THE SHOOTERS AS ERIC HARRIS AND [redacted]. ACCORDING TO ASHLEY, [redacted] WAS DRESSED IN A WHITE SHIRT WITH A BLACK TRENCH COAT OVER IT. SHE SAID THAT [student's name (not the Acne Shooter)] WAS ARMED WITH A HANDGUN WHILE HARRIS WAS ARMED WITH A SHOTGUN. ASHLEY SAID THAT SHE WAS NOT SURE ABOUT [redacted] IDENTITY UNTIL HER SISTER HEATHER SHOWED HER A COLUMBINE YEARBOOK AND SHE SAW HIS PICTURE IN THE BOOK. ASHLEY IS SURE THE TWO SHOOTERS SHE OBSERVED WERE ERIC HARRIS AND [redacted]."[46]

Ashley Egeland (reinterviewed May 6, 1999, by Investigator Dan Pfannenstiel, West Metro Fire Department): "Ashley stated that when she got home that day she told her sister, Heather (a Senior at CHS) and her father about [redacted]. She stated that her sister challenged her about [redacted] actually being Dylan. Ashley stated that she said 'no, Dylan has a broader nose and doesn't wear glasses like [redacted] does'. Ashley stated that Heather got the yearbook out (1998) and they looked up [redacted] to which she said 'that's him'. Ms. Egeland confirmed this conversation.

"Ashley stated that she is 'sure it was [redacted]'. She stated that it 'definitely was not Dylan Klebold'."[47]

Chris Wisher, student (written statement made 1:30 PM on April 20, 1999): "There was also another guy we saw in Weaver Park in the bushes ducking w/ a gun in his hand. We don't know if it was the same gunman from the school or a different one."[48] According to the official report, Harris and Klebold were never in Weaver Park, located near the high school.

Jake Apodaca, student (interviewed April 20, 1999, by Detective Brian Lynch): "...he saw a gunman ducked down with a shotgun in Weaver Park;"[49]

Dustin Gorton, student (written statement made at 3:15 PM on April 20, 1999): "[Redacted] was one of the shooters. I used to hang out with these guys. The group was made up of Nathan Dykman, Eric Harris, Dylan Klebold, and Christopher something. These guys had the capability to do this. Two of them had shotguns and nine millimeters."[50]

Jason Brehm, student (interviewed May 3, 1999, by Detective Terry Demmel): "Jason reported that on Tues. the 20th he had 5th period off and had retrieved his soccer ball out of his locker and was walking out of the west upper level entrance when he observed a party wearing a trench coat and black hat turned around backwards who was leaning against a green post that was anchoring a tree. John [sic] marked the exact location on the map. John [sic] stated that the person was a little shorter than himself, John [sic] is 5'11" or 6', and that he was wearing a black pair of boots that had black canvas between the sole and upper part and he noticed that one of the boots had the pant leg tucked into the boot which he thought was strange. Det. Demmel showed Jason photographs of Eric Harris and Dylan Klebold at that time with Jason reporting that the party he observed wearing a trench coat had a very round face and was neither Harris or Klebold. Jason said that the party appeared calm and relaxed and just appeared to be waiting for someone. Jason added that the party had a black nylon bag with straps at his feet. Jason described the bag as being approximately 1-1/2 to 2 feet long and appeared full."

"The party wearing the trench coat began shooting randomly as he walked down the stairs, got to the bottom, then turned around and walked back up the stairs. He then started shooting at a student that Jason knew as Denny Rowe. Jason reiterated that the guy in the trench coat was all alone and that he did not see anybody else with him. The gunman then started shooting into the windows of the Library. The individual then lobed [sic] several devices up onto the roof that caused explosions. He then ran back down the stairs to the bottom and fired off what Jason thinks was a shotgun that was louder than anything else that had been going off. Jason stated that he thinks that was when Lance Kirkland was shot in the face."[51]

Elisha Encinias, student (interviewed at 2:00 PM on April 20, 1999, during the SWAT evacuation of the school, by Agent Jerry Means, Colorado Bureau of Investigation): "Ms. Encinias stated she was in the cafeteria, eating her lunch at approximately 11:20 a.m., when the shooting started. She stated a student came into the cafeteria yelling 'Someone Just Shot Someone'. She stated everyone started screaming and she saw three people with guns coming into the cafeteria. Ms. ENCINIAS stated one of the gunmen had a long black coat, and she did not recognize him. She stated the other two students were a current student, and a student that had graduated last year. She did not know their names. She ran upstairs towards the science lab area."[52]

Devon Adams, student (interviewed May 12, 1999, by Jefferson County D.A. Office investigator G.B. Mumma and Sgt. J. Webb): "I asked Devon if she had ever been part of the TCM [Trench Coat Mafia] and she stated that she had not been a member, but she had been affiliated with them all." When asked to name members of the Trench Coat Mafia, she listed fifteen people, including Harris and Klebold.

"I asked Devon who else was involved directly in the Columbine Incident, and she, without hesitation stated, [redacted], [redacted] and [redacted]. I asked why she thought that, and Devon got quiet, and again looked down to the floor, then stated that she just knew....

"I concluded my interview with Devon at 1700 hours; However, I believe Devon needs to be reinterviewed for additional information about the bomb making and why she believes that the other three are directly involved."[53]

> "SHE STATED EVERYONE STARTED SCREAMING AND SHE SAW THREE PEOPLE WITH GUNS COMING INTO THE CAFETERIA."

When Devon was reinterviewed on May 26 (thirteen days later), she claimed that she didn't know the three were directly involved but named them because she knew they were violent and capable of taking part.[54]

Anthony Lacovetta, Denver police officer (written statement, May 4, 1999): "While clearing the initial rooms of the High School, I remembered a short conversation with a hostage which was found to be hiding in the school main office. She stated to me that she was the assistant principal of the school. I immediately began to debrief her in regard to the suspects. The brief time I talked to her she was in a state of shock and very friegthened [sic]. I asked her if she knew any of the suspects. She said yes, 'One was Ned, I don't know his last name.'"[55]

_SHOTS AND VOICES AFTER 1:00 PM

Harris and Klebold are officially said to have killed themselves around 12:08 PM.

Patricia Nielson, teacher (interviewed May 5, 1999, by Brice Moomaw): After being shot at by Eric Harris, Nielson ran into the library and dialed 911. She hid under a desk while the gunmen were in the library, and she crawled into the library's work room and hid inside a cupboard. "After she was in the cupboard for a long time, she heard someone in the room. As they walked by, she saw a purple dress. She opened the door and saw two people who she identified as Lois and Carol. She asked them if they knew if the suspects had been caught. They did not know. At around 1300 hrs. [i.e., 1:00 PM], Lois and Carol leave the room. Nielsen stayed in the room in the cupboard.

"Within minutes of Lois and Carol leaving, there was some more gunfire. The gunfire was very close. She described it as being a small short burst. Nielson believed the shooters had found Lois and Carol and shot them. Later after it was all over, Lois and Carol told Nielson they thought just the opposite. They believed the shooters found Nielson and shot her."[56]

Lois Kean, library assistant (interviewed May 27, 1999, by Obema): Kean and Carol Weld were hiding in the sound booth of the Rebel News Network Room, off of the library. After approximately a couple of hours, they went into the kitchen to retrieve their purses, then returned to the sound booth. "Kean estimates it was sometime between 1300 and 1330 hours [i.e., 1:00 PM and 1:30 PM] when she and Weld went back into the RNN sound booth. She stated that five minutes after getting back into the booth they heard more shooting. She stated it was a round of shots, definitely more than two, and had an automatic sound to it."[57]

Carol Weld, during her interview on June 1, 1999, recalled hearing the shots, too. She didn't note the time but said that "a good hour" later she looked at her watch. It was then 3:00 PM.[58]

Dorrain Salazar, student (written statement made at 4:10 PM on April 20, 1999): "At 11:25 we heard people screaming and running up the stairs and a few people came in the class room. We then ran to a back storage room and hid in their [sic]. For about 2 hours we heard gun shots and explosions."[59]

Lisa Kreutz, the only survivor who remained in the library until help arrived, said she heard the gunmen talking sometime after the 2:30 bell had sounded.[60]

_MORE INFORMATION THAT RAISES QUESTIONS

Crystal Archuleta, junior (interviewed April 27, 1999, by Detective Terry Demmel): In the midst of the shooting, Archuleta was in the parking lot. "Crystal remembers seeing an older full size dark brown pick-up truck circling the parking lot very slowly. The truck was described as having a very loud engine; slowly drove out of the lot approximately 2 minutes before a Jefferson County Sheriff wearing a yellow T-shirt and driving a gray car pulled into the parking lot."[61]

John Timothy Matteson, sophomore (interviewed May 10, 1999, by P.J. Doyle): "Tim said that he saw [redacted] in the back of a police car the day of the shooting, but had not seen him around the school. Tim said he had gone to school with [redacted] since Kindergarten. He knew [redacted] by sight."[62]

Lacey Smith, student (interviewed by phone May 9, 1999, by Officer [unclear, possibly "McHamen"]): "Smith said she has heard other students talking about up to 6 suspects at the school on 4-20-99, but

could not give any other details."[64]

Samantha Myers, school aid (interviewed by phone May 14, 1999, by Zimmerman): "Myers had provided information stating that she is an aid at the school and heard 'kids' talking about two separate groups of shooters, one speaking German and one speaking English."[65]

> "MYERS HAD PROVIDED INFORMATION STATING THAT SHE IS AN AID AT THE SCHOOL AND HEARD 'KIDS' TALKING ABOUT TWO SEPARATE GROUPS OF SHOOTERS, ONE SPEAKING GERMAN AND ONE SPEAKING ENGLISH."

Laura Farber, freshman (written answers to "Team Four Minimal Questions"): "Many people said they saw 3 people (not just 2)"[66]

Jana Stoloch, part-time teacher (English as a second language) (interviewed May 3, 1999, by J. Burkhalter): Between fourth and fifth period, Stoloch wrote a sentence on the chalkboard for the students to correct, then left the room. "When Mrs. Stoloch returned to the classroom the class bell had rung and she entered her small classroom. A student had written a sentence on the chalkboard along with hers. The sentence read, 'We should blow up the school.'" Minutes later, the gunfire and explosions started. Harris and Klebold were not in this class.[67]

_JUST THE BEGINNING

As powerful as these statements are, they represent only a fraction of the strangeness surrounding the Columbine massacre. Not even including the other important statements buried in the thousands of released documents, there is so much more to uncover. Why do the authorities continue to refuse to release full autopsies for Klebold and the majority of the victims? Why have they not released all of the ballistics information? A police officer who exchanged gunfire with Harris claims he never fired toward the library, yet three of his bullets were found inside the library. Some bullets recovered from the scene cannot be matched to the guns of Harris, Klebold, or law enforcement. The only mask officially acknowledged is a dark green ski mask perhaps worn briefly by Harris, yet numerous students report seeing more than one person in a mask, while others saw a gunman in a different kind of mask. Before the shooting, Dylan and Harris had several scrapes with the law; the family of student Brooks Brown even filed a complaint against Harris for threats, yet the cops never followed up in a meaningful way. Some Columbine students have died unsolved, violent deaths since the shooting, while many others report receiving death threats, usually by telephone. There are enough mysteries and secrets here to fill an entire book, which will hopefully happen someday, but until then the best place to look for answers is the Website of the Columbine Research Task Force <columbine.n3.net>.

Let's close this preliminary investigation with some quotes (taken from news stories) from those directly involved in trying to get at the truth:

Patty DePooter, mother of slain student Corey DePooter: "I gave up on getting a straight story from them. It changed every time we talked to them."[68]

Brian Rohrbough, father of slain student Danny Rohrbough: "It looks like going to court is the only way we're going to find out what happened."[69]

| "THEY'RE STILL LYING TO US ABOUT WHAT HAPPENED AND WITHHOLDING INFORMATION."

Randy Brown, father of Columbine student Brooks Brown: "They're still lying to us about what happened and withholding information."[70] "If people think this is the end, they are wrong. The sheriff's department is hiding a great deal of information."[71]

William Erickson, retired Chief Justice of the Colorado Supreme Court and chair of the Governor's Columbine Review Commission: "I've never seen such a great effort to withhold evidence that has material relevance to the work of the commission."[72]

Endnotes

Note: All page references are to the 11,000 pages of information released by Jefferson County, Colorado, on November 21, 2000. These documents are available online in Acrobat format at <www.boulderdailycamera.com/shooting/report.html>.

1. O'Driscoll, Patrick. "Students: Gunmen Belonged to Dark Group." *USA Today* 21 April 1999. **2.** p 1,262. **3.** p 654. **4.** p 653. **5.** Full names and affiliations of every interviewer aren't always given in the documents. **6.** p 660. **7.** pp 666-7. **8.** p 1,044. **9.** p 940. **10.** p 750. **11.** pp 3,131-4. **12.** p 829. **13.** p 3,433. **14.** p 4,677. **15.** pp 1,016-22. **16.** p 2,364. **17.** pp 2,365-6. **18.** pp 4,465-7. **19.** pp 813-4. **20.** pp 4,082-4. **21.** pp 2,183-4. **22.** pp 2,185. **23.** pp 2,189-90. **24.** p 2,242. **25.** p 2,222. **26.** p 1,881. **27.** p 4,931. **28.** p 2,185. **29.** Vogt, Katherine. "Security Videotapes at School May Show Whether Gunmen Had Help." Associated Press, 23 April 2001. **30.** p 4,691. **31.** p 2,794. **32.** p 4,682. **33.** p 5,212. **34.** p 1,508. **35.** pp 5,196-7. **36.** p 2,763. **37.** p 19. **38.** p 111. **39.** p 5,204. **40.** p 5,296. **41.** p 2,156. **42.** p 3,761. **43.** pp 1,927-8. **44.** pp 4,082-4. **45.** p 2,939. **46.** pp 5,248-9. **47.** p 5,253. **48.** p 1,262. **49.** p 653. **50.** p 3,161. **51.** pp 719-20. **52.** p 2,939. **53.** pp 10,615-7. **54.** p 10,618. **55.** p 5,792. **56.** p 76. **57.** p 453. **58.** p 603. **59.** p 2,156. **60.** p 64. **61.** p 2,364. **62.** p 3,694. **63.** p 4,190. **64.** pp 4,465-7. **65.** p 3,854. **66.** p 2,980. **67.** p 5,161. **68.** Prendergast, Alan. "The Bullet in the Backpack and Other Columbine Mysteries." *Westword* (Denver, Colorado) 25 Oct 2001. **69.** *Ibid.* **70.** *Ibid.* **71.** Nicholson, Kieran. "Parents' Claims Unearth Columbine Documents." *Denver Post* 23 May 2001. **72.** Pankratz, Howard. "Jeffco Won't Turn Over Harris-Klebold Tapes." *Denver Post* 3 Oct 2000.

CHARLIE MANSON'S IMAGE
PAUL KRASSNER

Proud to be a hippie and wearing my new, yellow, leather fringe jacket for the first time, I was on my way to the original Woodstock Festival along with half a million others on a musical pilgrimage. At the same time, newspapers were headlining the murder in Beverly Hills of Sharon Tate, the actress wife of director Roman Polanski, their unborn baby, and a few friends.

The killers turned out to be members of the Charles Manson family, the ultimate perversion of a hippie commune. Manson was portrayed by the media as a hippie cult leader, and the counterculture became a dangerous enemy. Hitchhikers were shunned. Communes were raided. In the public's mind, flower children had grown poisonous thorns.

But Manson was raised behind bars. His *real* family included con artists, pimps, drug dealers, thieves, muggers, rapists, and murderers. He had known only power relationships in an army of control junkies. Charlie was America's own Frankenstein monster, a logical product of the prison system—racist, paranoid, and violent—even if hippie astrologers thought his fate had been predetermined because he was a triple Scorpio.

In August 1969, he sent his brainwashed family off to slay whomever was at the Tate home: the pregnant Sharon; hairstylist and drug dealer to the stars Jay Sebring; would-be screenwriter Voytek Frykowski; and his girlfriend, coffee heiress Abigail Folger. The next night, Manson accompanied the killers to the home of supermarket mogul Leno LaBianca and his wife.

> **THE MURDERS WERE INTENDED TO IMPLY THAT THE VICTIMS HAD BEEN SELECTED AT RANDOM, BUT I HAD ALWAYS FELT THAT MANSON AND HIS KILLERS HAD SOME CONNECTION WITH THEM BEFORE THE MURDERS TOOK PLACE.**

And what a well-programmed family they were. A prison psychiatrist at San Quentin told me of an incident he had observed during Manson's trial. An inmate had said to Manson, "Look, I don't wanna know about your theories on race; I don't wanna hear anything about religion; I just wanna know one thing. How'd you get them girls to obey you like that?"

"I got a knack," Charlie replied.

His "knack" was combining LSD and mescaline with sing-alongs and games accompanying his perversion of techniques he'd learned in prison—encounter sessions, Scientology auditing, post-hypnotic suggestion, geographical isolation, subliminal motivation, transactional analysis, verbal probing, and the sexual longevity that he had practiced upon himself for all those years in the privacy of his cell.

Hal Lipset, San Francisco's renowned private investigator, informed me that not only did the Los Angeles Police Department seize pornographic films and videotapes they found in Roman Polanski's loft, but also that certain LAPD officers were *selling* them. Lipset had talked with one police source who told him exactly which porno flicks were available, a total of seven hours' worth for a quarter-million dollars.

Lipset recited a litany of those private porn flicks. There was Greg Bautzer, an attorney for Howard Hughes, with Jane Wyman, the ex-wife of Ronald Reagan, who was governor of California at the time of the murders. There was Cass Elliot in an orgy with Yul Brynner, Peter Sellers, and Warren Beatty, the same trio who, with John Phillips, had offered a $25,000 reward for the capture of the killers. There was Sharon Tate with Dean Martin. There was Sharon with Steve McQueen. And there she was with two bisexual black men.

"The cops weren't too happy about *that* one," Lipset recalled.

The murders were intended to imply that the victims had been selected at random, but I had always felt that Manson and his killers had some connection with them before the murders took place. I finally tracked down a reporter who told me that when she was hanging around with Los Angeles police, they showed her a porn video of Susan Atkins, one of Charlie's devils, with Voytek Frykowski, one of the victims, even though, according to legend, the executioners and the victims had never met until the night of the massacre.

But apparently the reporter mentioned the wrong victim, because when I wrote to Manson and asked directly, "Did Susan sleep with Frykowski?" he answered, "You are ill advised and misled. Sebring done Susan's hair and I think he sucked one or two of her dicks. I'm not sure who she was walking out from her stars and cages, that girl <u>loves</u> dick, you know what I mean, hon. Yul Brynner, Peter Sellers."

I continued to correspond with Charlie. He has become a cultural icon, the personification of evil. There are songs about him. In surfer jargon, Manson means a crazy, reckless surfer. For comedians, Manson is a generic joke reference. In 1992, I asked him how he felt about that.

He replied, "I don't know what a generic joke is. I think I know what that means. That means you talk bad about Reagan or Bush. I've always ran poker games and whores and crime. I'm a crook. You make the reality in court and press. I just ride and play the cards that were pushed on me to play. Mass killer. It's a job, what can I say."

> **"A FEW WEEKS PRIOR TO THE ARRESTS AT THE SPAHN RANCH RAID," HE SAID, "WE WERE TOLD THAT WE WERE NOT TO ARREST MANSON OR ANY OF HIS FOLLOWERS."**

I interviewed Preston Guillory, a former deputy sheriff in Los Angeles. "A few weeks prior to the arrests at the Spahn Ranch raid," he said, "we were told that we were not to arrest Manson or any of his followers. The reason he was left on the street was because our department thought that he was going to launch an attack on the Black Panthers."

And so it was that racism in the Sheriff's Department inadvertently turned them into collaborators in a mass murder. Yet Charles Manson is the only face you'll see glaring at you from some rebellious teenager's T-shirt. Because the killers left clues to imply that the victims had been slain by black militants, the media continue to infer that Manson's only motive was to start a race war.

However, on the evening of Friday, August 9, 1969, just a few hours before the slaughter took place, Joel Rostau, the boyfriend of Jay Sebring's receptionist and an intermediary in a cocaine ring, visited Sebring and Frykowski at the Tate house, to deliver mescaline and cocaine. During the Manson trial, several associates of Sebring were murdered, including Rostau, whose body was found in the trunk of a car in New York.

The media continue to perpetuate the myth that Manson's only motivation was to start a race war. Actually, his brainwashed so-called family unknowingly served as a hit squad for organized crime figures that he had met in prison. Three decades later, Manson continues to be a symbol for the end of the 1960s. One thing is certain, though. Charlie was never a hippie. Recently, *Variety*, the bible of Show Biz, reported that prosecutor Vincent Bugliosi's 1975 book about the Manson family, *Helter Skelter*, has been bought by, appropriately enough, Propaganda Films.

EVERYTHING YOU KNOW IS WRONG

FREE LAURIANE
FATHER CLAIMS DAUGHTER MOLESTED, HELD POLITICAL PRISONER IN FRANCE
JAMES RIDGEWAY WITH SANDRA BISIN

Supporters of a French girl believed by some to have been snared in a French sex ring marched across New York City during a UN summit on the rights of children in September 2001. The girl's father, Karim Christian Kamal, led the demonstration, designed to get the attention of UN Secretary-General Kofi Annan.

In June of that year, Kamal, a French pearl dealer, received a highly unusual granting of political asylum from a Los Angeles judge who slammed French officials for persecuting the man and his family. Kamal claimed prominent French judges and police brass trapped his daughter in a child-sex scheme and are now out to get him for exposing their pedophile racket.

It was a claim Judge Ronald N. Ohata found credible. "The French government's persecution has strong elements of personal revenge and vendetta, Mr. Kamal having complained about the corruption of the government and having been sued and persecuted following this complaint," Ohata stated. "It is pure abuse of power from individuals who are in control, and who are connected, against people who they feel are not."

The US very rarely grants political asylum to someone from a friendly nation. (It's hard enough for people who have a well-grounded fear of repressive regimes in their home countries.) In fact, Kamil is the first French citizen ever granted asylum in the US, according to Immigration officials. France has a lengthy tradition of respect for human rights, but that hasn't been enough to stave off a public furor. The French press has gone bananas over the case, with headlines screaming: "Save Lauriane."

The case itself is byzantine. During a rancorous divorce proceeding in 1993, Kamal charged that his wife, Guyot, had caused Lauriane, then five, to be abused by prominent pedophiles, including judges and other local political bigwigs, in the city of Nice. The judge assigned to the case in Nice threw it out. Kamal said that was no coincidence, since he claimed the judge himself was a member of the ring.

Later, child psychologists in the US examined Lauriane and reported that indeed she had been sexually abused.[1]

Claiming the French judges were out to get him, in 1994 Kamal took the little girl and fled to California where his sister, Dalila Kamal-Griffin, an L.A. attorney, launched court actions to protect both her brother and the girl by seeking political asylum for them in the US.

Two months later, the plot took a twist. French officials, accompanied by two Santa Monica detectives, appeared unannounced and without warrants at Kamal's home, seized the child, and headed for the airport to take her back to France. At this point, the FBI stepped in and ordered the kid off the plane. But the French didn't give up so easily, shunting Lauriane from the US to Mexico and back to France, where she lives with her mom in Nice. The French government says Kamal—who was convicted in absentia for abduction and malicious prosecution—is lying and that the daughter should have been sent home to begin with. US Immigration officials agree. Guyot, the former wife, accuses Kamal of failing to pay child support and denies the pedophile charges.

For Kamal's supporters, the removal of Lauriane to France was clearly wrong. "Can you imagine for a second, what the US and world reaction would have been if Elián González has been kidnapped by the Castro regime with the help of the Miami police instead of going through the courts?" asks his sister. She has founded a Website <www.lauriane.com> for the cause of missing and exploited children.

Race may also be a factor. Judge Ohata also agreed with Kamal's suspicion that he was a victim of discrimination because he is of Moroccan descent. "In this case you have a family that is being persecuted," Ohata declared, "and it is an Arab family. And it is a family that has become whistleblowers."

Endnote

1. According to Kamal-Griffin's Website: "Doctor [Nicole] Gilbert conducted clinical tests to determine whether Lauriane presented signs of physical and sexual abuse. Doctor Gilbert concluded that Lauriane presented all such clinical symptoms. Two other leadings experts in child abuse in Los Angeles reached the same conclusion. Doctor Gilbert's findings corroborated the findings of all the French experts who examined Lauriane while she was in France. Three French court-accredited Medical Doctors who examined Lauriane from late November 1993 to April 2, 1994 reported that she had been battered, as evidenced by, at times, up to 12 bruises on her body and face. These Medical Doctors are Eric El Baze, Eric Suquet and Gerald Quatrehomme. In 1993 and 1994, two French court-appointed psychologists recommended to the French courts that custody of Lauriane be transferred to Mr. Kamal (Doctors Catherine Caumont-Bonnet and Malek Santini). Expert Psychologist Malek Santini noted in her report to the French court that Lauriane expressed an unbearable distress in the presence of her mother while she was at peace and happy in the presence of her father. The French courts disregarded the opinions of their own appointed experts."

WHEN COPS BECOME THE GANGSTERS

JOSEPH D. McNAMARA

It may not be much comfort to Los Angeles, Detroit, and other cities involved in major police corruption scandals, but the pattern of small gangs of cops committing predatory crimes has occurred in almost every large city in the nation and in a great many less-populated areas, as well.

THROUGHOUT THE COUNTRY, SMALL GROUPS OF COPS *ARE* THE GANGSTERS.

Six years after retiring from 35 years in policing (which included tenures as Police Chief of San Jose, California, and of Kansas City, Missouri), I began research for a book on police administration. Studying the nation's police forces, I was stunned to discover that the old-type corruption uncovered when cops occasionally were caught taking payoffs from gangsters had been replaced by something considerably more ominous. Throughout the country, small groups of cops *are* the gangsters.

The lure of fortunes to be made in illegal drugs has led to thousands of police felonies: armed robbery, kidnapping, stealing drugs, selling drugs, perjury, framing people, and even some murders. These police crimes were committed on duty, often while the cop-gangsters were wearing their uniforms, the symbol of safety to the people they were supposed to be protecting.

Of course, only a small percentage of American police officers are recidivist felons. Sadly, however, these predatory criminals are protected by a code of silence. Otherwise honest officers who knew or suspected what was going on did not report the crooks, and at times even lied rather than testify against other cops.

A code of silence is not unique to police. It exists in the White House, among students, doctors, lawyers, business executives, and other groups. Indeed, even as children, our parents and peers admonish us not to tattle. Basic human characteristics of loyalty, trust, and security are involved. These motivations are even more intense in police work. If cops make an error of judgment, they or someone else may be killed, or they can be sent to jail for using too much force. And even the most ethical officers fear being falsely accused of brutality or other crimes and of being railroaded to prison because their chiefs or mayors will not support them in politically volatile cases.

Furthermore, the code of silence is strengthened because many cops chafe under the pressure from superiors to make petty arrests for drugs. State and local police made approximately 1.4 million drug-possession arrests in 2000. Very few took place with search warrants, although the Fourth Amendment, with few exceptions, requires the police to obtain a judicial warrant to search people or their homes. It is so common for police to lie about how they obtained drug evidence that the term "testilying" has replaced "testifying" in police jargon. Ambitious politicians and police brass calling for more arrests condemn the code of silence while ignoring widespread police perjury in drug cases. It is not surprising that many cops feel that the only one they can really trust is another cop.

Nevertheless, it is perverse when those sworn to enforce the law instead shelter predatory criminals who happen to carry a badge. Minorities tend to be the victims of the most grievous police crimes. The infamous Los Angeles police shooting scandal, like the thousands of cop crimes elsewhere, does immeasurable damage to the credibility of the criminal justice system. Mayors and police chiefs usually assure their citizens that there are only a few rotten apples when these scandals are publicized. Yet the number and similarity of police-gangster crimes nationally indicate a crisis in American policing.

Official corruption will be a major problem as long as we cling to the present drug policies. The code of silence cannot be totally eliminated. But the harm to good cops and to society can be reduced if politicians abandon their demagogic calls for a police war against drugs. Police officers who are true partners with the community in reducing crime will be far more likely to report thugs on the force than cops who think they're part of a warring occupation army.

IT IS SO COMMON FOR POLICE TO LIE ABOUT HOW THEY OBTAINED DRUG EVIDENCE THAT THE TERM "TESTILYING" HAS REPLACED "TESTIFYING" IN POLICE JARGON.

The perfect pathogen has arrived: Millions of people may be infected, and planet earth will never be the same. The advent of widespread mad cow disease—and the corresponding human epidemic of Creutzfeldt-Jakob disease (CJD)—has many nations on high alert. The US Department of Agriculture adamantly denies mad cows exist in America. However, leading private and government researchers, several key studies, and even statistical probability contradict these assertions. The agency itself has admitted that "the potential risk of amplification of the BSE agent is much greater in the United States" than in Britain. With 100 million head of cattle, America could soon be revealed as the planet's biggest mad cow sanctuary.

BOVINE BIOTERRORISM AND THE PERFECT PATHOGEN
MAD COW DISEASE IS SWEEPING THE WORLD—INCLUDING THE US

GABE KIRCHHEIMER

In the wake of terrorist attacks on America, public health threats from within have been increasingly ignored. A new awareness of bioterrorism has been sparked by the discovery of anthrax spores sent around the country. Yet right under the nose of America, a fatal, untreatable, and deeply hidden biological threat appears to be spreading virtually unchecked in the US. Harder to detect than anthrax and far more stealthy, the perfect pathogen was not engineered or spread by a terrorist group. It did not escape from a top-secret military facility. The agent is not a virus, nor a bacterium, and it contains no DNA. It is not even alive.

The perfect pathogen—which causes mad cow disease in cattle and Creutzfeldt-Jakob disease in humans—is a malformed protein molecule known as an infectious prion, and until recently, the unprecedented mechanism of its awesome destructive power was disbelieved by many of the world's leading biologists.

The presence of the infectious agent in livestock is assured in perhaps half the countries of the world, although only a fraction have admitted it (including the UK, Ireland, France, Germany, Italy, and Japan). While desperately denying the existence of mad cow disease on its own soil, America continues to profit from the honesty of its affected trade partners. This arrangement is quietly destroying the health of the nation, but business is booming.

Are you familiar with CJD? Welcome to a living hell. Take a brief walk with me while I tell you of the most horrifying disease known to mankind.
—Dolly Campbell, whose husband died of Creutzfeldt-Jakob disease

_IT'S A MAD, MAD, MAD, MAD WORLD

Every so often, a plague comes along with the power to shape nations. Such a plague is mad cow disease, or bovine spongiform encephalopathy (BSE), which first made international headlines in March 1996, when British authorities and the World Health Organization were forced to admit that ten human deaths from the apparently rare brain-wasting Creutzfeldt-Jakob disease (CJD) were "likely" to be directly related to eating tainted beef.

The increase in transmissible spongiform encephalopathies (TSEs)—which includes BSE and CJD—among livestock and people is now recognized as an expanding worldwide plague. Tests in Europe, where most countries routinely fed millions of recycled cattle corpses back to cows until the crisis broke, have revealed many cases of BSE, in addition to the 177,000 confirmed in Britain, which has incinerated nearly five million cows as a result. Consumption of British beef has plummeted; financial losses have been catastrophic.

The disease vector—tainted cattle feed containing the ground-up remains of cows harboring infectious prions—has been shipped all over the world, a million tons to Asia alone. In September 2001, Japan confirmed the presence of mad cow disease within its borders, devastating its domestic beef market almost overnight, while the world reacted with another round of import bans.

Nobody knows how many people have contracted new-variant Creutzfeldt-Jakob disease (nvCJD) through contaminated beef and byproducts. Not only meat, but many processed foods, drugs, vaccines, surgical instruments, dietary supplements, and even cosmetics may carry this plague, spread mainly through the forced cannibalism of millions of bovines. In Britain and beyond, maternal transmission of nvCJD presages generations of victims. There is no treatment or cure. Experimental tests for the living recently have been developed, but there is no indication of when they'll be available.

_A CLEVER, INDESTRUCTIBLE PROTEIN

Infectious prions represent truth stranger than science fiction. Virtually indestructible, they represent an entirely new class of pathogen. Not a living organism, the abnormal version of a protein known as a prion is able to withstand conditions which kill any other known pathogen, representing a biological threat never before seen on Earth. With unique abilities to survive temperatures upward of 1,100°F, jump species barriers, evade the immune system, and replicate themselves in victims whose very bodies remain infectious, these rogue proteins are sowing widespread devastation among animals and humans. Even HIV is neutralized by boiling water, but routine sterilization procedures are ineffective against this misfolded molecule, which destroys brain tissue by filling it with spongy holes.

The 1997 Nobel Prize in Physiology or Medicine was awarded to San Francisco scientist Stanley Prusiner for his discovery of "prions—a new biological principle of infection," even as others expressed incredulity at an infectious agent containing no genetic material whatsoever. Thought to replicate in the manner of crystals, abnormal prions malform neighboring prions upon contact, causing them to "fold" improperly and mutate their neighbors in a domino effect of devastation, until the host develops vacuoles in the brain, loses nervous system function, and dies. Unlike normal prions, mutants do not break down when meat is digested. The immune system is not provoked to attack the invader, because normal and rogue prions are almost chemically identical.

The long-term implications for the planet and its human and animal inhabitants are staggering. The number of vehicles which may harbor this hidden killer reads like a shopping list of common products. Not even vegetarians are immune: White sugar is bleached with cow bones, and McDonald's French fries, advertised as prepared in "pure vegetable oil," are seasoned—like many products with "natural flavors"—with beef fat.

_MAD DEER, SAD PEOPLE

In the Southwest, an outbreak of chronic wasting disease, the TSE affecting deer, elk, and other ungulates, is now raging, with 5 to 15 percent of elk in areas of Colorado and Wyoming reportedly infected. The case of Doug McEwen—a 30-year-old hunter who died of CJD in Utah on March 28, 1999—starkly illustrates the tragedy surrounding the illness. McEwen, who regularly ate deer meat, was diagnosed with classic CJD although, like many of the British victims, his youth might seem to indicate another, more virulent strain, as only 1 percent of classic CJD patients develop symptoms at his age. McEwen's situation was graphically reported by Mark Kennedy in the *Ottawa Citizen* the day before he died:

Tracie McEwen reaches over to the dying man... As he moans softly, she strokes his arm and kisses his forehead. "It's OK. Doug, it's OK."

Tracie married Doug exactly four years ago. She marked their anniversary by pouring sparkling cider into cups, making a toast, and lovingly dropping some into Doug's mouth....

It started slowly. First, there was the memory loss and the inability to do simple math, then the light tremors. Eventually came violent seizures as well as unexplainable outbursts of emotion—hysterical laughter, sometimes followed by uncontrollable crying. By late January, he could no longer speak in sentences....

"This is the worst thing I have seen," [Tracie McEwen] says. "I wouldn't wish it on my worst enemy."

Inexplicably, blood plasma donated by McEwen was cleared by the authorities and distributed during his illness and after his death. For nearly two years McEwen had donated blood plasma, which was processed by Bayer into fractionated blood products in Clayton, North Carolina, then shipped to 46 countries around the globe. "The scope of this is breathtaking," Dr. Tom Pringle says of the decision to release blood contaminated with CJD. "You've got a time bomb ticking in millions and millions of people. And as they become donors, it spreads further." Pringle is a molecular biologist and founder of the astonishingly extensive Official Mad Cow Website <www.madcow.org>, and his comments have appeared in mad cow articles in the *New York Times*.

> NOT A LIVING ORGANISM, THE ABNORMAL VERSION OF A PROTEIN KNOWN AS A PRION IS ABLE TO WITHSTAND CONDITIONS WHICH KILL ANY OTHER KNOWN PATHOGEN, REPRESENTING A BIOLOGICAL THREAT NEVER BEFORE SEEN ON EARTH.

EVERYTHING YOU KNOW IS WRONG

Of the infected deer which almost certainly led to McEwen's death, Pringle is unequivocal: "I think they have scrapie. Most cases trace back to Ft. Collins, Colorado, at the Foothills Research Station, an experimental facility which was contaminated," a contention shared by several other CWD researchers. Wild animals might also contract the disease by raiding contaminated feed meant for livestock.

_STATE OF EMERGENCY

Although the existence of mad cow disease is unconditionally denied by the American authorities, the prevalence of TSEs in other farmed livestock has been cause for two recent Declarations of Emergency by the USDA.

Effective February 1, 2000, then-Secretary of Agriculture Dan Glickman proclaimed a "Declaration of Emergency Because of Scrapie in the United States," due to a clear epidemic:

Scrapie, a degenerative and eventually fatal disease affecting the central nervous systems of sheep and goats, is present in the United States. Scrapie is a complicated disease because it often has an extremely long incubation period without clinical signs of disease. Currently, scrapie-free countries have an enormous competitive advantage over US sheep producers, who are unable to certify that their flocks originated from a scrapie-free country or region. Because importing countries are demanding that imported sheep come from scrapie-free regions and sheep producers in the United States are unable to make this certification, US producers are finding themselves locked out of the international market, a situation that is taking a serious financial toll on the US sheep industry.... Therefore...I declare that there is an emergency that threatens the sheep and goat industry of this country, and I authorize the transfer and use of such funds as may be necessary from appropriations or other funds available to the United States Department of Agriculture to conduct a program to accelerate the eradication of scrapie from the United States.

This admission was followed by a "Declaration of Emergency Because of Chronic Wasting Disease" issued by Secretary of Agriculture Ann Veneman, effective September 21, 2001:

Chronic wasting disease (CWD), a disease of deer and elk, is part of a group of diseases known as transmissible spongiform encephalopathies (TSEs), a group that also includes scrapie and bovine spongiform encephalopathy (BSE). While considered rare, the incidence of CWD is on the rise among both wild and domestic cervids. The disease, which occurs mostly in adult animals, is progressive and always fatal. The origin and mode of transmission of CWD are unknown. The disease has become of particular concern due to its fatal nature, lack of known prevention or treatment, its impact on the farmed cervid industry, and its pos-

sible transmissibility to cattle or other domestic livestock and humans.

Scrapie, the mad-sheep analogue suspected of infecting British cattle with BSE, has spread unchecked to 45 states.

On October 25, 2001, Reuters reported: "Companies that make amino acids used in pharmaceuticals and vaccines should not use cattle and sheep from mad cow-infected countries as a source, a US advisory panel said Thursday.... Current manufacturing processes cannot guarantee that prions, the infectious material thought to cause mad cow disease, would not be transmitted from amino acids to the end product."

SCRAPIE, THE MAD-SHEEP ANALOGUE SUSPECTED OF INFECTING BRITISH CATTLE WITH BSE, HAS SPREAD UNCHECKED TO 45 STATES.

A Reuters article published the next day, "FDA Urged to Consider Ban on Cow Brain Products," stated:

The US Food and Drug Administration (FDA) may soon consider banning the sale of any product containing cow brains or spinal tissue, whether made abroad or here in the US.

Expert advisors to the FDA voted 18 to 1 on Friday in favor of urging the federal agency to begin assessing the necessity and feasibility of passing regulations to either ban or restrict the use of products containing these tissues, due to the theoretical risk of "mad cow" disease.

These products range from soup stock and sausage casings to cosmetics, drugs, medical devices and dietary supplements....

But if the FDA should follow its committee recommendation, there are unlikely to be any immediate consequences. The FDA's rule-making process could take months and even years to complete, while the agency reviews the available data and upcoming studies.

_THE WSJ CHECKS IN

With the government issuing emergency decrees for sheep, goats, deer, and elk in response to widespread TSE infections among domestic and wild animals—and with the FDA considering a ban of products, including those containing *domestic* bovine nervous system tissue—it seems inevitable that mad cows will rear their spastic heads, even as big business desperately tries to bury the truth.

On August 29, 2001, none other than the *Wall Street Journal* ran an editorial, "Moo Over, Mad Cow Cometh" by Holman W. Jenkins, Jr., which admitted the futility of postponing the inevitable:

"Not a single case of mad cow" has been the proud

mantra of the US beef industry since the disease was discovered in Britain 15 years ago. Not finding a case, though, has been largely a function of not looking especially hard.... Looking is often finding, so this would seem to bode a consumer panic and economic disaster if mad cow is as widely spread as many experts believe. The US cattle industry long ago convinced itself that a single case would mean curtains for its $3.6 billion in annual beef exports, not to mention a bruising domestic whack as consumers defect to chicken, pork or—horrors—soy burgers....

Washington and the cattle lobby have spent a decade praying mad cow doesn't show up here, despite knowing it must sooner or later. Though 36 million head are slaughtered a year, the Agriculture Department has examined all of 12,000 brains since 1990. The time has come to gear up a real hunt for our first case, if only to get it over with.

_CJD AND NVCJD

CJD and BSE are both TSEs, which are invariably fatal. But not every case involves infection from contaminated material. Naturally occurring, or "sporadic," TSEs afflict humans, bovines, and many other animals at the rate of one in a million. Sporadic CJD, which primarily affects the elderly, can incubate for decades before leading to loss of coordination, horrific mental breakdown, and death.

The 100 British victims of nvCJD—which has a shorter incubation period than CJD—have been mostly younger people between 13 and 40 years of age. "Health officials say they've got mad cow under control, but millions of unaware people may be infected," warned a *Newsweek* cover story on March 12, 2001. "[O]nce a few cattle contracted it, 20th-century farming practices guaranteed that millions more would follow. For 11 years...British exporters shipped the remains of BSE-infected cows all over the world [to] more than 80 countries." The stakes are extremely high. One infected animal, whose remains are rendered, powdered, and mixed into feed, can infect thousands of other animals, plus the thousands of people who eat them.

All the British nvCJD victims express a genetic trait shared by 38 percent of the British population and all bovines. Jun Tateishi, professor emeritus of Japan's Kyushu University and an authority on prion study, explains: "Basically, there are differences in genes...between humans and animals. Humans have three types of [paired] gene structures: methionine, valine, and a combined type. On the other hand, a cow has only the methionine type," which apparently enables the effective transmission of BSE prions to humans carrying the same methionine pairing. "What we should

> "WASHINGTON AND THE CATTLE LOBBY HAVE SPENT A DECADE PRAYING MAD COW DOESN'T SHOW UP HERE, DESPITE KNOWING IT MUST SOONER OR LATER."
> —*WALL STREET JOURNAL*

note is that 91.6 percent of Japanese have the methionine gene type. Compared to British people, the rate is overwhelmingly high. I can't say so for sure yet, but my opinion is that Japanese are about 2.5 times more likely to get mad cow disease than British people." No test for this genetic trait is available.

_A DIFFERENT US STRAIN?

Over the last decade the USDA has tested over 12,000 cow brains, looking for the pathology seen in infected British cattle, and it continues to claim that not a single BSE-infected cow has been found. The US Centers for Disease Control and Prevention (CDC), which has refused to mandate CJD as a reportable disease in the face of many petitions, similarly asserts that only about 280 to 300 people a year die from it (about one for each million Americans, the standard rate for the naturally occurring variety), with no nvCJD detected in the US.

But what if America has been harboring a different and stealthy strain of BSE all along, with a corresponding variant of CJD, and neither were being detected by current methodology? "I don't expect the British strain of mad cow disease to be much of a problem here," says Dr. Pringle. "The main fear is that our own cattle may carry a different strain of the disease that is distinct from the British strain." TSEs are known to exist in numerous strains within a single species; sheep scrapie has at least 20 variants.

In Britain, speculates Pringle, "the top level of government itself does not know—nor want to know—the scope of the epidemic. This is to establish 'plausible deniability.'" It would appear the US is also burying its head in the sand.

_AMERICA'S EPIDEMICS

The evidence for epidemics of both BSE and CJD in America is persuasive:

1. In 1985, Dr. Richard Marsh, a TSE researcher at the University of Wisconsin investigating a mysterious outbreak of transmissible mink encephalopathy (TME) in that state, found that the minks' diet consisted almost exclusively of "downer" cows—animals too sick to stand.

In 1994, Marsh showed that when the brains of infected cattle were fed to healthy mink, they developed TME; healthy cattle inoculated with tissues obtained from TME-infected mink duly developed BSE. These experiments showed "the presence of a previously unrecognized scrapie-like infection in cattle in the United States."

The disease was different than that seen in Britain. Significantly, rather than exhibiting overt mad cow symptoms (European cattle with BSE usually act skittish and "crazy" before death), the US animals simply collapsed. In 1990, cows in Texas experimentally inoculated with American scrapie developed BSE, becoming lethargic and staggering to their deaths, just like downer cows. Some states, such as New York, don't send downer cows to the USDA for testing, leaving open the possibility that BSE in thousands of suspect animals is going undetected.

According to Prionics, which manufactures Europe's leading BSE test: "A study performed with Prionics-Check reveals that fallen stock...represent BSE high-risk categories."

2. Leading scientists aver that mad cows surely exist in the US. Dr. Clarence Gibbs—a preeminent TSE researcher who chaired a World Health Organization investigation into BSE and ran the laboratory of the National Institute of Neurological Disorders and Stroke until his death—had no doubts about domestic infection: "Do I believe BSE is here? Of course I do."

And Dr. Stanley Prusiner, who won the 1997 Nobel Prize in Medicine for his discovery of prions, expressed that contention to a congressional caucus in May 1996. That June, an article in *Food Chemical News* stated, "After more than two decades of research on prions, Stanley Prusiner of the University of California at San Francisco suggested that mad-cow disease must be present in US cows.... He said he agreed with [Richard Marsh] who believes mad-cow disease was linked to US cows in the mid-1980s."

"Thirty-seven million animals are slaughtered a year for consumption, and less than 1,000 are tested a year—it's too low," says Pierluigi Gambetti, the director of the CDC's National Prion Disease Pathology Surveillance Center. "If you don't look, you don't find it. Our testing is not on the cutting edge." Nearly one million animals are tested by both France and Germany every year.

What would the USDA do upon discovering a case of BSE? "Their first impulse would be to suppress it," asserts Dr. Michael Hanson, a senior research scientist at the Consumer Policy Institute of Consumers Union (publisher of *Consumer Reports*) and one of the country's leading food-safety experts. Of the government's TSE-detection program, Hanson reiterates, "Their strategy might be, act like you're looking, but really do a 'don't look, don't find.'"

As Pringle points out: "Absence of evidence is not evidence of absence."

3. In spite of the USDA's categorical denials, it's a scientific fact that one in a million cows naturally develops BSE. With about 100 million cattle in the US, that would mean approximately 100 mad cows exist on American soil at any given time. Many likely collapse before scheduled slaughter and are rendered into feed, with the potential to infect thousands of other animals.

4. The best evidence for widespread, hidden CJD is contained in a pair of revelatory university studies. Hanson has repeatedly pointed to the evidence: "A study at the University of Pittsburgh, in which autopsies were done on 54 demented patients diagnosed as having probable or possible Alzheimer's or some other dementia (but not CJD), found three cases (or 5.5 percent) of CJD among the 54 studied. A Yale study found that of 46 patients diagnosed with Alzheimer's, six (or 13 percent) were CJD at autopsy. Since there

are over two million cases of Alzheimer's disease currently in the United States, if even a small percentage of them turned out to be CJD, there could be a hidden CJD epidemic."

These shocking figures indicate that tens and perhaps hundreds of thousands of Americans are currently infected with a preventable variant of CJD. Since sporadic CJD occurs in only one in a million people, an infectious source must exist.

> "AFTER MORE THAN TWO DECADES OF RESEARCH ON PRIONS, STANLEY PRUSINER OF THE UNIVERSITY OF CALIFORNIA AT SAN FRANCISCO SUGGESTED THAT MAD-COW DISEASE MUST BE PRESENT IN US COWS."

_A RENDERED DISASTER

The common practice of feeding rendered protein supplements—the boiled-down, powdered remains of slaughterhouse and other animal waste—to domestic animals spread BSE in the UK. Surviving high heat and solvents, mutant prions from each BSE-infected cow infected thousands of other bovines, as huge batches of feed were mixed and fed back to cattle in a bovine version of *Soylent Green*'s forced cannibalism.

Feeding mammalian protein to ruminants (cud-chewing animals) was authoritatively banned in the UK in 1989. Eight years later, in August 1997, the FDA tardily issued weak regulations addressing this common practice. Consumers Union's Hanson explained the US ban: "All they said is that you've got to label it, 'Do not feed to cattle and other ruminants.' Farmers can walk in a feed store and still buy it. Nobody asks, 'Are you feeding it to cattle or pigs?' They have to keep records of where the material came from for one year, for a disease with an average incubation period of five years. It's a joke. The way the rule is written, you can take scrapie-infested sheep, CWD-infested deer, and BSE-infested animals and legally put that in animal feed and give it to pigs, chickens—anything but ruminants, as long as it's labeled. That's outrageous." On top of that, USDA feed-rule compliance among America's thousands of livestock farmers is virtually impossible to effectively monitor or enforce.

Incredibly, Hanson noted in 1999, "The new thing is to feed calves spray-dried bovine plasma. It's hardly processed, so you're not knocking down the infectivity—and you can put it right in the feed."

But calves are not the only hapless recipients; Hanson believes the industry is likely feeding cows "a huge amount of bovine blood products. Legally, you can take any blood product from cattle and feed it to cows. I've been told that cows won't eat feed with more than ten percent blood, because they can taste it, and that chickens will eat feed with up to thirty-five percent blood." Blood has been shown capable of containing infectious prions.

_WHAT GOES AROUND, COMES AROUND

In spite of the successful initiative by the European Union to ban all animal products in livestock feed, American animal agribusiness continues to make widespread use of rendered protein and feed containing animal parts.

Under current feed regulations, livestock often eat one another's remains. After inedible pig parts are rendered, they are often fed back to pigs, cows, and chickens; cow parts are fed to chickens and pigs; and pigs and chickens are still routinely fed rendered protein that includes the remains of downer cows, which are most suspect for harboring BSE.

Perhaps most repugnant, thousands of tons of fermented chicken manure are fed to millions of US cows each year in a bizarre loop of inexpensive husbandry. Hanson and Pringle believe that "cow to chicken manure to cow" could turn out to be a BSE vector path; infectious prions apparently survive ingestion and could plausibly make the round-trip on this perverse journey.

As for the question of whether fowl can contract TSEs from live-stock, the issue has "not really ever been investigated," says Pringle. "No one wanted to know, because so much cattle bone meal is fed to chickens. However, the chicken prion has a strong similarity to the mammalian amyloidogenic region, so it is theoretically possible."

It remains possible that all domestic animals may indeed be susceptible to TSE infection. According to Hanson, the USDA has "functionally ignored the potential TSE in pigs." Their very short factory-farm lifespan of six to eight months might hide any symptoms of TSE, which usually spends several years incubating in mammals. Dr. Paul Brown, a senior investigator for the National Institutes of Health and the author and coauthor of numerous TSE studies, also has indicated that poultry and especially pigs could harbor TSEs and pass them on to humans. "It's speculation," Brown has acknowledged, "but I am perfectly serious."

Pigs that were experimentally inoculated have developed BSE, and a suspected outbreak of porcine spongiform encephalopathy occurred near Albany, New York, in 1997. A 1973 study published in the *American Journal of Epidemiology* discovered that ten of 38 CJD patients had eaten hog brains.

_BIG BEEF AND THE USDA

Critics contend the $150 billion-a-year cattle industry is itself infected with agribusiness greed, preventing any possibility of truthful or timely disclosure of mad cows. Although American beef consumption has been cut nearly in half since 1980 (while chicken and pork have risen), the beef industry has rarely been as lucrative, with 85 percent of cattle farmers reporting profitability in 2000, up from only 15 percent in 1996. Ironically, Europe's crisis has been a huge boon to "BSE-free" American beef exports, which shot up 34 percent in 2000, with shipments to the Russian Federation increasing twenty-fivefold. Mad cow disease has clearly been great for business, although McDonald's has suffered large European and Japanese losses in the wake of widespread beef avoidance.

With America's sacred cow at stake, many doubt the USDA will voluntarily reveal the discovery of any BSE-infected cows—which would lead to certain market collapse and public panic. Dr. Michael Gregor—a physician who was one of the earliest critics of the US's handling of the BSE threat (and is the Webmaster of the successor to Pringle's mad cow site <www.purefood.org/madcow.htm>)—points out that the "USDA has a conflict of interest, as the agency is responsible both for consumer safety and the promotion of American agriculture, of which meat is the primary industry." He notes that industry groups have successfully lobbied against changes in the USDA's research program to accommodate the possibility that BSE is already present in the US.

In the absence of sufficient inspectors and vigorous monitoring, the agency puts its trust in the beef industry to implement its rules. Allegations that the relationship between the two entities is overly cozy were fortified with the appointment of President Bush's USDA staff. On February 11, 2001, the *New York Times* reported: "Although they have had a record year, cattle ranchers in the United States now face growing anxiety over mad-cow disease...which could drive down beef prices. But last week, they triumphed when Ann M. Veneman, the new agriculture secretary, named Dale Moore, a lobbyist for the National Cattlemen's Beef Association, as her chief of staff. Charles P. Schroeder, the association's chief executive, said the cattle industry was investing heavily in food safety and looking forward to working with its former advocate."

_FAILED REGULATIONS

The US has failed to close gaping loopholes in the firewall against mad cows, and the feeding of potentially infectious cow parts back to cattle continues largely unmonitored. In early 2001, the FDA charged livestock-feed producers and rendering plants—which powder a variety of animal waste for use as a cheap feed supplement—with widespread noncompliance with labeling and mixing regulations.

The next day, the *New York Times* followed with a front-page article describing the lapses: "Large numbers of companies involved in manufacturing animal feed are not complying with regulations meant to prevent the emergence and spread of mad-cow disease in the United States.... All products that contain rendered cattle or sheep must have a label that says, 'Do not feed to ruminants.'... Manufacturers must also have a system to prevent ruminant products from being commingled with other rendered material."

The issue of monitoring America's thousands of cattle farmers, the end-users of rendered feed, has not been addressed by the Food and Drug Administration, which primarily monitors interstate commerce.

Brain and spinal cord tissue are the primary—but not the only—reservoirs of infectious material in humans and animals. Current USDA and FDA regulations are designed to prevent this material from ending up on the American dinner plate, but the automatic meat-recovery (AMR) systems in wide use at modern slaughterhouses, which mechanically strip the spine of flesh, routinely include banned material in the meat. The USDA and the federal Food Safety and Inspection Service have found spinal-cord fragments and nervous-system tissue in AMR meat samples. It has also been shown that, upon impact on the skull, pneumatic slaughterhouse stun guns can force bovine brain matter into the bloodstream and edible tissues.

On August 10, 2001, the Center for Science in the Public Interest petitioned the USDA to ban AMR "meat" from the human food supply. Warning that cattle are better protected from mad cow disease than people, CSPI Food Safety Director Caroline Smith DeWaal stated:

Machines that strip meat from bones provide the best pathway for BSE to get into human food. While the Food and Drug Administration in 1997 banned the use of processed cattle parts in making cattle feed, USDA has not taken adequate precautions to protect the human food supply. US cattle aren't allowed to eat cattle spinal cord—and neither should people.

The CSPI press release notes:

AMR meat paste typically is used in the production of hundreds of millions of pounds of hot dogs, hamburgers, pizza toppings, and taco fillings, and although USDA has asked companies to remove spinal cord from the spinal column and neck bones before they enter the machines, the agency rarely checks the industry's compliance. Since 1998, USDA has tested approximately 100 samples of AMR meat for spinal cord. Of those, nine samples tested positive for this central nervous system tissue.

"Although the department [of Agriculture] classifies the tissues as being 'not meat,' their presence in a meat product is not a violation of food safety laws," notes reporter Lance Gay of the Scripps Howard News Service. "Much of the mechanically separated meat is sold to the school-lunch program, which the department also administers."

_THE ZOO LOOP

TSEs have been observed in numerous rodent, primate, and ungulate (hoofed) species, and in various felines such as cheetahs and domestic cats. During the late 1980s and the 1990s, numerous French zoo primates, felines, and hoofed animals were shown to have TSEs. "Large numbers of monkeys and lemurs in French zoos appear to be infected with the agent that causes 'mad cow disease,' according to a provocative study published today in *Proceedings of the National Academy of Sciences*," wrote the *New York Times*' mad cow reporter, Sandra Blakeslee, in March 1999. "The finding is bad news for people living in Britain who fear that a human form of mad cow disease, called new variant Creutzfeldt-Jakob disease, or CJD, may have similar underpinnings."

Tom Pringle commented on this study: "This is a huge scandal because it potentially affects the survival of many of the world's primate species. It also suggests very strongly that the nvCJD epidemic will indeed be a 'plague of biblical proportions'" (quoting a warning given by prominent neurogeneticist John Collinge, a member of the British government's Spongiform Encephalopathy Advisory Committee).

_GOT MAD MILK?

It's rarely mentioned, but infectious prions can be contained in milk, although it remains a remote vector. A 1992 Japanese study published in the *New England Journal of Medicine* showed that human breast-milk colostrum (the first milk a baby receives) is capable of transmitting prions, and the infection of lambs with scrapie through milk has also been demonstrated. It is not clear whether post-colostrum milk possesses this capacity. Some people have chosen to avoid cheese from the UK as a precautionary measure; many hard cheeses contain rennet, an enzyme extracted from the stomachs of calves.

_SUPPLEMENTS, VACCINES, BLOOD, AND MEDICAL INSTRUMENTS

Other routes of infection remain of grave concern. Direct inoculation presents the highest risk. Despite warnings from Pringle and others, US vaccines, which are often grown in bovine calf serum, are still being made from suspect materials. In February 2001, the *New York Times* finally picked up the story (curiously placed in the business section) under the headline, "5 Drug Makers Use Material With Possible Mad-Cow Link." The article stated, "For the last eight years the FDA has repeatedly asked pharmaceutical companies not to use materials from cattle raised in countries where there is a risk of mad-cow disease.... But regulators discovered last year that...some of the world's largest drug concerns were still using ingredients from those countries to make nine widely used vaccines...[which] include some regularly given to millions of American children, including common vaccines to prevent polio, diphtheria and tetanus." The list also includes flu shots and the hepatitis vaccine.

Numerous dietary supplements containing glandular material, brains, and other bovine ingredients are also at high risk. "Velvet Antler" capsules from General Nutrition Centers and many other retailers "come from the growing antlers of elk and can contain infectious agents," says Hanson. "They're filled with nerve tissue and blood. I wouldn't want to be the one to be experimented on."

"It's just insane not to have greater safeguards [for supplements]," the chair of the FDA's Advisory Committee on Mad Cow Disease, Dr. Paul Brown, told the *Times*. "The FDA is toothless."

The American Red Cross, which collects half the US blood supply but doesn't test for CJD, now bans blood donations from Americans who have spent three months in Britain or one year elsewhere in Europe. The strict ban has created a predicted national shortage of blood, especially in New York City, where 25 percent of the red-cell supply was until recently imported from FDA-approved European blood banks. The Red Cross estimates that the current ban will cut nationwide blood donations by 6 percent.

In the absence of strict government regulations, some medical organizations have voluntarily recalled large lots of fractionated blood products containing donations from people later found to have CJD, usually after some of the products have reached recipients. Over the past ten years, at least $100 million worth of plasma products has reportedly been destroyed.

Many drugs are derived from cattle, including growth hormones from pituitary glands, adrenaline products, cortisone, insulin for diabetics, and medications for the treatment of stomach ulcers. Thromboplastin, a common blood coagulant used in surgery, is derived from bovine brains. Pituitary extracts from mad cows (as well as human donors with CJD) have been traced as the cause of CJD infection in recipients.

"The thing that worries me is the immunization of the children," says Pringle. "Every kid in the United States can't go to school without their shots... They're growing vaccines out of fetal-calf serum. Then you're injecting four-year-old children—which is much worse than eating, 100,000 times more effective [at spreading the disease]. Every schoolchild in the UK has already been immunized with vaccine made from serum from infected bovines."

Surgical instruments are at high risk of transmitting the infection, as autoclave steam sterilization doesn't neutralize infectious prions. Blood, blood products, bovine extracts, and transplant organs—such as brain dura mater and corneas—are not usually screened for CJD, even though in Britain and around the world, infected organ recipients, who sometimes developed symptoms decades after treatment, have been traced to unwitting donors later found to have CJD. Effective prion sterilization protocols are not in wide use, but disposable surgical instruments are now used in many British procedures. It is inevitable that worldwide sterilization protocols will undergo drastic modification in the face of the prion.

_WHEN WILL WE GET THE TEST?

The spread of BSE has given birth to the emerging industry of prion diagnostics, which is rapidly growing to fill a demand for tests. Although postmortem tests for BSE are now widely used in Europe, antemortem (i.e., pre-death) tests for BSE and CJD are not yet commercially available.

A urine test developed by Israeli researchers at the Department of Neurology at Hadassah University Hospital, described in the *Journal of Biological Chemistry* (21 June 2001), promises to meet the need for a simple TSE test for live human and animal subjects. (The researchers note that the presence of infectious prions in urine indicates that they are being widely dispersed in soil, which has been experimentally shown to preserve prion infectivity over a period of years.) However, it is unclear how and when a viable CJD test will be released. In Britain,

the expected demand from millions of panicked individuals—concerned they may have a horrible brain-wasting disease—may delay screening while public policy for dealing with the results is formulated. A finding of thousands or even hundreds of thousands of cases, as has been projected by some researchers, could drastically alter British society. Already, several cases of suicide by the "worried well"—persons convinced they were developing CJD—have been recorded in Britain.

British public health officials have been widely castigated for incompetence, delays, and cover-ups in dealing with the BSE/CJD crisis. A crucial five-year study into whether British sheep have BSE was admitted to be ruined in mid-2001 by cross-contamination with bovine material. In the latest chapter of the cover-up, according to BBC News, the costly error wasn't announced until three months after its discovery.

The slow responses of Britain, the US, and other nations to the AIDS crisis are recalled by relatives of CJD victims, who hope this legacy of statistical obfuscation, delays in test availability, and poor dissemination of prevention information will not be repeated. Although Britain may be the first nation where widespread CJD testing occurs, testing in Japan, the US, and elsewhere will surely follow. It remains unclear which governments will promote or downplay the importance of CJD screening. With CJD, as with BSE, not looking is not finding.

_TIME WILL TELL

It has been proven experimentally that even fly larvae, after eating infected tissue, can transmit scrapie to hamsters; the larvae were still infectious after death. Nevertheless, the US government handbook *BSE Red Book—Emergency Operations* states: "Cleaning and disinfection is not necessary to prevent the spread of BSE."

Pringle is not optimistic. In the US, "it would be a wrenching experience to totally get away from the bovine economy, and realistically, they're only going to take half-measures. It's like a joke now to talk about containment. It's like locking the barn door after the horse is gone. WTO, NAFTA, has really helped globalize CJD. You don't know where your sutures are coming from, your shampoo, your sunscreen. The Pandora's box has been opened."

In the absence of a CJD test, the world can only guess the extent of the problem. As CBS *Evening News* relayed: "When asked if, in his darkest moment, he thought that this is the plague of the twenty-first century, [Dr. Prusiner] said, 'I don't need a dark moment to wonder if that's the case, because everybody's wondering that, not just me.'"

Interviews with Dr. Tom Pringle and Dr. Michael Hanson were conducted on several occasions between 1998-2001.

EVERY SCHOOLCHILD IN THE UK HAS ALREADY BEEN IMMUNIZED WITH VACCINE MADE FROM SERUM FROM INFECTED BOVINES.

FEAR OF A VEGAN PLANET
A CLOSER LOOK AT THE MEAT-BASED DIET
MICKEY Z.

"Until he extends the circle of compassion onto all living things, man will not himself find peace."
—Dr. Albert Schweitzer

The American Vegan Society defines veganism as "a way of living on the products of the plant kingdom to the exclusion of flesh, fowl, eggs, and animal milk and its derivatives. It encourages the study and use of alternatives for all commodities normally derived wholly or in part from animals."

I prefer to think of a vegan as someone who's a "vegetarian for ethical reasons." After all, the root of the word "vegetarian" is not vegetable; it is the Latin *vegetus*, meaning "full of life."

There are three primary reasons why one might opt to abstain from the standard American diet and be full of life: ethical, health, and environmental. In the name of provoking thought, here's a small taste of each.

_ETHICAL REASONS

"The time will come when men such as I will look on the murder of animals as they now look on the murder of men."
— Leonardo Da Vinci

The hidden ingredient in all animal-derived food (as well as clothing, entertainment, etc.) is cruelty. Whether it's chickens, horses, pigs, cattle, insects, deer, or any other exploited animal, the brutality inflicted by humans upon these creatures is seemingly without limit.

Chickens. Inside the hatchery, each chicken is confined to about 48 to 86 square inches of space (smaller than the page you're reading right now)[1] and these cages are piled tier upon tier. Due to the severe crowding, layer hens are kept in semi-darkness. The stressed birds are de-beaked using hot irons (without anesthesia) to prevent them from pecking each other to death. The wire cages rub off their feathers, and the mesh floor cripples their feet. Still, production proceeds apace. In 1888, the typical hen laid 100 eggs per year. By 1998, that number was 256.[2]

"Today's chickens are allowed no expression of their natural urges," says John Robbins, author of the vegan classic *Diet for a New America*. "They cannot walk around, scratch the ground, build a nest, or even stretch their wings. Every instinct is frustrated."[3] Twenty percent of layer hens die of stress or disease. Ninety percent of all commercially-sold eggs come from chickens raised on factory farms,[4] and 90 percent of those birds have chicken cancer (leukosis).[5] Those hens that survive see their egg production wane within two years and are promptly slaughtered. Under "normal" conditions, chickens may live 15 to 20 years.

Perhaps the finest illustration of what factory farming does to chickens has been presented by artist/writer Sue Coe. After her visit to a hatchery with Lorri Bauston from Farm Sanctuary (the activist organization focused on rescuing farm animals), Coe wrote about what they had found:

Around the back is a large dumpster. Lorri and I climb up to look inside. She is looking for live baby chicks. The male baby chicks are discarded as soon as they are hatched. They have no use, no value, since they cannot lay eggs. And it would cost too much to euthanize them. So they are tossed into the dumpster alive. But it is too late for us to rescue any chicks—the sun is just too hot. On the top layer of corpses, flies are eating the chicks' eyes. Lorri keeps digging under the corpses. There are layers upon layers, some chicks still half in the shells, having broken through with their beaks. I examine a chick, so perfect with its soft yellow down and tiny wings. The chicks are thrown in with other garbage: empty Coke cans, cigarette packs, computer printouts, samples of our throwaway society. Gene Bauston, cofounder of Farm Sanctuary, told me that sometimes the baby chicks are ground up alive and thrown on the fields as fertilizer. Walking along a plowed field, you can sometimes find a chick, still alive, with no legs or wings.[6]

Ducks. To some, the sight of a duck invokes images of *foie gras*. To produce this alleged delicacy, male ducks are force-fed six to seven pounds of grain three times a day with an air-driven feeder tube for 28 days. At that point, the ducks' livers, from which the pâté is made, will have bloated to six to twelve times their normal size. "About 10 percent of the ducks don't make it to slaughter," says vegetarian activist Pamela Rice. "They die when their stomachs burst."[7]

Cattle. The abhorrent treatment of cattle within the factory farm paradigm involves more than can be covered in an article. The castrating of bulls without anesthesia, the transporting of cattle in both extreme heat and cold, the butchering of cows that are still alive and conscious, and the rampant administration of antibiotics and hormones are just the beginning. The viciousness of the slaughterhouse industry has reached staggering proportions.

One of the more odious examples of cattle cruelty is the plight of the veal calf. "The newborn [male] calves are taken to veal sheds, and placed in what are euphemistically called 'stalls,'" explains Robbins.[8] The purpose of these stalls is to prevent the calves from developing their muscles—keeping their flesh "tender." Here's one description of the fate of a veal calf:

During their brief lives, they never see the sun or touch the earth. They never see or taste the grass. Their anemic bodies crave proper sustenance. Their muscles ache for freedom and exercise. They long for maternal care. About 14 weeks after their birth, they are slaughtered. The veal calf's permanent home is a veal crate, a wooden restraining device that is so small (22 inches by 54 inches) that the calves cannot turn around. Designed to prevent movement (exercise), the crate does its job of atrophying the calves' muscles, thus producing tender "gourmet" veal. The calves often suffer from open sores caused by the constant rubbing against the crates.[9]

The calves' diet is intentionally lacking in iron and other essential nutrients in order to promote anemia and create the whitish-pink color associated with veal. Craving iron, the abused calves lick urine-saturated slats and any metallic parts of their stalls. "Calves are born with stores of iron in their bodies, primarily in the form of extra hemoglobin in the blood, with lesser amounts stored in the liver, spleen, and bone marrow," says Robbins. "During the four months the veal calf is confined and 'special fed,' these reserves decline steadily."[10] Thus does modern science achieve the paradoxical achievement of breeding a calf whose flesh stays white as it gains weight.

Veal calves are a by-product of the dairy industry, which itself is an extension of the beef industry since used-up dairy cows are sent to the slaughterhouse after an average of four years—one-fifth their normal life expectancy. Those four years are usually not pleasant.

Rice notes, "Our modern dairy cow lives with an unnaturally swelled and sensitive udder, is likely never to be allowed out of her stall, is milked up to three times a day and is kept pregnant nearly all of her abbreviated life. Her young are usually taken from her almost immediately after birth."[11]

Bees. After a bee swallows floral nectar, it is partially digested in its primary stomach where the bee adds its own digestive secretion. It is then vomited up and named *honey* (or "bee puke," as Russ Kick calls it). Honey, of course, has become yet another animal product consumed by humans with predictably unfavorable results.

"In keeping with the usual animal agribusiness practice of wringing as much profit as possible from every captive being, many beekeepers have expanded their business to include taking in almost every substance found in the hive," writes Joanne Stepaniak, in the September/October 1996 issue of *The EarthHeart Message*. "Common methods used to evacuate bees include smoking or shaking the hives, chemical repellents, and forced air. Even the most careful keeper cannot help but squash or otherwise kill many of the bees in the process. During unproductive months, some beekeepers may starve their bees to death or burn the hive to avoid complex maintenance."

The beeswax industry isn't any less brutal. Beeswax is a substance

THE HIDDEN INGREDIENT IN *ALL* ANIMAL-DERIVED FOOD (AS WELL AS CLOTHING, ENTERTAINMENT, ETC.) IS CRUELTY.

secreted by honeybees to build their honeycombs. According to former American Vegan Society president H. Jay Dinshah, to obtain the wax "a fire is lit under the comb, the bees are driven away, then the comb is crushed along with all the eggs, larvae, and trapped bees. The honey is squeezed out and strained; then the crushed comb is heated, cleaned, and purified. For every honeycomb used to make beeswax, 5,000 to 35,000 lives are destroyed."[12]

Sheep. While sheep are yet another animal doomed to the slaughterhouse, they also face exploitation via the wool industry. The heavy, wool-bearing sheep that we see today are products of selective breeding over many generations. These "mutants" produce far more wool than they were designed to produce. Then, when this unnatural coat is shorn, the denuded sheep suffer from the cold. "Sometimes on the big runs of Australia," says Freda Dinshah, "thousands of newly-shorn sheep die of cold in one night when the weather turns unexpectedly cold."

There is a secondary manner in which the wool industry kills. Since domestic sheep are preyed upon by coyotes, farmers rely on poisoned bait to kill the predators. Coyotes are murdered for merely being coyotes, and countless other animals die from consuming the bait, including those who feed on poisoned carcasses. "These victims include golden eagles, bluebirds, hawks, falcons, badgers, bobcats, weasels, skunks, mink, martens, wild and domestic dogs, and bears," says Dinshah.[13]

The wool industry comes full circle back to the slaughterhouse, because the huge profit made from wool encourages further domestic breeding, which ultimately results in the butchery of animals for food. As a final component to this equation, the sizeable herds of sheep bred by the wool industry eventually make the land they graze on unfit for cultivation.

This is but a small sampling of human behavior towards animals. I didn't touch upon leather, silk, or fur; so-called entertainment or sports like circuses, rodeos, horse- and dog-racing, zoos, and hunting; animal experimentation; and the ever-expanding car culture (one million wild animals per week killed on US highways; antifreeze, bio-diesel fuel, hydraulic brake fluid, and asphalt binder are all made with ingredients culled from the carcasses of departed animals). A recent high-profile form of cruelty was the slaughtering of over two million animals in Great Britain during the hoof and mouth disease scare. Only 1,400 of those animals were actually sick.[14]

_HEALTH REASONS

> "Nothing will benefit health and increase the chances of survival of life on Earth as the evolution to a vegetarian diet."
> — Albert Einstein

There is no such thing as a vegetarian refrigerator. Try opening the nearest fridge and you'll find an egg rack along with a clearly marked butter tray and meat drawer. Eating animals and animal by-products is not just accepted, it's expected. Yet, contrary to popular opinion (and refrigerator manufacturers), human beings were not designed to consume animals.

"During 56 million years of primate evolution, the predecessors of man became bigger, smarter, and increasingly vegetarian, exploiting the fruits and leaves of their arboreal habitat," explains William Harris, M.D., in his book The Scientific Basis for Vegetarianism. Thus, Harris sees diet as an issue of kinetic energy.[15] For example, a gorilla would expend far more energy chasing, catching, and eating an insect that it would recover by eating it.

"Since no nutrients essential to man or any of his likely predecessors are synthesized by animals, the use of animal foods [by predecessors] must reflect other priorities," Harris continues.[16] Under conditions of scarcity, omnivorism may become necessary despite the fact that, unlike a true carnivore, Homo sapiens lack sharp teeth to tear through flesh, hide, and bones, and the human diges-

tive tract is quite long—22 feet—which means animal protein can sit for as much as fourteen days to putrefy and release dangerous carcinogens.[17]

Protein. There are many myths in circulation that contribute to contemporary human reliance on animal products as a dietary staple. The first is the protein myth. As any vegetarian can attest, the question most frequently posed to those who dine sans flesh is: Where do you get your protein?

The typical American adult ingests 100 grams of protein each day, roughly four to five times the amount recommended by scientists not affiliated with meat and dairy corporations.[18] How did we develop this idea that more is better when it comes to protein? The primary reason is the morally bankrupt and scientifically fraudulent institution of animal experimentation, which tries to set human diet standards by examining rats. Since trying to discern biological trends from human to human is often impossible, how can testing done on a rat lead to any knowledge about human anatomy and physiology? The breast milk of rats, for example, derives nearly half of its calories from protein. Human breast milk is 5.9 percent protein.[19] In addition, plaque (fatty deposits) is stored in the livers of rodents; in humans, plaque is regrettably deposited in blood vessels. Rats can manufacture vitamin C in their own bodies and obtain vitamin D by licking their own fur; humans must obtain both nutrients via diet. Unlike humans, rats cannot tolerate more than fifteen minutes of direct sunlight. Of utmost importance, the three-year lifespan of a rat requires massive doses of drugs for testing purposes—more than any human would ever ingest in his or her 70-plus years.[20] Since other differences between humans and the animals abused in laboratories could fill a book, there's clearly little functional information to be gained from monitoring the protein needs of rodents.

So, how much protein do we need? According to the World Health Organization, it's about 4.5 percent of our caloric intake.[21] That translates into a lot less grams than the US average of 100 a day. "An adult male on a fast only puts out 4.32 grams of urinary nitrogen

WE NEED LESS THAN 6 PERCENT OF OUR CALORIES FROM PROTEIN DURING A TIME OF INTENSE DEVELOPMENT, YET WE ARE CONSUMING VAST AMOUNTS OF PROTEIN AS FULL-GROWN ADULTS.

per day," says William Harris. "Each gram represents 6.25 grams of broken down protein, so under conditions in which some protein is actually being catabolized and used for fuel, only about 4.32 x 6.25 = 27 grams/day are actually needed." Twenty-seven grams.[22]

Which brings us back to mother's breast milk. We humans undergo our most rapid and significant growth during infancy. Human breast milk has evolved over hundreds of thousands of years to become the ideal food to facilitate such growth—deriving only 5.9 percent of its calories from protein. We need less than 6 percent of our calories from protein during a time of intense development, yet we are consuming vast amounts of protein as full-grown adults.

What about the athletes, those believed to need extra protein because they want to run faster, jump higher, or grow bigger muscles? As shown by Bergstrom, *et al.* in 1967, and reported by Reed Mangels, Ph.D., R.D., "Athletic performance is actually improved by a high carbohydrate diet, not a high protein diet." In addition, the decidedly mainstream National Academy of Sciences has declared, "There is little evidence that muscular activity increases the need for protein."[23]

Dairy Products. Another fashionable myth concerns the need to consume dairy products in order to stave off osteoporosis. The biochemical make-up of cow's milk is perfectly suited to turn a 65-pound newborn calf into a 400-pound cow in one year. It contains three times more protein and seven times more mineral content that human milk, while the human variety has ten times as much essential fatty acids, three times as much selenium, and half the calcium as bovine milk.[24]

Upon first glance, it may appear beneficial that cow's milk provides more calcium, but milk is actually a poor source for dietary calcium. Humans, like cows, get all the calcium they need from a plant-based diet. In fact, osteoporosis may be more the result of drinking cow's milk than eschewing. This is a classic example of the truth being diametrically opposed to the accepted reality. It is still widely accepted that the calcium in dairy products will strengthen our bones and help prevent osteoporosis, but studies show that foods originating from animal sources (like milk) make the blood acidic. When this occurs, the blood leeches calcium from the bones to increase alkalinity. While this works wonders for the pH balance of your blood, it sets your calcium-depleted bones up for osteoporosis.[25] As explained by John Robbins, "The only research that even begins to suggest that the consumption of dairy products might be helpful [in preventing osteoporosis] has been paid for by the National Dairy Council itself."[26]

Even if one were to ignore biology and continue indulging in cow's milk, there are other ingredients in this toxic bovine brew worth avoiding—man-made ingredients like bio-engineered hormones, antibiotics, and pesticides. Fifty-five percent of US antibiotics are fed to livestock.[27] "When researchers reviewed 500 medical articles on cows' milk," says Pamela Rice, "they found that none characterized the bovine secretion as an 'excellent food, free of side effects.'"[28]

"THERE IS LITTLE EVIDENCE THAT MUSCULAR ACTIVITY INCREASES THE NEED FOR PROTEIN."

Fish. Many who have accepted the health risks in consuming meat still buy into the myths surrounding fish. Plenty of so-called vegetarians eat seafood. For those who believe fish is a vegetable, here are a few facts:[29]

- A 3.5-ounce serving of salmon contains 74 milligrams of cholesterol, the same as in a comparable serving of T-bone steak or chicken.

- A six-month investigation by the Consumers Union found that fish are by far the biggest source of PCBs in the human diet. Forty-three percent of the salmon, 25 percent of swordfish, and 50 percent of lake whitefish had PCBs. (PCBs are a synthetic liquid once widely used in industry and banned as carcinogenic in 1976.) Nearly half the fish tested by the Consumers Union was contaminated by bacteria from human or animal feces.

- The Centers for Disease Control report an annual average of 325,000 cases of food poisoning from contaminated seafood in the US. One is left to wonder how many cases aren't reported or are mistakenly attributed to other causes.

Mad Cow Disease. A new meat-related myth is that mad cow disease cannot and will not happen in the US. First striking in 1985, bovine spongiform encephalopathy (BSE) has earned the caustic nickname "mad cow disease" thanks to the insidious symptoms presented in affected cattle (i.e., staggering, tremors, involuntary muscle spasms, bewilderment, hypersensitivity to auditory and tactile stimuli, and other examples of seemingly "mad" behavior).

Cases of BSE have been reported across the globe in France, Switzerland, Ireland, Portugal, Denmark, Canada, Italy, Oman, and the Falkland Islands. In the US, other forms of transmissable spongiform encephalopathy (TSE) have occurred in sheep (scrapie), mink (transmissible mink encephalopathy), and deer and elk (chronic wasting disease). Although not officially admitted, it seems certain that US cows have been hit with BSE. In Britain, nearly 100 people have died from the human form of BSE—Creutzfeld-Jakob disease (CJD)—most of whom have been in their twenties. Whether coming from infected cows or not, CJD has killed people in the United States, often being mistaken for Alzheimer's disease. (For more on BSE in the United States, see Gabe Kirchheimer's article elsewhere in this book.)

Because they contain no genetic material of their own, TSEs are not viruses, but are instead believed to be infectious proteins known as prions. Perhaps most disquieting about this hypothesis is the fact that, unlike viruses and bacteria, prions remain infectious even after being:

- baked at 680 degrees F for one hour (hot enough to melt lead),

- bombarded with radiation,

- soaked in formaldehyde, bleach, and boiling water.

"Cooking infected meat does not completely eliminate its infectivity," states environmentalist Peter Montague. Of course, this also means that forks, spoons, knives, or any other eating or cooking utensil cannot be sterilized. "BSE represents a big risk to the health of the [human] population," warns Stephen Dealler, a British microbiologist specializing in mad cow disease. "It is no use pretending that the danger is not there."

Edward L. Menning, D.V.M., editor of the *Journal of Federal Veterinarians*, agrees: "Potentially, this is one of the most frightening diseases the world has ever known."[30]

Other Health Problems. Besides the BSE risks, what price are humans paying for our illogical eating habits?[31]

> - Amount per year spent treating cardiovascular disease: $135 billion.
>
> - Every 25 seconds, an American has a heart attack.
>
> - Every 45 seconds, an American dies from a heart attack.
>
> - Risk of death by heart attack for average American male: 31 percent.
>
> - Risk of death by heart attack for average vegan: 4 percent.
>
> - Rise in blood cholesterol level from consuming one egg per day: 12 percent.
>
> - Associated rise in heart attack risk from consuming one egg per day: 24 percent.
>
> - Amount per year spent treating cancer: $70 billion.
>
> - Proportion of cancers that are diet related: 40 percent.
>
> - Food most likely to cause cancer from herbicide residue: beef.

"The plethora of degenerative diseases in the high animal-food countries reflects the failure of humans to adapt their 57-million-year vegetarian bodies to animal source food in the relatively short two to three million years since the hominids began to eat it," says Harris.[32]

In light of this self-inflicted health holocaust, can we expect anything of value in terms of help from the American medical community? There are 125 medical schools in the United States, of which only 30 require a nutrition course. As a result, the average physician receives 2.5 hours of nutrition training during four years in medical school.[33]

Perhaps the answer lies in the words of vaccination activist Sharon Kimmelman: "We are biologically accountable for our behavior."

Meatpacking Workers. There's another human health risk related to the standard American diet that could just as easily have been described in the "Ethical Reasons" section. Inside the slaughterhouses, the animals are not the only ones suffering. The meatpacking industry, along with its low wages, long hours, and dehumanizing work, has the highest job-related injury rate and by far the highest rate of serious injury. According to Eric Schlosser, author of *Fast Food Nation*, more than 25 percent of America's 150,000 meatpacking workers suffered an injury in 1999—and that may be a conservative estimate. "The meatpacking industry has a well-documented history of discouraging injury reports, falsifying injury data, and putting injured workers back on the job quickly to minimize the reporting of lost workdays," Schlosser says.[34] The situation is no better in the poultry industry. "Poultry workers typically make a single movement up to 20,140 times a day and suffer repetitive stress disorders at 16 times the national average," says Rice. As a result, the turnover rate is often as high as 100 percent per year.[35]

In a society where animals are routinely tortured, killed, and eaten, slaughterhouse workers occupy a position only slightly above our much-maligned feathered and furry co-inhabitants. "In some American slaughterhouses, more than three-quarters of the workers are not native English speakers; many can't read any language, and many are illegal immigrants," Schlosser reports. "These manual laborers [are] unlikely to complain or challenge authority, to file lawsuits, organize unions, fight for their legal rights. They tend to be poor, vulnerable, and fearful. From the industry's point of view, they are ideal workers: cheap, largely interchangeable, and disposable."[36]

In *Dead Meat*, Sue Coe describes her visit to a pig-slaughtering facility with Lorri Bauston:

> We go over to the pen holding cancerous pigs. These pigs have giant growths on their legs and sides. They hobble around and around on their stiff legs. One pig's eye is bleeding. When the men unload the pigs, they shock them in the eye to get them moving quickly. To the stockyard workers, it's just a job, a frustration. What is the alternative? To be unemployed? To have kids on welfare or maybe homeless? None of us can handle too many contradictions. Every dollar I get drips with blood.
>
> I look at the men again, "the guys," and see they are

ONE POUND OF HAMBURGER REQUIRES 2,500 GALLONS OF WATER TO PRODUCE, WHICH COULD INSTEAD HAVE BEEN USED TO GROW MORE THAN 50 POUNDS OF FRUITS AND VEGETABLES.

frightened. *Lorri and I are making trouble for them. They will be the sacrificial goats, the bosses can always diversify. The workers are expendable, replaceable in Mexico, where they import cruelty. The concealed labor will be concealed elsewhere. I ask the boss, "Are the workers upset by all the killing?" The boss says, "These workers see so much animal blood, they don't care, but if one man cuts his little finger, they all go crazy."*[37]

_ENVIRONMENTAL REASONS

> "While we ourselves are the living graves of murdered beasts, how can we expect any ideal conditions on this earth?"—George Bernard Shaw

Assessing the environmental cost of the meat- and dairy-based diet is an equally monumental and depressing task. For starters, consider Earthsave's calculations on the "real" price of a hamburger.[38]

- It takes twelve pounds of grain to produce one pound of hamburger. This same twelve pounds of grain could make eight loaves of bread or 24 plates of spaghetti.

- If the beef for your burger came from the rainforest, roughly 660 pounds of living matter is destroyed. This includes between 20 and 30 different plant species, over 100 insect species, and dozens of reptiles, birds, and mammals.

- One pound of hamburger requires 2,500 gallons of water to produce, which could instead have been used to grow more than 50 pounds of fruits and vegetables. Fifty percent of all water consumed in the US is used to grow feed and provide drinking water for cattle and other livestock.

- On a planet where a child starves to death every two seconds, fourteen times as many people could be fed by using the same land currently reserved for livestock grazing.

That Big Mac does more than just drain resources, it contributes to global warming. Two hundred gallons of fossil fuels are burned to produce the beef currently consumed by the average US family of four, while 500 pounds of carbon dioxide are released in the atmosphere for every quarter pound of rainforest beef.[39]

The standard American diet also pollutes the planet at an alarming rate. A 1997 Senate report declared that every year, US livestock produce 10,000 pounds of solid manure for every citizen. "In central California," Pamela Rice explains, "sixteen hundred dairies produce the feces and urine of a city of 21 million people." This is a problem

from coast to coast as "surplus cow sludge" is seriously polluting waterways.[40] Thanks in large part to run-off from animal agriculture, the Environmental Protection Agency has found 700 different pollutants in US drinking water.

Since 1945, overall pesticide use has increased by 3,300 percent with 1.5 billion pounds of pesticides applied to American farmlands annually. Despite the drastic increase in pesticide use, the USDA has found that prior to the 1950s, the overall annual crop loss due to "pest damage" was 7 percent. Today, it's 13 percent.[41] The bug spray may not be killing bugs, but it certainly has an impact on the human population. Studies have shown that 99 percent of non-vegetarian mothers in the US have significant levels of DDT in their breast milk. (For vegetarian mothers, the number is 8 percent.[42])

To the polluted air, water, land, and bodies, add in the devastation of topsoil and ensuing desertification and species destruction.

Over-fishing. Over-fishing is another diet-related environmental issue. A United Nations report stated that seventeen of the world's major fishing areas have reached or exceeded their natural limits. The World Conservation Union found 1,081 species of fish worldwide are threatened or endangered, while 106 Pacific salmon stocks are already extinct. "Industrial innovations permit fishers to scoop an astounding 80 to 90 percent of a given fish population from the sea in any one year," says Earthsave's Steve Lustgarden, who also reports on the "innocent bystanders" of the fishing industry. For example, for every pound of shrimp sold, roughly 20 pounds of other sea creatures are caught in the nets.[43] "In just one generation, human demand for fish has increased by 50 percent," says Pam Rice.[44]

Corporate Welfare. There's one more factor to consider when calculating the cost of a hamburger: the impact of corporate welfare of the planet. US farmers receive $22 billion in direct federal payments and subsidy aid,[45] and the total value of subsidized irrigation water used annually by animal feed growers in the US is $1 billion.[46]

"In the US we can buy a hamburger for 79 cents," explains cattle-rancher-turned-vegan Howard Lyman. "If the American taxpayer was not involved in subsidizing the beef industry, the same hamburger meat would cost over $12. Meat in America today would cost $48 a pound if it were not for the American taxpayers subsidizing the grain, the irrigation water, the electricity, the grazing on public lands. How many people—even in America—would go and spend that amount of money on meat if it wasn't subsidized? We can't afford roads, or schools, or health care, and yet we are paying $11.21 for every $12 of something that is helping kill one out of every two Americans today."[47]

"THESE PIGS HAVE GIANT GROWTHS ON THEIR LEGS AND SIDES."

> "I have no doubt that it is part of the destiny of the human race in its gradual development to leave off the eating of animals."—Henry David Thoreau

Like so many other aspects of American life, we've relinquished control of our eating habits to the corporate pirates and their well-paid propagandists, and in the process, surrendered part of our humanity. Thanks to decades of indoctrination, eating animals is as "normal" as breathing, while the consequent animal cruelty required to sustain this lifestyle is, at worst, considered a necessary evil on all sides of the political spectrum.

Before this issue can be addressed, it may help to explore the social conditioning that has lead to the prevalent belief that certain animals are to be eaten or used for overpriced clothes, others put in jail cells at a zoo, certain species bred as laboratory fodder, and still others force-fed cans of rendered roadkill in our studio apartments and called "pets."

"The conditioning starts early," proclaims anarchist author Larry Law. "We are taught to distinguish between different types of animals in the same way as we are taught to distinguish between different classes of people. Our first cuddly toys are animals, but usually little bears and lions, not cows or sheep. Our pets are our non-food animals, and well-conditioned people who eat white veal and battery chickens are often genuinely outraged that other people eat horses and dogs."[48]

Such conditioning enables us to perceive the breeding of animals for personal use as a natural outgrowth of being human. This perception, combined with the almost daily media mantra that those who oppose the use of animals as food or property are radical, out-of-touch tree-huggers, certainly helps keep the rabble in line (especially when progressives are a silent co-conspirator). Consequently, most of us not only see absolutely nothing wrong with eating certain animals and owning others, the very concept of wrong or right never even enters our thought process, vis-à-vis animals—even on the radical left.

Animals are not property. They are not entertainment, laboratory subjects, clothes, or shooting targets. Animals are not food. "It has nothing to do with being an 'animal lover'—some animals are not very lovable," Law concludes, "but would anyone expect that in order to be concerned about equality for a mistreated racial minority, you have to love each individual member of that minority—or regard them as cute and cuddly?"

Indeed, it's quite a psychological quantum leap to no longer perceive that adorable puppy as a commodity to be bought, spayed, and walked two times a day until death do you part (unless, of course, you meet up again thanks to pet food rendering), but this is precisely the type of emotional and cultural advance that may spur further introspection into our other illogical habits (i.e., operating health facilities on a for-profit basis, believing there's a difference between Republicans and Democrats, and renting oneself out eight hours a day).

The choice is ours.

"Everyone has a limited amount of time and energy," writes Peter Singer, author of *Animal Liberation*, "and time taken in active work for one cause reduces the time available for another cause; but there is nothing to stop those who devote their time and energy to human problems from joining the boycott of the product of agribusiness cruelty. It takes no more time to be a vegetarian than to eat animal flesh. When non-vegetarians say 'human problems come first,' I cannot help wondering what exactly it is that they are doing for humans that compels them to continue to support the wasteful, ruthless exploitation of farm animals."[49]

When you go vegan, you make a difference three times a day.

"MEAT IN AMERICA TODAY WOULD COST $48 A POUND IF IT WERE NOT FOR THE AMERICAN TAXPAYERS SUBSIDIZING THE GRAIN, THE IRRIGATION WATER, THE ELECTRICITY, THE GRAZING ON PUBLIC LANDS."

Suggested Reading

Coe, Sue. *Dead Meat*. Four Walls Eight Windows, 1995.
Eisnitz, Gail. *Slaughterhouse: The Shocking Story of Greed, Neglect, and Inhumane Treatment Inside the US Meat Industry*. Amherst, NY: Prometheus Books, 1997.
Francione, Gary L. *Rain Without Thunder: The Ideology of the Animal Rights Movement*. Temple University Press, 1996.
Harris, William, M.D. *The Scientific Basis of Vegetarianism*. Hawaii Health Publishers, 1995.
Law, Larry. *Animals*. Spectacular Times Pocket Book Series, 1982.
Lyman, Howard. *Mad Cowboy: Plain Truth from the Cattle Rancher Who Won't Eat Meat* New York: Scribner, 1998.
Moran, Victoria. *Compassion—The Ultimate Ethic: An Exploration of Veganism*. AVS, 1991.
Robbins, John. *Diet for a New America*. Stillpoint, 1987.
—*May All Be Fed*. New York: Avon Books, 1992.
—*Reclaiming Our Health*. HJ Kramer, 1996.
Wasserman, Debra. *Simply Vegan: Quick Vegetarian Meals*. Vegetarian Resource Group, 1991.

Suggested Websites

<www.madcowboy.com>, <www.earthsave.org>, <www.vivavegie.org>, <www.vegan.com>, <www.peta-online.org>, <www.vegsource.com/klaper>, <www.garynull.com>, <www.vegan.org>, <www.vegnews.com>, <www.satyamag.com>, <www.mad-cow.org>, <www.vegetariantimes.com>, <www.meatstinks.com>, <www.milksucks.org>, <www.veganoutreach.org>

Endnotes

1. Rice, Pamela. "101 Reasons Why I'm a Vegetarian"—pamphlet, 2001. **2.** "Why Vegan" pamphlet, published by www.veganoutreach.org. **3.** Robbins, John. *Diet for a New America*. Stillpoint, 1987: 60. **4.** PETA Website <www.peta-online.org>. **5.** Op cit., Robbins: 67. **6.** Coe, Sue. *Dead Meat*. Four Walls Eight Windows, 1995: 69. **7.** *Op cit.*, Rice. **8.** *Op cit.*, Robbins: 114. **9.** *Op cit.*, PETA Website. **10.** *Op cit.*, Robbins: 115. **11.** *Op cit.*, Rice. **12.** Dinshah, H. Jay. "Why Don't Vegans Use Honey?" *Ahimsa* (May 1961) **13.** Dinshah, Freda. "Don't Let Them Pull the Wool Over Your Eyes!" *Ahimsa*, #16-01. **14.** *Op cit.*, Rice. **15.** Harris, William, M.D. *The Scientific Basis of Vegetarianism*. Hawaii Health Publishers, 1995: 14. **16.** *Ibid.*: 16. **17.** Klaper, Michael, M.D., "A Diet for All Reasons," videocassette, 1992. **18.** *Ibid.* **19.** *Ibid.* **20.** People for the Ethical Treatment of Animals. "Can You Tell the Difference?" Pamphlet. **21.** Earthsave. "Realities for the 90's." Pamphlet. **22.** *Op cit.*, Harris: 40. **23.** *Op cit.*, Robbins: 188. **24.** Null, Gary. "Natural Living," radio show, WBAI 99.5 FM NYC, 1995. **25.** *Op cit.*, Klaper. **26.** *Op cit.*, Robbins: 193. **27.** *Op cit.*, Klaper. **28.** *Op cit.*, Rice. **29.** Lustgarden, Steve. "Fish: What's the Catch?" Earthsave Long Island newsletter (Summer 1997): 4-5, 13-4. **30.** See my article on mad cow disease: "Apocalypse Cow." *Gallery* (Aug 2001). **31.** *Op cit.*, Earthsave. **32.** *Op cit.*, Harris: 18. **33.** *Op cit.*, Earthsave. **34.** Schlosser, Eric. "The Chain Never Stops." *Mother Jones* (Aug 2001): 39-47, 86-7 **35.** *Op cit.*, Rice. **36.** *Op cit.*, Schlosser. **37.** *Op cit.*, Coe: 75. **38.** <www.earthsave.org>. **39.** Campbell, Susan and Todd Winant. "Food Choices and the Environment." Earthsave Long Island newsletter (Winter 1996): 10-1. **40.** *Op cit.*, Rice. **41.** *Op cit.*, Campbell and Winant. **42.** *Op cit.*, Earthsave **43.** *Op cit.*, Lustgarden. **44.** Rice, Pamela. "Extinction A to Z: Fish Stories We Wish Were Tall Tales" *Viva Vine* (Mar/Apr 2000): 3, 12 **45.** Rice, Pamela. "A Little Econ 101 for Vegetarians." *Viva Vine* (Jan/Feb 2000): 2. **46.** *Op cit.*, Earthsave. **47.** Lyman quoted in *Satya* magazine (Feb 1996). **48.** Law, Larry. *Animals*. Spectacular Times Pocket Book Series, 1982. **49.** *Ibid.*

"OUR PETS ARE OUR NON-FOOD ANIMALS, AND WELL-CONDITIONED PEOPLE WHO EAT WHITE VEAL AND BATTERY CHICKENS ARE OFTEN GENUINELY OUTRAGED THAT OTHER PEOPLE EAT HORSES AND DOGS."

In physics, we use the same laws to explain why airplanes fly, and why they crash. In psychiatry, we use one set of laws to explain sane behavior, which we attribute to reasons (choices), and another set of laws to explain insane behavior, which we attribute to causes (diseases). God, man's idea of moral perfection, judges human deeds without distinguishing between sane persons responsible for their behavior and insane persons deserving to be excused for their evil deeds. It is hubris to pretend that the insanity defense is compassionate, just, or scientific. Mental illness is to psychiatry as phlogiston was to chemistry. Establishing chemistry as a science of the nature of matter required the recognition of the nonexistence of phlogiston. Establishing psychiatry as a science of the nature of human behavior requires the recognition of the nonexistence of mental illness.

MENTAL ILLNESS: PSYCHIATRY'S PHLOGISTON

THOMAS SZASZ

■■■■■■■■■■

> There is no error so monstrous that it fails to find defenders among the ablest men.
> —Lord Acton[1]

People crave answers. Therefore, everyone may be considered a scientist, or at least a scientist manqué. The true scientist differs from the ordinary person in the depth, breadth, precision, and power of the account he accepts as the correct explanation for his observation, and in his willingness to revise it in the light of new evidence. In this essay, I show that mental illness is to psychiatry as phlogiston was to chemistry. Establishing chemistry as a science of the nature and composition of matter required the recognition of the nonexistence of phlogiston. Establishing "psychiatry" as a science of human behavior requires the recognition that "mental illness" does not exist.

_A BRIEF HISTORY OF PHLOGISTON

Chemistry began as alchemy which, in turn, was closely connected with medicine. Both Johann Joachim Becher (1635-1682) and Georg Ernst Stahl (1660-1734), two of chemistry's pioneers, were physicians, at a time when people believed that problems of health and disease are best explained in terms of the four basic Galenic humors.

One of the foremost problems early chemists tried to solve was combustion. What happens when a substance burns? Stahl proposed that all inflammable objects contained a material substance that he called "phlogiston," from the Greek word meaning "to set on fire." When a substance burned, it liberated its content of phlogiston into the air, which was believed to be chemically inert. The phlogiston theory dominated scientific thinking for more than a century.

However, it was observed that after a piece of metal was burned (oxidized), it weighed more than it did before, whereas according to the phlogiston theory it should have weighed less. This inconsistency was resolved by postulating that phlogiston was an immaterial principle rather than a material substance; alternatively, it was suggested that phlogiston had a negative weight. When chemists discovered hydrogen, they believed it to be pure phlogiston.

The phlogiston theory was overthrown by the work of Antoine Laurent Lavoisier (1743-1794). He named the fraction of air that supported combustion "oxygen," a term derived from the Greek words meaning "acid-producing," because he thought, wrongly, that oxygen was a necessary component of all acids. The major fraction of air that does not support combustion he called "azote," from the Greek words meaning "no life." Azote is now called "nitrogen." In an historic paper, titled "Memoir on the Nature of the Principle which Combines with Metals during their Calcination [Oxidation] and which Increases their Weight," delivered at the French Royal Academy of Sciences in 1775 and published in 1778, Lavoisier disproved the phlogiston theory and laid the framework for understanding chemical reactions as combinations of elements which form new materials.[2]

Once names and theories gain wide acceptance, they exercise a powerful influence on those inculcated to believe that their existence forms an integral part of the way the world is—in short, "reality." New observations are then "seen" through the lens of the prevailing system of mental optics. For example, Joseph Priestley (1733-1804), the great English chemist, could not relinquish the phlogiston theory, even after he himself had discovered oxygen and after Lavoisier's work swept the scientific world. He continued to view oxygen as "dephlogisticated air." In a pamphlet titled, "Considerations on the Doctrine of Phlogiston and the Decomposition of Water," published in 1796, he referred to Lavoisier's followers as "Antiphlogistians," and complained: "On the whole, I cannot help saying, that it appears to me not a little extraordinary, that a theory so new, and of such importance, overturning every thing that was thought to be the best established chemistry, should rest on so very narrow and precarious a foundation."[3]

_A BRIEF HISTORY OF MENTAL ILLNESS

While alchemy changed into chemistry, the soul changed into the mind, and sins became sicknesses (of the mind). The early alienists frankly acknowledged this metamorphosis. However, instead of recognizing that it was an early manifestation of a move from a religious to a secular outlook on human behavior, they attributed it to scientific advances and believed to have discovered a set of new brain diseases and called them "mental diseases."

What Georg Ernst Stahl was to early chemistry and phlogiston, Benjamin Rush (1745-1813) was to early psychiatry and mental illness. Rush was a physician and an American patriot. He signed the Declaration of Independence and served as physician general of the Continental Army and as professor of physic and dean of the University of Pennsylvania medical school. In 1812, he published *Medical Inquiries and Observations upon the Diseases of the Mind*, the first American textbook of psychiatry.[4] Rush is the undisputed father of American psychiatry; his portrait adorns the official seal of the American Psychiatric Association. In 1774, he declared: "Perhaps hereafter it may be as much the business of a physician as it is now of a divine to reclaim mankind from vice."[5]

WE HAVE ONE SET OF PRINCIPLES TO EXPLAIN THE FUNCTIONING OF THE MENTALLY HEALTHY PERSON AND ANOTHER SET TO EXPLAIN THE FUNCTIONING OF THE MENTALLY ILL PERSON.

To distinguish himself from the doctor of divinity, the doctor of medicine could not simply claim that he was protecting people from sin or "vice," as Rush put it. Badness remained, after all, a moral concept. As medical scientist, the physician had to claim that badness was madness, that his object of study was not the immaterial soul or "will," but a material object, a bodily disease. That is precisely what Rush did. His following assertions illustrate that he did not discover that certain behaviors are diseases; he decreed that "Lying is a corporeal disease. / Suicide is madness. / Chagrin, shame, fear, terror, anger, unfit[ness] for legal acts, are transient madness."[6] Today, some of these and many other unwanted human behaviors are widely accepted as real diseases, their existence ostensibly supported by scientific discoveries.

_THE CONGENITAL EPISTEMOLOGICAL ERROR OF PSYCHIATRY

Modern natural science rests on laws uninfluenced by human desire or motivation. We use the same physical laws to explain why airplanes fly and crash, the same chemical laws to explain the therapeutic and toxic effects of drugs, and the same biological laws to explain how healthy cells maintain the integrity of the organism and how these cells can become cancerous and destroy the host. We do not have one set of medical theories to explain normal bodily functions and another set to explain abnormal bodily functions.

In psychiatry, the situation is exactly the reverse. We have one set of principles to explain the functioning of the mentally healthy person and another set to explain the functioning of the mentally ill person. We attribute acceptable, "rational" behaviors to reasons, but unacceptable, "irrational" behaviors to causes. The mentally healthy person is viewed as an active agent: He makes decisions; he chooses, for example, to marry his sweetheart. In contrast, the mentally ill person is viewed as a passive body: As patient, he is the victim of injurious biological, chemical, or physical processes acting upon his body, that is, diseases (of his brain); for example, of an "irresistible impulse" to kill. "The epileptic neurosis," wrote Sir Henry Maudsley (1835-1918), the founder of modern British psychiatry, "is that it is apt to burst out into a convulsive explosion of violence.... To hold an insane person responsible for not controlling an insane impulse...is in some cases just as false...as it would be hold a man convulsed by strychnia responsible for not stopping the convulsions."[7] It is a false analogy. Killing is a coordinated act. Convulsion is an uncoordinated contraction of muscles, an event.

Because explanations of human behavior influence law and social policy much more pervasively and profoundly than do explanations of natural events, the mental illness theory of behavior has far-reaching implications for virtually every aspect of our daily lives. Law professor Michael S. Moore's following statement expresses a view now widely shared by lawyers, psychiatrists, and the general public:

Since mental illness negates our assumption of rationality, we do not hold the mentally ill responsible. It is not so much that we excuse them from a *prima facie* case of responsibility; rather, by being unable to regard them as fully rational beings, we cannot affirm the essential condition to viewing them as moral agents to begin with. In this the mentally ill join (to a decreasing degree) infants, wild beasts, plants, and stones—none of which are responsible because of the absence of any assumption of rationality.[8]

ATTRIBUTING ALL HUMAN ACTIONS TO CHOICE, THE BASIC BUILDING BLOCK OF OUR SOCIAL EXISTENCE, EXPLAINS HUMAN BEHAVIOR BETTER THAN ATTRIBUTING CERTAIN (DISAPPROVED) ACTIONS TO MENTAL ILLNESS, A NONEXISTENT DISEASE.

We are proud that we have all but abolished our prejudiced beliefs about the differences between the human natures of men and women or whites and blacks. At the same time, we are even prouder that we have created a set of psychiatric beliefs about the differences between the neuroanatomical and neurophysiological natures of the sane and the insane, the mentally healthy and the mentally ill. Oxidation, a real process, explains combustion better than does phlogiston, a nonexistent substance. Attributing all human actions to choice, the basic building block of our social existence, explains human behavior better than attributing certain (disapproved) actions to mental illness, a nonexistent disease.

A cause may operate momentarily or over time. A stationary billiard ball begins to move the moment another ball hits it. A broken hip makes walking impossible for days or weeks. Hence, it is not enough to say that a person pushes another in front of a subway train because he has schizophrenia and that schizophrenia is due to abnormal neurochemical processes in the brain.

We must also explain why he did so when he did so. The alleged condition, "schizophrenia," cannot do that, inasmuch as it has existed before the commission of the homicide and is said to exist in millions of persons who engage in no violence.

A person opens his umbrella when he goes out into the rain, because he does not want to get wet. A person pushes another in front of a subway train not because he "has" schizophrenia or because schizophrenia "makes" him do it; he does it because, like the man who opens an umbrella, he wants to improve his existence. We can explain a person's seemingly irrational act, too, by attributing it to a reason; for example, wanting to attract attention to himself or wanting to escape responsibility for housing and feeding himself.

In short, regardless of the condition of an "irrationally"-acting person's brain, he remains a moral agent who has reasons for his actions; like all of us, he chooses or wills what he does. People with brain diseases—amyotrophic lateral sclerosis, multiple sclerosis, Parkinsonism, glioblastoma—are persons whose actions continue to be governed by their desires or motives. The illness limits their freedom of action, but not their status as moral agents.

_ANSWERING OBJECTIONS

According to psychiatric theory, certain actions by certain people ought to be attributed to causes, not reasons. When and why do we seek a causal explanation for personal conduct? When we consider the actor's behavior unreasonable and do not want to blame him for it. We then look for an excuse masquerading as an explanation, rather than simply an explanation that neither exonerates nor incriminates.

There is a crucial difference between explaining the movement of objects and explaining the behavior of persons. Our explanation of the movement of planets is (today) devoid of moral implications, whereas our explanation of the behavior of persons is heavily freighted with moral implications. As a rule, we hold persons responsible for what they do, and do not hold them responsible for what happens to them. Agreement and disagreement, approval and disapproval, praise and blame are tacit elements of the vocabulary we use to explain personal conduct.

Holding a person responsible for his act is not the same as blaming or praising him for it—it means only that we regard him as an actor or moral agent. Blame or praise expresses judgment of his act, or of him as a person, as wicked or virtuous; in either case, it does not gainsay his authorship of his behavior. Conversely, holding a person not responsible for his act by reason of mental illness means that we do not regard him as a (full-fledged) actor or moral agent; instead, we regard him as a victim of his "illness." Although we pronounce such a person "not guilty" of the injurious act he has committed (say, murder), we nevertheless regard his act as deplorable, and we nevertheless deprive him of liberty. We have not proved that he lacks reasons for his behavior. We have merely offered a different explanation for his behavior (based on causes, not reasons) and provided a different justification for detaining him (based on medical rather than legal considerations). In short, the insanity plea, insanity verdict, and insanity disposition form a tactical package we use if we do not want to regard an actor as a moral agent and prefer to "treat" him as a mental patient.[9]

It is a mistake to believe that offering an excuse-explanation for an act is tantamount to showing that the actor has no reasons for his action. Offering an excuse for doing X—"God's voice commanded me"—is not the same as not having reasons for doing X. To the contrary, what we have shown is not that the actor has no reasons, but that his reasons are wrongheaded—"deluded," "mad," "insane." We conclude that his actions are caused by his being deluded, mad, insane. But we have not proven anything of the sort; we have postulated it.

Prior to the eighteenth century, people who committed heinous crimes and acted strangely were thought to resemble wild animals. Hence, the antiquated "wild beast" model of insanity and the defense based on it. Seeing the "deluded" person whose "voices" command him to kill as similar to an automaton or robot—that is, an object that performs human-like motions but is not human—is a modern idea. Accepting the assertion of a "schizophrenic" that he killed his wife because God's voice commanded him to do so is not evidence of the validity of the explanation. In my view, such a person kills his victim because that is what he wants to do, but he disavows his intention; instead of acknowledging his motive, he defines himself as a helpless slave obeying orders. As I have shown elsewhere, the so-called voices some mentally ill people "hear" are their own inner voices or self-conversations, whose authorship they disown.[10] This interpretation is supported by the fact that neuroimaging studies of hallucinating persons reveal activation of Broca's (speech) area, not activation of Wernicke's (auditory) area.[11]

The "mental patient" who attributes his misdeed to "voices"—that is, to an agent, other than himself, whose authority is irresistible—is not the victim of an irresistible impulse; he is an agent, a victimizer rationalizing his action by attributing it to an irresistible authority. The analogy between a person who "hears voices" and an object responding to information—say a computer programmed to play chess—is false. Mental patients responding to the commands of "voices" resemble persons responding to the commands of authorities with irresistible powers, exemplified by "suicide-bombers" who martyr themselves in the name of God. Both types of persons are moral agents, albeit both types represent themselves as slave-like objects, executing the wills of others (often identified as God or the devil).

These representations are dramatic metaphors that actors and audience alike may, or may not, interpret as literal truths. It is not by accident that, in all of psychiatric literature, there is not a single account of voices that command a schizophrenic to be especially kind to his wife. That is because being kind to one's wife is not the sort of behavior to which we want to assign a causal (psychiatric) explanation.

The facile, but fallacious, equation of mental illness with mental

> IT IS NOT BY ACCIDENT THAT, IN ALL OF PSYCHIATRIC LITERATURE, THERE IS NOT A SINGLE ACCOUNT OF VOICES THAT COMMAND A SCHIZOPHRENIC TO BE ESPECIALLY KIND TO HIS WIFE.

incompetence precludes an empirically valid and logically consistent psychiatric explanation of behavior. For example, a patient's belief that his wife is a witch may be a metaphor (for thinking that she is a bad person) or a "delusion" (similar to a false/self-serving/destructive religious belief, such as Abraham's belief that it is God's wish that he sacrifice Isaac). We do not view the person who acts on the basis of false information (say, a wrong time-table) as having no reason for his action. Similarly, we ought not to view the person who acts on the basis of false belief ("delusion") as having no reason for his action. We may, as I noted, want to treat such a person as not blameworthy. However, that is not the same as asserting that he acts without reason or that his deed is "meaningless" or "senseless," the terms typically used to dismiss the meaning or sense of heinous crimes.

The typical mental patient is a conscious adult who has not been declared legally incompetent. "Seriously mentally disordered patients neither lack insight, nor is their competency impaired to the degree previously believed," writes George Hoyer, a professor at the Institute of Community Medicine, University of Tromse, Norway.[12] Moreover, mental patients are regularly considered competent to do some things but not others—for example, competent to live independently, but not competent to reject psychiatric drug treatment; competent to stand trial, but not competent to represent themselves in court; competent to vote, but not competent to leave the hospital.[13]

Young children and senile persons engage, or may want to engage, in actions for which their reasons may be poor, indeed. But, again, that does not mean that their actions are not motivated by reasons. Bringing up children, "civilizing primitive people," forcibly converting people to the "true faith," rehabilitating criminals, and many other relations of domination-submission rest on the premise that the subject people's reasons for action are immature or erroneous and need to be "corrected," to enable them to enjoy "true freedom." As long as relations between psychiatrists and mental patients (especially "psychotics") rest on domination-submission, the idea of mental illness serves a similar set of functions—it explains the inferior person's (mis)behavior, exempts him from blame, and justifies his forcible control by psychiatrists.

"In 'The Myth of Mental Illness,'" observed University of Sussex professor Rupert Wilkinson, "the psychiatrist Thomas Szasz...did identify an important process—we might call it 'a chase through language.'... Our better natures, it seems, introduce words to promote compassion—but residual needs to despise and distance weakness will not be stopped.... [T]he terminology of mental illness substitutes labels of incompetence for labels of moral deficiency, and in a secular society this is no gift."[14]

_CONCLUSIONS

The word "mind" and the derivative term "mental illness" name two of our most important, but most confused and confusing, ideas. The Latin word "mens" means not only mind but also intention and will, a signification still present in our use of the word "mind" as a verb. Because we attribute intention only to intelligent, sentient beings, minding implies agency.

The concept of mind—as the attribution of moral agency to some persons but not others—plays a crucial role in moral philosophy, law, and psychiatry. Infants and demented old persons cannot communicate by language and are therefore typically excluded from the category of moral agents. In the past, persons able to communicate by language—for example, slaves and women—were also denied the status of moral agents. Today, many children and mental patients—possessing the ability to communicate—are denied that status. The point is that attributing or refusing to attribute moral agency to the Other is a matter of both fact and tactic—a decision that depends not only on the Other's abilities, but also on our attitude toward him. To be recognized as a moral agent, an individual must be able and willing to function as a responsible member of society, and society must be willing to ascribe that capacity and status to him.

PARADOXICALLY, THE OLD, PRESCIENTIFIC-RELIGIOUS EXPLANATION OF HUMAN BEHAVIOR IS MORE FAITHFUL TO THE FACTS THAN THE MODERN, SCIENTIFIC-PSYCHIATRIC EXPLANATION OF IT.

The dependence of moral agency on mindedness renders the judgment of impaired mindedness—that is, the diagnosis of "mental illness"—of paramount legal and social significance. Two common tactics characteristic of our age deserve special mention in this connection. One is treating persons as incompetent when in fact they are not—harming them under the guise of helping them. The other is treating persons as victims when in fact they are victimizers (of themselves or others)—excusing them of responsibility for their behavior (blaming their self-injury or injury of others on innocent third parties).

Paradoxically, the old, prescientific-religious explanation of human behavior is more faithful to the facts than the modern, scientific-psychiatric explanation of it. When man invents the Perfect Judge and calls Him "God," he creates an arbiter who does not distinguish between two kinds of conduct—one rational, for which man is responsible, and another irrational, for which he is not. Being held responsible for our actions is what renders us fully human—it is the glory with which God endows everyone, and the burden He imposes on everyone. Erroneous explanations of the material world lead to physical catastrophes, and false explanations of the human condition, to moral catastrophes.

Endnotes

1. Acton, JEED. *Essays in the Study and Writing of History*. Vol. 3. Ed. J.R. Fears. Indianapolis: Liberty Classics, 1988: 550. **2.** Donovan, A. *Antoine Lavoisier: Science, Administration, and Revolution*. Oxford: Blackwell, 1993. **3.** Priestley, J. *Considerations on the Doctrine of Phlogiston and the Decomposition of Water*. Philadelphia: Thomas Dobson, 1796. <www.web.lemoyne.edu/~giunta/priestley.html>. **4.** Rush, B. *Medical Inquiries and Observations upon the Diseases of the Mind*. 1812. New York: Macmillan - Hafner Press, 1962. **5.** Rush, B. Letter to Granville Sharp, July 9, 1774. Ed. J.A. Woods. "The Correspondence of Benjamin Rush and Granville Sharp, 1773-1809," *Journal of American Studies* 1.8 (1967). **6.** Rush, B. "Lectures on the Medical Jurisprudence of the Mind" 1810. Ed. G.W. Corner. *The Autobiography of Benjamin Rush: His "Travels Through Life" Together with His "Commonplace Book for 1789-1812"*. Princeton: Princeton University Press, 1948: 350. **7.** In Reynolds, E.H., and M.R. Trimble, eds. *Epilepsy and Psychiatry*. London: Churchill Livingstone, 1981: 4. **8.** Moore, M.S. "Some Myths About 'Mental Illness.'" *Archives of General Psychiatry* 32 (1975): 1483-97. **9.** Szasz, T.S. *Insanity: The Idea and Its Consequences*. New York: Wiley, 1987. **10.** Szasz, T.S. "'Audible Thoughts' and 'Speech Defect' in Schizophrenia: A Note on Reading and Translating Bleuler." *British Journal of Psychiatry* 168 (1996): 533-5. **11.** Szasz, T.S. *The Meaning of Mind: Language, Morality, and Neuroscience*. Westport, CT: Praeger, 1996: 124-9. **12.** Hoyer, G. "On the Justification for Civil Commitment." *Acta Psychiatrica Scandinavica* 101 (2000): 65-71. **13.** Alexander, G.J., and A.W. Scheflin. *Law and Mental Disorder*. Durham, NC: Carolina Academic Press, 1998. **14.** Wilkinson, R. "Word-Choosing: Sources of a Modern Obsession." *Encounter* (May 1982): 80-7.

Peter Breggin, M.D., Director of the International Center for the Study of Psychiatry and Psychology, testified on September 29, 2000, before the US House of Representatives, Committee on Education and the Workforce, Subcommittee on Oversight and Investigations.

PSYCHIATRIC DRUGGING OF CHILDREN FOR BEHAVIORAL CONTROL

PETER BREGGIN, M.D.

I appear today as Director of the International Center for the Study of Psychiatry and Psychology (ICSPP), and also on my own behalf as a practicing psychiatrist and a parent.

Parents throughout the country are being pressured and coerced by schools to give psychiatric drugs to their children. Teachers, school psychologists, and administrators commonly make dire threats about their inability to teach children without medicating them. They sometimes suggest that only medication can stave off a bleak future of delinquency and occupational failure. They even call child protective services to investigate parents for child neglect, and they sometimes testify against parents in court. Often the schools recommend particular physicians who favor the use of stimulant drugs to control behavior. These stimulant drugs include methylphenidate (Ritalin, Concerta, and Metadate) or forms of amphetamine (Dexedrine and Adderall).

My purpose today is to provide to this committee, parents, teachers, counselors, and other concerned adults a scientific basis for rejecting the use of stimulants for the treatment of attention deficit hyperactivity disorder or for the control of behavior in the classroom or home.

_ESCALATING RATES OF STIMULANT PRESCRIPTION

Stimulant drugs, including methylphenidate and amphetamine, were first approved for the control of behavior in children during the mid-1950s. Since then, there have been periodic attempts to promote their usage, and periodic public reactions against the practice. In fact, the first Congressional hearings critical of stimulant medication were held in the early 1970s, when an estimated 100,000 to 200,000 children were receiving these drugs.

Since the early 1990s, North America has turned to psychoactive drugs in unprecedented numbers for the control of children. In November 1999, the US Drug Enforcement Administration (DEA) warned about a record six-fold increase in Ritalin production between 1990 and 1995. In 1995, the International Narcotics Control Board (INCB), an agency of the World Health Organization, deplored that "10 to 12 percent of all boys between the ages of 6 and 14 in the United States have been diagnosed as having ADD and are being treated with methylphenidate [Ritalin]." In March 1997, the board declared, "The therapeutic use of methylphenidate is now under scrutiny by the American medical community; the INCB welcomes this." The United States uses approximately 90 percent of the world's Ritalin.

The number of children on these drugs has continued to escalate. A recent study in Virginia indicated that up to 20 percent of boys in the fifth grade were receiving stimulant drugs during the day from school officials. Another study from North Carolina showed that 10 percent of children were receiving stimulant drugs at home or in school. The rates for boys were not disclosed but probably exceeded 15 percent. With 53 million children enrolled in school, probably more than 5 million are taking stimulant drugs.

THE UNITED STATES USES APPROXIMATELY 90 PERCENT OF THE WORLD'S RITALIN.

A recent report in the *Journal of the American Medical Association* by Zito and her colleagues has demonstrated a three-fold increase in the prescription of stimulants to 2- to 4-year-old toddlers.

_LEGAL ACTIONS

Most recently, several major civil suits have been brought against Novartis, the manufacturer of Ritalin, for fraud in the over-promotion of ADHD and Ritalin. The suits also charge Novartis with conspiring with the American Psychiatric Association and with CHADD, a parents' group that receives money from the pharmaceutical industry and lobbies on their behalf. The attorneys involved, including Richard Scruggs, Donald Hildre, and C. Andrew Waters, have experience and resources generated in suits involving tobacco and asbestos. That they have joined forces to take on Novartis, the American Psychiatric Association, and CHADD indicates a growing wave of dissatisfaction with drugging millions of children. They have voiced their determination to pursue these kinds of suits regardless of any initial setbacks, exactly as they did before becoming victorious in the anti-tobacco suits.

The suits and the contents of the complaints are based on information first published in my book, *Talking Back to Ritalin*, and in my peer-reviewed articles.

_THE DANGERS OF STIMULANT MEDICATION

Stimulant medications are far more dangerous than most practitioners and published experts seem to realize. I summarized many of these effects in my scientific presentation on the mechanism of action and adverse effects of stimulant drugs to the November 1998

NIH [National Institutes of Health] Consensus Development Conference on the Diagnosis and Treatment of Attention Deficit Hyperactivity Disorder, and then published more detailed analyses in several scientific sources (see bibliography).

Table I summarizes many of the most salient adverse effects of all the commonly used stimulant drugs. It is important to note that the Drug Enforcement Administration (DEA) and all other drug enforcement agencies worldwide classify methylphenidate (Ritalin) and amphetamine (Dexedrine and Adderall) in the same Schedule II category as methamphetamine, cocaine, and the most potent opiates and barbiturates. Schedule II includes only those drugs with the very highest potential for addiction and abuse.

Table I: Harmful Effects Caused by Ritalin, Dexedrine, Adderall, and Other Similar Stimulants

Cardiovascular Function: palpitations; tachycardia; hypertension; cardiac arrhythmia; chest pain; cardiac arrest

Brain and Mind Function: mania, psychosis, hallucinations; agitation, anxiety, nervousness; insomnia; irritability, hostility, aggression; depression, emotional sensitivity, easy crying, social withdrawal; drowsiness, dopiness, reduced alertness; confusion, mental impairment (cognition and learning); zombie-like (robotic) behavior with loss of emotional spontaneity; obsessive-compulsive behavior; convulsions; dyskinesias, tics, Tourette's nervous habits (e.g., picking at skin, pulling at hair)

Gastrointestinal Function: anorexia; nausea, vomiting, bad taste; stomach ache, cramps; dry mouth; constipation; diarrhea; abnormal liver function tests

Endocrine and Metabolic Function: pituitary dysfunction, including growth hormone and prolactin disruption; weight loss; growth suppression; disturbed sexual function

Other Functions: blurred vision; headache; dizziness; hypersensivity reaction with rash, conjuctivitis, or hives

Withdrawal and Rebound Reactions: insomnia; evening crash; depression; overactivity and irritability; rebound (worsening of ADHD-like symptoms)

Animals and humans cross-addict to methylphenidate, amphetamine, and cocaine. These drugs affect the same three neurotransmitter systems and the same parts of the brain. It should have been no surprise when Nadine Lambert presented data at the Consensus Development Conference indicating that prescribed stimulant use in childhood predisposes the individual to cocaine abuse in young adulthood.

Furthermore, their addiction and abuse potential is based on the capacity of these drugs to drastically and permanently change brain chemistry. Studies of amphetamine show that short-term clinical doses produce brain-cell death. Similar studies of methylphenidate show long-lasting and sometimes permanent changes in the biochemistry of the brain.

All stimulants impair growth not only by suppressing appetite but also by disrupting growth hormone production. This poses a threat to every organ of the body, including the brain, during the child's growth. The disruption of neurotransmitter systems adds to this threat.

These drugs also endanger the cardiovascular system and commonly produce many adverse mental effects, including depression, anxiety, and obsessive-compulsive symptoms.

Too often, stimulants become gateway drugs to illicit drugs. As noted, the use of prescription stimulants predisposes children to cocaine and nicotine abuse in young adulthood.

EVENTUALLY, THESE CHILDREN END UP ON FOUR OR FIVE PSYCHIATRIC DRUGS AT ONCE, INCLUDING ANTIPSYCHOTIC AGENTS SUCH AS RISPERDAL, AND A DIAGNOSIS OF BIPOLAR DISORDER—ALL BY THE AGE OF EIGHT OR TEN.

Stimulants even more often become gateway drugs to additional psychiatric medications. Stimulant-induced overstimulation, for example, is often treated with addictive sedatives, while stimulant-induced depression is often treated with antidepressants. As the child's emotional control breaks down due to these combined medication effects, mood stabilizers may be added. Eventually, these children end up on four or five psychiatric drugs at once, including antipsychotic agents such as Risperdal, and a diagnosis of bipolar disorder—all by the age of eight or ten.

In my private practice, children can usually be taken off all psychiatric drugs with great improvement in their psychological life and behavior, provided that the parents or other interested adults are willing to learn new approaches to disciplining and caring for the children. Consultations with the school, a change of teachers or schools, and homeschooling can also help to meet the needs of children without resorting to medication.

_THE EDUCATIONAL EFFECT OF DIAGNOSING CHILDREN WITH ADHD

It is important for the Education Committee to understand that the ADD/ADHD diagnosis was developed specifically for the purpose of justifying the use of drugs to subdue the behaviors of children in the classroom. The content of the diagnosis in the 1994 *Diagnostic and Statistical Manual of Mental Disorders* of the American Psychiatric Association shows that it is specifically aimed at suppressing unwanted behaviors in the classroom.

The diagnosis is divided into three types: hyperactivity, impulsivity, and inattention. Under "hyperactivity," the first two (and supposedly most powerful) criteria are, "often fidgets with hands or feet or squirms in seat," and, "often leaves seat in classroom or in other situations in which remaining seated is expected." Clearly, these two "symptoms" are nothing more nor less than the behaviors most likely to cause disruptions in a large, structured classroom.

Under "impulsivity," the first criteria is, "often blurts out answers before questions have been completed." And under "inattention," the first criteria is "often fails to give close attention to details or makes careless mistakes in schoolwork, work, or other activities." Once again, the diagnosis itself, formulated over several decades, leaves no question concerning its purpose: to redefine disruptive classroom behavior into a disease. The ultimate aim is to justify the use of medication to suppress or control the behaviors.

Advocates of ADHD and stimulant drugs have claimed that ADHD is associated with changes in the brain. In fact, reports on ADHD from both the NIH Consensus Development Conference (1998) and the American Academy of Pediatrics (2000) have confirmed that there is no known biological basis for ADHD. Any brain abnormalities in these children are almost certainly caused by prior exposure to psychiatric medication.

_HOW THE MEDICATIONS WORK

Hundreds of animal studies and human clinical trials leave no doubt about how stimulant medication works. First, the drugs suppress all spontaneous behavior. In healthy chimpanzees and other animals, this can be measured with precision as a reduction in all spontaneous or self-generated activities. In animals and in humans, this is manifested in a reduction in behaviors such as exploration and curiosity, socializing, and playing.

Second, the drugs increase obsessive-compulsive behaviors, including very limited, overly focused activities.

Table II provides a list of adverse stimulant effects which are commonly mistaken for improvement by clinicians, teachers, and parents.

Table II: Harmful Stimulant Effects Commonly Misidentified as "Therapeutic" or "Beneficial" for Children Diagnosed With ADHD

Obsessive-Compulsive Effects: Compulsive persistence at meaningless activities (called stereotypical or perseverative behavior); increased obsessive-compulsive behavior (e.g., repeating chores endlessly and ineffectively); mental rigidity (called cognitive perseveration); inflexible thinking; overly narrow or obsessive focusing

Social Withdrawal Effects: socially withdrawn and isolated; generally dampened social behavior; reduced communicating or socializing; decreased responsiveness to parents and other children; increased solitary play and diminished overall play

Behaviorally Suppressive Effects: compliant in structured environments, socially inhibited, passive, and submissive; somber, subdued, apathetic, lethargic, drowsy, "dopey," dazed, and tired; bland, emotionally flat, humorless, unsmiling, depressed, and sad with frequent crying; lacking in initiative or spontaneity, curiosity, surprise, or pleasure

---

_WHAT IS REALLY HAPPENING

Children become diagnosed with ADHD when they are in conflict with the expectations or demands of parents and/or teachers. The ADHD diagnosis is simply a list of the behaviors that most commonly cause conflict or disturbance in classrooms, especially those that require a high degree of conformity.

By diagnosing the child with ADHD, blame for the conflict is placed on the child. Instead of examining the context of the child's life— why the child is restless or disobedient in the classroom or home—

the problem is attributed to the child's faulty brain. Both the classroom and the family are exempt from criticism or from the need to improve, and instead the child is made the source of the problem.

The medicating of the child then becomes a coercive response to conflict in which the weakest member of the conflict, the child, is drugged into a more compliant or submissive state. The production of drug-induced obsessive-compulsive disorder in the child especially fits the needs for compliance in regard to otherwise boring or distressing schoolwork.

_CONCLUSIONS AND OBSERVATIONS

Many observers have concluded that our schools and our families are failing to meet the needs of our children in a variety of ways. Focusing on schools, many teachers feel stressed by classroom conditions and ill-prepared to deal with emotional problems in the children. The classrooms themselves are often too large, there are too few teaching assistants and volunteers to help out, and the instructional materials are often outdated and boring in comparison to the modern technologies that appeal to children.

By diagnosing and drugging our children, we shift blame from our social institutions and ourselves as adults to the relatively powerless children in our care. We harm our children by failing to identify and to meet their real educational needs for safer school environments, better prepared teachers, more teacher- and child-friendly classrooms, more inspiring curriculum, and more engaging classroom technologies.

At the same time, when we diagnose and drug our children, we avoid facing critical issues about educational reform. In effect, we drug the children who are signaling the need for reform, and force all children into conformity with our bureaucratic systems.

Finally, when we diagnose and drug our children, we disempower ourselves as adults. While we may gain momentary relief from guilt by imagining that the fault lies in the brains of our children, ultimately we undermine our ability to make the necessary adult interventions that our children need. We literally become bystanders in the lives of our children.

It is time to reclaim our children from this false and suppressive medical approach. I applaud those parents who have the courage to refue to give stimulants to their children and who, instead, attempt to identify and to meet their genuine needs in the school, home, and community.

Abbeviated Bibliography

American Academy of Pediatrics. "Practice Guideline: Diagnosis and Evaluation of a Child With Attention-Deficit/Hyperactivity Disorder." *Pediatrics* 105.5 (May 2000): 1158-70. Also available at <www.aap.org/policy/ac0002.html>.

American Psychiatric Association. *Diagnostic and Statistical Manual of Mental Disorders*, Fourth Edition (DSM-IV). Washington, DC: author, 1994.

Breggin, P. *Talking Back to Ritalin: What Doctors Aren't Telling You About Stimulants for Children.* Revised edition. Cambridge, MA: Perseus Books, 2001.

Breggin, P. "Psychostimulants in the Treatment of Children Diagnosed With ADHD: Part I: Acute Risks and Psychological Effects." *Ethical Human Sciences and Services* 1 (1999): 13-33.

Breggin, P. "Psychostimulants in the Treatment of Children Diagnosed With ADHD: Part II: Adverse Effects on Brain and Behavior." *Ethical Human Sciences and Services* 1 (1999): 213-41.

Breggin, P. "Psychostimulants in the Treatment of Children Diagnosed With ADHD: Risks and Mechanism of Action." *International Journal of Risk and Safety in Medicine* 12: 3-35. By special arrangement, this report was originally published in two parts by Springer Publishing Company in *Ethical Human Sciences and Services* (above).

Breggin, P. *Reclaiming Our Children: A Healing Solution for a Nation in Crisis.* Cambridge, MA: Perseus Books, 2000.

Lambert, N. "Stimulant Treatment as a Risk Factor for Nicotine Use and Substance Abuse." Program and Abstracts, 191-8. NIH Consensus Development Conference, Diagnosis and Treatment of Attention Deficit Hyperactivity Disorder. 16-18 Nov 1998. William H. Natcher Conference Center. Bethesda, MD: National Institutes of Health, 1998.

Lambert, N., and C.S. Hartsough. "Prospective Study of Tobacco Smoking and Substance Dependence Among Samples of ADHD and Non-ADHD Subjects." *Journal of Learning Disabilities* (in press).

Zito, J.M., D.J. Safer, S. dosReis, J.F. Gardner, J. Boles, and F. Lynch. "Trends in the Prescribing of Psychotropic Medications to Preschoolers." *Journal of the American Medical Association* 283: 1025-30.

> BY DIAGNOSING AND DRUGGING OUR CHILDREN, WE SHIFT BLAME FROM OUR SOCIAL INSTITUTIONS AND OURSELVES AS ADULTS TO THE RELATIVELY POWERLESS CHILDREN IN OUR CARE.

EVERYTHING YOU KNOW IS WRONG

MYTHS ABOUT YOUTH
MIKE MALES

Interest groups and the news media routinely commodify American youth to the point where it is a shorter task to answer the question: Which of today's popularly-believed notions about adolescents is *not* a myth?

Are today's teenagers more violent than those of the past? No. Uniquely homicidal? Arguable. More criminal? Less so. More in danger of violent death? Safer than ever. Getting pregnant more? Less, actually. Smoking and drinking more? Less. Abusing more dangerous drugs? Far less. Spreading AIDS faster than adults? Not even nearly. More mentally ill? No. More suicidal? Far from it. Failing in school? No. Warped en masse by media images? Silly. More selfish? Dubious. Miserable, alienated, rebellious? Adults should be so optimistic. Eighty to 90 percent of youths consistently tell surveyors they're happy, self-confident, and get along with their parents.

Today's teens in general are more responsibly behaved than their Baby Boom parents were as kids or are as grownups today. This doesn't include every individual or subgroup, of course. For example, Columbine High School's Dylan Klebold and Eric Harris may have generated America's largest teen-killer body count, unless Charles Manson's youthful "creepy crawlies" have more 1960s victims buried. Further, there was a sharp, temporary spike in homicide and gun violence among poorer youth in the early 1990s.

> EIGHTY TO 90 PERCENT OF YOUTHS CONSISTENTLY TELL SURVEYORS THEY'RE HAPPY, SELF-CONFIDENT, AND GET ALONG WITH THEIR PARENTS.

Yet the many, many positive trends over the last 25 to 30 years have become taboo topics: the large declines in murder by grade-schoolers (down 40 percent from the 1970s to the 1990s), adolescent girls (down 35 percent), and middle-class and affluent youth (down 45 percent); the sharp declines in youthful drug abuse deaths (down 80 percent) and other violent deaths (down 20 percent); the general decreases in youth arrests (down 20 percent to 40 percent, depending on type). These figures refer to stable, long-term, population-adjusted rates. While choosing different base and comparison years would show worse trends for some measures and better ones for others, particularly cyclical ones, the results do not demonstrate that today's youth are uniquely at risk.

Thus, useful, nuanced analysis would explore which teenagers, which behaviors, and which time periods are being evaluated. American institutions and interest groups are well aware of the need to disaggregate "teenagers" into subgroups, to allow for individual differences, and to investigate multiple alternatives in order to make honest statements. Yet, virtually without exception, special interests choose to publicize only the particular "worst case" youths, measures, and time periods guaranteed to miscast modern adolescents as the worst generation ever. This isn't science or concern for young people, but transparent institutional self-interest founded in anti-youth biases.

How else can we explain why adult America, led by its most august experts such as Cornell psychologist James Garbarino, would anoint a dozen youths who conducted school shootings months and thousands of miles apart in the last five years as poster boys for an entire 25 million-member generation? Depict younger teenagers as more at risk today than at any time in recent decades, as the Carnegie Corporation does, when in fact they are safer than ever? Declare that teenagers display the biggest increases in serious crime while adult crime rates remain stable (according to Northeastern University's James Alan Fox and many others), when in fact teens display stable crime rates while adult felony rates have skyrocketed? Announce that teenagers show the biggest increases in HIV infections (White House Office of National AIDS Policy), when in fact they show among the slowest?

Major institutions, from the Heritage Foundation and Josephson Institute for Ethics to the Carnegie Corporation and Child Trends, regularly issue "studies" on youths, with redundant, always-alarming claims and remedies that would earn opprobrium if submitted in an undergraduate research methods class. Alarmingly often, "facts" (such as the repeated assertion that 5,000 teens commit suicide every year, 2.5 times the real number) are simply made up.

The universal ignoring of measures that dispute the "bad and getting worse" image of modern youth is not due to dictatorial censorship but to the suffocating consensus forged by a convergence of institutional interests. All sides, from those who would harshly punish to those who would reform by programs and education, require a continuing "youth crisis" to promote varied agendas advocating more prisons, police, after-school programs, nonviolence education, gun control, gun rights, legalized marijuana, zero tolerance for drug use, drug treatment, psychiatric treatment, censorship of objectionable cultural images, etc. No interest would benefit from admitting the massive, generation-long declines in youth risks or the socioeconomic bases for serious youth risks. No interest would benefit from admitting the massive increases in drug abuse, serious crime, imprisonment, and family disarray among Baby Boomers, the mainstream parents, voters, and consumers whom politicians and institutions seek to identify with and attract.

> ALL SIDES, FROM THOSE WHO WOULD HARSHLY PUNISH TO THOSE WHO WOULD REFORM BY PROGRAMS AND EDUCATION, REQUIRE A CONTINUING "YOUTH CRISIS" TO PROMOTE VARIED AGENDAS.

Whatever the lobby, two standard myths (several varieties of which are examined below) recycle endlessly. The most common is drastically exaggerating teenage problems to promote the need for the interest group's solutions; the other involves admitting improvements only for the purpose of claiming credit for them. This commodification of youth issues reflects a modern-American indifference toward the well-being of young people. They further reflect America's traditional institutional bias, one that hasn't changed in at least a century, that attributes social problems not to unhealthy social structures and mainstream values, but to the growth, bad behaviors, and lack of control of whatever unpopular demographic group is officially targeted at the time. These institutional biases produce faulty analyses and flawed policy, contributing heavily to America's inability to address its extraordinarily high rates of violence, gun casualty, drug abuse, unplanned pregnancy, poverty, and other social ills that set the US apart from peer Western nations.

_MYTH: TEENAGERS ARE MORE "AT RISK" TODAY

American youth do have some real problems. Thirteen million children and youths live in poverty (half of these in destitution, with family incomes less than half the poverty level); 350,000 are substantiated victims of violent or sexual abuses inflicted by parents and caretakers every year; and parents are a dozen times more at risk of drug abuse than their adolescent children. However, rigid political ground rules dictate that socioeconomics and adult behaviors are "off the table," drugs and violence may be discussed only as teenage issues, and all youths are "at risk" due to their own misbehaviors. Two major reports, by no means unique, serve as perfect examples.

The Carnegie Report. The October 1995 Carnegie Corporation study on younger adolescents, *Great Transitions*, is the epitome of modern "blue ribbon panel" reports. Like the 1987 *Risking the*

Future study of teenage pregnancy, the American Medical Association's 1990 *Code Blue* report on teenage health, and Child Trends' 1993 *Running in Place* study on families, the Carnegie report demonstrates the extent to which modern experts accept politically-driven "ground rules" that distort adolescent realities.

Carnegie's 135-page report, which claims to address the "underlying factors that contribute to problem behaviors," devotes two sentences and one chart to poverty, two sentences to child abuse, and one sentence to parents' drug and alcohol addictions. What do the other 134.5 pages of the report cover? Mostly a breathless roster of adolescent misbehaviors purportedly caused by adolescent attitude and developmental deficiencies in this dangerous modern age:

> Barely out of childhood, young people ages ten to fourteen are today experiencing more freedom, autonomy, and choice than ever at a time when they still need special nurturing, protection, and guidance. Without the sustained involvement of parents and other adults in safeguarding their welfare, young adolescents are at risk of harming themselves and others... [T]hreats to their well-being [include] AIDS and easy access to lethal weapons and drugs that were all but unknown to their parents and grandparents....

> The continuing decline in the health status of American adolescents is deeply disturbing. Since 1960, the burden of adolescent illness has shifted from the traditional causes of disease toward the "new morbidities" associated with health-damaging behaviors, such as depression, suicide, alcohol, tobacco and drug use, sexually transmitted diseases, including HIV/AIDS, and gun-related homicides... The vulnerability of young adolescents to health and educational risks is far greater than most people are aware of, and the casualties are mounting.

These statements show how freely modern experts fabricate complete nonsense about young people. In fact, adolescent health and behavior are improving, not declining.

First, the fact that "injury and violence have now replaced illness as the leading causes of death for adolescents" has been true since the mid-1950s not just for teens but also for adults up to age 40. It does not mean teenagers suffer rising violent death. Rather, it means many fewer teens die from infectious disease, such as influenza and tuberculosis, today than in the past, and many fewer teens than adults die from cancer and heart disease. These developments are highly positive, not cause for panic.

Second, let us compare risks among 10- to 14-year-olds in 1960 to those in the mid-1990s (the age group and time periods the Carnegie report chooses). In 1995, there were two million more American 10- to 14-year-olds than in 1960. Yet the National Center for Health Statistics reports there were 4,000 *fewer* deaths, including 600 fewer violent deaths, among ages 10-14 in 1995 than in 1960—a mortality decline of 45 percent! Further, the biggest declines in violent deaths among 10- to 14-year-olds were those likely to result from risky behaviors (drugs, guns, drownings, falls, hangings, etc., whether ruled suicide or accident). What might be called "society-inflicted" deaths (traffic wrecks, plane crashes, etc.) are down, but not as much. This pattern indicates that safer behavior, not just improved standards and medical technology, is a big reason for the death decline.

Homicide, a rare fate for this age group, rose. But most murders of 10- to 14-year-olds are inflicted by older teens or adults (often parents), not by peers. In fact, the Department of Justice and State of California cross-tabulations of ages of murder victims and offenders report that three-fourths of all murders of persons under age 18 are committed by adults. This crucial point has been almost completely omitted from the public discourse on "kids and guns."

Further, as discussed later, there are enormous disparities in gun deaths by economic status. White Anglo teens are less at risk than Hispanics over 40, blacks of any age, and white adults up to age 45. Thus, while authorities and the media deplore "children killing children," the fact is that the two most important factors in the murder of kids are both adult-caused: the imposition of high rates of poverty on youth, and the fact that most murderers of children and youths are adults.

Disease? In 1960, students missed an average of 5.3 school days due to illness, disability, or injury. In 1994, 4.5 days. Given the higher proportion of students with disabilities who attend public school today instead of being warehoused as in the past, this improvement is impressive.

Death, injury, illness, and disability should just about sum up "health status." Even by their own comparison criteria, Carnegie's portrait of grimly declining teenage health is erroneous on every count.

Third, lethal drugs and weapons were and are well-known to the parents of today's kids. In the late 1960s and early 1970s, when today's parents were that age, around 600 10- to 14-year-olds died from drugs or guns every year, about the same toll as among the same age group in the mid-1990s. Baby Boom youths suffered death rates from drugs, such as heroin and barbiturates, double to triple that of today's young people. AIDS was unknown in the childhoods of today's parents and grandparents, but at least 300,000 in these older generations contracted the disease in adulthood.

Fourth, having falsely posed a more dangerous world for teens,

Carnegie blames "youth culture" and innate teenage risks:

Today, information conveyed to adolescents comes largely from the media and peers. Much of it is incorrect or misleading or embodies values that are inimical to young people's self-image and health... Many parents see their teenagers drifting into an amorphous, risky peer milieu, popularly termed "the youth culture"... Often parents become perplexed, even angry, as they feel their authority weakened and their values challenged.

In fact, consistent research findings show powerful parallels between the values and behaviors of adolescents and those of their parents and adults around them. In one of many examples, the 1999 National Household Survey on Drug Abuse reports powerful correlations between rates of teenage binge drinking, smoking, and drug use and corresponding adult rates. However, while ignoring adult influences on youth, Carnegie's experts insinuate adults should blame adolescents for taking up "damaging patterns of behavior," since bad adult health is the result of "a time bomb set in youth."

THREE-FOURTHS OF ALL MURDERS OF PERSONS UNDER AGE 18 ARE COMMITTED BY ADULTS.

The Center for Adolescent Health Report. Carnegie's misrepresentations reappear in an influential 2001 report by the University of Minnesota Center for Adolescent Health, headed by Robert Blum. The Blum study claims that race, income, and family structure together explain only 1 percent to 2 percent of teenage risk variation, while individual behaviors (i.e., unsupervised time with peers) account for 20 percent to 40 percent.

The most astonishing aspects of the Blum study are how transparently the authors rigged it and that no major institutions protested. When evaluating the effects of race, income, and family structure on teenagers' behaviors, Blum study authors employed extremely broad definitions of "risk." Drinking one light beer on New Year's Eve was equated with getting drunk several times a week; having sex with a committed partner at age 17 was equated with doing the football team in sixth grade; carrying a pocketknife once was equated with shooting multiple victims; one fleeting thought about suicide in a year's time was judged equivalent to multiple real suicide attempts. Using such broad definitions erases differences between groups.

However, when evaluating individual characteristics such as hanging out with peers or difficulty in school, the Blum study authors switched to a detailed, 12-point scale which graded subtle behavior nuances. In this more realistic measure, one drink in a year's time was evaluated as far less risky than habitual drunkenness, and so on. Using detailed scales tends to enhance behavior differences between groups.

BABY BOOM YOUTHS SUFFERED DEATH RATES FROM DRUGS, SUCH AS HEROIN AND BARBITURATES, DOUBLE TO TRIPLE THAT OF TODAY'S YOUNG PEOPLE.

Then, the Blum study authors compounded their statistical malpractice by directly comparing social factors (race and poverty) evaluated by a procedure designed to minimize them with individual factors (too much free time, school failure) evaluated by a procedure designed to maximize them. This inconsistent method produced the authors' conclusion that poverty and racial issues were minimal factors, that concern about them represented backward thinking, and that attention should shift toward preventing individual teenage misbehavior through more controls, programming, and supervision.

The Blum study illustrates how far from real life modern institutional manifestos on adolescents have strayed, by design. In Blum's own state, Minnesota, dwell America's poorest African-American teens and near-richest white teens. Compared to white youth, Minnesota black youth are ten times more likely to have babies, eight times more likely to die violently, twelve times more likely to die by guns, and 40 times more likely to be murdered. So powerful is the effect of poverty that despite greater access to firearms (as shown in the General Social Survey), Minnesota white youth (like middle-class and affluent American youth elsewhere) have low homicide and gun-fatality rates similar to those of Canadian youth. Poverty and race (which is largely a surrogate for poverty) are correlated with 50 percent to 80 percent of these risk outcomes, not the 1-2 percent the Blum study predicts. Would Blum and colleagues seriously contend the biggest reason for these staggering disparities is that black kids have too much free time?

_MYTH: "YOUTH VIOLENCE" IS EPIDEMIC

Consider further the universal claim that youth today are more violent and are violent at younger ages than youth of prior decades. It is true that among the poorest segment of the teenage population, homicide arrests and deaths rose sharply in the late 1980s and early 1990s, a period in which adult murder was dropping. Beyond that, little stated on the topic of "youth violence" is accurate.

Several states keep consistent statistics over time for murder arrests by race and ethnicity, and these figures track homicide death trends in all states. They show the subgroups containing the vast majority of youth (suburban, rural, middle-class, affluent, and all females) experienced no increases, or declines, in murder. The "youth homicide" increase occurred only among a small segment of black, Hispanic, Asian, and poorer white youth mostly involved in gang warfare.

What caused this increase? The common explanations invoke combinations of natural teenage savagery, media violence, drug abuse, family breakup, gun availability, and gang battles. In fact, the chief

trigger was the explosion in hard-drug demand in the 1980s and 1990s, fueled by skyrocketing numbers of middle-aged, mostly suburban addicts. As drug abuse, hospital treatments, and deaths quadrupled among aging Baby Boomers, gang wars erupted among drug suppliers in inner cities plagued by high rates of poverty and unemployment. These resulted in temporary spikes in gun homicide and violence among young men at the street-level of drug distribution networks. As differences sorted out, homicide declined among inner-city males in the late 1990s to levels below those of the 1970s.

The contribution of each race to the increases in murders by youthful offenders in the above seven states from the trough in 1985 to the peak in 1991 (4 percent of the increase was by whites, 47 percent by Hispanics, 42 percent by blacks, 7 percent by Asians and other nonwhites) almost perfectly parallels estimates of gang membership by race. (This does not mean all youthful homicides are due to gangs, but that the *increase* in the late 1980s and decline in the mid-1990s were due to changes in gang killings).

Beyond the vastly oversimplified youth "gun violence epidemic," two 1990s manifestations in the commodification of "youth violence" are egregious. The first is the "adolescent superpredator," a creation of widely-quoted authorities such as UCLA's James Q. Wilson, Princeton's John DiIulio, Northeastern's James Alan Fox, and former Education Secretary William Bennett. The "superpredator," in DiIulio's description, was a new "fatherless, jobless, and godless" black or Hispanic gangster rogue whose vicious marauding would expand beyond traditional inner cities to menace suburban adults, creating an unprecedented "crime storm" (to use Fox's phrase).

When examined, the "superpredator" menace turned out to be a figment of crude statistical manipulations. The chief assertion by superpredator claimants, echoed widely in professional forums and in the media, is that while "overall crime rates are dropping, youth crime rates, especially for crimes of violence, are soaring" (DiIulio). This statement compares two incomparable measures: the National Crime Victimization Survey (which polls a representative sample of families about criminal victimization annually) and the FBI Uniform Crime Reports (which reports arrests for violent offenses reported by police agencies). If the Victimization Survey is cited, violence is down among all ages. If the FBI is cited, violence arrests are up among all ages. Part of the reason, the Office of Juvenile Justice and Delinquency Prevention (OJJDP) reports, is that police are making arrests for domestic violence and street offenses that were ignored in the past. Further complicating the problem is that the age of the offender is not known because only a small minority of violent offenses result in arrest; FBI "crime clearance" reports indicate adults commit more crimes per offender than youth do.

Fearsome forecasts of the coming "storm" of "superpredators" were equally vacuous. DiIulio simply multiplied the increase in America's general male youth population age zero to 17 from 1995 to 2005 (five million) by the 6 percent assumed in a *1948* study to engage in multiple offending to produce an estimate of 300,000 new juvenile "superpredators" who will "murder, rape, rob, assault, burglarize, deal deadly drugs, and get high...as long as their youthful energies hold out."

When it was pointed out by UC Berkeley criminologist Frank Zimring that the large majority of DiIulio's "superpredators" would consist of toddlers and gradeschoolers, and most would commit shoplifting and minor thefts rather than godless massacres, DiIulio reduced his projection to 30,000. Thirty thousand new thugs, even super ones, would hardly be noticed in a nation in which 12 million serious violent and property crimes are reported every year, in which one million more middle-aged adults ages 30-49 were arrested for violent, property, and drug felony offenses in 1996 than in 1980. The latter trend was completely ignored by all authorities, including Fox, who insisted that "mature" over-30 adults could not possibly commit much serious crime.

Fox, continuing his history of flatly-wrong 1970s and 1980s crime predictions based on overreliance on demographic trends, drew a straight line from the low point in juvenile homicide (1985) through 1994 and extended the trend to project a tripling in youth killers by 2005. Within two years of issuance, Fox's murder forecast was 250 percent too high. Contradicting Fox's and DiIulio's ever-upward predictions, homicide among black and Hispanic teenagers dropped 65 percent from 1993 to 1999, as it had after previous spikes in 1974 and 1980. In 2000, OJJDP chastised the youth-crime alarmists for their "fool's errand" and failure to mention the far more serious "middle aged superpredators."

The dramatic decline in inner-city gang killing in the late 1990s led to evolution of the "superpredator" theory. Now it was not the dark-skinned downtowner, but the white teenage "stone killer," who menaced the suburbs. Spectacular cases of brutal killings by upscale, icy-eyed white youths graced major media, from *People* and *Rolling Stone* to nightly newsmagazines, culminating in massive coverage of the school shootings of 1997 onward. The suburban-killer concept proved much more attractive to centrist and liberal interests, whose refutation to DiIulio's and Fox's racialized ghetto and barrio "superpredator" held that *all* teenagers *everywhere* were latent savages. If liberals thought such tactics, given the affluent white nature of the new menace, would head off draconian crackdowns and promote humane approaches, the result was the opposite.

The irony was that while the "superpredator" scare was attached to a real trend (as noted, gun murders and other violent crime temporarily doubled among black and Hispanic youths from the mid-1980s to the early 1990s), the suburban-killer furor contradicted clear trends. The seven states that kept long-term crime statistics by race and ethnicity—California, New York, Minnesota, Pennsylvania,

Oklahoma, Oregon, and Washington—all showed substantial increases in murder by black and Hispanic (and, where more detailed data were available, poorer white) youth in the early 1990s combined with very low rates and no increase among non-Hispanic white youth. By the late 1990s, states such as California and New York were reporting murder levels by Anglo white teens at their lowest levels since statistics were first kept, 30 percent below rates of the 1970s.

Thus, the school shootings and other killings by suburban and rural white youth in the late 1990s weren't manifestations of a rising violence trend but were rare anomalies amid generally declining violence. The only long-term survey of school violence, the Institute for Social Research's *Monitoring the Future*, reported both black and white youth in 1999 were safer from violence and weapons at school than at any time since the survey commenced in 1976. Even the supposedly new phenomenon of white school shootings was found to be an old one: Long forgotten school mass-shootings by white high schoolers occurred in the 1980s and 1970s (12 shot by a student at a rural New York high school in 1974; nine shot at a San Diego elementary school by a teen in 1979, for example) and perhaps earlier.

> FBI "CRIME CLEARANCE" REPORTS INDICATE ADULTS COMMIT MORE CRIMES PER OFFENDER THAN YOUTH DO.

The 1990s commodification of "youth violence" has devolved from propaganda to outright falsification. The motley pushers of the suburban-mayhem image (such as psychologists James Garbarino and David Elkind, the Josephson Institute of Ethics, the Heritage Foundation, the Carnegie Corporation, and a host of authorities) obliterated responsible analysis altogether. The new line, through the latest 2001 reports and commentaries, is that the "epidemic...of lethal youth violence...has spread throughout American society" (Garbarino). In fact, the opposite is true: Violence has become more concentrated. In the late 1990s, just 10 percent of California's inhabited zip codes accounted for four-fifths of its teenage gun toll and 90 percent of its teenage gun homicides. Occasional admissions that crime is diminishing and that schools are quite safe from serious violence are quickly dismissed by the non sequitur that violence "nowadays" can happen "anywhere, anytime."

_MYTH: TEEN SUICIDE IS "EPIDEMIC"

Other than children, teenagers are the least likely of any age group to commit suicide. Still, authorities—from the Centers for Disease Control to African-American physician Alvin Poussaint to media reports—assert today's teenagers (particularly black males) are blowing themselves away in record numbers. From these chilling statistics, theories abound: Modern youths are causing, and suffering, unprecedented dysfunction. More programs, more psychiatric interventions, more forced institutionalizations, and more abrogation of teenagers' rights are advanced in the name of protecting them from themselves.

In fact, the entire premise of a teen suicide epidemic, especially among blacks, is another lesson in misuse of statistics. The same references cited by interest groups actually show that modern teens, especially African Americans, are *less* likely to die by their own hand than at any time in at least half a century, and probably ever. How, then, have authorities manufactured the frightening image of rising adolescent self-destruction? By omitting massive changes in how deaths are classified. Consider the following numbers compiled by the National Center for Health Statistics:

> • In 1970, 1,352 black teens (ages 10-19) died from most-ly self-inflicted causes (drug overdoses, poisonings, falls, drownings, gunshots, hangings, suffocations, sharp instruments, and individual traffic crashes). Of these, 103 deaths were ruled suicides, 1,080 were ruled "accidents," and 169 were ruled "undetermined" as to intent (that is, the coroner couldn't figure out whether the person died accidentally or purposely).
>
> • In 1980, 767 black teenagers died from these same self-inflicted causes. Of these, 117 were ruled suicides, 596 were ruled "accidents," and 54 were ruled "undetermined."
>
> • In 1998, the latest year available, just 639 black teenagers died from these self-inflicted causes. Of these, 222 were ruled suicides, 375 were ruled "accidents," and 42 were ruled "undetermined."

On one hand, the total number of black teenage self-destructive deaths plummeted (1,352 in 1970, 639 in 1998). On the other, the number of black teenage deaths ruled as suicides leaped (103 in 1970, 222 in 1998). So, how can black teen suicide have "doubled" at the same time only half as many black teens are dying in accidents indicating suicidal intent? Consider a compelling possibility the experts overlooked.

In order to certify a death as a "suicide," a coroner must provide solid evidence (by a note or investigation) that the death was intentionally caused. For lack of resources or interest, pressure from families, religious concerns, insurance considerations, and other reasons, coroners are reluctant to rule a death (particularly a youthful death) as a suicide. A number of studies have found that coroners of past decades ruled hundreds of self-inflicted teenage deaths as "accidents" (or as "undetermined" as to intent) that, given today's more sophisticated diagnostic techniques, would now be ruled sui-

cides. Especially in Southern and rural areas, expending coroner time and money to investigate whether a black teen death was an accident or a suicide wasn't a priority. So, as Poussaint correctly suggests (refuting his own claim of a modern "crisis"), black suicide has been "historically underreported."

A startling example: In 1970, coroners ruled 169 black teenage deaths as "undetermined" because they couldn't (or didn't bother to) ascertain whether a suspicious, self-inflicted gunshot wound or drug overdose was accidental or intentional. In 1998, the number of black teenage deaths ruled as "undetermined" had fallen to just 42. Note that the supposed "increase" in black teen suicides (up 119 since 1970) almost perfectly matches the "decline" in black teenage "undetermined" deaths (down 127)—even without allowing for the bigger decline in mostly self-inflicted deaths ruled as "accidents" (down 705)!

More evidence: In California, where coroners traditionally consulted suicide experts to accurately certify questionable deaths, black teenage suicide *declined* by 40 percent over the last three decades. Meanwhile, in Southern states, black teen suicides "skyrocketed" from a scattering in 1970 to scores today. If some new, generational stressors are raising teen suicide, why is it falling sharply in California? These are the kinds of complications officials and experts are duty-bound to resolve before issuing alarming statements on emotional topics such as teen suicide—yet they did not.

Whatever the politics, the bottom line is straightforward. In 1998, there were 800,000 more black teenagers in the population than in 1970. Yet, among black teen males, suicidal deaths fell sharply, from 1,093 in 1970 to 549 in 1998. Among black teenage girls, the drop in self-demise was even larger: 259 deaths in 1970, and just 78 in 1998. By rate, then, today's average black teen male is 57 percent, and today's average black teen female is 73 percent, less likely to take his/her own life than their counterparts of 30 years ago. In fact, fewer black teens died by self-destructive means in 1998 than in 1950, when the black youth population was only one-third as large!

Among teenagers of all colors, similar but less dramatic improvements are evident. While teenage deaths ruled as suicides increased from 1,253 in 1970 to 2,054 in 1998, mostly self-inflicted deaths ruled as accidents plunged from 6,145 to 2,649 during that period, as did deaths ruled undetermined as to intent (518 in 1970, 190 in 1998). In 1998, teens had much lower rates of mostly self-inflicted death than teens in the supposedly tranquil 1950s.

Two conclusions are evident. First, the teenage suicide "epidemic" is an artifact of changes in death classification, not an increase in youthful self-dispatch. Second, teens display spectacular declines, not increases, in self-inflicted demise. Rarely do epidemiologists

MODERN TEENS, ESPECIALLY AFRICAN AMERICANS, ARE LESS LIKELY TO DIE BY THEIR OWN HAND THAN AT ANY TIME IN AT LEAST HALF A CENTURY, AND PROBABLY EVER.

record such rapid decreases in fatalities over such a short period. Yet the media and experts blare an incessant dirge that this increasingly healthy, resilient generation is killing itself at unheard-of rates.

Many groups justify their political tactic of "creating a crisis" as necessary to preserving support for the unquestionably fine, underfunded suicide prevention and mental health programs some youths need. But in the end, the myth of a teen suicide epidemic is not benign, no matter how humanely couched. It frightens the public that all young people are lethally out of control. It activates psychiatric industries (which a 1980s Congressional investigation found had unconscionably profiteered from spreading fear of teen suicide), programs gearing up to control, moralists eager to censor, police girding to suppress. We should be pondering why—despite more poverty, overcrowded schools, defunded services, dead-end jobs, family breakup, and incessant denigration by their elders—today's younger generation is *not* descending into self-hatred and suicide.

_MYTH: "MESSAGES" AND POLICIES DETERMINE "TEEN SEX"

In terms of reducing rates of pregnancy and HIV infection among American teenagers that far exceed rates in Europe or Canada, does it matter whether schools teach students "comprehensive sex and contraception education" or "abstinence only"? Not much. The evaluations that exist, mainly by ETR Associates and academic researchers, indicate the effects, if any, of sex education, abstinence education, and teen pregnancy prevention programs are small. The virulent sex education debate is another example of the way youth are commodified to serve conservative and liberal ideology.

> THE VIRULENT SEX EDUCATION DEBATE IS ANOTHER EXAMPLE OF THE WAY YOUTH ARE COMMODIFIED TO SERVE CONSERVATIVE AND LIBERAL IDEOLOGY.

Two factors, poverty and adult sexual behavior, can be used to create a formula that predicts rates of teenage birth, abortion, and miscarriage (that is, pregnancy) to within 10 percent of the true total. Ever since statistics were first compiled decades ago, and in every locale, trends in and rates of teenage birth, abortion, and miscarriage almost exactly parallel corresponding rates of adults around them. Not much room for all those other "messages" that preoccupy the left-right debate over "teen sex" today, such as TV and movie sex, comprehensive sex education or its lack, youthful ignorance, modern morality, or parents not "talking to their kids."

Part of the adult-teen statistical correlation stems from the fact that a large majority of what we call "teen pregnancy" involves adult partners. For example, California's comprehensive age-of-parent figures show a 23-year-old is more likely to father a baby with a junior-high mother (age 15 or younger) than is a junior-high boy. The Center for Disease Control's HIV/AIDS surveillance and STD surveillance show rates of infection among teenage girls from hetero-

sexual relations are three times higher for gonorrhea and syphilis, and nine times higher for HIV, than corresponding rates among teenage boys would predict. This indicates a large majority of sexual outcomes such as pregnancy and disease among teenage girls results from sex with men age 20 and older. These patterns, in turn, indicate teenage boys and girls are not sexual peers in the sense the media and programs depict. After a brief flurry of angry attention in the mid-1990s surrounding the welfare reform debate, the fact that most "teenage" sexual outcomes could better be termed "adult-teen" has largely been forgotten. As with many other impolitic realities youths face, this one did not suit political or program needs.

Nor does the overriding issue of socioeconomics. Where American teenagers enjoy the low rates of poverty common among European teens, American teens show the low rates of pregnancy and HIV rates found among European teens. For example, California's most affluent counties contain half a million white teenagers. Their annual birth rate (3 per 1,000 females ages 10-17) is similar to those of Sweden or Germany. A few hours' drive away, black, Hispanic, and Asian youths in the state's poorest migrant-labor counties have birth rates exceeding 50 per 1,000 females, similar to Ethiopia or Bangladesh. Race is not the factor. White-teen birth rates vary five-fold from richer to poorer counties, as do birth rates for other races.

When major teen-pregnancy lobbies acknowledge poverty as a factor at all, they imply that middle-class and affluent teens have similar pregnancy rates as poorer youth but were more likely to obtain abortions. However, surveys of abortion clinics by the Guttmacher Institute found abortion rates considerably higher among poorer youth as well, as are miscarriages. When the adult determinants of teenage sexual outcomes are considered, it is questionable whether "teenage sex" exists as a distinct behavior.

Despite strenuous, post-1975 efforts to reduce teenage childbearing, the birth rate among teens age 15-19 in 1999 versus the birth rate among adults age 20-44 remains exactly the same ratio (0.73) as it was in 1970 and 1950. So, while the late-1990s boom economy created more jobs and access to higher education that helped reduce birth rates among teens and adults to their lowest levels in decades, no fundamental reforms have occurred that would prevent youthful birth rates from rising again when conditions worsen.

Pointing out that family planning, sex education, and contraception provision are not "solutions" to "teenage pregnancy" and disease does not mean they're useless. To the contrary, these services have been connected for nearly a century to enormous reductions in pregnancy, birth, and disease throughout the world. But they only work in conjunction with political reforms that improve the status of women, young people, and poorer populations—that is, by supplementing the "incentive" to reduce births with the "means" to do so. But, by claiming their programs can reduce or eliminate unwanted teenage sexual outcomes without the necessity of socioeconomic reform, liberal sex-education and family-planning advocates sabotage effective policy by letting politicians off the hook for their failure to address youth poverty.

_MYTH: "MESSAGES" AND POLICIES DETERMINE TEEN DRUG USE

When I asked an assembly of 300 youths locked in Chicago's mammoth juvenile prison why so few kids are dying from drugs (only seven of the city's 900 overdose deaths in 1999 were teens), several shouted: "Because you can't die from weed!" Therein lies a powerful point both "War on Drugs" officials and those who would reform drug policy are missing. Drug reformers like the Lindesmith Center now insist that stopping teenage drug use should be the Drug War's most urgent priority, and decriminalizing marijuana for adult pleasure, as the Netherlands does, is the best way to do it. Their logic is that American teens who now acquire marijuana and other drugs freely through unregulated, illicit dealers would find drugs harder to get in a legal, adults-only market regulated (like cigarettes and beer) to forbid underage use.

> PART OF THE ADULT-TEEN STATISTICAL CORRELATION STEMS FROM THE FACT THAT A LARGE MAJORITY OF WHAT WE CALL "TEEN PREGNANCY" INVOLVES ADULT PARTNERS.

Lindesmith Center researcher Robert Sharpe recently wrote columnist Ann Landers that the Netherlands' policy of legalizing marijuana with "age controls" has "reduced overall drug use" and "protect[ed] children from drugs." Common Sense for Drug Policy sensibly argues for making drug treatment the top priority but obtusely urges a tripling in spending to promote teenage abstinence. The National Organization for the Reform of Marijuana Laws (NORML) states, "Marijuana smoking is not for kids," but that "it's time to stop arresting adults who smoke marijuana responsibly." Change the Climate advises parents that they can indulge their own pot pleasures while raising just-say-no kids. Drug reform groups showered accolades on the pro-Drug War, Drug Enforcement Administration-endorsed movie Traffic, largely because one young character absurdly said teenagers can get heroin easier than legal, "regulated" alcohol.

Before their new "save the children" campaign, reformers used to argue that legal, government-regulated alcohol and tobacco were the big teenage drugs-of-choice. They were, and still are, right. Consistent surveys show American teens use legal, age-regulated alcohol and tobacco 2.5 to 100 times more than illicit marijuana, ecstasy, or heroin. The 2000 Monitoring the Future survey shows that teens at every age find alcohol and tobacco far easier to obtain than every type of illicit drug, a pattern confirmed by use surveys.

The "save the children" crusades of both the Drug Warriors and the drug reformers distort Dutch and American drug realities. In fact,

American drug reformers who raise popular fears of mild teenage drug experimentation in order to win legal highs for today's dangerously drug-abusing grownup generation are pursuing tactics diametrically opposite of the Dutch strategy, which calms fear of youthful soft-drug use to redirect attention to treating middle-aged hard-drug addicts.

Contrary to Lindesmith's argument that protecting teenagers from their own drug use should be the "primary mandate" of drug policy, the Dutch enacted successful reforms precisely because they didn't panic over whether teenage marijuana use rose or fell. Conversely, American drug-reform groups don't seem to perceive that Drug Warriors stymie reform by whipping up America's moralistic terror over whether a youth smokes a joint now and then.

Those exercised over teenage pot-smoking must be horrified at the increase after the Dutch decriminalized marijuana. The Netherlands' Trimbos Research Institute found marijuana use in the previous month by Dutch 12- to 18-year-olds more than tripled from 3 percent in 1988 to 11 percent in 1996, then fell to 9 percent in 1999. American drug reform groups dodge that fact when they should be declaring, "So what?" Teenage marijuana use also soared in the 1990s in the United States and other prohibitionist countries, where "zero tolerance" ads, policies, arrests, imprisonments, and other punishments escalated. The US's National Household Survey on Drug Abuse found that 12- to 17-year-olds' monthly pot-smoking rose from 5 percent in 1988 to 8 percent in 1996, where it remains in 1999.

On the other side, Drug Warriors have shamelessly demonized the Dutch experiment. The worst (but by no means the only) distortion was former Drug Czar Barry McCaffrey's fib that "the murder rate in Holland is double that of the United States" and "the overall crime rate in Holland is probably 40 percent higher than in the United States. That's drugs." As European media and political ridicule mounted (US murder rates actually are eight times the Dutch rate, and the US crime rate is well above the Netherlands'), McCaffrey was forced to half-heartedly recant.

Today, Dutch teens use marijuana, heroin, cocaine, and ecstasy at about the same rates as US teens. Dutch teens use legal alcohol and cigarettes at much higher rates, as they always have.

Statistics on use don't matter, however. The important issue is that neither Dutch nor American teens show increasing or appreciable drug abuse. In both countries in the 1990s, for example, teens under age 20 comprised only about 3 percent of drug abuse deaths, with the vast bulk of drug abuse occurring among adults 35 and older.

Ignoring small differences in trends, levels, and age groups surveyed, it's a wash. Neither libertarian Dutch legalization nor draconian US prohibition has had any material effect on teenage drug proclivities. Obsession over "messages" drug policies "send" to teenagers reflects the exaggerated self-importance that Drug War combatants attach to their irrelevant squabble over "children and drugs."

What the Dutch decriminalization and harm-reduction reforms did achieve (in conjunction with comprehensive health care systems) is far more important: dramatic reductions in drug abuse among mostly older addicts. Heroin deaths dropped by 40 percent there from late 1970s to the late 1990s at the same time they were tripling in the US. Indeed, as the latest Dutch statistics show drug casualties falling, the newest US Drug Abuse Warning Network reports (1999 and 2000) show hospital emergency treatments and deaths involving drug overdoses soaring to their highest levels ever. From 1999 to 2000 alone, US cocaine emergencies increased 4 percent, heroin emergencies rose 15 percent, and methamphetamine emergencies leapt 29 percent, all reaching record peaks. Today, Americans are dying from heroin, cocaine, and methamphetamine at rates seven times higher than the Dutch are.

TEENS UNDER AGE 20 COMPRISED ONLY ABOUT 3 PERCENT OF DRUG ABUSE DEATHS, WITH THE VAST BULK OF DRUG ABUSE OCCURRING AMONG ADULTS 35 AND OLDER.

Both the appalling failure of America's War on Drugs to stem drug abuse and the encouraging realities of Dutch experience uphold harm-reduction reforms far more convincingly than the distorted claims about "protecting children" reformers make. Teenagers are not waiting with bated bong for the latest official "message" or "policy." Rather, teenagers' moderate patronage of soft drugs in Western nations appears to be a generally healthy reaction to the alarming damage they see hard-drug abuse causing among adults around them.

The Lindesmith Center's excellent 1997 research compendium, *Marijuana Myths, Marijuana Facts*, thoroughly reviews hundreds of studies. Though there are individuals of all ages who can't handle drugs and others who reasonably choose abstinence, the research findings report no medical, developmental, or other reason that adults should be allowed to use marijuana responsibly that would not also apply to teens. Young age is not a valid criterion for discrimination; it is merely a politically convenient target.

_MYTH: TOUGHER CONTROLS PRODUCE BETTER KIDS

Increasingly over the last 25 years, panaceas have reigned. Teenage drinking? Raise the drinking age and ban it. School discipline? Impose zero tolerance and uniforms. Drugs? Zero tolerance, and mass-test kids. Youth crime? Curfews, adult trials, adult imprisonment, even execution.

Initiated with increasing fervor during the 1990s, panaceas have three main features: They don't cost much, they do nothing to affect the larger values and conditions that powerfully affect youth behavior, and they never apply to the panacea's perpetrator. Youth curfews, school uniforms, student drug-testing, "zero tolerance," V-chips, music and movie labeling, Internet censorship, youth firearms bans, character education, and other cure-alls are wildly popular with policy makers precisely because they don't disturb grownup freedoms. But do they work?

Consider the panacea acclaimed as the most effective: The National Highway Traffic Safety Administration claims in its 1999 report that outlawing under-21 alcohol use "saved 19,121 lives" since 1975. The number is junk. The NHTSA multiplied 2.5-fold the small reduction in teenage traffic fatalities from an outdated Insurance Institute for Highway Safety study that used 1984 data. This study found that in states that raised drinking ages, traffic deaths fell 9 percent more among 18- to 20-year-olds than among drivers age 21-24.

But even if the NHTSA number is embellished, didn't the bulk of research summarized in a General Accounting Office report find the drinking age of 21 saves some lives? Yes, at first. However, more comprehensive, long-term research reports more complex results. The 21 drinking age has a "seesaw" effect: Teen deaths go down a bit, but adult deaths rise. Rutgers and Baltimore University economists Peter Asch and David Levy (consultant for safety lobbies) reported that raising the drinking age to 21 slightly reduced fatal crashes by 18- to 20-year-old drivers at the expense of more deaths among 21- to 24-year-olds. The "legal drinking age has no perceptible influence on fatalities," their exhaustive, federally-funded study concluded, "but inexperience in drinking is an apparent risk factor independent of age."

Their findings were confirmed in a 2001 paper by Swarthmore and University of Maryland economists Thomas Dee and William Evans. "The nationwide increases in MLDA (minimum legal drinking age) may have merely shifted some of the fatality risks from teens to young adults," they conclude after examining multiple factors. Raising drinking ages from 19 to 21 cut 18- and 19-year-olds' traffic deaths by 5 percent but increased fatalities among 22- and 23-year-olds by 8 percent. "The magnitude of mortality redistribution," Dee/Evans report, "is quite large."

These findings suggest the 21 drinking age doesn't save lives; it merely postpones deaths, perhaps even increases them. Why? Because "learning by doing" is "an important component of teens' maturation," Dee and Evans note. To the extent that age-based prohibition prevents adolescents from accomplishing their necessary task of practicing adult behaviors in adult settings, risks accumulate in more perilous young-adult years where family and peer controls are weaker. (Nor is risk-taking an "adult right"; in 40 percent of the drunken accidents that kill teens and 90 percent that kill children, the drunk driver at fault is over age 21.) Experimentation with adult behaviors is an essential part of adolescence that adults can guide or hamper, but not prevent.

Recent panaceas, initially greeted with glowing political accolades, aren't even surviving the first round of research. Controlled studies of youth curfews in New Orleans, Cincinnati, Connecticut, New Jersey, and California cities find them either ineffective or contributory to higher crime rates. Large-scale reports by Notre Dame University and staid Educational Testing Service researchers found school uniforms were not associated with improvements in student behaviors, attendance, or attitude—but they did accompany reduced academic achievement. ETS also found schools' "zero tolerance" policies ineffective in combating drug use or gangs.

In short, the fear, mythmaking, and repressive policies governing American attitudes toward youth are interfering with improvements that young people are making on their own. The question now is, how much more harm are institutions willing to inflict on adolescents in their futile crusade to abolish adolescence?

CONTROLLED STUDIES OF YOUTH CURFEWS FIND THEM EITHER INEFFECTIVE OR CONTRIBUTORY TO HIGHER CRIME RATES.

Sources

Youth risk, suicide, drug abuse, and violent death data are from:
Asch, P., and D.T. Levy. "Does the Minimum Drinking Age Affect Traffic Fatalities?" *Journal of Policy Analysis & Management* 6.2 (1987): 180-92.
Blum, R., *et al. Protecting Teens: Beyond Race, Income, and Family Structure*. Minneapolis: University of Minnesota, Center for Adolescent Health, 2001.
Carnegie Corporation on Adolescent Development. *Great Transitions: Preparing Adolescents for a New Century*. New York: Carnegie Corporation, 1995.
Dee, T.S. and W.N. Evans. "Behavioral Policies and Teen Traffic Safety." *AEA Papers and Proceedings* (May 2001): 91-6.
Drug Abuse Warning Network. *Annual Emergency Department Data* and *Annual Medical Examiner Data*. Washington, DC: Substance Abuse and Mental Health Services Administration, US Department of Health and Human Services, 1980-1999.
National Institute on Drug Abuse. *National Household Survey on Drug Abuse*. Washington, DC: US Department of Health and Human Services, 1975-2000.
Johnston, L., *et al. Monitoring the Future*. Ann Arbor: Institute for Social Research, University of Michigan, 1975-2000.
National Center for Health Statistics. *Vital Statistics of the United States*, Part I, Mortality (annual report), and US Mortality Detail File (electronic data file). Washington, DC: US Department of Health and Human Services, 1968-98.

National crime, victimization, and policy data are from:
Bureau of Justice Statistics. *Criminal Victimization in the United States*. Washington, DC: US Department of Justice, 1973-2000.
Bureau of Justice Statistics. *Sourcebook of Criminal Justice Statistics*. Washington, DC: US Department of Justice, 1973-99.
Criminal Justice Statistics Center. *Crime & Delinquency in California* (1970-1999), and its annual supplement, *California Criminal Justice Profiles* (1977-1999). Sacramento: California Department of Justice.
Donohue E., V. Schiraldi, J. Ziedenberg. *Schoolhouse Hype: School Shootings and the Real Risks Kids Face in America*. Washington, DC: Justice Policy Institute, 1998.
Federal Bureau of Investigation. *Uniform Crime Reports for the United States*. Washington, DC: US Department of Justice, 1970-1999.
Males, M. "Vernon, Connecticut's, Juvenile Curfew: The Situations of Youths Cited and Effects on Crime." *Criminal Justice Policy Review* 11.3 (Sept 2000): 254-67.
School-Associated Violent Deaths. National School Safety Center. Continually updated 2001 <http://www.nssc1.org>.

Office of Juvenile Justice and Delinquency Prevention. *Juvenile Offenders and Victims, 1999 National Update*. Washington, DC: US Department of Justice, 2000.

"Things started out pretty good the first couple of years. Then, she slowly changed. She always had a temper, but then we got into some money problems, and it got worse. She would get mad, and it would escalate all out of proportion. She'd start hitting. She'd slap at my face, and then keep slapping and try to scratch me. I'd put up my arms, or just grab and hold her hands. I never hit her back. I was just taught that you never hit a woman."
—Joe S.

THE WHOLE TRUTH ABOUT DOMESTIC VIOLENCE

PHILIP W. COOK

Joe S. is one of 40 male victims of domestic violence whom I interviewed over a two-year period. Canadian researcher Lesley Gregorash and Dr. Malcolm George in England have interviewed a similar number of such men. This apparently represents the sum total of all such men who have been the subject of in-depth published interviews. Despite this scarcity of field research, some common patterns of behavior by victims and abusers have emerged; perhaps the most striking is the similarity between female and male victims and their abusers. Of the differences, the biggest is one of public and personal perception. In most cases, male victims are stuck in a time warp; they find themselves in the same position that women were in nearly 30 years ago. Despite the overwhelming number of male victims of domestic abuse, their problem is viewed as of little consequence, or they are seen to be somehow to blame for it.

With support from the National Institute of Mental Health, two researchers—Murray Straus, Ph.D., and Richard Gelles, Ph.D., from the Family Research Laboratory at the University of New Hampshire—conducted a nationally representative survey of married and cohabiting couples regarding domestic violence. The results were first published in 1977, followed by a book, with coauthor Suzanne Stienmetz, Ph.D., in 1980. Straus and Gelles followed up the initial survey of more than 2,000 couples with a larger 6,000-couple group in 1985.

By 1985, the incident rates for minor violence (slap, spank, throw something, push, grab, or shove) were equal for men and women. In severe violence (kick, bite, hit with a fist, hit or try to hit with an object, beat up the other, threaten with a knife or gun, use a knife or gun), more *men* were victimized than women. The first survey had shown an equal amount of domestic violence for each gender, but the 1985 results showed a decrease of female victims, while the number of male victims remained the same. Projecting the 1985 study onto the national population of married couples, the results showed more than eight million couples a year engaging in some form of domestic violence, with 1.8 million female victims of severe violence and 2 million male victims of severe violence.[1] To put this another way: A woman is assaulted by a domestic partner every eighteen seconds; a man, every fifteen seconds.

If couples not currently living together were included, the figure would likely be higher. These totals come with a qualification that is rarely mentioned, however; the surveys asked only if a particular type of violence occurred at least once in the past year. Other studies indicate severe repeated battering attacks to be much less common.

These figures for abused women—especially the "one woman every eighteen seconds" statistic—are the most often quoted numbers regarding domestic violence in support of funding and attention for the problem. Almost always, the equal or greater number of male victims, which were found in the *same* surveys, is simply ignored. But accepting the Family Research Laboratory results for women should mean having to accept the same source for male victimization.

US Justice Department and other crime surveys show a much lower rate of domestic violence for both men and women. The Family Research Laboratory surveys are recognized, however, as being more accurate since they are based on a nationally representative sample, are not labeled a crime survey, and cover a range of violent actions that Justice Department surveys neglect. The Family Research Laboratory results have been upheld by other studies in the US, Canada, and Britain. In fact, a review of published academic literature by Martin Fiebert, Ph.D., at the University of California Long Beach found 70 empirical studies, fifteen reviews and/or analyses, and 85 scholarly investigations which demonstrate that women are as physically aggressive, or more aggressive, than men in their relationships with their spouses or opposite-sex partners.[2]

The number of studies coming to the same conclusion continues to grow. This author, R.L. McNeely, Ph.D., and Jose Torres, Ph.D., at the University of Wisconsin recently published a review and discussion of the history and results of such studies in *The Journal of Human Behavior in the Social Environment*.[3] The evidence from all over the world is there for anyone choosing to look. For example, Terrie Moffitt, a University of Wisconsin psychology professor, performed a New Zealand study that supported the Family Violence survey data, showing that wives hit their husbands at least as often as husbands hit their wives. Even in the pro-feminist, progressive magazine *Mother Jones*, the results of this study were given prominent play: "In addition, Moffit found that her in-depth survey of more than 800 couples found that, 'female perpetrators of partner violence differed from nonviolent women with respect to factors that could not be solely the result of being in a violent relationship.' Her research disputes a long-held belief about the nature of domestic violence: If a woman hits, it's only in response to her partner's attacks. The study suggests that some women may be prone to violence—by nature and circumstance—just as some men may be."[4]

In the UK, the British Home Office, in yet another nationally representative sample, found the same thing, as have researchers in Canada.[5] In fact, when one considers all the peer-reviewed, published sociological studies of domestic violence in which both men and women are surveyed in random or nationally representative samples, there is not a single one that does not conclude that men make up a highly significant number of domestic violence victims.

■ ■ ■ ■ ■ ■ ■ ■ ■ ■

Most domestic violence is mutual, and most would not happen if there were not a history of such violence in the family of origin.

By their own admission in the sociological surveys, women hit first at about the same rate as men do. About half of all incidents of violence is one-sided; the rest is mutual combat (the woman who slaps or throws things greatly increases her chances of being hit in return). More important, the sons of violent parents have a rate of wife-beating 1,000 percent greater than those of nonviolent parents. The daughters of violent parents have a husband-beating rate 600 percent greater. Only about 10 percent of violent couples have a nonviolent family history. Ignoring violent women, and concentrating solely on inhibiting violent men, contributes to the cycle of violence for the next generation.

Certainly, a man slapping or shoving a woman is much more likely to inflict injury than a woman slapping or shoving a man. Since much more domestic violence falls into the "general violence" category, there should be more injuries for women. An examination of 6,200 police and hospital reports by Maureen McLeod, Ph.D., however, found that men suffered severe injuries more often than women did in domestic encounters. Seventy-four percent of the men reported some injury, while injuries among women averaged 57 percent.[6] The reason being that when domestic violence falls into the "severe" category, women are more likely to use a weapon than are men. In McLeod's study, 63 percent of the men faced a deadly weapon, while only 15 percent of the women did. A report published in the *Annals of Emergency Medicine* at one inner-city emergency room found a slightly higher number of males than females seeking treatment for domestic violence injuries.[7]

BY THEIR OWN ADMISSION IN THE SOCIOLOGICAL SURVEYS, WOMEN HIT FIRST AT ABOUT THE SAME RATE AS MEN DO.

It may seem surprising, but accurate data about domestic violence injuries is actually hard to come by. There is, in fact, only one nationally representative survey of injuries from domestic violence in which emergency-room personnel were specifically asked to denote the cause of injury from assaults. (Other surveys depend on respondents to reveal what happened to themselves or, as in McLeod's survey, on what is reported to police). This 1994 Justice Department report found that out of all injury assaults being treated in the ER (including partner rape), 17 percent was due to domestic violence (14 percent women and 3 percent men).[8] Even this large-scale hospital survey, however, has deficiencies. The relationship to the assailant was unknown for one-fifth of the cases involving women and fully one-third of the cases involving men. Thus, underreporting of possible domestic violence injuries in the ER is significant for women victims and substantial for male victims.

As with any significant social problem, it is important to look at the large body of research in order to determine the extent of the issue. When it comes to domestic violence data, particularly when dealing with injury rates, it is critical that advocacy-based statements be noted. I can think of no other significant social issue in which advocates' statements are so frequently taken as factual without question, then repeated by the news media and government officials.

Here is a perfect example. Former Secretary of Health and Human Services Donna Shalala told the American Medical Association's National Conference on Family Violence: "We do know that 20 to 30 percent of the injuries that send women to the emergency room stem from physical abuse by their partners."[9] These high figures are not supported by the research. The notion that they are tenable comes from the same source that proclaims that domestic violence is a more frequent cause of injury to women than heart attacks, muggings, rape, and even car accidents! That source, specifically, is the duo of Evan Stark and Anne Flitcraft, who examined ER records and classified *any* injury caused by another person (stranger or not) as a case of domestic violence.[10] In questioning from one reporter, Stark finally admitted: "Maybe domestic violence is the leading cause of injury and maybe it isn't."[11]

Nevertheless, the "one-third of all injuries in the ER" myth is repeated frequently not only in advocate literature, but also by the AMA, the American Bar Association, US Surgeons General, and many others. But even if we assume that all of the unknown relationship assaults in the Justice Department ER survey were due to domestic violence, that *still* would not approach 30 percent, or even 20 percent, of all ER admissions for women. Remember, the 14 percent of female domestic-violence injuries were out of all *assaults* in the ER, not out of total treatments for all causes, as Shalala and other advocates want the public and professionals to believe.

The rule seems to be that the more unbelievable the statement about the number of female victims of domestic violence, the more likely that same source is to ignore the existence of male victims. I devote most of a chapter to the many examples of this selective inattention in my book, *Abused Men: The Hidden Side of Domestic Violence*, so I can't do it justice in this essay, but I will mention a very important example that occurred after publication of that book.

"Every twelve seconds another woman is beaten. That's nearly 900,000 victims every year."[12] When President Clinton made this statement, I guess the calculators were already packed. Nine hundred thousand victims a year does not equal one every twelve seconds. What is really hilarious is that the figure of 900,000 is closer to the number of *male* victims each year, according to the survey funded by the very act he was signing into law. That law was the reauthorization of the Violence Against Women Act (providing nearly $5 billion over five years). The resulting survey found 1.5 million female victims each year—and 835,000 male victims. To put it another way, well over a third of the victims were found to be men.[13]

The authors of this survey went to great pains to justify a greater attention to female victims due to their findings regarding injuries. They found that women were twice as likely to report being injured in the most recent assault compared to men (41.5 percent vs. 19.9 percent). However, lead researcher Patricia Tjaden, in a recorded interview, stated the obvious: "Clearly there are a significant number of male victims. The study should not be taken to mean there should be no concern or resources for them."[14]

"CLEARLY THERE ARE A SIGNIFICANT NUMBER OF MALE VICTIMS."

Apparently, when it comes to inflicting injury, it's just a matter of style. Women probably suffer a greater amount of total injuries, ranging from mild to serious, because they are struck with the most ready instrument, the human hand, which will cause greater damage coming from a man than from a woman. But when it comes to serious injuries where weapons and objects come into play, the injury rate is about the same or perhaps greater for men. Stylistic differences aside, the result is the same for their partners: injury and intimidation.

■ ■ ■ ■ ■ ■ ■ ■ ■ ■

A discussion of domestic violence and injury would not be complete without examining the ultimate form of abuse—murder.

The numbers show that a woman is nearly 25 percent more likely to be killed by her husband than a man is to be killed by his wife (however, the rate is virtually equal for black couples).[15] In the last 20

THE WHOLE TRUTH ABOUT DOMESTIC VIOLENCE
PHILIP W. COOK

years, there has been a remarkable stability in the average spousal murder rate. What is important to note, though, is that prior to this period there was no difference between the sexes: Wives killed husbands at about the same rate that husbands killed wives. Why the change? In a review of my book on Amazon.com, Katherine Van Wormer from the University of Northern Iowa wrote, "What people need to realize is that women's shelters are saving the lives of more men than women. Women are not murdering men like they were due to the fact that they were killing out of fear. Now they have the shelter option." She said that because of this and another factor which I will address later, my book has "misleading conclusions."[16] The misleading conclusion, however, may be Van Wormer's.

A COMPREHENSIVE EXAMINATION BY CORAMAE MANN IN *JUSTICE QUARTERLY* FOUND THAT MOST FEMALE SPOUSE-KILLERS DO NOT MURDER OUT OF FEAR OR SELF-DEFENSE.

First, while it is certainly true that many women murder their spouses out of fear, that is not the case a majority of the time. A comprehensive examination by Coramae Mann in *Justice Quarterly* (explored in detail in my book, which I guess Van Wormer chose to ignore) found that most female spouse-killers do not murder out of fear or self-defense.[17] Some murder out of greed, others because they have taken a new lover, and for a variety of other reasons. There are many such cases in the anecdotal newspaper record. For example, there is Donyea Jones of Seattle, who was shot by his wife in the *back* of the head (not a case of imminent fear) in front of their children, and then was dragged out of the house and set on fire. This murder took place during October 2000—National Domestic Violence Awareness month—but, of course, neither Seattle newspaper nor any domestic violence advocate in Seattle pointed to this case as an example. The murder of famous comedian Phil Hartman by his wife is another case of this double standard: When it happens to a man, it's not even labeled as an example of domestic violence by the news media.

Regardless of the anecdotal evidence, Dr. Mann's analysis and others show that a different conclusion can be drawn from the same set of data that Van Wormer cites. The resources for women (shelters and crisis lines) do seem to be saving men's lives, which should only lead us to establish the same types of resources for men, so more women's lives could be saved. To put it another way, shelters and crisis lines offer an opportunity for someone to cool off (along with fulfilling other needs). They offer a place to go and someone neutral (i.e., not a friend or family member) to talk to. Crisis lines and shelters, legal system advocates, and other helping systems provide an essential mechanism that aids in defusing a family-violence situation. Anger management courses available to men (but not very often to women) may also be helpful. (Their effectiveness or lack of

effectiveness has not been adequately studied.) Thus, it is little wonder that the rate of women murdering their spouses has fallen somewhat over the last 20 years, while the rate of men doing the same to women has remained constant.

■ ■ ■ ■ ■ ■ ■ ■ ■ ■

Van Wormer's analysis of the change in murder statistics is not unique. In her critique she cites another factor which leads her and many others to downplay the amount of domestic violence against men: "Also on the battering statistics these figures include a lot of women slapping men who get fresh with them. Or self-defense assaults. So the facts revealed in this book and carried by the media are false."

I'll leave readers to their own conclusions as to whether a woman should always be given the liberty to slap a man for getting fresh. For myself, I tend to be an absolutist about violence and don't think it is acceptable except in self-defense.

Besides, a woman who slaps a man only increases her chances of getting hit in return—it ultimately does not make her feel very good, either. Be that as it may, had Van Wormer and other apologists for violent women actually taken the time to look at the data in my book—and many other sources—they would find that self-defense as an explanation for domestic violence has been studied. Indeed, it is this aspect of such situations that gives us the clearest picture of the whole truth about domestic violence. The research also squares with the experience of veteran police officers. Half of domestic violence involves mutual combat. Even if we look at only what women reveal and discount what men say, there is agreement: A quarter of the time only the man was violent; a quarter of the time only the woman was violent. In the 50 percent of cases in which the violence was two-way, women struck the first blow half the time.[18]

In other words, the research mirrors the reality of couples' lives in general: Both sexes engage equally in both physical and verbal abuse.[19]

A case in point involves a well-known example of just how messy and complex domestic violence is, and how it is not limited to one gender. A very prominent public figure has several sexual encounters with a young intern in his office. He denies the affair publicly and to his wife. Upon discovery of his lie, his wife hits him on the side of the head. He appears the next day on television with a visible red mark on the left side of his head.[20]

I conducted a series of on-the-street interviews, asking people for their reactions to this alleged incident involving Bill and Hillary Clinton. The overwhelming majority of those questioned didn't seem surprised; they laughed and said, "Well, he deserved it," or, "He should have expected that kind of reaction." I then asked if it's OK for a man to attack his wife after finding out that she's having an affair; does she deserve to be hit? As you can imagine, the reactions were quite different.

The last question I put to people goes to the heart of the messy issues surrounding domestic violence: Most states have mandatory arrest laws for domestic violence. Regardless of how light the injury, someone would have to be arrested. If this incident is true, do you think Hillary Clinton should have been arrested? The overwhelming majority of people—both men and women—said no. Most people thought it was a minor one-time thing, a simple case of a couple fighting and not a real case of abuse.

The general public is perhaps smarter than many domestic violence awareness advocates. They sense what the majority of the research does in fact show: About 5 percent (being generous to the high end of things) of all couples experience an incident of minor to severe physical violence between them at least once a year. Repeated physical attacks, or what we most commonly think of as battering, are rarer. My best estimate, given the relatively scanty long-term (longitudinal) research on frequency, is that battering occurs in less than 1 percent of all couples. This is not to say, of course, that domestic violence is not a significant social problem. The psychological as well as the physical damage can be severe to both men and women, and as we have already discussed, the effects on children are devastating and demonstrably lead to a similar pattern of behavior in their adult lives, either as victim or perpetrator.

■ ■ ■ ■ ■ ■ ■ ■ ■ ■

What I find amazing is the disingenuous use of children to focus only on women as victims of domestic violence. President Clinton—in his radio address with the wrong data—gave as good an example as any: "And statistics tell us that in half the families where a spouse is beaten, the children are beaten, too." Remember, this is a presidential address upon the signing of the Violence Against Women Act, and the entire speech focuses on women as the only victims of domestic violence. The clear implication is that only men beat their spouses and that they then beat their children. The reality is quite different. Mothers kill their own children more often than fathers do, and the rate of physical child abuse is about equal, with mothers more likely to commit criminal child neglect.[21] When one excludes

stepfathers from the equation, men are *less* likely to physically abuse their children than are women.

Former President Clinton is not to be singled out in this regard, as most literature from domestic violence coalitions and shelters makes similar statements or alludes to men being the primary or exclusive perpetrators of child abuse. The question that should be asked is this one: If mothers can abuse and kill their own children, why in the world is it so difficult to believe that some women can also physically attack someone they also purport to love—their husbands?

"IF THERE HAD BEEN A CRISIS LINE FOR MEN IN THIS SITUATION, I WOULD HAVE CALLED IT TO FIND OUT WHAT TO DO, WHAT THE OPTIONS WERE, HOW TO STOP IT."

Another argument for ignoring the true nature of most domestic violence is the claim that because of financial reasons, women have a much more difficult time than men do in leaving an abusive relationship. This does not hold up to scrutiny, either; in fact, low-income women are *more* likely, not less likely, to leave an abusive relationship than are affluent women.[22]

Indeed, if there are children involved, men may be less likely to leave an abusive relationship than women. Men know one thing: Their chances of getting custody of the children are not very good. Their chances of unblocked visitation with the children from a possibly vindictive and abusive spouse aren't very good, either. Losing a relationship with one's own children, possibly forever, can certainly be seen as a big factor in a man's decision to stay in an abusive relationship.

Men also face another factor that abused women don't face as much—ridicule and isolation. Whom can they talk to about their problem?

"The cops show up, and they think it's a big joke," Tim S. explained after his live-in girlfriend hit him in the head with a frying pan, which resulted in severe bleeding from a deep cut. "I never did tell anyone [of my friends and family] about all this while it was going on, because they would assume that I had done something to her, or that I deserved it. If there had been a crisis line for men in this situation, I would have called it to find out what to do, what the options were, how to stop it."

Not having any resources to turn to for help with their situation—no victim advocates, no crisis lines, no support groups, no media recognition, no shelters—and a pervasive macho attitude of "I can handle it...I must be the strong and responsible one," further inhibits a man from leaving an abusive relationship, or even acknowledging it.

Even if a man seeks out a therapist for help, he is likely to find none, contends counselor Michael Thomas of Seattle, Washington. "In talking with other therapists, I find that they rarely even ask questions of their male clients about the possibility of the client being abused. I think a great many clinicians are still resistant to seeing certain types of female behavior as abusive. If the client can't talk about it, it becomes internalized, and it increases the danger of the men exploding in rage themselves, getting depressed or suicidal, withdrawing from relationships, and other kinds of effects. I have also heard from female abusers who can't get help. There are very few resources out there, for either victim or abuser."[23]

■ ■ ■ ■ ■ ■ ■ ■ ■ ■

It should come as no surprise that national surveys show a significant drop in public approval of a man slapping his wife under any circumstances, but no change at all in approval for a woman slapping her husband.[24]

Still, the apologists for women who are violent in the home are legion, despite the overwhelming amount of data.[25] When all else fails, they fall back on patriarchy as an excuse. In other words, this is the prime mover. It is the historical subjugation of women by men and the societal and economic acceptance of this subjugation that leads to domestic violence. Men don't have to face the patriarchy, this school of thought says, and in fact this patriarchy gives them the power and excuse to perpetrate domestic violence. Unfortunately for this quasi-Marxist viewpoint, there are methods by which we can test the theory—and it doesn't hold up.

First, consider this: Traditional, conservative, Christian men who attend church regularly do not have a greater incidence of domestic violence than other groups.[26] What is remarkable, however, is that researchers found that women who strongly subscribe to traditional, very conservative Christian theology have a higher rate of being physically abusive. The researchers don't say why this is so, but based on my interviews with abused men, I think I know the answer. Women like this believe that their man must appear to be macho when dealing with people (taking charge, for example, in dealing with a sales or trade person, particularly another male), then may become violent when the couple is behind closed doors because the man wasn't being macho enough.

HAVE YOU EVER SEEN A BILLBOARD OR PUBLIC SERVICE ANNOUNCEMENT TARGETING LESBIAN VICTIMS?

Second, the armed forces can certainly be seen as a hierarchical, macho patriarchy machine. Despite several erroneous press reports (most notably a *60 Minutes* segment in which very different kinds of research were compared), a huge, comprehensive survey of the US Army found that its rate of domestic violence is not significantly higher than that of the general population.[27]

Lastly, the patriarchy and the economic and social forces that support it fall down as a causative factor for domestic violence when we consider that some lesbians assault their lesbian partners. There is no man involved. Where's the patriarchy? The rate of lesbian domestic violence compared to the heterosexual population is debatable, as more research needs to be done. The Violence Against Women Act survey, for example, found a slightly lower rate, while other studies found an equal or higher incidence.[28] In an essay in *Naming the Violence: Speaking Out About Lesbian Battering*, the female authors comment about what this means: "Many women in the broader battered women's movement are affected by the public acknowledgment of lesbian violence. This acknowledgment forces a deepening of the analysis of sexism and male/female roles as contributors to violence in relationships. To understand violence in lesbian relationships is to challenge and perhaps rework some of these beliefs."[29] Indeed!

Unfortunately, because many in the domestic violence movement are wedded to the Marxist-type, patriarchal theory of domestic violence and its usefulness in establishing a powerful, exclusive victimhood, outreach to lesbian victims is limited. Have you ever seen a billboard or public service announcement targeting lesbian victims? Even simple brochures are rare. Thus, women end up not helping other women because they don't want to publicly admit that women can be violent toward their partners. Such an admission might mean losing power. Exclusive victim status translates into control, both politically and with regard to funding. Many in the domestic violence movement fear that if the messy reality of domestic violence gets into the public consciousness, they'll lose the power to set the agenda—men are always the perpetrators or potentially evil, while women are always the victims. Even when women are bad, this philosophy goes, there's an excuse or reason that makes their violence more understandable and sympathetic. This agenda pays off in power and money. For example, the Violence Against Women Act is written in such a way that there is no funding—out of $5 billion—available for programs to serve male domestic violence victims.

■ ■ ■ ■ ■ ■ ■ ■ ■ ■

The irony is that many (but not all) in the established domestic violence movement use power, control, and intimidation to a remarkable degree in making sure that their agenda is the only one heard. These are the very tactics that domestic violence abusers use. Researcher Suzanne Steinmetz was the subject of bomb threats before presenting a speech to the ACLU, and her children's lives were threatened. Canadian Senator Anne Cools was the subject of physical intimidation by protesters in Vancouver, and police whistles were used to prevent her from speaking. Posters were also stolen at that event, and when one person attempted to grab a whistle out of one of the women's hands, the group proclaimed to the news media that they were assaulted. Researchers such as Murray Straus, Ph.D., and Richard Gelles, Ph.D., have received death threats, as well. The most remarkable example of intimidation is Erin Pizzey, the founder of the battered women's movement. She has needed a police escort for speaking engagements, and her home in the US has been fired upon.

Her open letter to those in the movement (published here, in part, for the first time) is worth sharing:

An Open Letter to Women in the Domestic Violence Movement From the Founder and Author of the First Modern Book About Domestic Violence

When I first tried to open the refuge [Chiswick Women's Refuge, the world's first shelter for battered women], the police, the charities, the social service agencies, the newspapers, all said it would stand empty. They said it wasn't a significant problem, that it happened only rarely, and when it did it was already being handled by the existing agencies. Domestic violence against women was only a minor problem, and very few women were getting seriously hurt anyway. Of course, when we finally did open and got a little support to make women aware of our existence, we were filled to overflowing, and the phone was ringing off the hook.

It's the same exact attitude now with attempts to have domestic violence resources for men. However, it's even more difficult now to open something for men, or raise awareness, than it was when I opened the first shelter for women.

There is now an established domestic violence industry which fears any acknowledgment of the well-established scientific fact that women can be as violent as men with their intimate part-

ners and are not always the victim or acting only in self-defense. This fear is based on a false premise, that acknowledging this fact or speaking publicly about it, or offering services, will take away funding and hurt established resources for women. That's nonsense. I proved and others can, too, that offering help for abused men can be done within an existing system set up originally to help women.

The charities and the social service system and government told me when I opened the first refuge for women that there wasn't enough money, that resources were stretched too thin, that police have to focus on where the majority of the crime is, and so on. Nonsense. Where there's a will, there's a way. The trouble is, there's no will. But there should be, and women should take the lead, not men. After all, not only is it our brothers, fathers, and friends who are being abused, by not helping men, we're not effectively helping women who are having trouble dealing with their own violence against their partners and against their children.

Women have the power in the established domestic violence movement now. We should take the lead in taking the movement to the next step. Economic circumstances for many women have changed, so that while it was important to focus first on women when I started things, women now have more economic opportunities and more government support, as well as refuge resources to get help. As women, we cannot claim perfection and ask to be put on a pedestal any longer, and most women no longer desire that, but to make that change, we must also accept responsibility for our own actions or lack of action.

Because of these views, and daring to speak out, I've been vilified and physically threatened many times by women in the domestic violence movement. Don't tell me that women can't be violent! Nowadays, you won't even find my name or my domestic violence books mentioned in the established domestic violence literature.... I've been erased because of heresy, for daring to speak the truth. But when I can, I still take the opportunity to speak out, because we'll never break

| "BECAUSE OF THESE VIEWS, AND DARING TO SPEAK OUT, I'VE BEEN VILIFIED AND PHYSICALLY THREATENED MANY TIMES BY WOMEN IN THE DOMESTIC VIOLENCE MOVEMENT." |

the chain of domestic violence until we accept the truth: Domestic violence is a complex issue; there are many elements involved in intimate partner relationships; it takes hard work and investigation to deal with it in a truly effective manner; and finally, no one sex, just because of their sex, is less capable of it.

—Erin Pizzey, author of *Scream Quietly or the Neighbors Will Hear* and founder of the world's first shelter and crisis line for battered women

Pizzey's point, and mine, is not to excuse violence. It should not matter who started it or what the provocation was. True self-defense is one matter; however, research clearly shows that in the overwhelming majority of domestic violence incidents, a direct threat to one's life is not involved. If we excuse violent acts by women by saying that they must have been provoked or were responding to violent acts by men, that would put us in the position of accepting violent acts by men under the same circumstances.

■ ■ ■ ■ ■ ■ ■ ■ ■ ■

As Pizzey has pointed out, the solution for dealing with domestic violence on a realistic and factual basis does not constitute a threat to funding for shelters or crisis lines as they currently exist. I don't believe we need a second set of funding for men's shelters. Rather, a change in attitude can accomplish the same goals. The Valley Oasis Shelter of Lancaster, California, for example, treats each call from those seeking help—whether a man or a woman—with dignity and respect. It has a separate facility for men with children in need of shelter. The Kelso, Washington Emergency Shelter also handles crisis calls from men and has a male support worker, though it doesn't provide shelter services. A small but growing number of domestic violence crisis lines have obtained a newly available male-victim brochure in an attempt to reach out to this underserved population.

A little creative thinking and configuration could provide actual shelter services—or hotel vouchers at the very least—for males and their children in many circumstances. Training professionals is the first step. When we train the professionals who provide domestic violence services—social workers, health care providers, law enforcement, and legal professionals—in how to help and reach out to all victims, then real progress will have been made. Stop Abuse For Everyone <www.safe4all.org> has a distinguished list of available trainers; the problem is, they're not being called upon nearly enough. The messy problems of how to identify primary perpetrators, single victims, and mutual combat situations and how to effectively provide help on a case-by-case basis can be dealt with if effective and inclusive training and education is widespread.

No program to combat domestic violence will be very effective unless the true nature of such violence is recognized. Unless all the factors for domestic violence are considered, women seeking help for their anger problems, lesbians and gay men with partner problems, and heterosexual men who are being abused will continue to be discriminated against and told that their problem isn't real. The facts show otherwise; their problem is real and it affects millions of people.

For nearly 30 years, we have been presented with only one part of the equation. Given the legal and societal history of discrimination and oppression against women in many areas, this was appropriate, but it is not appropriate today. It has become an us-against-them battle. The reality of domestic violence, however, tells us that it is more complex than that. Some cases can be attributed to mental illness, but most are due to family upbringing, poor self-esteem, substance abuse, and/or uncertain employment combined with low anger-management and communication skills. Domestic violence is a human problem, not a gender problem.

If we fail to put resources and effort into dealing with the total reality of domestic violence, instead of just one part of this phenomena, we only encourage a group-against-group effect, which is a disservice to everyone. The sociologists tell us that domestic violence at some level affects a significant minority of couples in Britain, Canada, Australia, New Zealand, and the US. It is a criminal tragedy that must be dealt with on economic, social, legal, and spiritual levels, but these problems shouldn't encourage us to declare that the family is a bankrupt construct. If we can move forward to a better understanding of the benevolent and malevolent nature of each gender, we increase the opportunity for constructive rather than destructive relationships.

DOMESTIC VIOLENCE IS A HUMAN PROBLEM, NOT A GENDER PROBLEM.

Endnotes

1. Straus, M., and R. Gelles. "Societal Change and Change in Family Violence from 1975 to 1985 as Revealed by Two National Surveys." *Journal of Marriage and the Family* 48 (Aug 1986). **2.** Fiebert, M., Ph.D. "References Examining Assaults by Women on their Spouses/Partners: An Annotated Bibliography." <www.csulb.edu/~mfiebert/assault.htm> (updated 2000). **3.** McNeely, R.L., P. Cook, and J. Torres. "Is Domestic Violence a Gender Issue or a Human Issue?" *Journal of Human Behavior in the Social Environment* 4.4 (2001). **4.** Updike, Nancy. "Hitting the Wall." *Mother Jones* (May/June 1999). **5.** The best source for the British Home Office Study is <www.home-office.gov.uk/rds/pdfs/hors191.pdf>. In Canada, the nationally representative sample was reported in Brinkerhoff, M., and E. Lupri. "Interspousal Violence." *The Canadian Journal of Sociology* 13.4 (Fall 1988). **6.** McLeod, M. "Women Against Men: An Examination of Domestic Violence Based on an Analysis of Official Data and National Victimization Data." *Justice Quarterly* 1 (1984): 171-93. **7.** Ernst, Amy, M.D., Todd G. Nick, Ph.D., Steven Weiss, M.D., Debra Hours, and Trevor Mills, M.D. *Annals of*

Emergency Medicine. 20.2 (1997). **8.** "Violence-Related Injuries Treated in Hospital Emergency Departments." US Department of Justice, Office of Justice Programs, Bureau of Justice Statistics. (1997). NCJ-156921. See also: National Center for Health Statistics. "National Hospital Ambulatory Medical Care Survey 1992. Emergency Department Summary." Hyattsville, Maryland (March 1997). **9.** Shalala, D. Oral remarks. American Medical Association National Conference on Family Violence. Washington, DC (11 March 1994). **10.** Stark, E., and A. Flitcraft. "Spouse Abuse." *Surgeon General's Workshop on Violence and Public Health Source Book* (1985). See also: *Journal of the American Medical Association* 267.23 (17 June 1992): 3190. **11.** Hallinan, J. Newhouse News Service. Note: Nationally syndicated article to Newhouse newspapers, it appeared in *The Oregonian* (7 July 1994), but also in other Newhouse newspapers around the US on or near that date. **12.** Radio address of the President to the nation on signing Victims of Trafficking and Violence Protection Act of 2000 (Nov 2000). **13.** Tjaden, P., and N. Thoennes. "Extent, Nature, and Consequences of Intimate Partner Violence: Findings from the National Violence Against Women Survey." National Institute of Justice, Centers for Disease Control (July 2000), NCJ 181867. **14.** Interview with Patricia Tjaden by Philip Cook (Oct 2000). **15.** "Murder in Families." US Department of Justice, Office of Justice Programs (July 1984), NCJ-143498. See also: subsequent Justice Department five-year reviews. **16.** Amazon.com customer review (16 June 2001). **17.** Mann, C., Ph.D. "Getting Even? Women Who Kill in Domestic Encounters." *Justice Quarterly* 5.1 (1988): 33-50. **18.** Straus, M. "Physical Assaults by Wives: A Major Social Problem." *Current Controversies on Family Violence.* Ed. R.J. Gelles and D.R. Loseke. Newbury Park, CA: Sage, 1993. See also: O'Marain, Padraig. "Domestic Violence More Likely From Women—Report." *Irish Times* 14 June 2001: "Women are more likely than men to perpetrate domestic violence, according to new research on Irish couples who seek marriage counselling. The report, published yesterday, also found that domestic violence was one of the less important factors in marriage breakdown in the largely middleclass group studied. It was produced by a team led by Dr Kieran McKeown, who has a distinguished reputation in social research and was commissioned by Marriage and Relationship Counselling Services, one of the main counselling organisations in the country. In a survey of 530 clients of MRCS, the researchers found domestic violence occurs in almost half (48 per cent) of all relationships which are sufficiently troubled for one or both partners to seek counselling. Where there is violence, about one-third (33 per cent) inflict violence on each other, 'while female-perpetrated violence occurs in about four out of 10 couples (41 per cent) and male-perpetrated violence in a quarter of couples (26 per cent), leading us to conclude that women are more likely than men to be the perpetrators of domestic violence,' the report's authors say.... They cite research from the US, Britain, Canada and New Zealand which, they say, shows that the 'prevalence of domestic violence among men and women, both as victims and as perpetrators, is broadly similar for all types of violence, both psychological and physical, minor and severe. In addition, both men and women are about equally likely to initiate domestic violence and seem to give broadly similar reasons for doing so.'" **19.** From Steinmetz, S.K. *The Cycle of Violence: Assertive, Aggressive and Abusive Family Interaction.* Praeger, 1977: "93% of all husbands and wives employed verbal aggression against each other, at least once in the prior year. The verbal aggression was defined as arguing, yelling, screaming and insulting each other, sulking, stomping out of the room." From Straus, M., and S. Sweet. "Verbal/symbolic Aggression in Couples: Incidence Rates and Relationships to Personal Characteristics." *Journal of Marriage and the Family* 54 (May 1992): 346-57: "At least once in a prior year, 74% of men and 75% of the women engaged in verbal/symbolic aggression. Defined in the survey of 5,232 American couples as insulting, swearing at, sulking, refusing to talk, stomping out of the room or yard, saying things to spite a partner, threatening to strike a partner, threatening to throw something at a partner, and actually throwing, hitting, kicking or smashing something." **20.** From Drudge, Matt. "White House Fight!" *Drudge Report* (4 Jan 1999): "The *National Enquirer* is set to report in its January 5, 1999 edition: The First Lady has physically attacked the President, hitting him so hard she left a visible mark on his face—and Secret Service agents had to separate them. The Drudge Report trusts the account to be accurate and non-libelous because the *National Enquirer* and President Bill Clinton use the same law firm, Williams and Connolly. In fact, Clinton's private lawyer, David Kendall, has directly done work for the tabloid through the years." Author's note: I twice called the office of the Press Secretary for First Lady Hillary Clinton shortly after this report appeared, saying that I was planning to write articles on the subject and asking the office to confirm or deny this report—and earlier report—of her throwing ashtrays. The office refused to deny it or reply. **21.** From "Murder in Families." US Department of Justice (1993): "55% of parent to child murders were by women." Note: Homicide rates of mothers vs. fathers have remained fairly constant. However, there is not a consensus among the research about which gender is more responsible for child abuse. That is, some researchers believe that mother's boyfriends are responsible for the act of child abuse, but the mother is also responsible for allowing the abuse to occur. See: Margolin, L. "Child Abuse by Mother's Boyfriends: Why the Overrepresentation?" *Child Abuse & Neglect* 16 (1992): 451-551. In The National Family Violence Survey (Straus, Gelles), mothers had a 62 percent greater rate of child abuse than fathers. Child abuse rates can also vary by state depending on enforcement and reporting. For example, in Oregon for 1993, the perpetrators of child abuse of all types were: mother (38.3 percent); father (20.7 percent); neighbor/friend (8.2 percent); stepfather (6.4 percent); live-in companion (4.9 percent); brother (3.2 percent); uncle (2.4 percent); other relative (2.1 percent); grandfather (1.7 percent); stepsibling (1 percent); grandmother (0.8 percent); stepmother (0.7 percent). Source: Oregon Department of Human Resources, Children's Services Division. **22.** McNeely, R.L., and G. Robinson-Simpson. "The Truth About Domestic Violence: A Falsely Framed Issue." *Social Work* (Nov/Dec 1987): 485-90. **23.** Interview of Michael Thomas by Philip Cook. **24.** Straus, M., and G. Kaufman-Kantor. "Cultural Norms Approving Marital Violence: Changes from 1968 to 1992 in Relation to Gender, Class, Cohort and Other Social Characteristics." Family Research Laboratory, University of New Hampshire (1997). **25.** Here are three more sources: i) Morse, B.J. "Beyond the Conflict Tactics Scale: Assessing Gender Differences in Partner Violence." *Violence and Victims* 10.4 (1995): 251-72. Over twice as many women as men reported assaulting a partner who had not assaulted them during the study year. ii) Arias, I., M. Samios, and K.D. O'Leary. "Prevalence and Correlates of Physical Aggression During Courtship." *Journal of Interpersonal Violence* 2: 82-90. Thirty percent of men and 49 percent of women self-reported using some form of aggression in their dating histories, with a greater percentage of women engaging in severe physical aggression. iii) Cascardi, M., J. Langinrichsen, and D. Vivian. "Marital Aggression: Impact, Injury, and Health Correlates for Husbands and Wives." *Archives of Internal Medicine* 152 (1992): 1178-84. Women and men were equally likely to perpetrate violence. **26.** Brinkerof, M., M. Grandine, and E. Lupri. "Religious Involvement and Spousal Violence." *Journal for the Scientific Study of Religion* 31.1 (1992): 15-31. **27.** Heyman, R., and P. Neidig. "A Comparison of Spousal Aggression Prevalence Rates in US Army and Civilian Representation Samples." *Journal of Consulting and Clinical Psychology* (forthcoming). For a Freedom of Information Act release of the data, see: Cook, P. *Abused Men: The Hidden Side of Domestic Violence.* Westport, CT: Praeger, 1997: 5. **28.** Renzettie, C. *Violent Betrayal: Partner Abuse in Lesbian Relationships.* Newbury Park, CA: Sage, 1992. See also: Lie and Gentlewarrior. "Intimate Violence in Lesbian Relationships." *Journal of Social Science Research* 15 (1987): 41-59. Card, C. "Lesbian Battering." *Newsletter on Feminism and Philosophy* (Nov 1988): 3. **29.** Lobel, K., ed. *Naming the Violence: Speaking Out About Lesbian Battering.* Seattle, WA: Seal Press, 1986: 98-102.

DESPITE THE OVERWHELMING NUMBER OF MALE VICTIMS OF DOMESTIC ABUSE, THEIR PROBLEM IS VIEWED AS OF LITTLE CONSEQUENCE, OR THEY ARE SEEN TO BE SOMEHOW AT BLAME FOR IT.

POSTCARDS FROM THE PLANET OF THE FREAKS

LUCY GWIN

_WATCH OUT!

This could turn out to be the worst day of your life. At the peak of your pain, when the child you've labored all night to bring into the world is moments away from its first breath, the doc, unaccountably, puts you under. When you awaken, your child is not in evidence but the pediatrician is, delivering very bad news with a complicated Latin name. Every pregnant woman's nightmare has landed on you. You've given birth to a freak, and they don't even want you to see it.

Or, alternately, here's you, barely awake, sipping a morning cup of coffee when the lovely old tree that shades your porch groans once, shears vertically down the length of its secret, rotten core, and sets off a chain of collapsing catastrophes that, milliseconds later, severs your spine at the C-5 vertebra. Ka-whomp. You're a monster now.

Or, more likely, your gentle but noisy middle child is expertly assessed as being ADHD or ADD or some other signifier of not-quite-human status from the DSM (*Diagnostic and Statistical Manual of Mental Disorders of the American Psychiatric Association*). You have a maniac in the family.

Welcome to second-class citizenship. While there is no known limit to variations on the human form or manifestations of the human mind, possession of quite a number of them will brand you or yours as defective. Only when your life as presently constituted goes to pieces are you likely to learn that everything you know about freaks, monsters, and maniacs is wrong.

First off, they lie. What everybody says about disability, the storehouse of conventional wisdom? It ain't so, starting with the big one: "We only want to help you." Fact is, we want you outta here. You give us the creeps.

But maybe, if you could be cured....

> **WHILE THERE IS NO KNOWN LIMIT TO VARIATIONS ON THE HUMAN FORM OR MANIFESTATIONS OF THE HUMAN MIND, POSSESSION OF QUITE A NUMBER OF THEM WILL BRAND YOU OR YOURS AS DEFECTIVE.**

_POSTCARD FROM THE INCURABLY MONSTROUS

The editor of this book, Russ Kick, believes that what would most surprise you about freaks, monsters, and maniacs is their scorn for the "cure." Joe Ehman, a Denver housing activist with muscular dystrophy, notes that there are plenty of things in this world which cry out for fixing. He wants to know, "How come everybody wants to fix *me*? I ain't broken." Ehman has been subjected to the laying on of hands by god-fearing total strangers. Waitresses do him the same variety of favor when Joe and I dine together, asking me, "And what would he like on his salad?" Once demoted to monsterhood, your companions are presumed to know what you want. And of course what you really want is a fix.

You're right. Superman and that leftover Mouseketeer go all pitiful for the cameras, "confined to their wheelchairs," suffering, begging shamelessly for the fix. Monsters who aren't wired for stardom don't give it a second thought. A postcard from the Freak Planet shows Jerry Lewis and says, *Piss on pity*.

_FREAK PREVENTION ESSENTIAL

For the record: Jonas Salk did not cure polio but created a vaccine to prevent it. Should a real cure come, it won't change what freaks have learned about rejection. Dan Wilkins, engaged in the struggle for disability rights, says that before he lost the use of his legs, "I sympathized with the African-American civil rights movement and the women's movement, but I was a white guy. I have come to understand and appreciate rather than sympathize. No cure is going to take that away. I wouldn't want one if it did."

Prevention is the cure Jerry's charity provides: a dose of genetic screening. Josie Byzek, writer and Freak Planet theorist, notes that "Americans seem to believe they have a constitutional right to normalcy." There's progress on that front. In all 50 states and four territories, abortion is legal right up to the moment of birth—and for days or even weeks after, but only if the fetus is disabled. From time beyond immemorial, mommies, daddies, and medicine men who lacked the luxury of amniocentesis "exposed" baby monsters to the elements, as if a stiff breeze rather than a pack of dogs would waft them away. Call it choice. Call it selective breeding. Call it preserving the family unit. Call it malpractice insurance or a real-world resolution of the ancient academic debate over what constitutes personhood. Fact is, we don't want them around. Live babies with Down Syndrome are on the verge of extinction among the health-insured middle and upper classes. As-yet-unidentified chromosomal peculiarities may soon help us to detect and prevent the queer or even the future felon. We don't want them around either.

_FIVE-INCH NAILS

David Apocalypse, a very special guy who's more a geek than a freak, hammers five-inch nails up his nose for a living. What he said about it to *Erie Times-News* reporter Scott Westcott identifies him as hailing from the Planet of the Freaks. "Thank God as a young boy I saw someone sticking a nail up their nose, or I would have a terrible life. You want to see a freak show? A guy sitting in a cubicle, staring into a computer all day with a 'Thank God it's Friday' mug on his desk, there's your freak show."

Here sits the writer, no trace of TGIF in her soul, her office yay-deep in notes and clippings for a new book, *Freaks, Monsters, Maniacs and Their History on Planet Earth*. The headline of a prize *Denver Post* clip says, "Teacher Caters to the Disabled." The accompanying photograph shows a hefty white woman in a bright plaid shirt, eyebrows arching above a burlesque grimace, a blubbery rubber dog's nose masking her own. All in fun, she holds up menacing, claw-like hands.

Here come the special people. Send in the clowns.

And here's a fold-out postcard from Freak Planet. In the first panel he leaps tall buildings with a single bound. In the second he requires a machine to draw breath. Next panel he's swarmed by grimacing fussbudgets who actually *condescend*...to Superman! The final panel wishes you a special day.

_GOING PLACES

Getting Reeve back into superhero mode would be a challenge; getting him on a cross-town bus is all but impossible.

There was a time when white kids like I was back then got their social change cherries busted in America's South, sitting beside our black friends on public buses, all of us determined, all of us terrified. People got themselves killed for doing what we did. For the African Americans leading us it was ten years at the center of a storm of invective and violence. Set upon by dogs, jailed, hosed off the

streets with 90 pounds-per-square-inch-pressure fire hoses, they were also, occasionally, hung out like forgotten laundry. A great and fateful controversy played itself out in television news beamed from tedious places: voter registration offices, lunch counters, city buses.

Folks with disabilities still can't get on the bus. On the hottest day of the summer of 2001, I stood at a bus stop in Chicago's loop with playwright Mike Ervin, who uses a wheelchair, as four Clark Street buses passed us by. Rush hour was over. All four were nearly empty. If we could have inquired, the drivers would have told us their lifts were broken. That would have been a lie. Like disability rights activist Roy Posten has said more than once, "I think I just been niggerized." I got loud and furious about it, but Ervin, one of the original Jerry's Orphans of the telethon protests, stayed cool, wary of what he referred to in a recent magazine column as "that deeply suppressed primal urge to throttle an uppity cripple."

> **FOLKS WITH DISABILITIES STILL CAN'T GET ON THE BUS.**

We gave up and hoofed it to his place. With curb cuts blocked in two places, lacking in others, we had a sweaty, roundabout trek. His power wheelchair had more pep than I did. As Dan Wilkins says, "Walking is overrated." Another bus whipped past us, a postcard in itself. Through the cloud of fumes it trailed, I caught the ad on its tail: "Chicago Transit Authority—Going Places."

Come to think of it just this minute, hanging with the freaks, monsters, and maniacs, I hear bitches aplenty about places they can't get into, bureaucratic-professional quagmires they can't get out of. Searching years of memory, I find no record of a single bitch about the thing itself, the disabling condition. That thought gives me the chills, of anticipation and of certainty. The disabling condition is real. It can't be fixed. It's a drag and they live with it. But being exiled as non-persons? They're going to change that.

Standing with Mike as dusk gathered and the buses roared past, it was the same old me, the odd kid who hangs with the outcasts, bent on changing the world. Out with the outcasts again, I could feel it in the air. Their time has come.

Not that you'd know it from watching the nightly news.

_ST. MEANSWELL AND THE SHOCKING TRUTH

Here's a newsworthy postcard from the Center for Economic and Policy Analysis. They shook out state spending on disability and found that only eight cents on the dollar spent on disability goes either directly *to* a person with a disability or into projects where the theoretical beneficiaries had a say in the setup of that theoretical benefit. The other 92 cents of your tax dollar are wasted not on bureaucracy but on missionary-professionals of St. Meanswell. Billy Golfus, the brain-damaged writer-producer of *When Billy Broke His*

Head, reminds us that "a professional is somebody who does it for the money, remember." Let's follow the money to what your kids call "speds," the victims of special education. The money we spend per student on special education, for instance, would send that student to Harvard if we spent it with her rather than for her.

Eight cents on the dollar, or even less, is also true of charitable donations. Charity reports depart from this truth because they label certain fundraising activities *public education*. So well-educated, yet everything the public knows is wrong. Here's a virtual reality live-action postcard from the Planet of the Freaks. And look—it's you!—phone in one hand, credit card in the other, all sweet and unsuspecting, pumping your dollars down the 1-800 pipeline to Jerry's Kids. *But, Mother, those aren't kids!* They're PLODs (People Living Off the Disabled), aka fundsuckers, sucking hard at their end of the pipeline from high atop an *Architectural Digest* spread in Tucson, Arizona. Watch them play Lady Bountiful with your dollars, endowing certain overpromising researchers with the means to publish rather than perish. Now watch as Jerry's Kids get to where they can't breathe without mechanical assistance. And listen as the fundsuckers recite their official policy not to provide breathing apparatus.

money tree. Billing the state or your insurance company for a treatment, the shrink appends the DSM code number for your diagnosis. Presto, you're crazy.

On the Planet of the Freaks, maniacs rue the day we granted them the very first exception to the Bill of Rights. Protections granted to you and me, such as those against unwarranted search and seizure, don't apply to maniacs. They can be hustled off to a lockup on your complaint, or mine for that matter, and kept under lock and key until they repent of their eccentricities, their sad-bad-mad thoughts, their wild inspirations. Otherwise they must prove their sanity, a neat trick with a money tree blocking the light.

But we make it up to them, right? If charged with a crime, they might not be locked up in a lousy county jail but in the prison of euphemism instead, a mental hospital. The next postcard is a no-Miranda rights warning. Anything you admit to a shrink will be held against you; an attorney will not be provided; all sentences are indeterminate and rehabilitation is forcibly applied. No "real" prison—not that

> "YOU DON'T WANT TO BE PITIED BECAUSE YOU'RE A CRIPPLE IN A WHEELCHAIR? STAY IN YOUR HOUSE!" —JERRY LEWIS

As for Jerry, the freaks would love to burst your bubble one more time. On camera for the 'thon, he makes much of "not taking a penny for my work on behalf of these kids." Not a penny in salary, no, but travel expenses. According to a reluctant mole at Jerry's Charity, "He could travel to Mars, round trip, first class" on that expense account. Now add insult to injury. While traveling he has called his kids "only half a person." In the spring of 2001, on *CBS News Sunday Morning*, Jerry revealed the secret for his pitch to cure their demi-humanhood: "If it's pity, we'll get some money. Pity? You don't want to be pitied because you're a cripple in a wheelchair? Stay in your house!"

Mike Ervin, who left his house to protest the 2000 telethon and got roughed up by some ardent fundsuckers, warns his fellow freaks, "Don't ever tell them you don't want their stinkin' charity. It brings out the beast."

_MRS. PLUM, IN THE KITCHEN, WITH A BONK

We interrupt the pity postcard for one about maniacs. But first we must isolate exactly what makes them the way they are, that being the DSM, the *Diagnostic and Statistical Manual*. Characterized as "nonsense on stilts" in an August 2001 *Wall Street Journal* editorial, the DSM determines which designer shrink label will be applied to a person whose activities another person, probably a relative and presumably more powerful, cannot abide. From the corresponding Freak Planet postcard, headlined "Mental health drives me crazy," we learn that a listing in the DSM is the magic that shakes the

I'm recommending one—can force Schedule II drugs down your throat, let alone fasten electrodes to your temples so as to impart to flabby gray matter the crispiness known as "normalcy," all in the name of help.

Judi Chamberlin, a leader among psychiatric survivors, says, "When I hear somebody say, 'We just want to help you,' I run the other way, fast." Another champion of the maniacs, Justin Dart, Jr., Chair of the Equal Employment Opportunity Commission under President Reagan, thunders, "No forced treatment, ever!" I hear you scoffing. If a maniac is not forcibly medicated, he's liable to rave up behind you on the subway platform and make you very late for dinner. Forced treatment saves lives—right?

Sorry, but the 1998 MacArthur Foundation Risk Assessment Study found that nut cases are no more likely than anyone else in the general population to commit violent crimes, perhaps less so. "Violence," it concluded, "committed by people discharged from a [mental] hospital is very similar to violence committed by other people living in their communities in terms of type (hitting), target (family members), and location (at home)." Mrs. Plum, in the kitchen, with a bonk on the head. Rule one, then: Put your bodyguards on duty at your house. Since law enforcement can't yet lock up your friends and relatives even if they're most likely to put you in harm's way, perhaps we should allow every citizen who hasn't committed a crime to run around loose? Nope. In the name of prevention, that old dog again, we expect shrinks to predict if a citizen could be "a danger to himself or others," then hold the malpractice insurer to it. Trouble is that in study after study, shrinks' predictions are no better than we'd get from tea leaves. Worse, actually, since tea leaves don't worry over insurance rates and thus don't over-predict the likelihood of violence. Here's a postcard with a peculiar message. *Beware depression screening day*. Wonder what that means...

As for the compensating exception we grant, where we send certifiably loony lawbreakers to hospitals and not prisons, maniacs turn up their noses there, too. You want to help? Treat a citizen like a citizen, fair weather or foul.

_LIP-BUTTONING AND TYPECASTING

The press will someday see what I see: a new and vital desegregation struggle, with more than 50 million Americans, the poorest among us by the way, trying and most of the time failing, through no fault of their poverty or their disabling condition, to go where every other American has gone before. Why won't the press see it now? Reporters I know say they're "too senior now to work the disability beat." (Even John Hockenberry told me he doesn't want to be "typecast as the disability guy.") Reporters on that beat are lowly feature-page beginners, recent graduates from the obits and the brides' pages, desperate just to fit in. They go into tragic-brave mode to cover disability, just as their editors once did, editors who learned it under the same stifling conditions. Editors, however, do know what I'm only now sniffing out, that so far as we're concerned, disabled people are not really people at all. Half-person, half-animal-vegetable-criminal, they ruin the ratings. Mama taught us not to stare. Here comes one now. Quick, change the channel.

Josie Byzek, a monster and a queer who considers herself doubly blessed, told me recently, "I couldn't climb stairs last week, and I was pissing my pants every five minutes. I am a woman, not a monster. But look it up in *Webster's*. I could have qualified. Since the MS [multiple sclerosis] comes and goes, a couple hundred years ago I coulda been burned at the stake for it." That's an interesting take. Just don't count on reading it anywhere else.

Me, I can't complain. I have what writers love best—rich, juicy material, an unexplored continent all to myself. Just one gripe: Three times so far, network TV producers have sent me on fact-gathering missions so they could win an Emmy exposing sheltered workshops. None of the stories made it to broadcast. A *60 Minutes* producer told me why. "We are, after all, the top-rated newsmagazine show. We can't put...well...*unattractive* people on camera. A wheelchair? We could probably shoot around *that*." Here comes another one. Look away.

_THE HISTORY OF STARING

Rosemarie Garland-Thomson, author of *Extraordinary Bodies* and

BILL CLINTON'S WORST FEAR, HE CONFIDED TO GENNIFER FLOWERS, WAS OF "CRIPPLES CHAINING THEMSELVES TO THE WHITE HOUSE GATES."

disability studies maven (think black studies, women's studies) at Howard University, writes that "the history of disabled people in the Western world is in part the history of being on display. We are visually conspicuous while we are politically and socially erased." She adds that "disabled people have variously been objects of awe, scorn, terror, delight, inspiration, pity, laughter, or fascination—but we have always been stared at." These days certain political freaks use our rude staring behavior to advantage.

Bill Clinton's worst fear, he confided to Gennifer Flowers, was of "cripples chaining themselves to the White House gates." The specific cripples he feared are the disability rights warriors of ADAPT. They haunted him in Arkansas, kept after him in DC. Nonpartisan, they dogged George Dubya all the way from Austin to the White House gates.

An ADAPT action is where you are free at last to stare at freaks, monsters, and maniacs. But prepare for the shock of the real. First thing you notice is people in shorts with see-through plastic pee bags strapped to wasted legs. Pee bags with actual pee in them! These characters are chaos on hot wheels, making speed to their next target. You won't know which way to look first. One guy absently scratches his itchy stump, another's twisted arms flail, a gal pumps food direct to her belly through a plastic tube, another flies by, flat on her back on a power gurney. Medical monster prostheses and hideo-science appliances, hooked to backpacks, fly along behind. The Freak Planet has dropped out of orbit for a day, from out of sight and out of mind, chanting *Free Our People* in robo-speak with reverb, in low grunts and manic shrieks clobbered up on spastic tongues. There's laughter on that soundtrack, too, the unbridled lunatic variety with snorts at the end of it. It's weird. It is.

When ADAPT gathers, freaks are liable to barricade the doors they can't get through, like at the 2000 Republican National Convention. "Just like a nursing home," they chant, "you can't get out." If they have to crawl to get in, you have to crawl over them to get out. The theory in operation, according to Josie Byzek, is, "We are the untouchables. We make them touch us to get where they're going."

_THERE'S GOLD IN THEM THERE REJECTS

Are you listening? Because the United States of America now jails and imprisons more citizens (just short of two million in 2000), in total and per capita, than any other industrialized nation. Here's the freak part: An equal number of Americans (just short of two million in 2000) is locked up for the crime of having a disability. And all but a handful of those unlucky millions are incarcerated, just like your standard criminals, at taxpayer expense.

Now, we don't call it incarceration any more than we call slow people retards. There are complex, pretty euphemisms: For slow we say developmentally delayed; for lockup we say nursing home, developmental center, rehab facility, mental hospital. Most of them are holdovers, relics of the progressive-colonial nineteenth century when the Western world was caught in the grip of the industrially revolutionized social-Darwinian panic. If society pampers the unfit, or lets them run around loose, the unfit will survive and breed like cockroaches. Upstanding white folks, keeping the monsters in porridge and breeding at a far more conservative pace, would fall first into bankruptcy, then minority status.

The Third Reich had its Final Solution, exterminating freaks, monsters, and maniacs years before it got around to the Jews. Segregation (that's what we called it) and sterilization (that, too) were America's humane, semifinal solutions. We appeared to believe that, once sterilized, monsters would appear on our earth no more. Tax-funded asylums for freaks, monsters, and maniacs popped up on the rural landscape the way Wal-Marts do now. It was said that asylums would provide care for the unfit. It was meant that segregation and sterilization would prevent their beastly breeding. State taxpayers footed the bill for the asylum boom; they pay for madhouses to this day. A similar boom, in nursing homes this time, got underway when the feds opened the Medicare/Medicaid pipeline in 1965. There's gold in them there rejects.

You think nobody goes to a nursing home unless they're "too old"? Sorry again. People of all ages, even infants, get dumped there when they're disabled and require some assistance. You think almost no one goes there unless they have to? You're right about that, but why would anyone have to? There are two answers to that, one acute and one chronic.

1. Hospitals rush to discharge acute-care patients before their DRGs run out. (DRG—Diagnostic Related Group, the insurance industry box scores on cost-effective recovery times.) If the DRGs on your condition run out before the hospital discharges you, the hospital gets stranded with an unpaid bill. The pressure is on to "place" you in a less costly setting. Not wanting to appear unreasonable, you sign on their bottom line and presto, you're captive of a nursing home, or a rehabilitation facility (pretty name, same license). For future reference: No matter how they press, you do not have to go. Don't argue; just say, "No, thanks."

2. Chronic cases, disabled people, sooner or later wear out their everyday helpers or don't have cash to purchase assistance on the open market.

Folks sure don't get themselves locked up for their health. "Congregate settings" do not, repeat do not, supply medical care, as in physicians rushing to the bedside. Should Aunt Sally or Uncle Sam in the nursing home have an episode of something actually medical, they go to an ER, just as they would from their own homes, only maybe not so fast. The leading causes of death in congregate settings are not what you're thinking but are iatrogenic (the medical term for professionally-induced). Those are: starvation, preventable accident, incorrectly administered medication, iatrogenic infections which run rampant in ersatz homes (don't even pronounce *methicillin-resistant staphylococcus aureus* or you'll catch it), suicide, fire, allergic reaction, and manslaughter. Why would American taxpayers send poor Uncle Sam to a deathtrap? Follow the money. The pipeline operators, our legislators, dine with fat-pocket lobbyists for corporate wealth and welfare. The nursing home lobby, called the American Health Care Association, is bigger than the NRA, and way wealthier.

_NO ONE WILL EVER KNOW

I have before me another news clipping, this one from the August 2001 *Columbus Dispatch*. The headline says, "Woman, 88, dies in three-story fall at nursing home." The story, by Bruce Cadwallader, leads off with: "No one will ever know what was going through Mary Dowe's confused mind when she tied several bedsheets together and climbed out of a third-floor window at a Near East Side nursing home." Freaks aren't mind-readers, but the one who sent this postcard to me, Woody Osburn, thinks Mary may have had escape in mind. She wouldn't have lived long in any event. Fifteen months of ensqualidation in a congregate setting is the average for healthy, young, male quadriplegics like Osburn, whose escape succeeded. "Relatives had transferred her there because they thought she would be safer," the article says. And everything they thought they knew was wrong.

THE THIRD REICH HAD ITS FINAL SOLUTION, EXTERMINATING FREAKS, MONSTERS, AND MANIACS YEARS BEFORE IT GOT AROUND TO THE JEWS.

We spent 133 billion tax dollars in 1999, more by now, on the safety of long-term care. Four out of five of those tax dollars go for care—as if care can be bought and sold—not in people's homes, where they'd have some control, but in congregate settings where they have none. The life of an unwelcome guest. Think Bates Motel, even if it changed its name to Assisted Living. You might prefer Club Med. And it would be cheaper.

The billions keep rolling; care corporations multiply fiercely. Meanwhile, for those billions, three times as many Americans could receive assistance, e.g., get their medications sorted out, their butts wiped, their checkbooks balanced, even get out to the movies without a recreational therapist attached. There probably aren't three times as many Americans who need personal assistance, but on what we're spending now, that's how many could get the assistance required to live, albeit modestly, in the safety of their own homes.

THE NURSING HOME LOBBY, CALLED THE AMERICAN HEALTH CARE ASSOCIATION, IS BIGGER THAN THE NRA, AND WAY WEALTHIER.

This assistance deal is not terribly medical. While I have never been present for what veteran freaks call a "bowel program," I have it on good authority that quads, people like Chris Reeve, may require some assistance to stick a suppository up their butts. No special training required. The cure required for that to happen in people's homes instead of congregate death traps won't be discovered in laboratories but in legislatures.

_TINY TIM FELL DOWN THE WELL

While more than three million people in the US are on court-ordered probation or work-release programs, twice as many freaks, monsters, and maniacs are similarly monitored, only moreso—supervised and overseen 24-7 in nonprofit group homes and the like, nonprofit sheltered workshops and the like. Note: Nonprofit orgs are like for-profit coms, just not taxable. They can't lose money for long or, like any other business, they'd go under. Wages in nonprofits aren't appreciably lower, nor is overhead. But from my observations, busy-work takes up longer stretches of company time.

Nobody's got a count on the number of nonprofit overseers. The people at *Mouth* magazine made an I-think conservative estimate that eight million PLODs ride on the backs of the disabled, noting that they are likely to be "liberals." (Translation: registered Democrats whose neighbors call them saints for having the patience to work with *those people*.) Freaks see them as minor-league missionaries for middle-class values, crusaders and conquistadors who draw their living from the bottomless well of sentimentality inspired by, oh, say Tiny Tim. Meantime, down in the well, how is Timmy faring at the hands of the saints? No one looks, or wants to, or is allowed to. Outsiders and cameras are barred on grounds of client confidentiality, as if confinement to such a setting is cause for shame, as of course it is.

_GOING UNDERCOVER

But now, through the magic of the printed page, we present the horrible, hidden truth of (insert ooo-eee-ooo effect here) sheltered workshops. I went undercover as a client (that's what the saints call them, that or *consumers*, as in *useless eaters*) at a big one in Rochester, New York, being extruded after not quite three days. No, my secret identity went undiscovered. Clients are clients, subhuman clods. PLODs don't look at clods unless they make a sudden move or a loud shrieking sound, both of which behaviors are strictly forbidden. Workshops, and their even more evil twin, day programs, inhabit a planet in the black hole of space, delivering for six million Americans what is termed "work hardening," "habilitation," or "day treatment." The six million have been, or have a history of being, dis-labeled. Here are translations for earthlings of some technical-

sounding workshop dis-labels: slow on the uptake; speaks so haltingly that people in a hurry can't understand; publicly eccentric or demented but nonetheless well-behaved; as spastic as Michael J. Fox; as blind as Stevie Wonder; "in recovery"; noticeably buggered up by psychiatric drugs or shock; not wanted at home. And once he gets in there, not even Stevie will get out.

Ian Stanton, a British amputee, singer and songwriter for the Tragic But Brave Show, was prisoner of a workshop for eight years. His poem "S.O.S." paraphrases a case manager for the Spastics Society, a British charity. "You're safe in here/not like out there/People laugh/and people stare/They don't mean harm/they're just not used to/seeing someone *jerk*...like you."

He'd been there. I've been there, and to more than one. I found that workshops aren't sweatshops but assembly or disassembly lines. People sit or stand, quietly, at tables, often in a basement or other windowless room with no means of egress to the world at large, putting doohickeys together or pulling them apart. Charity obtains remuneration for this work through its account reps, who flog "outsourcing" to local industry at everyday low prices. Most such work, according to Ruby Moore of New England Business Enterprises, a former workshop, is garbage-related: e.g., winding garbage bags on rolls; separating used, disposable camera parts for recycling; disassembling stereo components that flunked quality control. At one Northwest Indiana workshop with the wistful name of Tradewinds, clients labor at industrial sewing machines, on contract to the Pentagon, creating extravagant costumes for germ warfare epics.

Generally, though, sheltered work is the indoor equivalent of stoop labor. It's farmed out because it's degrading, poorly paid, even dangerous. Dangerous as in disassembling used hypodermic syringes. For $4.15 per month, net take-home. Yes, month. The take-home is no better at Tradewinds where, no matter what you call the workers, their labor is skilled.

NBC News once called me, planning a hidden camera exposé of the sheltered work industry. I was assigned to find a truly egregious case, "one that even a television viewer can understand." I located, in Alabama, prisoners for the crime of disability working in a tin-roofed shed where they (are you ready?) bag deer urine. You bet I asked. Hunters use it to entice Bambi's papa into the line of fire. I didn't think to ask how deer urine is collected. "Heeeere, Bambi.... No, no, over *here*!" I dunno.

The NBC producer had hoped for a Porsche, but the bag o' urine workshop's front man drives a Lincoln Town Car. Two clients get a daily break from the hot, stinking shed to wash and polish it. Human bondage! Corruption! Leather interiors! Even so, the story was not produced.

_THE CASE OF THE 99-CENT PAYCHECK

What's striking about a tour of a sheltered workshop, were you able to reach this faraway planet, is the near-silence of its beneficiaries. In the one where I worked, clients were forbidden to speak until the break bell rang. ("Inappropriate behavior," such as talking on the job, is punishable by exile to the dreaded Time Out Room.) Trips to the bathroom were similarly forbidden until the bell rang. When the shop ran out of contract work, clients were to sit in place, in silence, until the bell rang. Even Nike's outsource shops in China can't tell workers to shut up and hold their water until the bell rings. Or maybe they can. Clients on my line advised me, "Be careful! They'll write you up!"

Avoided even more strenuously than Time Out was a room around the corner from our bench called the Day Program. Day programming in this context consisted of a television set mounted on a clamp, up high by the fluorescents, tuned to *Sesame Street* or soap operas. Programmed, the clods huddled under flickering blue light, nearly silent, nearly unmoving until the bell rang. I have heard day programs defended by industrial missionaries who say, "But if they stay home, they'll just watch television all day." And if they stay home, the charity won't earn your tax dollars for keeping the freaks out of our sight.

A fellow client arrived at work one morning, sick with something wet and communicable. It wasn't the work ethic prompting her to show. Staying at home was not allowed. "There's no day staff at the residence," a PLOD informed me. When the client vomited, staff called 911. An ambulance took her, PLOD attached, to the hospital emergency room. Clients, silent clients, mopped up after her. Mustn't grumble.

Mike Auberger, leader of ADAPT, has a framed 99-cent paycheck hung up over his desk. A guy he knows earned it for a month's labor in a sheltered workshop. My own extrusion came long before my first paycheck, but I was to be paid some percentage of the hourly minimum wage, a percentage determined by a junior-college maybe-graduate during a formal assessment of my abilities versus normal abilities. I saw some first-rate workers there; none of them earned more than 20 percent of minimum wage.

Our workshop was lodged beneath the headquarters of a number of local offices of national charities. To be assessed, I had to go upstairs, as in The Man Upstairs. My trip required a special pass. A PLOD directed me to proceed "without no runnin' or foolin' around." Upstairs, all the charity presidents' offices stood in a freak show row, the fabled Hall of Presidents. Each top dog was male, white, distinguished-looking, graying at the temples, wearing a blue suit and a power tie. Seated behind an impressive desk, each was power-positioned before a wall of diplomas, photos, awards. None appeared to have any actual work to do. I've worked in business offices, even been a boss. I know the telltale signs of look-busy-ism. TGIF.

My paycheck, like theirs, would have shown the usual deductions, plus one for my fair share to United Way. (This was a United Way agency. We had a duty to kick back.) Unlike theirs, mine would have shown two big deductions: one for charity-provided transportation to and from the job ($16 per day), the other for my required daily lunch ($3) in the workshop's cafeteria. I could have spent what was left of my pay in the workshop vending machines, at break time, on payday. Everybody else did. Our postcard to Earth would have read, *We owe our souls to the company store. Have a nice day!*

_THEY HAVE WORDS FOR US

The Freak Planet term for congregate settings is handicaptivity. For the business of congregate settings, handicapitalism. For sellout freaks, Tiny Tim. For Jack Kevorkian, serial crip killer.

The bigotry earthpeople express in regard to disabled people is termed able-ism, as in racism or sexism. *Able*-ism: the belief that one is superior because one is, e.g., able to speak clearly, wipe one's own butt, climb stairs. The hyphen is there to assist the non-disabled in pronunciation. For the record, that's what they call us, non-disabled. Queers call me "straight." I resent that, too.

_CHEAPER DEAD THAN ALIVE

"Don't bother with a funeral," Verna B. Gwin, my mama, always said. "Just toss me in a garbage can and walk away." Trouble is, she didn't just up and die; she got Alzheimer's. A resolute iconoclast who in consequence struggled with poverty most of her adult life, she shopped at the Goodwill but wore her findings as if she were Coco Chanel. She had this thing about shame. By 1987 Verna was drooling, blabbering, feeling neither pain nor shame. I'm the one who felt shame, shame *for* her, I thought. She wouldn't have wanted anyone to see her like that. We're kinder to dogs, I remember thinking, putting them out of their misery when the moment comes. (Well, maybe our misery, not theirs.) I entertained a tragic fantasy of drowning her, gently, in her beloved Ohio River. I meant well. As usual, that's no excuse for sloppy thinking.

Fast-forward ten years to 1997, when I stood with more than a thousand members of Not Dead Yet at the US Supreme Court to deliver a postcard in person: *We want to live!*

The case before the Court that day was *Vacco v. Quill*—Dennis Vacco, then Attorney General of New York State, versus Timothy Quill, M.D. Quill wanted the right to kill his patients without Vacco bringing him up on criminal charges. The press had long been projecting non-disabled America's death wish for freaks and monsters. When we asked America to think about it, we hit the front pages for once. Let's recap: 1) Calling alcoholism a disease is somebody's ticket to ride your health insurance into the medical system. The "right to die" is somebody's ticket to kill a monster and get out of jail free. 2) If the fifty-some-odd million Americans with disabilities wanted to die, they'd be flying off rooftops, pounding the sidewalks like hard rain. Getting dead is easy, requiring no medical intervention. 3) Oregon, a state which proffers compassion in dying, bolsters its argument with economic rationales, as do many medical ethicists. Freaks are cheaper dead than alive.

State Farm Insurance operates with a similar philosophical bent. Its actuaries having discovered that fatality rates involving sport utility vehicles have a real upside. "SUVs," they told stockholders, "may actually save insurers money...by killing people who might otherwise have survived with serious injuries. Severe injuries tend to produce larger settlements than deaths." It's not just freaks, monsters, and maniacs who are cheaper dead than alive. It's all of us. Take a moment to envision the last man left alive marking down Planet Earth for quick sale.

> **IF THE FIFTY-SOME-ODD MILLION AMERICANS WITH DISABILITIES WANTED TO DIE, THEY'D BE FLYING OFF ROOFTOPS, POUNDING THE SIDEWALKS LIKE HARD RAIN.**

Now, one dying postcard. The standard advance medical directive dictates that one does not wish for "heroic measures" to be taken to preserve one's paltry life. This card from the Planet of the Freaks says: *Spare no expense. Keep me alive.*

_CALL OFF THE ATTACK DOGS

Freaks, monsters, maniacs chained to society's gates, howling for freedom—they're coming soon to a gate near you. I'm in favor and hope you don't sic your dogs on them. Standing with them, I get a rush like I do when the ideal deal is being hammered out. Another rush, too. When they win their long-lost freedom to run around loose, when we finally move over, loosen up, and make room for them, then we non-freaks, non-monsters, non-maniacs can breathe a little easier, even take five from the conformity that, c'mon, admit it, hurts so bad. We could, just imagine it, let a little more of our own freaky, monstrous, maniacal selves out to play. I know how good it is because I have a piece of it now, hanging with the freaks on their planet. Don't be afraid to come visit.

TOXIC TV SYNDROME
KALLE LASN

A few recent psychosocial studies may change the way we think about television, advertising, and our consumer culture.

If you reduced all of history's best advice on living well to two fridge-magnet-worthy goals, they would probably be 1) pursue excellence or 2) pursue balance. In other words, either drill down—work with obsessive focus in one area, try to create something new and valuable and lasting; or go wide—learn to surf or meditate, read good books, tend a garden, raise a kid or two, try to be neighborly. You know, all the stuff that makes life worth the price if your job itself isn't all that fulfilling.

TV-watching doesn't exactly top either list. When you sit down in front of the box—not occasionally, but on a regular basis, as a lifestyle choice (and we North Americans watch four hours a day, on average, making TV-watching the lifestyle of choice)—you're basically choosing neither path. You're neither rounding yourself out in any appreciable way, nor are you sharpening some art or skill or craft. You're just dropping out. Chronic TV-watching is like wearing sweatpants in public. It's a public declaration: "I give up."

Write me off as a scold if you like; I won't be hurt. We TV-turnoff proponents are forever being chided by hip critics as joyless, clueless prudes, the Carrie Nations of the media age. But have you ever noticed how these same critics often sound more earnest in their support of television than anyone on the turnoff side does questioning it? There are the predictable hymns to *The Simpsons* and *The Sopranos* (a show you don't even get where I live without an expensive extension to your already expensive cable package). And the oh-but-the-cream-of-TV-is-high-art shtick. It may be true. But "the cream" is an ever-diminishing portion of the grand, bland banquet of commercial programming. Anyway, the cream isn't what most people watch.

There are so many great reasons to go on a TV-fast for a week that the case can be won without resorting to the merely good reasons. But I'm not going to go that route. Jerry Mander (author of *Four Arguments for the Elimination of Television*, Morrow Quill, 1978)

pretty much covered it over 20 years ago. Besides, it doesn't make sense these days to talk about TV in isolation. The media environment is one big, complicated mass of connected componentry, of which TV is but one element. You can't really pull out one part and hold it to the light. You have to step back far enough to get a picture of how the whole thing works. And when you do that, something interesting and a little bit scary happens. You start to discover things you might have been better off not knowing.

Recently some very credible researchers have taken just that wide view, publishing some pretty powerful studies. Their work suggests that there's something extremely wrong with our hyper-mediated way of life. That something psychologically corrosive is happening. The strong implication is that not just television and the Internet, but our whole commercial culture is toxic.

Social epidemiologist Myrna Weissman of Columbia University published two such studies in 1992 and 1996 in the *Journal of the American Medical Association*.[1] She found a depression explosion in America. Not only are more Americans becoming depressed each year, they're becoming depressed at a younger age, and the severity and frequency of their depression is rising. Each of the last four generations has suffered more depression than its predecessor. Since World War II, the overall rate of depression has more than doubled. A more recent study, published in the *Archives of General Psychiatry* in 2000,[2] showed more than a doubling of depression in women from 1970 to 1992. Martin Seligman, University of Pennsylvania psychology professor and head of the American Psychological Association, flatly claims the United States is in the throes of an "epidemic" of clinical depression.[3]

What's going on? No one really knows. Probably a complex set of related causes is involved. Could some little-understood virus be making us genetically vulnerable? Or might it be something in the environment—microwaves, electromagnetism, or a chemical in our food or water? The accelerating pace of life is forcing breakneck adjustments; maybe that's stressing us out. Or maybe it's corporate identity branding? Or growing isolation, the "bowling alone" syn-

> **MEXICAN MEN BORN IN THE US WERE FIVE TIMES AS LIKELY AS RECENT IMMIGRANTS TO EXPERIENCE A "MAJOR DEPRESSIVE EPISODE."**

drome? Depression is "significantly more common" among people who live alone, reports the National Institute for Healthcare Research (NIHR)[4]—and nightly face-time with Regis, strangely, doesn't seem to fill the void.

I've always had trouble convincing some people that culture itself is one of the prime culprits in our malaise, but the task has been much easier since William Vega's 1998 study was published in the *Archives of General Psychiatry*.[5] A public health researcher at Rutgers University, Vega followed recent immigrants from Mexico as they tried to integrate into American society. When they first arrived in the US, they were much better adjusted than the Americans they settled among (they had half the incidence of psychological dysfunction). But as they Americanized, they got sicker and sicker. After thirteen years Stateside, their rates of depression, anxiety, and drug problems had almost doubled (from 18 percent to 32 percent), to the point where they were now on par with the average American's.

Mexican-Americans born in the US got the full brunt of American toxic culture from the get-go, and their still-higher rates of psychological affliction show that just about half suffered a disorder, as defined by the standard tests. Mexican men born in the US were five times as likely as recent immigrants to experience a "major depressive episode." Drug misuse among Mexican women born in the US was seven times as high as that of recent immigrants. Other studies have both replicated William Vega's findings and extended them to other ethnic groups. Vega's conclusion: "Socialization into American culture and society [will] increase susceptibility to psychiatric disorders." That's a damning indictment—and hard to rebut.

Except that it doesn't tell us which part of the culture is toxic. Is it the lack of community and family life? The junk food? The thousands of commercial messages the mass media pumps into our brains every day? The gradual blunting of emotions that comes from growing up in a violent and erotically-charged media environment? It could be any or all of these, but a 1992 study published in the *Journal of the American Medical Association*[6] laid some of the blame on the atomizing effects of television and mass communications, which the study's authors suggested "have turned us into a single competitive group while destroying our intimate social networks." Watching TV is the very opposite of an affiliating exercise—we finish up isolating ourselves by watching nature shows instead of going hiking with a friend, laughing at TV jokes instead of joking around ourselves, drooling over video sex and porno Websites instead of having sex ourselves.

The authors of a Stanford University study released in 2000 found that the Internet also steals time normally spent with other human beings. "If I go home at 6:30 in the evening and spend the whole night sending email and wake up the next morning, I still haven't talked to my wife or kids or friends," the study's principal investigator, Norman Nie, told the *New York Times*.[7] "When you spend your time on the Internet, you don't hear a human voice and you never get a hug." An online "community" can't possibly substitute for a real community, because the essential things that make a community are absent.

David Korten, author of *When Corporations Rule the World*, points the finger at the whole capitalist rat race. He argues that we are all caught to some degree in "a downward spiral of deepening alienation." Our incessant quest for money widens the gulf between ourselves and our family/community. This separation creates an inner sense of social and spiritual emptiness. Advertisers then get into the act by assuring us that their products can make us happy and whole again. So we go out and buy their stuff, which of course puts us right back at the beginning of the vicious cycle—our incessant quest for money.

> IN 1999, A TEAM OF HARVARD RESEARCHERS LOOKED AT CHRONIC TV-WATCHING AND FOUND IT CORRELATED POSITIVELY WITH LOW PUBLIC ENGAGEMENT, LACK OF SOCIABILITY, AND JUST GENERAL LOUTISHNESS.

Have any studies isolated the toxicity of TV specifically? Actually, yes. In 1999, a team of Harvard researchers looked at chronic TV-watching and found it correlated positively with low public engagement, lack of sociability, and just general loutishness.[8] It "even correlates positively with 'giving the finger to people,'" said David Campbell, a member of the research team. (The question remains, of course, whether chronic TV-watching creates louts, or whether louts tend to watch a lot of tube. Either way, the results don't say much for TV.)

These studies tend to contradict the prevailing narrative that evermore-electronic stimulation is a good thing and that mediated living is our inevitable future. Maybe that's why these studies haven't got much play outside scientific journals. But for my culture-jamming friends and me, these statistics mean something; they explain something; they are fascinating, alarming, revolutionary.

Think about the average mental state of the average millennial serf steeped in electronic media. Always, always on the go, with never a quiet time to reflect, persistent low-level anxiety, rapid emotional swings from euphoria to boredom, daily bouts of frustration that threaten to tip into despair. And all the while we have this unshakable conviction that happiness is right around the corner, as soon as the next raise comes or the Hawaiian vacation happens or the guy delivers the Bowflex. This is dire stuff. Put enough people who feel this way together, get them sharing the intimate details of their disease, and what you have is a recipe for revolution.

Once people start making the connection between advertising/TV/culture and their own mental health, I think we'll see a politicization of the mental environment and the birth of a mental-environmental movement every bit as potent and far-reaching as the physical environmental movement of yesteryear. As this "environmental movement of the mind" gathers momentum, it will alter the way information flows, the way TV stations are run, the way meaning is produced. Every bit of our mediated lives will be up for grabs. Parents will teach their kids new rhymes like, "A bit less TV a day keeps the blues at bay." Activists will challenge a TV system that delivers fifteen minutes per hour of station hype and ads, and, in the name of democracy and a free marketplace of ideas, they will demand that the six media megacorporations that now control over half of all the news and entertainment around the planet be broken into smaller parts. And then, just about everybody will suddenly get into the act, demanding all the media start paring back their usual celebrity gossip and consumer hype and start providing some, well...balance.

These, I'd say, would be most excellent pursuits.

Endnotes

1. Cross-National Collaborative Group. "The Changing Rate of Major Depression: Cross-national Comparisons." *Journal of the American Medical Association* 268.21 (2 Dec 1992): 3098(8); Weissman, Myrna M., *et al*. "Cross-national Epidemiology of Major Depression and Bipolar Disorder." *The Journal of the American Medical Association* 276.4 (24 July 1996): 293(7). **2.** Murphy, Jane M., Nan M Laird, *et al*. "A 40-year Perspective on the Prevalence of Depression: The Stirling County Study." *Archives of General Psychiatry* 57.3 (March 2000): 209. **3.** Mattox, William R., Jr. "Bawling Alone." *Policy Review* (Sept/Oct 1998). **4.** *Ibid*. **5.** Alderete, Ethel, William Armando Vega, *et al*. "Lifetime Prevalence of and Risk Factors for Psychiatric Disorders Among Mexican Migrant Farmworkers in California." *The American Journal of Public Health* 90.4 (April 2000): 608. **6.** Centerwall, Brandon S. "Television and Violence: The Scale of the Problem and Where to Go From Here." *Journal of the American Medical Association* 267.22 (10 June 1992): 3059(5). **7.** Markoff, John. "A Newer, Lonelier Crowd Emerges in Internet Study." *New York Times* 16 Feb 2000. **8.** Campbell, David E., *et al*. "The American Viewer: Television's Impact on Social Capital." Presented at the 1999 Annual Meeting of the American Political Science Association.

PARENTS WILL TEACH THEIR KIDS NEW RHYMES LIKE, "A BIT LESS TV A DAY KEEPS THE BLUES AT BAY."

TREATMENT OR JAIL
IS THIS REALLY A CHOICE?
PRESTON PEET

> "Madness is not enlightenment, but the search for enlightenment can easily be mistaken for madness."
> —Martin (Asylum 1996-1997)[1]

Some people take drugs to escape difficult life situations. Some take drugs to assist in treating pain, physical or psychological. Some take drugs simply to get high. The reasons for taking drugs are legion. But under the War on Some Drugs prohibition, the US government has given itself the right to dictate which drugs and highs are acceptable. Now a movement is growing in the US to push those convicted of drug charges into drug treatment instead of jail.

Although US jails can be hellish and cruel, a certain percentage of people willfully continue to get high on any assortment of illicit (and licit) substances no matter what the law says. So they must be crazy or sick and therefore in need of behavior modification and mind control. In other words, drug treatment.

While living in Florida in 1987, I was arrested on a misdemeanor charge completely unrelated to drugs. Sitting in jail unable to make bail, I was taken from my cellblock one morning to meet with a man from TASC (Treatment Alternatives to Street Crime).[2] Naïve and unsuspecting, I was open with him about my drug use, listing all the drugs I had ingested up to that point in my life. It was a long list.

A week or so later, when I finally got to court, I was stunned when the same TASC evaluator stood up before the judge and told her I had a "drug problem" and needed to be placed into treatment. The judge sentenced me to a year of probation and to successful completion of the TASC program.

I fought it all the way. I was using some drugs then, abusing some others, and dealing with other problems, as well. I was told that the TASC program lasted twelve to eighteen months on average and that my probation would not be finished in twelve months unless I'd graduated from TASC. After a couple of months in the outpatient treatment program, I was being urine-tested each week—Monday, Wednesday, and Friday, then Tuesday and Thursday on alternating weeks. After dodging these testing sessions as much as possible, and repeatedly trying to fool the tests, marijuana and cocaine turned up in my urine. I was taken to see the head of the program, who told me he was notifying my probation officer and would be in court to recommend the maximum jail time for me, as I was "incorrigible and untreatable."

Basically, he was right. I was, and still am, incorrigible but not necessarily untreatable. This doesn't mean that I personally want or need treatment now, nor do I support treatment for others unless it is entirely voluntary. Under current US War on Some Drugs policies, how often is drug treatment really voluntary?

_THE THERAPEUTIC STATE

"Coerced treatment is an oxymoron. Government intrusion by police and arrest is anti-treatment. I am not against treatment; I am against government-compelled treatment," said ACLU Executive Director Ira Glasser at the Lindesmith Center-Drug Policy Foundation's[3] international drug policy reform conference.[4] Continuing with a dire prognostication, Glasser said, "Fusing the police power of the State with medicine corrupts medicine and makes it a tool of the State. Then we get the therapeutic State and pretend that is progress. The worst danger is an ever-expanding net of social control. The 'benevolence' of coerced treatment is a trap. It will allow the State to define acceptable treatment, and that means abstinence and piss-testing."

Deborah Small, Director of Public Policy and Community Outreach at Lindesmith-NYC, countered Glasser's statements by asking, "How can you question anything that gets people out of the living death of prison? We have to engage with what is actually happening in the criminal justice system, and coerced treatment is an alternative to incarceration."

I can personally vouch for the fact that jail is not healthy or fun, nor did spending time inside ever keep me from wanting to get high.

"COERCED TREATMENT IS AN OXYMORON. GOVERNMENT INTRUSION BY POLICE AND ARREST IS ANTI-TREATMENT."

When the judge first mandated me into treatment, I thought it was a far better choice than a trip through jail. Not by any means do I support incarceration for any drug offense (which I hadn't been charged with at that time, anyway), but treatment at that point wasn't better for me. It merely exacerbated my already high stress levels by focusing on immediately eradicating my drug use to the exclusion of all else, which I in turn dealt with by doing more drugs. This was when I first heard that I had a disease called "addiction," that I had no control, that all substance use was substance abuse, that any drug use would lead me straight to jails, institutions, or death. As I wouldn't accept this, even daring to question these assertions, I was in "denial." Coerced drug treatment ordered by the court did nothing but prolong my legal and personal difficulties.

"In thinking about linkages between drug treatment and criminal sanctions, it is important to distinguish between questions of effectiveness and fairness," explains a recent report from the National Academy of Sciences.[5] "Supporters of using the criminal justice system for therapeutic leverage typically view treatment participation offered to offenders as an ameliorative device—an opportunity for mitigating the sentence they would otherwise receive (i.e., probation with treatment is offered in lieu of incarceration, using the threat of incarceration for noncompliance). Others worry that programs of mandated treatment will actually have the effect of increasing the severity of punishment compared with what the offenders would otherwise have received. As an example, offenders who otherwise would have been sentenced to traditional probation could be subject to treatment conditions that create a risk of imprisonment (for noncompliance) that otherwise wouldn't have existed. Or an offender whose case might otherwise have been dismissed could be sentenced to conditional probation. These are classic 'net-widening' concerns, because they widen the reach and deepen the intensity of punishment. This issue should be kept in mind in considering research on coerced treatment."

_LOCK 'EM UP, ONE WAY OR THE OTHER

"Because when the smack begins to flow I really don't care anymore, about all the Jim-Jims in this town, and all the politicians making crazy sounds, and everybody putting everybody else down, and all the dead bodies piled up in mounds." —Lou Reed[6]

Reading through the statistics, the numbers of people being arrested and going on to jail in the US for drug offenses are offensive. At first glance, it would seem that putting people into treatment programs instead of sending them to jail with hardened, sometimes violent, predatory criminals simply makes good sense. At the time of this writing (August 2001), the US is about to surpass one million people arrested for drug offenses this year, with someone being arrested every 20 seconds. The US is locking up nearly 648 people a day for drug offenses. A new report from the US Justice Department shows the number of adult Americans under "correctional supervision" rose 2 percent in 2000. In the US, federal and state prisoners, plus those on probation or parole, now number 6.5 million.[7] The federal and state governments are spending, in 2001, approximately $19 and $20 billion, respectively, on the War on Some Drugs.[8] As with any war, this means all kinds of established profit potential in conducting all facets of this war.

With the new push for drug treatment, there comes a lucrative new business and means of control that can be instituted without giving up the profits currently pulled in by the War on Some Drugs industries. When announcing his resignation as head of the White House Office of National Drug Control Policy (ONDCP), then-US Drug Czar Gen. Barry McCaffrey bemoaned the use of war terminology in the fight against drug use, saying that perhaps when discussing the situation in the Andes, "war" is an apt term, but not when discussing efforts in US cities. This might seem an odd stance for such a stalwart proponent of US military and law enforcement involvement in waging the War on Some Drugs, but McCaffrey "agreed" on July 24, 2001, to join the board of directors at DrugAbuse Sciences Inc., "the world's first pharmaceutical company worldwide devoted solely to developing medications for the treatment of addiction."[9] McCaffrey's newfound love of treatment is now explained.

"DrugAbuse Sciences has the potential to make a historic difference in the health of Americans through its understanding of treatment and its broad portfolio of new medications under development," asserted the retired general. "They have created a company consisting of the leading medical researchers, clinicians and most exciting new product candidates. This combination offers the promise of developing highly effective medical treatment options for addictions. Addiction is a disease that costs our country over 100,000 lives and over $250 billion per year."[10] Which is odd, as McCaffrey said only the year before, in July 2000: "Each year 52,000 Americans die from drug-related causes. The additional societal costs of drug use to the nation total over $110 billion per year."[11]

Spouting spurious numbers to promote and justify repressive (and profitable) anti-drug policies has been a favorite ploy of prohibitionist Drug Warriors since President Nixon first uttered his declaration of a War on Drugs in 1968. As related by author Dan Baum, by 1972, "The conservative Hudson Institute estimated that New York City's 250,000 heroin addicts were responsible for a whopping $1.7 billion in crime, which was well more than the total amount of crime in the NATION. 'Narcotics addiction and crime are inseparable companions,' said presidential candidate George McGovern in a speech on the Senate floor. 'In 98 percent of the cases [the junkie] steals to pay the pusher...that translates into about $4.4 billion in crime.' Senator Charles Percy of Illinois saw McGovern's bid and raised him. 'The total cost of drug-related crime in the US today is around $10 billion to $15 billion,' he said.

"In fact, only $1.28 billion worth of property was stolen in the US in 1972 (the figure had actually fallen slightly from the previous year). That includes everything except cars, which junkies don't usually steal because they can't easily fence them, and embezzlement, which isn't a junkie crime. The combined value of everything swiped in burglaries, robberies, and muggings, everything shoplifted, filched off the back of a truck, or boosted from a warehouse was $1.28 billion. Yet during the heroin panic of Nixon's War on Drugs, junkies would be blamed for stealing as much as fifteen times the value of everything stolen in the United States."[12] As the original fallacious numbers bandied about by prohibitionists convinced the nation to support mass-jailing of druggies, so too do they steer us toward coerced treatment today.

_IS IT REALLY WORTH IT?

"Humanity has advanced, when it has advanced, not because it has been sober, responsible, and cautious, but because it has been playful, rebellious, and immature."
—Tom Robbins[13]

According to public hearings for "Changing the Conversation: A National Plan to Improve Substance Abuse Treatment," sponsored by the US Center for Substance Abuse Treatment: "Over the last decade, spending on substance abuse prevention and treatment has increased, albeit more slowly than overall health spending, to an estimated annual total of $12.6 billion in 1996. Of this amount, public spending is estimated at $7.6 billion.... One of the main reasons for the higher outlay in public spending is the frequently limited coverage of substance abuse treatment by private insurers. Although '70 percent of drug users are employed and most have private health insurance, 20 percent of public treatment funds were spent on people with private health insurance in 1993, due to limitations on their policy.'"[14]

If the current "rush to rehab is indeed going to ease our nation away from the disasters of addiction, we must first determine if treatment indeed keeps addicts off drugs," notes author and photojournalist Lonny Shavelson when discussing US treatment efforts, primarily San Francisco's September 1997 plan of treatment on demand for any addict who said he or she was ready to stop using drugs. "If, as the data seem to show, treatment doesn't actually keep addicts clean, this new push for rehab will simply become another dogma-based government strategy doomed to failure.

"Rehab has to work for the hardest-core of the dope fiends—those who create the vast majority of troubles we've artificially lumped into a single set phrase: the drug problem. The US Department of Justice has concluded that only a small percentage of the nation's drug abusers create 'an extraordinary proportion of crime.' Yet those most destructive addicts are the least likely to enter or be helped by rehab. This latest push towards treatment, then, may do nothing more than get the 'better' addicts off drugs, leaving the hard-core troublemakers still disastrously addicted.... Those hard-core addicts (10 to 20 percent of users) have, depending on your point of view, either brought on the drug war, or are the tragic casualties of its battles. But if frenzied addictions are indeed responses to lives often complicated by irresolute ghetto-poverty or psychological disturbances, then rehab programs that fail to address these underlying conditions will barely make a dent in our nation's drug disasters."[15]

Rather than addressing the root causes of hardcore drug abuse, the prohibitionists have a much easier time directing attention to that most benign of plants, marijuana. The Office of National Drug Control Policy estimates the numbers of hardcore drug abusers between 1988 and 1998 at 3.2 million to 3.9 million (cocaine), 630,000 to 980,000 (heroin), and 300,00 to 400,000 (methamphetamine). With these numbers, the Warriors should be hard-pressed to justify the billions spent on the war—unless they drag pot into the picture.

"Marijuana is the gateway drug for the growth of state-mandated drug treatment. This important policy issue deserves greater public scrutiny and debate," writes Jon Gettman, Ph.D.[16] Admissions for treatment of adolescent marijuana abuse increased 155 percent, from 30,832 in 1993 to 78,523 in 1998, according to the Substance Abuse and Mental Health Services Administration of the Department of Health and Human Services. Total marijuana admissions increased 88 percent, from 111,265 in 1993 to 208,671 in 1998. Almost half of those admitted to treatment for marijuana abuse were under the age of 20.

All marijuana arrests increased 93 percent, from 380,689 in 1993 to 734,498 in 2000. Arrests for simple marijuana possession rose by 107 percent, from 310,859 in 1993 to 646,042 in 2000 (in other words, of those arrested on pot charges in 2000, nearly 88 percent were charged with simple possesion).[17] Out of a reported 208,671 admissions to treatment for pot use in 1998, slightly more than half (53.4 percent) were referred by the criminal justice system, all of which goes a long way toward "explaining a great deal of the increase in marijuana treatment admissions," notes Gettman. "Police and drug treatment specialists are caught up in an economic system. When criminal justice system referrals provide over half of admissions for treatment of marijuana abuse, it is clear that in this economic sector arrests move the market. Marijuana can be abused and the source of dependency, and these problems can be alleviated with medical treatment. Most debate focuses, with good reason, on whether the actual abuse liability of marijuana justifies arrest and criminal sanctions. A more fundamental question though is whether law enforcement and/or judicial personnel should be making medical decisions and enforcing them with the power of the state. At what point does the state dictate the treatment as well as provide the patients?"[18]

_THE ASSASSINS OF YOUTH

> "The young do not know enough to be prudent, and therefore they attempt the impossible, and achieve it, generation after generation." —Pearl S. Buck[19]

"With America's Number One Drug Problem [marijuana] identified as the one teenagers are most likely to use, and every sneer, slammed door, and blast of Joan Jett pegged as evidence of a 'drug problem,' the War on Drugs became a powerful weapon for parents to use in their struggle with their teenagers," writes Dan Baum about the shift in emphasis by Drug Warriors to marijuana under Carlton Turner, President Reagan's first Drug Czar, in September 1981.[20] "Blaming drugs for kids' troubles also worked in wider society: it obviated concern for 'root causes' and let parents take their own behavior off the hook. If drugs were, as the Florida pediatrician Ian McDonald liked to assert, a problem teenager's 'only' problem, then parents needn't examine their own role in their children's troubles—divorce, career obsession, neglect—or for that matter failing wages, the need for both parents to work long hours, and slashed funding for education and after-school programs. While some nasty kids *did* have drug problems that required intervention, the parents of *all* nasty kids were urged—in magazine articles, PTA handouts, TV spots, and exhortations from the White House—to band together and 'fight back.' And in 1982, the most bellicose pro-parent, anti-child manifesto of them all rocketed up the best seller list: *Tough Love*."[21, 22]

Saving our children is one of the most oft-quoted justifications given by rabid anti-drug warriors and supporters for continuing the War. As Arnold Trebach, chairman of the Trebach Institute, so eloquently put it at the Saving Our Children From Abusive Drug Treatment conference: "Anything for the kids. Like the phrase in Vietnam, we had to destroy the village to save it,[23] some people say I've got to destroy my kid to save it." Scores of both now-adult and adolescent survivors—whose parents, under the influence of "Tough Love" philosophy and anti-drug hysteria, forced them into adolescent drug treatment programs such as Straight Inc.,[24] Safe, Kids, and many more—came together to relate individual experiences of being beaten, starved, spit on, deprived of sleep, subjected to constant surveillance, and isolated from schools and communities while in these so-called treatment programs. They also tried to figure some way to

stop this industry from continuing. Many of these people were forced into long-term, confrontational drug treatment over minor experimentation with drugs or natural adolescent rebellious behavior, finding themselves locked in horrific programs that aim to tear people down and rebuild them as contributing members of society (as the treatment programs define it).

"During my involvement with the Seed and Straight, extreme physical violence was not very much a part of the Program," says survivor Ginger Warbis.[25] "Physical coercion, such as restraint, which sometimes resulted in injury and forced exercise, were. But these were not everyday occurrences. I don't think I ever saw more than one person pinned to the floor at a time and very rarely any obvious and serious physical injury." Until witnessing a severe incident of terror perpetrated against another Straight inmate, Warbis notes that, "I knew it was all theatre designed to intimidate and coerce sincere, internal compliance. I'd thought that eventually we'd each get out one way or another and either live as good little Straightlings or just shake it off. But I've come to realize that 1) the very basic thought reform methods used in these programs are extremely harmful psychologically and emotionally in themselves and 2) escalation to more extreme physical and psychological abuse is just about an eventuality under these conditions.

"The most important message that I wanted to deliver [at the conference] is that many of the most influential people in public policy, the drug war, juvenile justice and child protective services are big believers in using these very harmful methods. Some of them, I believe, should be in prison right now. Others just need a better understanding of what they're advocating."[26]

A few parents attending the conference said that having put their children into a confrontational therapy-based behavior modification program had "saved their kids' lives."

"I think the parents are sincere. But they're confusing the issue," says Warbis. "If you'll remember, Brian Seeber [a parent who put his child in SAFE, yet another drug treatment program for adolescents] talked about how much his son hated him before and how much he loves him now. They're not saving their children; they're saving their own egos. They're not aware of this, though, as they cloister themselves with people who constantly reassure them that they're right and they demonize all others. I wish I'd gotten my hands on the mic to answer the question, 'Well, what do we do if not this?' Basically, there comes a time when you have to realize that, as a parent, you don't have any guaranteed right to your child's affection. They're always your babies and you'd do anything to help or protect them; that never changes. But there comes a time when they're also young adults who may not want your help or advice or even your company. Whatever you do you have to respect that, even when you know they're making horrible mistakes. These people are doing great harm by crushing their children's egos. If I could find a way to make them understand that, I'd try it on my mother. I haven't spoken with her in years for just this reason."

Stockbroker Stoney Burke sent his two sons, Scott and David, into treatment with Teen Help,[27] the umbrella name for a consortium of companies headquartered in St. George, Utah, that operates behavior modification camps in the US, Mexico, Western Samoa, Jamaica, and the Czech Republic. According to a news series by Lou Kilzer,[28] Burke sent Scott into treatment "because 'he was the extreme picture of what you didn't want your kid to be at 13 years old.' He said he sent David 'because he wouldn't stay with me. The court granted me custody, and he kept running back to his mother. He was not functioning properly in life.'"

The boys' mother, Donna Burke, is suing Teen Help for its treatment of the boys while they were at its Tranquility Bay facility in Jamaica, alleging: "Both are changed from the wonderful, spontaneous young men they were before Tranquility Bay into robotic victims, afraid of any authority figure. They have lost their individuality, their spirits are broken, and their characters ruined. Instead of independent men, they are afraid, haunted by nightmares, subject to panic attacks and refuse to go anywhere near a beach."[29]

■ ■ ■ ■ ■ ■ ■ ■ ■ ■

"She may have been thinking, 'Well maybe I'll injure myself, hurt myself, and that way I can manipulate and get home,'" said Teen Help spokesman Ken Kay to reporter Kilzer,[30] offering several possible reasons why Valerie Ann Heron, a 17-year-old Alabama girl, plunged to her death from a 35-foot-high balcony at Tranquility Bay in August 2001. Heron had been taken against her will from her parents' home at 4:00 AM the previous day by a Teen Help "transportation team," then shipped to Tranquility Bay, where she bolted from a room, jumped the balcony, and died. Kay refuses to entertain the notion that Heron was trying to commit suicide, while simultaneously acknowledging that Heron was not at Tranquility Bay of her own free will.

sent from Washington to the US Embassy in Apia, Western Samoa. The State Department asked the Western Samoan government to investigate."

Authorities in Mexico and the Czech Republic raided and closed Teen Help facilities over allegations of mistreatment and abuse, but Teen Help still exists, running a booming business elsewhere. They unfortunately are not the only ones, with scores of these programs continuing to open around the world.

_UN-AMERICAN DOGMA

> "Without deviation, progress is not possible." —Frank Zappa[32]

I am not arguing that drug treatment never helps anyone, but I am strongly asserting that coerced drug treatment by courts and government is not the answer to incarceration for recreational, or even abusive drug use. In my own experience, I did eventually come to a point where I felt I could use help and tried numerous times without success to get myself into one drug treatment program or another, both medical and non-medical modalities. Heroin withdrawals are harsh, and while living the life of a street-bound junkie, I was unable to arrest the cycle of self-abuse on my own. At that point, my drug use was no longer simply recreational. Maintaining the financial and physical costs of my habit, inflated beyond all rhyme or reason by prohibition, was a full-time job. After detoxing more than once, normally a five-day spell, only to find I couldn't enter immediately into any sort of long-term treatment facility, I would find myself back on the streets, homeless, jobless, and soon strung out again. The couple of long-term residential treatment programs I did experience weren't offering the help I needed, and I soon left.

"THE ABUSE ALLEGED TO HAVE OCCURRED INCLUDES BEATINGS, ISOLATION, FOOD AND WATER DEPRIVATION, CHOKE-HOLDS, KICKING, PUNCHING, BONDAGE, SPRAYING WITH CHEMICAL AGENTS, FORCED MEDICATION, VERBAL ABUSE AND THREATS OF FURTHER PHYSICAL ABUSE."

"The State Department said it received 'credible allegations' in 1998 of abuse against American teens at Paradise Cove [Teen Help's facility in Western Samoa] about the time that Corey Murphy's stay there was coming to an end," writes Kilzer.[31] Seventeen-year-old Corey committed suicide when his mother, Laura Murphy, threatened to send him back to Teen Help, where he previously had been sequestered for 22 months. "'The abuse alleged to have occurred includes beatings, isolation, food and water deprivation, choke-holds, kicking, punching, bondage, spraying with chemical agents, forced medication, verbal abuse and threats of further physical abuse,' according to a September 1998 State Department cable

Finally, after swearing up and down for years that I would never do so, I took an opportunity presented to me while in jail on Riker's Island, requesting entrance to a methadone maintenance program. Substituting a legal, officially sanctioned yet much more addictive drug that didn't get me high for an illicit other that did enabled me to avoid withdrawal symptoms (until I decided to kick methadone five years later) and remove myself from contact with the worst of the black-market dope scene.[33]

I was one of the hardcore drug abusers committing petty crimes that Drug Warrior politicians rant about when allocating ever more taxpayer money to waging the war. Yet I was not mandated into methadone maintenance; methadone did nothing to assist my successful attempt to stop using cocaine, nor did I receive treatment when I kicked methadone. Though still feeding my head on occasion, I'm no longer abusing drugs nor committing real crimes. There are undoubtedly some uses and even benefits to be had by drug abusers and those around them by offering a vast assortment of voluntary treatment options for drug abusers who desire a change.

Use of illicit drugs is the currently accepted stigma in American society. It is no longer considered socially proper or politically correct to hate one's neighbor for their skin color or their sexual preferences (not to say it doesn't happen), but it is perfectly okay to advocate harsh jail sentences or behavior modification for those who have an innate "drive to transcend consensus reality," as Dr. Andrew Weil phrased it.[34]

"Hunger is not volitional. Neither are inebriative instincts and urges," says author and researcher Dan Russell.[35] "That's why it is not controllable by law. It's like trying to control sex by law. It can't be done, and has never been done. It has to do with the process of enslavement. When you take a free tribe and enslave it, if you destroy the central sacrament of its culture, it's how you commit cultural genocide, and how to domesticate them."

I WAS ONE OF THE HARDCORE DRUG ABUSERS COMMITTING PETTY CRIMES THAT DRUG WARRIOR POLITICIANS RANT ABOUT.

Indeed, the War on Some Drugs has much more to do with controlling culture than it does with health. Baum writes: "In an article titled 'White House Stop-Drug-Use Program: Why the Emphasis Is on Marijuana,' the magazine Government Executive profiled [Carlton] Turner and summarized his views this way: marijuana, like 'hard-rock music, torn jeans, and sexual promiscuity,' was a pillar of 'the counter culture.'" Turner was quoted: "'Point is, illegal, i.e. non-prescription, use of drugs...is not only a perverse, pervasive plague, though it is that. But drug use also is a behavioral pattern that has sort of tagged along during the present young-adult generation's involvement in anti-military, anti-nuclear power, anti-big business, anti-authority demonstrations; of people from a myriad of different racial, religious or otherwise persuasions demanding rights or entitlements politically while refusing to accept corollary civic responsibility.'"[36]

While many countries around the world are beginning not only to debate but also to implement decriminalization and legalization of some drugs,[37] and while yet others lean toward harm reduction methods to help their hardcore drug abusers and society at large,[38] US police, courts, and government continue to dogmatically deem all use of currently illicit drugs, whether recreational or abusive, to be morally reprehensible and criminal, as well as a sign of a disease that requires treatment with or without the patients' cooperation. This is simply dangerous and even, dare I say, un-American.

Endnotes

1. Jansen, Karl L.R., M.D., Ph.D. "Ketamine: Dreams and Realities." *Multidisciplinary Association for Psychedelic Studies* (2001): 260. **2.** See: <www.uwsrq.com/First_Call/7y12yg7a.HTM>. **3.** Lindesmith Center-Drug Policy Foundation: Broadening the Debate on Drugs and Drug Policy <www.lindesmith.org>. **4.** Held in Albuquerque, New Mexico, 30 May - 2 June 2001. "Conference Report: As Drug Reform Edges Closer to Mainstream (or Vice Versa), Fractures Emerge Over Politics of Treatment." *Week Online With DRCNet* 189 (8 June 2001). **5.** Committee on Data and Research for Policy on Illegal Drugs, Charles F. Manski, John V. Pepper, and Carol V. Petrie, Editors. "Informing America's Policy on Illegal Drugs: What We Don't Know Keeps Hurting Us." Committee on Law and Justice and Committee on National Statistics, National Research Council (2001): 238. **6.** Reed, Lou. "Heroin." Performed by the Velvet Underground. *The Velvet Underground and Nico*. Verve, 1967. **7.** Unsigned. "US Jail Population Hits Record 6.5 Million." Reuters, 26 Aug 2001. **8.** For up-to-the-minute statistics, see DrugSense.org's Drug War Clock at <www.drugsense.org/wodclock.htm>. **9.** DrugAbuse Sciences, Inc. Press release. 24 July 2001 <www.drugabusesciences.com/Articles.asp?entry=123> **10.** *Ibid.* **11.** McCaffrey, Barry. Letter to *Los Angeles Times* 14 July 2000. **12.** Baum, Dan. *Smoke and Mirrors: The War on Drugs and the Politics of Failure.* New York: Little, Brown and Company, 1996: 69-70. **13.** Craven, Cyndi. "A Journey in Word: A Collection of Quotes." <www.spiritsong.com/quotes>. **14.** "Changing the Conversation: Improving Substance Abuse Treatment: The National Treatment Plan Initiative: Panel Reports, Public Hearings, and Public Acknowledgements." US Department of Health and Human Services (Nov 2000): 12. <www.natxplan.org>. For ease of reading, internal references in the quote have been left out. **15.** Shavelson, Lonny. *Hooked: Five Addicts Challenge Our Misguided Drug Rehab System.* New York: The New Press, 2001: 7. **16.** Gettman, Jon. "Marijuana and Drug Treatment: An Introduction." From an article presented at the Saving Our Children From Abusive Drug Treatment conference held by the Trebach Institute, Bethesda, Maryland, 21-22 July 2001. For conference details, see: <trebach.org/conference.html>. **17.** Statistics come from the FBI's Uniform Crime Reports and were highlighted by NORML. **18.** *Op cit.*, Gettman. **19.** *Op cit.*, Craven. **20.** *Op cit.*, Baum: 155-6. **21.** *Ibid*. **22.** York, David, Phyllis York, and Ted Wachtel. *Tough Love.* New York: Doubleday, 1982. See: Tough Love International <www.toughlove.org/default.htm>. **23.** In Bethesda, Maryland, 21-22 July 2001. <trebach.org/conference.html>. Also see: Peet, Preston. "Drug Treatment for Teens: A Secret Shame." High Times Online, 1 Aug 2001. **24.** The man who founded Straight Inc. in 1976—Florida real estate developer and Republican power broker Melvin Sembler—was nominated in July 2001 by President Bush to be Ambassador to Italy. Sembler was Ambassador to Australia under the former President Bush, and resigned in January 2001 as head of the Republican Party's national finance committee. Unsigned. "Florida Developer Tapped to be Ambassador to Italy." Associated Press, 28 July 2001. **25.** For more info about Warbis and adolescent treatment programs, see Anonymity Anonymous <fornits.com/anonanon>. For more treatment survivor tales also see: <pub70.ezboard.com/fstraightincsurvivors30607frm1> **26.** Warbis, Ginger. Email correspondence with author, 25 July 2001. **27.** Teen Help Adolescent Resources: Support for Families with Teen Challenges. <www.vpp.com/teenhelp>. **28.** Kilzer, Lou. "Desperate Measures: 'I Call it Teen Torment'." *Rocky Mountain News*, no month or day, 1999 <www.denver-rmn.com/desperate/site-desperate/day2/pg5-desperate.shtml>. **29.** *Ibid.* **30.** Kilzer, Lou. "Teenager Leaps to Her Death at Compound in Jamaica." *Rocky Mountain News* 18 Aug 2001. **31.** Kilzer, Lou. "Desperate Measures: Lost Boy." *Rocky Mountain News*, no day or month, 2000. <www.denver-rmn.com/desperate/site-desperate/0702desp1.shtml>. **32.** *Op cit.*, Craven. **33.** For more on methadone, see: Peet, Preston. "M Is for Methadone." Disinformation Website, 7 Feb 2001. <www.disinfo.com/pages/dossier/id838/pg1>. **34.** Weil, Andrew, M.D. *The Natural Mind: A New Way of Looking at Drugs and the Higher Consciousness.* Boston: Houghton Mifflin, 1972. As noted in Jansen: 150. **35.** Russell, Dan. Interview with author (Feb 2001). <www.disinfo.com/pages/article/id911/pg1>. Dan Russell is the author of *Drug War: Covert Money, Power and Policy* (Kalyx.com, 2000) and *Shamanism and the Drug Propaganda* (Kalyx.com, 1998). **36.** *Op cit.*, Baum: 154. **37.** As of August 2001, Jamaica, Canada, and Great Britain were debating decriminalizing and even legalizing personal use of marijuana; Spain, Italy, Switzerland, and Portugal had decriminalized all personal possession of drugs; Colombia, Bolivia, Peru, and Venezuela were calling for rational debate on regulating the commerce of drugs in order to do away with problems of violence and corruption, both results of current US-exported War on Some Drugs policy (which are much more damaging to society at large than any drug use and dependency). Even nine US states have passed laws allowing the use of medical marijuana, although the US government is insisting it will enforce federal anti-marijuana laws anyway, denying even the terminally ill legal use of marijuana. **38.** Germany, Switzerland, and the Netherlands all have safe injection rooms for heroin, as does Australia. For more information on international harm reduction methods and implementations, see: <www.harmreduction.org>, especially the links section.

EVERYTHING YOU KNOW IS WRONG

PORNOGRAPHY
WENDY McELROY

To approach pornography, it is necessary to struggle with the most fundamental question that anyone can ask about anything: What is it?

I propose a value-neutral definition: Pornography is the explicit artistic depiction of men and/or women as sexual beings. Take the definition in two sections, first—"Pornography is the explicit artistic depiction..." The word "explicit" excludes such gray areas as women's romance novels. The word "artistic" distinguishes pornography from psychological or political analyses of sex, which might be graphic. The term "depiction" includes a wide range of expression, from paintings to literature to videos, while excluding live sex acts.

The second part of the definition is that pornography depicts "men and/or women as sexual beings." This means that pornography is the genre of art or literature which focuses on the sexual nature of human beings, just as murder mysteries is the genre that focuses on the criminal nature of man. This does not mean pornography cannot present people as full, well-rounded human beings or have secondary themes that are non-sexual. But in order for the piece of art to be pornography, it must explicitly emphasize sexuality and not just include it as a secondary component.

My definition bears little resemblance to that of radical feminism, which has become—often in watered-down form—the most popular approach to pornography within the feminist movement.

> ## WHAT I ARGUE FOR IS FREEDOM OF SPEECH, A WOMAN'S RIGHT TO CHOOSE, AND THE VALIDITY OF WOMEN'S SEXUAL CONTRACTS.

The politically correct definition derives largely from the 1983 Minneapolis Anti-Pornography Ordinance drafted by Catharine MacKinnon and Andrea Dworkin. After failing to eliminate "adult" shops through zoning, the city of Minneapolis turned to these radical feminists for assistance. Because the resulting definition constituted a watershed in the definition of pornography, it is quoted in full:

Pornography. Pornography is a form of discrimination on the basis of sex. Pornography is the sexually explicit subordination of women, graphically depicted, whether in pictures or in words, that also includes one or more of the following:

(i) women are presented as dehumanized sexual objects, things or commodities; or
(ii) women are presented as sexual objects who enjoy pain or humiliation; or
(iii) women are presented as sexual objects who experience sexual pleasure in being raped; or
(iv) women are presented as sexual objects tied up or cut up or mutilated or bruised or physically hurt; or
(v) women are presented in postures of sexual submission; [or sexual servility, including by inviting penetration] or
(vi) women's body parts—including but not limited to vaginas, breasts, and buttocks—are exhibited, such that women are reduced to those parts; or
(vii) women are presented as whores by nature; or
(viii) women are presented being penetrated by objects or animals; or
(ix) women are presented in scenarios of degradation, injury, abasement, torture, shown as filthy or inferior, bleeding, bruised, or hurt in a context that makes these conditions sexual.

This is not a definition—it is a conclusion, and a conclusion I argue against. What I argue for is freedom of speech, a woman's right to choose, and the validity of women's sexual contracts.

But, first, some history.

In the 1960s, pornography flourished as one of a collection of new freedoms that became collectively known as sexual liberation. Sex had been liberated by a new political awareness. In a groundswell of protest against the Vietnam War, an entire generation questioned the rules and rewards of their parents' world. Young people dropped out, pursued alternate lifestyles, and wanted everything to be "meaningful." Drugs seemed to open doors of consciousness; sex lost its aura of guilt and obligation; government lost its automatic authority.

In 1966, the National Organization of Women (NOW) was founded with a basically liberal political slant, and it explicitly defended the right to pornography and to prostitution. The next year, the first radical feminist group, the New York Radical Women, was established.

Meanwhile, pornography was also undergoing a transformation, especially in its legal status. In 1966—perhaps as a reflection of society's growing tolerance—the Supreme Court loosened the standard of what was considered pornography to exclude anything that had any "redeeming social value."

Since it is difficult to establish that anything is "utterly without redeeming social value," this provided a legal loophole that pornographers quickly exploited. The late 1960s saw a flowering of adult films and books. Many of them included a tacked-on social message or a discussion of hygiene to skirt prosecution. One of the results could be described as the "democratization" of pornography. Soon, magazines such as *Playboy* were available in convenience stores across America. As pornography flourished, it became part of the changing view of sexuality that also allowed lesbianism and "feminist" issues, such as rape, to be discussed openly.

In 1973, feminism won a tremendous victory when the Supreme Court's decision on *Roe v. Wade* ensured legal access to abortion. For years, mainstream feminists had focused on the abortion crusade with a single-minded determination. Now that this goal had been achieved, they focused instead on an effort to pass a federal Equal Rights Amendment. The long, exhausting campaign was a disaster and was definitively over by 1984.

Women felt discouraged, tired, and betrayed by both men and the system. This is the point at which radical feminist voices—voices that considered men and women to be separate, antagonistic classes and wanted to reconstruct society rather than reform it—began to dominate.

Pornography became the primary target of their rage.

Pornography was and is attacked on many fronts but, arguably, the most important accusation hurled is that pornography is violence against women. It is violence in several ways, including but not limited to the claims that:

1. women are physically coerced into pornography;
2. women involved in the production of pornography are so psychologically damaged by patriarchy that they are incapable of giving informed or "real" consent;
3. capitalism forces women into pornography by restricting other remunerative alternatives;
4. pornography leads to violence against women on the street.

Do these accusations stand up?

_CLAIM #1: WOMEN ARE COERCED INTO PORNOGRAPHY

My empirical research into the realities of the industry, which has been extensive, indicates the contrary.

But if a claim of "coercion into pornography" is proven true, then those who used force or threats to make a woman perform should be charged with kidnapping, assault, and/or rape. In short, those who use force are not engaging in pornography (words and images)—they are committing a crime.

_CLAIM #2: WOMEN CAN'T GIVE "REAL" CONSENT

This claim says that women in porn who have not been physically coerced, have been so traumatized by patriarchy that they cannot give real consent. And the absence of real consent is the equivalent of coercion.

Women in the industry are said to be victims of violence because they are so brainwashed by white male culture that they cannot render consent. They are *de facto* coerced.

Consider how arrogant this statement is.

Although women in pornography appear to be willing, anti-porn feminists see through this charade. They know that no psychologically healthy woman would agree to the degradation of pornography. If agreement seems to be present, it is only because the women are so emotionally beaten down that they have fallen in love with their own oppression. If a woman enjoys performing sex acts in front of a camera, it is not because she is a unique human being who reasons and reacts from a different background or personality. It is not because she has a different definition of what is degrading or humiliating. No, it is because she is psychologically damaged and no longer responsible for her actions.

This is more than an attack on the right to pose for pornography. It is a denial of a woman's right to choose anything that is considered demeaning by some dominant standards. But radical feminists are going one step farther: They deny that the women involved in pornography have the ability to choose. They are too brainwashed to be able to reach a "correct" conclusion.

What does this do to a woman's right to contract—the established manner in which our society forms economic relationships? Consider again the Minneapolis Ordinance. In that document, the following factors did *not* indicate the presence of a contract between a producer of pornography and an actress:

(cc) that the person has attained the age of majority; or...
(hh) that the person actually consented to a use of the

performance that is changed into pornography; or
(ii) that the person knew the purpose of the acts...; or
(jj) that the person showed no resistance or appeared to cooperate actively...; or
(kk) that the person signed a contract, or made statements affirming a willingness to cooperate; or
(ll) that no physical force, threats, or weapons were used in the making of the pornography; or
(mm) that the person was paid or otherwise compensated.

Even if a woman in pornography signed a contract with full knowledge and was fully paid, she could later sue on the grounds of coercion. Again, what legal implications does this have for a woman's right to contract?

For centuries, women have struggled against tremendous odds to have their contracts taken seriously. At great personal expense, they stood up and demanded the right to own land, to control their own wages, to retain custody of their children...in other words, to become legally responsible for themselves and for their property. A woman's consent must never be reduced to a legal triviality.

And yet cultural pressures are now said to "force" women into pornography.

Consider one fact: Everyone is formed by his or her culture. And certainly there are times when cultural pressures lead people to make bad choices. But to say that any woman who poses nude does so only because she has been indoctrinated by patriarchy, is to eliminate the possibility of anyone ever choosing anything.

In other words, to invalidate one choice because it was culturally influenced leads to invalidating all choices. Why? Because all choices include cultural influences. Every decision is made in the presence of cultural pressures. To invalidate a woman's choices—and her contracts—because she grew up in an unhealthy environment is to deny her the one protection she has against that environment: namely, the right to decide for herself how to change things for the better.

_CLAIM #3: CAPITALISM FORCES WOMEN INTO PORNOGRAPHY

According to this view, capitalism is a system of "economic coercion" that forces women into pornography in order to make a living. This is actually a continuation of the last point.

The anti-porn argument here runs like this: Because women in our society are paid less than men and have fewer opportunities, they are forced to enter unsavory professions in order to make a decent living. Women go into pornography because they need money.

When radical feminists deny the validity of porn contracts, they are not attacking pornography—they are denying the validity of any contract. Most people enter labor contracts—that is, get a job—because they need money. But, to radical feminists, this is economic coercion. If they reject porn contracts because the woman needs money and is influenced by culture, then they are logically constrained to reject many, if not most other labor contracts, as well.

_CLAIM #4: PORNOGRAPHY LEADS TO VIOLENCE AGAINST WOMEN

Radical feminists claim there is a cause-and-effect relationship between men viewing pornography and men attacking women, especially in the form of rape.

But studies and experts disagree as to whether there is a relationship of any kind between pornography and violence. Or, more broadly stated, between images and behavior. Some studies, such as the one prepared by feminist Thelma McCormick (1983) for the Metropolitan Toronto Task Force on Violence Against Women, found no pattern to indicate a connection between pornography and sex crimes. Incredibly, the Task Force suppressed the study and reassigned the project to a pro-censorship male, who returned the "correct" results. His study was published.

Even generously granting the assumption that a correlation does exist between pornography and violence, what would such a correlation tell us? It would certainly not indicate a cause-and-effect relationship. It is a fallacy to assume that if A can be correlated with B, then A causes B. Such a correlation might indicate nothing more than that both are caused by another factor, C. For example, there is a high correlation between the number of doctors in a city and the number of alcoholics there. One doesn't cause the other; both statistics are proportional to the size of the city's population.

Those researchers who draw a relationship between pornography and violence tend to hold one of two contradictory views on what that connection might mean. The first view is that porn is a form of catharsis. That is, the more pornography we see, the less likely we are to act out our sexual urges. The second view is that porn inspires imitation. That is, the more pornography we see, the more likely we are to imitate the behavior it represents.

I favor the first theory.

■ ■ ■ ■ ■ ■ ■ ■ ■ ■

Moving away from counterarguments, what are the arguments *for* pornography?

I contend the presence of pornography benefits women, both personally and politically. The benefits are many but, in the interests of space, I can list only two in each category.

_PORNOGRAPHY BENEFITS WOMEN PERSONALLY

1. Pornography gives a panoramic view of the world's sexual possibilities; it allows women to "safely" experience sexual alternatives.

Pornography provides women with a visceral sense of the wide variety of sexual possibilities without their having to venture into the real world to experiment. One of the most benevolent aspects of pornography is that it provides women with a safe environment in which they can satisfy a healthy sexual curiosity. The world is a dangerous place. Reaching out for real-world experience—through dating, frequenting a bar, etc.—often involves putting yourself in a vulnerable position.

By contrast, pornography can be a source of solitary enlightenment. This cornucopia is served up in the privacy of a woman's own bedroom, on a television set that can be turned off whenever she has had enough. She does not have to defend herself against persistent advances or "give in" rather than be hurt by a man who will not accept "no."

Pornography is also safe sex, a safe way to experiment. No diseases. No violence. No pregnancy. No infidelity. No one to apologize to the next morning. Pornography is one of the most benevolent ways a woman can experience pleasure, can learn about who she is sexually, including which practices she does not like.

2. Pornography opens windows so that each woman can interpret sex for herself.

I remember hearing a lesbian explain how she had grown up in agony over her sexual identity because she felt like a freak, a biological aberration. Only when she stumbled across lesbian pornography did she understand that many others shared her preferences. Only then did she have the courage to acknowledge who she was and to pursue a relationship with another woman.

_PORNOGRAPHY BENEFITS WOMEN POLITICALLY

1. Historically, pornography and feminism have been fellow travelers and natural allies.

Through much of their history, women's rights and pornography have had common cause. Both have risen and flourished during the same periods of sexual freedom; both have been attacked by the same political forces, usually conservatives. Laws directed against pornography or obscenity, such as the Comstock Law in the late 1880s, have always been used to hinder women's rights, such as

access to birth control information. Although it is not possible to draw a cause-and-effect relationship between the rise of pornography and that of feminism, it seems that they both demand the same social conditions—namely, sexual freedom.

They also both benefit from freedom of speech, which is the ally of those who seek change, and the enemy of those who seek to maintain control. Pornography is nothing more or less than freedom of speech applied to the sexual realm. It is the freedom to challenge the sexual status quo. And sexual heresy should have the same legal protection as political heresy.

This protection is especially important to women, whose sexuality has been controlled by censorship through the centuries.

2. Legitimizing pornography would protect women sex workers, who are stigmatized by our society.

The law cannot eliminate pornography but it can drive the industry underground, where the working conditions of women are miserable and dangerous. Women who were involved in pornography in the 1950s, when it was illegal, tell horror stories of abuse by employers and of police raids in which they were made to lie naked, face-down on the floor, with guns pressed against their heads. Such raids made the women in porn reluctant to go to the police when other abuses occurred.

> **PORNOGRAPHY IS NOTHING MORE OR LESS THAN FREEDOM OF SPEECH APPLIED TO THE SEXUAL REALM.**

Because of the semi-legal status of pornography, the contracts of porn actresses—when such exist—are often treated unfairly if brought to court and are often dismissed as "frivolous." Women need the protection of having their contracts taken seriously by the legal system, and this will come only when those contracts are recognized on the same level as any other labor agreement.

_CONCLUSION

Is there no form of pornography that should be prohibited?

On a political/legal level, the answer is "no." Pornography is words and images over which the law should exercise no jurisdiction. Moreover, the law has no business telling women what to do with their own bodies in both producing and consuming pornography. "It is a woman's body, it is a woman's right."

On a personal level, every woman has to discover for herself what is unacceptable. Every woman has to act as her own censor, her own judge of what is appropriate or degrading.

"A woman's body, a woman's right" also carries responsibilities.

PROSTITUTION
WENDY McELROY

Prostitution consists of taking money in exchange for sex. It is one of the few crimes that involves an entirely legal act—sex—that is made illegal simply by the exchange of money.

This article consists of an analysis of prostitution between consenting adults in the context of North America. It applies the principle "a woman's body, a woman's right" to the choice to sell sex. If choice and consent are not present, then the sex act ceases to be an exchange and becomes an act of violence. At that point, it should be condemned as kidnapping, rape, and battery, not punished as prostitution, which it has ceased to be.

To radical or gender feminism, however, prostitution is an act of violence against women whether or not choice and consent appear to be present. Andrea Dworkin captures the anti-prostitute view of whoredom well: "The only analogy I can think of concerning prostitution is that it is more like gang rape than it is like anything else.... The gang rape is punctuated by a money exchange. That's all. That's the only difference."[1]

To prostitutes who insist that they consent and benefit from the exchange, the philosopher Laurie Shrage explains that they are being duped by the patriarchal system: "Because of the cultural context in which prostitution operates, it epitomizes and perpetuates pernicious patriarchal beliefs and values and therefore is both damaging to the women who sell sex and, as an organized social practice, to all women in our society."[2]

At a feminist conference, a representative of CORP (Canadian Organization for the Rights of Prostitutes) related the emotional impact that anti-prostitution feminists were having on prostitutes: "They find it necessary to interpret prostitutes' experience of their lives and then feed it back to the prostitutes to tell them what's really happening, whereas they wouldn't dare be so condescending or patronizing with any other group of women. Why is that?"[3]

Prostitutes have good reason to feel such animosity. The International Committee for Prostitutes' Rights explains:

"Historically, women's movements...have opposed the institution of prostitution while claiming to support prostitute women. However, prostitutes reject support that requires them to leave prostitution; they object to being treated as symbols of oppression and demand recognition as workers."[4]

At issue here is the question, "Who speaks for the prostitute?" Feminists who are for prostitutes' rights, feminists who are against them, self-described "liberated whores," or ex-sex workers who have been damaged by prostitution? Or do all of them have something valuable to say?

Unfortunately, the voices are drowning each other out. The International Congress on Prostitution that occurred in 1997 was cosponsored by Cal-State Northridge and the national sex workers' rights organization COYOTE (Call Off Your Old Tired Ethics). The conference was attended by about 200 researchers and academics, some 300 sex workers from around the world, and several vice cops. (Because I was a presenter, I was privy to backstage dramas.) The prominent anti-prostitution feminist Kathleen Barry had been invited to the conference as a featured speaker in order to represent an alternative view. Barry canceled because the prostitute activist who was organizing the conference could not guarantee she would not be booed and heckled while at the podium. Had she attended, I have no doubt that a significant minority of the sex workers attending would have done that and more to make her uncomfortable. As a result, no exchange of views occurred or was possible.

_HISTORY LESSON: PROSTITUTES AND FEMINISTS AS PARTNERS

It may seem natural to assume that conflict is a natural state between prostitutes and feminists, but this assumption is incorrect, as a brief overview of the history of the Prostitutes' Rights Movement demonstrates. (This movement is a loose coalition of organizations and individuals who advocate the rights of women who sell sex.)

The Prostitutes' Rights Movement first appeared through the organization COYOTE, which emerged in 1973 in San Francisco from a preceding group, WHO—Whores, Housewives, and Others. The "Others" referred to were lesbians—a word no one even whispered aloud at that political juncture. The willingness of prostitutes to embrace the cause of lesbian rights was one of their early and strongest links with many feminists of that time.

The founder of COYOTE, Margo St. James, became convinced that a prostitute-based group was necessary because the feminist movement would not take the issue of prostitution seriously until whores themselves spoke out, in very much the way lesbian groups needed to speak out for themselves before feminism would embrace them.

The mid-1970s was a propitious time for prostitute rights. The 1960s had created sympathy toward decriminalizing victimless crimes. The abortion crusade had embedded the principle of "a woman's body, a woman's right" into American society. The Gay Rights Movement in San Francisco had highlighted police abuse of sexual minorities. Pornography was thriving as an industry.

Originally COYOTE's intentions were modest and limited to providing services to prostitutes in San Francisco. St. James was as surprised as anyone when a national Prostitutes' Rights Movement began to coalesce around the local San Francisco model. Within one year, COYOTE claimed a membership of over 1,000, despite the fact that working prostitutes—the members—were criminals and understandably reluctant to become visible in a political organization. By the end of 1974, COYOTE boasted a membership of over 10,000, and three COYOTE affiliates had emerged.

The feminist movement reacted with applause. In 1973, for example, the National Organization for Women (NOW) endorsed the decriminalization of prostitution, and this is still the "official" policy—on paper. But NOW's most prominent chapters, including Los Angeles and New York, came to be headed by extremely vocal anti-prostitution feminists.

As late as 1979, prostitutes and feminists were actively cooperating. For example, COYOTE aligned with NOW in what was called a Kiss and Tell campaign to further the Equal Rights Amendment effort. A 1979 issue of *COYOTE howls*, the organization's newsletter, declared:

COYOTE has called on all prostitutes to join the international "Kiss and Tell" campaign to convince legislators that it is in their best interest to support the decriminalization of prostitution, the Equal Rights Amendment, abortion funding, lesbian and gay rights, and all other issues of importance to women. The organizers of the campaign are urging that the names of legislators who have consistently voted against those issues, yet are regular patrons of prostitutes, be turned over to feminist organizations for their use.

_THE CURRENT BREACH BETWEEN PROSTITUTION AND FEMINISM

In the mid-80s, the Prostitutes' Rights Movement was decisively killed by an unexpected assassin: the AIDS virus. In the understandable social backlash that surrounded AIDS, prostitution came to be seen as a source of contagion every bit as virulent as I.V. needle use. Around this time, feminism underwent an ideological shift from liberal to radical ideology, and the mainstream of feminism publicly began to excoriate prostitution as a form of patriarchal abuse of women, dismissing self-described liberated whores as deluded victims. In 1985, St. James left the United States to live in France. She cited the sexually conservative swing in the American feminist movement as one of her motives in leaving. (She has subsequently returned.)

AS LATE AS 1979, PROSTITUTES AND FEMINISTS WERE ACTIVELY COOPERATING.

The view of radical feminists came to dominate. In essence, they denied that prostitutes had truly chosen "the life." They had been coerced into whoring in two ways.

First, radical feminists argue that women become street prostitutes through a brutal process by which they are kidnapped and forced to perform sexual acts. This is the "white slavery" that Gail Sheehy's influential book *Hustling* portrays.

White slavery is clearly a serious problem in Third World countries—especially Asian countries—but no convincing evidence has established that a similar problem exists in the United States. That is, although individual women may be coerced into sex acts, there is no trafficking in women in the same way as there is elsewhere. If white slavery were flourishing in the US, however, it would be an activity quite distinct from prostitution; it would be a criminal activity already prohibited by laws against kidnapping. White slavery involves kidnapping women and forcing them to perform sexual acts. Prostitution involves consenting adults performing sexual acts for mutual profit. If white slavery were swept away, prostitution would continue.

Second, radical feminists claim that, under capitalism, women's choices are limited to wage slavery, domestic slavery, or sexual slavery (prostitution). None of these alternatives could be called choices in any meaningful sense of that word, it is argued. The "alleged" choices are simply rules dictated by a male-dominated culture. As Alison Jaggar explains, "[I]t is the economic coercion underlying prostitution...that provides the basic feminist objection to prostitution."[5]

As for women who appear to "choose" prostitution, radical feminists maintain that, in a male-dominated world where most women must choose between wage labor and domestic labor, some women will say "no" to both and "choose" prostitution instead. Prostitution is now seen as a paradigm of woman's dilemma under patriarchy.

Evelina Giobbe explains how white males in the conservative right and the liberal left "collude" to keep women in prostitution: "[T]he right by demanding that women be socially and sexually subordinate to one man in marriage, and the left by demanding that women be socially and sexually subordinate to all men in prostitution and pornography."[6]

_A REALISTIC PICTURE OF PROSTITUTION IN AMERICA

The first step toward understanding the breach between current feminists and prostitutes' rights activists is to sketch a realistic picture of prostitution in America. The National Task Force on Prostitution estimates that, of the entire female prostitute community in America, only 5 to 20 percent are streetwalkers. The percentage spread depends on the size of the city. Eighty to 95 percent of prostitutes work either in-call (e.g. escort services) or outcall (e.g. massage parlors). But because streetwalkers are the most visible of all prostitutes—in terms of public awareness, arrest records, and social work programs—they are incorrectly perceived as being the paradigm of a prostitute. In reality, streetwalkers form the smallest portion of the community, and they are, by far, the portion of the community with whom the problems associated with prostitution—drug abuse, police harassment, violence, disease—are likely to occur.

The anti-prostitute feminists Melissa Farley and Norma Hotaling have conducted an interesting study of streetwalkers from street areas of San Francisco, particularly the strolls frequented by homeless, drug-using prostitutes or by particularly young prostitutes. These prostitutes are targets for violence, but they are not necessarily representative even of the streetwalking community. Yet this study and others like it have been used by anti-prostitution groups to present a portrait not simply of the most vulnerable of streetwalkers, but of "the prostitute."[7]

Farley and Hotaling entered the study to test the hypothesis that streetwalkers suffered from posttraumatic stress disorder, comparing the psychological states of prostitutes to those of hostages and torture victims. From a sample of 130 prostitutes, which included some male and transgendered ones, Farley and Hotaling came up with disturbing statistics: 82 percent reported having been physically assaulted since entering prostitution; 75 percent stated that they had or did have a drug problem; 88 percent wanted to leave prostitution.

These figures are distressingly high, but—remember—the sampling is from the streetwalking segment of the prostitute community, and usually from the further subcategories of streetwalkers who are in prison, who seek treatment for drug problems, or who otherwise enter programs to get off the street. In other words, these samples self-select for the women who are most likely to have been victimized by prostitution and most likely to want out of the profession. Moreover, a woman seeking treatment or leniency in prison is likely to give authority figures—the researchers—whatever answer she believes they wish to hear.

In 1995, I conducted an intensive study of about 60 female members of COYOTE. Thirty-four of the respondents were, or had been, prostitutes. Out of this sample, 71 percent of the women reported having experienced no violence over their years of sex work, while 29 percent had experienced violence, more often from the police or a coworker than from a client. None of the women stated, or evidenced, a drug problem. And 17 percent of the women wished to leave sex work, with 24 percent not being sure.[8] Needless to say, there is discrepancy between my results and those of such researchers as Farley and Hotaling. One of the reasons is probably that my survey also self-selects. I selected from the highest rung of the prostitute community, the women least likely to experience the negatives.

I don't dismiss the work of anti-prostitution researchers, nor do I discount the voices of ex-prostitutes who feel they have been damaged by sex work. What I am saying is that truth is usually more complicated than any one perspective can capture. Prostitution is not a monolith. Each woman experiences the profession in a different manner. And nothing can be gained by having different groups of feminists or prostitutes—all of whom are probably telling the truth of their own experiences—attempting to discredit each other.

The day-to-day realities of a streetwalker cannot be extended to say anything that is necessarily, or even probably, true of the daily routine of a woman in a massage parlor or of an exclusive call girl or of a stripper who hooks on the side. About the only political and personal interest that all women in prostitution seem to share is that—whatever their circumstances—it is better for every woman *not* to be arrested and legally persecuted for the choices she makes with her own body. It is better for prostitution to be decriminalized.

_TERMS AND APPROACHES

I want to clarify some terms. Traditionally, society has approached "the problem" of prostitution in one of three ways: abolition, legalization, or decriminalization.

The meaning of abolition is fairly clear. It refers to the State prohibition of prostitution.

Legalization, or regulation, refers to some form of State-controlled prostitution, for example, the creation of red light districts. It almost always includes a government record of who is a prostitute—information which is commonly used for other government purposes. For example, some countries in Europe indicate whether someone is a prostitute on her passport, and other countries automatically refuse entry to her on that basis.

Decriminalization is the opposite of abolition and legalization. The latter two positions acknowledge that the State has proper authority over the sexual activity of consenting adults. Decriminalization says that the State has no right to intervene in private sexual matters. It refers to the elimination of all laws against prostitution, including laws against those who associate with prostitutes—madams, pimps, and johns.

With startling consistency, the Prostitutes' Rights Movement calls for decriminalization. You will sometimes hear anti-prostitution feminists describe their position as "decriminalization with the goal of abolition." But, in using the term "decriminalization," each side means something very different. Prostitute activists mean that all aspects of prostitution must be legally tolerated. Anti-prostitution feminists mean that the police should not arrest the prostitutes, only the men (the pimps and johns) and the women who act as pimps (madams). And—with the support of such feminists—there has been a sea change in the way many police departments in North America legally address the nitty-gritty of streetwalking. Namely, they are now arresting the men. In discussions with the vice cops who were invited speakers at the International Congress on Prostitution, all but one of them said that arrests now ran about 50/50 for prostitutes and for johns. This is opposed to something like 2 percent for the men in the past. Some police departments go even further, like the Edmonton Police Services in Canada, which declared 1992 the Year of the John and concentrated on charging clients.

When I speak of active cooperation between anti-prostitution feminists and vice cops, I am referring specifically to the Schools for Johns, a phenomenon that seems to be sweeping North America, city-by-city. It began in San Francisco, when Norma Hotaling teamed up with the vice department to formulate new policy on prostitution. Instead of ignoring johns as they normally did, police arrested them and gave first-time johns an option: They could erase the arrest from their records by paying a fee and by attending a one-day seminar during which they would be lectured, usually by feminists and damaged ex-prostitutes, on the turpitude of their ways. Some cities, like Chicago, have added the touch of publishing the names and addresses of men so arrested in major newspapers.

Prostitutes' Rights advocates are appalled. One of their reasons is that the School for Johns is making the streets *less* safe for prostitutes. Such laws will not determine, and never have determined, how many women will turn to the streets. In other words, there are as many women out there as before. But such laws will and have discouraged a certain class of men from seeking out streetwalkers. It has reduced the number of men on the street purchasing sex, but the men who are vanishing are the married ones, with respectable careers and a good reputation to protect. These are the men who are just out for the sex thrill of something new. But the new risk of being publicly exposed as a john isn't worth it to them.

> **PROSTITUTION IS NOT A MONOLITH. EACH WOMAN EXPERIENCES THE PROFESSION IN A DIFFERENT MANNER.**

The men who are *not* discouraged by such laws are those who are criminally inclined toward prostitutes, men who are otherwise unstable, men with nothing much to lose socially by being picked up and fined. Thus, the thrust of police/feminist policy keeps peaceful johns off the streets, while leaving about as many women out there. The women have to compete more vigorously and screen less rigorously for the johns who still approach them. Is it any wonder that violence against streetwalkers is rising sharply in many North American cities?

_PIMPS AND MADAMS

To the women who chose prostitution as a profession, arresting the men on whom they rely to make a living is a direct attack upon them. When I say "the men," I mean not only the johns but also the most reviled of all people in prostitution—the pimps. It is precisely because pimps are so hated that I want to present arguments against current anti-pimping laws on the assumption that, if I call these measures into question, doubt will be cast on other laws prosecuting "the men." Consider an email exchange—a discussion that occurred between myself and three female prostitutes—on the subject of pimps and madams. The first woman wrote:

I would like the movement [Prostitutes' Rights] to be *less* oriented toward social work and *more* about giving people the skills (and other things they need) to be professionally successful. Key to this is supporting madams and business owners instead of trashing them (whether subtly or directly). Because in order to succeed and have staying power a prostitute eventually has to become more entrepreneurial. [Emphasis in the original.]

The second prostitute commented electronically:

I think madams are a great asset to the industry— they're women who usually have first-hand experience, and tend to be thorough when it comes to protecting their underlings. I have a bit of a problem with pimps, though...especially men whose only experience in the biz is from the demand side.

The third prostitute voiced a dissenting opinion:

What is the big fuss about pimps?... If you are talking about people who (but for a penis) might be called madams, I don't see a problem. I might prefer to work with another lady but that's a personality thing. When I was younger, I worked for an agency that was owned by two guys and one woman. They were all about the same—sometimes nice, sometimes annoying, like anyone else in the world.

It is interesting to note that the discussion of pimps does not even touch upon the issue of violence. It dwells entirely upon economics, and that is because the most commonly used legal definition of pimp is an economic one. As the Canadian ex-prostitute Alexandra Highcrest commented in her book, *At Home on the Stroll*: "In simple legal terms a pimp is someone who lives off the earnings of a prostitute. Such a broad definition can include many people most of us don't think of when we hear that word. Children live off the earnings of prostitute mothers; husbands, lovers, siblings, perhaps even parents, can all meet the basic requirements for being classified as pimps by the courts."[7]

Such economic laws do not punish men for beating, raping, or stealing from a prostitute. The police do not generally define a pimp as a man who kidnaps a woman and coerces her onto the streets. Overwhelmingly the part of the law that is enforced refers to financial arrangements and targets those who receive money from or give money to prostitutes. And, so, it becomes illegal for a prostitute to form the economic associations that most women take for granted. Whenever she gives money to her husband, family, manager, or friend, she legally endangers them.

The public widely perceives anti-pimping laws as protecting prostitutes from abusive men. But if this were so, the Prostitutes' Rights Movement would support the measures, instead of adamantly opposing them. In a resolution entitled "Statement on Prostitution and Human Rights," the International Committee for Prostitutes' Rights (ICPR) declared: "[A]nti-pimping laws violate a prostitute's right to a private life by putting all of her personal associates...under even more risk of arrest than exploiters and physical violators. Confiscation of personal letters or literary work of prostitutes...is a clear denial of respect for home..."

In a COYOTE release, the veteran prostitute activist Carol Leigh— "the Scarlot Harlot"—pleaded on behalf of her husband:

You want to make laws against the pimps? Make sure that you make the distinction between forced prostitution, and those who want to be in prostitution by choice. Go after those who actually abuse us. Just as in marriage, some husbands are abusive of women. Not all husbands are that way. Don't take away my husband because he's really, really good to me. But if you want to help women, go after those people who actually abuse us, but be very, very careful how you word legislation that goes after those who you think exploit and abuse us, because those laws ultimately get used against us.

How do allegedly protective laws get used against prostitutes? For example, in both the United States and Europe, it's common practice for the police to use anti-pimping laws to ignore a prostitute's right to privacy. In pursuit of pimps, the police may break into the home of a known prostitute, rifle her possessions, and harass anyone they find on the premises. The fear of such laws makes many prostitutes reluctant to speak out or to become involved in community affairs. In turn, this makes them more alienated and less likely to break out of prostitution by acquiring other work.

Anti-pimping laws also act as a barrier to those prostitutes who wish to get out of the business. The husband—even of an ex-prostitute— becomes automatically vulnerable to charges of pimping. This is true even of husbands who do not live primarily off their wives' whoring but who share household expenses with her.

But what of the husbands or lovers who are fully dependent on profits from prostitution? Are they not parasites living off the sexual wages of their wives? Prostitutes are quick to point out that other women have the right to support their husbands and lovers. No one passes laws forbidding waitresses, lawyers, or secretaries from having dependent men in their lives. Why are prostitutes the only women legally singled out in this manner?

> "CHILDREN LIVE OFF THE EARNINGS OF PROSTITUTE MOTHERS; HUSBANDS, LOVERS, SIBLINGS, PERHAPS EVEN PARENTS, CAN ALL MEET THE BASIC REQUIREMENTS FOR BEING CLASSIFIED AS PIMPS BY THE COURTS."

Yet pimps continue to be excoriated. There are two main reasons for this.

First, pimps—but not madams—are associated with streetwalking, which is the most violence-prone and stigmatized form of prostitution. Second, pimps—as men—have been systematically portrayed as exploiters and oppressors by modern feminism. As the gender-feminist Kathleen Barry explains in her influential book *Female Sexual Slavery*:

Together, pimping and procuring are perhaps the most ruthless displays of male power and sexual dominance.... Procuring is a strategy, a tactic for acquiring women and turning them into prostitution; pimping keeps them there. Procuring today involves "convincing" a woman to be a prostitute through cunning, fraud, and/or physical force, taking her against her will or knowledge and putting her into prostitution.[10]

How can this image of the pimp be reconciled with the following observation by a prostitute who chooses to remain anonymous?

Many of the men who get described...as "pimps" are boyfriends, lovers, license-plate-number takers, and managers. Many girls seek out pimps and even love their "man." A girl has a right...even if she is a bit dumb and is being taken. And the venom of the law is another way to get at prostitutes—by busting their lovers. If a bank teller's husband beats her, he is charged with assault, not with being a bank teller's husband.

The best explanation of the schism between these two portraits of the pimp is that, like prostitution, pimping is not a monolithic institu-

tion. Some pimps are husbands and friends, who offer protection and partnership. But, especially on the street level of prostitution, other pimps are kidnappers, batterers, and rapists who deserve to be taken to a back alley where feminism can be more graphically explained to them.

But such criminals are effectively protected by the law and the court system. Barry reports talking to a street prostitute who had been raped and kidnapped by pimps, and another who had been slashed by a razor the night before. Barry mentions in passing that they "didn't consider reporting to the police." Barry details many horrifying cases of women being abused by pimps, but not one case that would be tolerated if committed by a man against straight women. Regular women are protected by laws that prosecute rapists and kidnappers, but the illegal status and stigma attached to prostitution renders the women defenseless against such men. Even worse, they are persecuted by a legal system that protects other women. The police become just another layer of abuse.

I have not yet met a prostitute activist who comes out for laws that penalize the economic associates of prostitutes. And there is a necessary logic to their position. If it should be legal for a woman to sell a sexual service, then it should be legal for someone to buy it or be a partner in the sale.

The best way—and, perhaps, the only way—to protect the women is to decriminalize all aspects of prostitution, including economic association with a prostitute.

Endnotes

1. Dworkin, Andrea. "Prostitution and Male Supremacy." Speech delivered at Prostitution: From Academia to Activism, a symposium sponsored by the Michigan Journal of Gender and Law, University of Michigan Law School (31 Oct 1992). **2.** Shrage, Laurie. "Should Feminists Oppose Prostitution?" *Ethics* 99 (1989): 347-61. **3.** Bell, Laurie, ed. *Good Girls, Bad Girls: Sex Trade Workers and Feminists Face to Face.* Toronto: The Women's Press, 1987. **4.** The International Committee for Prostitutes' Rights. Brussels (1-3 Oct 1986): 192. **5.** Jaggar, Alison. "Prostitution." Ed. A. Soble. *The Philosophy of Sex: Contemporary Readings.* Totowa, NJ: Rowman and Littlefield, 1980: 360. **6.** *Op cit.,* Bell: 76. **7.** Presented at the NGO Forum, Fourth World Conference on Women, Beijing (4 Sept 1995). **8.** McElroy, Wendy. *XXX: A Woman's Right to Pornography.* New York: St. Martin's Press, 1995: appendix. **9.** Highcrest, Alexandra. *At Home on the Stroll: My Twenty Years as a Prostitute in Canada.* Toronto: Knopf, 1997: 121. **10.** Barry, Kathleen. *Female Sexual Slavery.* New York: Avon, 1981: 73.

EVERYTHING YOU KNOW IS WRONG

TWO'S TOO TOUGH
TRISTAN TAORMINO

Following in the footsteps of some of our great politicians, stars, and sports heroes, former New York Mayor Rudy Giuliani apparently couldn't keep it in his pants, either. Or so said his wife, Donna Hanover, who claimed his cheating was the reason they separated. He denies actually doing the deed with his former communications director, Cristyne Lategano, but the statistics are not on his side. (And by the way, there is no image—none—that skeevs me out more than that of the hypocritical, hairline-challenged mayor having sex with anyone.) Matrimonial polls reveal that 40 to 60 percent of people cheat on their spouses at least once, and half of all marriages topple. Haven't we learned anything from Monica's mouthwork, Frank Gifford's elevator shenanigans, and all the other scarlet-letter activities? Let's face it, folks: Monogamy is dead.

Maybe not completely dead, but goddess knows, it's barely breathing. These high-profile couples, as well as many others, might benefit from breaking the pattern of one-ball-plus-one-chain-equals-love. Look, the hair-pulling caveman is gone, and the Cleavers seem oh-so-retro. In May 2000, when the state of Vermont legalized civil unions (read: gay marriages), that single act struck fear into the hearts of conservatives everywhere and signaled the downfall of the American marriage as we know it. We're all going to hell now anyway, so why not expand the possibilities of our intimate relationships? Let's explore polyamory!

I am not recommending you all go Mormon on me. Fundamentalist Mormons practice their own brand of polygamy, which involves men marrying multiple women at a very young age, marrying their new wives' relatives, and making way too many babies. Mormon polygamous lifestyles have also been known to include coercion and abuse, and there is that whole religion thing. So, let's just leave the Mormons out of this discussion.

> **WE'RE ALL GOING TO HELL NOW ANYWAY, SO WHY NOT EXPAND THE POSSIBILITIES OF OUR INTIMATE RELATIONSHIPS? LET'S EXPLORE POLYAMORY!**

Polyamory, a catchall term for many different practices, encompasses relationships that fall outside the traditional, sexually faithful, two-person model known as monogamy. Think of it as a postmillennial antidote to chronic serial monogamy, which includes an abundance of cheating, embarrassment, deception, scandal, separation, and divorce. Many polyamorous couples practice nonmonogamy—the partners are emotionally committed to one another, but their relationship isn't sexually exclusive. Some poly people have multiple partners with whom they have both sexual and emotional/love relationships. Some polyamorous couples expand to become a triad or a group.

It may be every red-blooded American man's dream come true (finally, that threesome with your wife and her best friend legitimized!), but that doesn't mean it's a free-for-all. Polyamory for couples requires honesty, communication, boundaries, mutual respect, and rules—rules based on your individual relationship, desires, needs, and goals, rules that everyone can agree on, rules that you need to stick to. You may decide that having the occasional *ménage à trois* to spice things up is okay by both of you. Or you may allow each other to have fuckbuddies as long as you two remain the primary relationship. Your rules are whatever you need (no sleepovers? no anal sex? no blondes?) to feel secure, sane, and satisfied. One member of a poly dyke couple told me, "Say I am going through this phase where I want to be spanked and tied up, and my lover's not really into it. What about if we just go find someone that I could do that with? It could be safe, fun, and hot. It doesn't mean I am going to go run off and marry that person."

I know one polyamorous couple that comes to the table as a package deal: If you want to get jiggy with him, you have to boink her, too. Another duo bases their sanctioned dalliances on geography; when either or both are out of town, they have free rein to do the nasty with whomever they choose. While in the same zip code, they remain true-blue. A rad bisexual couple works the gender angle. She's allowed to muffdive with other girls, but he's the only XY in her equation. He can suck all the cock he wants, but must remain loyal to one and only one pussy—hers. Two leatherwomen in a Daddy/boy relationship have a rule based on s/m roles: They're allowed to play with other tops and bottoms as long as the boy has only one Daddy and vice versa.

My freaky friends are not the only ones expanding their horizons—there are plenty of people doing it, trust me. If you're looking for them, a good place to start is a magazine called *Loving More* <www.lovemore.com>, which has a wealth of information on the subject and celebrates alternative arrangements of all kinds. At the risk of sounding like my fellow *Village Voice* columnist Michael Musto, I have it on good authority that a certain married couple of actors who starred in a late-1980s drama has a three-way marriage with another woman; they all live and have Tantric sex together in Northern California. Dude, everything's way cooler on the West Coast.

While it may seem reminiscent of 1970s free love without the drugs, polyamory today encompasses a greater consciousness of safer sex and everyone's feelings and boundaries than it did in the days of wife-swapping and key parties. It's a surefire way to challenge your sexual and emotional boundaries and explore your feelings about jealousy and possessiveness. If you were allowed to stray within the confines of your relationship—the illicit naughtiness of an affair no longer present—would it still be desirable? Could you live with the knowledge that your partner was fucking someone else but still loved you? Polyamory is not a tool to avoid issues in your marriage, not an excuse to act out irresponsibly, and it's not for everyone. It takes just as much work as monogamy, and probably more honesty.

IT'S A SUREFIRE WAY TO CHALLENGE YOUR SEXUAL AND EMOTIONAL BOUNDARIES AND EXPLORE YOUR FEELINGS ABOUT JEALOUSY AND POSSESSIVENESS.

The sneers "slut," "swinger," and "sex addict" may be vaulted your way by others, but check the source—they're probably just jealous. Who says there can't be a president, two first husbands, and a first girlfriend in the White House?

HOW TO RID THE WORLD OF GOOD
NICK MAMATAS

On September 11, 2001, two airliners crashed into the Twin Towers of New York City's World Trade Center, obliterating the buildings and killing thousands of working people, tourists, executives, and passers-by. A third plane crashed into the Pentagon, killing a couple hundred more people, and a fourth plane crash-landed in Pennsylvania, presumably short of its target somewhere in Washington, DC. At press time, this unprecedented disaster was believed to be the work of terrorists under the aegis of Osama bin Laden, the Saudi millionaire and former CIA asset.[1] The perceptual reaction was swift. The terrorists were evil, perhaps evil lunatics, who attacked the US only because of a hatred of freedom, a jealousy of the United States' way of life. The US, victim of this attack, was good. President George W. Bush was explicit: "This will be a monumental struggle of good versus evil," he explained to the shocked nation. The little AOL news zipper was even more succinct: "Bush promises to 'rid world of evil.'"

"Good versus evil" was shorthand obscuring all the complexities of the last 50 years of US foreign policy in the Middle East and the near-inevitable "blowback" of the September 11 attacks. The very notion of good versus evil is not an artifact of material reality (there is neither good nor evil in the real world), nor is it some deep, hardwired set of archetypes squirming around the human brain. Ironically enough, it is an artifact of the Persian domination of the cradle of civilization, and this apocalyptic worldview that so neatly splits all experience, thought, and imagination into two categories has been with the Western world ever since. So it wasn't always like this. Many of the greatest works of antiquity, for example, do not involve the conflict between good and evil. The epic poems and tragedies of ancient Greece are not concerned with such a struggle, and even the earliest books of the Bible posit evil as an overdetermined force—God, through a variety of agents, creates evil as an obstacle or mile marker on a path toward a closer relationship with the Divine.

> THE VERY NOTION OF GOOD VERSUS EVIL IS NOT AN ARTIFACT OF MATERIAL REALITY (THERE IS NEITHER GOOD NOR EVIL IN THE REAL WORLD), NOR IS IT SOME DEEP, HARDWIRED SET OF ARCHETYPES SQUIRMING AROUND THE HUMAN BRAIN.

In Homer's *Illiad*, Hektor, the breaker of horses and the hero of Troy, was as respected and admired, and as much of a protagonist, as any of the Greek heroes. In *Odyssey*, the capriciousness of the gods was not a reflection of their evil, and Odysseus was neither good nor evil in his attempts to stay alive and get home to Ithaca. He was simply noble, intelligent, wise, crafty, and wily; the best a human being could be. He manifested *arete*.[2]

Further, good and evil as we know them don't appear as concepts in any work by Sophocles, Euripides, or Aeschylus. Good does not rise up and conquer evil; evil is not inexplicable, animal, unfair, or inescapable. Even in *The Eumenides*, which features the Greek spirits of vengeance, the Furies, there is no final apocalyptic conflict between good and evil. Instead, the Furies are encouraged to turn Orestes, who killed his mother, over to Athenian judges for trial. Athena declares Orestes acquitted and then turns to the Furies themselves. She asks them to end their bitterness and live with her as goddesses. She will bear their anger and their role, and she asks them not to infect the hearts of young men with evil and the thirst for revenge.

She tells them, "Do good, receive good, and be honored as the good are honored. Share our country, the beloved of god."[3] Initially, the Furies balk at this request, and repeat their old grievances against the new gods and their commitment to reason, and threaten to punish the land. Athena continues reasoning with the Furies, offering them both the classic carrot—offerings from the people—and the stick—the wrath of Zeus and his thunderbolts. The Furies initially don't believe that the people of Athens could ever accept them as part of the civil society of democracy, rather than as symbols of vengeance and fear, but Athena convinces them otherwise through logical argument and personal empathy.

In Aeschylus' worldview, the ferocity of the Furies can be integrated into a peaceful society, and the primal nature of emotion can be reconciled into the world of reason without being cast out or destroyed. This is done through the democratic process and through reasoned debate between equals—there is no apocalyptic battle, no utter destruction or negation of the primitive side of human nature, and no essentialist arguments about the nature of good and evil. And indeed, the Furies finally accept Athena's offer and become Eumenides, or the kindly ones, whose mission is to keep Athens from civil war and to provide prosperity and blessings for the democracy.

The notion of good versus evil as the underlying theme of some übernarrative that informs all human thought and behavior cannot be found even in the earliest books of the Old Testament, the foundation of Judeo-Christian mythology. The "original sin" of Adam and Eve was a relatively late invention, and understandably so. One needn't be a theologian to point to the massive plot and consistency holes in the well-known story of Man's Fall. Why was the fruit in the Garden? Why would God allow the serpent into the Garden? Isn't knowledge a good thing, and if so, why would God prevent eating from the Tree of Knowledge? There are many explanations, and the earliest don't use the concept of good versus evil. "One source assures us that [the serpent] was the angels' emissary; they had concluded that man would represent too formidable a challenge unless he could be made to stray and sin."[4] In other legendary Jewish commentaries—the texts of the Midrash—surrounding the event, "Adam and Eve *had* to defy God so that their descendants might sing His praises."[5]

> THE NOTION OF GOOD VERSUS EVIL AS THE UNDERLYING THEME OF SOME ÜBERNARRATIVE THAT INFORMS ALL HUMAN THOUGHT AND BEHAVIOR CANNOT BE FOUND EVEN IN THE EARLIEST BOOKS OF THE OLD TESTAMENT, THE FOUNDATION OF JUDEO-CHRISTIAN MYTHOLOGY.

What about the serpent? Wasn't he the Devil in disguise, looking to tempt the unwary and thwart the (necessarily) good plans of God? Not necessarily. Much of the Old Testament, including the entire Book of Job, shows Satan (and, more generally, satans) as an angel with a special task, that of obstacle. "The root *stn* means 'one who opposes, obstructs, or acts as adversary.' (The Greek term *diabolos*, later translated 'devil,' literally means 'one who throws something across one's path.')"[6] And the obstacle doesn't necessarily take the form of a test or temptation, either; Satan appears in some stories in order to be an obstacle on the path to some event or circumstance. And if the path or circumstance is bad, then the obstacle is beneficial.

The etymology of *diabolos* provides further clues. "Devil" isn't quite a translation of *diabolos*; it has even older roots:

The Devas of the [Hindu] Veda are the bright gods who fight on the side of Indra; in the [Zoroastrian] Avesta the word has come to mean an evil spirit, and the Zoroastrian was bound to declare that he ceased to be a worshipper of the daevas...

[T]he word devil passed into an immense number of forms, the Gothic *tieval, diuval, diufal*, the Icelandic *djofull*, Swedish *djevful*, all of them, together with the Italian, French, and Spanish forms carrying back the word [diabolos] to the same root which furnished the Latin *Divus, Djovis*, and the Sanskrit *deva*.[7]

The word "demon" has some noble ancestors, as well. In Greek, the *daemon* was the divine force that engendered and informed the character of men (women had their own spirits). In Latin, this concept was adopted and called *genius*. The genius was eventually separated from the self as a concept and was identified with household gods and ancestral spirits, the Manes.[8] *Daemon* was well-known enough as a term describing an internal creative spirit, or as a set of natural skills and inclinations, to make it into Shakespeare, as per this discussion between an Egyptian seer and Antony:

Thy daemon, that thy spirit which keeps thee, is Noble, courageous, high, unmatchable, Where Caesar's is not. But near him thy angel Becomes afeard, as being o'erpowered.
(*Antony and Cleopatra* 2.3.17-20)

The inclusion of artifacts of the personality within the greater rubric of evil also suggests that some transcultural, transhistorical fear of the Other is not to blame for the modern ubiquity of good/evil narratives. Before the good/evil split, it wasn't unusual for the Other to be widely respected, up to and including adopting gods and heroes from neighboring cultures, incorporating them into the local pantheon. As seen in Homer, it was simple enough to have an extensive, bloody war with a neighboring kingdom, with little more than freely admitted acrimony over property and honor at stake; all the Greek and Trojan heroes were fully realized as human beings with human drives and circumstances. The Trojans are not dehumanized as the Other.

The Bible isn't even consistent on who the Other is and what its role was, even up to offering different agents of change for different accounts of the same incident. In 2 Samuel 24, for example, God influences David to take a census, then punishes him for doing so. In 1 Chronicles 21:1, the same event is described, with one difference. Rather than God directly influencing David's behavior, and then unleashing a plague, an evil emissary is credited with having David take the forbidden census. Chronicles, written about a century after Samuel, still doesn't demonstrate a good/evil duality. Rather, God performs evil actions indirectly. In neither case, it should be noted, is evil in opposition to good. Both work hand-in-hand to achieve a natural and ultimately good result, namely the will of God.

The Persian occupation, circa the fifth century BC, led to interaction between Judaism and Zoroastrianism, and the duality of the latter religion—plus other concepts, like angels and the immortality of the soul—was picked up from Zoroastrianism by Jewish sects.[9] Founded by the Persian prophet Zarathustra, Zoroastrianism offered a monotheistic creed to a polytheistic region. The religion posits a single, all-powerful god, Ahura Mazda, who created the material world and communicated with humanity via the Amesha Spentas, the personifications of certain abstract concepts. Angra Mainyu, the hostile spirit, is a finite, evil being who brought ruin, death, and destruction upon the material world, but who will eventually be destroyed through the good actions of human beings. Additionally, Zoroastrianism posits the eventual arrival of a savior, Saoshyant, who will be born of a virgin. This savior will raise the dead and lead them all to a final judgment.

Sound familiar? One or more of the Jewish sects impacted by Zoroastrianism happened to become Christianity, which eventually took over most of the world. And indeed, it was Christianity that put the final nail in the coffin of religious pluralism. Clement of Alexandria declared, contra the practice of Roman paganism and most of the public cults of the day, that "the gods of all the nations are images of demons."[10] Previously, the commonalties of neighboring pantheons were highlighted, and most worshippers assumed that foreign gods were variants on their local gods.

Once Christianity became the public cult, the success of the good/evil dichotomy in both explaining the natural world and in creating cross-ethnic unity across Christendom was quite handy. If illness and disaster were the work of the Devil, the victims could be blamed for their own misfortune, since God would clearly protect them otherwise. The successful, of course, were owed their success thanks to their piety. Evil was then applied to certain other cultural groups in order to limit trade, encourage war-making, engage in land grabs, and undercut internal ethnic communities that might have had foreign allegiances. The strategy of obscure Iranian prophets had made the big time.

Today the secular world doesn't need Satan. Good and evil, however, are in great demand. The old Iranian dualism of good versus evil is entirely an arbitrary one, but it's effective for maintaining social order. In US history, the good/evil dualism was projected onto the continent itself. The undiscovered countries of Africa and North America were cast in the role of evil, conveniently enough, as they were both un-Christian and ripe for exploration and exploitation in a way that much of seventeenth-century Asia was not. In 1676, Bacon's Rebellion, which saw both black and white indentured servants rise up against their masters, threatened the power of the fledgling Virginia colony and led directly to the "divide and conquer" strategy that split poor whites from poor blacks politically, socially, and spiritually. Poor whites were favored over blacks and granted a level of citizenship (an arbitrary concept that boils down to, "You are within this set of dotted lines and you are good.") that put them on the good side of the dualism of Christianity/savagery, white/black, and worker/slave.

This dualism also informed the slavery of blacks in the United States for the next two centuries, as well as the three centuries of genocide of various Native American tribes in the continental United States and Hawaii. The United States also emerged as a world power and used its newfound influence over the West's mass culture to offer a thoroughly revisionist history of both slavery and the Indian Wars through popular fiction and motion pictures. This same revisionism can be found across fiction generally; everything from the hundreds of Tolkien-inspired fantasy novels to the modern technothriller utilize the same duality of the Western frontier combat narrative. The Western itself was in turn influenced by the heroic Romances, which had the explicit lessons of the good/evil duality as their primary thematic/narrative goal.[11]

This dualism now informs the Muslim world as the propaganda enemy of the United States. Currently, the United States is bombing the already shattered landscape of Afghanistan in order to root out the ruling Taliban and find the arch-terrorist and media-proclaimed "evil mastermind" Osama bin Laden. At the same time, anonymous individuals are sending anthrax-tainted materials through the mails to government officials and media outlets. At the time of this writing, the terror campaigns of (presumably) bin Laden and the anthrax letters are widely considered to be linked, but the reactions to the two elements of terrorism are entirely divorced.

It is publicly acknowledged that most Afghans are "innocent" in that they support neither the Taliban nor Osama bin Laden. Decades of war and interventions by both the United States and the USSR have left the country shattered. Accompanying the US bombing runs are food drops, which have been roundly criticized by most observers as a simple propaganda move, and a White House fundraising scheme wherein American children are asked to send dollar bills to the White House in order to feed Afghan children.[12] These moves are tactical media events, not real attempts to ease the suffering of the Afghan people. Rather, they exist to ensure the United States public that they are on the side of good.

The vast majority of people in Afghanistan are innocent, but in order to root out the evil bin Laden's hiding place (which may not even be in Afghanistan), they must suffer through terrible bombings. The US is also hiding parts of bin Laden's terror network, as can be seen by the existence of our anonymous Anthrax Mary and his or her (or their) busy mailing campaign. And yet, the United States is not bombing parts of Florida or Trenton, New Jersey, much less Texas-sized areas around these locations.

Both the Afghans and the Americans are equally innocent.

HOW TO RID THE WORLD OF GOOD
NICK MAMATAS

But only one is "good." Only one exists within the magic circle. The Afghans need not be guilty for the United States government, and much of the American public, to chalk up their despair to poor luck or the sacrifices that one (typically someone else) needs to make in order for good to triumph over evil. The United States and its citizens, inherently good, intrinsically innocent, and in a blessed, free land, are immune from the consequences of their actions. It was George W. Bush who coined the phrase-cum-demand, "May God continue to bless America," at about the same time that he swore to "rid the world of evil." And thanks to a long-ago Iranian prophet, even the slaughter of the universally-acknowledged innocent can be called good. The recognition of the false duality that allows innocent deaths to be called good should be sufficient, dear reader, to allow the good to fold in on itself and disappear in a puff of logic. Consider yourself liberated.

Won't go very far toward eliminating the evil, however.

Endnotes

1. In 1987 alone, the US government gave Afghani terrorists-cum-freedom fighters $500 million, and bin Laden and his Saudi allies matched this largesse dollar for dollar. See Weaver, Mary Anne. "The Real bin Laden." *The New Yorker* 24 Jan, 2000: 32. **2.** Manifesting *arete* is a tricky thing to write, because *arete* is a tricky concept to grasp. Generally, the concept of *eudaimonia*, following Aristotle, refers to the constant, excellent activity of those parts of the soul that are peculiar to human beings. However, since the soul is ineffable, the only way to be aware of this excellence is to observe it in other human beings. *Arete* refers both to excellence in taking actions dictated by reason, and a variety of virtues (moderation, courage, practical wisdom, etc.) that are developed through habit, not through nature. *Arete*, is thus "excellence of being" and is conceptually designed to replace simple pleasure as the goal of life. Needless to say, English doesn't have a word for this concept. **3.** Aeschylus, *The Eumenides*. Tr. Richmond Lattimore, 868-9. **4.** Wiesel, Elie. *Messengers of God*. New York: Simon and Schuster (A Touchstone Book), 1994: 17. **5.** *Ibid.*: 27. **6.** Pagels, Elaine. *The Origin of Satan*. New York: Random House, 1995: 39-41. **7.** Cox, George. *Mythology of the Aryan Nations*. Longmans, 1870: 355, 363. **8.** Remember those really weak devils from Dungeons & Dragons? That's them. **9.** For more on this incredibly complex subject and the roots of Zarathustra's own ideas of good/evil duality and how they relate to Hinduism and its spread thanks to the Indo-European invasion of circa 2000 BC, check out Messandé, G. *The History of the Devil*. London: Newleaf, 1986. **10.** *Ibid.*: 262. **11.** For a further discussion of genre as an outgrowth of the Romantic period, see: Olsen, Lance. *Rebel Yell: A Short Guide to Fiction Writing*. Cambrian Publications, 1998. **12.** Afghanistan has several million starving residents, many of whom were being fed by a

THE OLD IRANIAN DUALISM OF GOOD VERSUS EVIL IS ENTIRELY AN ARBITRARY ONE, BUT IT'S EFFECTIVE FOR MAINTAINING SOCIAL ORDER.

variety of relief organizations until the bombing began. The airdrops of individual Meals Ready to Eat would not provide sustenance for even a tenth of the people in need in Afghanistan, even if every meal landed on the lap of a starving person. Additionally, most of the food is being dropped in the best-fed area in the country; there is no infrastructure on the ground to collect and distribute the food; and much of the food is landing in minefields. As far as the cash to Afghan children, the notion of converting a pile of dollar bills into useful funds for Afghan children and only Afghan children, most of whom do not participate in a cash economy, should be obviously foolish to even the densest observer.

WHY WOMEN NEED FREEDOM FROM RELIGION

ANNIE LAURIE GAYLOR

"You should give up your pen and take up your position as a woman, speak only when spoken to, stay pregnant and barefoot, do the chores and submit to your man whenever he feels the need for it. This is a man's world, let men run it."

This email, posted to me after my appearance representing the freethought point of view on a Fox News Network talkshow in September 2001, initially struck me as a comical atavism. Then I had a moment of shocked recognition. The misogynist missive, in fact, is an accurate summary, albeit vulgarly worded, of the view of women still shared by fundamentalists worldwide. Patriarchal Christianity, Judaism, and Islam—all claiming the same Abrahamic root—consider women's inferiority to be divinely decreed.

Many Jews, Christians, and Muslims ironically claim that each other's religions have oppressed woman, while their own has uplifted her. But Jews, Christians, and Muslims have a common denominator. She is Eve, whose "transgression" has been used to keep even her modern daughter in the proper biblical position: prone, with the foot of one of Adam's descendants resting on her neck. For causing the downfall of the human race, womankind is sentenced by a supreme deity to bring forth children in sorrow: "[T]hy desire shall be to thy husband, and he shall rule over thee" (Genesis 3:16).

The New Testament continues the holy war against women's rights:

But I would have you know, that the head of every man is Christ; and the head of every woman is the man; and the head of Christ is God. (I Corinthians 11:3, 8-9)

Let your women keep silence in the churches; for it is not permitted unto them to speak; but they are commanded to be under obedience, as also saith the law. (I Corinthians 14:34-35)

Let the woman learn in silence in all subjection. But I suffer not a woman to teach nor to usurp authority over the man, but to be in silence. For Adam was first formed, then Eve. And Adam was not deceived, but the woman being deceived was in the transgression. (I Timothy 2:11-14)

The Bible wastes no time establishing woman's inferior status, her uncleanliness, her transgressions, and her God-ordained master/servant relationship to men (all by the third chapter of Genesis). Women in the Bible, when they are mentioned, are appendages. According to the favored version of creation, woman was created from a spare rib—quite an exercise in patriarchal reversal! Biblical women are possessions: Fathers own them, sell them into bondage, sometimes have sex with them (as with Lot, described in II Peter 2:8 as "that righteous man"), and even sacrifice them, as in the cruel story of Jephthah and his nameless daughter.

The Bible sanctions rape under many circumstances and denies its existence under others, specifically ordaining the taking of virgins as war booty. Wives are subject to Mosaic-law-sanctioned bed-checks as brides and later, as wives, to deadly tests for faithfulness, as well as no-notice divorce. The Bible characterizes many women as "harlots" and "whores." When the biblical Lord is displeased with a nation, it is referred to as a "lewd" woman, with graphic descriptions of sexually sadistic punishment. The few Bible heroines to be found are generally glorified only for their obedience and battle spirit. The New Testament decrees that women must submit to their husbands in the same manner that men must submit to the biblical Lord. For these reasons and more, Elizabeth Cady Stanton, the great nineteenth-century founder of the feminist movement, wrote: "The Bible and the Church have been the greatest stumbling blocks in the way of women's emancipation."

■ ■ ■ ■ ■ ■ ■ ■ ■ ■

The Koran, written some 700 years after Christianity began, and embracing much of the Old and New Testaments, embroidered on biblical themes, such as polygamy, advising: "Marry as many women as you like, two, three, or four" (Koran 4:3). The result in many Islamic nations today is that men are permitted four wives at a time. The Koran states that women are worth half as much as men: "The male shall have the equal of the portion of two females" (4:11).

Domestic violence plagues Arab countries, such as West Bank-Gaza Strip, Israel, Jordan, Egypt, Tunisia, and Kuwait, according to a 1994 Associated Press report. Providing divine justification for beatings is the Koranic verse: "Men are the maintainers of women... the good women are therefore obedient, guarding the unseen as Allah has guarded; and [as to] those on whose part you fear desertion, admonish them, and leave them alone in the sleeping-places and beat them..." (4:34). The instruction to beat wives is fortified by a verse advising to "take in your hand a green branch and beat her with it" (38:44) (a green branch is specified since it will hurt more). *The Muslim's Handbook*, published in Turkey in 2000, advises its readers "not to strike the woman's face" but to hit her "gently" elsewhere. The Imam Mohamed Kamal Mostafa, a Koranic scholar in Spain, outraged many when his book, *Women in Islam* (2000), included tips on wife-beating.

The biblical story of Noah and Lot is invoked to teach women what happens to disobedient wives—they go to hell (66:10). Likewise, Hebrew Testament verses mandating death for fornication and adultery are taken literally across much of the Arab and Muslim world, taking the form of "honor killings" by male family members against transgressing female relatives. Statistics on honor killing for Jordan, considered the most credible, reflect that they account for one in four homicides a year, with the lightest of sentences meted out for prosecuted murderers. Until 1999, Egyptian law promised a pardon to any rapist who agreed to marry his victim, another variation straight out of Mosaic law, with its overarching value upon "chastity" in females. Stoning women to death for adultery has become routine in Islamic Iran.

■ ■ ■ ■ ■ ■ ■ ■ ■ ■

The Mormon religion, a bizarre nineteenth-century American permutation of Christianity, and today the fastest-growing religion in the world, dipped back into Hebrew Bible stories to make polygamy its controversial linchpin—until forced to abandon it by the expediency of seeking statehood for Utah. ("True believers," calling themselves fundamentalist Mormons, continue the practice, however, leading to charges of widespread welfare fraud, child marriages, and sexual abuse in isolated polygamous pockets.) While polygamy is officially eschewed, the doctrine of "celestial marriage" specifically mandates eternal polygamy. Mormon Church doctrine permits men to sign up future wives to possess in Mormondom's polygamous heaven. A Mormon wife is destined to become an eternal breeder of "spirit" babies, surely making the Mormon Church's vision of heaven one of the most unappetizing afterlives for women—a place of unrelieved reproductive servitude.

The Church's original nineteenth-century position on marriage was not the equal-opportunity heaven promised by Jesus in Galatians. Instead it taught that only through men could women be ensured entry to heaven: "No woman will get into the celestial kingdom, except her husband receives her, if she is worthy to have a husband; and if not, somebody will receive her as a servant," preached Erastus Snow in 1857 (*Journal of Discourses*, volume 5, p 291). The doctrine of women's salvation only through marriage is underplayed today, with the current Church emphasizing the importance of temple marriages and "sacred ordinances and covenants" to ensure eternal life for both women and men.

Even sanitized, the Mormon Church is among the most patriarchal, conferring the "priesthood" upon all Mormon men and continuing to emphasize women's role as subservient mother and wife in a patriarchal family. In his 1995 "Proclamation to the World" on the family, Mormon president Gordon B. Hinckley decreed:

By divine design, fathers are to preside over their families in love and righteousness and are responsible to provide the necessities of life and protection for their families. Mothers are primarily responsible for the nurture of their children.... Further, we warn that the disintegration of the family will bring upon individuals, communities, and nations the calamities foretold by ancient and modern prophets.

The Mormon Church exerts special control over everyday matters—its underwear requirements, for instance, dictate women's fashions by ruling out short skirts, sleeveless dresses, and shorts. The Mormon Church maintains its role as a leading opponent of abortion and gay rights, with Hinckley parroting the Catholic Pope by decreeing: "We declare that God's commandment for His children to multiply and replenish the earth remains in force. We further declare that God has commanded that the sacred powers of procreation are to be employed only between man and wife, lawfully wedded as husband and wife."

■ ■ ■ ■ ■ ■ ■ ■ ■ ■

While apologists for religion will argue that many teachings out of "holy books" have been "taken out of context" or can no longer be taken literally, the historic harm of religious power over women cannot be denied. It can be demonstrated by the consequences of one

"NO WOMAN WILL GET INTO THE CELESTIAL KINGDOM, EXCEPT HER HUSBAND RECEIVES HER, IF SHE IS WORTHY TO HAVE A HUSBAND; AND IF NOT, SOMEBODY WILL RECEIVE HER AS A SERVANT," PREACHED ERASTUS SNOW IN 1857.

Bible verse alone, Exodus 22:18: "Thou shalt not suffer a witch to live," which is responsible for the deaths of tens of thousands, if not millions, of innocent women. Today only oddballs take the verse seriously, yet the horrors it inflicted upon women in the name of God and the Bible cannot be textproofed away.

Similarly, one Koranic passage (24:30-31) has imposed *purdah* on whole nations of women (known as "submitters," since Islam means "submission"): "And say to the believing women, that they should cast down their eyes and guard their private parts, and reveal not their adornment save such as is outward; and let them cast their veils over their bosoms, and not reveal their adornment save to their husbands..."

In some Islamic cultures a headscarf and long garments suffice. But others, such as theocratic Iran, impose the *chador* (a tent-like robe) and police the streets looking for transgressors, who are harassed, beaten, or even jailed. During the reign of the Taliban Islamic government, Afghan women were literally enshrouded in the claustrophobic *burqua*, which covers the entire body and face. In some cultures militant Muslims throw acid in the uncovered faces of women; a 15-year-old Kashmir girl was disfigured for life in a September 2001 attack for defying an informal imposition of the Islamic dress code on women. Earlier that year, a Kashmir girl was shot dead for wearing "fashionable" clothes in Pahalgam.

IN SOME CULTURES MILITANT MUSLIMS THROW ACID IN THE UNCOVERED FACES OF WOMEN.

In traditional Islamic cultures the verse 24:30-31 has also been used to confine daughters and wives to their homes, such as in Jordan, where a woman cannot leave the home without the permission of her family. The imposition of *sharia*, or religious law, in parts of Nigeria in 2000 immediately resulted in an edict banning the transportation of women on motorbike taxis, since Islamic rules call for segregating men and women on public transportation. Saudi Arabia bars women from driving cars for the same reason. At its most repressive, Islam places women under virtual house arrest.

■ ■ ■ ■ ■ ■ ■ ■ ■ ■

Whether declared or undeclared, there is nothing new in the religious war against women's freedoms. After the organized women's movement was launched in the 1800s, Elizabeth Cady Stanton recalled how the "Bible was hurled at us on every side." In remarks to the 1885 National Woman Suffrage Association Convention, Stanton analyzed religion's unique power over women:

You may go over the world and you will find that every form of religion which has breathed upon this earth has degraded woman. There is not one which has not made her subject to man. Men may rejoice in them because they make man the head of the woman. I have been traveling the old world during the last few years and have found new food for thought. What power is it that makes the Hindoo woman burn herself on the funeral pyre of her husband? Her religion. What holds the Turkish woman in the harem? Her religion. By what power do the Mormons perpetuate their system of polygamy? By their religion. Man, of himself, could not do this; but when he declares, "Thus saith the Lord," of course he can do it. So long as ministers stand up and tell us that as Christ is the head of the church, so is man the head of the woman, how are we to break the chains which have held women down through the ages?... We want to help roll off from the soul of woman the terrible superstitions that have so long repressed and crushed her.

The Bible and other "holy books" continue to be hurled at women working for their freedom. Christian holy men have invoked the Bible to oppose reproductive freedom—from the YMCA-backed nineteenth-century postal censor and religious fanatic Anthony Comstock, and the powerful Archbishop Patrick Hayes of New York, who used the law to shut down Margaret Sanger's public meeting on birth control in 1921—to the clergy ringleaders of today's terrorism against abortion clinic personnel and patients. The Catholic, fundamentalist, and Mormon churches organized their congregations against the Equal Rights Amendment, defeating the ratification process, just as a century before they ensured the suffrage amendment took several generations of struggle to achieve. The religious war against women's rights continues unabated today around the world. Whether the issue is birth control, abortion, ordination, education, political office, employment, or dress reform, the message against freedom for women is the same from the fundamentalist branches of patriarchal religions.

Up until 150 years ago, the biblical subjugation of women was the operative norm of Western society, the prevailing dogma and custom, even in the United States, a land with a secular government and constitution. Not only could women not vote, they could not speak in public and certainly not before "mixed" (or "promiscuous") assemblies. They could not make contracts, sue or be sued, sit on juries, attend colleges or universities, or enter most trades or professions. A married woman could not maintain control of the property she brought into marriage or earned during marriage. By law her husband could even pick up her paycheck and spend it. She was not recognized as the legal guardian of her own children. Women were classed with children and, in the parlance of the day, "idiots." Thanks to the edict in Genesis, when they married, they utterly lost their identities, not just their names, with the male identity totally subsuming the woman's ("flesh of my flesh"). The term for it was "civil death," but its origin was strictly biblical.

■ ■ ■ ■ ■ ■ ■ ■ ■ ■

Every freedom won for women in the United States, small or large—wearing bloomers, riding bicycles, not wearing bonnets in church, and being permitted to speak in public, to attend universities, to enter professions, to vote and own property—was opposed by the churches. Therefore it is no surprise that the first to speak out for women's rights were the secularists, the freethinkers, and the unorthodox. Mary Wollstonecraft, a freethinking Deist, wrote the first significant call for women's rights, *A Vindication of the Rights of Woman*, in 1792. The first woman in North America to defy the New Testament ban on public speaking was freethinker Frances Wright, during her unprecedented lecture series on "free inquiry," women's education, and freethought in 1828-1829, during which she was attacked by mobs and labeled the "Red Harlot of Infidelity."

When Sarah and Angelina Grimke began speaking before female audiences against slavery in 1837, the Congregational Church of Massachusetts sent out a Pastoral Letter censuring them. ("The appropriate duties and influence of woman are clearly stated in the New Testament.... If the vine, whose strength and beauty is to lean upon the trellis-work, and half conceal its clusters, thinks to assume the independence and the overshadowing nature of the elm, it will not only cease to bear fruit, but fall in shame and dishonor into the dust.") The sisters' notorious speaking tour lasted less than a year. Other women rose to their places, including abolitionist Abby Kelley, who eventually left the condemning Society of Friends (aka, the Quakers) to do abolition and suffrage work without benefit of clergy. Nearly 300 men walked out of the American Anti-Slavery Society meeting in 1840 in New York to protest Abby's presence on the business committee, then formed a rival society forbidding women to vote or hold office. The silencing of women at the 1840 World's Anti-Slavery Conference in London, in which men voted on the basis of scriptural edicts to exclude women from participation, was the feminist awakening of young Elizabeth Cady Stanton. She and four Quaker friends went on to organize the 1848 Seneca Falls Convention, the first public gathering calling for suffrage and rights for women, which sparked the wrath of clergy around the continent.

As the activism of American women increased, on their own behalf

and on behalf of slaves, and in defiance of the New Testament, so did the clergy resistance. Delegates at the May 12, 1853, "Brick Church Meeting" in New York voted 34-32 against women being recognized as temperance delegates. "Throughout this protracted, disgraceful assault on American womanhood, the clergy baptized each new insult and set of injustice in the name of the Christian religion, and uniformly asked God's blessing on proceedings that would have put to shame an assembly of Hottentots," wrote Stanton reprovingly in *The History of Woman Suffrage*. The mainly clerical speakers condemned any public role for women, "quoting Scripture and the Divine will to sanction their injustice," Stanton added. The annual woman's rights convention at the Broadway Tabernacle in September 1853 went down in history as the "mob convention," when throngs of men, mainly clergymen or religionists acting on biblical precepts, sabotaged the convention with hisses, groans, stamping, and ridiculing remarks, forcing it to shut down. The religion-incited mobs continued wherever women spoke in public.

> EVERY FREEDOM WON FOR WOMEN IN THE UNITED STATES, SMALL OR LARGE—WEARING BLOOMERS, RIDING BICYCLES, NOT WEARING BONNETS IN CHURCH, AND BEING PERMITTED TO SPEAK IN PUBLIC, TO ATTEND UNIVERSITIES, TO ENTER PROFESSIONS, TO VOTE AND OWN PROPERTY—WAS OPPOSED BY THE CHURCHES.

Freethinking Judge Thomas Hertell of the New York legislature was the first to introduce legislation to protect the property rights of women. Ardent atheist Ernestine L. Rose, a Polish immigrant, became the first to lobby for passage of the Married Woman's Property Act, as well as becoming the first canvasser for women's rights. Like Wollstonecraft and Wright, Rose was an object of vituperation, libeled by clergy as "a thousand times lower than a prostitute." Fledgling freethinker Elizabeth Cady Stanton, who had been the first to call for women's suffrage, took the lead in calling for marriage and divorce reform, becoming the Bible's sharpest critic by the time she penned the *Woman's Bible* nearly 50 years later. "My heart's desire is to lift women out of all these dangerous, degrading superstitions, and to this end will I labor my remaining days on earth," she wrote in 1896. Stanton's "coadjutant," Susan B. Anthony, was an agnostic, and their feminist partner, Matilda Joslyn Gage, author of the influential *Woman, Church and State* (1893), was a freethinker who in 1890 formed the first national feminist organization to work for the separation of church and state.

Freethinking women unafraid to defy holy scripture filled the ranks of state and national suffrage organizations and were the catalysts challenging the position of woman as the proverbial drudge and "helpmeet," pushing the exploration of broader questions, such as marriage, sexual rights and wrongs, and divorce reform. Freethinking women pioneered what woman's rights lecturer Lois

Waisbrooker called woman's "natural, inherent right to herself." Poet and radical freethinker Voltairine de Cleyre wrote in 1890: "The question of souls is old—we demand our bodies, now. We are tired of promises, God is deaf, and his church is our worst enemy." She harpooned the "virtuous" drudge of Proverbs in her address "Woman Versus Orthodoxy," and wrote searingly of the issue of battered women a century before US law addressed the issue. British iconoclast Annie Besant, anarchist atheist Emma Goldman, and targets of censor Anthony Comstock, such as Elmina Slenker, were among the freethinkers who helped pave the way for "woman rebel" Margaret Sanger to ignite the birth control movement worldwide. Sanger wrote in her autobiography: "I wanted each woman to be a rebellious Vashti, not an Esther." Freethinker Charlotte Perkins Gilman, one of the most famous woman writers of the early twentieth century, addressed the "family values question" by writing in her book *His Religion and Hers*: "One religion after another has accepted and perpetuated man's original mistake in making a private servant of the mother of the race."

While unorthodox women were defying religion to its face by claiming their freedoms, they also, in self-defense, have been among the most ardent supporters of secularism. With her followers, Anne Hutchinson, who was banished and excommunicated by the Massachusetts Bay Colony in 1637, adopted the first civil secular government, making a declaration of religious freedom in America during their brief settlement of Aquidneck, Rhode Island. Anne Royall, a nationally-known eccentric author and passionate defender of the Enlightenment, fearlessly dedicated herself to fighting the God-in-the-Constitution party, organized in the 1820s. Royall's motto was, "Good works instead of long prayers." Stanton led the campaign to ensure that Sabbatarians would not close the World's Fair of 1893 on Sundays. Vashti McCollum brought the first lawsuit successfully challenging religious instruction in public schools in the US, winning a landmark Supreme Court decision in 1948 that is still prevailing law. Sonia Johnson was excommunicated by the Mormon Church in 1979 for exposing the political role the tax-exempt church was playing in defeating the Equal Rights Amendment. Secularist Taslima Nasrin of Bangladesh, who has a *fatwa* hanging over her head from Muslim fundamentalists, is a modern-day freedom fighter in the international battle of "woman versus orthodoxy."

■ ■ ■ ■ ■ ■ ■ ■ ■ ■

Islamic fundamentalist theocrats openly talk of *jihad*, a holy war, and seek to impose *sharia* upon women. But are they so different from their Christian cousins? Radical political personality Patrick Buchanan, an arch-enemy of women's rights, has called for a Christian "holy war" against secularism in this nation. The infamous remarks of the Rev. Jerry Falwell in the wake of the terrorist attacks on the US on September 11, 2001, reveal his sympathies with Osama bin Laden, who also eschews the United States because of its secularism.

"I really believe," said Rev. Falwell, "that the pagans, and the abortionists, and the feminists, and the gays and the lesbians, who are actively trying to make that an alternative lifestyle, the ACLU, People For the American Way, all of them who tried to secularize America, I point the finger in their face and say you helped this happen."

In Alabama, the "Army of God" bombed an abortion clinic in early 1998. In Algeria, it is terrorists from similarly-named groups who have shot schoolgirls on the streets for not wearing veils. Orthodox Jews attack Israeli women for wearing sleeveless dresses in public and for daring to pray at the Wailing Wall. Whether in the name of God, Allah, or Yahweh, the surge in fundamentalism, and its attempts to destroy or encroach on secular life, remains women's greatest threat.

■ ■ ■ ■ ■ ■ ■ ■ ■ ■

"Do you tell me that the Bible is against our rights? Then I say that our claims do not rest upon a book written no one knows when, or by whom... [B]ooks and opinions, no matter from whom they came, if they are in opposition to human rights, are nothing but dead letters...." said Ernestine L. Rose during a debate over the Bible at an 1856 women's rights convention.

Women today would do well to heed Stanton's admonition in her 1896 essay, "The Degraded Status of Woman in the Bible":

For fifty years the women of this nation have tried to dam up this deadly stream that poisons all their lives, but thus far they have lacked the insight or courage to follow it back to its source and there strike the blow at the fountain of all tyranny, religious superstition, priestly power, and the canon law.

Why do women remain second-class citizens? Why is there a religion-fostered war against women's rights? Without question, it is because the Bible and other "holy works" are handbooks for the subjugation of women. When attempts are made to base laws on these holy books, women must beware. The principle of separation between religion and government first espoused in the US Constitution is the only sure barrier standing between women and religion.

FISSION STORIES
NUCLEAR POWER'S SECRETS
DAVID LOCHBAUM

I graduated in June 1979 from the University of Tennessee with a degree in nuclear engineering. The meltdown at Three Mile Island had occurred less than three months earlier. For the next seventeen years, I worked at nuclear power plants in Georgia, Alabama, Mississippi, Kansas, New Jersey, Pennsylvania, New York, and Connecticut. This prompted me to join the Union of Concerned Scientists, where, as their nuclear safety engineer, I monitor safety performance of all US nuclear power plants. In more than two decades, I've studied literally thousands of reports on nuclear plant accidents and near-misses. Many of these reports are publicly available, but they're very obscure and their information is veiled in technical jargon and acronyms called "nukespeak." The following stories, which examine some basically unknown and unpublicized problems since 1968, provide a glimpse behind the nuclear curtain.

_ERROR JORDAN

In 1968, operators shut down a nuclear research reactor to modify its cooling system, and a pipe connected to the water-filled pool containing the reactor core had to be cut open. There were two options: Remove the irradiated fuel assemblies from the pool so the water level could be dropped below the point where the pipe connected to its wall, or block the pipe at a point between the pool and the proposed cut. To save time, workers decided to block the pipe. To do this, they wrapped tape around a basketball until it was about two inches larger. They lowered the basketball into the pool and inserted it into the pipe's opening. They inflated the basketball to seal it firmly within the pipe, then cut into the pipe and started working.

They didn't work for long. Water pressed against the basketball until it popped out the open end of the pipe. Nearly 14,000 gallons of water drained into the basement in five minutes. A gate inside the reactor pool, which was supposed to have been removed during this work but fortunately remained in place, kept more water from draining. Had this gate been removed, the water level would have dropped below the top of the irradiated fuel assemblies in the reactor core. According to the official report, two-thirds of the fuel assemblies would have been uncovered.[1]

Actually, *all* of the fuel assemblies would have been uncovered for the upper two-thirds of their length. Water performs two vital functions: It cools the fuel assemblies that produce substantial amounts of heat long after the reactor is shut down, and it shields workers from the intense radioactivity emitted by the fuel assemblies. Uncovering the fuel assemblies in the reactor core could have triggered a meltdown or, at the very least, produced an extremely serious radiation hazard for plant workers.

The nuclear industry has made tremendous improvements in safety since 1968. Redundancy and defense-in-depth are key elements in the nuclear industry's safety program. *Two* basketballs would be used today.

_INDOOR POOL

In early July 1981, workers at Nine Mile Point Unit 1 in central New York faced a problem. All of the radwaste system's tanks were filled, yet waste water continued to be generated. So they deliberately flooded the basement of the waste building with about four feet of water.

Nearly 150 metal drums, each containing 55 gallons of highly radioactive solid waste, were stored in the basement. The rising water caused many of these drums to float. Several drums tipped over and spilled their radioactive contents into the water.

On July 8 of the same year, workers pumped 50,000 gallons of contaminated water from a tank into Lake Ontario. They discharged this radioactive water to make room for the water from the waste building basement. Workers tried decontaminating the basement for the next three months. In October, these attempts were abandoned with about a foot of water still covering the basement floor.

The plant's owner told the Nuclear Regulatory Commission (NRC) on October 31, 1981, about the 50,000 gallons of contaminated water discharged to the lake in July. The flooded basement and the spilled waste drums were not mentioned.

In 1989, the plant's owner was harshly criticized by the Institute for Nuclear Power Operations (INPO)—the nuclear industry's own watchdog organization—for the *still-flooded* waste building basement. INPO's secret report leaked to the media. After NRC officials watched the story on the TV news, they dispatched a special team to investigate. The NRC inspectors estimated that the radiation fields in the basement approached 500 rem per hour. A lethal radiation dose is 450 to 600 rem. Thus, an employee would have received a fatal dose by working in that basement for only an hour.

The NRC censured the plant's owner for failing to tell them about the flooded basement.[2]

When the INPO report leaked to the public, the plant was on the NRC's "Watch List," meaning that it received heightened regulatory attention. In addition, NRC Resident Inspectors were stationed at the plant from 1981 through 1989. In eight years, including several months when the plant was on the "Watch List," *no* NRC inspector ever ventured into the waste building basement. What *were* they watching all that time? Good fortune that it included the TV news.

_LIFE IMITATES ART

In the beginning of the 1979 movie *China Syndrome*—starring Jane Fonda, Jack Lemmon, Michael Douglas, and James Hampton—control room operators confront an unexpected situation at the fictional nuclear plant. The extremely tense situation ends when an operator taps an instrument gauge for water level. The stuck indicator moves to its true position. The operators feel much, much better.

This scene was ridiculed within the nuclear industry as pure Hollywood fiction. Gauges never stick like that in real life, and even if they did, backup gauges would be used.

On New Year's Day 1986, operators were starting up the Grand Gulf Nuclear Station in Mississippi. An operator monitored the water level in the reactor vessel using a nearby recorder as he increased the plant's power output. Moments later, much to his surprise, the plant automatically tripped (i.e., shut down) because of low water level in the reactor vessel. The recorder pen had stuck in the normal range, providing a false sense of comfort while the actual water level gradually dropped until it reached the trip setpoint. A backup gauge showed the water level dropping, but the operator had not checked it.[3]

Maybe if operators spent less time critiquing movies and more time cross-checking instrument gauges with their backups, incidents like this Mississippi mess might become fictional. Until then, they'll remain all too real.

> **A PORTION OF THEIR GARDEN HAD TO BE CLEARED AND DISPOSED OF AS HAZARDOUS WASTE BECAUSE OF THE RADIOACTIVE PIGEON DROPPINGS.**

_JELLYFISH PUT NUCLEAR PLANT IN A JAM

Jellyfish appear fairly harmless. Despite an occasional tale about swimmers being stung by jellyfish, Hollywood movies always feature shark attacks. No *National Geographic* special featured cameramen being lowered into the sea in heavy steel cages to film voracious jellyfish.

Nevertheless, a flotilla of jellyfish attacked the Turkey Point nuclear plant in Florida on September 3, 1984. They stormed the plant in such numbers and with such ferocity that they clogged the flow of cooling water to the plant's main condensers. A metal screen designed to keep debris from being pumped into the plant was bent inward nearly two feet during the assault. Both of the nuclear reactors at Turkey Point had to be shut down. The reactors remained shut down for eleven days until Hurricane Diana swept the rampaging jellyfish back out to sea.[4]

_THE OL' PIGEON DROPPINGS

In March 1998, the Ministry of Agriculture, Fisheries and Food cautioned residents of the English village of Seascale not to eat pigeons. It seems that a couple of dead pigeons removed from the garden of two sisters were found to have high levels of radioactivity. The pigeons had roosted on buildings at the nearby Sellafield nuclear plant, where they had become contaminated. British Nuclear Fuels, Limited, which runs the plant, checked for contamination around the sisters' home. A portion of their garden had to be cleared and disposed of as hazardous waste because of the radioactive pigeon droppings.[5]

_NEAR MISS AT OYSTER CREEK

A technician testing switches on May 2, 1979, at the Oyster Creek plant in New Jersey caused a false signal of high pressure inside the reactor vessel. This false signal automatically tripped the reactor, which caused the turbine to be shut down seconds later. The turbine trip caused the plant's internal power supplies to transfer from the auxiliary transformers to the startup transformers.

However, one of the two startup transformers was unavailable due to maintenance. Two of the three feedwater pumps were powered from the unavailable startup transformer and stopped running when the auxiliary transformers de-energized. The third feedwater pump automatically tripped during the feedwater system transient. Operators couldn't restart this feedwater pump because its auxiliary oil pump was broken.

With the loss of all three feedwater pumps, the only water supply to the reactor vessel was provided by the two control rod drive pumps, which didn't provide enough water to the reactor vessel to make up for the all the steam being pumped out. Consequently, the water level dropped until it was a mere twelve inches above the top of the irradiated fuel assemblies in the reactor core. The normal water level is more than ten feet above the core.

About 36 minutes after the scram (i.e., the rapid shutdown of a reactor by insertion of its control rods), the operators restarted one of the feedwater pumps, and reactor vessel water level was quickly restored to the normal operating band. A few minutes' delay would've probably caused the reactor core to be uncovered. As at Three Mile Island Unit 2 just 35 days earlier, uncovering the reactor core could've triggered its meltdown.[6]

_PLEASE DON'T FLUSH THE TOILET WHILE THE REACTOR IS RUNNING

A sign on the bathroom door at the University of Florida's research reactor in the 1980s warned:

Please Don't Flush the Toilet While the Reactor is Running.

The cooling water system for the reactor was connected to the city water main. This connection also supplied water to the toilet. The reactor automatically shut down at least five times because a flushing toilet had affected its cooling water flow.

The good news, on a relative basis, was that this research reactor was equipped with a direct connection to a well-supplied cooling water system for "risky" experiments.[7]

How could a conscientious person in the bathroom really tell whether the reactor was running? To flush or not to flush, that's the question.

_FATAL ACCIDENTS

On December 9, 1986, the reactor at the Surry Unit 2 facility in Virginia scrammed from full power. A pipe going to one of the main feedwater pumps ruptured, releasing about 30,000 gallons of hot water into the turbine building. Some of the water flashed to steam. Eight workers were scalded by the water and steam. Four workers later died from their injuries.

The pipe's metal walls were originally about half an inch thick, but they had been eroded over the years to less than 10 percent of their original thickness by the water flowing through the pipe. This thinning weakened the piping until it broke.

The high temperature in the turbine building following the pipe rup-

ture caused 62 fire sprinklers to discharge. After the sprinklers activated, water from the pipe rupture and sprinklers flowed into a control cabinet for the Halon fire-suppression systems in the emergency switchgear rooms. As a result, both Halon systems discharged. Water from the sprinklers also entered the control cabinet for the fire-suppression systems in the cable tray rooms. Both systems discharged carbon dioxide into the cable tray rooms located directly above the control room.

Water also got into a security card reader. The water caused this reader to send a continuous signal to the security computer, which overloaded the system and locked all areas controlled by card readers. This lockout enabled personnel to leave these areas, but prevented anyone from entering them.

Halon and carbon dioxide leaked into the control room. Carbon dioxide, which is heavier than air, flowed down the turbine building hallway. The control room door to the turbine building had been blocked open to allow personnel to enter the room. Due to the security computer lockout, the card reader at this door was not working properly. Because the pressure in the emergency switchgear room was higher than that in the control room, Halon leaked through floor penetrations into the control room. Operators in the control room reported shortness of breath, dizziness, and nausea from inhaling the Halon and carbon dioxide.[8]

This was not the first time that steam mortally injured nuclear plant workers. In fact, it wasn't even the first time at the Surry plant. On July 27, 1972, three workers manually opened valves to allow steam to bypass the turbine and go directly to the condenser. After adjusting several valves, steam shot into the area through a small gap in a vent line. Two workers were badly scalded and rushed to the hospital. Both later died of their injuries.[9]

_'BAMA BOO-BOO

Workers at Farley Nuclear Plant Unit 2 in Alabama first achieved a nuclear chain reaction on May 8, 1981. They ran the plant through its initial operating cycle uneventfully. The plant was shut down on October 24, 1982, for its first refueling outage.

Four days later, personnel discovered that the containment spray header isolation valves were locked in the closed position. This system sprays borated water into the containment following an accident to reduce the pressure and temperature. The system also sprays sodium hydroxide into the containment following an accident to remove radioactive iodine from the air.

Or at least that's what the system could do if its isolation valves were open. A check of the records revealed that the valves had always been closed. Calculations determined that the radiation doses to the thyroids of plant workers and members of the public would have exceeded federal limits had an accident occurred with containment spray disabled.

The reason for the valves being in the locked closed position instead of locked open position was attributed to a modification during the plant's construction. The modification lengthened the stem of the valves, which made the valves appear open when they were actually closed. That excuse lost favor when further research discovered that the same modification had been made to the valves on Unit 1. The Unit 1 valves were found to be in the locked open (i.e., proper) position.[10]

The plant's owner paid a $40,000 fine to the NRC for this 'Bama boo-boo. Put another way, for exposing the public to undue risk over a 17-month period, the NRC penalized the plant's owner less than $80 per day! The General Accounting Office reports that it costs a plant owner around $250,000 each day that a nuclear plant is shut down. Therefore, a plant owner finding broken safety equipment can either shut down to fix it—and incur a quarter-million dollar tab each day of the shutdown—or continue running and risk an $80 fine. It doesn't take a Harvard MBA to figure out which is the better business decision.

_MYSTERY PLUG

On Saturday night, June 28, 1980, operators reduced power at Browns Ferry Unit 3 in Alabama for a scheduled maintenance outage. Tradition called for the plant to be manually tripped when power dropped to about 30 percent. An operator depressed the trip pushbuttons, and control rods raced into the reactor core. But not all of them—76 of the 92 control rods on half of the core were not fully inserted. In fact, many of these control rods had hardly moved in at all. The reactor was still running.

About two minutes later, the operator depressed the trip pushbuttons again. This time, 59 of the stubborn rods remained withdrawn. The operator depressed the pushbuttons again. There were still 47 control rods withdrawn.

> **HENCE, THE NUCLEAR REGULATORY COMMISSION REPORTED ABOUT A 50-50 CHANCE OF A CORE MELTDOWN OCCURRING BY 2004.**

The third time may be a charm, but it was the fourth time at Browns Ferry that night. When the operator depressed the pushbuttons a fourth time, all of the control rods fully inserted. It had taken four tries and about fifteen minutes to shut down the Unit 3 reactor.

No one knows what happened that night. The theory is that something plugged one of the scram discharge headers. The fourth scram attempt allegedly dislodged this mystery plug and blew it into the reactor building's sump, where it hid amid considerable other gunk and grime.[11]

_SAFETY IN NUMBERS?

What *are* the chances of a nuclear accident? Here's what the NRC said in 1984:

> The most complete and recent probabilistic risk assessments suggest core-melt frequencies in the range of 10^{-3} [one in one thousand] per reactor year to 10^{-4} [one in ten thousand] per reactor year. A typical value is 3×10^{-4} [three in ten thousand]. Were this the industry average, then in a population of 100 reactors operating over a period of 20 years, the crude cumulative probability of [a severe core melt] accident would be 45 percent.

Hence, the Nuclear Regulatory Commission reported about a 50-50 chance of a core meltdown occurring by 2004. Time is running out![12]

_POWER PLANT PORNO

Pornography may or may not have social value, but a skin magazine may have damaged important equipment at a California nuclear plant in March 1984:

> A misplaced magazine was sucked into a crucial cooling water system at Diablo Canyon Nuclear Power Plant, breaking a giant pump, a Pacific Gas and Electric Co. spokesman said yesterday. A plant worker apparently set the magazine too close to a pipe that sucks in air to cool the pump engine, said startup engineer John Sumner. Sumner said it was rumored the offending magazine may have been a forbidden 'girlie' publication that a plant worker hastily stashed near the air intake.[13]

The NRC should not adopt regulations protecting nuclear power plant equipment from pornography. If it did, testing and inspections would be required to verify that the regulations were being satisfied.

Nuclear plant owners essentially banned pornography in the late 1980s when they placed restrictions on non-technical materials in the workplace. The "nudie" magazines were replaced with "nukie" magazines.

_ASLEEP AT THE SWITCHES

On March 24, 1987, the NRC heard from a whistleblower that operators at the Peach Bottom plant were sleeping on duty in the control room. The NRC immediately sent inspectors out to the

Pennsylvania facility to investigate. The inspectors reported:

At times during various shifts, in particular the 11:00 pm to 7:00 am shift, one or more of the Peach Bottom operations control room staff (including licensed operators, senior licensed operators and shift supervision) have for at least the past five months periodically slept or have been otherwise inattentive to licensed duties.[14]

During a midnight shift, NRC inspectors found all three operators asleep and the shift supervisor reading a magazine. On another shift, the shift superintendent, the shift supervisor, and two operators were asleep while the remaining operator was awake, but he was not in the control room. Finally, the NRC inspectors found the operators on another shift gathered around a console playing a computer game.[15]

Although sleeping operators make fewer mistakes than awake operators, the NRC still became disenchanted. They ordered Peach Bottom shut down.

A spokesman for the nuclear industry's trade group explained why operators sleep on duty: "The problem is that it's an extremely boring job."[16]

Before a gathering of local townspeople, an NRC staffer complimented the Peach Bottom operators: "If they are awake, they can do the job very well."[17] Glowing praise, indeed.

The two units at Peach Bottom remained closed for over two years. Then, with a brand new management team—and very well-rested operators—the plant owner restarted the reactors.

_PATRIOT GAMES

On February 5, 1997, the owners of the Palo Verde nuclear plant in Arizona informed the NRC that a plastic bag containing material believed to be marijuana had been found in November 1996. The bag fell out of the folds of an American flag which had been stored since 1980. Workers threw the bag in the trash. When supervisors later learned of the discovery, a search of the trash failed to locate the bag.[18]

Coincidentally, there are unconfirmed reports that all of the bags of potato chips and pretzels in the vending machines at the site also disappeared.

_COFFEE BREAK

An employee allegedly tried to kill his supervisor at the Browns Ferry Nuclear Plant in Alabama in 1980. Reportedly, the employee became disenchanted with his supervisor over some real or imagined slight. When the supervisor sat down for his mid-morning coffee break, fumes spewed from his coffee thermos as soon as he opened it. The supervisor, in charge of the chemistry group, had the contents of the thermos analyzed. The results showed that the coffee contained high amounts of hydrochloric acid.

A security investigation quickly determined who did what to whom and why. The plant's owner elected to downplay the situation. It's rather poor public relations to have it widely known that workers at a nuclear plant are trying to kill each other, so they convinced the supervisor not to have the employee arrested or otherwise disciplined. But the supervisor, rightly so, didn't want the individual working for him anymore. Management transferred the employee to another group at the plant.

> DURING A MIDNIGHT SHIFT, NRC INSPECTORS FOUND ALL THREE OPERATORS ASLEEP AND THE SHIFT SUPERVISOR READING A MAGAZINE.

Imagine being a fly on the wall when management explained to the new supervisor that this individual was being transferred to his group because of the attempted murder of another supervisor.

_HOW HAVE I FAILED THEE? LET ME COUNT THE WAYS, AGAIN

Thursday April 7, 1994, began with both units at the Salem Generating Station in southern New Jersey operating at about 75 percent power. Operators had reduced power in case one of the circulating water (CW) pumps tripped. Five of the six CW pumps for each unit were running, with the sixth pump in standby. These pumps take water from the Delaware River, send it through the condenser to cool the steam leaving the turbine, then discharge it back to the river. Since the beginning of March, dead reeds and marsh grass floating on the tides had clogged the debris screens for the CW pumps several times each day. This was more than inconvenience—cooling water from the bay was needed to remove heat from the reactor core.

At 10:14 AM, debris began accumulating on the screens. Within ten minutes, two of the five operating CW pumps automatically tripped on high differential pressure across the debris screens (failures #1 and #2). An attempt to start the standby CW pump failed because its breaker had been improperly positioned after maintenance (failure #3).

By 10:30, operators were reducing power by injecting boric acid and inserting control rods. They rushed to get power down to the point where three circulating water pumps could handle the heat load.

At 10:36, an operator restarted one CW water pump. The pump's discharge valve, which had to be closed to restart the pump, began slowly re-opening.

At 10:39, two other CW pumps automatically tripped because of high differential pressure (failures #4 and #5). One other CW pump was restarted.

At 10:40, the plant's power level had been reduced to 57 percent. Although three CW pumps were running, only one was actually providing cooling water flow to the main condenser, since the discharge valves for the two other running CW pumps were still opening.

At 10:44, the power level was 24 percent. Three CW pumps were running, until another CW pump tripped because of high differential pressure (failure #6).

A minute later, with power down to 18 percent, an operator left the reactor controls to transfer electrical loads in the plant (failure #7).

At 10:46, power had dropped to 8 percent. The reactor coolant system temperature was too low, so a supervisor stepped to the reactor controls and withdrew control rods to bring it back up (failure #8). Another operator restarted a CW pump while another CW pump tripped again (failure #9).

At 10:47, reactor power was about 7 percent. The reactor coolant system temperature was below legal limits (failure #10). The supervisor stepped back from the reactor controls and directed an operator to restore the temperature to the legal range.

The operator withdrew control rods for 55 seconds to increase the plant's power level (failure #11). At 10:50, the reactor automatically scrammed because of high neutron flux at 25 percent power (failure #12).

By 11:19 AM, the pressurizer had completely filled with water, and its power-operated relief valve (PORV) was opening periodically to relieve the rising pressure (failure #13). The atmospheric dump valves (ADVs) should have opened to control pressure on the secondary side, but they failed due to a longstanding problem (failures #14 and #15).

At 11:26, all four main steam line safety relief valves opened to protect the secondary side from overpressurization. Operators tried but failed to reset the ADVs so they would automatically open (failure #16). The operators manually opened the ADVs to reclose the safety relief valves.

The open ADVs caused the pressure on the primary side to drop rapidly. The decreasing pressure resulted in another safety injection signal (failure #17). The safety injection flow increased primary side pressure until the PORV began cycling again (failure #18). The PORV discharged steam and water to the pressurizer relief tank until it overfilled (failure #19) and spilled contaminated water into containment.

Operators realized that primary side was water-solid and secondary side pressure was being loosely controlled by the open ADVs. They were in a situation not even close to being covered by their procedures. They allowed the PORV to open and close for the next 20 minutes (failure #20).

At 3:11 PM, operators restored a steam bubble in the pressurizer. They were back in a condition covered by their procedures. A "routine" plant shutdown using normal procedures followed.[19]

The NRC was less than pleased by this event. They fined the plant's owners $600,000.[20] That's $30,000 per error. Since the NRC was allowed to assess penalties of $50,000 for each day of each violation, Salem's owners must have received the volume discount.

"Two wrongs don't make a right" is an old cliché. The folks at Salem tried to figure out just how many wrongs it does take to make a right.

_NOT SO SLICK

The Big Rock Point plant near Charlevoix, Michigan, shut down permanently in August 1997 after nearly 35 years of operation. A year later, as the plant was being decommissioned, workers couldn't empty the sodium pentaborate tank in the standby liquid control (SLC) system. They found the pipe that carried the sodium pentaborate solution to the reactor vessel was completely severed. They concluded that for at least the last *13 years* of the plant's operation, this safety system would not have functioned had there been an accident.[21]

The acronym SLC is pronounced "slick" within the industry. In this case, it was actually not so slick.

_WRONG PLACE, WRONG TIME

The following events demonstrate the value of the adage, "If it ain't broke, don't break it!"

On March 14, 1981, a worker de-energized five motor-operated valves on the safety injection system at the DC Cook Unit 1 plant in Michigan. Unfortunately, he had been told to de-energize the valves on Unit 2. The operator disabled a vital emergency system on an operating nuclear plant, instead of disabling an unneeded safety system on a shut down plant.

On April 22, 1982, an operator drained reactor water from Point Beach Unit 1 in Wisconsin. Problem was, he had been assigned to perform this activity on Unit 2, which was shut down at the time. Unit 1 was operating and had an urgent need for *all* of its reactor coolant.

On August 17, 1982, an operator at Hatch Nuclear Plant Unit 2 in Georgia took the "A" train of the residual heat removal service water system (RHRSWS) out of service. Unfortunately, the "B" train of RHRSWS was already out of service for maintenance. The total loss of RHRSWS meant that the entire residual heat removal system was also disabled, since that system is cooled by RHRSWS. Had there been an accident, things could have gotten very ugly, very quickly.

On April 14, 1983, operators closed the steam supply valves for the "B" and "C" auxiliary feedwater (AFW) pumps at the Turkey Point Unit 3 plant in Florida for maintenance. Too bad the maintenance was scheduled on the "A" AFW pump, so the operators had isolated the wrong pumps instead. All three AFW pumps remained disabled for five days. Had there been an accident, the entire AFW system would have been unavailable. The AFW system at Three Mile Island—also unavailable due to valves mistakenly closed for maintenance—had contributed to its partial core meltdown four years earlier.

On October 2, 1983, an operator closed manual valves on the containment spray pumps at the Turkey Point Unit 4 in Florida, which was standard procedure as the plant prepared for a refueling outage. Unfortunately, Unit 4 was at full power; Unit 3 was entering a refueling outage. The operator had been sent to close the Unit 3 valves but mistakenly closed the Unit 4 valves (the valves look remarkably similar). Had there been an accident on Unit 4, the closed valves would have disabled *all* of the containment spray pumps. Since these valves could not be opened from the control room, these vital emergency pumps would have been unavailable during the important mitigation stage of an accident.

On February 7, 1984, a technician calibrated the turbine speed instrumentation for the reactor core isolation cooling (RCIC) system at the FitzPatrick nuclear plant near Oswego, New York, following maintenance. Sadly, the maintenance had been performed on the high pressure coolant injection (HPCI) system, not the RCIC system. By calibrating the RCIC turbine speed instrumentation with the HPCI calibration procedure, the technician disabled the RCIC system at a time when the HPCI system was already disabled. A supervisor reviewed the completed procedure and discovered the error. The RCIC turbine speed instrumentation was recalibrated, this time with the proper procedure. Had there been an accident, the disabled HPCI and RCIC systems would have left the plant without its high pressure makeup systems for reactor core cooling.[22]

_NUCLEAR POWER'S DIRTY LITTLE SECRET

One June 17, 1970, an operator at the LaCrosse nuclear plant near Genoa, Wisconsin, used a dust cloth to clean the control room. The cloth snagged the identification tag attached to one of the key switches and moved it around to the OFF position. The reposition-

ing of this single switch caused the reactor to automatically shut down.

To prevent this unfortunate event from happening again, the control room operators were instructed to use a feather duster when cleaning.[23]

The training program for operators consists of more than a year's worth of classroom instruction and simulator exercises. The proper techniques for feather-dusting are not covered during this otherwise comprehensive training.

_EASY DOESN'T DO IT

In late May 1990, the Brunswick nuclear plant in North Carolina was shut down because the operators flunked their requalification exams. In early May, fourteen of 20 operators and three of four operating crews had failed the test. On May 19-20, all four crews and eight of 27 operators failed re-tests.

A spokesman for the plant attributed the failures to a change in the retraining program requested by the NRC. According to the spokesman: "The NRC exam is very difficult."[24]

Hopefully, nuclear power plants will only have easy accidents. *Hard* accidents can be so darned inconvenient.

_AERIAL DISASTER

In January 1971, an Air Force B-52 bomber crashed about 20 seconds short of the Big Rock Point nuclear plant in Michigan. All nine crew members on board the plane died in the crash. The plane had been on a routine training mission.[25] The Air Force (luckily, ours) conducted low altitude simulated bombing runs near the plant for years.

_THIS PICTURE'S WORTH A THOUSAND CUSS WORDS

On the morning of August 7, 1997, an instructor at the Haddam Neck plant in Connecticut took a picture inside the fire detection panel in the control room. The camera used its flash to light up the darkened interior of the cabinet. An alarm sounded. Three to five seconds later, the fire suppression system discharged Halon into the control room from overhead nozzles. The Halon gas, which functions like carbon dioxide to extinguish fires by displacing oxygen, blew into the control room, scattering papers and dislodging ceiling tiles. A falling ceiling tile struck, but did not seriously injure, an operator on his way out of the room. Within 30 seconds, the control room was abandoned.

After the operators left the control room, they assembled in an adjacent room where they could monitor the control panels through a window. When an alarm light blinked on and off, an operator would rush back into the control room, without self-contained breathing apparatus, and respond to it. About 35 minutes later, the ventilation system had removed enough of the Halon gas to allow operators back into the control room.

Subsequent investigation determined that the flash from the camera affected a microprocessor in the initiation circuit for the Halon system. The fire suppression system was supposed to have a one-minute delay between warning alarms and Halon discharge to enable workers to safely exit the area, but the flash caused a premature discharge. It happens. Or so they say.

IN LATE MAY 1990, THE BRUNSWICK NUCLEAR PLANT IN NORTH CAROLINA WAS SHUT DOWN BECAUSE THE OPERATORS FLUNKED THEIR REQUALIFICATION EXAMS.

To prevent future occurrences, the plant's owners posted signs on all fire system control panels warning folks that photography is prohibited inside the cabinets.[26]

It's been said that a picture is worth a thousand words. In this case, the majority of them were probably expletives.

_NUCLEAR-SIZED SINK STOPPER

On December 28, 1994, a bolt dropped into the Unit 1 spent fuel pool at the Hatch Nuclear Plant in Georgia. An overhead crane was carrying this bolt over the pool when the sling holding the bolt broke. The bolt, 17 feet long by three inches in diameter and weighing 365 pounds, glanced off the side wall and fell to the bottom of the spent fuel pool without hitting the storage racks or irradiated fuel assemblies. The bolt tore a three-inch gash in the stainless steel liner. Approximately 2,000 gallons leaked through the hole and through a drain line before workers closed valves in the drain line.

The spent fuel pool water level dropped nearly two inches, causing the fuel pool cooling system pumps to trip. Operators restored the water level after the leakage path was isolated, then returned the fuel pool cooling system to service. Workers removed the bolt and placed a large rubber mat (i.e., a nuclear-sized sink stopper) over the hole to limit leakage until underwater welding repairs were completed.

The Hatch incident occurred less than a year after a screwdriver fell into the spent fuel pool at a European nuclear plant with similar results. On January 31, 1994, workers at Tricastin Unit 1 in France were removing the control rod cluster guide tube from a spent fuel assembly. A 15-foot-long screwdriver weighing 44 pounds fell into the spent fuel pool and punctured the stainless steel liner. The level in the spent fuel pool dropped nearly four inches. A stainless steel plate was welded over the hole.

_LUCKIEST MEN IN TENNESSEE

On April 19, 1984, eight workers entered the seal table room at the Sequoyah Unit 1 facility in Tennessee to clean the incore probe thimble guide tubes.

The incore probe is a neutron detector on the end of a long, flexible cable that is normally stored outside the reactor core. Periodically, the probe is inserted through a number of thimble guide tubes located within the reactor core to determine the power distribution.

The workers disconnected the thimble tubes and inserted a cleaning brush. While the brush was being hand-cranked up one of the thimble tubes, workers noticed water leaking around the fitting holding the guide tube.

The eight workers immediately evacuated the seal table room. Seconds later, the fitting broke loose, ejecting the entire thimble guide tube and cleaning assembly from the reactor core. An unisolatable reactor coolant leak ensued. The hot reactor water flashed to steam as it shot into the room. The leakage, initially about 30 gallons per minute, continued for approximately eleven hours until the reactor was shut down and the reactor water level was reduced to below the seal table. Approximately 16,000 gallons of reactor coolant leaked into the containment during this period.

Radiation surveys conducted the following day indicated two to three rem per hour at the entrance to the seal table room, 200 to 300 rem at the end of the thimble tube near the seal table and greater than 1,000 rem in the center of the ejected tube. The tip of the thimble tube was reading approximately 4,000 rem.[27] A lethal radiation dose is 450 to 600 rem.

The investigation of this incident revealed how close it came to being a disaster. While the workers were inside the seal table room, another group of workers arrived to perform maintenance on an airlock door, which happened to be the outer door on the airlock into the seal table room. They disabled the outer door for nearly 30 minutes while doing some welding. With the outer airlock door disabled in the open position, the inner door was interlocked closed. The workers inside the room wouldn't have been able to leave the room quickly during this time. The steam conditions and the radiation levels inside the room would have threatened their lives.

When the workers got into the airlock, one of the workers picked up the telephone to inform the control room operators about the leaking reactor water. The phone line was dead.[28]

Luckily, *only* the phone line was dead this time.

On Halloween, 1996, the NRC reported the following event for the Davis-Besse plant in Ohio:

On October 30, 1996, plant personnel discovered what appeared to be undetonated explosive ordnance in the owner controlled area. The ordnance involved 11 shells/projectiles that were found in a marsh area near the edge of Lake Erie, the closest shell being approximately 500 yards from the plant's [allegedly] protected area. The ordnance was identified during an emergency preparedness drill when a radiation monitoring team (RMT) entered the marsh area to collect samples and noted the shells/projectiles. The licensee postulates that the ordnance was from nearby Camp Perry's artillery test range. Since World War II, artillery has been fired from Camp Perry to a target area in Lake Erie a short distance from Davis-Besse. As a result, shrapnel and unexploded ordnance occupy the lake bottom near the plant site. Because of lake currents, etc., some of the submerged ordnance has gradually shifted towards the shoreline. In addition, due to high wind conditions at the time of discovery, Lake Erie water level had receded sufficiently to expose the subject ordnance. Similar findings along the lakeshore or in the nearby Toussaint River have been made in the last several years.

Following discovery of the shells/projectiles, plant security cordoned off the areas, conducted additional inspections of the shoreline, and restricted access to the marsh. The explosive ordnance disposal (EOD) unit at Wright-Patterson Air Force Base was contacted and a group of explosives experts were dispatched to disposition the discovered items. Upon arrival, the EOD unit was able to characterize the 11 rounds as follows: 2-106mm, 2-155mm, and 7 bazooka (rocket) type rounds. The ordnance was subsequently detonated in 5 separate explosions, indicating that at least several of the rounds were live.[29]

Maybe nuclear plant owners should bring in those metal detector guys from the beaches to check around their sites. It also seems reasonable to ask that proposed sites for nuclear plants be checked for buried ordnance *before* construction begins.

■ ■ ■ ■ ■ ■ ■ ■ ■ ■

These stories suggest why nuclear power is like sausage: The more you know about how it's made, the less likely you are to like it. They also explain why so many people around the world are nuclear vegetarians.

Endnotes

1. Union of Concerned Scientists. *The Nugget File*. Cambridge, MA: UCS, 1979 **2.** Knapp, Malcolm R. (Director of Radiation Safety and Safeguards, Nuclear Regulatory Commission) to Lawrence Burkhardt, III (Executive Vice President, Nuclear Operations, Niagra Mohawk Power Corporation). "NRC Region I Augmented Inspection Team (AIT) Inspection (50-220/89-90) of the use of the Radwaste Building's sub-basement as a long-term liquid retention facility at Nine Mile Point Unit 1," 2 Oct 1989; Russell, William T. (Regional Administratior, Nuclear Regulatory Commission) to Lawrence Burkhardt, III. "Notice of Violation (NRC Inspection Report No. 50-220/89-90)," 23 Feb 1990; Wald, Matthew L. "Study Says A-Plant's Handling of Waste Left Costly Mess." *New York Times* 23 Feb 1990. **3.** Mississippi Power and Light Company. "Failed Level Recorder Contributes to Operational Error Causing a Reactor Scram" (Licensee Event Report No. 50-416/96-001-00). 30 Jan 1986. **4.** May, John. *The Greenpeace Book of the Nuclear Age: The Hidden History, the Human Cost.* New York: Pantheon Books, 1989. **5.** Unsigned. "Flying Nuke Storm Comes Back to Roost." *Belfast News Letter* 12 March 1998. **6.** Nuclear Regulatory Commission. "Indication of Low Water Level in the Oyster Creek Reactor" (Information Notice No. 79-13). 29 May 1979. **7.** United Press International. "Fla. Nuclear Reactor's Cooling System Sabotaged by Toilets." *Washington Post* 19 Aug 1977. **8.** Nuclear Regulatory Commission. "Feedwater Line Break" (Information Notice No. 86-106). 16 Dec 1986; Nuclear Regulatory Commission. Information Notice No. 86-106, Supplement 1. 13 Feb 1987; Nuclear Regulatory Commission. Information Notice No. 86-106, Supplement 2. 18 March 1987; Virginia Electric and Power Company. Licensee Event Report No. 50-281/86-020-00. 8 Jan 1987; Virginia Electric and Power Company. Licensee Event Report No. 50-281/86-020-01. 14 Jan 1987; Virginia Electric and Power Company. Licensee Event Report No. 50-281/86-020-02. 31 March 1987; Nuclear Regulatory Commission. Inspection Report No. 50-280/86-42 and 50-281/86-42. 10 Feb 1987. **9.** Bertini, H.W. "Descriptions of Selected Accidents That have Occurred at Nuclear Reactor Facilities" (ORNL/NSIC-176). Oak Ridge National Laboratory, Nuclear Safety Information Center. April 1980. **10.** Nuclear Regulatory Commission. "Report to Congress on Abnormal Occurrences: October - December 1982." (NUREG-0900, Vol. 5 No. 4.). May 1983. **11.** Nuclear Regulatory Commission. "Failure of 76 of 185 Control Rods to Fully Insert During a Scram at a BWR" (Bulletin No. 80-17). 3 July 1980; Buslik, A.J., and R.A. Bari. "System Interaction, with Applications to D.C. Power Systems in Nuclear Reactors." Brookhaven National Laboratory. January 1981. **12.** Nuclear Regulatory Commission. "Delayed Access to Safety-Related Areas and Equipment During Plant Emergencies" (Information Notice No. 86-55). 10 July 1986. **13.** Radin, Patricia. "Magazine Breaks Pump at Diablo Canyon Plant." *Oakland Tribune* 6 March 1984. **14.** Nuclear Regulatory Commission. "NRC Staff Orders Shutdown of Peach Bottom Nuclear Power Plant" (Press Release No. 87-53). 31 March 1987. **15.** Morrison, Don. "NRC Claims Peach Bottom Is Among Nation's Most Safe Plants." *The Agegis* 25 June 1987. **16.** Gruson, Lindsey. "Reactor Closing Shows Industry's People Problem." *New York Times.* 3 April 1987. **17.** *Op. cit.,* Morrison. **18.** Nuclear Regulatory Commission. Daily Event Report No. 31736. 6 Feb 1997. **19.** INPO Significant Operating Experience Report 94-01. "Nonconservable Decisions and Equipment Performance Problems Result in a Reactor Scram, Two Safety Injections." 14 July 1994. **20.** Unsigned. "Salem I, II Operator Find $600,000." *Asbury Park Press* 18 Oct 1995. **21.** Nuclear Regulatory Commission. Daily Event Report No. 34125. 15 July 1998. **22.** Nuclear Regulatory Commission. "Inadvertent Defeat of Safety Function Caused by Human Error Involving Wrong Unit, Wrong Train, or Wrong System" (Information Notice No 84-58). 25 July 1984. **23.** Nuclear Regulatory Commission. "Integrated Plant Safety Assessment Systematic Evaluation Program: La Crosse Boiling Water Reactor" (NUREG-0827). June 1983. **24.** Unsigned. "CP&L Shuts Plant After Its Crew Flunk NRC Test." *The Energy Daily* 22 May 1990. **25.** CER Corporation. "History of 10CFR50, Appendix B, and Its Impact on Nuclear Power Plant Performance." CER Corporation, November 1993. **26.** Nuclear Regulatory Commission. "Control Room Evacuation Due to Inadvertent Halogen Actuation" (Preliminary Notification of Event of Unusual Occurrence PNO-I-97-049). 8 Aug 1997; Nuclear Regulatory Commission. "Inadvertent Control Room Halon Actuation Due to a Camera Flash" (Information Notice No. 97-82). 28 Nov 1997. **27.** Nuclear Regulatory Commission. "Seal Table Leaks at PWRs" (Information Notice No. 84-55). 6 July 1984. **28.** Tennessee Valley Authority. "Sequoyah Nuclear Plant: Investigation of Unit 1 Incore Instrumentation Thimble Tube Ejection Accident on April 19, 1984" (Nuclear Safety Review Staff Investigation Report No. I-84-12-SQN). 1 Aug 1984. **29.** Nuclear Regulatory Commission. "Explosive Ordnance Discovered in Owner Controlled Area" (Morning Report No. 3-96-0114). 31 Oct 1996.

> "ON OCTOBER 30, 1996, PLANT PERSONNEL DISCOVERED WHAT APPEARED TO BE UNDETONATED EXPLOSIVE ORDNANCE."

"CALL IT OFF!"
NEW REVELATIONS ABOUT THE WACO INCIDENT
DAVID T. HARDY

Millions of Americans know the story. We saw it everyday on the news, as the events unfolded—it was the media event of the year. For almost two solid months it seemed that every time we turned on our television sets, there it was, the distant cluster of buildings set in the background as reporters gave us the latest news about an obscure religious group and their standoff with federal agents.

On February 28, 1993, the Bureau of Alcohol, Tobacco and Firearms (ATF) tried to raid a communal church, known as Mt. Carmel, located just outside Waco, Texas. The church was operated by the Branch Davidians—an offshoot of the Seventh Day Adventist Church—who were led by one David Koresh.

By the time the affair ended some 51 days later, over 80 civilians and four federal agents were dead. It was the bloodiest law enforcement debacle in the history of the United States.

It may come as a surprise to many that the same media that were providing coverage of these events actually had very little firsthand knowledge of them—federal officials confined the reporters to a "media compound" miles away and arrested the few that ventured closer. As a result, the news coverage was little more than a relay of the FBI's daily press conferences.

From these, we learned that the Davidians were a cult, blindly following the orders of self-styled messiah David Koresh, a madman with a hatred for law enforcement and a lust for women and violence. The standoff began, we heard, when the ATF learned that the Davidians were amassing illegal machine guns. Since Koresh was a reclusive paranoid who never left the building, ATF had to root him out with a daring SWAT-type raid. Unfortunately, Koresh was tipped that the ATF was coming, and the Davidians planned a murderous ambush. Agents approaching the compound walked into a hail of machine-gun fire. Koresh and his fanatical followers then barricaded themselves within the fortress-like building, and for 51 days refused to leave.

Finally, a tear gas assault became the only hope for ending the siege without bloodshed. But the Davidians responded to the negotiators' pleas with gunfire. Then Koresh ordered the compound put to the torch, and he and his followers died in a fiery suicide.

Eight long years later, we know there is one small problem with the above account.

Scarcely a word of it is true.

Let us look at the accusations one at a time.

_CLAIM: THE DAVIDIANS WERE A CULT

A cult has been defined as a religion without sufficient political power. It is hard to see how the Davidians fit any other definition—in fact, one might even question whether they were regimented sufficiently enough to be called an organized religion.

The Davidians began, 70 years ago, as an offshoot of Seventh Day Adventism. Their religious focus was upon the Seven Seals, set out in the biblical Book of Revelation, which describes what is commonly denominated as the end of the world. Revelation is, to say the least, a complex and symbol-laden text. Among its *dramatis personae* are Babylon (the bad guys), the Lamb (the good guy), and a beast with ten horns and seven heads, who with other entities act along intricate timetables keyed to sundry occurrences, usually described in allegory. The Davidians evolved a number of interpretations keying these to past events, with those beliefs being adjusted, improved, or discarded from time to time as better explanations appeared.

By 1993, most of what we call Davidians simply called themselves students of the Seven Seals, and their organization seemed as loose as a group of students. At many points the group had several contending leaders. Members were free to challenge any interpretation, to leave if they desired, or even to try to prove status as a prophet themselves (at one point, Koresh was only one of three contenders for such recognition).

IT WAS THE BLOODIEST LAW ENFORCEMENT DEBACLE IN THE HISTORY OF THE UNITED STATES.

Nor did the Davidians look upon non-Davidians as a hostile force. Quite the contrary: They believed that as the final days approached, and divine portents became obvious, the vast majority of humanity would be converted to their understanding. Revelation 7, after all, said that the 144,000 "sealed" by God would be joined by a multitude of the chosen which number past all counting. Non-Davidians were neither enemies nor damned; they would just be Johnny-come-latelies.

In short, far from being regimented cult automatons, the Davidians were less organized and less dogmatic than most large religions.

_CLAIM: KORESH AND THE DAVIDIANS THOUGHT THE END OF WORLD WAS IMMINENT

Here we meet a question of definitions. In the Davidian view, we were in something of the end stages, about midway through the Seven Seals, the precise point being subject to debate. But the end process was not the sudden cataclysm that most of Christianity envisions. It would certainly take decades, perhaps centuries. One step, for example, would require 144,000 of the righteous to gather at Mt. Zion in Israel, an event obviously not on the immediate horizon. And at that point there would still be seven of the 22 chapters of Revelation awaiting fulfillment!

_CLAIM: KORESH AND THE DAVIDIANS HATED GOVERNMENT AND LAW ENFORCEMENT

Not even close. The Davidians responded to the outbreak of gunfire by...calling 911. They begged the dispatcher to stop the shooting and actually asked the Sheriff to "come on out and arrest these people." After the gunfight died down, they agreed that the ATF could remove its wounded, and when ATF supervisors said that the agents would not come if they had to lay down their arms, the Davidians agreed that the agents could come up (which involved climbing on the Davidians' roof) while armed.

After the shooting stopped, ATF supervisor Jim Cavanaugh called David Koresh. Koresh was at this point painfully wounded. Yet he was friendly to Cavanaugh and started their remarkable conversation with a mention of his fondness for ATF agent Robert Rodriguez (cover name Gonzales):

Koresh: …. Just like, uh, just like I told, uh… Jerry—Jerry Gonzales?…. Robert Gonzales. I really liked that guy, too. I've always loved law enforcement, because y'all guys risk your lives every day, you know.

Cavanaugh: I understand. Let me—

Koresh [*sadly*]: I'm so sorry that—

Cavanaugh: Aw, David, we know that.

Koresh apparently believed he was dying at this point. He asked Cavanaugh to tell (former) Sheriff Thorn that he had always liked him, and to tell Sheriff Harwell (who fished in the Davidians' ponds) that "after we're gone, he can still come out here fishing."[1]

The negotiation tapes show the same side of Koresh. He banters and commiserates with the ATF and the FBI. He and the Davidians even play the occasional practical joke. At one point the Davidians are negotiating to get milk for the children. The FBI calls for Koresh on the negotiation telephone line, and a Davidian responds that "he's not home right now." After a pause for the punch line, the Davidian states: "He went to town for some milk." At another point, according to the FBI transcripts, the Davidians discovered an FBI "bug" and pondered what to do with it. Koresh cheerfully quips, "I'll preach to it," and has it brought to his room where he delivers a long sermon to the electronic device and its listeners.

If anything is abnormal about Koresh's approach to law enforcement agents, it seems to be his fondness for them even after they shot him!

_CLAIM: A VIOLENT RAID WAS NECESSARY BECAUSE KORESH NEVER LEFT THE BUILDING AND COULD NOT BE ARRESTED PEACEFULLY

Weeks before the raid, the ATF had established an undercover position in a house across the road from the Davidians. The Davidians quickly deduced that they were agents[2] and...sent over beer and pizza as housewarming presents. A few days after the raid, Koresh told an FBI negotiator: "I sent some of the boys over there, and I said, 'Well, this is the way the system is working,' and I said, 'Remember that these guys don't know us, they don't know me, and we're going to treat them just like we treat everybody else.' And we sat over there and all that; we gave them beer."[3]

ATF internal reports show that nine days before the raid, two of the agents went shooting...*with David Koresh.* As the Report of Investigation notes:

On February 19, 1993, Special Agents Robert Rodriguez and Jeffrey Brzozowski, in an undercover capacity, went to the Davidian Compound and met with leader David Koresh and two other male members for the purpose of shooting the AR-15 rifles…. Before the shooting started, David Koresh went back inside the compound and brought some .223 caliber rounds for the agents to shoot…. After shooting the rifles, Special Agent Rodriguez allowed David Koresh and the two males to shoot Rodriguez's .38 Super pistol….[4]

If David Koresh could be lured out with no more than, "We got some rifles, Dave—let's go shooting," why use a raid team of 80 heavily-armed agents backed by three military helicopters? The answer is simple: The ATF desperately needed publicity. It was reeling from a *60 Minutes* series on sexual harassment (indeed, near-rapes) of female agents, stinging from a racial discrimination class-action lawsuit (which it soon lost), and was only ten days away from its appropriations hearings in the House of Representatives. Internally, agents were referring to the Waco raid a "ZBO," slang for "Zee Big One," the publicity stunt that would ensure the agency went into the hearings with headlines and national media coverage behind it.[5] A quiet arrest in the countryside would not make for ZBO.

_CLAIM: KORESH AND THE DAVIDIANS AMBUSHED THE APPROACHING ATF AGENTS

Not even close. Both the ATF and the Davidians agree that as the agents ran out of their vans, Koresh appeared at the front door, alone, unarmed, and in the line of fire. Depending upon the witness, he either asked what was going on or told everyone to calm down because "there are women and children in here." Shooting began, not near Koresh, but at the other end of the building, somewhere far to the agents' left.[6] Only after shots were heard did Koresh stop trying to talk things out and instead took cover inside. Men who plan ambushes do not step into the line of fire and try to work things out peacefully.

In the first minute of firing, Davidian Wayne Martin called the Sheriff's 911 line and began with: "There are 75 men around our building and they're shooting at us, at Mount Carmel. Tell 'em there are women and children in here and to call it off! Call it off!" He begged for a ceasefire and, upon the dispatcher's mere assurance that he was "working on it," began to shout for the Davidians to stop shooting, saying that, "If we stop shooting, they'll stop shooting."[7] This is hardly the conduct of cop-killers springing an ambush.

_CLAIM: THE DAVIDIANS FIRED FIRST

This is a trickier question, since the shooting could've been begun by panicking Davidians without Koresh's instructions. But it does seem unlikely that the Davidians would have begun a battle, without provocation, while Koresh, their prophet, was standing helpless in the line of fire.

It is generally assumed that the fight began in the front of the building. But all the agents who were there testified that *before* the fighting began at that location, there was a string of single shots in the distance, to their left.

The ATF's plan for the raid called for three National Guard helicopters, some carrying ATF agents, to make a run at the rear of the building as a distraction; the helos showed up late, made a run, took fire, and broke off to the agents' left. In short, the helos were in the direction assigned by the agents to the first gunshots.

Through an FOIA lawsuit, I secured a videotape made by an ATF agent in one of the helicopters. The soundtrack contains the clear sound of gunshots occurring at a point when the choppers were still several hundred yards out and gunshots from the building would probably have been drowned out by the helicopter's engine and rotor sounds. Moreover, a careful time analysis ruled out gunshots from the ground as the source of the sound.[8] The gunshots' source is, in short, not the Davidian position, but something much closer to the helicopters and to the camera. For which there is one likely candidate: the helicopters themselves.

Once those shots were heard, the ATF may also have been the first to fire in front of the building. Both the Davidians and the ATF agreed that the gunfight here began with bullets flying through the left half of Mt. Carmel's front double doors; each, of course, claims that the other fired those shots. What is significant here is not the evidence we have but the evidence which has vanished.

During the siege, Davidians told FBI negotiators that the double doors were the best evidence of who fired first: The bullet holes through the left one were all pointing inward. After the fire, the left door (which, it should be stressed, was made of sheet metal, not wood) simply vanished. Although the scene was sealed off to all but the ATF and the FBI, divided into squares and searched as if it were an archaeological site, the left door somehow went missing and remains so to this day.

Two clues point to its fate. First, the soundtrack of an FBI video picked up radio transmissions as the fire was burning down: They reveal "T-1" asking: "Shall we begin taking this place apart?"[9] Second, Jim Brannon, attorney for some of the Davidian survivors, located a home video made by one of the fire department personnel as the fire died down. This shows agents backing up a rented moving truck to the ruins and hastily loading a door-sized object, wrapped in black plastic, into it.

The evidence, in short, strongly suggests that the government knew the door's bullet holes would incriminate the ATF as the initiator of the gunfight in front, and accordingly made its disappearance a high priority.

AFTER THE FIRE, THE LEFT DOOR (WHICH, IT SHOULD BE STRESSED, WAS MADE OF SHEET METAL, NOT WOOD) SIMPLY VANISHED.

"CALL IT OFF!"
DAVID T. HARDY

_CLAIM: THE DAVIDIANS DELUGED THE AGENTS WITH MACHINE-GUN FIRE

This was the ATF story from the beginning—it had to be the explanation for why 80 supposedly crack SWAT agents, fresh from military close-combat training, had been beaten by an oversized Sunday School class. At the criminal trial of the surviving Davidians, agents vied with each other in describing the battery of machine guns raking them. Agent Jim Curtis claimed to have heard five-shot bursts from a .50 caliber heavy machine gun in the center of the building.[10] Agent Bill Buford stated under oath that he heard a Browning Automatic Rifle (a WWII-vintage light machine gun) or perhaps an M-60 belt-fed machine gun.[11] Agent Gerry Petrelli testified that he had heard full-automatic fire from multiple M-16s and AK-47s, plus a .30 or .50 caliber belt-fed machinegun.[12] Seven Davidians were given additional ten-year "no parole" sentences for use of machine guns.

In 1999, after doggedly resisting, and losing, a Freedom of Information Act lawsuit, the ATF released tapes made in its "radio van." The van had handled radio communications during the raid and was within hearing range of the gunfight. The tapes revealed exactly *one* burst of machine-gun fire, lasting less than a second. The burst comes over twelve minutes after the fight begins, and the radio van crew is so shocked that one exclaims: "Fuck, a machine gun!" A few seconds later the tape reveals a triumphant chuckle and an agent exclaiming: "Hey, hey, we got the machine gun."

The agents' sworn testimony of being raked by batteries of machine guns was perjury, pure and simple. The agents had just invented whatever tale was necessary to convict as many Davidians as possible.

_CLAIM: FBI NEGOTIATORS TRIED FOR 51 DAYS TO TALK THE DAVIDIANS INTO SURRENDERING

The negotiators did try to talk the Davidians out. But the foundation of any negotiation is trust, and the FBI's Hostage Rescue Team consistently sabotaged the negotiations. Whenever the Davidians and negotiators reached an agreement, the HRT immediately did something that could only be construed as a government double-cross.

In early and mid-March, negotiators made substantial progress: On March 12, one woman departed, and the next day, one man; Davidians told the negotiators that three men would be leaving soon. That night, for no apparent reason, the FBI's Hostage Rescue Team cut the electricity to the building.

The departures stopped for a week, then resumed. On March 19, two Davidians left, and on March 21, eight more. The FBI's negotiation coordinator considered that day "the most positive day they

had experienced. There were indications...that 20 people would come out the next day."[13]

That evening, for no reason that has ever been explained, the Hostage Rescue Team sent tanks to bulldoze and smash the Davidians' vehicles on the right end of the building; shortly thereafter, it began blasting the building with random noise in order to disrupt the Davidians' sleep. The exodus promptly halted.

Six years later, it was revealed that the FBI's negotiation coordinator had warned that the decision to bulldoze the Davidians' property after ten Davidians had come out would ensure that no one else left...and that the Hostage Rescue Team admitted in response that the bulldozing "was just to 'piss them off.'"[14]

_CLAIM: THE GASSING ASSAULT WHICH CULMINATED IN THE FIRE WAS NECESSARY BECAUSE THE DAVIDIANS REFUSED TO COME OUT

Actually, the Davidians had *already* agreed to come out. In early April, two theologians who specialized in apocalyptic religions had approached the FBI; they believed that they understood the Davidian belief system and that they could demonstrate, using the Davidians' own beliefs and values, that they must come out in order to fulfill the divine purpose.

The FBI rejected their aid, but they arranged to appear on a radio program to which the Davidians were known to listen. They outlined their argument that if Koresh was the "Lamb" who opens the Seals, he could only fulfill the applicable prophecies by writing a "little book" mentioned in Revelation, then surrendering and using that opportunity to explain his understanding to the world. This was, literally, a heaven-sent opportunity to convert the 144,000 followers cited in Revelation; Koresh had misunderstood the subtlety of the divine plan.

THE TAPES REVEALED EXACTLY ONE BURST OF MACHINE-GUN FIRE, LASTING LESS THAN A SECOND.

The effects were speedy. On April 14, Koresh sent out a note: He was writing the booklet that would explain the Seven Seals, and he wanted it to be given to the two theologians. He would then surrender: "I hope to finish this as soon as possible, and to stand before man to answer any and all questions regarding my actions."

Koresh immediately began churning out his booklet. On April 16, Davidians told the FBI negotiators that he had finished the First Seal, and on April 17, that he was well into the Second Seal.[15] FBI bugs picked up sounds of Davidians rejoicing and packing their bags.[16]

On the evening of April 18, Davidian Steven Schneider explained to an FBI negotiator that as a show of good faith, Koresh would send out each chapter as soon as it was written. The FBI negotiator agreed, adding: "I know he's sensitive about deadlines being put on him, and we're not doing that."[17]

It was a lie. The next morning the FBI's Hostage Rescue Team hit them with gas.

_CLAIM: THE GAS INJECTED WAS "TEAR GAS," HARMLESS EVEN TO INFANTS

The "gas" was actually a powder, known as CS (from the initials of its inventors). Upon contact with a wet surface (eyes, throat), the compound releases a nitrile group—a polite term for cyanide. The result is excruciating burning pains and a feeling of suffocation—a chemical asthma attack. The effect on civilians is usually sheer panic.

The form used on the Davidians, "liquid CS," was still more dangerous. In it, the CS powder is dissolved in the industrial solvent methylene chloride, or MeCl. Pounds of MeCl were injected for every ounce of CS.

MeCl was once a popular paint stripper—until it was banned because of deaths resulting from its use. Its fumes have a rapid anesthetic effect, causing disorientation, coma, and death. Within an hour, the body metabolizes MeCl into carbon monoxide, doing so at a high rate of return. The Standard Data Safety Sheet on the substance notes that workers should only enter its fumes using a self-contained breathing apparatus, accompanied by an observer, and with medical backup available.

At Waco, the FBI went wild with the liquid CS. It was poured in, several gallons at a time, from tanks mounted on the armored vehicles. Other vehicles shot it in from projectiles known as Ferret rounds. One or two Ferrets are adequate to gas a large room; the FBI shot off nearly 400 in the first hour.

ONE OR TWO FERRETS ARE ADEQUATE TO GAS A LARGE ROOM; THE FBI SHOT OFF NEARLY 400 IN THE FIRST HOUR.

In an after-action analysis, Failure Analysis Associates found that the gassing had exceeded "Immediately Dangerous to Life and Health" concentrations for both CS and MeCl, often surpassing those levels by 60 percent.[18] MeCl concentrations over large areas inside the building, they calculated, would have ranged from 6,000 to 9,000 parts per million;[19] Dow Chemical, a manufacturer of MeCl, warns that levels over 1,000 ppm can cause dizziness and intoxication, while "concentrations as low as 10,000 ppm can cause unconsciousness and death."[20] These figures assume adults are involved; two of the Davidian children were later found to have died of suffo-

cation *before* the fire; neither had any signs of smoke inhalation.

_CLAIM: ATTORNEY GENERAL JANET RENO APPROVED THE GASSING ONLY AFTER SHE WAS INFORMED THAT THE GAS WAS HARMLESS TO CHILDREN AND THAT THE SIEGE COULD NOT BE CONTINUED

This is Reno's story; unfortunately for her, it conflicts with all the hard evidence. Two military advisors summoned to her meeting with the FBI prepared a detailed written report of what went on. Although she later implied that they approved the plan, they actually warned her: "Some people would panic," and that due to this, "mothers may run off and leave children."[21]

The claim that CS gas had been found harmless to children was based on a medical journal article relating the case of a toddler who had been exposed to it. Following two hours' exposure (at Waco, the exposures would last six hours), the toddler developed chemical pneumonia, suffered skin burns, went into respiratory failure, and had to be placed on a respirator.[22] Unless Reno was grossly misinformed, she had to have known that "CS has in the past not permanently harmed children" was more like, "CS has in the past very nearly killed children."

Reno later claimed that the gassing was necessary because she agreed with the military advisors that the FBI Hostage Rescue Team was losing its "perishable skills" due to lack of retraining. The military officers' memo notes that when they brought up this issue, it was only in the context of suggesting that the HRT should be pulled off for retraining, and the FBI in fact denied that there was any problem: "The FBI response was that the HRT agents were in fact training in the Waco area... They were strongly opposed to leaving the target."[2]

Koresh was proceeding rapidly with his booklet, and the Davidians were already rejoicing at the coming surrender. All that was required was a wait of a week or two. Reno certainly was on notice that the FBI plan involved serious risks to the children, and her excuse for taking the risks, rather than waiting a bit, appears to be a later invention.

_CLAIM: THE DAVIDIANS STARTED THE FIRE AND THEN SHOT THEMSELVES

We may never know for certain who started the fire. We do know that the Davidians shared the common Christian view that suicide is a grave sin, and that they were exceptionally serious about their religious beliefs. We know that some survived, and none of them has ever expressed misgivings over survival. We know that the FBI had multiple bugs inside the building, listening to Davidians' private conversations for weeks preceding the fire, and the FBI itself insists there is nothing in this record that suggests suicide. The FBI does point to recordings of voices talking about "spreading fuel" and saying, "We only light it if they come in, right?"—but these come from around 6 to 7 AM, five hours before any fire broke out. We nonetheless cannot rule out the possibility that some Davidians started a fire without the others knowing (by midday, tanks crashing into the building had split the Davidians into several separated groups).

For years, the FBI vehemently denied use of any pyrotechnic rounds at Waco. In 1999, documentary maker Mike McNulty found Texas Ranger photos which showed two fired pyrotechnic rounds near the burned building. The FBI thereupon admitted to using pyrotechnics...but only those two, and not at the building itself. This is inconsistent with Doyle's description of the projectiles that did enter the building.

DEPARTMENT OF THE TREASURY- BUREAU ALCOHOL, TOBACCO AND FIREARMS — INVESTIGATION IS — Page 1 of
REPORT OF INVESTIGATION (Law Enforcement) — ROUTINE / SENSITIVE / SIGNIFICANT — 2 pages

Special Agent in Charge
ton Field Division Office

3. MONITORED INVESTIGATION INFORMATION (Number and Branch)
CIP: HOUSTON FY-93
FIREARMS VIOLATIONS
REPORT 039 Monitor No. F53192-09

TITLE OF INVESTIGATION
Howell, Vernon Wayne et.al...

5. INVESTIGATION No. (Include Suspect No.)
53110-92-1069-X

TYPE OF REPORT (Check applicable boxes)

			7. BUREAU PROGRAM		8. PROJECT(S)
PRELIMINARY	COLLATERAL (Request).	X	TITLE I		TARGETED OFFENDER
		X	TITLE II	FIREARMS	TERRORIST/EXTREMIST
STATUS	COLLATERAL (Reply)		TITLE VII		OCD
			TITLE II	EXPLOSIVES	ITAR
FINAL	INTELLIGENCE	X	TITLE XI		SEAR
			TOBACCO		OMO
SUPPLEMENTAL	REFERRAL (Internal)		ALCOHOL	X	OTHER (Specify) GENERAL

DETAILS:

(X) MONTHLY STATUS - LAST REPORT DATE: 02/18/93
( ) 90 DAY SUPPLEMENTAL----------DATE:
( ) CASE REPORT SUBMITTED--------DATE:
( ) PROPERTY IN CUSTODY

PENDING: ( ) US ATTORNEY ACTION; ( ) TRIAL; ( ) SENTENCE ( ) FUGITIVE
( ) FILE CLOSED – ALL ACTIONS INCLUDING PROPERTY HAVE BEEN CONCLUDED.

's report relates to the status of a sensitive investigation initiated response to a "Referral" from the McLennan County Sheriff's Department, Waco, Texas, concerning the alleged illegal possession and or illegal conversion/manufacturing of Title II, NFA weapons and explosives by Vernon W. Howell, A/K/A David Koresh, Route 7, Box 471-B, Waco, McLennan County, Texas.

SYNOPSIS OF SURVEILLANCE - FEBRUARY 19, 1993; FRIDAY

On February 19, 1993, Special Agents Robert Rodriguez and Jeffrey Brzozowski; in an undercover capacity, went to the Davidian Compound and met with Leader David Koresh and two other male members for the purpose of shooting the AR-15 rifles. When both agents arrived at the compound they were asked to enter the compound and wait for David Koresh. When David Koresh arrived, he examined the two AR-15 rifles very carefully. It was obvious that David Koresh had a lot of knowledge about the two firearms. After examining the firearms, Special Agents Rodriguez and Brzozowski followed David Koresh and two males through the inside of the compound towards the back. Special Agents Rodriguez and Brzozowski, walked through the halls of the compound and through the kitchen.

SUBMITTED BY (Name) Davy Aguilera	11. TITLE AND OFFICE Special Agent Austin, Texas	12. DATE 02/22/
REVIEWED BY (Name) Earl K. Dunagan	14. TITLE AND OFFICE ARAC, Austin Field Office	15. DATE
APPROVED BY (Name) Phillip J. Chojnacki	17. TITLE AND OFFICE Special Agent in Charge	18. DATE

(16)

DEPARTMENT OF THE TREASURY
BUREAU OF ALCOHOL, TOBACCO AND FIREARMS
REPORT OF INVESTIGATION - CONTINUATION SHEET
(Law Enforcement)
PAGE 2 OF 2 PAGES

TITLE OF INVESTIGATION
Howell, Vernon Wayne et.al...

INVESTIGATION NO.
53110-92-1069-X

(Continued)

Numerous women were observed working in the kitchen and then observed numerous males working in the back at the shelter area. Before the shooting started, David Koresh went back inside the compound and brought some .223 caliber rounds for the agents to shoot. Special Agents Rodriguez and Brzozowski, along with David Koresh shot the AR-15 rifles. David Koresh displayed an ability to shoot the rifles very well. After shooting the rifles, Special Agent Rodriguez allowed David Koresh and two males to shoot Rodriguez' .38 super pistol. The two males did not display an ability to shoot the pistol. During this time, David Koresh returned to the compound and returned two Sig-Sauer pistols. He returned with a model 226 and a 220. David Koresh provided the 9mm and .45 caliber ammunition. David Koresh also stated that he owned a Ruger, 10-22 caliber rifle and other weapons. Mr. Koresh stated that he believed that every person had the right to own firearms and protect their homes.

As Special Agents Rodriguez and Brzozowski left the compound a quick observation of the east side of the compound was made as requested by the SRT Leader, Ken Latimer. The side wall appeared to be approximately 16 to 18 feet high.

No photographs were taken during this meeting.

Special Agents Steve Seal and James O'Flaherty provided assistance from the undercover house.

Investigation continues......

(17)

The smoking gun. This ATF report proves beyond a shadow of a doubt that the authorities could've peacefully arrested Koresh. The raid did not have to take place.

There are, on the other hand, indications that the FBI may have had a role in the fire. The FBI had ended earlier confrontations by "burning them out": A 1983 standoff had been ended by pouring fuel down a chimney, and a later one by firing a magnesium flare into a cabin.[24] At Waco, the FBI belatedly admitted to having fired what are known as pyrotechnic CS projectiles. These release the CS by burning a gunpowder-like compound; they spew flames and are well known for starting residential fires (pyrotechnic rounds started the fire in which the Symbionese Liberation Army members were incinerated in the 1970s). In 1995, before he could have known the significance, Davidian Clive Doyle stated that he had heard the "Ferrets" hissing as they landed inside the building and that they were too hot to pick up. Ferrets neither hiss nor heat up; pyrotechnic rounds do both.

Other mysteries remain about the projectiles used by the FBI. For instance, McNulty also found photographs of two strange 40 mm projectiles at the scene, which the Texas Rangers determined were part of a tiny lot made for the Army by a German company some ten years before. The projectiles were "flash-bangs," designed to penetrate a building and explode with a flash and stunning report inside. How these specialized military rounds came to be used at Waco has never been explained.

There is also a deeper question: Regardless of who started the fire, did the FBI deliberately initiate a chain of events which would cause one? Getting rid of the incriminating front door appears to have been a high priority. It would have been the most solid of evidence that the

ATF began the gunfight, and coming after 51 days of government spokesmen blaming the Davidians, would have been stunning evidence that they were victims rather than cop-killers. The Davidians had been insisting that the door would prove them right and that the building bore bullet holes from above, as a record of the helicopters' gunfire, as well. A fire provided the only convenient way of making the door and all the bullet holes in the walls vanish. A disastrous fire would, in short, be uncommonly convenient to the federal agencies.

_CLAIM: ONCE THE FIRE BROKE OUT, AGENTS WATCHED IN HELPLESS DISMAY AS THE DAVIDIANS DIED

Actually, the evidence suggests that the FBI took measures to ensure that the fire was as lethal and destructive as possible. As the fire trucks responded to the fire, the FBI ordered them stopped at its roadblocks, even as women and children burned. The FBI On Scene Commander Jeff Jamar told Congress: "[W]hen the fire did start and the fire trucks did arrive, I didn't let them in. I held them at the checkpoint because I didn't want the firemen to drive into gunfire. I just wasn't going to permit it."[25]

But there is little evidence that the Davidians were shooting. FBI photographs show that, as the fire spread, armored vehicle crews opened their hatches and stuck their heads out to watch. FBI aerial photos show that somewhat earlier, when debris fell atop a tank and blocked its viewing prisms, two crewmen dismounted within easy rifle range to clear the debris.

Fire was known as a risk: The operations plan given to the Attorney General had separately itemized hospitals with burn units. But FBI phone logs show that on April 9, ten days before the fire, the two highest FBI commanders had decided that "there would be no Federal plan to fight a fire should one develop in the Davidian compound."[26] Although the FBI had alerted local fire departments on certain occasions during the siege, on the day of the fire it gave no such alert.[27] And when the fire engines did arrive, they were held at FBI checkpoints until after the building had collapsed.

There is additional, and more sinister, evidence that the FBI viewed the fire as a tool of vengeance. The soundtrack of an infrared videotape, made from an FBI aircraft, recorded the radio transmissions audible in the cockpit. These picked up conversations between "SA-1" and "HR-1," the two top FBI commanders at the scene. SA-1, the Special Agent in Charge, was the official responsible for holding the fire engines at the FBI roadblock; HR-1 was the leader of the Hostage Rescue Team, watching the fire from his M-1 tank.

Shortly after the burning building collapsed, HR-1 is heard transmitting: "If you have any fire engines, get them out here right now." Four minutes pass with no response from SA-1.

The FBI had anticipated that the Davidians would put the children in

a salvaged school bus, partially buried as an improvised tornado shelter. SA-1 finally transmits: "Our people focused on the bus area for the kids, is that what we're doing?"

HR-1 replies: "That's what we're trying to do."

SA-1 coldly responds: "No one else, I hope."[28]

At that, the fire engines were still not allowed to move. After a long pause, perhaps shocked at the response, HR-1 snaps back: "What's the ETA on the fire engines, SA-1?"

SA-1 replies: "They'll be there momentarily." But (although they are being held barely a half-mile away), they don't arrive.

Two minutes later, HR-1 is reduced to screaming in frustration: "If you have any fire engines down there, pull them up immediately!"

The aerial photos show that by the time the fire engines finally were allowed onto the scene, the building was a pile of hot coals. In the midst of the coals stands a concrete room, smoke pouring from a hole in its ceiling. Inside the room are the remains of 24 children.

_CLAIM: THE DAVIDIANS CHOSE TO STAY INSIDE AND BURN

The largest cluster of dead Davidians was composed of the women and children, whose bodies were found in the room known to the Davidians as "the vault" and to the FBI as "the bunker." This was the one concrete room inside the building, and it had a single doorway, facing forward.

Some minutes before the fire, an armored vehicle drove into the area in front of the vault, penetrated deep into the building, and discharged two bottles of the CS/MeCl mixture. The concentration was enough to put the area well over the "Immediately Dangerous to Life and Health" level for MeCl.[29] As noted above, MeCl acts as a potent anesthetic, and chemists, most notably Dr. Edward Larsen, have opined that the women and children were probably unconscious from MeCl inhalation before the fire broke out.

Of the remaining dead, it can be noted that the tank incursions appear to have demolished the stairwells and pushed wreckage into the hallways, which the Davidians would've had to negotiate with CS gas in their eyes and methylene chloride in their bloodstreams. Whether they chose to remain and die, or simply were unable to escape, will never be known. Most of the survivors came from the first floor, where stairwells were no impediment, on the right, upwind, side of the building, where the fire spread most slowly. This at least suggests that where Davidians were able to escape the fire, they had no hesitation doing so.

_CLAIM: THE FBI SHOWED RESTRAINT AND DID NOT FIRE A SINGLE SHOT ON THE DAY OF THE FIRE

Over the last eight years, this consistently has been the FBI's position. There are a few problems with it, the biggest of which is the FBI's own videotape.

Overhead, an FBI aircraft was filming the events using an infrared or FLIR (forward looking infrared) sensor, which shows an image of radiated heat, rather than light. A number of infrared imaging experts—including Dr. Edward Allard and Ferdinand Zegel (both retired from the Army's Night Vision Laboratory), two analysts with Infraspection Institute, and the late Carlos Ghigliotti (an expert who had in the past been retained by the FBI)—have opined that heat flashes which appear on the tape are indicative of FBI gunfire before and during the fire. Ghigliotti managed to piece together evidence of a hatch opening on one of the FBI tanks, a person exiting, and gunfire erupting from his new position.

Among the Davidian dead was one Jimmy Riddle. Riddle's autopsy showed that he was killed by a single shot to the head, from a distance, and had died *before* the fire broke out; there was no carbon monoxide in his blood nor soot in his lungs. Why a Davidian would have shot himself (from a distance, no less) before the fire broke out seems beyond understanding.

There were other anomalies. Riddle's right arm and shoulder blade had been "traumatically amputated"—sheared or torn off, as if run over by a tank. And although his body was found inside the building, with even the floor underneath him reduced to ashes, his clothing was intact, with only bits burned. The most likely explanation seems to be that his body was moved before it was cataloged.

One other anomaly: The FBI recorder was set to make two simultaneous copies of its imaging. Both copies have a four-minute gap at the same point, which the FBI to this day has not explained.

In 1999, former Senator John Danforth was appointed as a Special Counsel to investigate the gunfire issue. Danforth retained a firm he described as completely independent and qualified, Vector Data Systems, or VDS. VDS in turn certified that the flashes were not gunfire, based on a comparison with known gun flashes filmed during a test at Ft. Hood.

When the VDS analysts were questioned, however, it was discovered that they were neither independent nor qualified. Their company was a tiny, seventeen-man division of the Anteon Corporation. Anteon did 80 percent of its business with the US government and had sales representatives detailed to the ATF and the FBI.[30] Moreover, the analysts had to admit, VDS had never before been hired to analyze FLIR footage: "This is basically the first job that Vector has actually performed as an analysis-type function."[31] It is hard to understand why, in seeking a qualified and neutral expert,

Danforth went across the Atlantic to hire a British firm with no experience and for whom the US government was its largest customer.

_CLAIM: THE GOVERNMENT WAS CLEARED OF WRONGDOING BY THE VERDICT IN A CIVIL WRONGFUL DEATH SUIT

It is correct that the jury found in favor of the government. But it is also true that the court refused to permit the jury to hear evidence relating to whether a violent raid was necessary, whether a peaceful arrest could have been made, whether the gasses were injected in dangerous quantities, and whether the gassing assault was required—in short, all of the major arguments against the agency's conduct. The Davidians were required to present their case in six days, whereupon the government was given two weeks to attack it, and the court then announced that the Davidians would have one afternoon in which to reply.

■ ■ ■ ■ ■ ■ ■ ■ ■ ■

In short, virtually nothing that we "know" to be true about the Waco incident is, in fact, true. When put into their proper context, we may well wonder whether the operations resemble more an ethnic cleansing than a law enforcement operation.

Endnotes

1. ATF audiotapes, produced in response to author's FOIA lawsuit. The tapes are more fully discussed in Hardy, David T. *This Is Not An Assault*. Philadelphia: Xlibris, 2001: 208-35. **2.** The agents claimed to be students at a local college but were middle-aged, drove large, new cars, and when asked, knew little of the campus or its courses. **3.** FBI Negotiation transcripts, 3 March 1993, p 16. **4.** Report of Investigation, Agent Davy Aquilera, dated 22 Feb 1993 **5.** Vinzant, Carol. "BATF Troop." *Spy* (March 1994): 49. **6.** This was the position taken by all ATF witnesses on the point during the civil wrongful death trials. **7.** *Op cit.*, Hardy: 220-6. **8.** Several seconds after the gunshots, three dull thumps are heard, which the helicopter pilot identified as bullets hitting his aircraft. The helicopter does in fact show three bullet holes. Rifle bullets at any but very long ranges are supersonic; they arrive before the sound of the shot that launched them. At 300 yards, rifle bullets of the type owned by the Davidians would have arrived in about a half second, and the sound in about three-quarters of a second. But no gunshots are audible after the impact sounds, nor at any time for several seconds around them. This would indicate that even when shots were certainly fired directly at the helos, they could not be heard over engine noise. **9.** Audio track of FBI FLIR videotape, 13:01:10 hours. **10.** *United States v. Branch*, No. 93-CR-046 (W.D. Texas), trial transcript, p 1744. **11.** *Ibid.*: 2689. **12.** *Ibid.*: 2331. **13.** Hancock, Lee. "FBI Missteps Doomed Siege Talks, Memos Say." *Dallas Morning News* 30 Dec 1999. **14.** *Ibid.* **15.** *Op cit.*, Hardy: 260 **16.** Kopel, David, and Paul Blackman. *No More Wacos: What's Wrong With Federal Law Enforcement and How To Fix It*. Amherst, NY: Prometheus Books, 1997: 150-1. **17.** FBI negotiation transcripts, 18 April 1993, p 3. **18.** Failure Analysis Associates. "Investigation of the April 19, 1993 Assault on the Mount Carmel Center." (July 1995). **19.** *Ibid.* **20.** Dow Chemical. Material Safety Data Sheet, p 3. **21.** "Memorandum for Commander, US Army Special Operations Command." Dated 13 May 1993. **22.** Park, Sungmin, and Samuel Giammona. "Toxic Effects of Tear Gas on an Infant Following Prolonged Exposure." *Amer. Diseases of the Child* 245 (1972): 123 **23.** *Op cit.* note 21. **24.** The incidents are summarized by the FBI HRT founder, Danny Coulson, in his book *No Heroes* (Pocket Books, 1999): 192, 206. **25.** House of Representatives Waco hearings, 26 July 1995. Transcript p 44. **26.** Hancock, Lee. "FBI Didn't Plan To Fight Waco Fire." *Dallas Morning News* 2 March 2000. **27.** CNN "raw feed," 19 April 1993. **28.** FBI FLIR videotape, 12:35:00 hours. **29.** *Op cit.*, Failure Analysis Associates. FAA found that this gassing, taken alone, caused MeCl concentrations of 120 percent of the "Immediately Dangerous to Life and Health" level, and CS concentrations over *500 percent* of that necessary to break trained soldiers. **30.** Deposition of Nicholas Evans, pp 68, 81-2. **31.** Deposition of Peter Ayers, p 87.

THE BOMBING OF PANAM FLIGHT 103
CASE NOT CLOSED
WILLIAM BLUM

The newspapers were filled with pictures of happy relatives of the victims of the December 21, 1988, bombing of PanAm 103 over Lockerbie, Scotland. A Libyan, Abdelbaset Ali Mohmed al Megrahi, had been found guilty of the crime the day before, January 31, 2001, by a Scottish court in the Hague, though his codefendant, Al Amin Khalifa Fhimah, was acquitted. At long last there was going to be some kind of closure for the families.

But what was wrong with this picture?

What was wrong was that the evidence against Megrahi was thin to the point of transparency. Coming the month after the (s)election of George W. Bush, the Hague verdict could have been dubbed Supreme Court II, another instance of non-judicial factors fatally clouding judicial reasoning. The three Scottish judges could not have relished the prospect of returning to the United Kingdom after finding both defendants innocent of the murder of 270 people, largely from the UK and the United States. Not to mention having to face dozens of hysterical victims' family members in the courtroom. The three judges also well knew the fervent desires of the White House and Downing Street as to the outcome. If both men had been acquitted, the United States and Great Britain would have had to answer for a decade of sanctions and ill will directed toward Libya.

One has to read the entire 26,000-word "Opinion of the Court," as well as be very familiar with the history of the case going back to 1988, to appreciate how questionable was the judges' verdict.

The key charge against Megrahi—the *sine qua non*—was that he placed explosives in a suitcase and tagged it so it would lead the following charmed life: 1) loaded aboard an Air Malta flight to Frankfurt without an accompanying passenger; 2) transferred in Frankfurt to the PanAm 103A flight to London without an accompanying passenger; 3) transferred in London to the PanAm 103 flight to New York without an accompanying passenger.

To the magic bullet of the JFK assassination, can we now add the magic suitcase?

This scenario by itself would have been a major feat and so unlikely to succeed that any terrorist with any common sense would have found a better way. But aside from anything else, we have the first step, loading the suitcase at Malta: There was no witness, no video, no document, no fingerprints, nothing to tie Megrahi to the particular brown Samsonite suitcase, no history of terrorism, no forensic evidence of any kind linking him or Fhimah to such an act.

And the court admitted it: "The absence of any explanation of the method by which the primary suitcase might have been placed on board KM180 [Air Malta] is a major difficulty for the Crown case."[1]

Moreover, under security requirements in 1988, unaccompanied baggage was subjected to special X-ray examinations, plus—because of recent arrests in Germany—the security personnel in Frankfurt were on the lookout specifically for a bomb secreted in a radio, which indeed turned out to be the method used with the PanAm 103 bomb.

Requiring some sort of direct and credible testimony linking Megrahi to the bombing, the Hague court placed great—nay, paramount—weight upon the supposed identification of the Libyan by a shopkeeper in Malta, as the purchaser of the clothing found in the bomb suitcase. But this shopkeeper had earlier identified several other people as the culprit, including one who was a CIA asset.[2] When he finally identified Megrahi from a photo, it was after Megrahi's photo had been in the world news for years. The court acknowledged the possible danger inherent in such a verification: "These identifications were criticised *inter alia* on the ground that photographs of the accused have been featured many times over the years in the media and accordingly purported identifications more than 10 years after the event are of little if any value."[3]

There were also major discrepancies between the shopkeeper's original description of the clothes-buyer and Megrahi's actual appearance. The shopkeeper told police that the customer was "six feet or more in height" and "was about 50 years of age."

Megrahi is 5'8" tall and was 36-years-old in 1988. The judges again acknowledged the weakness of their argument by conceding that the initial description "would not in a number of respects fit the first accused [Megrahi]" and that "it has to be accepted that there was a substantial discrepancy."[4] Nevertheless, the judges went ahead and accepted the identification as accurate.

Before the indictment of the two Libyans in Washington in November 1991, the press had reported police findings that the clothing had been purchased on November 23, 1988.[5] But the indictment of Megrahi states that he made the purchase on December 7. Could this be because the investigators were able to document Megrahi being in Malta (where he worked for Libya Airlines) on that date but cannot do so for November 23?[6]

There is also this to be considered: If the bomber needed some clothing to wrap up an ultra-secret bomb in a suitcase, would he go to a clothing store in the city where he planned to carry out his dastardly deed, where he knew he'd likely be remembered as an obvious foreigner, and buy brand new, easily traceable items? Would an intelligence officer—which Megrahi was alleged to be—do this? Or even a common boob? Wouldn't it make more sense to use any old clothing, from anywhere?

Furthermore, after the world was repeatedly assured that these items of clothing were sold only in Malta, it was learned that at least one of the items was actually "sold at dozens of outlets throughout Europe, and it was impossible to trace the purchaser."[7]

The "Opinion of the Court" placed considerable weight on the suspicious behavior of Megrahi prior to the fatal day, making much of his comings and goings abroad, phone calls to unknown parties for unknown reasons, the use of a pseudonym, etc. (It was later reported by Fhimah that Megrahi's mysteriousness was due in part to his involvement in trying to obtain parts for Libya Airlines on the black market in the face of sweeping international sanctions.)

The three judges tried to squeeze as much mileage out of these events as they could, as if they had no better case to make.

But if Megrahi was indeed a member of Libyan intelligence, we must consider that intelligence agents have been known to act in mysterious ways, for whatever assignment they're on. The court, however, had no idea what assignment, if any, Megrahi was working on.

There is much more that is known about the case that makes the court verdict and written opinion questionable, although credit must be given the court for its frankness about what it was doing, even while it was doing it. "We are aware that in relation to certain aspects of the case there are a number of uncertainties and qualifications," the judges wrote. "We are also aware that there is a danger that by selecting parts of the evidence which seem to fit together and ignoring parts which might not fit, it is possible to read into a mass of conflicting evidence a pattern or conclusion which is not really justified."[8]

It is remarkable, given all that the judges conceded was questionable or uncertain in the trial—not to mention all that was questionable or uncertain that they *didn't* concede—that at the end of the day they could still declare to the world: "There is nothing in the evidence which leaves us with any reasonable doubt as to the guilt of [Megrahi]".[9]

The *Guardian* of London later wrote that two days before the verdict, "[S]enior Foreign Office officials briefed a group of journalists in London. They painted a picture of a bright new chapter in Britain's relations with Colonel Gadafy's regime. They made it quite clear they assumed both the Libyans in the dock would be acquitted. The Foreign Office officials were not alone. Most independent observers believed it was impossible for the court to find the prosecution had proved its case against Megrahi beyond reasonable doubt."[10]

_ALTERNATIVE SCENARIO

There is, moreover, an alternative scenario, laying the blame on Palestinians, Iran, and Syria, which is much better documented and makes a lot more sense, logistically and otherwise.

Indeed, this was the original Official Version, delivered with Olympian rectitude by the US government—guaranteed, sworn to, scout's honor, case closed—until the buildup to the Gulf War came along in 1990, and the support of Iran and Syria was needed.

Washington was anxious as well to achieve the release of American hostages held in Lebanon by groups close to Iran. Thus it was that the scurrying sound of backtracking became audible in the corridors of the White House.

> "WE ARE AWARE THAT IN RELATION TO CERTAIN ASPECTS OF THE CASE THERE ARE A NUMBER OF UNCERTAINTIES AND QUALIFICATIONS," THE JUDGES WROTE.

Suddenly—or so it seemed—in October 1990, there was a new Official Version: It was Libya—the Arab state least supportive of the US build-up to the Gulf War and the sanctions imposed against Iraq—that was behind the bombing, after all, declared Washington.

The two Libyans were formally indicted in the US and Scotland on November 14, 1991.

"This was a Libyan government operation from start to finish," declared the State Department spokesman.[11]

"The Syrians took a bum rap on this," said President George H.W. Bush.[12]

Within the next 20 days, the remaining four American hostages in Lebanon were released, along with the most prominent British hostage, Terry Waite.

The original Official Version accused the PFLP-GC, a 1968 breakaway from a component of the Palestine Liberation Organization, of making the bomb and somehow placing it aboard the flight in Frankfurt.

The PFLP-GC was led by Ahmed Jabril, one of the world's leading terrorists, and was headquartered in, financed by, and closely supported by Syria. The bombing was allegedly done at the behest of Iran as revenge for the US shootdown of an Iranian passenger plane over the Persian Gulf on July 3, 1988, which claimed 290 lives.

The support for this scenario was, and remains, impressive, as the following sample indicates:

In April 1989, the FBI—in response to criticism that it was bungling the investigation—leaked to CBS the news that it had tentatively identified the person who unwittingly carried the bomb aboard. His name was Khalid Jaafar, a 21-year-old Lebanese-American. The report said that the bomb had been planted in Jaafar's suitcase by a member of the PFLP-GC, whose name was not revealed.[13]

In May, the State Department stated that the CIA was "confident" of the Iran-Syria-PFLP-GC account of events.[14]

On September 20 of that year, the *Times* of London reported that "security officials from Britain, the United States and West Germany are 'totally satisfied' that it was the PFLP-GC" behind the crime.

In December 1989, Scottish investigators announced that they had "hard evidence" of the involvement of the PFLP-GC in the bombing.[15]

A National Security Agency electronic intercept disclosed that Ali Akbar Mohtashemi, Iranian interior minister, had paid Palestinian terrorists $10 million to gain revenge for the downed Iranian airplane.[16] The intercept appears to have occurred in July 1988, shortly after the Iranian plane was shot down.

Israeli intelligence also intercepted a communication between Mohtashemi and the Iranian embassy in Beirut "indicating that Iran paid for the Lockerbie bombing."[17]

Even after the Libyans had been indicted, Israeli officials declared that their intelligence analysts remained convinced that the PFLP-GC bore primary responsibility for the bombing.[18]

In 1992, Abu Sharif, a political adviser to PLO chairman Yasser Arafat, stated that the PLO had compiled a secret report which concluded that the bombing of 103 was the work of a "Middle Eastern country" other than Libya.[19]

In February 1995, former Scottish Office minister Alan Stewart wrote to the British Foreign Secretary and the Lord Advocate, questioning the reliability of evidence which had led to the accusations against the two Libyans.

This move, wrote the *Guardian*, reflected the concern of the Scottish legal profession, reaching into the Crown Office (Scotland's equivalent of the Attorney General's Office), that the bombing may not have been the work of Libya, but of Syrians, Palestinians, and Iranians.[20]

We must also ask why Prime Minister Margaret Thatcher, writing in her 1993 memoirs about the US bombing of Libya in 1986, with which Britain had cooperated, stated: "But the much vaunted Libyan counter-attack did not and could not take place. Gaddafy had not been destroyed but he had been humbled. There was a marked decline in Libyan-sponsored terrorism in succeeding years."[21]

_KEY QUESTION

A key question in the PFLP-GC version has always been: How did the bomb get aboard the plane in Frankfurt or at some other point? One widely disseminated explanation was in a report, completed during the summer of 1989 and leaked in the fall, which had been prepared by a New York investigating firm called Interfor. Headed by a former Israeli intelligence agent, Juval Aviv, Interfor—whose other clients included Fortune 500 companies, the FBI, IRS, and Secret Service[22]—was hired by the law firm representing PanAm's insurance carrier.

The Interfor Report said that in the mid-1980s, a drug- and arms-smuggling operation was set up in various European cities, with Frankfurt airport as the site of one of the drug routes. The Frankfurt operation was run by Manzer Al-Kassar, a Syrian, the same man from whom Oliver North's shadowy network purchased large quantities of arms for the contras. At the airport, according to the report, a courier would board a flight with checked luggage containing innocent items; after the luggage had passed all security checks, one or another of PanAm's Turkish baggage handlers, acting as an accomplice, would substitute an identical suitcase containing contraband; the passenger then picked up this suitcase upon arrival at the destination.

The only courier named by Interfor was Khalid Jaafar, who, as noted above, had been named by the FBI a few months earlier as the person who unwittingly carried the bomb aboard.

The Interfor report spins a web much too lengthy and complex to go into here. The short version is that the CIA in Germany discovered the airport drug operation and learned also that Kassar had the contacts to gain the release of American hostages in Lebanon. He had already done the same for French hostages. Thus it was that the CIA and the German Bundeskriminalamt (BKA, Federal Criminal Office) allowed the drug operation to continue in hopes of effecting the release of American hostages.

According to the report, this same smuggling ring and its method of switching suitcases at the Frankfurt airport were used to smuggle the fatal bomb aboard flight 103, under the eyes of the CIA and BKA.

In January 1990, Interfor gave three of the baggage handlers polygraph tests, and two of them were judged as being deceitful when denying any involvement in baggage switching. However, neither the US, UK, nor German investigators showed any interest in the results or in questioning the baggage handlers. Instead, the polygrapher, James Keefe, was hauled before a Washington grand jury, and, as he puts it, "they were bent on destroying my credibility—not theirs [the baggage handlers']." To Interfor, the lack of interest in the polygraph results and the attempted intimidation of Keefe were the strongest evidence of a cover-up by the various government authorities who did not want their permissive role in the baggage switching to be revealed.[23]

Critics claimed that the Interfor report had been inspired by PanAm's interest in proving that it was impossible for normal airline security to have prevented the loading of the bomb, thus removing the basis for accusing the airline of negligence.

The report was the principal reason PanAm's attorneys subpoenaed the FBI, CIA, NSA, DEA, State Department, and National Security Council, as well as, reportedly, the Defense Intelligence Agency and Federal Aviation Administration, to turn over all documents relating to the crash of 103 or to a drug operation preceding the crash. The government moved to quash the subpoenas on grounds of "national security" and refused to turn over a single document in open court, although it gave some to a judge to view privately.

The judge later commented that he was "troubled about certain parts" of what he'd read, that he didn't "know quite what to do because I think some of the material may be significant."[24]

_DRUGS REVELATION

On October 30, 1990, NBC-TV News reported that "PanAm flights from Frankfurt, including 103, had been used a number of times by the DEA as part of its undercover operation to fly informants and suitcases of heroin into Detroit as part of a sting operation to catch dealers in Detroit."

The TV network reported that the Drug Enforcement Administration was looking into the possibility that a young man who lived in Michigan and regularly visited the Middle East may have unwittingly carried the bomb aboard Flight 103. His name was Khalid Jaafar. "Unidentified law enforcement sources" were cited as saying that Jaafar had been a DEA informant and was involved in a drug-sting operation based out of Cyprus. The DEA was investigating whether the PFLP-GC had tricked Jaafar into carrying a suitcase containing the bomb instead of the drugs he usually carried.

The NBC report quoted an airline source as saying: "Informants would put [suit]cases of heroin on the PanAm flights apparently without the usual security checks, through an arrangement between the DEA and German authorities."[25]

These revelations were enough to inspire a congressional hearing, held that December, entitled, "Drug Enforcement Administration's Alleged Connection to the PanAm Flight 103 Disaster."

The chairman of the committee, Rep. Robert Wise (Democrat - West Virginia), began the hearing by lamenting the fact that the DEA and the Department of Justice had not made any of their field agents who were most knowledgeable about Flight 103 available to testify; that they had not provided requested written information, including the results of the DEA's investigation into the air disaster; and that "the FBI to this date has been totally uncooperative."

The two DEA officials who did testify admitted that the agency had, in fact, run "controlled drug deliveries" through Frankfurt airport with the cooperation of German authorities, using US airlines, but insisted that no such operation had been conducted in December 1988. (The drug agency had said nothing of its sting operation to the President's Commission on Aviation Security and Terrorism, which had held hearings in the first months of 1990 in response to the 103 bombing.)

The officials denied that the DEA had had any "association with Mr. Jaafar in any way, shape, or form." However, to questions concerning Jaafar's background, family, and his frequent trips to Lebanon, they asked to respond only in closed session. They made the same request in response to several other questions.[26]

NBC News had reported on October 30 that the DEA had told law enforcement officers in Detroit not to talk to the media about Jaafar.

The hearing ended after but one day, even though Rep. Wise had promised a "full-scale" investigation and indicated during the hearing that there would be more to come. What was said in the closed sessions remains closed.[27]

One of the DEA officials who testified, Stephen Greene, had a reservation on Flight 103, but he canceled because of one or more of the several international warnings that had preceded the fateful day. He has described standing on the Heathrow tarmac, watching the doomed plane take off.[28]

There have been many reports of heroin being found in the field around the crash, from "traces" to "a substantial quantity" found in a suitcase.[29] Two days after the NBC report, however, the *New York Times* quoted a "federal official" saying that "no hard drugs were aboard the aircraft."

_THE FILM

In 1994, American filmmaker Allan Francovich completed a documentary, *The Maltese Double Cross*, which presents Jaafar as an unwitting bomb-carrier with ties to the DEA and the CIA. Showings of the film in Britain were canceled under threat of lawsuits, and venues were burglarized or attacked by arsonists. When Channel 4 agreed to air the film, the Scottish Crown Office and the US Embassy in London sent press packs to the media, labeling the film "blatant propaganda" and attacking some of the film's interviewees, including Juval Aviv, the head of Interfor.[30]

Aviv paid a price for his report and his outspokenness. Over a period of time, his New York office suffered a series of break-ins, the FBI visited his clients, his polygrapher was harassed (as mentioned above), and a contrived commercial fraud charge was brought against him. Even though Aviv eventually was cleared in court, it was a long, expensive, and painful ordeal.[31]

Francovich also stated that he had learned that five CIA operatives had been sent to London and Cyprus to discredit the film while it was being made, that his office phones were tapped, that staff cars were sabotaged, and that one of his researchers narrowly escaped an attempt to force his vehicle into the path of an oncoming truck.[32] Government officials examining the Lockerbie bombing went so far as to ask the FBI to investigate the film. The Bureau later issued a highly derogatory opinion of it.[33]

The film's detractors made much of the fact that the film was initially funded jointly by a UK company (two-thirds) and a Libyan government investment arm (one-third). Francovich said that he was fully aware of this and had taken pains to negotiate a guarantee of independence from any interference.

On April 17, 1997, Allan Francovich suddenly died of a heart attack at age 56, upon arrival at Houston Airport.[34] His film has had virtually no showings in the United States.

_ABU TALB

The DEA sting operation and Interfor's baggage-handler hypothesis both predicate the bomb suitcase being placed aboard the plane in Frankfurt without going through the normal security checks. In either case, it eliminates the need for the questionable triple-unaccompanied baggage scenario. With either scenario the clothing could still have been purchased in Malta, but in any event we don't need the Libyans for that.

Mohammed Abu Talb fits that and perhaps other pieces of the puzzle. The Palestinian had close ties to PFLP-GC cells in Germany which were making Toshiba radio-cassette bombs, similar, if not identical, to what was used to bring down 103. In October 1988, two months before Lockerbie, the German police raided these cells, finding several such bombs. In May 1989, Talb was arrested in Sweden, where he lived, and was later convicted of taking part in several bombings of the offices of American airline companies in Scandinavia. In his Swedish flat, police found large quantities of clothing made in Malta.

Police investigation of Talb disclosed that during October 1988 he had been to Cyprus and Malta, at least once in the company of Hafez Dalkamoni, the leader of the German PFLP-GC, who was arrested in the raid. The men met with PFLP-GC members who lived in Malta. Talb was also in Malta on November 23, which was originally reported as the date of the clothing purchase, before the indictment of the Libyans, as mentioned earlier.

After his arrest, Talb told investigators that between October and December 1988 he had retrieved and passed to another person a bomb that had been hidden in a building used by the PFLP-GC in Germany. Officials declined to identify the person to whom Talb said he had passed the bomb. A month later, however, he recanted his confession.

Talb was reported to possess a brown Samsonite suitcase and have circled December 21 in a diary seized in his Swedish flat. After the raid upon his flat, his wife was heard to telephone Palestinian friends and say: "Get rid of the clothes."

In December 1989, Scottish police, in papers filed with Swedish legal officials, made Talb the only publicly identified suspect "in the murder or participation in the murder of 270 people"; the Palestinian subsequently became another of the several individuals to be identified by the Maltese shopkeeper from a photo as the clothing purchaser. Since that time, the world has scarcely heard of Abu Talb, who was sentenced to life in prison in Sweden but never charged with anything to do with Lockerbie.[35]

In Allan Francovich's film, members of Khalid Jaafar's family—which long had ties to the drug trade in Lebanon's notorious Bekaa Valley—are interviewed. In either halting English or translated Arabic, or paraphrased by the film's narrator, they drop many bits of information, which are difficult to put together into a coherent whole. Amongst the bits: Khalid had told his parents that he'd met Talb in Sweden and had been given Maltese clothing ... someone had given Khalid a tape recorder, or put one into his bag ... he was told to go to Germany to see friends of PFLP-GC leader Ahmed Jabril, who would help him earn some money ... he arrived in Germany with two kilos of heroin ... "He didn't know it was a bomb. They gave him the drugs to take to Germany. He didn't know. Who wants to die?"

It cannot be stated with certainty what happened at Frankfurt airport on that fateful day, if, as seems most likely, that is the place where the bomb was placed into the system. Either Jaafar, the DEA courier, arrived with his suitcase containing heroin and a bomb and was escorted through security by the proper authorities, or this was a day he was a courier for Manzer al-Kassar, and the baggage handlers did their usual switch.

Or perhaps we'll never know for sure what happened. On February 16, 1990, a group of British relatives of Lockerbie victims went to the American Embassy in London for a meeting with members of the President's Commission on Aviation Security and Terrorism. After the meeting, Britisher Martin Cadman was chatting with two of the commission members. He later reported what one of them had said to him: "Your government and our government know exactly what happened at Lockerbie. But they are not going to tell you."[36]

_COMMENTS ABOUT THE HAGUE COURT VERDICT

"The judges nearly agreed with the defense. In their verdict, they tossed out much of the prosecution witnesses' evidence as false or questionable and said the prosecution had failed to prove crucial elements, including the route that the bomb suitcase took." —*New York Times*[37]

"It sure does look like they bent over backwards to find a way to convict, and you have to assume the political context of the case influenced them." —Michael Scharf, professor, New England School of Law[38]

"THE JUDGES NEARLY AGREED WITH THE DEFENSE."

"I thought this was a very, very weak circumstantial case. I am absolutely astounded, astonished. I was extremely reluctant to believe that any Scottish judge would convict anyone, even a Libyan, on the basis of such evidence." —Robert Black, Scottish law professor who was the architect of the Hague trial[39]

"A general pattern of the trial consisted in the fact that virtually all people presented by the prosecution as key witnesses were proven to lack credibility to a very high extent, in certain cases even having openly lied to the court.

"While the first accused was found 'guilty,' the second accused was found 'not guilty.'... This is totally incomprehensible for any rational observer when one considers that the indictment in its very essence was based on the joint action of the two accused in Malta.

"As to the undersigned's [Koechler's] knowledge, there is not a sin-

gle piece of material evidence linking the two accused to the crime. In such a context, the guilty verdict in regard to the first accused appears to be arbitrary, even irrational....

"This leads the undersigned to the suspicion that political considerations may have been overriding a strictly judicial evaluation of the case... Regrettably, through the conduct of the Court, disservice has been done to the important cause of international criminal justice." —Hans Koechler, appointed as an international observer of the Lockerbie trial by UN Secretary-General Kofi Annan[40]

So, let's hope that Abdelbaset Ali Mohmed al Megrahi is really guilty. It would be a terrible shame if he spends the rest of his life in prison because back in 1990 Washington's hegemonic plans for the Middle East needed a convenient enemy, which just happened to be his country.

Endnotes

1. "Opinion of the Court," Par. 39. **2.** Perry, Mark. *Eclipse: The Last Days of the CIA*. New York: William Morrow, 1992: 342-7 **3.** *Op cit.*, "Opinion," Par. 55. **4.** *Ibid.*, Par. 68. **5.** See, e.g., *Sunday Times* (London), 12 Nov 1989: 3. **6.** For a detailed discussion of this issue see: "A Special Report from Private Eye: Lockerbie—the Flight from Justice," *Private Eye* (May/June 2001): 20-2; *Private Eye* is a magazine published in London. **7.** *Sunday Times* (London), 17 Dec 1989: 14. Malta is, in fact, a major manufacturer of clothing sold throughout the world. **8.** *Op cit.*, "Opinion," Par. 89. **9.** *Ibid*. **10.** *Guardian* (London) 19 June 2001. **11.** *New York Times* 15 Nov 1991. **12.** *Los Angeles Times* 15 Nov 1991. **13.** *New York Times* 13 April 1989: 9; Johnston, David. *Lockerbie: The Tragedy of Flight 103*. New York: St. Martin's Press, 1989: 157, 161-2. **14.** *Washington Post* 11 May 1989: 1. **15.** *New York Times* 16 Dec 1989: 3. **16.** Department of the Air Force—Air Intelligence Agency intelligence summary report, 4 March 1991, released under a FOIA request made by lawyers for PanAm. Reports of the intercept appeared in the press long before the above document was released; e.g., *New York Times* 27 Sept 1989: 11; *NYT* 31 Oct 1989: 8; *Sunday Times* (London) 29 Oct 1989: 4. But it wasn't until January 1995 that the exact text became widely publicized and caused a storm in the UK, although it was ignored in the US. **17.** *Times* (London) 20 Sept 1989: 1. **18.** *New York Times* 21 Nov 1991: 14. It should be borne in mind, however, that Israel may have been influenced because of its hostility toward the PFLP-GC. **19.** Reuters dispatch, datelined Tunis, 26 Feb 1992. **20.** *Guardian* (London) 24 Feb 1995: 7. **21.** Thatcher, Margaret. *The Downing Street Years*. New York: HarperCollins Publishers, 1993: 448-9. **22.** *National Law Journal* 25 Sept 1995: A11, from papers filed in a New York court case. **23.** *Barron's* 17 Dec 1990: 19, 22. A copy of the Interfor Report is in the author's possession, but he has been unable to locate a complete copy of it on the Internet. **24.** *Ibid.*: 18. **25.** *Times* (London) 1 Nov 1990: 3; *Washington Times* 31 Oct 1990: 3. **26.** Government Information, Justice, and Agriculture Subcommittee of the Committee on Government Operations, House of Representatives, 18 Dec 1990, passim. **27.** *Ibid.* **28.** *The Maltese Double Cross* (film) (see below). **29.** *Sunday Times* (London) 16 April 1989 ("traces"); *op. cit.*, Johnston, 79 ("substantial"). *The Maltese Double Cross* film mentions other reports of drugs found by a Scottish policeman and a mountain rescue man. **30.** *Financial Times* (London) 12 May 1995: 8; article by John Ashton, leading 103 investigator, in *Mail on Sunday* (London) 9 June 1996. **31.** *Op. cit.*, Ashton; *Wall Street Journal* 18 Dec 1995: 1; *WSJ* 18 Dec 1996: B2. **32.** *Guardian* (London) 23 April 1994: 5. **33.** *Sunday Times* (London) 7 May 1995. **34.** Francovich's former wife told the author that he had not had any symptoms of a heart problem before. However, the author also spoke to Dr. Cyril Wecht, of JFK "conspiracy" fame, who performed an autopsy on Francovich. Wecht stated that he found no reason to suspect foul play. **35.** Re: Abu Talb, all 1989: *New York Times* 31 Oct: 1; *NYT* 1 Dec: 12; *NYT* 24 Dec: 1; *Sunday Times* (London) 12 Nov: 3; *ST* 5 Dec; *Times* (London), 21 Dec: 5. Also, the Associated Press 11 July 2000. **36.** Cadman in *The Maltese Double Cross*. Also see: *Guardian* 29 July 1995: 27. **37.** *New York Times* 2 Feb 2001. **38.** *Ibid.* **39.** *Electronic Telegraph* (London) 4 Feb 2001. **40.** All quotations are from Koechler's report of 3 Feb 2001, easily found on the Internet.

LEADERS AGAINST THE DRUG WAR
RUSS KICK

The forces trying to keep certain substances illegal would have us believe that the only people calling for changes in drug laws are radical, out-of-touch hippie-freaks who are only interested in being able to ingest massive quantities of drugs without fear of arrest. The reality is that over 70 political officials—some of them very high-ranking—have gone on record to support the relaxation of drugs laws. Their number includes sitting Presidents of the US, Mexico, Uruguay, Portugal, and Colombia, a former Canadian Prime Minister, a former US Vice President, a former Secretary of State, a sitting Mexican Foreign Minister, other Cabinet-level officials, three US governors, several mayors, legislators, federal judges, police chiefs, and others. They hail from all over the political spectrum. The most radical argue for the complete legalization of all drugs. Others believe that penalties for using a specific drug—most often marijuana—should be struck off the books. A few push only for the acceptance of cannabis for medical purposes, while others want to shift the focus of drug policy from arrests and incarceration to education and medical help for addiction. No matter what approach they favor, though, they all have in mind a radical change of the laws governing what we can put into our bodies.

Perhaps we're witnessing the birth of a new movement—Leaders for Drug Law Reform.

Bill Clinton, former President of the United States
"I think that most small amounts of marijuana have been decriminalized in some places, and should be."[1]

Jimmy Carter, former President of the United States
"Penalties against a drug should not be more damaging to an individual than the use of the drug itself. Nowhere is this more clear than in the laws against possession of marijuana in private for personal use. The National Commission on Marijuana...concluded years ago that marijuana use should be decriminalized, and I believe it is time to implement those basic recommendations."[2]

> "I THINK THAT MOST SMALL AMOUNTS OF MARIJUANA HAVE BEEN DECRIMINALIZED IN SOME PLACES, AND SHOULD BE."
> —THEN-US PRESIDENT BILL CLINTON

Vicente Fox, President of Mexico
"My opinion is that in Mexico it is not a crime to have a small dose of drugs in one's pocket."

When a reporter asked President Fox what he thought of the notion that crime and violence result from the illegality of drugs, not the drugs themselves, Fox replied: "That's right! That's true! That's true! But the day that the alternative of freeing the consumption of drugs from punishment comes, it will have to be done in the entire world because we are not going to win anything if Mexico does it, but the production and traffick of the drugs to import them to the United States continues. Thus, humanity will some day view it [legalization] as the best in this sense."[3]

Jorge Batlle, President of Uruguay
"Why don't we just legalize the drugs?"[4]

"The day that it [all drugs] is legalized in the United States, it will lose value. And if it loses value, there will be no profit. But as long as the US citizenry doesn't rise up to do something, they will pass this life fighting and fighting." Comparing current drug policy to the days of alcohol prohibition in the US, Batlle said the problem "will be resolved on the day that the consumers announce that this cannot be fixed by any other manner than changing this situation in the same way that was done with the 'Dry Laws.'"[5]

Andres Pastrana, President of Colombia
"The moment has arrived to evaluate world policy against drugs."[6]

Percival Patterson, Prime Minister of Jamaica
"I want to make it absolutely clear that we are not considering legalising [marijuana] in the sense of making it legal for people to grow, to sell, to export. It is for private use, and, of course, it will have to be confined to adults.... That process [of decriminalization] we intend to begin shortly."[7]

Jorge Sampaio, President of Portugal
"Policies conceived and enforced to control drug-related problems and effects, have led to disastrous and perverse results. Prohibition is the fundamental

principle of drug policies. If we consider the results achieved, there are profound doubts regarding its effectiveness. Prohibitionist policies have been unable to control the consumption of narcotics; on the other hand, there has been an increase of criminality. There is also a high mortality rate related to the quality of substances and to AIDS or other viral diseases."[8]

Joe Clark, former Prime Minister, current head of Tory Party, Member of Parliament, Canada
"I believe the least controversial approach is decriminalization [of marijuana], because it's unjust to see someone, because of one decision one night in their youth, carry the stigma—to be barred from studying medicine, law, architecture or other fields where a criminal record could present an obstacle."[9]

Luis Eduardo Garzon, presidental candidate (2001), Colombia
"[T]he best way to end this problem and the war it has brought us is to legalize drugs."[10]

Dan Quayle, former Vice President of the US
"Congress should definitely consider decriminalizing possession of marijuana.... We should concentrate on prosecuting the rapists and burglars who are a menace to society."[11]

George Schultz, Secretary of State under President Reagan
"The conceptual base of current programs is flawed.... [W]e need at least to consider and examine forms of controlled legalization of drugs."[12]

Peter Bourne, Drug Czar under President Carter
"We [the Carter Administration] did not view marijuana as a significant health problem—as it was not—even though there were people who wanted to construe it as being a public health problem. Nobody dies from marijuana smoking. Marijuana smoking, in fact, if one wants to be honest, is a source of pleasure and amusement to countless millions of people in America, and it continues to be that way."[13]

Jorge Castañeda, Foreign Minister, Mexico (the equivalent of the US Secretary of State)
"In the end, legalization of certain substances may be the only way to bring prices down, and doing so may be the only remedy to some of the worst aspects of the drug plague: violence, corruption and the collapse of the rule of law. To many in the United States, for good reasons and bad, legalization remains anathema; but its costs and benefits must be assessed in the light of the pernicious, hypocritical and dysfunctional status quo. Using present tactics, the war on drugs is being lost; it is long past time to reassess a failed policy."[14]

Miguel Angel de la Torre, chief of Mexico's federal police force
"It seems like this is the only possible solution, although it is utopian, to combat narco-trafficking, because the corrupting power that the narco generates is tremendous and in the consumer arena of money it is more important than the moral principles that the drug laws instill. The drug problem is so grave that I don't see any other solution than this one [legalization]. Every kind of drug would have to be included..."[15]

Gustavo de Greiff, former Attorney General, Colombia
"We should legalize drugs because we here are providing the dead, and the consumers are there in the US."[16]

Jaime Ruiz, senior adviser to President Andres Pastrana, Colombia
"From the Colombian point of view, [legalization] is the easy solution. I mean, just legalize it and we won't have any more problems. Probably in five years we wouldn't even have guerrillas. No problems. We [would] have a great country with no problems."[17]

Peter Lilley, former Social Security Secretary, Britain
"In the final analysis, the reason the law on cannabis is unenforceable is that it is indefensible—especially in a country where alcohol and nicotine are legal.... The arguments for prohibition crumble on close analysis.... Short of legalising trade in cannabis entirely, the only way to stop driving soft drug users into the arms of the criminals who push hard drugs is to license some legal outlets to retail cannabis. Holland's so-called 'coffee shops' (which allow consumption of cannabis on the premises and sales of retail amounts of cannabis) are the best known legal outlets. But there is no need to go that far. We could let the licensing justices give premises off-licences to sell retail amounts."[18]

> "[W]E NEED AT LEAST TO CONSIDER AND EXAMINE FORMS OF CONTROLLED LEGALIZATION OF DRUGS." —GEORGE SCHULTZ, SECRETARY OF STATE UNDER PRESIDENT REAGAN

Mo Mowlam, former Cabinet Minister responsible for drug policy, Britain
"From my time [of being] concerned [with] the government's drug policy I have come to the conclusion that we must decriminalise cannabis. The trade needs to be legalised so it can be sensibly regulated."[19]

Philip Oppenheim, former Treasury Minister, Britain
"Criminalising drugs hands massive profits to organised crime.... [L]egalisation looks like the lesser evil."[20]

Sir Keith Morris, Britain's former Ambassador to Colombia
"I have come to realise that the [drug] war is unwinnable, costly and counter-productive.... Decriminalisation, which is often mentioned, would be an unsatisfactory halfway house, because it would leave the trade in criminal hands, giving no help at all to the producer countries, and would not guarantee consumers a safe product or free them from the pressure of pushers. It has been difficult for me to advocate legalisation because it means saying to those with

whom I worked, and to the relatives of those who died, that this was an unnecessary war. But the imperative must be to try to stop the damage."[21]

Georges Papandreou, Minister of European Affairs, Greece
"As Minister of European Affairs, I can officially state that my Government and myself believe that all over Europe we need to open a debate on the 'Drug Question' in order to create more coherent and human policies with better perspectives.... The policy of criminalizing consumers has failed, creating many problems to our society: a criminal environment that accumulates enormous amounts of money and that undermines our democratic institutions, whether it is the police, the judiciary or politicians themselves;... social problems that start when we turn ill people into criminals, obliging them to become the involuntary army of the criminal environment of illegal drug trafficking."[22]

Allan Rock, Health Minister, Canada
"I think there's a lot to think about here. I'm glad that the committee is going to be working on it [changing marijuana's legal status]. I'm glad that people are going to be asking these questions and looking at different approaches. I think it's time for a discussion in Canada about all this. And I look forward to the results.... And I've got to tell you—I've got an open mind."[23]

Ron Paul, US Congressman (Republican - Texas)
"When we finally decide that drug prohibition has been no more successful than alcohol prohibition, the drug dealers will disappear."[24]

House of Lords, Great Britain
"We consider it undesirable to prosecute genuine therapeutic users of cannabis who possess or grow cannabis for their own use. This unsatisfactory situation underlines the need to legalise cannabis preparations for therapeutic use."[25]

Australian Parliament
"Over the past two decades in Australia we have devoted increased resources to drug law enforcement, we have increased the penalties for drug trafficking and we have accepted increasing inroads on our civil liberties as part of the battle to curb the drug trade. All the evidence shows, however, not only that our law enforcement agencies have not succeeded in preventing the supply of illicit drugs to Australian markets, but that it is unrealistic to expect them to do so. If the present policy of prohibition is not working then it is time to give serious consideration to the alternatives, however radical they may seem."[26]

Keith Martin, Member of Parliament, Canada (also a former corrections officer and ER doctor)
"For far too long, police and court resources have been wasted arresting and prosecuting people possessing small amounts of pot. While our resources are squandered in this futile effort, the House of Commons has been quiet and has refused to untie the hands of police so they can go after the real criminals."[27]

Dick Procter, Member of Parliament, Canada
"We intend to have a pretty wide-open discussion on how to proceed. Everything has to be on the table, including the possibility of decriminalizing recreational drugs like marijuana for personal use."[28]

National Commission on Ganja, Government of Jamaica
"It is the view of the Commission that the punitive sanctions administered by the justice system to users of small quantities is not only unjust but is a major source of disrespect and contempt for the legal system as a whole.... Accordingly the Commission recommends as follows: that the relevant laws be amended so that ganja be decriminalised for the private, personal use of small quantities by adults..."[29]

> "WE SHOULD LEGALIZE DRUGS BECAUSE WE HERE ARE PROVIDING THE DEAD, AND THE CONSUMERS ARE THERE IN THE US."
> —GUSTAVO DE GREIFF, FORMER ATTORNEY GENERAL, COLOMBIA

Gary Johnson, Governor of New Mexico
"Make drugs a controlled substance like alcohol. Legalize it, control it, regulate it, tax it. If you legalize it, we might actually have a healthier society."[30]

Jesse Ventura, Governor of Minnesota
"That's consensual crime. People who commit consensual crimes shouldn't go to jail. We shouldn't even prosecute them. That's crime against yourself. Drugs and prostitution, those should not be imprisoning crimes. The government has much more important things to do.... In the end it's the individual's decision to make. The prohibition of drugs causes crime. You don't have to legalize it, just decriminalize it. Regulate it. Create places where the addict can go get it."[31]

Ben Cayetano, Governor of Hawaii
"I just think it's a matter of time that Congress finally gets around to understanding that the states should be allowed to provide this kind of relief [medical marijuana] to the people. Congress is way, way behind in their thinking."[32]

Patricio Martínez García, Governor of Chihuahua, Mexico
"I believe that this proposal [legalization] must be studied seriously, because if the war is going to continue being lost, with the deterioration of the life of communities and even the nation, and with the deterioration of the quality of life for the citizens of the country, well, then, where are we heading?... There has to be a remaking of the law."[33]

Guillermo Gaviria, Governor of Antioquia, Colombia
"Colombia cannot go on being the victim of the wrong, shortsighted

attitude of countries that judge us superficially. Our society didn't choose to be part of the conflict."[34]

"We cannot keep our heads between our legs and continue with the same strategies of 30 years ago.... There are no magic solutions, and legalization is not necessarily the solution, but I believe in a controlled legalization."[35]

Hernando Emilio Zambrano, Governor of Amazonas, Colombia
"The entire world is asking for this solution [the legalization of drugs] because we know that it is the only way to end the high price."[36]

Viviane Morales, state Senator, Colombia
"From the 1990s onwards, the guerrillas and paramilitaries have grown incredibly because of the money coming from narco-trafficking. The main ally of narco-trafficking is prohibition." (According to the *Financial Times*, Senator Morales is the "author of a bill that calls for drug legalisation.")[37]

"[I'm trying to] create political deeds to open a debate about legalization because the prohibitionist alternative is not the solution for Colombia."[38]

Edward Lawson, Senator, British Columbia, Canada
"Maybe we should tie [drugs, including heroin and cocaine] together with the liquor stores, have it government controlled and have them quality controlled."[39]

Kurt Schmoke, former Mayor of Baltimore, Maryland
"I asked the US Conference of Mayors last month to adopt a resolution calling upon Congress to hold hearings on whether to decriminalize narcotics....

> "[I]F THE COCAINE INDUSTRY HAD COMMISSIONED A CONSULTANT TO DESIGN A MECHANISM TO INSURE PROFITABILITY, IT COULDN'T HAVE DONE BETTER THAN THE WAR ON DRUGS."
> —NANCY GERTNER, US DISTRICT COURT JUDGE

"The time has come to admit that the emperor has no clothes. The war on drugs is being lost, notwithstanding President Reagan's recent claim that we are digging our way out. And continuing our present policy—even with more money—is unlikely to make any difference.... Decriminalization would take the profit out of drugs and greatly reduce, if not eliminate, the drug-related violence that is currently plaguing our streets. Decriminalization will not solve this country's drug abuse problem, but it could solve our most intractable crime problem."[40]

Willie Brown, Mayor of San Francisco, California
"The debate over medical marijuana is, above all else, about compassion for people in pain.... Rather than censure this public health

crisis with a lawsuit, the Justice Department should urge the Clinton Administration to work with local and state governments to implement a plan for distributing medical marijuana that complies with both federal and state law and that puts the needs of patients first."[41]

Frank Jordan, former Mayor of San Francisco, California
"I have no problem whatsoever with the use of marijuana for medical purposes. I am sensitive and compassionate to people who have legitimate needs. We should bend the law and do what's right."[42]

Sue Bauman, Mayor of Madison, Wisconsin
The Drug War is "a failed strategy.... Do I think we should continue to build prisons and put people [who use drugs] in them? No way."[43]

Philip Owen, Mayor of Vancouver, British Columbia
"It is not if we will do it [decriminalize marijuana]; it is when will we do it."[44]

Juan Torruella, Chief Judge of the First Circuit US Court of Appeals
"Drug use, legal and illegal, is principally a health problem which is best dealt with not by driving it underground with prohibition tactics, but by having it out in the open to allow for treatment and education.... There is a need for pilot tests of some types of limited decriminalization, probably commencing with marijuana, and obviously not including minors."[45]

Donald P. Lay, US Court of Appeals Judge, Eighth Circuit
"Present policies breed further crime, dehumanize individuals and require gross expenditures of tax dollars needed for other purposes. With our nation facing both societal and fiscal crises of unrivaled proportions, we must move quickly and forcefully to overhaul the current system."[46]

John Curtin, US District Court Judge, New York
"In spite of throwing more men and millions of dollars into the fray, we finally concluded that negotiation was the only solution. The use of the word 'legalization' has been demonized, just like 'negotiation' was before Henry Kissinger met with the Viet Cong in Paris.... Education, counseling, less use of criminal sanctions, partial legalization, and legalization are all alternatives. It is a hard road, but the present course has failed."[47]

Nancy Gertner, US District Court Judge, Massachusetts
"By attempting to restrict the supply [of drugs], we have increased the profits and therefore created enormous incentives for people to continue this business no matter what.... [I]f the cocaine industry had commissioned a consultant to design a mechanism to insure profitability, it couldn't have done better than the war on drugs."[48]

John Kane, US District Court Judge, Colorado
"If the resources now spent on criminalization of drugs were devoted instead to education and treatment, the cost and dangers of drug use would be greatly reduced."[49]

Robert Sweet, US District Court Judge, New York
"Finally, the fundamental flaw, which will ultimately destroy this prohibition as it did the last one, is that criminal sanctions cannot, and should not attempt to, prohibit personal conduct which does no harm to others."[50]

James Jarvis, US District Court Judge, Tennessee
"It [the Drug War] is an exercise in futility."[51]

James P. Gray, Superior Court Judge, Orange County, California
"In short, the drug policy our government has pursued for decades has worked directly against the people of this country, and actually stregthens the things that it attempts to destroy. Most people agree that our War on Drugs is not working, but most people are simply not aware that we have viable options."[52]

Eugéne de Montgolfier, district attorney for Nice, France
"We no longer prosecute cannabis users because we are in tune with social evolution."[53]

Ray Kendall, Secretary General of Interpol
"[I am] entirely supportive of the notion of removing the abuse of drugs from the penal realm in favour of other forms of regulation such as psycho, medical, social treatment."[54]

Edward Ellison, former head of Scotland Yard's anti-drug unit, Britain
"I want all drugs legalized.... I say legalize drugs because I want to see less drug abuse, not more. And I say legalize drugs because I want to see the criminals put out of business."[55]

Joseph D. McNamara, former chief of police in San Jose, CA, and Kanasas City, MO
"We should immediately stop arresting people whose only crime is possessing small amounts of drugs for their own use."[56]

Kevin Morris, Chief Superintendent, president of the Superintendent's Association, Britain
"I would say there are far more important things which cause real harm to the community in the way that ecstasy does not cause real harm to the community."[57]

Francis Wilkinson, former chief of police in Gwent, Britain
"The only way to reduce the problem...is to supply heroin officially to users in a way that will minimise the leakage of those supplies."[58]

Andy Hayman, Deputy Assistant Commissioner of the Metropolitan Police, London, Britain
"If you've got someone for personal use [of ecstasy], one tablet, maybe two, with no other previous convictions...then rather than just push them through the criminal justice process—which could have negative effects on that individual—let's go about it in a different way." (The *Observer* reports: "One of Britain's most senior police officers reignited the debate over the policing of drugs last night when he revealed that first-time offenders caught with ecstasy are not being prosecuted, even though it is a Class A drug punishable by up to seven years in prison.")[59]

Brian Paddick, Metropolitan Police commander, London, Britain
"There are a whole range of people who buy drugs, not just cannabis, but even cocaine and ecstasy, who buy those drugs with money they have earned legitimately. They use a small amount of these drugs, a lot of them just at weekends. It has no adverse effect on the rest of the people they are with, either in terms of people they socialise with, or within the wider community, and they go back to work on Monday morning and are unaffected for the rest of the week. In terms of my priorities as an operational police officer, they are low down."[60]

"I WANT ALL DRUGS LEGALIZED."
—EDWARD ELLISON, FORMER HEAD OF SCOTLAND YARD'S ANTI-DRUG UNIT

Grant Obst, head of the Candian Police Association
"In real terms, the police in this country don't spend resources or time or energy focused on the individual who has one or two joints in his pocket."[61]

_OTHERS

Alejandro Gertz Manero, Public Safety Czar, Mexico. Former Mexico City Police Commissioner Manero has said he would like to see "a Holland-style drug policy" in Mexico.[62]

Ewart Brown, Transport Minister, Bermuda. Wants to see marijuana decriminalized.[63]

Carlos Holguin Sard, president of the National Conservative Board, Colombia. Wants to see the legalization of all drugs.[64]

Tom Campbell, US Congressman (Democrat - Michigan). Has suggested "experiments in supplying drugs to addicts the way Zurich, Switzerland, tried."[65]

Chris Davies, Member of European Parliament. British newswire Ananova reports: "[Davies] has called for a Royal Commission to be set up to examine the practicalities of licensing hard drugs and selling them over the counter."[66]

Jon Owen Jones, Member of Parliament, Britain. Favors the legalization of marijuana.[67]

Carlos Infanta, Congressman, Peru. Wants to see regulated legalization.[68]

Richard Posner, Chief Judge of the Seventh US Circuit Court of Appeals (1993-2000). Reagan-appointee who argued in favor of legalizing marijuana and psychedelics. He was the highest-ranking US judge ever to do so.[69]

Warren Eginton, US District Court Judge, Connecticut. Wants to see marijuana and cocaine legalized.[70]

James C. Paine, US District Court Judge, Florida. Thinks all drugs should be decriminalized and regulated.[71]

Julian Fantino, Chief of Police, Toronto, Ontario. Wants to decriminalize small amounts of pot.[72]

Canada: "Several Canadian police and health organizations, including the Canadian Association of Chiefs of Police, the Royal Canadian Mounted Police, the Canadian Medical Association and the Council of Churches, support relaxing the country's marijuana laws. In addition, 76 percent of Canadians agree that marijuana possession should not be a criminal offense."[73]

Britain: "Cannabis should be sold at licensed outlets such as pubs, cafes and shops, according to a confidential survey of police forces, courts, probation officers and drug care workers. Eighty-one per cent of the 300 groups surveyed said that a system of licensed distribution should be introduced as soon as possible."[74]

■ ■ ■ ■ ■ ■ ■ ■ ■ ■

Finally, we shouldn't forget the headline-grabbing letter sent to Kofi Annan as the UN's General Assembly commenced a special session on drugs in June 1998. Penned by the Lindesmith Center and signed by an international roster of luminaries, it declared: "We believe that the global war on drugs is now causing more harm than drug abuse itself.... Persisting in our current policies will only result in more drug abuse, more empowerment of drug markets and criminals, and more disease and suffering."

Among the political leaders putting their signatures on the letter were George Schultz, Willie Brown, Joycelyn Elders, Kurt Schmoke, several former members of Congress (including Senator Alan Cranston), two former US Attorneys General, a former Assistant Secretary of State, two federal judges, the mayor of San Jose,

California, a former police commissioner of New York City, a former Secretary General of the UN, 28 Spanish judges, past presidents of Bolivia, Guatemala, Colombia, Costa Rica, and Nicaragua, and current legislators from Australia, Britain, Canada, European Parliament, Mexico, Peru, and elsewhere.

Non-politicos who signed on include Kweisi Mfume of the NAACP, Walter Cronkite, Stephen Jay Gould, Andrew Weil, Isabel Allende, Günter Grass, a slew of professors at top-notch universities, several CEOs, various clergy, and around a dozen Nobel Laureates, including conservative economist Milton Friedman.[75]

> "CANNABIS SHOULD BE SOLD AT LICENSED OUTLETS SUCH AS PUBS, CAFES AND SHOPS, ACCORDING TO A CONFIDENTIAL SURVEY OF POLICE FORCES, COURTS, PROBATION OFFICERS AND DRUG CARE WORKERS."

Endnotes

1. Interview by Jan Wenner. *Rolling Stone*, 6 Oct 2000. Thus, this comment was made while Clinton was still the sitting President of the US. **2.** Address to Congress, 2 Aug 1977. **3.** *Unomasuno* (Mexico City), 17 March 2001. Trans. NarcoNews. **4.** *NRC* (The Netherlands), 19 Dec 2000. **5.** *El Observador* (Uruguayan), 1 Dec 2000. Tr. NarcoNews **6.** Wilson, James. "Colombia Calls For Drugs Summit." *Financial Times* 7 Sept 2001. **7.** Unsigned. "Jamaican PM Wants to Decriminalize Ganja." *Japan Today* 28 Aug 2001. **8.** *El País* (Madrid) 7 April 1997. **9.** *Globe and Mail*, 23 May 2001. **10.** Medellín, Octavio Gómez V. "Distant Positions Over Legalization of Narcotics." Tr. NarcoNews. *El Colombiano* 23 Aug 2001. **11.** Baum, Dan. *Smoke and Mirrors: The War on Drugs and the Politics of Failure*. New York: Little, Brown, 1996. Quoting Quayle from March 1977. **12.** *Wall Street Journal* 27 Oct 1990. **13.** Public Broadcasting System. *PBS Frontline: Drug Wars*. October 2000. **14.** Castañeda, Jorge. "How We Fight a Losing War." *Newsweek*, 6 Sept 1999 **15.** Loyola, Arturo. "Federal Police Chief Proposes Legalizing Drugs in Mexico to Solve the Narco-Trafficking Problem." Tr. NarcoNews. Notimex News Agency, 15 March 2001. **16.** *El Diario-La Prensa* 8 April 1994. **17.** Gardner, Dan. "Losing The War On Drugs, Part 2." *Ottawa Citizen* 6 Sept 2000. **18.** Lilley, Peter. "Cannabis Should be Legally Sold in Special Off-licences." *Daily Telegraph* (London) 6 July 2001. **19.** Bowcott, Owen. "Ex-envoy to Colombia Says Legalise Drugs." *Guardian* (London) 4 July 2001. **20.** Bowcott, Owen. "Ex-envoy to Colombia Says Legalise Drugs ." *Guardian* (London) 4 July 2001. **21.** Morris, Keith. "This War Is Unwinnable." *Guardian* (London) 4 July 2001. **22.** Transnational Radical Party's Anti-Prohibitionist Days, Brussels, 11 Dec 1997. **23.** Kennedy, Mark. "Rock 'Open' to Legal Marijuana." *Ottawa Citizen* 3 Aug 2001. **24.** "A Republic, If You Can Keep It," statement of Hon. Ron Paul, 2 Feb 2000. **25.** House of Lords, Select Committee on Science and Technology. "Therapeutic Uses of Cannabis." 14 March 2001. **26.** Joint Committee on the National Crime Authority (Australia), 1988. **27.** NORML. "Canadian Parliament Ponders Decriminalizing Marijuana." *Weekly News Bulletin* 8 Nov 2001. **28.** MacKinnon, Mark. "MPs Set To Debate Legalizing Marijuana." *Globe and Mail* (Toronto), 18 May 2001. **29.** "A Report of the National Commission on Ganja to Rt. Hon P.J. Patterson, Q.C., M.P. Prime Minister of Jamaica." Quoting Barry Chevannes, Chairman. 7 Aug 2001. **30.** Jackson, Derrick Z. "From New Mexico's Governor, Rare Candor On Drugs." *Boston Globe* 13 Oct 1999. **31.** Interview in *Playboy*, November 1999. **32.** Unsigned. "Legalization Of Pot For Medical Purposes Will Be Sought." Associated Press in *Honolulu Star-Bulletin* 15 May 2001. **33.** "'Drug Legalization Must be Supported'." Tr. NarcoNews. *El Universal* (Mexico City) 27 March 2001. **34.** Wilson, James. "Colombia Faces Strong Push To Legalise Drugs." *Financial Times* 2 Sept 2001 **35.** Roa, Élber Gutiérrez. "Governors Seek Legalization." Trans. NarcoNews. *El Espectador* 24 Aug 2001. **36.** Roa, Élber Gutiérrez. "Governors Seek Legalization." Trans. NarcoNews. *El Espectador* 24 Aug 2001. **37.** Wilson, James. "Colombia Faces Strong Push To Legalise Drugs." *Financial Times* 2 Sept 2001. **38.** Unsigned. "The Debate Over Drug Legalization Opens in Colombia." Tr. NarcoNews. Associated Press (in Spanish). 23 Aug 2001. **39.** Unsigned. "BC Senator Wants Drugs In Liquor Stores." *London Free Press* (Ontario, Canada) 8 Nov 2001. **40.** Schmoke, Kurt. "Decriminalizing Drugs: It Just Might Work—And Nothing Else Does." *Washington Post* 15 May 1988. **41.** Brown, Willie. "Don't Bar a Pain Killer OK'd by Voters." *Los Angeles Times* 8 April 1998. **42.** Paddock, Richard C. "Is Smoking Pot Good Medicine?" *Los Angeles Times* 26 Feb 1995. **43.** Callender, David. "Bauman Wants To End Drug War." *Capital Times* (Wisconsin) 18 July 2001. **44.** Lee, Jeff. "Decriminalize

Marijuana, Vancouver Mayor Says." *Vancouver Sun* 8 Nov 2001. **45.** Torruella, Juan. "One Judge's Attempt at a Rational Discussion of the So-called 'War on Drugs'." Spotlight Lecture at Colby College, Waterville Maine, 25 April 1996. **46.** Gray, Judge James. P. *Why Our Drug Laws Have Failed and What We Can Do About It: A Judicial Indictment of the War on Drugs*. Philadelphia: Temple University Press, 2001, referencing Lay, Judge Donald P. "Our Justice System, So-called." *New York Times*, 22 Oct 1990. **47.** "Federal Judge Concludes Drug Legalization Is the Way to Go." *Buffalo News* (New York) 2 March 1997. **48.** Gray, Judge James P. *Why Our Drug Laws Have Failed and What We Can Do About It: A Judicial Indictment of the War on Drugs*. Philadelphia: Temple University Press, 2001. **49.** Kane, John L., Jr. "Prisoner to Drugs." *Denver Post* 2 Nov 1997. **50.** Robert Sweet, *et. al.* "The War on Drugs is Lost." *National Review* 12 Feb 1996: 44. **51.** Ayo, Laura. "Judge Calls Drug War an 'Exercise In Futility'." *Knoxville News-Sentinel* 2 Sept 2001. **52.** Gray, Judge James P. *Why Our Drug Laws Have Failed and What We Can Do About It: A Judicial Indictment of the War on Drugs*. Philadelphia: Temple University Press, 2001. **53.** Smith, Sam. Progressive Review Undernews, 5 Oct 2001. **54.** "Drugs and Our Community: Report of the Premier's Advisory Council 1996." Victoria, Australia. **55.** Ellison, Edward. *Daily Mail* (London) 10 March 1998. **56.** McNamara, Joseph D. "Stop the War: A Former Police Chief's Plea to Clinton's New Drug Czar." *Washington Post* 19 May 1996. **57.** Unsigned. "Senior Officers Back 'Softer' Drug Laws." BBC News, 21 Nov 2001. **58.** White, Michael. "Legalise Heroin, Says Former Police Chief." *Guardian* (London) 7 Nov 2001. **59.** Ahmed, Kamal. "We Don't Prosecute Ecstasy Users—Police Chief." *Observer* (London) 25 Nov 2001. **60.** Travis, Alan. "Police Chief: Cocaine OK at Weekends." *Guardian* (London) 21 Nov 2001. **61.** Unsigned. "Pot Smokers No Longer a Police Target, Top Cop Says." Canadian Press in *Toronto Star*, 30 Aug 2001. **62.** Giordano, Al. "Fox Calls for Drug Legalization." Narco News, 20 March 2001. **63.** Regan, Nigel. "A 'Degree Of Decriminalization' Exists In Bermuda." *Bermuda Sun* 31 Aug 2001. **64.** Medellín, Octavio Gómez V. "Distant Positions Over Legalization of Narcotics." Tr. Narco News. *El Colombiano* 23 Aug 2001. **65.** Page, Clarence. "Nonviolent Drug Abusers Need Treatment, Not Jail." *Chicago Tribune*, reprinted in *The Blade* (Ohio) 9 Dec 2000. **66.** Unsigned. "Euro-MP Demands Study into Hard Drugs 'Over the Counter'." Ananova (UK) 23 Sept 2001. **67.** Morris, Nigel. "Former Minister Launches Attempt to Legalise Sale, Supply and Use of Cannabis." *Independent* (London) 18 July 2001 **68.** Unsigned. "Andean Parliament Opens Debate About Drug Legalization." Tr. NarcoNews. *El Tiempo* 18 Aug 2001. **69.** Herhold, Scott. "Posner Best Known for Melding Law, Economics." *San Jose Mercury News*, reprinted in SiliconValley.com, 20 Nov 1999. **70.** Mayko, Michael P. "Judge: Legalize 2 Drugs." *Bridgeport Post* (Connecticut) 8 Oct 1985. **71.** Paine, James C. Speech Before the Federal Bar Association. Miami, Florida, 8 Oct 1997. **72.** Unsigned. "Toronto Police Chief Calls for Softer Marijuana Penalties." Canadian Broadcasting Corporation, 10 Sept 2001. **73.** NORML. "Canadian Parliament Ponders Decriminalizing Marijuana." *Weekly News Bulletin*. 8 Nov 2001 **74.** Walsh, Nick Paton. "Police Say: Sell The Drug in Shops and Pubs." *Observer* (London) 11 Nov 2001. **75.** "Public Letter to Kofi Annan." 1 June 1998.

> "PERSISTING IN OUR CURRENT POLICIES WILL ONLY RESULT IN MORE DRUG ABUSE, MORE EMPOWERMENT OF DRUG MARKETS AND CRIMINALS, AND MORE DISEASE AND SUFFERING."
> —PUBLIC LETTER TO KOFI ANNAN

VOTESCAM 2000

JONATHAN VANKIN

The electoral insanity of the year 2000 confirmed something that I and a small number of people who have occasionally thought about these things over the past decade or so, had known for a while: Over the past three and a half decades, we in the United States have sold out our election process—which, unless I'm very much mistaken, is the foundation of our democracy (such as it is)—to a small but lucrative cadre of for-profit businesses and their wildly defective products, which they manufactured, in some cases, many years ago but which are still used to tally votes today.

The real scandal of this election is that most of the problems in the voting and vote-counting systems have been well-known for years, and no one has done a damn thing about them.

More than eleven years earlier, I wrote a detailed article titled "Vote of No Confidence" for the Silicon Valley weekly *Metro* (28 Sept 1989). In the article, I discussed how, "The next president of the United States may not be chosen by the voters. Instead, he may be the choice of whoever controls or manipulates the computer systems that tally the votes." The now famous "hanging chad" was but one small aspect of this story. (Until November 2000, I was one of the few citizens of the United States who had actually heard, much less uttered, the words "hanging chad.")

A deeper problem lay in the security and integrity of the software used to run the vote count. The software for most of the machines, I learned, was incomprehensible—what computer scientists described as "spaghetti code" and "a bucket of worms," prone to error and vulnerable to deliberate manipulation in a way that would be, for all purposes, undetectable. An ethically challenged software engineer could write a little program to make the count come out however he wanted it to, and no one would ever know. Even if a fraudulent program were detectable, someone would have to look at it to detect it. And that was impossible, because the private companies that owned the software considered the code a protected trade secret.

In fact, there are today two companies that dominate the industry. Election Systems & Software, whose machines count about 60 percent of the votes nationwide, and Sequoia

Pacific Voting Equipment of Jamestown, New York. In 1993, Sequoia Pacific won a $60 million contract from New York City to take the city into the electronic voting age—only to have the contract ditched in 2000.

No one is saying that those companies, or any of their much smaller would-be competitors, don't try their best—and certainly not that they're dishonest. The flaws are inherent to computerized voting systems. I found, eleven years before the 2000 election, that there was no particular reason to trust the outcome of any election in the United States anymore. At least not those counted by computer, which is most of them.

Since 1989 there has been no reason to update that opinion. Despite having authored that prescient article, filled with startling facts about the iffy nature of American elections, I have not, over the past decade, spent an undue amount of time waiting by the mailbox for my Pulitzer Prize. Why not? Because I was hardly the first person to make note of these facts. No less a source than the *New York Times* ran a series about the vulnerability of elections in 1985, by reporter David Burnham, who also wrote the book *The Rise of the Computer State*.

As early as 1974, the US General Accounting Office commissioned a study that found significant accuracy and security problems in the methods used to count votes by computer. In 1986, the California Attorney General's office released a report criticizing computerized vote-counting systems for "lacking a reliable audit trail and having a program structure that is very difficult even for computer professionals to understand." In 1988, the National Bureau of Standards (now called the National Institute of Standards and Technology) released a study by computer scientist Roy G. Saltman that concluded, in the typically understated language of government documents, that "it has been clearly shown that audit trails that document election results, as well as general practices to assure accuracy, integrity and security, can be considerably improved."

> AS EARLY AS 1974, THE US GENERAL ACCOUNTING OFFICE COMMISSIONED A STUDY THAT FOUND SIGNIFICANT ACCURACY AND SECURITY PROBLEMS IN THE METHODS USED TO COUNT VOTES BY COMPUTER.

Somewhat more bluntly, Computer Professionals for Social Responsibility followed up on Saltman's report in their fall 1988 newsletter, declaring: "America's fundamental democratic institution is ripe for abuse... It is ridiculous for our country to run such a haphazard, easily violated election system. If we are to retain confidence in our election results, we must institute adequate security procedures in computerized vote tallying, and return election control to the citizenry."

Also in 1988 (something of a watershed year for computer-voting exposes), the journalist Ronnie Dugger, founder of the *Texas Observer*, authored a staggeringly long and meticulously researched essay for *The New Yorker* (when *The New Yorker* was still publishing staggeringly long and meticulously researched essays) in which he singled out the "Vote-o-Matic" system in particular—still a popular computer voting system, and the very one used in those disputed Florida counties—as possibly "disenfranchising hundreds of thousands of voters."

Dugger explained how computer systems that tabulate elections are shot through with error and wide open to what, more recently, James Baker might call "mischief." I talked to Dugger back in 1989, when I was writing my own article. Freed from the genteel strictures of *New Yorker* house style, he told me, "The whole damn thing is mind-boggling. They could steal the presidency."

Computerized vote-counting is a terrible system. This is only news to those who haven't been paying attention. Every problem that arose in the 2000 election had been on the public record for more than a decade. Yet here we are. Why?

My first thought was that less-wealthy counties couldn't afford the latest technology. They're stuck with outdated systems like the Vote-o-Matic for reasons of pure economics. But David Lublin doesn't think so. He teaches in the American University School of Public Affairs' Department of Government, and is now on his second grant from the National Science Foundation to collect election data from around the country.

"I wouldn't say the wealthier places always have better or well-conducted elections," he says. "Often that is the case, but there are surprising exceptions. It depends on the willingness of the local county authority to spend the money, or the state to require them to do it."

Nor, for that matter, is increasingly sophisticated computer technology the answer. In fact, it may only make the problems even worse. For example, the next generation of voting computers are known as DREs ("Direct Recording Electronic"), kind of like ATMs that allow voters to cast ballot-free votes on a video monitor by pressing buttons, or even on a touch screen.

"DREs are even worse," says Rebecca Mercuri, a computer scientist at Bryn Mawr College who's studied computerized elections for more than ten years and recently finished her doctoral dissertation on that exact topic at the University of Pennsylvania. DREs leave no "audit trail" (paper trail) whatsoever, she points out. Votes are recorded directly onto a memory cartridge. There is absolutely nothing to ensure that the vote that registers on the screen is the vote that gets recorded on the cartridge, or that the vote that is recorded on the cartridge is the vote that prints out on paper.

"Unless the voter sees that paper trail, how do they know?" she says. "I could teach a 12-year-old to write a program that shows one thing on the screen and another thing on the printout."

While some newer election computing companies say they've figured out how to create a foolproof electronic audit trail, Mercuri dismisses such claims as "preposterous." There's no way to make sure that software is 100 percent pure. "If we could do that in computer science, we'd have the virus problem solved," she says.

Since computers were first used to count votes in the early 1960s, there have been dozens of instances of computer error in elections. And that's counting only the known errors. There have been no verified frauds, but that may be only because computer fraud is nearly impossible to verify. Former Florida Governor Kenneth "Buddy" MacKay suggested to Carl Bernstein (in an article on the website Voter.com) that computer fraud may have been behind his highly suspicious 1988 Senate loss to Connie Mack. MacKay lost by 33,000 votes out of four million. In a development that foreshadowed what happened in 2000, the TV networks "called" a MacKay victory, only to later tell their viewers: "Never mind."

Funny thing was, in four large counties—Miami-Dade, Broward, Palm Beach, and Hillsborough—200,000 fewer voters registered votes in the Senate race than in the presidential race. That's a 20 percent drop-off. In other counties, and in earlier elections, the drop-off was around 1 percent. Computer error or tampering remains the most likely explanation for the alarming discrepancy, though none was ever proved. MacKay tried to get a look at the source code for the vote-counting software but was rebuffed by the election equipment companies, who declared it proprietary.

"What could have happened in 1988," MacKay told Bernstein, "was that the machines could have been programmed so that in my big precincts every tenth vote got counted wrong."

Another "Sore Loserman," perhaps? Maybe—but MacKay was echoing what Peter Neumann, principal scientist at SRI International's Menlo Park, California, computer lab (and author of the 1995 book *Computer-Related Risks*), said back then. Writing about the MacKay-Mack election in *Risks Digest*, Neumann noted,

"Remembering that these computer systems reportedly permit operators to turn off the audit trails and to change arbitrary memory locations on the fly, it seems natural to wonder whether anything fishy went on."

Here are a few other amusing anecdotes from the annals of wacky election computing:

• In Middlesex County, New Jersey, also in the year 2000, a DRE vote-counting computer went on the fritz. It recorded votes for both the Republican and Democratic candidates in the county freeholder's race but simply wiped out all votes for their respective running mates.

• In the 1985 Dallas, Texas, mayor's race, Starke Taylor defeated Max Goldblatt in an election so controversial that it led the Texas legislature to investigate flaws in the state's computerized vote-tabulation process. Allegedly, according to the *Dallas Morning News*, a computer had been shut off and given "new instructions" after it showed Goldblatt leading by 400 votes.

• During the Democratic presidential primary of 1980, in Orange County, California, a "programmer's error" gave about 15,000 votes cast for Jimmy Carter and Ted Kennedy to Jerry Brown—and, of all people, Lyndon LaRouche.

There are many more such tales. Computers in Oklahoma skipped 10 percent of the ballots in a 1986 election. A power surge in San Francisco switched votes from one candidate to another. A Moline, Illinois, city alderman actually took office in 1985 only to step down three months later when someone figured out that a machine had misread hundreds of ballots due to a bad "timing belt."

A MOLINE, ILLINOIS, CITY ALDERMAN ACTUALLY TOOK OFFICE IN 1985 ONLY TO STEP DOWN THREE MONTHS LATER WHEN SOMEONE FIGURED OUT THAT A MACHINE HAD MISREAD HUNDREDS OF BALLOTS DUE TO A BAD "TIMING BELT."

You get the picture. The Dallas case prompted the Texas Secretary of State to direct that, in future elections, a "manual recount" could be ordered to "ensure the accuracy of the count." The actual ballots, the computer punch cards themselves, are the only existing "audit trail" to document how people actually voted.

With all of these well-documented facts, it seemed to me that the idea set forth by the Bush contingent, that machine counts are better than human counts, is patently absurd. So I called up Bob Swartz, founder of Pennsylvania-based Cardamation, one of the nation's largest makers and sellers of computer punch cards and card-reading machines. (Not many companies are in that field anymore.) Swartz has been in the punch-card business for 40 years, though he doesn't do elections anymore. I thought that made him a good person to ask.

Turns out, in his line of work, looking at computer cards with your own eyes is standard procedure. "We didn't call it a 'hand count.' We just called it 'looking at the cards,'" he says. "We read the cards through the machine twice, and if there are differences we look at the cards. If our goal is to get 100 percent accuracy, there's no question that's the way to achieve it."

Swartz fully expects card-reading machines to make mistakes. It's when they do not make mistakes that he gets suspicious. "If you recount 400,000 votes and there's no difference," he says, "someone fudged the figures."

No election system can ever be fraud-proof or error-free. That doesn't mean we shouldn't try to improve on the dismal systems we're using today. It just seems that casting votes on paper ballots, then counting and recounting them by hand, is the surest way to figure out who really won an election. Assuming mostly honest personnel, and barring breathtaking acts of ineptitude, human vote-counters will not, generally speaking, discard ballots by the thousands on a mere whim. Nor will they, unless they are severely reading-deficient or insane, record votes cast for one candidate as votes cast for another candidate.

Further, it is much more conspicuous for a dishonest election official to issue new instructions to a group of human beings midway through a counting session than it is for a dishonest computer programmer to type a few new lines of code into a machine. Perhaps most important, there is nothing "proprietary" about a person picking up pieces of paper and going, "One for this guy, one for that guy."

If Americans, or at least the television networks Americans like to watch, weren't so damned impatient, conducting elections completely on paper ballots would be the most sensible solution. Non-computerized elections take a lot longer to produce results, there's no denying that. But we don't hold elections all that often in this country. We wait four years to vote for president. We can't wait another week or two to find out who won?

If the tortuous election of 2000 taught us anything, it's that we can indeed wait it out for a while without untoward consequences. To quote the instant cliché uttered *ad infinitum* by the pundits: "There are no tanks in the streets." I guess it's a little unsettling when "there are no tanks in the streets" is the most reassuring bromide they can come up with. But the fact is, nothing really terrible happened between the inconclusive evening of November 7, 2000, and the election's conclusion at the hands of the Supreme Court five weeks later.

If America returned to the paper ballot system, fraud and error in elections definitely would not end. They would, however, be much easier to detect and correct. Elections would be run by people, not corporations. There are enough vested interests trying to influence every election. Why do we need the extraneous interest of profit-making companies?

_POSTSCRIPT

On November 12, 2001—more than a full year after the disputed presidential election that ended with a Supreme Court decision placing George W. Bush in the White House—the National Opinion Research Center released results from the most extensive recount of Florida ballots yet conducted. The NORC project was carried out at the behest of, and paid for by, a consortium of major media organizations that included the *New York Times*, CNN, the *Wall Street Journal*, the *Washington Post*, and a number of other, less prominent news outlets.

Even before the results were announced, representatives of the media consortium declared that the purpose of their recount project was not to determine a "real winner" of the 2000 election but simply to compile a database of disputed ballots. That was probably wise, because the results of the recount....

Well, the best that can be said is that the NORC count proved that Bush won the election, unless Gore did. Or vice versa.

The NORC did establish one fact definitively: Computerized voting is even more flawed than it looked to be before. The NORC reported its results based on nine different "standards." As it turned out, Al Gore would have been the winner under six of the nine standards, with Bush winning under the other three. That looks like a pretty good score for Gore. But really, it proves nothing. Except that the entire process is hopelessly confusing and subjective. None of the standards produced a difference of more than 493 votes (in that case, for Bush) and went as low as 42 votes (for Gore).

There is one other conclusion I would draw from the NORC investigation. The universal principle "simplify everything" applies nowhere as much as in elections. It was not only the elderly voters of Palm Beach County who were befuddled by "butterfly ballots." The NORC showed that voting precincts with the highest error rates were actually dominated by younger voters, not the old folks who provided talkshow callers with so many chuckles. Most mistakes turned up in counties where the ballot split the ten presidential candidates between two pages. In Duvall County (which includes the city of Jacksonville) ballot instructions told voters to "vote all pages" even though presidential candidates were on two pages of the ballot. Not surprisingly, almost 22,000 voters cast more than one presidential vote, thus invalidating their ballots.

After poring over the NORC results, I ended up with the same thought that I had a year earlier. Computers have no place in the voting process. While no voting system is foolproof, plain old paper and pen still provide the clearest, simplest means of casting and counting votes.

WELL, THE BEST THAT CAN BE SAID IS THAT THE NORC COUNT PROVED THAT BUSH WON THE ELECTION, UNLESS GORE DID. OR VICE VERSA.

UNTOUCHABLES IN THE TWENTY-FIRST CENTURY
THE PLIGHT OF DALITS IN INDIA
DR. K. JAMANADAS

It has been my experience that it is difficult to explain to my Irish and British friends what Untouchability is. These friends, brought up under egalitarian Christianity, cannot comprehend that there could be people who are not allowed to touch others, people whose touch pollutes. They were more surprised that there are some whose sight or approach also pollutes, the Unseeables and Unapproachables. There are some tribals (Adivasis) who live in forests and hills, most of whom have not even seen a railway train. Today the Untouchables, Unseeables, and Unapproachables come under the general term of "Dalit," and together they form about a quarter of India's population of one billion.

But my friends knew about slavery, both in ancient Rome and antebellum America. Millions of slaves in ancient Rome were treated with the greatest cruelty, beaten, and sent to prison, had to work in fetters, and were branded. English society also had its servile classes. In America, Africans suffered great miseries during their capture, travel, and toil. What is of importance is that these unfree, unprivileged classes have disappeared as a separate class and have become part and parcel of the greater society. The question is: Why has Untouchability not disappeared?

Contrary to claims by some, slavery is a very ancient institution of the Hindus. It is recognized by Manu, and the other *Smriti* writers. It applied to both the touchables, as well as the Untouchables, and continued throughout all history till the year 1843, when it was abolished by the British government. But slavery is different than Untouchability, and less cruel. Some Untouchables hid their caste in order to become slaves; those who were discovered were punished during Peshava rule.

Legally defined either as a piece of property or as one who is not a person, *de jure*, it might appear that the slave was worse off than the Untouchable. But, *de facto*, the condition of slaves was better than Untouchables.

Unlike a Dalit, slaves did not have to worry about availability of work. Slaves got their bread, clothes, and shelter whether it was boom or depression. The slave was property, and being valuable, the master took great care of the health of the slave. In Rome, the slaves were never employed on marshy and malarial land. Untouchability carries no security as to livelihood. None of the Hindus is responsible for the feeding, housing, clothing, or health of a Dalit.

Roman religion was never hostile to slaves. It did not close the temple doors against them; it did not banish them from its festivals. The slave informally formed a part of the family, and was considered under the protection of the same gods. The law insisted that a slave's grave be regarded as sacred. Roman mythology provided no different heaven or hell for slaves. However, inequality is the official doctrine of the Hindu religion. Every Hindu must observe caste, including Untouchability, throughout his daily life, as long as he lives. This is not mere tradition or custom; it is religion.

SOME UNTOUCHABLES HID THEIR CASTE IN ORDER TO BECOME SLAVES; THOSE WHO WERE DISCOVERED WERE PUNISHED DURING PESHAVA RULE.

A person was "permitted" to hold another as his slave. There was no compulsion on him if he didn't want to. A Hindu, on the other hand, is "enjoined" to hold another as Untouchable. There is compulsion on the Hindu which he cannot escape not matter what his personal wishes in the matter may be.

There is no freedom from Untouchability, no way to buy freedom or to be set free.

The cruelties and atrocities practiced by the Hindus against the Untouchables were more cruel than those practiced by the Americans upon their slaves. They are not known to the world, unlike the African slaves' plight, because there is no Hindu who will not do his best to conceal truth in order to hide his shame. These are not matters of the distant past. That is why we have recently seen how hard the Upper Caste (UC) Indian government tried to keep the discriminations of caste away from the World Conference Against Racism, held in September 2001 in Durban, South Africa.

_THE HISTORY OF UNTOUCHABILITY

Recently, Brahmanic scholars tried to blame Muslims for the start of

Untouchability. This is false and mischievous. As a matter of fact, Untouchability existed before Islam came to India. The real cause of Untouchability, as proved by Dr. Ambedkar, lies in the hatred and contempt of Buddhists felt by the Brahmins, the leaders of the Hindus. Therefore, we have to peep through the pages of history to find instances of persecutions of Buddhists.[1]

The persecution really started with the counterrevolution against Buddhism by Pushyamitra Shunga, around 185 BC. He had ordered the genocide of Buddhists and offered a hundred *dinars* for the head of a *Bhikku* (i.e, a monk). There was religious persecution by Nara, a Kashmir ruler of the first century BC and by the Huna ruler Mihirkula (510-530 AD). The persecution by Gauda King Sashanka (seventh century AD) is well known: He uprooted the *Bodhi* tree (under which Buddha achieved enlightenment), destroyed footprints of the Buddha, and killed thousands of *Bhikkus*. After Harshavardhana, in the seventh century, the Rajput Age was the darkest period in the history of India, for Buddhist persecution was at its peak. Untouchability had started as a religious persecution.

When the Muslims came, they annihilated the Buddhist external symbols, such as idols and monasteries, and gave a final blow to Buddhism, causing its fall. But the Buddhist population, which by this time had become Untouchables, found great relief from Brahmanic hostility by converting to Islam.

There remained a large population among the "Untouchable" Buddhists who did not get converted to Islam, and they now had to face double persecution. On one hand, they were already under Brahmanic oppression, and on the other, the Muslims considered all the non-Muslims as "Hindus," so they tortured the Dalits.

Medieval Saints. During 800 years of Muslim rule, till the British came, there was no relief to those Dalits who did not convert to Islam. Even the movement of non-Brahmin saints did not remove their inequalities during the medieval period, because these saints preached equality "in the eyes of god," not necessarily in the eyes of man, and thus they remained indifferent to the practice of Untouchability.

Kindhearted Brahmin Saint Eknath touched Untouchable children, not because he disliked Untouchability but because he believed that a bath could wash away the sin from this type of touch. Even then, Eknatha's sons severed all relations with their father. Brahmin Saint Ramdas has averred that even a corrupt Brahmin is greatest among three worlds, and an Untouchable, though learned and wise, is of no use.

Shivaji's Rule. The rule of Shivaji (1630-1680) was egalitarian, treating all on equal footing, neither anti-Muslim nor pro-Brahmin. The Untouchables were given a place in his army. He was not a "*go brahman pratipalak*" (protector of cows and Brahmins), contrary to Brahmanic propaganda.

One of Shivaji's wives was an Untouchable, and this Untouchable wife was given due respect at the time of his coronation, says Keluskar in his "Shiv Charitra." Sharad Patil has proved this.[2]

Condition of Dalits During the Peshava Rule. Peshava rule was a Brahmanic rule: The Dalits could not enter town when shadows were long, i.e. in morning and evening, as the shadow of a Dalit was polluting. Dalits had to tie to their waists a small earthen pot as a spittoon and a branch of a thorny tree to wipe the ground, so that their spit and footmarks didn't pollute others. Brahmins always ensured that everyone followed their caste rules, and any transgression was severely punished.

> DALITS HAD TO TIE TO THEIR WAISTS A SMALL EARTHEN POT AS A SPITTOON AND A BRANCH OF A THORNY TREE TO WIPE THE GROUND, SO THAT THEIR SPIT AND FOOTMARKS DIDN'T POLLUTE OTHERS.

The practice of slavery was different during Peshava rule. Usually the Untouchables were not even allowed to be slaves. Those who were wrongly appointed as slaves, if detected later, were punished. In 1795, when a woman of the Untouchable subcaste Chambhar tried to become a domestic maid servant, the whole family had to be purified by *prayaschita* (punishment). S.R. Tikkekar explains: "The slaves were clothed and fed, some times much better than the free man of their standing and were allowed to possess property."[3]

When a Mahar (another subcaste of Untouchability) tried to buy and sell fish, which was prohibited by royal order, he was admonished and threatened with the death penalty if the offense was repeated, says a note in *Peshava Rojnishi*.[4]

Dalits were buried alive in foundations of forts and public buildings and sacrificed during the digging of wells, during medieval times, to bring good fortune to the completion of the work.

During India's Struggle for Independence. The famous Sepoy Mutiny against the British in 1857, which Brahmin scholars arrogantly glorify as "the first war of independence," was in fact for the liberation of Brahmins. All the leaders—including Tatya Tope, Laxmibai, and Nanasaheb—were Brahmins, and even the soldier Mangal Pande, who fired the first shot, was a Brahmin. In fact, the cause of the mutiny was caste: In the British army, soldiers from high and low castes had to intermingle, even dining together, which Brahmins felt was degrading.

Mahatma Jotirao Phule. Phule was the first to struggle for the upliftment of Untouchables, starting the first school for Dalit girls in 1848.

Periyar Ramasami Naikkar. Naikkar started the Self Respect Movement in South India for the upliftment of non-Brahmins, and he led the *Vaicom satyagraha*, which pushed for allowing Dalits to walk over a particular street near a Hindu temple.

Gandhi and Dalits. It is incorrect to say that Gandhi was a friend of Dalits, who consider him their number-one enemy. He deprived Dalits of the political rights given by Communal Award by the British. To protest the separate electorates granted to Untouchables, he "fasted till death," and to save his life, Dr. Ambedkar, the real savior of Dalits, had to sign the Poona Pact, which did not include a provision for Dalit electorates. A Jain philosopher said about the glass of orange juice given to Gandhi to break his fast: "But this orange juice, this one glass of orange juice, contains millions of people's blood." Gandhi gave Dalits a new name, *Harijan*, which literally means "sons of god," but traditionally was applied by a Gujarati medieval saint to children of temple prostitutes. Gandhi once advised a Dalit graduate to scavenge in a better way, rather than take up a white-collar job.

After Independence. As Dale Carnegie has said, "Nobody kicks a dead dog." Only those Dalits who struggle for their rights are targeted. The murders, rapes, and arsons are matters of everyday life.

Dr. Babasaheb Ambedkar—the human rights champion and the main architect of India's Constitution—remarked that no Untouchables are engaged in intellectual occupations, such as rhetoricians, grammarians, philosophers, tutors, doctors, and artists. None is engaged in trade, commerce, or industry.

There is still a "two glass" system in town restaurants; Dalits are not allowed in temples; Dalit students are not allowed to sit with others; Dalits have to get down from a bicycle after seeing a UC (Upper Caste) person. It is only recently that Dalit women in South India started using clothes to cover their breasts if a UC person was approaching. Even now there are killings if a Dalit bridegroom rides a mare. Even now there is bonded labor. Even now Dalit girls are forced into religious temple prostitution. Even now there are starvation deaths.

_ATROCITIES AGAINST DALITS

If one wishes to make a list of only the reported and documented atrocities (the majority of them are not reported to authorities, and all those reported are not registered), the list would run into volumes bigger than the *Encyclopedia Britannica*. Hence, it is futile to make such an attempt. It is not necessary to list all the gory instances to understand the plight of these hapless people. Suffice it to mention a few representative instances from different times and different regions, their different immediate reasons, and the different forms such atrocities can take.

Kambalapalli Carnage in Karnataka.[5] Kolar is a district headquarters of Karnataka State, with three out of twelve Assembly seats, and one out of two Parliament seats, reserved for Dalits. Kolar has the highest population of Dalits and Scheduled Tribes (the official name for Adivasis, indigenous peoples)—around 30 percent, mostly landless agricultural laborers, most being bonded laborers, working under the feudal landlords of the Vokkaliga (a middle caste who now consider themselves a UC).

The Vokkaligas could not tolerate the passing with distinction of a Dalit boy in Kolar College, so they murdered him. As usual, in the murder case all the accused were acquitted, with political pressure, for want of evidence.

Then there was a gang rape and murder of a Dalit girl, Chinnamma, by Vokkaligas in a nearby village. The dead body—with injuries on the face, breasts, and genitals—was thrown into a well. The Dalits agitated, got the body exhumed, and a postmortem was conducted. But the accused was not convicted for want of evidence. In 1975, a

> A DALIT WAS HACKED TO DEATH, 50 PEOPLE WERE INJURED, AND 50 HUTS TORCHED.

Dalit woman, Nagamma, was gang-raped by about six men (one Brahmin and five Vokkaligas) in the presence of her husband. In this case, too, there was no conviction.

In 1978, there was an armed attack on a Dalit colony by about 200 Vokkaligas, who set houses on fire. One Dalit was stabbed to death, and 30 to 35 Dalits sustained injuries. The police could not control the situation, and the chief of police sustained grievous injuries. The case ended in the acquittal of the accused.

In 1979, one OBC (Other Backward Castes) was brutally murdered by a Taluk Board President and other Vokkaligas because he opposed the Vokkaligas trying to snatch away his piece of land. They also raped his daughter. The police did not arrest all the accused because of political clout.

The Marathwada Caste War. A very destructive caste war was started after the Maharashtra government passed a resolution to rename Marathwada University after Dr. Ambedkar, as the Dalits wished. A fortnight of violence changed the face of Marathwada. It is reported:

> The violence against Dalits was unprecedented. The attackers were from upper, middle and even lower castes. They belonged to all strata of the peasantry: the rich, the middle and the poor. The attacks were well planned, and well organized....

> They set fire to huts and pucca houses, and destroyed

the Mahars' flour shops, sewing machines, bicycles, bullock carts, food grains, utensils etc. etc. They damaged the standing crops with a vengeance. They broke into pieces the photographs of Dr. Ambedkar and Buddha.... "This would be a lesson for lifetime."—the attackers warned.[6]

Atrocities were highest in Nanded District, affecting 780 families from 55 villages. Two ghastly incidents were reported. In August 1978, in Sugaon village, the Dalits' colony was attacked by a mob of 1,500 with weapons. A Dalit was hacked to death, 50 people were injured, and 50 huts torched. In a second incident, Kochiram Kamble, a Mang by caste, was chased by 150 people for five kilometers, stabbed with a *barchi* (spear), and while he was groaning with pain, was burnt alive. Why? Because he was supporting Neo-Buddhists.

Madhukar Taksande wrote that only Buddhists were victims of the attack, because only they are conscious and living with self-confidence and dignity. Due to Ambedkar's inspiration, they have abandoned their dependent ways of living and are fighting for their rights. Atrocities were not committed on the subcastes Mang, Dhor, or Chambhar, because they believe in Hinduism and its traditions of inequality. Those from above who helped or cooperated with Buddhists were also subjected to atrocities.

Pucca houses of Dalits were demolished or burnt. In Eklara village alone, 81 concrete houses, some double-storied, were razed to the ground. In Parbhani district, 1,400 families from 124 villages suffered, and 508 houses and 557 huts were destroyed. In Osmanabad district, Bhurewar—a police sub-inspector sent to maintain law and order—was cornered by the mob. When he jumped into a well to escape, he was pulled out and burnt alive.

The slogans of attackers were:

1. Why do you want to wear clothes better than ours?
2. Why do you want brick houses?
3. Why do you want metal pots and pans?
4. Why do you want to keep cattle?
5. Why do you send your boys and girls to schools and colleges?
6. Why do you want electric lamps in your rooms?
7. Why do you hang these pictures of Ambedkar and Buddha?

They ordained that Dalits must live like their forefathers did, scavenging the streets, collecting dung and excreta.

The Notorious Billandla Halli Incident. Dalits in Billandla Halli village wanted to start a village unit of DSS, the Dalits' rights organization. State DSS leader N. Shivanna and others were invited. On the day of inauguration in 1997, the police asked N. Shivanna to cancel the program for fear of violence, which he did. The police went to the village to prevent any untoward incident. Thinking that N. Shivanna

and other leaders of DSS would come to attend the function under police protection, the Vokkaligas had created road blocks with stones and boulders.

WHY DO YOU WANT BRICK HOUSES? WHY DO YOU WANT METAL POTS AND PANS?

Sudhakarreddy, a Vokkaliga Yuva Vedike activist who was sitting in a tree with a loaded gun to shoot DSS leaders, fired at police who started removing the road blocks, killing one constable. In the return of fire by the police, Sudhakarreddy was killed. Vokkaligas hiding behind the bushes to attack Dalits instead attacked the police, killing one constable on the spot. Another was chased into a school and murdered. Only the non-Vokkaliga police constables were killed.

The Belchi Massacre. Caste wars in Bihar have their own peculiarities and are fought on a regular basis. The population is mostly rural, and the oppressors have organized themselves into private armies, heavily armed with guns. The attacks and counterattacks are a regular feature of Bihar life, with casualties on both sides. Like other areas, the culprits used to be higher castes, but nowadays it is the middle castes who have grown rich and commit atrocities. We will mention only one incident, which got into the limelight because Indira Gandhi visited the scene on an elephant, as other modes of transport could not reach it. In what is known as the Belchi Massacre, in May 1977, eight Dalits were burnt alive by rich Kurmi landlords.

Ghatkopar Carnage. After the conversion to Buddhism, the Neo-Buddhists erected statues of Dr. Ambedkar and the Buddha in practically all Dalit localities. The desecration and dismantling of these is one of the main techniques the UCs use to start atrocities, riots, and massacres against Dalits. Such incidents have taken place all over Maharashtra, but the incident at Bombay in Ghatkopar on July 11, 1997, broke the tolerance of Dalits. Ambedkar's statue was founded garlanded by sandals and *chappals* (a type of footwear). A mob of Dalit protesters assembled and demonstrated. Police sub-inspector Kadam, without any warning, ordered police to open fire. Thirty-two were injured, and ten people died (eight of the dead were below 22 years of age; one of them was a 14-year-old who was sitting over a gutter to answer the call of nature).

The report of the Indian Peoples Human Rights Commission, by Justices Dawood and Suresh, declared that there had been no riots or unlawful assembly near the statue. It held Kadam responsible for the bloodbath.

Consequently, there was *bundh* (a general strike) all over Maharashtra and in some parts of Gujarat. Questions were raised in Parliament. Demonstrations were held all over India. On March 12, two were killed and eight injured in Nagpur. Police beat protestors with wooden clubs in Kamptee, and there was violence in Akola, Amravati, Yevatmal, Buldhana, and the suburbs of Bombay. One person was killed in Kurla, 100 people were arrested in Nasik, and three were injured by police at Kamptee. An artist, Vilas Ghogre in Mulund, committed suicide as a protest. *Bundh* was observed all over the state. In Amravati, 72 houses of Dalits were burnt. Two Dalit higher Officers resigned in protest.

During a protest in Karanja Ghatge in Vidarbha, on July 14, 1997, local leaders of Hindutva forces targeted Ramatai, a junior female Dalit worker in Khadi Office. She wore clean clothes, a fact intolerable to UCs, so she was dragged by her hair from the office to the street, where she was beaten. Shouting slogans that the *maharin* has gone arrogant, Ramatai's attackers paraded her naked through the streets after a crowd had torn off her clothes.[7]

Gang rape and Murder in Lucknow. On July 9, 1999, the *New Indian Express* reported: "A 42-year-old Dalit woman was gang-raped by nearly 14 people, of a Yadav family, and then burnt alive in full public view yesterday. Her 'crime': her son eloped with the daughter of one of the culprits.... Police have still not arrested the culprits at Kabraha village under Chaubeypur police station of Kanpur. Three policemen, including the station incharge, have been suspended for 'abetting' the offenders."[8]

_SOME RECENT HEADLINES

Some illustrative cases from more recent times are reproduced below. It makes for gory reading, but demonstrates the causes, the "crimes" committed by Dalits, and the "punishments" given by upper castes throughout the length and breadth of the country.

These are some of the crimes committed on Dalits from March to September 2000, reported primarily in national daily newspapers and archived at <www.ambedkar.org>. Hundreds of such crimes go unreported.

Lucknow, March 17: "Days ahead of Bill Clinton's visit to Agra, a Dalit woman was stripped and beaten to death by two men in broad daylight even as villagers stood by helplessly and watched the gory spectacle to its tragic end. Twenty-three-year-old Sukhviri Devi of Nagla village in Agra district made the mistake of crossing the path of Virendra Pal and Vijay Pal, carrying an empty matka [i.e., a pot for carrying water]. The price she paid for it was death."[9]

Cuddapah, April 19: "Upper caste landlords have attacked dalits and set ablaze 30 houses belonging to the latter, near Rajupalem in B. Kodur mandal. A dalit, Penchalaiah, sustained injuries when he was attacked with an axe. Forty goats perished in the fire and all the belongings of the dalits were gutted.... The dalits of Rajupalem vil-lage and a farmer, O. Venkatarami Reddy, were engaged in a land dispute for some time and the issue is pending in court, according to the B. Kodur Sub-inspector, Mr. Ramana." No one was arrested.[10]

Patna, April 26: "According to information reaching the state headquarters, a strong contingent of armed upper caste Rajputs attacked the Dalit village, pulled out seven male members and shot them. Four of them died on the spot while three others are struggling for life in the hospital. Later the armed men set fire to a dozen huts, which later spread in the entire village and gutted almost all the houses rendering at least 25 families homeless."[11]

Uttar Pradesh, May 2: "The scene at the wheat fields along the national highway in Basai village was gory on May 2 morning. Villagers going for work saw five bodies soaked in blood. Vijay Singh, Jaipal Singh, Satbir Singh and Sugreev, all Dalits of the village were dead, but another Dalit, Santhosh was still hanging on to life, though his neck had a deep gash. He was rushed to hospital. The five men had gone to the neighbouring Alai village for work on May 1. 'It looks like they were tortured before they were killed,' said Nihal Singh, an elderly villager, pointing to the marks on the bodies. When a police constable's cap was found under Vijay Singh's body, all hell broke loose. To make things worse, a group of policemen turned up and began lathicharging the crowd [i.e., beating them with wooden clubs]. They did not let the relatives take the bodies for funeral. When the villagers refused to move, the police opened fire killing one person. Varsha, Jaipal's wife, broke her arm in the melee. Even the pregnant wife of Sugreev was not spared. 'We were kicked on the abdomen and pulled by the hair and we fell unconscious,' said Varsha."[12]

Lucknow, May 8: "Angry at his daughter eloping with a Dalit, a police sub-inspector avenged the humiliation by killing four of the latter's family.... The family had just settled down when Ramnath along with his two sons Ankit Singh and Pradeep Singh, armed with firearms, barged into the house and started firing. Rustam and his son Rakesh died on the spot. His brother-in-law Puttulal and cousin Vijaypal died in the hospital while two others are battling for life."[13]

Faridkot, May 31: "A married, Dalit woman was gang-raped and paraded naked in the village Tharajwala of Muktsar district because of her brother's alleged involvement with a girl of the village."[14]

Ahmedabad, June 7: "Tension mounted at Bhilwada in Amraiwadi area on Wednesday evening, after a 19-year-old youth of dalit community was murdered in broad daylight by four members of the upper caste."[15]

Betul, June 9: "'What could I have done?' asks Madani (not her real name), a woman panch of Boregaon village in Betul district of Madhya Pradesh. Raped repeatedly by a young member of the village's afflu-

"A 42-YEAR-OLD DALIT WOMAN WAS GANG-RAPED BY NEARLY 14 PEOPLE, OF A YADAV FAMILY, AND THEN BURNT ALIVE IN FULL PUBLIC VIEW YESTERDAY."

ent OBC caste of Kunabis last week, she found harsher punishment waiting for her when she returned to her village and lodged a complaint against the rapist. With her hands tied behind her back and a garland of shoes strung around her neck, Madani was stripped and paraded through the streets of her village by the members of her own community for 'getting herself raped' and bringing a stigma on the family."[16]

Chennai, June 24: The National Public Hearing on Dalit Human Rights in Chennai gave many lower caste individuals a chance to tell their stories. "The emaciated old man recalled in broken sentences the gruesome details of the recent carnage in Kambalapalli village in Kolar district, Karnataka. His wife, daughter and two sons were burnt alive, along with three others, when members of the Reddy community set fire to three huts belonging to Dalit families. His eldest son, the first graduate from the village, was murdered two years ago, also by caste Hindus. With folded hands, he pleaded that protection be given to his daughter-in-law and two grandchildren, the only other survivors in his family."[17]

Karnataka, June 25: "You can tell the 'servants of God' from the other Dalit women outside the Hindu temple in Manvi, a village in northern Karnataka, by their jewelry. They're wearing red beaded necklaces with silver and gold medallions. The necklaces symbolize the bondage that defines devadasis girls from the lowest caste whose parents have given them to local goddesses or temples as human 'offerings.' Married to God before puberty, the devadasis, many of whom live in the temples, become sexual servants to the villages' upper-caste men after their first menstrual period. In some villages, devadasis are kept as concubines by the men who bought them. In others they are public chattel, who can be used by men free of charge. 'Only in this aspect do Untouchables suddenly become touchable,' says Sister Bridget Pailey, a nun who does social work among devadasis in Karnataka. 'The upper castes wouldn't drink from the same glass as a devadasi but they make use of her body.'"[18]

"MARRIED TO GOD BEFORE PUBERTY, THE DEVADASIS, MANY OF WHOM LIVE IN THE TEMPLES, BECOME SEXUAL SERVANTS TO THE VILLAGES' UPPER-CASTE MEN AFTER THEIR FIRST MENSTRUAL PERIOD."

Dehli, June 25: "On paper, the people in the slum on Delhi's Lodi Road don't even exist. The Dalits, or literally 'broken people,' as members of India's Untouchable castes are now called, don't show up on electoral rolls, ration cards or water bills. Huddled in the shadow of India's Housing and Urban Development Corporation, the slum huts are made of mud, cardboard and plastic bags. Kids play with pigs in the mud; mothers wash clothes in sewer water. These Kabariwallahs, or scavengers, sort through garbage or haul human sewage to earn a few rupees."[19]

Roorke, July 1: "A 40-year-old man allegedly 'sacrificed' a four-year-old [Dalit] girl on Monday in Miragpur village, 30 km from Roorke. Only the head of the victim has been recovered so far."[20]

Kerala, July 2: "The shocking revelations of sexual exploitation of some inmates of the Government-run Agali Tribal Girls Hostel in the tribal heartland of Attappady in Palakkad district resulting in a few of them becoming pregnant has rocked Kerala, the most literate State.... The girl who delivered a child last month in her complaint to the police said that five other girls of her hostel were exploited sexually by outsiders with the help of some of those who were in-charge of running the hostel. These girls were taken out of the hostel to a nearby theatre for late night show and there they were allegedly handed over to the sex racketeers.... The political interference, official apathy and the helplessness of the tribals helped the culprits to go scot free despite their involvement in the gruesome incidents of exploitation of the minor girls sexually."[21]

Patna, July 10: "Embarassed by the charges of torture of two Dalits by Minister of State for Cooperatives Lalit Yadav, Chief Minister Rabri Devi on Monday promptly sacked him.... Mr Yadav has been charged with torturing and confining a truck driver Deenanath Baitha and cleaner Karoo Ram in the outhouse of his official residence here for over a month.... According to reports, the Minister and his cousin, Surendra Yadav, also removed the nails of the driver and made him drink urine."[22]

Hyderabad, July 28: "In a gruesome incident, five Dalits were hacked to death at Surampalli village under Tekmal police limits of Medak district, some 100 km from here, on Thursday night.... [A] minor tiff between Ravinder and his neighbour Pochaiah over sharing water for agricultural lands prompted the murders."[23]

Eastern Uttar Pradesh, August 1: An 18-year-old Dalit woman was abducted by a dozen members of a high caste, who tortured her and set her on fire in front of their entire village. Police ruled her death a suicide.[24]

Bareilly, August 4: "A teenaged Dalit boy was allegedly beaten to death by the President of the locality of Fateh Ganj for plucking some flowers from his garden. The boy and his brother were plucking flowers from the garden of Shabbir Ahmad when he caught both of them, police said today. They added that one of the boys was beaten to death while the other managed to escape."[25]

Barabanki, September 10: "In a gruesome incident, policemen allegedly poured petrol on a Dalit farmer's body and burnt his private parts after torturing him continuously for three days inside the Ram Sanehi Ghat police station, about 30 km from here."[26]

Bhubaneswar: "Four members of a tribal family were stripped, beaten up and made to parade naked before their fellow villagers in Chhatam, in Orissa's tribal-dominated Sundergarh district. Their crime—trying to chase away some hens that were pecking at their paddy crop."[27]

Mumbai: "Following a raid by police officials along with Samarthan, a Mumbai-based NGO, 32 children were rescued from Walope village near Chiplun in Ratnagiri district. Most of the children were Dalits and under 14 years. The children, who were rescued on Friday morning from a local sweetmeat shop, were working in extremely harsh conditions and were poorly fed. The Ratnagiri case is symptomatic of the widespread use of child labour in the state."[28]

"A TEENAGED DALIT BOY WAS ALLEGEDLY BEATEN TO DEATH BY THE PRESIDENT OF THE LOCALITY OF FATEH GANJ FOR PLUCKING SOME FLOWERS FROM HIS GARDEN."

Mysore: Five Dalits were rescued after having been shackled and forced to work in a stone quarry for two years. Their leg irons had been welded shut so that they could never be removed, and they were routinely beaten and tortured.[29]

Sonepat: "More than 100 *kutcha* and *pucca* houses were razed to the ground by officials of the demolition squad with the help of the police in RK Colony on the GT Road about eight km from here, on Wednesday night.... Residents alleged officials did not give them time to carry out their household articles."[30]

Meerut: "A 40-year-old Dalit agricultural labourer was tortured and humiliated before being shot dead in front of his wife and others at Kabaraut village, 35 km from Muzaffarnagar, allegedly by some influential persons, on Tuesday evening.... The denial by the agricultural worker, Samendra Sain, to hand over his *patta* (land), on which he had grown wheat and was harvesting the crop, to members of an upper caste family apparently provoked the latter to torture him to death. Sain had been reportedly given the land along with other landless dalits during the chief ministership of Mayawati."[31]

Endnotes

1. This matter is dealt with in detail in my "Decline and Fall of Buddhism" on <www.ambedkar.org> and <www.dalitstan.org>. **2.** Ashok Rana. "Bhumiputrachi hak," 15 Sept 2001. **3.** Gawai P.A. *Peshave Kalin Gulamgiri va Asprushta*, 1990: 112. **4.** *Ibid*.: 113. **5.** The following account is condensed from the booklet *Kambalapalli Carnage* by Oruvingal Sreedharan and R. Muniyappa <www.ambedkar.org>. **6.** Punalkar, S.P. *Caste, Caste Conflict and Reservation*. Surat, 1985: 172. **7.** Habir, Angar E. *Dr. Ambedkar Aur Miniorities Nation*. Samta Sangar prakashan, Nagpur, 2000: 36 ff. **8.** Unsigned. "Dalit Mother Raped for Son's 'Criminal' Affair." *New Indian Express* 9 July 1999. **9.** Soondas, Anand. "Woman Stripped, Killed." *The Telegraph* (Calcutta) 17 March 2000. **10.** Unsigned. "Landlords Attack Dalits, Burn Houses." *The Hindu* 19 April 2000. **11.** Unsigned. "Four Dalits Gunned Down in Bihar." DHNS, 26 April 2000. **12.** Unsigned. "Nailing Evidence—Police Cap Under a Dead Man." ambedkar.org Dalit E-forum, 2 May 2000. **13.** Unsigned. "SI Guns Down Four Dalits in Uttar Pradesh." DHNS, 8 May 2000. **14.** Garg, Balwant. "Dalit Woman Gang-Raped, Paraded Naked." *Times of India* 31 May 2000. **15.** Unsigned. "Dalit Killed in Amraiwadi by 4 Upper Caste Persons." ambedkar.org Dalit E-forum, 7 June 2000. **16.** Vajpeyi, Yogesh. "Two Cases of Rape." *Indian Express* 9 June 2000. **17.** Devi, V. Vasanthi. "A Cry for Justice." *Frontline* (India) 17.13 (24 June - 7 July 2000). **18.** Power, Carla. "Becoming a 'Servant of God'." *Newsweek* 25 June 2000. **19.** Power, Carla. "Caste Struggle." *Newsweek* 25 June 2001. **20.** Unsigned. "Four-year-old Girl Beheaded for Sacrifice." *Hindustan Times* 1 July 2001. **21.** Prabhakaran, G. "Dalit Girl Hostel for Sexual Exploitation." ambedkar.org Dalit E-forum. **22.** Unsigned. "Bihar Minister Sacked." *Hindustan Times* 7 July 2000. **23.** Unsigned. "Five Dalits Hacked to Death Over Minor Dispute." *Times of India* News Service, 28 July 2000. **24.** Pradhan, Sharat. "Girl Tortured, Burnt to Death in UP." *India Abroad* 1 Aug 2000. **25.** Unsigned. "Dalit Boy Beaten to Death for Plucking Flowers." *Indian Express* 4 Aug 2000. **26.** Naqvi, Bobby. "Dalit Tortured by Cops for Three Days." *Hindustan Times* 11 Sept 2000. **27.** Unsigned. "Tribal Family Stripped for Shooing Away Hens." *Times of India*, no date. **28.** Iyer, Srinivas. "32 Kids Rescued From Bonded Labour." *Times of India*, no date. **29.** Prakash, Soorya. "Life in Chains." ambedkar.org Dalit E-forum, no date. **30.** Unsigned. "Dalit Colony Razed in Sonepat." *Times of India* News Service, no date. **31.** Unsigned. "Dalit Farm Worker Killed in Caste Conflict." *Times of India* News Service, no date.

EVERYTHING YOU KNOW IS WRONG

VIVA KADAFFI!
ROBERT STERLING

On October 3, 1993, the US military faced its most violent combat firefight since the Vietnam War. On that day, eighteen members of the US Army were killed in Somalia, and 84 were wounded, in a battle with supporters of General Mohamed Farah Aidid, a warlord who was the main target of the US forces. Soon after, the US slinked out of the African country, humiliated by the experience. That what was called a peacekeeping mission—the US operation was known as "Operation Restore Hope"—could have caused such misfortune for US troops created both confusion and mass outrage from the public and the pundits. The anger was fueled by pictures of the corpse of a naked American soldier being dragged through the Mogadishu streets by a cheering mob. How dare these ungrateful people perform such a monstrous act on soldiers there solely for humanitarian reasons? (The results of "Operation Restore Hope" justified to many the apathetic disregard in the Western world toward the genocide that occurred in Rwanda the following year.) The blame—as Rush Limbaugh and his mouth-foaming reactionary clones often repeated—was laid at the feet of foolish bumpkin Bill Clinton, whose liberalism had put American soldiers at risk over a nation-building operation that left them defenseless.

The reality was much different. In the first place, the operation—which was, incidentally, conceived by George Bush I—included US Army Rangers and the Delta Force, both elite-trained commando units. All told, Bush had sent 25,000 troops into the country, hardly a poor, oppressed brigade. Furthermore, whatever the legitimate purposes of the original UN operation in the area were—to assure the delivery of food and medicine to a country in internal turmoil thanks to a bloody civil war—they were obsolete by the time the US military forces came in. In perfect Orwellian logic, the American "peacekeeping" operation involved commando raids on the nation to rid it of Aidid, the supposed outlaw menace who was blamed for the whole tragedy.

(Summarizing the utter hypocrisy and moral bankruptcy of the conservative spin on the Somalia operation are the writings of pundit Charles Krauthammer. His first article on the subject, in the October 9, 1992, edition of the *Washington Post*, was titled "Trusteeship for Somalia: An old—colonial—idea whose time has come again." In it, he argued that it would be best if the US took over the Somali government since those backward Africans obviously couldn't govern

themselves. The opinion was both blatantly racist and evasive of the true causes of civil war in the country. Krauthammer later became one of the harshest critics of the Clinton Administration's actions in Somalia.)

The results speak for themselves, but fortunately for the military-industrial complex, the true results were rarely spoken. A perfect example of the slanted discussion of events was offered in a 1995 *New Yorker* article. The author, William Finnegan, described the raid that killed US commandos as "disastrous"; it was not termed disastrous earlier in the same paragraph when it was mentioned, almost as an aside, that "remaining American airborne units led the increasingly violent search for Aidid, bombing and strafing suspected hideouts, and killing more than a thousand civilians." As noted by Ken Gaillo of the libertarian-bent *The Revolution*:

During the weeks from June 5 to October 3, 1993, UN/US forces inflicted 6,000 to 10,000 casualties on the Somali resistance, said Eric Schmitt in the December 8, 1993 *New York Times*. Schmitt confirmed the account with US military intelligence, relief workers, UN officials and the US special envoy to Somalia. US Marine Corps General Anthony Zinni estimated that two-thirds of the casualties were women and children.

Considering the fact that the "peacekeeping" force of benevolent Delta Force and Army Ranger commandos had caused such carnage, the glee of an angry mob over the solitary naked soldier paraded through the streets becomes more understandable.

Defenders of foreign policy would object, stating that the mass deaths, while tragic, were unfortunate, but part of a well-meaning operation gone haywire. After all, Bush had involved troops because Aidid was the warlord who had caused all the damage: over 350,000 dead (the vast majority due to famines) during the civil war, and as many as 30,000 reputed to have died in a single three-month shelling duel.

To blame the deaths all on Aidid as the singular cause, however, ignores that deaths and famine are often tragic effects of a civil war. And to turn him into a bogeyman ignores that, as he was decidedly elected (by a two-thirds vote) chairman of the United Somali Congress, the leading group behind the revolution, he had as legitimate of a claim to head of state as anyone in the country. Even the United Nations agreed on this point.

Why would Aidid lead a civil war that led to such bitter ends? Western media consistently portrayed petty politics and greedy self-enrichment as his motivation, and there likely was some self-interest involved in the decision. But overlooked in nearly all coverage of the civil war were the policies of dictator Mohamed Siad Barre, the man whom Aidid helped to overthrow. As noted in a Project Censored citation for excellence in suppressed journalism:

Investigative authors Rory Cox, in *Propaganda Review*, and Jim Naureckas, in *EXTRA!*, wondered whether the decision to send US troops to Somalia was based more on potential oil reserves there than on the tragic images of starving Somalis that dominated major media outlets in late 1992 and 1993. The US/UN military involvement in Somalia began in mid-November 1992, but it wasn't until January 18, 1993, two days before George Bush left office, that a major media outlet, the *Los Angeles Times*, published an article that revealed America's oil connection with Somalia. *Times* staff writer Mark Fineman started his Mogadishu-datelined article with, "Far beneath the surface of the tragic drama of Somalia, four major US oil companies are quietly sitting on a prospective fortune in exclusive concessions to explore and exploit tens of millions of acres of the Somali countryside. That land, in the opinion of geologists and industry sources, could yield significant amounts of oil and natural gas if the US-led military mission can restore peace to the impoverished East African nation."

According to Fineman, nearly two-thirds of Somalia was allocated to the American oil giants Conoco, Amoco, Chevron, and Phillips before Somalia's pro-US President Mohamed Siad Barre was overthrown. The US oil companies are "well positioned to pursue Somalia's most promising potential oil reserves the moment the nation is pacified." Oil industry spokesmen, along with Bush/Clinton Administration spokespersons, deny these allegations as "absurd" and "nonsense." However, Thomas E. O'Connor, the principal petroleum engineer for the World Bank, who headed an in-depth three-year study of oil prospects off Somalia's northern coast, said, "There's no doubt there's oil there... It's got high (commercial) potential...once the Somalis get their act together."

Fineman would add: "Conoco, whose tireless exploration efforts in north-central Somalia reportedly had yielded the most encouraging prospects just before Siad Barre's fall, permitted its Mogadishu corporate compound to be transformed into a de facto American embassy a few days before the US Marines landed in the capital, with Bush's special envoy using it as his temporary headquarters." They wouldn't have done this if Aidid had been in their pocket. Considering that two-thirds of the country's richest natural resources were given to American energy barons, Aidid (and his revolutionary network) was rightfully objecting the plundering of the nation's wealth by a corporate oligopoly while the people suffered in abject poverty. The more one looks at Somalia, the more it appears a better moniker for the Bush-Clinton plan would be "Operation Destroy Hope."

In August 1996, Aidid was pronounced dead, a victim of assassin's bullets. Western media cheered this event, announcing that his death would potentially lead to a greater "peace" in Somalia. For what it's worth, Aidid's Washington spokesman, Ahmed Mohamed Dahman, told the British Broadcasting Corporation (BBC) in regard to his death: "It was a conspiracy by a certain group...who fired on him. They were in the services of an international conspiracy... They were forces against Aidid and his ideals. His supporters had always been protecting him.'"

Aidid was dead, but his image had been destroyed in the Western world long before by mass media attacks. There is nothing new, of course, in demonizing political enemies. But after the widespread sympathy received in the West to Third World revolutionary leaders such as Ho Chi Minh, Che Guevara, and Salvador Allende—who, most frighteningly of all, was a democratically elected Marxist in Chile before he was ousted by a CIA-supported junta and death squads led by General Augusto Pinochet—it would be clear to any political analyst that the US was slipping in the propaganda war. And that war, of course, is ultimately the most important of all. In his 1990 magnum opus on socio-economics and politics, *Powershift*, Alvin Toffler lists the three prime sources of power in the world: violence, wealth, and knowledge. The United States establishment, with its Pentagon and titanic corporate megaliths, has the first two decidedly wrapped up, but it is in the transmission of ideas and values where there's ultimately an Achilles' heel.

> THE MORE ONE LOOKS AT SOMALIA, THE MORE IT APPEARS A BETTER MONIKER FOR THE BUSH-CLINTON PLAN WOULD BE "OPERATION DESTROY HOPE."

Fortunately for elites, control of information and knowledge is heavily concentrated in decreasingly fewer hands. According to Ben Bagdikian in *The Media Monopoly*, six corporations dominate most every mass medium today. (When he first wrote his book of dire warning on information concentration, the number of media titans was a near utopian number in comparison, totaling 50.) With the increased concentration comes an increased control over the minds of the masses. With that control, significant resources have been used to smear the images of anyone from the Third World who suddenly develops an uppity atto.

Not that demonizing Third World leaders is usually difficult. The reason most enemies of the Western establishment are so easily attacked is that in order to get to a position of power, they usually need to be dirty themselves. Saddam Hussein, Manuel Noriega, Slobodan Milosevic, and Che's buddy Fidel Castro are noteworthy examples of men whose claims of anti-imperialism are extremely tainted by their own repressive and autocratic rule. (And then there are the sordid histories of the USSR and China, two faux "anti-imperialist" nations that were and are as repressive as any during the twentieth century.)

Then again, perhaps looking at things in such Manichean, "good versus evil" terms is a bit simplistic. Even in the cases listed above, it appears that these leaders (who were all previously backed by the US powers that would later attack them) are demonized because of their most positive features: Their refusal to follow the mammon-tainted edicts of Western governments and corporations has made them pariahs.

When it comes to American foreign policy, the bogeymen tend to be quasi-communist or socialist in ideology. This is more out of convenience than any commitment to ideological purity; communist or socialist groups have traditionally received their funding from enemies of the United States—most notably the Soviet empire or China. Meanwhile, in Russia, the enemies list starts with the Chechnyans, and in China it is the Tibetans. Beneath all the slogans, the uniting theme of demonization campaigns is not some abstract political philosophy, but to attack groups that resist the exploitation of resources by the imperial powers.

That said, this would be a good time to look at the more noted US campaigns of Third World bogeyman currently in effect.

Jean-Bertrand Aristide, Haiti. The radical former Catholic priest is a proponent of liberation theology and opponent of imperialism and International Monetary Fund (IMF) policies—he once declared: "Capitalism is a mortal sin." He is perhaps the most Allende-esque of all the current bogeymen. When he won an overwhelming election victory in 1990, the *New York Times* declared that he "can now become either the father of Haitian democracy, or just one more of its many betrayers." Unsurprisingly, it was the CIA—who worked with those connected to the bloody Duvalier family (which long held Haiti in an iron grip)—who betrayed democracy. The CIA teamed with the nation's military and the Haitian death squad FRAPH (whose leader, Emmanuel "Toto" Constant, was on the CIA payroll) to overthrow Aristide less than a year later. More than 4,000 civilians were killed in the bloody coup.

The mainstream media, rather than express outrage at this subversion of popular will, created a chorus that blamed Aristide, claiming he had become power-hungry and alluding to CIA documents which alleged he was "mentally unstable" and a "murderer and psychopath." He was reinstalled later, but only after he promised not to run for reelection and thus became an impotent lame duck. Nonetheless, he is quite popular among the people of Haiti and was overwhelmingly reelected (with 92 percent of the votes) on November 26, 2000, less than a month after the Florida Votescam. Right-wing forces in both Haiti and the US declared his election a "sham"—including those supporting "president" George W. Bush (making the charge both amusing in its irony and repulsive for its duplicity).

Hugo Chavez, Venezuela. In marketing his platform, the former paratrooper and lieutenant colonel combines machismo (he often appears dressed in combat fatigues) and leftist economic nationalism to promote a manly form of radical populism inspired by Simon Bolivar. Considering that his nation is oil-rich yet mired in poverty, such programs don't endear him to US officials. In 1992, he led a failed coup against the corrupt government in place; by 1998 he had won it by election, destroying the corrupt twin parties that had maintained power for over 40 years. (Both Accion Democratic and Copei had traditionally received 90 percent of the vote between them, but in 1998 it was only 9 percent, compared to Chavez's 56 percent.) In April 1999, 90 percent of the public voted in favor of Chavez's proposal for a Constituent Assembly, through which he plans to change the nation's political system.

> WHEN IT COMES TO AMERICAN FOREIGN POLICY, THE BOGEYMEN TEND TO BE QUASI-COMMUNIST OR SOCIALIST IN IDEOLOGY.

A critic of IMF austerity programs in Venezuela, he was quoted by the Workers World News Service: "So much riches, the largest petroleum reserves in the world, the fifth largest reserves of gas—God, the immensely rich Caribbean Sea. All this, and 80 percent of our people live in poverty. What scientist can explain this?" He rejected the demands of business and political interests to evict squatters from abandoned and unused buildings in the nation's capital. "I'm not going to send in troops," he stated in a *New York Times* interview on the controversy. "I will not rest until every human being who lives in this land has housing, employment, and some way to manage his life." It also doesn't help that he is resistant to the US Plan Colombia. Despite (or because of) his rampant popularity, he is regularly accused of being a would-be Castro in Western newspaper articles (including the supposedly liberal *Salon*, who stated that Fidel is "his idol"), and rumors of a military coup and assassination plague his leadership.

Revolutionary Armed Forces of Colombia (FARC), Colombia. Speaking of Plan Colombia, the ultimate target of the supposed "anti-drug" operation is the extermination of this organization.

Founded in 1964 as the military wing of the Colombian Communist Party, FARC is the oldest insurgency group in Colombia and the most powerful group of guerrilla fighters in all of Latin America. (Two other groups, the National Liberation Army (ELN) and the Popular Liberation Army (EPL) also have large followings.) Currently they control close to half of the country. The organization is hampered by charges of terrorism; the charges are completely true. They have been involved in bombings, murders, kidnappings, extortion, and hijackings, as well as guerrilla and conventional military action against Colombian political, military, and economic targets. Of course, so have the right-wing paramilitary death squads tied to the Colombian government. As Amnesty International put it in a pull-no-punches report: "All parties to the conflict were responsible for serious human rights violations—including massacres—but the majority were carried out by illegal paramilitary groups which systematically targeted the civilian population."

What is truly dangerous to American foreign policy regarding FARC and its ilk is their refusal to do business with corporations. Rather than hand over the rights to vast amounts of natural resources (mainly oil) to gigantic conglomerates, such as Occidental Petroleum, they expect any deals to be worked out with a bigger slice of the pie for Colombia. The so-called "War on Drugs" against Colombia is really an excuse for American corporations to destroy these organizations, which collect a "tax" on all drug production that comes through their controlled areas.

Zapatista Movement, Mexico. Named after famed revolutionary Emiliano Zapata and led by the mysterious masked man Subcomandante Marcos, the group has perhaps the most romantic image of all. Made up primarily of Mayan Indians in the Chiapas area, they became famous on New Year's Day 1994, with a declaration of war against the Mexican government. Along with their outlaw image, intellectuals admire Marcos for both his passionate writings and persuasive philosophy. According to resolutions of support by the National Indigenous Congress, a majority of Mexico's 10 million Indians supports the ideals espoused by the rebels, such as self-government and a new Charter for Indian Rights. The Zapatista National Liberation Front (FZLN) promotes the transition to full democracy on a national level.

Naturally, the Zapatistas have been slammed as terrorists for their actions, but their followers have been the main victims of massacres, caused by government-backed paramilitary organizations. Narco News states that "the Zapatistas have explicit revolutionary laws against drug use or trafficking. They have, in fact, driven the drug cartels off their jungle and mountain lands—where governments had previously failed to do so. Alcohol, too, is banned in their villages." Combined with their stated opposition to the neoliberal agenda, it makes them a very dangerous enemy to US interests. The mass popularity of the movement (and its vast control of the Chiapas) has led to negotiations with the Mexican government to legitimize the organization.

Tupac Amaru, Peru. Though often lumped together with the Shining Path, or *Sendero Luminoso*, these two revolutionary movements are actually quite separate. The Shining Path is an organization that follows the Marxist-Leninist-Maoist ideology, with the emphasis on Mao. Tupac Amaru representative Isaac Velazco has stated, "There's more that separates us from than unites us with *Sendero Luminoso. Sendero* is a profoundly dogmatic, sectarian movement.... They don't seek to win hearts and minds, but impose their direction on the people, which is why they don't hesitate to kill to achieve their domination.... I would hesitate to describe *Sendero* as a revolutionary group because their Pol Pot concept of life and revolution is a long way from what we think of as revolution."

Meanwhile, the Tupac Amaru Revolutionary Movement, founded in 1984, is named after an Incan leader who led an anti-colonialist rebellion that almost shook off Spanish domination in South America before he was caught and killed in Cuzco. "We try to put Peruvian reality ahead of any pre-defined ideology," Velazco says. "We don't want state centralism or the bureaucratization of Peruvian society. Life has taught us that is not the way.... We want it to be a participatory democracy with the people as actors." The numbers back up the distinction: According to Amnesty International, while 53 percent of extra-judicial assassinations have been committed by the brutal Peruvian government and 45 percent by the Shining Path, only one percent is by Tupac Amaru, and there appears to be no organizational backing of these deeds.

These leaders and movements have much in common. They are at least partially socialist in philosophy. They are decidedly opposed to the agenda of the World Bank and International Monetary Fund. (Indeed, their stocks in the mainstream press all seem to rise and fall depending on how closely they toe the line of the neoliberal agenda.) Perhaps most disturbing to the US State Department, they are all Latin American and thus in the US's backyard.

Still, besides Castro—a man who serves Pentagon interests by having a communist menace so close to US borders, which makes him a very worthwhile bogeyman to keep around—the longest and most extensive bogeyman campaign still in existence isn't against any of these fine groups or fellows. Nor is it against Daniel Ortega and the Sandinistas. (After overthrowing the corrupt Somoza regime in Nicaragua, the Sandinistas instituted elections and did come out victorious in the first contest. Years of economic battering fueled by US embargoes and illegal minings of harbors finally did them in after the 1990 election, yet they became the first revolutionary organization to give up power by democratic means. Ortega nearly returned to the

> WHAT IS TRULY DANGEROUS TO AMERICAN FOREIGN POLICY REGARDING FARC AND ITS ILK IS THEIR REFUSAL TO DO BUSINESS WITH CORPORATIONS.

presidency during a November 2001 election.) In fact, like Aidid in Somalia, it isn't even against a Latin American. The winner of this dubious honor is, instead, Libya's Moammar Kadaffi, a man who has been relentlessly defamed, insulted, mocked, and smeared for most of his history as the symbolic leader of his country.

Even among radical critics of American politics and policy, there is deep suspicion of the man. Underground writer Alex Constantine noted both his ties to defense contractor Fiat and financial support of the pedophile religious cult Children of God. Meanwhile, in his excellent exposé, *The CIA's Greatest Hits*, Mark Zepezauer makes the argument that Kadaffi is actually a CIA provocateur, citing the supply of 21 tons of C4 explosives to his regime by supposed "renegade" CIA agents Ed Wilson and Frank Terpil.

In the mainstream press, the image projected in the United States of Kadaffi totters between him being (at best) an amusing madman to a diabolical monster. Indeed, thanks to the continuous assaults on his motives and character, he rivals Saddam Hussein as a top nominee among Nostradamus buffs as the reputed Third Anti-Christ following Napoleon and Hitler. Bringing up Mo is always a good way for Jay Leno, David Letterman, or some other smirking wiseass to get a cheap laugh; he was once referred to as "Daffy Kadaffi" on *Saturday Night Live*. Nobody can even agree on how to spell his name. (Among the alternate spellings: Khadafy, Kadafi, Kaddafi, Gadafy, Gadhafi, Gadaffi, Gaddafi, Qadhafi, Qaddafi, al-Qadhafi, Quaddaffi, Qadahfi. And that's just a few for his *last* name.)

If he is crazy, he's crazy like a fox. Middle Eastern and African politics are notoriously cutthroat; to survive over 32 years in such an environment requires a crafty instinct. As for his supposed status as a vile evil-doer, it is more promoted because it's an easy sell. The Middle East, it goes without saying, is a hotbed of religious fundamentalism, and thus the charge of "terrorist mastermind" is an easy smear to make. (Though Libya is actually a North African nation, because of its oil and 97 percent Sunni Muslim population, it is often viewed as a Middle Eastern nation.)

In fact, Kadaffi has supported terrorism. Of course, one man's terrorist is another man's freedom fighter. The terrorist/freedom fighters he has supported with money and weapons include both the Irish Republican Army (the leading resistance movement against the United Kingdom), the PLO (who, for whatever the organization's many noted acts of violence, are now considered by most of the world as the legitimate leaders of a persecuted people), the Sandinistas and El Salvadoran guerrillas (who fought US-backed death squads in Latin America), and the African National Congress (back in the 1980s, when they were officially viewed as an outlaw terrorist organization during US support for South Africa's racist apartheid system).

For most of his years as the symbolic

Libyan head of state, Kadaffi has thrown his support towards numerous anti-Western government causes. That would include practically every group fighting the US and UK governments, or one of their allies—the most notable Western ally, of course, being Israel. (This explains his support for the Children of God, who declared victimhood by the CIA, though they are likely connected to the outfit themselves.) Some of the organizations he has supported have deservedly notorious histories (most notably Abu Nidal's Black September, the PLO, and the Red Brigade). In that capacity, yes, Libyan money, weapons, and training went to groups which did commit acts of terror against civilians. In that club of terrorist leaders, of course, is the leader of nearly every country in the world, starting with the US (the most notorious exporter of terrorism) and the UK, plus Syria, Saudi Arabia, and Pakistan (three Middle Eastern countries which have fairly strong ties to the West). There's a term for giving aid to dubious groups because they serve some political interest foreign policy.

Others may scoff at this point, insisting that Kadaffi has personally been involved in terrorist operations. However, the two cases of terrorism he's been charged with by the US government are made of thin air, at best.

In 1986, President Reagan claimed Tripoli was behind the bombing of a West Berlin discotheque frequented by American servicemen. The US has yet to supply any evidence to back this up, and Libya never claimed responsibility. In Victor Ostrovsky's book on the history of the Mossad (*By Way of Deception*), he claims the Israeli intelligence agency provoked America into this conclusion by making it appear that terrorist orders were transmitted from the Libyan government to its embassies around the world. But the messages originated in Israel and were retransmitted by a special communication device—a "Trojan horse"—that the Mossad had placed inside Libya. (Previously, the Mossad had passed disinformation of a bogus Kadaffi plot to assassinate Reagan. The story was subsequently admitted to be false.) Of course, that may be giving Mossad too much credit; the Reagan Administration didn't need to be provoked at all. They were quite ready to pin the blame on Libya for anything, and the discotheque bombing provided an easy—if flimsy—excuse.

Though there isn't any evidence linking Libya to the Berlin bombing, what followed is not in doubt: Team Reagan ordered US aircraft to bomb several targets in Tripoli and Benghazi, including Kadaffi's residence. Forty civilians, among them Kadaffi's adopted daughter, were killed in an intentional act of terror. The administration had already written a letter of regret for the accidental death of Kadaffi, whom they naturally wouldn't have been targeting for assassination, since that would be illegal.

IN THE MAINSTREAM PRESS, THE IMAGE PROJECTED IN THE UNITED STATES OF KADAFFI TOTTERS BETWEEN HIM BEING (AT BEST) AN AMUSING MADMAN TO A DIABOLICAL MONSTER.

VIVA KADAFFI!
ROBERT STERLING

As for PanAm 103 (the infamous bombing of a 747 that killed 270 over Lockerbie, Scotland, on December 21, 1988), the story is even more of the same. The official story originally pinned the blame on Syrian-backed terrorists—Ahmed Jabril of the Popular Front for the Liberation of Palestine-General Command. (Members of the PFLP had already been arrested in West Germany in possession of a bomb similar to the one used over Lockerbie.) This explanation became quite inconvenient in 1990, when Syria was needed as part of the coalition to massacre Iraq. Soon after, evidence which was claimed to be undeniable linked the tragedy firmly on two Libyan intelligence agents, Abdel Basset Ali al-Megrahi and Lamen Khalifa Fhimah. UN sanctions were imposed against Libya in April 1992. (Libya refused to extradite the duo, claiming the prosecution was politically motivated and that US-UK courts couldn't be trusted.)

HE NATIONALIZED THE OIL INDUSTRY AND REQUIRED WESTERN COMPANIES WHO HAD SWEETHEART DEALS COURTESY OF IDRIS TO NEGOTIATE NEW CONTRACTS THAT GAVE LIBYA MORE THAN HALF OF THE PROFITS.

The amazing evidence which proved the guilt of Libyan intelligence? A timing fragment used on the bomb was supposedly discovered (eighteen months after the bombing), being a type that was sold only to Libya. Or so the US government claimed in 1991. In court Edwin Bollier, head of the Swiss manufacturer Mebo Telecommunications, stated that the original identification of the timer as one sold to Libya was based solely on photographs. When he saw the actual evidence (something that investigators waited nine years to show), he firmly stated that "the fragment does not come from one of the timers we sold to Libya." He then testified instead that the timers were sold only to East Germany's Institute of Technical Research (a front for the Stasi secret police—who had heavy links to the PFLP-GC). Nobody has ever bothered to explain the differences between what Bollier was originally shown and the actual evidence.

After a long extradition battle, the two stood trial in 1999, with al-Megrahi found guilty and Fhimah acquitted. The World Socialist Web Site provided some of the best reporting on the trial. On the verdicts, they reported:

In their 82-page verdict, the Scottish judges-Lords Sutherland, Coulsfield and Maclean-expose the weakness of the prosecution case and how they ignored, or simply dismissed, a mass of contradictory forensic and circumstantial evidence in order to bring a guilty verdict against Al Megrahi.

Significantly they rejected in its entirety the defence argument that other individuals and groups—namely the Popular Front for the Liberation of Palestine-General Command (PFLP-GC)—were responsible for the bomb, on the grounds that the evidence against them was circumstantial and inconclusive.

This raises the question, why was there such a discrepancy between the standards applied to the defence's arguments seeking to implicate others for the bombing and those employed by the prosecution against Al Megrahi? The case against the two Libyans was no less circumstantial and flimsy, a fact acknowledged in part by the acquittal of Al Amin Khalifa Fhimah. Under Scottish law, moreover, it was possible to return a verdict of "not proven" that would free but not completely exonerate Al Megrahi on the basis that the court could not accept his guilt "beyond reasonable doubt".

(For much more on the PanAm sham, see "The Bombing of PanAm Flight 103," elsewhere in this book.)

So why the hard-on for Mo? Kadaffi earned ill will at the ripe age of 27, soon after he engineered the bloodless Libyan revolution against the corrupt and plutocratic monarchy of King Idris on September 1, 1969. Soon after, he instituted a program which normally earns a death certificate: He nationalized the oil industry and required Western companies who had sweetheart deals courtesy of Idris to negotiate new contracts that gave Libya more than half of the profits. (For those interested in symbolism, the date is the start of the seventh week following the moon landing, making it the first great revolution of the Lunar Age.) (An ironic note: The most notable beneficiary of Idris' plundering was Occidental Petroleum, headed by Armand Hammer. Hammer has in recent years been revealed to be a major KGB-Soviet agent and asset in the West. Kadaffi would also denounce communism for its atheism. It is possible, then, that the ease with which Kadaffi took over Libya was due to support by anti-communist elements in the Central Intelligence Agency. This also explains the curious links to the CIA which Constantine and Zepezauer have noted.)

Kadaffi didn't leave it at that; he nationalized the banking industry and closed all five US Air Force bases in Libya, as well. Rather than use the money merely to swindle the Libyan people for his own benefit, he invested heavily in housing, medicine, agriculture, and education (the literacy rate has increased tenfold). In short, Kadaffi has created what is as close to a pure socialist state as there is. The results are telling: In 1951, Libya was the poorest nation in the world, with a per capita income of $50. Today, despite bombings and heavy sanctions imposed by the West, it is the richest nation in Africa and among the top in the Middle East, boasting a standard of living comparable to the US and Western European countries—without any homeless citizens. In short, Libya challenges the ideology promoted by Western elites as the final solution to Third World poverty.

(Some may point out that no oil was known to exist in Libya in 1951, but the fact remains that, under the "deals" made by King Idris, the oil revenues would have been siphoned off from the Libyan people.)

Though often described as a dictatorship, Libya has perhaps more democracy and local participation in government than the leading so-called democracies in the West. This was achieved through the formation of *Jamahiriya* (state of the masses)—direct democracy on the local level that is anti-hierarchical in nature. In fact, Kadaffi has no actual governmental title besides "Leader of the Revolution," and his power and influence continue solely because of his mass popularity. (The nation has a unicameral legislature, a president, and a Supreme Court.) And, in contrast to the image of the Middle East as some universally repressed Islamic fundamentalism enclave, Libya is actually an extremely liberated society, with emancipation of women (complete with equal employment opportunities and relaxed Western dress codes) and the embrace of social secularism.

Of course, Kadaffi's progressive populism would be bad enough if Libya merely kept it to itself. Instead, Kadaffi has diligently pushed his nationalist ideology toward a pan-national union. Kadaffi is merely following in the footsteps of his idol, Gamel Abdel Nasser, the Egyptian revolutionary who openly dreamed of an Arab Union. Nasser died in 1970, and Kadaffi quickly took up the mantle. His most insidious fantasy, according to Western elites? A plan for a "Third World Bank," where the richest nations of the Third World would pool resources and loan money to their more impoverished members at minimal interest—and without the strings attached by the IMF and the World Bank. Such a scheme would destroy what is perhaps the greatest lie of all promoted by the Western world, that the IMF and World Bank are trying to help the Third World. As Nick Mamatas succinctly notes on the Disinformation Website: "Not one country has successfully developed thanks to the World Bank's system, and those few Third World countries that have become industrial or trade powers (South Korea, Taiwan, the OPEC states) have done so by doing the exact opposite of what the World Bank prescribes." Zero for fifty-plus years isn't an accident; it's a pattern of a very successfully destructive design. (For more info on this, see "Burn the Olive Tree, Sell the Lexus," elsewhere in this book.)

Most of Kadaffi's vision and ideology is presented in his manifesto, *The Green Book*. While the image of Kadaffi as a dispenser of wisdom earns snickers in the West, the actual work, in this writer's view, is passionate and compelling, if a tad naïve and idealistic. (It can be found at Mathaba.net, a Website run by admirers of the Kadaffi vision.) Rather than noble, some may call his plan an extension of intense megalomania. Kadaffi appears to be a fairly narcissistic fellow, but, as anyone who has seen *Citizen Kane* would know, in the finest of egotists the ego is served by acts of benevolence to flatter the individual's own self-worth. Kadaffi would more than likely fit into such a category.

His naïvete is underscored with the roadblocks to his regional union plans. He originally intended to create a Pan-Arab pact but has since resigned that vision in disgust, having the dream thwarted by the corruption and back-stabbing mistrust among the Middle Eastern states. Middle Eastern leaders showed little interest in joining a federation that would bear fruits only for their people and earn Western wrath.

Now he has modified his plan for a Pan-African union, and though it seems a dubious plot when viewing history, it has at least a plausible future. Money talks, and Libya does have the cash that Kadaffi's neighbor nations need.

At this point, his plan is more than a mere dream: He has given tangible aid to fellow African nations in need, earning much gratitude for it. He has helped prop up the battered nation of Zimbabwe by pushing a $360-million oil deal to end the nation's major fuel crisis. The sale of the oil comes at "knock-down prices," according to the BBC, which added: "Libyan oil wealth is bolstering the economies of countries in the African Sahara." In July 2001, Kadaffi personally delivered 1,000 tons of drought aid to Kenya. On the statesman front, he has been at the center of a peace initiative with Egypt aimed at ending the civil war in Sudan, and he thwarted a coup in the Central African Republic by sending troops to quash an army rebellion.

Meanwhile, in a bid to create ties with another Third World bloc, he has offered to buy all the bananas produced in the Caribbean region at above-market prices. According to Kadaffi, the current deals with Europe and the World Trade Organization have led to an "economic stranglehold" on the region.

While it has moderated its public image through sharp PR, Libya has started to play hardball again with the US, threatening to strip US corporations of operating licenses on oil fields abandoned after the 1986 sanctions. "We have agreements with the American companies, and those agreements need our cooperation," said Libya's Foreign Minister, Abdel Rahman Shalqam. Europe is salivating over the fields, which would provide ample funds for the African Union. Libya's threat seems to be intended to spark the US to drop its sanctions before it gets cut out of a lucrative deal.

IN MARCH 2001, KADAFFI ANNOUNCED PLANS FOR THE AFRICAN UNION.

In March 2001, Kadaffi announced plans for the African Union, under which boundaries between states would be eliminated, national armies merged, and a single passport introduced. Surprisingly, his plan has been largely accepted by his fellow African leaders. There are plans for the first AU summit in 2002, which would likely be held in Pretoria (a wise political choice). The central parliament building has already been constructed—in Tripoli, no less. There will also be a court of justice, a central bank, and a common currency. The ultimate vision, of course, is that the African Union will become a regional superpower and break the shackles of Western control. Perhaps Kadaffi's dreams seem impractical and unlikely, but, if they do succeed, he would be among the most important revolutionaries of history.

Of course, his vision and actions are far from perfect. He is, after all, still a politician. With vast political power comes abuse and corruption. He may be utopian and idealistic in theory, but he can be ruthless and cynical in practice. Recently, in a shameless ploy to support his Pan-African vision, Kadaffi praised and defended the race-baiting and larceny of Zimbabwe's Mugabe, whose policies seem doomed to lead the nation towards mass starvation. (While Mugabe correctly claims that Zimbabwe's land is unjustly concentrated in the hands of a few white Africans, he has had 20 years to deal with this issue and only chose to when his placation of neoliberalism led to overwhelming desperation.) Kadaffi's embrace of Mugabe follows his pattern of befriending Idi Amin and other thugs who feigned victimhood. There is also a serious question of Libya's tolerance of Jewish populations; their shrinking numbers in Libya speak volumes. And, while the Libyan state is hardly the worst human rights abuser, it has a history of police-state tactics that, while better than most major cities in the US, hardly follows his own self-proclaimed vision.

That said, these criticisms seem to miss the point. Kadaffi is promoted as a demon in the West not for his vices but for his virtues, and hated by elites not for his villainy but for his heroism. In politics, it is said, you can best judge a man by the enemies he has earned. If that be the case, there is no greater tribute than can be given to the guy. If Kadaffi is doomed to hell for what he has done as a leader, he definitely will have lots of familiar company.

Sources: Websites

Amnesty International <www.amnesty.org>
CIA World Factbook <www.odci.gov/cia/publications/factbook>
Committee to Support the Revolution in Peru <www.csrp.org/index.html>
From The Wilderness Publications <www.copvcia.com>
The Konformist <www.konformist.com>
Mathaba.net <www.mathaba.net>
New Dawn magazine <www.newdawnmagazine.com>
Nexus magazine <www.nexusmagazine.com>
Project Censored <www.projectcensored.org>
Sendero Luminoso: A Pathfinder <ils.unc.edu/~marsc/sendero.htm>
Tupac Amaru Revolutionary Movement Solidarity Page <burn.ucsd.edu/~ats/mrta.htm>
World Socialist Web Site <www.wsws.org>
Zapatista Network <www.zapatistas.org>

Sources: Articles and Books

Al-Kurdi, Husayn. "Libya: The Perpetual Target." <www.geocities.com/Athens/8744/kurdi.htm>. Al-Kurdi is a senior editor of News International Press Service.
Bagdikian, Ben H. *The Media Monopoly* (6th edition). Boston: Beacon Press, 2000.
Bailey, Blake. *Zapatista*. Bloomington, Indiana: 1stBooks, 2000.
Bainerman, Joel. *Crimes of a President: New Revelations on the Conspiracy and Cover Up in the Bush and Reagan Administration*. New York: S.P.I. Books (Shapolsky Publishers), 1992.
Bainerman, Joel. "Bush Administration's Involvement in Bombing PanAm 103." *Portland Free Press*, May/June 1997.

Bamford, David. "Gaddafi: Africa's New Sponsor." BBC News, 23 July 2001.
Bamford, David. "Libya 'to Buy All Caribbean Bananas.'" BBC News, 10 Sept 2001.
Blum, William. "PanAm 103 & The Charge Against Libya: Case Closed or More Disinformation?" *Covert Action Quarterly* 66 (Winter 1999).
Constantine, Alex. *Psychic Dictatorship in the USA*. Los Angeles: Feral House, 1995.
Dupuy, Ben. "The Attempted Character Assassination of Aristide." Project Censored, Censored 1999.
Fineman, Mark. "The Oil Factor in Somalia." *Los Angeles Times* 18 January 1993.
Finnegan, William. "Letter from Mogadishu: A World of Dust." *The New Yorker* 20 March 1995.
Gaal, Chris. "Who Are The Peruvian 'Terrorists'?" Jay's Leftist and "Progressive" Internet Resource Directory <www.neravt.com/left>.
Gaillo, Ken. "The Civil War In Somalia." The Revolution <www.boogieonline.com/revolution>.
Giordano, Al. "The Narco-State of Chiapas." Narco News Bulletin <www.narconews.com>, 5 June 2000.
Ighneiwa, Ibrahim. "Libya: The US Air and Sea Attacks on Libya in 1986." Libya: Our Home <ourworld.compuserve.com/homepages/dr_ibrahim_ighneiwa>.
Johnson, R.W. "Gaddafi Bids to Be Leader of Africa." *Sunday Times* (London) 22 July 2001.
Johnstone, Diana. "The Man We Love to Hate." *New Internationalist* 161 (July 1986).
Keith, Jim, and Kenn Thomas. *The Octopus*. Los Angeles: Feral House, 1997.
Mamatas, Nick. "A16: The World Bank v. the World." Disinformation <www.disinfo.com>, 29 May 2001.
Norton, James. "Hugo Chavez." *Flak* magazine <www.flakmag.com> (2001).
Ostrovsky, Victor. *By Way of Deception: The Making and Unmaking of a Mossad Officer*. Toronto: Stoddart, 1990.
Overbeck, Charles. "War Is Peace." Parascope.com (Feb 1997).
Patterns of Global Terrorism, 2000. United States Department of State (April 2001).
Peet, Preston. "Ed Wilson Got Shafted." Disinformation, 18 Oct 2000.
Public Broadcasting System. "Ambush in Mogadishu." *Frontline* (1998).
Rowan, Roy. "PanAm 103: Why Did They Die?" *Time* 27 April 1992.
Sterling, Robert. "Occidental Petroleum v. the U'wa Indians: The Ooze Surrounding Al Gore." Disinformation, 14 Dec 2000.
Toffler, Alvin. *Powershift*. New York: Bantam Books, 1990.
Trigos-Gilbert, Maria L. "Venezuela and Hugo Chavez Frías." Goinside.com, 31 October 1999.
Vankin, Jonathan. *The Big Book of Scandal*. New York: Paradox Press, 1997.
Vankin, Jonathan. *Conspiracies, Cover-Ups, and Crimes: Political Manipulation and Mind Control in America*. Lilburn, Georgia: IllumiNet Press, 1996.
Vankin, Jonathan, and John Whalen. *The Seventy Greatest Conspiracies of All Time: History's Biggest Mysteries, Coverups, and Cabals*. Secaucus, New Jersey: The Citadel Press, 1998.
Wernick, David A. "Venezuela's President Is Playing With Fire." Salon, 17 Aug 2000
Zepezauer, Mark. *The CIA's Greatest Hits*. Monroe, ME: Odonian Press, 1994.

Much thanks to author Jim Hogshire, who helped inspire this article. Thanks as well to Duncan Roads of Nexus *magazine, David Jones of* New Dawn, *and Mathaba.net for their information.*

EVERYTHING YOU KNOW IS WRONG

WILL THIS BE THE CHINESE CENTURY?
HOWARD BLOOM AND DIANE STARR PETRYK-BLOOM

In the nineteenth century, Britain ruled the waves, presided over an empire on which the Sun never set, and held the world in the grip of an uneasy peace. After World War I and World War II, it became America's turn to spread its influence wherever a ray of earthly sun could reach, to stride in and police many an international mess, and to proclaim, in the words of Time/Life publisher Henry Luce, that the twentieth was the "American Century." Will the coming decades see the scepter fall from America's hands? And if so, who will grab it before it hits the ground? Which nation, if any, will keep the peace and be the reigning power of this still-young twenty-first century? One country nominated itself for this position back in the 1990s. The people who would be king are the Chinese. China has called for "a new world order," a new "peace" over which it would presumably preside.

Periods of peace imposed by a single superpower have often produced substantial benefits to nations roped into the sphere of influence of the overlord. Conquered, cowed, or allied countries have been able to take down their fortress walls, open up their societies, and concentrate on productivity instead of devastation. But there have also been considerable disadvantages for those who are squashed under the thumb of the megapower. The nation running the world gets to influence—or dictate—how its vassals think, govern, eat, and speak. It has the privilege of sending its troops into lesser lands at the slightest sign that the underling states are getting out of hand.

This means that life can become quite cheap. The Athens of ultimate democracy—that of Pericles' Golden Age—annihilated populations of entire city-states and razed their buildings to the ground when Athens' leader felt such punishment was necessary to make a point. Cities in the Athenian League were allegedly independent allies, but woe be unto to the ally that got out of line. Rome in the golden days of the Pax Romana crucified 6,000 rebellious slaves alongside one of its greatest highways—the Appian Way. The victims acted as writhing, moaning billboards advertising the penalties of civic unrest. Russia, when it imposed its version of peace on a good part of Europe and Asia in the twentieth century, did without Rome's theatrical flair. It sent tanks into the streets of Prague, ran secret police operations and torture chambers in its subject states, encouraged ordinary citizens to spy on their neighbors, taught kids to rat on their

parents, and sent inconveniently vocal citizens of its puppet nations to gulags or to the executioners. The USSR drove a stake of terror into the hearts of those who had dissenting or creative ideas. Even the US, probably one of the most benevolent hegemons of all time, trampled on others in its pre-superpower days. Over a century ago, it wreaked havoc in the Philippines, Cuba, and snatched territory from Mexico and Spain. Some claim it's continuing equal atrocities to this day.

The lesson of these histories is simple. The tight grip of a monolithic superpower frequently allows us normal folks to go about our daily business without fear that any passing auto may explode in our face and shrapnel us into hamburger. But if we're going to maximize our freedoms, the central power should be us.

China disagrees with this evaluation. The Chinese are calling for an end to "hegemonism"—the Chinese and Soviet codeword for domination of the world by a single power. Yet all the signs are that China is positioning itself to be the next great hegemon. China has been recruiting nations in South America, the Middle East, and Asia for what it has specifically told each of them will be the "new world order," one that will put an end to the "gunboat diplomacy," "neo-colonialism," and the "hegemonism" of an unnamed rival power. That unmentioned power is the United States.

What the nature of a Chinese global peace would be, we will have to see, but here are the signs that the Chinese are laboring to make it a reality.

The Chinese have put big bucks into what Jane's Information Group, the world's top gatherer of military hardware data, calls "leapfrog" military technologies. The Chinese have long had a large nuclear arsenal mounted on some of the world's most powerful Intercontinental Ballistic Missiles and packaged in sophisticated MIRVed warheads (MIRV stands for "multiple independently-targeted reentry vehicle"—a device that allows one rocket to carry a cluster of nuclear bombs, each aimed at a different city). But the Chinese count on this nuclear arsenal as a deterrent—a way of keeping the US's nuclear forces at bay.

The Chinese know that America's military ability to operate overseas is totally dependent on just twelve aircraft carriers (the *Kitty Hawk*, *Constellation*, *Enterprise*, *John F. Kennedy*, *Nimitz*, *Dwight D. Eisenhower*, *Carl Vinson*, *Theodore Roosevelt*, *Abraham Lincoln*, *George Washington*, *John C. Stennis*, *Harry S. Truman*, and the still-unfinished *Ronald Reagan*). China's clincher is a missile designed to destroy every single one of these floating flight-decks. An expert at Jane's Information Group says China's ship-obliterating cruise missile—code-named SS-N-22, the "Sunburn"—was a dangerous aircraft-carrier-killer in its Soviet version, capable of flying at supersonic speed just over the water's surface and evading detection by following an unpredictable zigzag course while carrying a nuclear warhead. With modifications made by the Chinese—whose experience in manufacturing consumer semiconductor devices has put them far ahead of the Russians in microelectronics—the missile goes into what the Jane's experts call a "gray" category, which means it's nearly impossible to detect and destroy. China originally purchased at least sixteen of the missiles from cash-hungry Russian sellers. Each is capable of delivering an explosive punch six times more powerful than the atomic bomb used on Hiroshima.

We do not know how many additional Sunburns the Chinese have manufactured, and we do not know what sort of upgrades the Chinese have made. However, we do know that the Chinese started their own cruise missile program in 1977, reverse-engineered the US Tomahawk missile in the early 1990s, and had nuclear-tipped cruise missiles by 1995. We also know the Chinese created one of the most advanced anti-ship missiles of the late twentieth century, the Silkworm (referred to in China as the Hai Ying-2), were working on a cruise missile with an astonishing 1,500-mile range in the year 2000, and at that point had long since perfected mass production of the devices, cranking them out in sufficient abundance to allow for high-quantity exports to other nations. No wonder Chinese military documents proudly announce that "the strategic superiority which can be claimed by the US is close to zero. It does not even enjoy a sure advantage in terms of the foreseeable scale of war and the high-tech content which can be applied to combat."

The Chinese initially installed their Sunburn strike weapons on two new Russian-built, Sovremenny-class guided-missile destroyers. Their next plan was rumored to be one of greater simplicity—building vessels roughly the size of a PT boat capable of carrying one Sunburn missile each.

Here's where the Tom Clancy stuff comes in. By skimming the water and using violent end maneuvers that throw off defenses, Sunburn missiles have the capacity to put the US military totally out of business in the Western Pacific. At its current detection capability, the Navy would have to plot a response in 2.5 seconds. Impossible.

In other words, as of 2001, China was capable of turning any soldiers, sailors, or pilots sent to Japan, Korea, the Philippines, or Taiwan into chopped meat. Chinese political and military leaders are not the least bit afraid that nuclear war would follow. They've leaked the word to Reuters that, to quote an unnamed "source close to China's military": "Americans can't tolerate death." Says this Asian Deep Throat, China's generals "look at your yellow ribbons for these servicemen and your casualty-free Kosovo and they think you don't have the will." A 1999 document from China's Office of the Central Military Commission backs this up. "Our principle," it says, "is [one of being] 'willing to sustain major losses of our armed forces to defend even just one square inch of land.' If the US forces lose thousands or hundreds of men under our powerful strikes, the anti-war sentiment within their country will force the US government to take the same path as they did in Vietnam."

BY SKIMMING THE WATER AND USING VIOLENT END MANEUVERS THAT THROW OFF DEFENSES, SUNBURN MISSILES HAVE THE CAPACITY TO PUT THE US MILITARY TOTALLY OUT OF BUSINESS IN THE WESTERN PACIFIC.

All through the 1990s and the first years of the twenty-first century, the Chinese slowly and patiently intensified demands that Taiwan be returned to their control. China has also declared sovereignty over virtually everything in the South China Sea, an area rich in natural gas and oil...and an area dotted with landmasses six other countries call their own. The Chinese have bragged in their military documents that they have "conquering-all operational capacity." With the Sunburn missile, they have the magic bullet with which to take what they want. But that is not the Chinese way. They are likely to advance on their prey with the same patience they showed in swallowing Hong Kong back in 1997 and Macau in 1999.

■ ■ ■ ■ ■ ■ ■ ■ ■ ■

Weaponry is just one sign that China is increasing its potential for hegemony—its readiness for a global sway that sidelines the United States. China is eating America's socks economically, too. According to some analysts—like those at the *Japan Times*—China's economy is already the second largest in the world...and it's sprinting fast to catch up with the US's. China's officially-reported gross domestic product is almost twice that of the third-place runner-up, Japan. While the US ran a trade deficit of over $360 billion in the year 2000 alone, China pocketed an annual $84 billion surplus with the US and another $24.9 billion surplus with Japan. In other words, China has become an economic vacuum cleaner emptying the wallets of America and its allies. Pick almost any shopping mall, discount chain, or local store in America and you'll find evidence of major dependency on Chinese goods. A staggering percentage of the clothing, toys, and electronic devices on sale originate in China. Take away all items that say "made in China," and the average American wouldn't make it through the week.

But that's just the beginning. China has made huge profits on export goods by doing what social theorist Jane Jacobs calls "import replacement"—cranking out items once made by American, Japanese, Korean, or Thai workers at a price no American, Japanese, Korean, or Thai can beat. The next step, as the *People's Daily* says, is to "intensify the content of high-technology." Which means the Chinese want to outsprint the US in the race toward twenty-second-century innovations.

The nation that holds the innovative high ground is usually the one that rules the world. But what are China's chances of actually outpacing Bill Gates and America's other techno-leaders in the sprint toward next-generation wonders? Very good, indeed.

CHINA HAS BECOME AN ECONOMIC VACUUM CLEANER EMPTYING THE WALLETS OF AMERICA AND ITS ALLIES.

Green parties stoking fears of "Frankenfoods" and other new agricultural technologies are trying to drag Europe and the US into the agro-past. Meanwhile China has jumped enthusiastically into genetically-modified seed use. A million Chinese farmers now grow genetically-modified cotton, saving $100 billion on pesticides and losses to insects and rodents, and giving China—the former land of famine—an increasingly potent agricultural export industry...one capable, in the words of Japan's Agricultural Ministry, of "flooding" Japan with cheap vegetable imports.

Then there's optoelectronics—a $10-billion business for the Chinese as of 2001, and growing at the rate of 50 percent a year. And computer education—a million Chinese a year are learning to use Microsoft software (poor things). And consumer software creation. Microsoft, which very seldom plants research and development operations on foreign soil, established a software R&D center in Beijing way back in 1998. Not to mention artificial intelligence—where one investor feels Guangzhou's Hua Ling Group "is a step ahead of foreign scientists."

China stands a good chance of becoming the world's top semiconductor manufacturer by 2006. Project 909 is an effort to lure high-tech manufacturers to China so the Chinese can suck up foreign expertise in military and civilian semiconductor development and fabrication, then eventually imitate, borrow, and outpace it. Once the bait was laid out, the number of those who happily stumbled into the trap was remarkable. Motorola, which as of November 2000 had already seeded China with eight semiconductor design houses and at least one mobile-handset plant, announced that it would spend close to $2 billion on a new Chinese chip production complex. Japan's NEC, the world's fourth-largest chipmaker, built a $1.2-billion chip plant in China's Zhangjiang High-Tech Industrial Park. Meantime, investors from Taiwan and a variety of other international locations were building a $1.6 billion chip foundry in the same park.

In the early 1990s, 70 percent of foreign direct investment in the Asian nations went to the Southeast Asian tigers and only 30 per-

cent to China. By 2001, the tigers had been declawed and defanged by their Chinese neighbor, which now swallowed 70 percent of foreign investment funds. Further dollars and high-tech investment will continue to flow in. One reason—the Chinese are graduating more students with information technology training than any other low-cost-labor nation in sight. "Their mathematics background is excellent. It's disciplined and thorough in a way that you often can't find in the West," says Microsoft's head of research in China, American-born Kai-fu Lee (one of many highly-skilled Asians the Chinese have lured back to fuel the high-tech climb of their homeland). But education and intelligence are not the only Chinese edge. By 2000, Intel had a $400-million flash memory assembly plant up and running in Shanghai and a research and development center near Beijing. Then, when the world economy crashed in 2001, Intel defied logic and invested an additional $302 million. The money was used to expand a Shanghai-based Intel plant dedicated to the manufacture of Intel 845 chipsets for the Pentium 4 processor. The move was not as daft as it may have seemed.

While the consumers in the rest of the world were up to their ears in computers and were snapping their purses shut, China's 1.2 billion buyers were expected to increase their purchase of PCs by 20 percent a year. In the long-run, Intel, NEC, Microsoft, and the others rushing to build plants and other facilities in China may regret their eagerness. China steals the technologies of outsiders, then becomes the outside-firms' most ferocious competitor. The US did this in the nineteenth century when it sent industrial spies to England to ferret out the secrets of Britain's top-secret industrial devices—mechanized weaving machines. Though it was illegal to take drawings or plans for these machines out of the UK, Americans smuggled sketches and blueprints to New England and built their own mass-production textile mills. From the 1950s to the 1980s, the Japanese did the same to the US—gutting the consumer electronics industry and pummeling auto companies into a sorry state.

Now it's China's turn. The Chinese already show signs of turning the tables on America in such fields as robotics. In 1988, the Shenyang Institute of Automation paid a firm called Perry Tritech in Florida a million dollars for an unusual package deal: a deep-sea robot, spare parts, and training in robot technology. By 1991, the Chinese had upgraded the undersea rover—a device that comes in handy for inspections of floating oil rigs and dams. In fact, they'd improved its qualities and lowered its price so much that they were able to sell their new version of the ROV (remote-operated vehicle) to several American companies. Intel China President Wee Theng Tan is extremely open about this form of techno-theft when he says proudly: "We [Intel] will continue to bring our leading edge technical and manufacturing expertise to China to help the country develop a leadership role in high-end, value-added manufacturing technologies."

But the real crunch will come when China takes advantage of its people's ingenuity and respect for education by out-innovating the

US. China—the nation that created the world's first modern paper, first encyclopedias, first magnetic compass, first gunpowder, and first cannon—held the high ground in technology from roughly 200 BC until 1600 AD. Now the Chinese are working hard to get back to the leading edge and beyond, moving into such fields as nanotechnology. A team of four scientists at Jiaotong University in Shanghai announced in 2001 that they'd created a micro-motor a quarter the size of a sesame seed. The device, they said, was smaller and lighter than any developed in the US, Europe, or Japan. It was exactly the sort of thing the medical equipment industry was looking for. In another area, telecommunications, Dr. Wei Chen—an American-born Chinese—started a company in China to manufacture and sell his pioneering wireless local-loop equipment. And the Institute of Developmental Biology in Beijing is working on beyond-the-envelope genetic engineering.

Boast the writers of one 1999 Chinese document from the Office of the Central Military Commission: "In the five thousand years of outstanding civilisation, our country has commanded a predominant position in the whole world." And they're right. To the Chinese, dominance of the world's economy would simply mean a return to the way things used to be. Balance of payments deficits between China and the West go back at least 2,000 years, to the days when the Romans nearly depleted the product of their Laurium and Pangaeum silver mines to pay for Chinese silk. Eighteen-hundred years later, the Chinese delusion began—the notion that one could make vast sums of money by selling goods to China's masses. This was a dream, a fantasy. China sold goods the world wanted—silk, porcelain (called "China" because it became a necessity in Western homes), and tea (another daily necessity in the British lifestyle). But the West had nothing the Chinese needed.

CHINA STEALS THE TECHNOLOGIES OF OUTSIDERS, THEN BECOMES THE OUTSIDE-FIRMS' MOST FEROCIOUS COMPETITOR.

The balance of trade deficits threatened to drain the coffers of Britain and America until the puritanical Empire of Queen Victoria began an official policy of breaking Chinese law by selling and promoting opium from England's Indian territories. Leading American families—from the Forbes to the Delanos—made millions smuggling illicit drugs into the Chinese market. When the Chinese, under Lin Tse-hsü, Yeh Ming-ch'en, and Hsü Kuang-chin, mounted several potentially successful internal wars on the drug trade, the West responded with the Opium Wars of 1839 and 1856. To be specific, Europeans and Americans used steam-powered gunboats to shove opiates down China's throat. To get an idea of how this felt to the Chinese, imagine what would happen if Colombia, impatient with America's resistance to its export trade in cocaine and heroin, mounted a war against the US, won, forced America to legalize narcotics, then went on a mass-marketing campaign to put an addict in every home, a line of coke up every nostril, and a needle in every American teenager's arm.

Despite this experience, the delusion that one could make millions selling legitimate goods and services to the Chinese continued. Douglas MacArthur's father was dazzled by it in the nineteenth century. MacArthur himself continued with it. What American auto makers and others who made huge investments in Chinese joint ventures failed to realize was China's new economic strategy for the twentieth and twenty-first centuries: Let the foreign barbarians build their plants; make sure those factories are under the control of Chinese co-owners; study the manufacturing machinery, organizational techniques, and patented technologies the Western investors so gracefully provide; imitate them, improve on them, steal those under patent or licensing protection; then undercut the American and US industries that had been foolish enough to offer themselves on the altar of sacrifice to the new China.

■ ■ ■ ■ ■ ■ ■ ■ ■ ■

The payoff will come on the geopolitical side of the equation. China's President Jiang Zemin took a six-nation trip to the strategic backyard of the United States—Latin America—in April 2001, calling on Latin Americans to work with China toward building, to use his catchphrase, a "new international order" (the six nations were Uruguay, Brazil, Chile, Argentina, Cuba, and Venezuela). Jiang found enormous eagerness in anti-American Venezuela (where Chinese have invested $530 million and have interests in two oil fields), in Chile, in Argentina, and in Cuba, to which the Chinese are lending $400 million.

Meanwhile, Chinese power showed itself in many another international nuance. The new Japanese Prime Minister Junichiro Koizumi put improving relations with China at the top of his international agenda when he rose to power in May 2001. Mexican President Vicente Fox visited Jiang in China in June. Fox was wary of the impact of cheap Chinese imports on Mexican industry. (In just two months—January and February 2001—China sold $465-million worth of products to Mexico but bought only $32-million worth of Mexican products.) Yet Fox felt it necessary to make a pilgrimage to Beijing.

Chinese businesses have been exploring the potential of Africa as a market for their goods—the Chinese have built Africa's biggest supermarket in Johannesburg, a power-generating equipment plant in Nigeria, and methane tanks in Uganda (with plans for solar energy and hydropower projects to follow). Cambodia's Hun Sen has urged other nations to follow an anti-Taiwan, one-China policy to keep Beijing happy and deliver Taiwan into China's hands. On July 15, 2001, Jiang Zemin headed for Moscow, where he signed a friendship treaty. The Bush Administration said it was not afraid of the agreement because China still needs the US for investment and technology—meaning that George W. Bush intends to continue the policy of letting China suck America dry.

President Jiang Zemin has also taken his message of a world

"peace" led by China to his neighbors, the ASEAN states: Thailand, Myanmar, Cambodia, Laos, Vietnam, Malaysia, Brunei, Singapore, the Philippines, and Indonesia. In September 1999, Jiang visited Thailand to repeat his standard message, that "China and countries of the Association of South East Asian Nations (ASEAN) wanted a new international order to counter the power politics of some big world powers."

China has frequently railed against what it calls "encirclement," but its diplomatic maneuverings seem carefully designed to encircle Europe and the US. Take China's Islamic connection. In 1999, Egypt's Hosni Mubarak and China's Jiang Zemin signed an agreement establishing a strategic cooperative relationship. Reported China's government mouthpiece *People's Daily*, the Egyptian ambassador to China said Egypt "opposes certain countries which use the human rights issue to interfere in the internal affairs of China and other countries" and "supports China's just struggle against power politics and hegemonism." Meanwhile, the Chinese and Egyptian news media—both noted for their lack of free expression—are engaged in active exchanges.

China is building "a special economic zone" in the northwest Suez. And China has close ties with the Palestinians. Far more important, China makes a considerable amount of money by selling high-tech weapons—including nuclear and missile parts and instructions—to "rogue nations" like Iran and Iraq. China also had a hand in helping Pakistan build "the Islamic bomb."

In one sense, this is reassuring. It shows that the Chinese can be as shortsighted as the US. From 1980 onward, the CIA and the Peoples' Liberation Army backed the Taliban in Afghanistan. China cooperated with the US and Saudi Arabia in arming and training 50,000 militant Muslims from 30 countries for this "freedom-fighting" *jihad*. The Chinese joined America in giving Osama bin Laden his troops, and sent 300 officers to train the *mujahideen* in the use of sophisticated weapons—like Chinese-made anti-tank missiles. When the Taliban took over in 1995, support for it had been a bipartisan affair in the US, beginning in the Carter Administration and continuing under Reagan and Bush. The US helped build the very force that would come back to strike it on September 11, 2001. The resulting worldwide war of the US and its allies against "terrorism" could theoretically weaken both the West and the Islamic militants and help world domination slip easily into Chinese hands.

However, once the smoke of battle between Islamic extremism and the West has cleared, bin Laden-style blowback could prove equally dangerous to Beijing. There is an extremely active *jihad*—an Islamic holy war—taking place in China's "wild west" province, Xinjiang. It is part of a widespread military campaign to take all of Central Asia—including Xinjiang, Chechnya, Dagestan, Tajikistan,

Kyrgyzstan, Kashmir, and Uzbekistan—thus "liberating" this enormous sweep of territory to be part of *dar el Islam* (the Islamic World).

The holy warriors' fervor to make all the world Islamic could easily go further than China's border provinces and strike at the Chinese heart. China has the second-largest Islamic population in the world. The Islamic *mujahedin* that the US and the Chinese have trained and armed are idealists of the highest degree. They cannot rest until justice and purity have been given as a gift to all the citizens of this world. Justice can be obtained only by imposing Islamic law—*shari'a*. Purity and propriety are only possible when a people has been freed from false idols and taught to worship the one and only god (Allah) and his one true prophet (Mohammed). China, too, should be ruled by the laws of the Koran.

The jostling for position between China, Islam, and the US is part of a standard hierarchical game that dates back to the dawn of life 3.5 billion years ago. It has involved all forms of beings, from microbes to mammals. If an animal or a social group doesn't see an opportunity to move up, it lets the top dog rule without challenge. But if things change, if the alpha male begins to slip, weakened by age or battle, if the underdog goes from a puny adolescent to a muscular adult, or if the subordinate grows stronger by discovering a new source of energy or food, the former inferior seizes the opportunity to knock the head honcho out of his number-one slot.

The most overtly belligerent underdog in today's world is fundamentalist Islam. But the real power working on the sidelines to pick up the pieces of authority when Islam and the US exhaust themselves in battle is China.

Chinese President Jiang Zemin sums up his goals this way: "The world is far from being tranquil. Hegemonism and power politics still exist and have even developed in the international political, economic, and security fields. The new 'gunboat policy' and the economic neo-colonialism pursued by some big powers has severely undermined the sovereign independence and development interest of small and medium-sized countries and has threatened world peace and international security. China firmly opposes hegemonism and power politics and will never seek hegemony—that is a solemn commitment that the Chinese government and the people have made to the whole world."

Any nation that buys that line is putting a down payment on a seat at the bottom of the Chinese heap.

SCENES FROM A SECRET WAR
THE IMPORTANCE OF PERU'S COMPLICITY IN PLAN COLOMBIA AND HOW IT HAS BEEN ASSURED

PETER GORMAN

Even before Bill Clinton unveiled his massive military aid package known as Plan Colombia, his intelligence had identified Peru as the key to making it work because of its location. Peru shares the southern border of Colombia for 995 miles (1,600 kilometers), along the Putumayo river, a remote jungle region in which there are very few villages and fewer potential witnesses.

Peru's strategic location is vital to Plan Colombia's success for two reasons. First, the Peruvian side of the border—toward which the FARC rebels will be pushed once Colombia's offensive is initiated—gives the US and Colombia an easily protected resupply and repair area away from the long reach of rebel ambush; second, the Putumayo river provides a clearly defined southern point to the fighting about to commence. The river will be utilized as the containment line that marks the end of the road for retreating rebels or coca growers.

Simply put, while rebels may flee into the unprotectable mountainous jungle of Ecuador to the west, or into the unprotectable jungles of Venezuela and Brazil to the east (though the latter two are anticipated to be quite a distance from the heart of battle and neither border represents a FARC stronghold), Peru offers the US a definitive line in the sand, the sort of line it didn't have in either Vietnam or Korea.

Because of that strategic importance, it is necessary that Peru be a willing partner in Plan Colombia. Through a series of three reports that were written and published—in slightly different form—in the months leading up to battle, this article deals with the successful machinations of the US government to insure Peru's compliance with the US's needs. The first deals with the reasons the CIA had to eliminate Peru's former president Alberto Fujimori, as well as how it was done. The second deals with how Peru is actively preparing for the war through the use of CIA and State Department contractors. The third article discusses the possibility that the decision to implement Plan Colombia, as well as the location of its military target zone, might have been decided by the discovery of a potentially massive oil bed beneath FARC territory. Taken as a body, the evidence clearly demonstrates that several disturbing but apparently unassociated events that have occurred in Peru during the past year have in fact been a very well-orchestrated plan by the US intelligence community to force Peru into compliance with Plan Colombia.

The reports are presented here in the time frame during which they were published.

_ANATOMY OF A COUP: CIA OPERATION IN PERU OPENS DOOR TO PLAN COLOMBIA

(December 2000) For more than 50 years, the history of US involvement with South America has been one of often bloody interference in social, economic, and political affairs. From setting up dictatorships to the movement of drugs, the CIA has been the puppeteer behind the scenes when US interests are at stake. Peru in 2000 was no exception. When its longtime president, Alberto Fujimori, refused to cooperate with Clinton's Plan Colombia, he had to go. Enter the CIA; exit Fujimori. In what has all the earmarks of a bloodless coup arranged by the CIA, Fujimori was forced from office, and his right-hand man and Pentagon-trained CIA informant, Vladimiro Montesinos, is in hiding and faces criminal charges. A little-known lifetime politician, Congressman Valentin Paniagua, after a series of resignations by several people in line for the post, has ascended to Peru's presidency, albeit only on an interim basis until new elections can be held in April 2001.

> FOR MORE THAN 50 YEARS, THE HISTORY OF US INVOLVEMENT WITH SOUTH AMERICA HAS BEEN ONE OF OFTEN BLOODY INTERFERENCE IN SOCIAL, ECONOMIC, AND POLITICAL AFFAIRS.

How and why the popular, though dictatorial Fujimori so suddenly lost his autocratic grip on the government, and what will undoubtedly happen soon—as well as who will benefit—make for a scenario straight out of a Tom Clancy novel.

In truth, Fujimori was forced from office by the CIA in a coup so smoothly arranged that no major Western press outlet has even hinted at it being such. The reason was because Fujimori was vocal in his dislike of the military components in US President Bill Clinton's Plan Colombia, and particularly in his refusal to allow the US to use

Peru as a staging ground for the US advisors and Colombian troops needed to make Plan Colombia work.

Plan Colombia. The plot has roots that go back more than a year, to the time when Plan Colombia was first unveiled. That plan calls for a $1.3-billion effort by the US to rid Colombia of its burgeoning coca-producing fields, although conspiratorialists would say its real purpose is to wrest control of that trade from the Colombian rebels and return it to the Colombian armed forces and known narco-traffickers who put their proceeds in American banks. The plan centers on elite US Special Forces' training of three Colombian military battalions—equipped with more than half-a-billion dollars in US-made helicopters and arms—in jungle warfare. Once trained, the Colombian military will move into the vast jungle in southern Colombia, controlled by the FARC rebels, calling for them to lay down their arms, while simultaneously destroying the coca fields they depend on to generate funds for their rebellion.

> THE PLAN CENTERS ON ELITE US SPECIAL FORCES' TRAINING OF THREE COLOMBIAN MILITARY BATTALIONS—EQUIPPED WITH MORE THAN HALF-A-BILLION DOLLARS IN US-MADE HELICOPTERS AND ARMS—IN JUNGLE WARFARE.

Though the US is calling on the Colombians to refrain from engaging the rebels in conflict, most observers expect that heavy fighting will occur. Colombia's civil strife—fueled by cocaine money—has already been raging for 35 years, leaving 35,000 dead and nearly half a million people displaced, so there appears little chance that a new government offensive will end it without further casualties. Tens of thousands more people—mostly agrarian peasants and indigenous peoples—are expected to become refugees, with many seeking asylum in neighboring countries.

Which is where Plan Colombia ran into an unexpected stumbling block. To make the plan work, the US needed the approval of at least some of Colombia's neighbors, both to willingly accept the anticipated refugees and to provide a military base for use by the Colombians and the new fleet of battle-ready Blackhawk and Huey helicopters with which the US is arming them. Specifically what was needed was a base outside of Colombia, which would considerably lessen the chance of a rebel strike on those choppers, as the FARC forces are not considered strong enough to fight a war against both their own government and a foreign government (which would surely be the result of an attack on a base in a neighboring country).

At the time of the plan's unveiling in early 2000, the US already knew that Venezuela, with a socialist government, would not be a party to it. Brazil, whose little-populated northwest corner is likely to see an influx of refugees from the fray, was also unwilling to build a base there. Ecuador, a US ally, is neither strong enough nor stable enough to offer much. It has leased a large base to the US at Manta,

on the Pacific coast, but to reach it from the expected area of battle, the helicopters would need to fly over the Andes mountain range, an impossible task, particularly if they were hit by enemy fire. Bolivia—under the leadership of its newly-elected president, General Hugo Banzer, a Pentagon-trained former cocaine baron—volunteered to build a large airbase for the US to use, but like Ecuador's Manta, it is too far away from Colombia to be of much assistance as an immediate repair and resupply point. Which left Colombia's immediate neighbor to the south, Peru, as the anticipated key ally of Plan Colombia.

Peru's then-president, Alberto Fujimori, while not always an ally of US policy, was already dependent on the US and the International Monetary Fund to keep its foreign loan-cycles floating. Additionally, Fujimori's closest advisor was Vladimiro Montesinos—Peru's spy-chief and, like Bolivia's Banzer, trained by the Pentagon—who is considered by the international press to be a CIA operative. With those two in the primary seats of power, the US expected Peru to herald the plan and volunteer its jungle city of Iquitos and environs as a staging ground for the coming conflict. Moreover, during 1998 and 1999, the US had helped Peru build a large military post outside of Iquitos near Colombia's southern border—where much of the fighting produced from Plan Colombia is expected to take place. But Fujimori threw the US a curve when, after the base was completed, he announced that it would be utilized exclusively by the Peruvian military. He then further enraged the US when he publicly and repeatedly decried the military components of Plan Colombia in spring 2000.

Which meant, in CIA parlance, that he had to go. Unfortunately for the US, he was about to be elected to a third term as president (which, though illegal under Peruvian law, didn't seem to matter much to the Peruvian populace, which gave him a 42 percent approval rating—very high in that country), so any overt attempt to remove him would've drawn severe political backlash just as Clinton was pushing for approval (read: funding) for Plan Colombia.

Worse, in April 2000—when Colombia President Andres Pastrana was set to come to the US to push for emergency passage of the plan—many Republicans, including Senate majority leader Trent Lott, were pressing for a postponement of allocating emergency funds for the plan, instead suggesting that it ought to wait until 2001 and the normal federal budgetary timetable. If that happened, if the funding were not approved while Clinton was still in office, it would no longer be considered Clinton's Plan Colombia, something that would've pleased the Republicans no end. But Clinton and his Drug Czar—former head of the Southern Command, General Barry McCaffrey—would have none of that. And so on April 9, just days before Pastrana's visit, the State Department leaked a story to MSNBC—in other words, the State Department was MSNBC's source—that Russian planes were picking up used Kalishnakov rifles in Aaman, Jordan, which were being delivered by air drop to the FARC rebels in southern Colombia. After they dropped their cargo, according to MSNBC, the planes were being refueled in Peru, in nearby Iquitos' airport, where they were being filled each time with as much as 40 tons of FARC-made cocaine for distribution in Europe.

The story was a fake on the face of it. First off, while the FARC rebels are known to tax cocaine producers, they have never been known as traffickers. Also, the airport at Iquitos is in a very public location that borders on a Peruvian Air Force base where several US Drug Enforcement Administration agents work—which means it would have taken overt complicity by both the DEA and the Peruvian military with the FARC rebels for the story to have merit.

Nonetheless, the story had its desired effect: Trent Lott and the other Republicans, who just days earlier were saying "no" to Plan Colombia, quickly changed their positions, and on April 12, Lott, in the face of looking soft on drugs, assured Pastrana that Plan Colombia would pass. One month later, on May 18, Clinton got his plan and the monies approved.

First Hope to Eliminate Fujimori. Plan Colombia went into effect almost immediately. The first battalion of vetted and screened elite Colombian soldiers were flown to Fort Bragg, North Carolina, in August 2000 and are expected to graduate in late December, offering a potential timetable for the fighting to begin as early as January 2001. To the US, that meant Fujimori would either quickly decide to get with the program and let the US use the new base, or he would have to go. Whichever it was, it had to be done by the time the first offensive started. Fujimori wouldn't budge.

The first hope to remove Fujimori was to have him simply lose his bid for a third term in office to the previously unknown, Stanford-trained World Bank economist and former shoeshine boy Alejandro Toledo. That failed when Fujimori and Toledo wound up in an election runoff in which Toledo refused to participate, leaving Fujimori the winner of his third term. But the bitter election, with talk of Fujimori having stolen it through vote-rigging, left Fujimori politically vulnerable. There were even rumors that he would be publicly denounced at a South American presidential summit in August, leading many political observers to think he might voluntarily step down rather than face international disgrace.

Instead of stepping down, however, just prior to the summit meetings Fujimori cleverly resurrected the State Department story of the Russian guns making their way to the FARC rebels. His version left out the part about the planes loading up with cocaine in Iquitos, though. In his version it was his spy chief, Montesinos, who had discovered and busted the ring of arms dealers. Unlike the State Department story, which was invented to pass Plan Colombia and

then quickly die, Fujimori's version made the international wire services; photos of Fujimori and Montesinos with part of the arms shipment appeared in every major media outlet, and subsequently, at the August summit, Fujimori was lauded for his work against the FARC rebels rather than ridiculed for stealing the election.

Unfortunately, the story quickly blew up in Fujimori's face when the Aaman arms dealers acknowledged the arms sales but said that they'd all occurred a year earlier, that the buyers were Peruvian Generals, and that all the paperwork was in order. Vulnerable again, Fujimori quickly announced that jailed American Lori Berenson—convicted in Peru in 1996 of treason for her association with the Peruvian rebel group Tupac Amaru—would get a new trial, a story which the Western press jumped on, while all but dropping the fake FARC arms bust.

By early September, with Fujimori firmly in place for his third term, the US was getting desperate. The first US-trained Colombian military forces were set to stage their initial offensive into FARC territory in early January 2001—Pastrana's timetable for peace-or-else—and Fujimori was still not going along with the idea of the US using the new military base near Colombia's southern border.

The Coup. That's when the CIA stepped in with a classic maneuver. In mid-September, a video was widely released throughout Peru—and subsequently through worldwide media outlets—showing Montesinos giving Peruvian Congressman Alberto Kouri US$15,000 during the previous April. Shortly after the money changed hands, Kouri, from Peru's opposition party, switched allegiances and joined Fujimori's party, one of several Congressmen who had done so at that time, giving Fujimori a congressional majority. But while the media went wild over the apparent bribe, none asked the logical question: Who released the tape to the media?

Broadcasters acknowledged that the tape was made by Montesinos in his own offices, something we later learned he routinely did, apparently to use as blackmail. But who could have gotten into his incredibly well-protected offices in the heart of the Peruvian presidential palace and located a short segment of tape made months earlier among the thousands of other hours of tape that Montesinos made of all his office doings? Unless something comes to light in the future to disprove it, it's reasonably safe to say Montesinos did not release the tape himself, which means someone close to him did. And whoever did it knew it would bring the spy chief down, and, eventually, Fujimori with him. Which means, though it has yet to be proven, that someone got to a person close to Montesinos and promised something big in the new administration that would take over after Fujimori fell. Who the promiser and promisee were, we don't yet know. We do know that in an unscheduled flight on October

> "THE POSSIBLE US USE OF THE STRATEGIC NEW MILITARY BASE NEAR THE COLOMBIAN BORDER HAS COME UP IN EARLY DISCUSSIONS RELATED TO THE REFINANCING OF PERU'S DEBT STRUCTURE."

EVERYTHING YOU KNOW IS WRONG

27, Alberto Kouri, the receiver of the alleged bribe, fled to Dallas, where he was greeted with open arms and currently remains. That suggests that Kouri may well have been aware that the tape was going to be released and offered himself up as a sacrificial lamb in exchange for asylum in the US. All of which points to CIA involvement and arrangements.

As to the tape of the apparent bribe, it immediately disgraced Montesinos, who fled to Panama, where he has extensive landholdings, seeking political asylum. That bid failed, and he returned to Peru in late October. It is thought that he has fled to Venezuela since then. Fujimori tried to ride out the tide of public opinion which rose against him after his advisor was caught bribing Kouri by publicly going after Montesinos. But when he did not locate him, Fujimori announced that he would hold new elections in April 2001, in which he would not run, and he promised to step down when the new president took office on July 28, 2001.

Unfortunately, that timetable simply did not work with the US need for a military base near Colombia's southern border by January 1, 2001. By chance, Peruvian congressional investigations were started into both Montesinos and Fujimori in early November, and allegations of millions of dollars in secret Swiss bank accounts in Montesinos' name—alleged to be from illegal arms and drug transactions—surfaced within mere days.

Those allegations, coupled with the sudden instability of Peru's presidential administration, had an immediate and dire effect on Peru's economy. On November 3, Standard and Poor's—the arbiter of international finance—downgraded Peru's long-term foreign currency rating to a level four notches below investment-grade status, leaving the country in a position of not being able to make good on major international loans due at year's end.

Again trying to cleverly avoid the Peruvian public reaction to the burgeoning corruption scandal, Fujimori traveled to Brunei for a Pacific Rim summit and then on to Japan to try to secure loans, which were desperately needed by Peru by the end of 2000 in order to keep their loan-cycles floating. But while he was there, political opposition party leaders wrested control of the Congress from Fujimori's party, leading to Fujimori faxing in a resignation "for the good of the country."

The resignation was refused, with Peru's Congress instead choosing to oust Fujimori in late November on the grounds that he was "morally unfit" to lead the country. He is currently in Japan, where he has claim to citizenship because both his parents were Japanese.

Beyond Fujimori, the next two vice presidents in line for the presidency abruptly resigned because of the scandal. The head of Peru's Congress, Martha Hildebrandt, a close Fujimori ally, would have been the natural next choice for the vacated presidency, but she had just been ousted by Congressional vote when she refused to call for

an investigation of Montesinos' criminal activity. The void in Peru's presidential succession order was filled when Peru's Congress elected Valentin Paniagua, a political moderate, to take the empty Hildebrandt seat, and shortly thereafter he was chosen by Congressional consensus to take over as interim President until the April elections. Paniagua, 64, is a lawyer with the Popular Action Party who twice served at cabinet level, both as Justice Minister in the 1960s and as Education Minister in 1984, during the two administrations of former Peruvian President Fernando Belaunde.

Belaunde was widely loved in Peru, but critics faulted him for being in the pocket of the US. Paniagua is from the same mold. So while Paniagua's accession to the presidency does not automatically mean that Peru will change its position and sign on to Plan Colombia, it probably does. And if Paniagua should decide not to allow the US to use the new military base near Colombia's border, the financial turmoil the country finds itself in and the pressing obligations it must fulfill make him vulnerable to fiscal pressure from the US. In fact, a senior finance official at the Peruvian Consulate in Washington, DC, told this reporter on December 3—on condition that his name not be used—that "the possible US use of the strategic new military base near the Colombian border has come up in early discussions related to the refinancing of Peru's debt structure."

If that indeed takes place, then we might well have seen one of the most clever CIA-engineered coups in South America in some time. Bloodless and clean as a bone.

Aftermath. On January 16, 2001, Valentin Paniagua—through his Interim Prime Minister Javier Perez de Cuellar, the former UN Secretary General—announced that Peru had rethought its commitment to Plan Colombia and would now assist in its implementation in any way possible. Standard and Poors has not yet changed the long-term currency rating.

On May 14, the Narco News Bulletin <narconews.com> published the translated transcript of one of the Vladimiro Montesinos' tapes. The original transcript was published in Spanish on that day by the Peruvian daily *La Republica*. The tape has Montesinos speaking with the owner of Global Television of Peru, Genaro Delgado Parker. It was made on April 21, 2000, just days after Plan Colombia was approved and Peru's President Alberto Fujimori had once again decried it, this time in Washington, DC.

Delgado: "I saw the other day that the President [of Perú, Alberto Fujimori] had a chat in Washington."

Montesinos: "Yes, on the theme of Colombia? Clearly, that was coordinated with the Americans."

Delgado: "Yes, but I think that behind this is the idea of making a kind of NATO in Latin America."

Montesinos: "Do you know why that could not happen? Because, in first place, [Ecuador President Jamil] Mahuad doesn't agree. That lunatic from Venezuela, [President Hugo] Chávez, doesn't agree either. And the only one that supports is [Argentina President Carlos] Menem, but Menem is very far from the stage; and [Brazil President Fernando] Cardoso doesn't want it either. Then, the only alternative that the Americans have in order to solve the problem of Colombia, is the invasion, that they are going to do this year. They are preparing half a million Marine infantry troops in order to invade Colombia and they asked us for the President to make declarations because they could not say it themselves. Then, the President [Fujimori] made declarations at the Interamerican School. Here we are making preparations in order to close the entire zone that we have, 1,600 kilometers of border. When the infantry of the Marines does enter, what are they going to make the FARC and the drug dealers do? They are going to come to Perú. And if we don't close the border now and adopt security measures, we will bring the problem here."

Montesinos himself was captured in Venezuela in late June 2001 and returned to Peru. He is currently awaiting trial on more than 100 counts of criminal activity, and the Peruvian courts are trying to establish the specific origins of $256 million said to be in accounts under his name. At least $10 million of that came from the CIA, which has admitted paying him $1 million a year during Fujimori's ten-year administration, which they claim was to help fight drug trafficking.

Fujimori remains in Japan, though he is currently under indictment in Peru on several criminal counts.

Alejandro Toledo, elected to office over former President Alan Garcia in April 2001, officially took office on July 28, 2001. He, like former interim-President Valentin Paniagua, has promised whatever support Peru can give to both the original Plan Colombia—which will mean the use of the military base near the Colombian border—as well as to US President George W. Bush's new Andean Initiative, which will intensify US presence throughout the region.

_COLOMBIA'S PASTRANA READIES FOR BATTLE, JANUARY 2001: AMERICAN MERCENARIES VOLUNTEER FOR KILL FEES

IQUITOS, PERU — By the time this goes to press in early February 2001, Colombia's President Andres Pastrana will have met for the first time since November with Manuel "Sureshot" Marulanda, the leader of the Revolutionary Armed Forces of Colombia (FARC). It is

possibly the last chance at the peace tables for the rebels before he unleashes his US-trained and US-armed jungle fighters on them, and follows four extensions of the peace-table-or-else ultimatum that Pastrana set for early January. Most people observing the ongoing civil war in that country view Pastrana's unwillingness to forego the peace process in favor of all-out war as a sign of enlightened leadership. Cynics, however, see it more as a sign that his US-trained troops are not quite ready for action. In fact, before heading into war, Pastrana has several pieces of his military puzzle to line up, a process that may take several more months. If the cynics are right, until those pieces are in place, additional olive-branches—extending the already passed January 1 deadline for peace talks—will be offered to the FARC as a cover for preparing for battle.

Preparing for the Coming War. Pastrana needed four things to occur before he could feel confident that a war with the FARC could be won in a decisive manner. First, of the three battalions of hand-picked and US-vetted Colombian military troops to be trained by US Special Forces personnel, only one has finished its training and is fully prepared for battle in the dense jungle of southern Colombia, the FARC stronghold. The two additional battalions won't be ready until April and late May, leaving Pastrana currently shorthanded in well-trained jungle troops.

Secondly, while the 46 armed Blackhawk and Huey helicopters promised as part of Clinton's initial $1.3 billion Plan Colombia are starting to be delivered, Colombia has insufficient troops to fly them. So Pastrana, by stalling the commencement of hostilities against the FARC, is also buying time for US advisors to train Colombian chopper pilots.

> THEY CLAIM—QUITE OPENLY TO THOSE IN IQUITOS, INCLUDING THIS REPORTER—THAT THEY ARE HIRED BY A COMPANY CALLED VIRGINIA ELECTRONICS, THAT THEY EARN MONEY PER KILL, AND THAT SINCE THEY ARE RETIRED, THEY AREN'T BOUND BY MILITARY CODES.

A third element that Pastrana needed to have in place before going to war recently has been handled: Peru, which under former President Alberto Fujimori had refused to permit either the US or Colombian troops to use Peruvian military bases near the Colombian border (leading to the US-arranged coup of Fujimori), has changed its stance since new interim President Valentin Paniagua has taken over the reins. Paniagua, through his interim Prime Minister Javier Perez de Cuellar, the former UN Secretary General, announced on January 16 that Peru has done an about-face and will now back Plan Colombia in any way it can. Since then, the US has quietly been moving advisors—and is preparing to move military equipment—to a base near the Putumayo river, the Peru-Colombia border adjacent to the spot where the heaviest fighting is expected to take place.

Mercenaries: Last Piece of the Puzzle. There is one more piece to the puzzle that Pastrana needs in place before taking on the 17-

20,000-strong FARC in the jungle turf they know so well: Someone to clean up the mess and eliminate them as they flee. That piece of the puzzle is also falling into place, though both the US and Colombia, along with now-complicit Peru, deny it. During the past two months, the Peruvian jungle city of Iquitos, the closest Peruvian city to southern Colombia with an international airport, has become the receiving point for several gunboats said to be part of the US-backed Peruvian Riverine Program. That program is one in which the US provides boats and training to Peru's military in order to help them better intercept coca base making its way through the Peruvian Amazon to the Colombian port of Leticia, just a five-minute boat ride across the Amazon from Peruvian soil.

But while the Riverine Program has been in place for several years, it is only during the past few weeks that those boats have begun to be moved from Peru's Amazon to the Putumayo. The boats, as large as 38 feet with four guns, are equipped with cutting-edge marine electronics, from radar to listening devices, and armed with anti-aircraft guns along with mounted machine guns. But unlike the times when they genuinely were used as part of the Riverine Program, they are no longer going to be manned by Peruvian forces but by teams of retired Navy SEALS, often considered the Pentagon's best stealth fighting force.

ON FEBRUARY 18, 2001, RETIRED US SPECIAL FORCES TROOPS FLYING HELICOPTER COVER FOR A CROPDUSTER SPRAYING HERBICIDE ON COCA FIELDS IN FARC TERRITORY IN SOUTHERN COLOMBIA CAME UNDER FIRE AND WAS FORCED DOWN.

The retired SEAL teams—who have also been arriving in Iquitos during the past several weeks—have been brought in ostensibly to work the boats' complicated electronics devices and systems. In truth, their job will be to ply the Putumayo river and kill any FARC rebels—or anyone else, for that matter—trying to retreat onto Peruvian soil. They claim—quite openly to those in Iquitos, including this reporter—that they are hired by a company called Virginia Electronics, that they earn money per kill, and that since they are retired, they aren't bound by military codes. Neither can they be traced back to the US, though the paychecks cut for their mercenary work will undoubtedly be signed by a company doing business with the military. A Web search doesn't show the existence of a military-connected company called Virginia Electronics. There is, however, a Virginia Electronics Expo site which touts itself as being approved by the Department of Defense, deals in part with cutting edge marine-electronics technology, and is sponsored by a who's who list of military defense contractors. Whether there is a genuine connection between the two or whether it is simply the invented name of the company that hired them is anyone's guess.

Calls to the US embassy in Lima, Peru, produced only heated denials from someone who refused to give his name that "we would ever be involved in the use of mercenaries" and that "it's unimaginable that former Navy SEALS would ever be mercenaries." The legitimate US Special Forces troops working various programs out of Iquitos, however, claim the men are just who they say they are: mercenaries—hired to kill retreating FARC troops—who were culled for the black-bag operation because of their SEAL backgrounds and the quality of their work in Southeast Asia, the Middle East, Central America, and Africa.

Once Pastrana has all four of these military components in place—three US-trained battalions of specialized jungle fighters; chopper pilots to move the new Plan Colombia Blackhawks and Hueys; a jungle base in Peru near the planned region of battle to repair military equipment and bring in new supplies; and a team of killers waiting to pick off those who try to escape through the backdoor into Peru as the Colombians push them southward—there will probably be no more peace-talk deadline extensions. It simply will be war. Two of those four objectives have already been met; there remains only a matter of months before the final two objectives have been met, as well.

Aftermath. Despite the denials of the US embassy in Lima, we shortly learned that much of the dirty work connected with Plan Colombia has already been outsourced to retired US Special Forces whose covert activities are not bound by military code and who are protected by the State Department from civil sanctions. On February 18, 2001, retired US Special Forces troops flying helicopter cover for a cropduster spraying herbicide on coca fields in FARC territory in southern Colombia came under fire and was forced down. A second chopper, also manned by retired US Special Forces, came to the the first chopper's rescue. Surprisingly, the crew members announced that they were working for DynCorp, which is under contract to provide manpower and services to the State Department.

It was the first time the US public became aware of the use of such mercenaries. Shortly thereafter, it became public knowledge that Military Professional Resources, Inc. (MPRI) of Alexandria, Virginia, had just completed a year-long contract to help restructure Colombia's Ministry of Defense to fight the War on Drugs. MPRI, owned by former US Army Chief of Staff Carl Vuono, used retired US Special Forces for the Department of Defense contract.

Two months after these outfits came to light, another company, Aviation Development Corporation—which operates out of a single hangar at Maxwell Air Force Base in Montgomery, Alabama—was also discovered to be working with retired US Special Forces, this time under contract with the CIA. This disclosure came when one of their planes, being used to locate potential drug-carrying aircraft in Peru, misidentified a missionary craft as a potential drug runner on April 20. The missionary plane was shot out of the air, and two of its passengers were killed in the incident.

As of August 2001, the mercenaries in Peru aren't known to have been used as killers on the Putumayo river. They remain in Iquitos, however, and have been supplemented by several-dozen young US Marines, none of whom would discuss their role in Iquitos with this writer.

_THE SCUTTLEBUTT IN IQUITOS: PLAN COLOMBIA MIGHT REALLY BE ALL ABOUT OIL

IQUITOS, PERU (February 1, 2001) — Though the stated objectives of Plan Colombia are to end the 30-year-old civil war that has cost the lives of more than 35,000 Colombians and to end the production of cocaine and heroin, there may be a simpler reality: oil. Rumors have long swirled that somewhere between the vast oilfields of Venezuela and the third-rate shale-oil fields of the Peruvian Amazon's northwest there might lie the mother lode of South America's oil. Recently, geologists have been tying those rumored deposits to the southeastern foothills of Colombia's Andes. While the scientists passing the story on to this reporter are not yet willing to put their names on the record, if they are correct, then Plan Colombia has an even more wretched face than previously thought. Could it be possible that Plan Colombia is simply a cover for eliminating the people in the region who stand between oil exploration and the potential riches it would produce? Of course, that begs the question: If we already know there are unimaginably rich oil fields in the region, why not simply move in as businessmen and purchase the rights?

The answer, if such oil fields exist, is twofold. First, Colombia is in the midst of a civil war, and US oil companies are already having tremendous difficulty maintaining qualified men there because it's such an extremely dangerous job. Most US companies are paying a premium of $1,000 a day to men who, in other countries, would be earning $200 or less per day for the same work. And they are still short of men willing to risk their lives in the ongoing civil war. Exploring for oil in the heart of rebel-held territory would simply be impossible in the present political climate.

> RUMORS HAVE LONG SWIRLED THAT SOMEWHERE BETWEEN THE VAST OILFIELDS OF VENEZUELA AND THE THIRD-RATE SHALE-OIL FIELDS OF THE PERUVIAN AMAZON'S NORTHWEST THERE MIGHT LIE THE MOTHER LODE OF SOUTH AMERICA'S OIL.

There is also the question of public relations. Several indigenous peoples live in the region in question, including the Cofan tribal group, and drilling for oil in traditional indigenous territory has already proven to be a political and public relations nightmare in South America. It has cost companies years of work and millions upon millions of dollars in legal battles, most recently in the Waorani territory in Ecuador. If, however, those traditional peoples, as well as the FARC, were moved from the region because of war, they would largely lose their claims to the "traditional territory." Imagine the

FARC and locals in the region slaughtered or displaced in a US-backed war, after which US oil companies quickly move into the now-vacated territory and discover terribly rich oilfields. Rather than being a public relations debacle for the oil companies, they would appear as proverbial White Knights rushing in to help rebuild a decimated land.

If such fields exist, it is not difficult to imagine the possibility of some people in the US State Department knowing of them and subsequently pushing for the passage of Plan Colombia under the guise of fighting the War on Drugs. As noted, to date the existence of the oil motherload is just a rumor, but it would explain why the US position went from one of having no interest in Colombia's civil war—even at the height of the cocaine epidemic in the US—to the billion-dollar-plus Plan Colombia with all of its war components, *after* the FARC agreed to peace talks.

It would also explain why nearly all of those war components of Plan Colombia are aimed at the FARC demilitarized zone and not at the paramilitary (AUC)-held regions, which are the primary sources of finished cocaine and the exclusive regions of distribution and export of same.

Aftermath. In February 2001, writers Than Dunning and Leslie Wirpsa published a story called "Oil Rigged" on the americas.org Website. The story details the oil industry's interest in Plan Colombia, noting, among other things, that Colombia's biggest foreign investor is BP Amoco and that Colombia's state oil company, Ecopetrol, awarded a record thirteen new exploration and production contracts in 2000. Moreover, lobbying for Plan Colombia was particularly fierce among oil giants such as Los Angeles-based Occidental Petroleum and the Houston-based Enron Corporation.

"Oil Rigged" quotes a former US Special Forces intelligence sergeant (Stan Goff, who retired in 1996 from the unit that trains Colombian anti-narcotics battalions) who says that Plan Colombia's purpose is "defending the operations of Occidental, British Petroleum, and Texas Petroleum and securing control of future Colombian fields." Goff's comments were originally made in an October 2000 issue of the Bogota daily *El Espectador*. They also note that in 1998, General Charles Wilhelm, then head of the US Southern Command, told Congress that oil discoveries had increased Colombia's "strategic importance."

To date, no one has confirmed the "mother lode" story this reporter was told by geologists in Iquitos. But with all of the interest Big Oil has in Plan Colombia—and with the aiming of force toward the southern FARC-held states, rather than the cocaine-finishing and -exporting paramilitary states in the north—there is reason to believe it may well prove more than just a rumor.

One more interesting oil-related note with regard to Colombia: Beginning in 1997, Brown and Root, the engineering and construction unit of Halliburton Corporation—for which Vice President Dick Cheney was CEO until he took office—purchased more than 800,000 square feet of warehouse space in Colombia and has recently leased an additional 122,000 square feet. In addition to working oil, Brown and Root contracts for the military of several countries.

_POSTSCRIPT

In the summer of 2001, the Colombian military launched an unprecedented offensive on two columns of FARC rebels who had left their protected areas. Hundreds died, though it has never been made clear exactly how many of those were FARC rebels, how many were Colombian military (and paramilitary soldiers working with them), and how many were civilians caught in the crossfire.

US attention to the Colombian situation shifted abruptly, however, following the events of September 11, 2001, and the subsequent war in Afghanistan. Colombia's President Pastrana took advantage of the momentary lull in outside interest to try once more to bring the FARC rebels to the peace table. Colombia's hardliners saw the move as giving too much to the rebels, particularly in light of the recent offensive, which saw at least half a dozen high-ranking FARC rebels die.

AT LEAST SOME PEOPLE CLOSE TO THE SCENE THINK THAT PASTRANA WILL STALL ON ANOTHER MAJOR OFFENSIVE UNTIL THE US TURNS ITS ATTENTION BACK TO COLOMBIA, THIS TIME WITH THE REBELS BEING DEFINED AS TERRORISTS.

At least some people close to the scene think that Pastrana will stall on another major offensive until the US turns its attention back to Colombia, this time with the rebels being defined as terrorists. Such a definition would permit the Colombian military, backed by US advisors, money, equipment, and contract soldiers, to advance a genuinely major offensive against the FARC. That offensive may not be long in coming.

THE ACCIDENTAL OPERATIVE
FORMER CIA DIRECTOR'S AFGHAN NIECE LEADS CORPS OF TALIBAN REPS
CAMELIA FARD AND JAMES RIDGEWAY

WASHINGTON, DC, June 6, 2001—On this muggy afternoon, a group of neatly attired men and a handful of women gather in a conference room at the Johns Hopkins School of Advanced International Studies. The guest list includes officials from the furthest corners of the world—Turkmenistan, Kazakhstan, Pakistan, and Turkey—and reps from the World Bank, the Uzbekistan chamber of commerce, the oil industry, and the Russian news agency Tass, along with various individuals identified only as "US Government," which in times past was code for spook.

At hand is a low-profile briefing on international narcotics by a top State Department official, who has recently returned from a United Nations trip to inspect the poppy fields of Afghanistan, source of 80 percent of the world's opium and target of a recent eradication campaign by the fundamentalist Taliban. The lecture begins as every other in Washington: The speaker politely informs the crowd he has nothing to do with policymaking. And, by the way, it's all off the record.

Lecture over, the chairman asks for questions. One man after another rises to describe his own observations while in the foreign service. The moderator pauses, looks to the back of the room, and says in a scarcely audible voice: "Laili Helms." The room goes silent.

For the people gathered here, the name brings back memories of Richard Helms, Director of the CIA during the tumultuous 1960s, the era of Cuba and Vietnam. After he was accused of destroying most of the agency's secret documents detailing its own crimes, Helms left the CIA and became President Ford's Ambassador to Iran. There, he trained the repressive secret police, inadvertently sparking the revolution that soon toppled his friend the Shah.

Laili Helms, his niece by marriage, is an operative, too—but of a different kind. This pleasant young woman who makes her home in New Jersey is the Taliban rulers' unofficial ambassador in the US, and their most active and best-known advocate elsewhere in the West. As such, she not only defends but promotes a severe regime that has given the White House fits for the past six years—by throwing women out of jobs and schools, stoning adulterers, forcing Hindus to wear an identifying yellow patch, and smashing ancient statues of Buddha.

In meetings on Capitol Hill and at the State Department, Helms represents a theocracy that harbors America's Public Enemy No. 1: Osama bin Laden, the man who allegedly masterminded the bombing of American embassies in Tanzania and Kenya and is suspected of blowing up the USS *Cole*. From his Afghan fortress, bin Laden operates a terrorist network reaching across the world.

All of which is highly ironic since bin Laden is the progeny of a US policy that sought to unite Muslims in a *jihad* against the Soviet Union, but over a decade eroded the moderate political wing and launched a wave of young, radical fundamentalists. The Taliban, says the author Ahmed Rashid, "is the hip-hop generation of Islamic militants. They know nothing about nothing. Their aim is the destruction of the status quo, but they offer nothing to replace it with."

Now the Bush Administration is lowering its sights, viewing the Taliban within a broader context of an oil-rich central Asia. The chaotic region is strewn with crooked governments, terrorist brotherhoods, thieving warlords, and smugglers. Against this backdrop, the Taliban sometimes seems to be the least of America's problems.

The mullahs would like to take advantage of the Bush Administration's own fundamentalist leanings, complete with anti-drug, pro-energy, and feminist-rollback policies. Their often comic efforts to establish representation in the US took off when they found Helms. For them, she is a disarming presence, the unassuming woman at the back of the room.

After spending most of her life in the States, Helms has impeccable suburban credentials. She lives in Jersey City and is the mother of a couple of grade-school kids. Her husband works at Chase Manhattan.

> **THIS PLEASANT YOUNG WOMAN WHO MAKES HER HOME IN NEW JERSEY IS THE TALIBAN RULERS' UNOFFICIAL AMBASSADOR IN THE US, AND THEIR MOST ACTIVE AND BEST-KNOWN ADVOCATE ELSEWHERE IN THE WEST.**

A granddaughter of a former Afghan minister in the last monarchy, she returned home during the war to work on US aid missions. "Everyone thinks I'm a spy," she said in a recent *Village Voice* interview. "And Uncle Dick thinks I'm crazy."

■ ■ ■ ■ ■ ■ ■ ■ ■

Helms' home across the Hudson has become a sort of kitchen-table embassy. She says she patches together conference calls between the Taliban leadership and State Department officials. A recent one cost more than $1,000, an expense she covered from her own checking account.

One moment she's packing up a used computer for the foreign ministry in Kabul, the next driving down to Washington for a briefing or meeting with members of Congress. Her cell phone rings nonstop. "These guys," she says, referring to the Taliban leaders, "are on no one else's agenda. They are so isolated you can't call the country. You can't send letters out. None of their officials can leave Afghanistan now."

Indeed, the Taliban government is virtually unrecognized by most others. It has no standing at the UN, where it has come under scathing indictment for human rights abuses. In February, the US demanded that Taliban offices here be closed.

Helms may be just another suburban mom in the States, but last year in Afghanistan she got movie-star treatment, driving around downtown Kabul in a smart, late-model Japanese car, escorted by armed guards waving Kalashnikov rifles, rattling away in English and Farsi as she shot video footage to prove that Afghan women are working, free, and happy.

She stands at the public relations hub of a ragtag network of amateur Taliban advocates in the US. At the University of Southern California, economics professor Nake M. Kamrany arranged last year for the Taliban's Rahmatullah Hashami, ambassador at large, to bypass the visa block. He even rounded up enough money for Hashami to lecture at the University of California, both in Los Angeles and Berkeley. The trip ended at the State Department in DC, with a reported offer to turn Osama bin Laden over to the US.

Kamrany hardly looks the part of a foreign emissary, showing up for an interview recently in Santa Monica dressed in a Hawaiian shirt and shorts, and insisting on a tuna fish sandwich before getting down to defending the *burqa*, the head-to-toe covering required for Afghani women. In addition to Kamrany, there's the erstwhile official Taliban representative, Abdul Hakim Mojahed, in Queens, whom Helms dismisses with a wave of her hand as a do-nothing, not worth talking to. Mojahed's voice line has been disconnected, and his fax number never picks up.

Dr. Davood Davoodyar, an economics professor at Cal State in San Francisco, joined the *jihad* to fight against the Soviets in the early 1980s. Today he keeps in touch with the elusive Mojahed, who seems to have gone underground since his office was shuttered. Davoodyar thinks the Taliban is helping to stabilize Afghanistan, but concedes, "If I asked my wife to wear the *burqa*, she'd kill me."

Also in San Francisco, Ghamar Farhad, a bank supervisor, has served as host to the Taliban's visiting deputy minister of information along with the ambassador at large. She generally likes the Taliban because she believes they have cut down on rape, but got very upset when they blew up the Buddha statues. When the Taliban explained to her that these satanic idols had to go, Farhad says, she changed her mind.

■ ■ ■ ■ ■ ■ ■ ■ ■

Led by Helms, these people have answers for all the accusations made against the Taliban, starting with its treatment of women. To a visitor it might seem as if women had just disappeared, as if by some sort of massive ethnic cleansing. Though they made up 40 percent of all the doctors and 70 percent of teachers in the capital, women were forced to abandon Western clothes and stay indoors behind windows painted black "for their own good." Ten million reportedly have been denied education, hospital care, and the right to work.

The Taliban insists that a woman wear a *burqa*, stifling garb with only tiny slits for her eyes and no peripheral vision. Even her voice is banned. In shops or in the market, she must have her brother, husband, or father speak to the shopkeeper so that she will not excite him with the sound of her speaking.

Helms argues that foreign observers have forgotten conditions in the country following the war against the Soviets. "Afghanistan was like a *Mad Max* scenario," she says. "Anyone who had a gun and a pickup truck could abduct your women, rape them.... When the Taliban came and established security, the majority of Afghan women who suffered from the chaotic conditions were happy, because they could live, their children could live."

But a current Physicians for Human Rights poll taken in Afghanistan reports that women surveyed in Taliban-controlled areas "almost unanimously expressed that the Taliban had made their life 'much worse.'" They reported high rates of depression and suicide.

Last year a group of Afghan women gathered in Tajikistan made a concerted demand for basic human rights, citing "torture and inhumane and degrading treatment." Their address noted that "poverty and the lack of freedom of movement push women into prostitution, involuntary exile, forced marriages, and the selling and trafficking of

> THE TRIP ENDED AT THE STATE DEPARTMENT IN DC, WITH A REPORTED OFFER TO TURN OSAMA BIN LADEN OVER TO THE US.

their daughters."

The Taliban drew more worldwide criticism for its abuse of other religious and ethnic minorities. It required that Hindus wear yellow clothing—saris for women and shirts for men, so they could be distinguished from Muslims—a move that immediately brought back images of Jews in Nazi Germany wearing the Star of David. There are 5,000 Hindus living in Kabul and thousands more in other Afghan cities. An Indian external affairs spokesman condemned the new requirements as "reprehensible" and told the *Times of India* it was another example of the Taliban's "obscurantist and racist ideology, which is alien to Afghan traditions."

Helms argues outsiders don't understand the import of the yellow tags. "We asked them to identify themselves [to protect] their religious beliefs. Everyone has identity cards. The intention is to protect people." She shrugs. "Here you have labels for handicapped people. So you can have special parking."

Blowing up the ancient statues of Buddha, hewn from cliffs in the third and fifth centuries BC, was another matter. "That was a very big deal," she says. "That was them thumbing their nose at the international community."

■ ■ ■ ■ ■ ■ ■ ■ ■ ■

Helms has little regard for Osama bin Laden, whom she sneeringly refers to as a "tractor driver." She says he was inherited by the Taliban and is widely viewed as a "hangnail."

In 1999, Helms says, she got a message from the Taliban leadership that they were willing to turn over all of bin Laden's communications equipment, which they had seized, to the US. When she called the State Department with this offer, officials were at first interested but later said, "No. We want *him*."

In the same year, Prince Turki, head of Saudi intelligence, reputedly came up with a scheme to capture bin Laden on his own; after consulting with the Taliban, he flew his private plane to Kabul and drove out to see Mullah Omar at his HQ. The two men sat down, as Helms recounts the story, and the Saudi said, "There's just one little thing. Will you kill bin Laden before you put him on the plane?" Mullah Omar called for a bucket of cold water. As the Saudi delegation fidgeted, he took off his turban, splashed water on his head, and then washed his hands before sitting back down. "You know why I asked for the cold water?" he asked Turki. "What you just said made my blood boil."

Bin Laden was a guest of the Afghans, and there was no way they were going to kill him, though they might turn him over for a trial. At that the deal collapsed, and Turki flew home empty-handed.

Early this year, the Taliban's ambassador at large, Hashami, a young man speaking perfect English, met with CIA operations people and State Department reps, Helms says. At this final meeting, she says, Hashami proposed that the Taliban hold bin Laden in one location long enough for the US to locate and destroy him. The US refused, says Helms, who claims she was the go-between in this deal between the supreme leader and the feds.

A US government source, who spoke on condition of anonymity, made clear that the US is not trying to kill bin Laden but instead wants him expelled from Afghanistan so he can be brought to justice. Acknowledging that Laili Helms does a lot of lobbying on behalf of the Taliban, this source said Helms does not speak to the Taliban for the US.

In the *realpolitik* of Bush foreign policy, the Taliban may have improved its chances for an opening of relations with the rest of the world. As it now stands, there seems little question that Afghanistan has indeed stopped the production of poppies in the areas under its control. Partly as a result, its farmers are destitute, their lives made more miserable by drought.

But that's not likely to faze the powers that be in Afghanistan, since most of the country's real money comes from taxing non-dope trade. Nor will it bother the drug traffickers, who swarm the region and are shifting production north and west into such places as Turkmenistan. As of last month, the US had committed $124 million in aid to Afghanistan, according to the State Department. Meanwhile, Iran, which harbors some 2 million Afghan refugees and is fighting massive drug addiction, has sent agricultural engineers north to help repair Afghanistan's irrigation systems.

HELMS HAS LITTLE REGARD FOR OSAMA BIN LADEN, WHOM SHE SNEERINGLY REFERS TO AS A "TRACTOR DRIVER."

Last week Milt Bearden, the former CIA station chief in Pakistan and Sudan, argued in the *Wall Street Journal* that the Bush Administration should take a "more restrained approach" to bin Laden. "There may be a realization that the two years of unrestrained rhetoric of the Clinton administration following the 1998 attacks in Africa may have done little more than inflate the myth that has inspired others to harm Americans," he wrote.

None of this has changed the impression most people here have of the Taliban. Helms and her cohorts have a lot of work to do. As she freely admits, the Taliban leaders "are considered fascists, tyrants, Pol Pots. They can't do anything right. We perceive them as monsters no matter what they do."

Additional reporting: Ariston-Lizabeth Anderson and Rouven Gueissaz

A CANTICLE FOR OSAMA BIN LADEN
ALEX BURNS

_DILUVIUM IGNIS (THE FLAME DELUGE)

Walter M. Miller's classic science fiction story *A Canticle for Leibowitz* (1959) depicts a post-apocalyptic world where the Roman Catholic Church has become the custodian of civilization's remaining knowledge-base. After the Great Simplification, the priesthood regards the remnants of nuclear weaponry as sacred icons that possess heterodox powers, the archaic symbols of fading memories.

Miller's evocative study of complex moral and social issues cast the die for Russell Hoban's *Riddley Walker* (1980) and J.G. Ballard's *Hello America* (1981), two novels that explore how nuclear weaponry may be fetishized within post-apocalyptic religions. Miller's vision has now become a terrifying reality, a geopolitical wild card that may shape the future of Afghanistan, India, and Pakistan.

_NEGOTIUM PERAMBULANS IN TENEBRIS (THE PESTILENCE THAT STALKS IN DARKNESS)

While researching Osama bin Laden's background for a *New York Times* piece (June 25, 1998), journalist Jeffrey Goldberg interviewed Samiul Haq, a 17-year-old Muslim teacher who taught 9-year-old students to worship the Koran and the Muslim Bomb.

After explaining to Goldberg that Muslims should wage *jihad* against Israel, Russia, and Serbia, Haq then retorted, "Listen, if you Americans don't stop pestering us about the Taliban, we'll give them the nuclear bomb. How would you like that?"

The national holiday Yaum-e-Takbeer celebrates Pakistan's first nuclear test on May 28, 1998. The nuclear test took US intelligence by surprise. Goldberg describes how monuments to the test have been built throughout the major cities, complete with eerie lightshow recreations of the fiery blast. Celebrants worship the radioactive fragments as religious artifacts that can bestow their powers upon families and country.

Goldberg interviewed Fazlur Rahman Khalil, a real-life reversal of Father Leibowitz, who vowed, if necessary, to use nuclear weapons to end the conflict over Kashmir. Khalil's pro-nuclear stance—that God bestowed Pakistan with the nuclear bomb to enlighten a corrupted world—fulfills the macrohistorian and philosopher Oswald Spengler's unnerving prediction that the West would be eclipsed by hordes who used its knowledge and technology against it.

The rise-to-globalism of Osama bin Laden also recalls Muslim macrohistorian Ibn Khaldun's thesis that the cultural elites would corrupt themselves and be displaced by triumphant Bedouin tribes (the thesis was explored in Frank Herbert's *Dune* series).

These macrohistorical theories don't confer legal or moral legitimacy upon Osama bin Laden's terrorist campaign, yet they do suggest that the campaign is an opening gambit in a War on Terrorism that will be shaped, in turn, by the apocalyptic style of geopolitics. This apocalyptic style encompasses new biochemical warfare technology, resource shortages, operations-other-than-war, insights from complex adaptive systems research, and an appreciation of weapons as religiopolitical tools to inflame the populace and deter sworn enemies.

> CELEBRANTS WORSHIP THE RADIOACTIVE FRAGMENTS AS RELIGIOUS ARTIFACTS THAT CAN BESTOW THEIR POWERS UPON FAMILIES AND COUNTRY.

_SIC TRANSIT MUNDUS (THUS PASSES THE WORLD)

The looming clash between the West and militant forms of Islam embodies more than Samuel P. Huntington's *Clash of Civilizations* model. Social cycles and technological innovation have created a fractal sense of time: We simultaneously live in different psychological spaces. Osama bin Laden reveals this fractal complexity, fusing a reverence for family and tribal order with absolutistic thinking and an appreciation of technology. A terrorist does not need to have developed the systems of thinking that built the technology in order to use it against a civilization.

While they fulfill their purpose to galvanize their audiences to take action, media stereotypes of terrorists largely fail to capture this fractal complexity, increasing the difficulty of successfully profiling and outwitting the opponents who endanger our society. They overlook the individual's psychohistory, ignore the cultural imprinting points, and obscure personal motivations. And stereotypes ignore the gaps in our own cultural and societal evolution, such as the widening post-seventeenth-century gap between democratic ideals and reason, that may be seized upon by others to justify their actions.

A TERRORIST DOES NOT NEED TO HAVE DEVELOPED THE SYSTEMS OF THINKING THAT BUILT THE TECHNOLOGY IN ORDER TO USE IT AGAINST A CIVILIZATION.

Walter M. Miller's brooding vision was fiction, but terrorists like Osama bin Laden are intent on making this religiopolitical apocalypse a frightening reality, an intent that may imprint on the generations of fundamentalist Muslim warriors to come. Will the War on Terrorism become a "Forever War" that never really ends?

Author's Note: Special thanks to Howard Bloom for providing notes on New York Times *reporter Jeffrey Goldberg's research.*

BATTLE BORING
WHY REAL SECURITY CAN'T BE CORDONED OFF
NAOMI KLEIN

Just hours after the terrorist attacks on the World Trade Center and the Pentagon, Republican Representative Curt Weldon went on CNN and announced that he didn't want to hear anyone talking about funding for schools or hospitals. From here on out, it was all about spies, bombs, and other manly things.

"The first priority of the US government is not education, it is not health care, it is the defense and protection of US citizens," he said, later adding: "I'm a teacher married to a nurse—none of that matters today."

But now it turns out that those frivolous social services matter a great deal. What is making the US most vulnerable to terrorist networks is not a depleted weapons arsenal but its starved, devalued, and crumbling public sector. The new battlefields are not just the Pentagon, but also the post office; not just military intelligence, but also training for doctors and nurses; not a sexy new missile defense shield, but the boring old Food and Drug Administration.

> THE NEW BATTLEFIELDS ARE NOT JUST THE PENTAGON, BUT ALSO THE POST OFFICE; NOT JUST MILITARY INTELLIGENCE, BUT ALSO TRAINING FOR DOCTORS AND NURSES; NOT A SEXY NEW MISSILE DEFENSE SHIELD, BUT THE BORING OLD FOOD AND DRUG ADMINISTRATION.

It has become fashionable to wryly observe that the terrorists use the West's technologies as weapons against itself: planes, email, cell phones. But as fears of bioterrorism mount, it could well turn out that their best weapons are the rips and holes in the US's public infrastructure.

Is this because there was no time to prepare for the attacks?

Hardly. The US administration has openly recognized the threat of biological attacks since the Gulf War, and President Clinton renewed calls to protect the nation from bioterror after the embassy bombings in 1998. And yet shockingly little has actually been done.

The reason is simple: Preparing for biological warfare would have required a cease-fire in America's older, less dramatic war—the one against the public sphere. It didn't happen. Here are some snapshots from the front lines.

The Health System. Half the states in the US don't have federal experts trained in bioterrorism. The Centers for Disease Control and Prevention are buckling under the strain of anthrax fears, their underfunded labs scrambling to keep up with the demand for tests. Little research has been done on how to treat children who have contracted anthrax, since Cipro—the most popular antibiotic—is not recommended.

Many doctors in the US public health-care system have not been trained to identify symptoms of anthrax, botulism, or plague. A recent US Senate panel heard that hospitals and health departments lack basic diagnostic tools and that information-sharing is difficult since some departments don't have email access. Many health departments are closed on weekends, with no staff on call.

If treatment is a mess, federal inoculation programs are in worse shape. The only laboratory in the US licensed to produce the anthrax vaccine has left the country unprepared for its current crisis. Why? It's a typical privatization debacle. The lab, located in Lansing, Michigan, used to be owned and operated by the state. In 1998, it was sold to BioPort, which promised greater efficiency. Instead, the new lab has failed several Food and Drug Administration inspections and has so far been unable to supply a single dose of the vaccine to the US military, let alone to the general population.

As for smallpox, there are not nearly enough vaccines to cover the population, leading the US National Institute of Allergy and Infectious Diseases to experiment with diluting the existing vaccines at a ratio of 1/5 or even 1/10.

The Water System. Internal documents show that the US

Environmental Protection Agency is years behind schedule in safeguarding the water supply against bioterrorist attacks. According to an audit released on October 4, 2001, the EPA was supposed to have identified security vulnerabilities in municipal water supplies by 1999, but it hasn't yet completed even this first stage.

The Food Supply. Another federal agency, the Food and Drug Administration, has proved unable to introduce measures that would better protect the food supply from "agroterrorism"—deadly bacteria introduced into the food supply. With agriculture increasingly centralized and globalized, the sector is vulnerable to the spread of disease, both inside the US and outside (as the hoof-and-mouth epidemic demonstrated most recently). But the FDA, which only managed to inspect 1 percent of food imports under its jurisdiction in 2000, says it is in "desperate need of more inspectors." Tom Hammonds, chief executive of the Food Marketing Institute, an industry group representing food sellers, says, "Should a crisis arise—real or manufactured as a hoax—the deficiencies of the current system would become glaringly obvious."

■ ■ ■ ■ ■ ■ ■ ■ ■ ■

After September 11, 2001, George Bush created the position of "Homeland Security," designed to evoke a nation steeled and prepared for any attack. And yet it turns out that what "homeland security" really means is a mad rush to reassemble basic public infrastructure and resurrect heath and safety standards that have been drastically eroded. The troops at the front lines of America's new war are embattled indeed: the very bureaucracies that have been cut back, privatized, and vilified for two decades, not just in the US but in virtually every country in the world.

"Public health is a national security issue," US Secretary of Health Tommy Thompson observed in October 2001. No kidding. For years, critics have argued that there are human costs to all the cost-cutting, deregulating, and privatizing—train crashes in Britain, *E. coli* outbreaks in Ontario, food poisoning, substandard health care. And yet until September 11, "security" was still narrowly confined to the machinery of war and policing, a fortress built atop a crumbling foundation.

If there is a lesson to be learned out of this mess, it is that real security cannot be cordoned off. It is woven into our most basic social fabric, from the post office to the emergency room, from the subway to the water reservoir, from schools to food inspection. Infrastructure—the boring stuff that binds us all together—is not irrelevant to the serious business of fighting terrorism. It is the foundation of all of our future security.

EVERYTHING YOU KNOW IS WRONG

SEPTEMBER 11, 2001: NO SURPRISE
RUSS KICK

The US has the Central Intelligence Agency, the Federal Bureau of Investigation, the National Security Agency, the Defense Intelligence Agency, the National Reconnaissance Office, the Secret Service, and a host of other intelligence and security agencies. These agencies employ Echelon, which monitors the majority of electronic communication in the world; Carnivore, which intercepts email; Tempest, a technology that can read a computer monitor's display from over a block away; Keyhole satellites that have a resolution of four inches;[1] and other spy technologies, probably most of which we don't know about. In 2001, the US spent $30 billion on intelligence gathering and an additional $12 billion on counterterrorism.[2] With all of these resources, and more, we're supposed to believe that the government didn't have the slightest inkling that terrorists were planning to attack the United States, much less hijack four planes and send them careening into major landmarks as they did on September 11, 2001.

As we'll see in this article, the facts just don't support the ignorance excuse. At the very least, the success of the 911 attacks reveals gross incompetence, criminal negligence, and general stupidity on the part of intelligence and other aspects of the government. Remember, this is truly the most charitable interpretation that can be given, and a fuller accounting of the facts reveals an even more unwholesome scenario: Some parties in the government knew what was about to happen but failed to act.

Let us build the case slowly, starting with the more general warning signs that were allegedly missed. Gradually, we shall move up the evidence ladder, to the indications that the US knew what was about to happen.

_CONGRESSIONALLY-MANDATED REPORTS WARNED OF TERRORISM AND BIN LADEN IN THE US[3]

In December 2000, a committee appointed by Congress—the Advisory Panel to Assess Domestic Response Capabilities for Terrorism Involving Weapons of Mass Destruction—released its second annual report. It flatly stated: "We are impelled by the stark realization that a terrorist attack on some level inside our borders is inevitable."

Even more to the point, on September 10, 2001—the day before the attacks—the Congressional Research Service issued a report titled "Terrorism: Near Eastern Groups and State Sponsors." This prescient report stated: "Signs continue to point to...a rise in the scope of threat posed by the independent network of exiled Saudi dissident Osama bin Laden.... Osama bin Laden's network, which is independently financed and enjoys safe haven in Afghanistan, poses an increasingly significant threat to US interests in the Near East and perhaps elsewhere."

Finally, the clincher comes when the report reveals ominous signs "that the network wants to strike within the United States itself."

_DEFENSE DEPARTMENT-COMMISSIONED REPORTS WARNED OF ATTACKS ON THE US[4]

Chartered by the Department of Defense and supported by Congress and the White House, the US Commission on National Security/21st Century (originally called the National Security Study's Senior Advisory Board) is a blue-ribbon panel charged with examining how the US can best protect itself and its citizens, both at home and abroad. Chaired by two former Senators, the Commission includes a who's who of the military-industrial complex: a former CEO of Lockheed Martin, a retired general and former NATO commander, the president of the Council on Foreign Relations, a former Secretary of Defense and Director of the CIA, a former US Ambassador to the UN, and many others. They spent several years traveling to 25 countries, interviewing over 100 experts, and otherwise conducting important research, which was completely ignored.

Their first report, released on September 15, 1999, flat-out warned: "Americans will likely die on American soil, possibly in large numbers." In fact, the first of the fifteen major conclusions it listed was, "America will become increasingly vulnerable to hostile attack on our homeland, and our military superiority will not entirely protect us."

The Commission's final report, released on March 15, 2001, was longer and even more emphatic. Among its findings:

The combination of unconventional weapons proliferation with the persistence of international terrorism will end the relative invulnerability of the US homeland to catastrophic attack. To deter attack against the homeland in the 21st century, the United States requires a new triad of *prevention*, *protection*, and *response*.

...

America's present global predominance does not render it immune from these dangers. To the contrary, US preeminence makes the American homeland more appealing as a target, while America's openness and freedoms make it more vulnerable.

...

This Commission believes that the security of the American homeland from the threats of the new century should be the primary national security mission of the US government.

...

Since the occurrence of even one event that causes catastrophic loss of life would represent an unacceptable failure of policy, US strategy should therefore act as far forward as possible to prevent attacks on the homeland.

Although the Commission focused primarily on weapons of mass destruction, it also recognized the threat of cheap, low-tech methods when it noted that those who want to cause terror are now "less obliged to gain large industrial capabilities in order to wreak havoc.... Clearly, the threshold for small groups or even individuals to inflict massive damage on those they take to be their enemies is falling dramatically."

As if all this foreshadowing weren't enough, one of the Senators who headed the Commission mentioned the possibility of "a weapon of mass destruction in a highrise building" to a reporter from the London *Guardian*.

_DEFENSE DEPARTMENT REPORT WARNED OF BOMBING US TARGETS

A report commissioned by the Defense Department's Office of Special Operations and Low-Intensity Conflict discussed the possibility of terrorists using a plane to bomb national landmarks. The date of this report? 1993.[5]

_TERRORISM EXPERT WARNED OF SIMULTANEOUS TARGETS, INCLUDING THE WTC[6]

In 1994, Marvin J. Cetron wrote of possible terrorist attacks in *The Futurist* magazine:

Targets such as the World Trade Center not only provide the requisite casualties but, because of their symbolic nature, provide more bang for the buck. In order to maximize their odds for success, terrorist groups will likely consider mounting multiple, simultaneous operations with the aim of overtaxing a government's ability to respond, as well as demonstrating their professionalism and reach.

Cetron led a group of military officials and experts in a terrorism conference at Langley Air Force Base in 1993. They discussed the use of planes to ram targets, and Cetron told the group: "Coming down the Potomac, you could make a left turn at the Washington Monument and take out the White House, or you could make a right turn and take out the Pentagon."

_TERRORISM EXPERT TALKED OF SIMULTANEOUS US ATTACKS IN 1997[7]

Steven Emerson is an investigative journalist whose 1994 PBS documentary *Jihad in America* exposed the existence of Muslim terror networks in the US. In early 1997, Emerson said: "[The threat of terrorism] is greater now than before the World Trade Center bombing [in 1993] as the numbers of these groups and their members expands. In fact, I would say that the infrastructure now exists to carry off twenty simultaneous World Trade Center-type bombings across the United States."

With Daniel Pipes, Emerson plainly wrote at the end of May 2001 that bin Laden's group, al Qaeda, is "planning new attacks on the US." This information appeared in the *Wall Street Journal*, which is read by all manner of politicians, executives, and other movers and shakers.

_YOSSEF BODANSKY ISSUED WARNINGS STARTING IN 1993

When it comes to experts who predicted attacks on the US, no one was more on-target than Yossef Bodansky, who has deep contacts in the world of intelligence and counterterrorism. In early 1995 he warned that a federal building in America's heartland was going to be attacked. That April, the Alfred P. Murrah Federal Building in Oklahoma City was blown to smithereens.

Bodansky's 1999 book *Bin Laden: The Man Who Targeted America* became a bestseller after the 911 attacks, but a book he wrote all

"AMERICANS WILL LIKELY DIE ON AMERICAN SOIL, POSSIBLY IN LARGE NUMBERS."
—US COMMISSION ON NATIONAL SECURITY/21ST CENTURY, SEPTEMBER 1999

the way back in 1993 has proven downright scary in its foresight regarding suicide bombers on American soil. In *Target America: Terrorism in the US Today*, Bodansky wrote in depth about the Muslim terrorists who were not only targeting America but were already in the country.

He devoted much space in the first chapter to the training of hijackers and pilots to commandeer airliners and crash them into targets in furtherance of the *jihad*:

> "THE TRAINING OF SUICIDE PILOTS STARTED IN BUSHER AIR BASE IN IRAN *IN THE EARLY 1980S,* WITH SOME 90 PILATUS PC-7 AIRCRAFT PURCHASED FROM SWITZERLAND."

The training of suicide pilots started in Busher air base in Iran *in the early 1980s*, with some 90 Pilatus PC-7 aircraft purchased from Switzerland... Tehran decided to send experienced pilots, including Hushang Morteza'i, to the Won San air base in North Korea, where they would "be trained under the supervision of Korean instructors, known for their kamikaze flights" for one year....

For the disruption of aerial traffic in the West, from airport attacks to hijacking, Iran maintained two major installations for terrorist training. The first installation was established in Wakilabad near Mashhad. The entire Western-built airport was given over to the terrorist training program. The latest Western airport equipment was purchased and transferred to the training facility. Iran Air maintained a Boeing 707 and a Boeing 727 jet in the airport, and could send a Boeing 747 for special classes. There were several former Iran Air and Iranian Air Force pilots among the staff and students, including some who were trained in the United States.

According to a former trainee in Wakilabad, one of the exercises included having an Islamic Jihad detachment seize (or hijack) a transport aircraft. Then, trained air crews from among the terrorists would crash the airliner with its passengers into a selected objective.

You might want to read that again to let it truly sink in. As you do, recall that this information was published *eight years* before the attacks on the WTC and the Pentagon.

Here are some other important and relevant extracts from *Target America*:

One of the main objectives of the Iranian terrorist system was to launch daring operations in the West, especially *in the United States.*
...

The February 26, 1993 bombing of the World Trade Center in New York was but one of the first events in a new phase of the Islamist Jihad against the West, one that if carried out as planned, will be characterized by a spate of terrorism throughout America and Western Europe.
...

The leading terrorists are known as '*Afghans*,' having been trained with the mujahideen in Pakistan. Some fought in Afghanistan.... Muslim volunteers from several Arab and Asian countries were encouraged to come to Pakistan and join the Afghan Jihad.
...

The states controlling the Islamist terrorist network, primarily Syria and Iran, are committed to extending their struggle into the US and are willing to withstand the consequences. Therefore, in the early 1980's they began a lengthy, prudent, and professional process of consolidating a stable and redundant infrastructure in America based on a myriad of dormant networks and using established methods for the insertion of experts and trigger-men. This approach is derived from, and essentially similar to, the successful terrorist build-up in Western Europe in the 1980s and incorporates many of the lessons learned from the rich operational experience accumulated there.
...

By the mid-1980s, the Iranian-sponsored Islamist network in the US and Canada had markedly expanded and become better organized. The Islamist infrastructure already included all the components of a mature terrorist support system. These included safe houses in major cities, weapons, ammunition, money, systems to provide medical and legal aid, false identity papers and intelligence for the operative. The network was also large in scale and spanned the United States.
...

These very acts of terrorism testify to the existence of a vibrant Islamist communal structure in the US identical to that of numerous Islamist communities in Western Europe that have been harboring, supporting, and recruiting Islamist terrorists, both individuals and networks. Now that the masters of Islamist international terrorism have given the order to strike, there should be no doubt that the bombing of the World Trade Center was, indeed, only the beginning.[8]

After *Target America*, Bodansky continued to sound the alarm. His 1996 report "Islamic Terrorism in the United States" opens:

The explosion that shook New York, and the rest of America, was only the beginning. The World Trade

Center bombing and the second terrorist network exposed in late June are but a prelude to an escalation of Islamic terror in the United States.

The Islamic world has embarked on a Holy War—Jihad—against the West, especially the United States, that is being waged primarily through international terrorism. Unlike past terrorist campaigns, this war will be waged on American soil.

The terrorist plots in New York clearly demonstrated that it was now both permissible and possible to strike at the heart of America. In essence, the primary legacy of the bombing is the encouragement for the like-minded to follow. Indeed, French experts believe that the New York bombing amounts to "the beginning of a 'war' between radical Islam and the United States."[9]

So, who is Bodansky? What does it matter if some guy warned of what would happen in a little-known book published in 1993 by a small, independent publisher? Because he's not some obscure, self-proclaimed expert—he happens to be the Director of the Task Force on Terrorism and Unconventional Warfare in the US House of Representatives. He works for and has the ear of the US Congress. Yet somehow the government had absolutely no idea that terrorists would strike the US or that they'd use hijacked planes as weapons.

_THE DIRECTOR OF THE CIA WARNED OF THE US BEING ATTACKED

Like the rest of the government, CIA Director George Tenet has claimed to be shocked and amazed by the attacks on the US. Then perhaps he'd care to explain why he said this in a speech on December 7, 2000:

Today, Americans must recognize that ours is a world without front lines. That the continental United States—and not just our embassies and forces abroad—is itself susceptible to attack. And that the potential method of assault goes well beyond a terrorist with a truck full of conventional explosives....

When you take the sheer number and variety of people out in the world who would do harm to our country, its interests, or its allies, and if you add to that the wild card of technology—which enables, drives, and magnifies dangers to us—you will understand why we in the

Intelligence Community believe that the chances for unpleasant—even deadly—surprise are greater now than at any time since the end of the Second World War.[10]

On February 2 of that year, Tenet discussed bin Laden in front of the Senate Select Committee on Intelligence:

Usama Bin Ladin is still foremost among these terrorists, because of the immediacy and seriousness of the threat he poses. Everything we have learned recently confirms our conviction that he wants to strike further blows against America. Despite some well-publicized disruptions, we believe he could still strike without additional warning.[11]

But Tenet was specifically talking about bin Laden's threat to the US even before that. On February 2, 1999—exactly one year earlier—he told the Senate Armed Services Committee:

Looking out over the next year, Mr. Chairman, let me mention two specific concerns. First, there is not the slightest doubt that Usama Bin Ladin, his worldwide allies, and his sympathizers are planning further attacks against us. Despite progress against his networks, Bin Ladin's organization has contacts virtually worldwide, *including in the United States*—and he has stated unequivocally, Mr. Chairman, that all Americans are targets....

We have noted recent activity similar to what occurred prior to the African embassy bombings, Mr. Chairman, and I must tell you we are concerned that one or more of Bin Ladin's attacks could occur at any time.[12]

As we'll see toward the end of this article, Tenet knew even more than he admitted openly, although these public statements by themselves are quite telling.

_ARABIC NEWSPAPER IN LONDON WAS WARNED OF ATTACKS

Less than two hours after the first plane plowed into the World Trade Center's north tower, Abdel-Bari Atwan—editor of the *al-Quds al-Arabi* newspaper in London—told Reuters: "Osama bin Laden warned three weeks ago that he would attack American interests in an unprecedented attack, a very big one.... Personally we received information that he planned very, very big attacks against American

> "TODAY, AMERICANS MUST RECOGNIZE THAT OURS IS A WORLD WITHOUT FRONT LINES. THAT THE CONTINENTAL UNITED STATES—AND NOT JUST OUR EMBASSIES AND FORCES ABROAD—IS ITSELF SUSCEPTIBLE TO ATTACK."
> —CIA DIRECTOR GEORGE TENET, DECEMBER 2000

interests. We received several warnings like this."[13]

Atwan chose not to alert the authorities, though, cryptically adding: "We did not take it so seriously, preferring to see what would happen before reporting it." Reuters sheds a little light on the topic by slyly noting, "Atwan has interviewed bin Laden and maintains close contacts with his followers." In a report prior to the attacks, the FBI said that *al-Quds al-Arabi* has published violent *fatwas* (Islamic edicts) from bin Laden, including one which "stated that Muslims should kill Americans—including civilians—anywhere in the world where they can be found."[14]

Perhaps this explains why Atwan wasn't anxious to let everyone know about bin Laden's unprecedented threats. What we definitely know from this is that bin Laden wasn't keeping quiet about his plans. If the staff of a paper in Britain knew, why didn't any intelligence agencies?

_STATE DEPARTMENT ISSUED WARNING[15]

On September 7, 2001, the State Department issued a "worldwide caution" which said: "American citizens may be the target of a terrorist threat from extremist groups with links to Osama bin Laden's al Qaeda organization."

It went on to warn, "Such individuals have not distinguished between official and civilian targets. As always, we take this information seriously. US Government facilities worldwide remain on heightened alert."

The warning was supposedly directed at Americans overseas—particularly in Asia—though in a press conference held the Friday before the attacks, State Department spokesman Richard Boucher said that the warning was issued "to ensure that the *general American public* is aware of this potential danger to their safety."

Days after the attacks, former US Secretary of State George Schultz said he was "startled" by the State Department's memo. "I have no idea what intelligence lies behind the warning, but they put this out because they had some sort of intelligence," he said. "They had some sort of rumbling of something, even if they didn't pinpoint it in the right direction.... [S]omething was cooking."

_AIRLINE INDUSTRY NEWS SERVICE WARNED OF ATTACKS

"US Airlines May Be a Terror Risk Over Next 3 Days," read the headline of a story from Airjet Airline World News. Dated June 23, 2001,

the news release is worth quoting at length:

With US Gulf forces already on high alert, the US State Department is expected to issue a travel advisory shortly warning Americans traveling overseas to be on their guard.

Videotapes allegedly show Osama bin Laden threatening to attack US interests in the region. Indictments against 13 Saudi nationals and one Lebanese, charging them with killing 19 US servicemen at a military base in Saudi Arabia in 1996 appears to be the catalyst.

With the announcement of the indictments, *US Attorney General Ashcroft noted how terrorists are targeting the United States. "Americans are a high-priority target for terrorists," he said....*

The Arabic satellite television channel MBC has reported, "the next two weeks will witness a big surprise."

A reporter of MBC said, "A severe blow is expected against US and Israeli interests worldwide." MBC said the reporter met with Osama bin Laden two days ago in Afghanistan.

"There is a major state of mobilization among the Osama bin Laden forces. It seems that there is a race of who will strike first. Will it be the United States or Osama bin Laden?" the correspondent said....

Bob Monetti, President of the Victims of Pan Am Flight 103 said, "I hope the airlines are watching this situation closely."

Mr. Monetti, who lost his son Rick on Pan Am 103 is also a special advisor to the FAA on security related matters. Monetti is hopeful about the progress that has been made since the bombing of Pan Am 103.

SAN FRANCISCO MAYOR WILLIE BROWN WAS SCHEDULED TO FLY FROM HIS HOMETOWN TO NEW YORK ON THE MORNING OF SEPTEMBER 11. THE NIGHT BEFORE, THOUGH, HE RECEIVED A CALL TELLING HIM THAT HE NEEDED TO BE VERY CAREFUL ABOUT FLYING.

However, Monetti expressed serious concern about the abilities of the airlines to stop a terrorist organization from carrying out their plans as promised. Monetti noted that Osama bin Laden has had several terrorist targets over the years and not all of them have been military.

"The airlines are at risk — They need to take all appropriate measures and counter-measures to ensure the safety of their passengers," Monetti said.[16]

_SAN FRANCISCO'S MAYOR AND MULTIPLE FAA WARNINGS[17]

San Francisco Mayor Willie Brown was scheduled to fly from his hometown to New York on the morning of September 11. The night before, though, he received a call telling him that he needed to be very careful about flying. Though Brown has tried to downplay the warning, he received it around 10 PM Pacific time—not exactly business hours, indicating that the warning could be considered urgent. Further adding to the mystery, the mayor refuses to say exactly who warned him, referring only to "my security people at the airport."

INVESTIGATORS FOUND EVIDENCE THAT THE TERRORISTS WERE ALSO PLANNING KAMIKAZE ATTACKS ON THE WHITE HOUSE, THE SEARS TOWER IN CHICAGO, THE TRANSAMERICA TOWER IN SAN FRANCISCO, AND—BRACE YOURSELF—*THE WORLD TRADE CENTER.*

When the assistant deputy director of the San Francisco International Airport was contacted, he admitted that the FAA had issued two or three security warnings in the past two months. Too bad none of the people on the four flights had been apprised of these multiple warnings.

_SALMAN RUSHDIE GROUNDED A WEEK BEFORE THE ATTACKS

From the *Times* of London:

The author Salman Rushdie believes that US authorities knew of an imminent terrorist strike when they banned him from taking internal flights in Canada and the US only a week before the attacks.

On September 3 the Federal Aviation Authority made an emergency ruling to prevent Mr Rushdie from flying unless airlines complied with strict and costly security measures. Mr Rushdie told *The Times* that the airlines would not upgrade their security.

The FAA told the author's publisher that US intelligence had given warning of "something out there" but failed to give any further details.

The FAA confirmed that it stepped up security measures concerning Mr Rushdie but refused to give a rea-
son.[18]

The reason almost certainly is that Rushdie is famously hated by Muslims for his novel *The Satanic Verses*, and US intelligence (and probably the FAA) knew that Islamic terrorists were preparing to hijack planes.

_ISLAMIC MILITANT WHO MASTERMINDED THE 1993 WTC BOMBING HAD PLANS FOR CRASHING PASSENGER JETS INTO US BUILDINGS[19]

A small fire broke out in an apartment in Manila in 1995. The place turned out to be a veritable bombmaking factory, and authorities quickly realized it was a hideout for Ramzi Yousef, the terrorist mastermind who has since been convicted for his role in the 1993 WTC bombing. Yousef evaded the Philippine authorities, but they nabbed his accomplice, Abdul Hakim Murad, who had been trained as a pilot in the US. Both men are believed to be part of bin Laden's network.

An investigator with Philippine intelligence said: "Murad narrated to us about a plan by the Ramzi cell in the continental US to hijack a commercial plane and ram it into the CIA headquarters in Langley, Virginia, and also the Pentagon."

Investigators found evidence that the terrorists were also planning kamikaze attacks on the White House, the Sears Tower in Chicago, the Transamerica Tower in San Francisco, and—brace yourself—*the World Trade Center*.

A search of Yousef's computer also yielded a plan to blow up eleven or twelve US airliners during international flights in a two-day period. The terrorists had even mapped out which flights to target and when to set the timers on the bombs. As the third facet of their plan, they intended to assassinate the Pope and President Clinton when they arrived in the Philippines. This orgy of death and destruction was named Project Bojinka by the terrorists.[20]

Discussing the 911 attacks, an unnamed official admitted the obvious to the *World Tribune*: "What we saw was the completion of Yousef's plans. The resemblance is too strong to ignore."

_FEDS KNEW ABOUT PILOT TRAINING[21]

FBI Director Robert Mueller has repeatedly pleaded ignorance about the fact that terrorists were training to be pilots in the US. When this training was first announced in the days following the attacks, he pretended that this was "news, quite obviously," and said: "If we had understood that to be the case, we would have—

perhaps one could have averted this." Several facts show that Mueller is a bald-faced liar.

First, while investigating the simultaneous 1998 bombings of US embassies in Kenya and Tanzania, federal authorities discovered that two of bin Laden's associates had been trained as pilots. This revelation even became part of the public record in the first half of 2001, when these two men testified during trial in New York.

Second, the vice president of Airman Flight School in Oklahoma has revealed that the FBI twice interviewed him about suspected terrorists training at his school, once in August 2001 and once in 1999. In the earlier incident, investigators asked about Ihab Ali Nawawi—charged in the embassy bombings—who had trained at Airman.

In the later incident—taking place just three weeks before the 911 attacks—the feds asked questions about Zacarias Moussaoui, an Algerian now being held in New York over his suspected ties to the hijackers. They wanted to know if Moussaoui had made "extreme comments" about the US during his time training at Airman. When asked why they were inquiring, the agents said "he had done something very bad."

It turns out that Moussaoui had been arrested over an alleged passport violation when he tried to take flying lessons at a *second* school, this one in Minnesota. According to Europe 1 radio, he "had several passports, technical information on Boeing aircraft and flight manuals." He was being held in a county jail.

Several things had made the Algerian extraordinarily suspicious. He wanted to learn to fly a Boeing 747 even though he had negligible experience or training in air travel, and he was offering thousands of dollars in cash if someone would teach him. Moussaoui was openly interested only in how to steer the plane in the air; he didn't care about learning to take off or land. To top it off, he specifically asked about flying in New York City airspace and about opening cabin doors while in flight.

At least ten days before the 911 attacks, French intelligence warned the FBI that Moussaoui had connections to Muslim militants and may have

ITALIAN INTELLIGENCE HAD UNCOVERED A PLAN TO ASSASSINATE PRESIDENT BUSH DURING THE EVENT BY CRASHING A HIJACKED COMMERCIAL AIRLINER EITHER INTO AIR FORCE ONE OR ONE OF THE BUILDINGS BEING USED FOR THE SUMMIT.

been trained at terrorist camps in Afghanistan. The FBI then confirmed that Moussaoui was involved with bin Laden's group, yet they still didn't take him into federal custody, and the Justice Department wouldn't give permission to examine his hard drive.

(Moussaoui is considered likely to have been the missing "twentieth" hijacker. Each of the four 911 planes was hijacked by five men, except for United Flight 93, which crashed in Pennsylvania. Some authorities believe Moussaoui was the fifth man but couldn't make

his date with destiny because he was locked up.)

Even further back, operators of two other flight schools—Coastal Aviation in North Carolina and Richmor Aviation in New York—said that the FBI questioned them about Islamic terrorist Abdul Hakim Murad (caught in the Philippines, as mentioned above) and several Arab pilots connected to him. This took place in *1996*.

In the end, 37 of the hijackers and their associates are known to have trained as pilots in the US. *Newsweek* and the *Washington Post* even unearthed evidence that three of the hijackers received pilot training at a US military facility, specifically the Naval Air Station in Pensacola, Florida, considered the "cradle of US Navy aviation." (It also appears that Mohamed Atta graduated from US International Officers School at Maxwell Air Force Base, Alabama.) Clearly, the authorities' claims that they were unaware of Muslim terrorist suspects training as pilots is completely bogus.

_PREVIOUS ATTEMPTS TO TURN PLANES INTO WEAPONS[22]

NBC News put it as well as anyone could: "The World Trade Center and Pentagon attacks with hijacked airliners have been called 'unimaginable,' 'without precedent' and 'impossible to predict.' But were they? In 1994, in a strikingly similar plan, suicidal Algerian hijackers plotted to use an Air France jetliner, loaded with fuel and dynamite, as a deadly weapon—and to aim it at the Eiffel Tower."

Air France Flight 8969 was hijacked by four Muslim militants—believed to have ties to bin Laden—as it got ready to take off from Algiers for Paris on Christmas Eve 1994. The terrorists loaded the plane with explosives and, stopping in Marseilles, had it filled with extra fuel to make it highly combustible for ramming into the Eiffel Tower. Before the plane took off again, though, commandos stormed it, killing the hijackers.

In an unrelated incident earlier that year, a disgruntled Federal Express employee broke into the cockpit of a DC-10 and brained all three members of the flight crew with a hammer. Luckily, despite their serious injuries, they fended him off and kept control of the plane. According to the man's coworkers, he planned to crash the plane into FedEx's corporate headquarters in Memphis, Tennessee.

It turns out that even these harbingers of the 911 attacks weren't completely unprecedented. A somewhat similar plan was hatched by Muslim militants to hijack Pan Am Flight 76 in Pakistan in 1986, and blow it to pieces over Tel Aviv, raining debris and fuel onto the Israeli city. Luckily, the Palestinian hijackers were captured before the plane had taken off.

And let's not forget that the White House has been attacked kamikaze-style by a small plane. In the early morning hours of September 12, 1994, a down-on-his-luck truck driver stole a small plane—a single-engine Cessna 150—and flew it directly at the White House. Not one shot was fired by the Secret Service as the plane instead hit a 160-year-old magnolia tree on the South Lawn, careened end over end, and came to rest against the White House, causing only minor damage.

The *Chicago Tribune* noted that the pilot "shattered the myth of an impregnable White House and showed how easily someone, perhaps a determined terrorist, could strike again.... Terrorism experts said the White House's vulnerability to attack by air, using readily available technology, is greater than believed."

Unprecedented? Not even close.

_SECURITY AT THE 1996 OLYMPICS[23]

When the 1996 Olympics were held in Atlanta, authorities put into place security measures designed to thwart any attempt to crash a plane into the proceedings. The *Los Angeles Times* reports: "In an extraordinary aerial dragnet, launched quietly that summer and kept largely under wraps ever since, Black Hawk helicopters and US Customs Service jets were deployed to intercept suspicious aircraft in the skies over the Olympic venues, officials said."

Regional airports were monitored, and a no-fly zone was instituted. "From July 6 through the end of the Games on Aug. 11, the FAA banned all aviation within a one-mile radius of the Olympic Village that housed the athletes," says the *Times.* "It also ordered aircraft to stay at least three miles away from other sites beginning three hours before each event until three hours after each event ended."

_PLANE TERROR AT THE G8 SUMMIT[24]

Lest you somehow still think the authorities didn't know Islamic terrorists were planning on using hijacked planes as weapons, let's turn our attention to the G8 Summit in Italy. This meeting of the world's eight economic superpowers, which took place in Genoa in July 2001, became infamous when police shot and killed an unarmed protestor.

Security at the event was tight and included surface-to-air missiles, as well as the shutting down of airspace over the city. This seemed ridiculously excessive at the time, but Italy's Deputy Prime Minister Gianfranco Fini revealed the actual reason for the heightened state of alert: Italian intelligence had uncovered a plan to assassinate President Bush during the event by *crashing a hijacked commercial*

airliner either into Air Force One or one of the buildings being used for the summit. According to three sources—Deputy Prime Minister Fini, Egyptian President Hosni Mubarak, and Russian President Vladimir Putin's bodyguard service—the threat to kill Bush (and possibly other leaders) came from none other than Osama bin Laden.

The claim that authorities couldn't possibly have foreseen kamikaze airplane attacks is obviously untenable.

_FAA PLEADS IGNORANCE, DESPITE ITS OWN REPORTS[25]

In spite of the incidents mentioned above, the Administrator of the Federal Aviation Administration, Jane F. Garvey, had the nerve to tell a House subcommittee nine days after the attacks: "This is a whole new world for us." Making this and other related claims of industry surprise look even more silly are the FAA's annual "Criminal Acts Against Aviation" reports. The 2000 report said that while bin Laden "is not known to have attacked civil aviation, he has both the motivation and the wherewithal to do so.... Bin Laden's anti-Western and anti-American attitudes make him and his followers a significant threat to civil aviation, particularly to US civil aviation."

FROM JANUARY TO MAY 2000, MOHAMED ATTA —CONSIDERED THE RINGLEADER OF THE HIJACKING TEAMS—LIVED IN FRANKFURT, GERMANY, WHERE THE CIA HAD HIM UNDER SURVEILLANCE.

The *New York Times* notes: "The previous year's edition of that report said that an exiled Islamic leader in Britain proclaimed in August 1998 that Mr. bin Laden would 'bring down an airliner, or hijack an airliner to humiliate the United States.'"

Administrator Garvey might want to try reading her own agency's reports.

_TWO HIJACKERS WERE BEING INVESTIGATED (HALF-HEARTEDLY) BEFORE THE ATTACKS[26]

As of August 21, 2001, the CIA, the FBI, and the Immigration and Naturalization Service knew that two associates of bin Laden were in the country. One of them had been seen on videotape talking to a suspect in the bombing of the *USS Cole* in Yemen (also thought to have been the work of al Qaeda). These two men—Khalid Al-Midhar and Salem Alhamzi—are listed as two of the hijackers of American Flight 77, which hit the Pentagon.

The FBI was unable to trace the two men in time. Not that they gave it their all. The suspects were known to have lived in the San Diego area (one of them even attended college there), yet the agents didn't ask the Los Angeles field office for help until one or two days before the 911 attacks. And according to FBI Special Agent Jeff

Thurman in San Diego, they didn't contact the San Diego office itself until two days *after* the attacks.

_AUTHORITIES DETAINED MEN PLOTTING TERROR IN NEW YORK IN JUNE[27]

In June 2001, Federal Protective Service officers in New York arrested three Middle Eastern men who were engaged in photographic reconnaissance of federal buildings in New York City. In another stunning display of incompetence, after the FBI and INS interrogated the men, they were let go. When the men's film was finally developed days later, the feds were beside themselves. "The photos were of security checkpoints, police posts and surveillance cameras at 26 Federal Plaza, two federal courthouses and the federal building at 290 Broadway," according to the *New York Post*.

Their intentions were so obvious that even the FBI could understand. The *Post* wrote that "anxious authorities expressed concern that plans for a terror attack were under way." They tried to apprehend the three again, but according to a leaked US Marshals memo: "Further investigation by the FBI showed that the three have left their last known residences, leaving behind paychecks from their employment."

The FBI and military intelligence now believe that the three are part of bin Laden's network.

_AL QAEDA ATTEMPTED TO TOPPLE THE SPACE NEEDLE[28]

In December 1999, a Montreal-based cell of al Qaeda was foiled in its apparent attempt to bring down Seattle's Space Needle with explosives around the time of the millennium celebrations. According to a United Press International story filed in March 2001: "The plot fell apart when a courier from the ring, a 32-year old Algerian man, Ahmed Ressam, was stopped Dec. 14 by US Customs officials at Port Angeles, about 60 miles northwest of Seattle after crossing the Canadian border. He was carrying more than 1,000 pounds of explosives and four timers similar to those that had been used in a 1994 Philippines-based plot allegedly aided by bin Laden to blow up 11 US airliners simultaneously."

Could there have been any doubt that bin Laden was actively trying to topple tall buildings in the US?

_THE CIA WAS SURVEILLING THE LEAD HIJACKER IN GERMANY[29]

From January to May 2000, Mohamed Atta—considered the ring-

leader of the hijacking teams—lived in Frankfurt, Germany, where the CIA had him under surveillance. (According to the German news magazine *Focus*, the agents didn't tell German authorities about Atta, who came to the US in June 2000 to take flying lessons.) This is in stark contrast to the statements of authorities, who claim that as of Atta's January 2001 entry into the US, they had no idea he was involved in terrorist activity.

On a related note, German security officials say they had been observing Said Bahaji—a prime suspect under warrant for the 911 attacks—at some point before September 11. They refuse to say when their investigation of him began or ended. Bahaji is now believed to have arranged travel documents and accommodations for some of the hijackers.

_COMMUNICATIONS OF BIN LADEN AND HIS TERRORISTS WERE BEING MONITORED BY US INTELLIGENCE FOR YEARS[30]

What are we to make of the fact that the FBI intercepted bin Laden's men making a celebratory phone call just after the attacks? Had the US been unable to monitor al Qaeda's calls before September 11, but miraculously managed to start intercepting calls on that very

THE NATIONAL SECURITY AGENCY USED ITS ECHELON SYSTEM TO LISTEN IN ON CONVERSATIONS BETWEEN AL QAEDA OPERATIVES AND BIN LADEN HIMSELF IN AFGHANISTAN, KENYA, YEMEN, NAIROBI, BRITAIN, AND THE US.

day? Of course not. Based on just this information, we can deduce that US intelligence had been monitoring the terrorists' communications before the crashes.

We also have direct proof that this is so. On September 10, 2001, US intelligence agencies intercepted a call between "bin Laden supporters in the United States and senior members of bin Laden's al Qaeda terrorist organization" in which they discussed an impending "big attack." This comes from an unnamed source the *Washington Times* identified as "a senior administration official."

Unfortunately, though the call was made on the 10th, it wasn't analyzed by intelligence until several days after September 11. The administration official said that this time-lag is an unfortunate part of intelligence gathering.

However, there's no time-lag excuse with another intercepted message from a member of al Qaeda, who declared that bin Laden was preparing a "Hiroshima" against the US. This message was uncovered sometime in 2000.

But let's go back even further. The New York trial in 2001 of some of bin Laden's acquaintances for the 1998 attack on US embassies in Africa was based almost completely on intercepted cell phone calls.

The National Security Agency used its Echelon system to listen in on conversations between al Qaeda operatives and bin Laden himself in Afghanistan, Kenya, Yemen, Nairobi, Britain, and the US. United Press International quoted multiple intelligence officials saying that the encryption used by the terrorists had been broken. Furthermore, they admitted that al Qaeda doesn't always use secure channels of communications, since doing so is burdensome. Tellingly, these stunning admissions were made in February 2001, seven months before it would become too embarrassing to admit such things.

(Furthermore, the *Wall Street Journal* revealed that bin Laden was under limited *physical* surveillance by the US prior to September 11. In September and October 2000, unarmed Predator drones were flying over terrorist camps in Afghanistan, sending back real-time video to Washington. On several occasions, the planes spotted "a very tall man with a beard and flowing white robes who was surrounded by a large security operation," according to a senior intelligence official. It was generally believed that this was bin Laden.)

A *Time* magazine columnist has claimed that when documents presented at the embassy bombing trials made it clear that al Qaeda's messages were being intercepted, bin Laden's organization stopped using satellite phones, the result being, "We lost him." Then how can we explain the fact that US intelligence intercepted the terror organization's calls on September 10 and 11? Obviously, despite official claims to the contrary, the US *was* monitoring the conversations of al Qaeda and bin Laden around the world up to and including the day of the attacks. And so were other countries, as we'll see in the next section.

_BIN LADEN HIMSELF WAS BEING MONITORED BY FOREIGN INTELLIGENCE AGENCIES[31]

"In two days you're going to hear big news and you're not going to hear from me for a while." That was the tip-off bin Laden gave to his stepmother on September 9, 2001. According to NBC News, this phone call was intercepted by a "foreign intelligence service."

We also know, based on a report from CNN, that bin Laden's people were being monitored by German intelligence even on the fateful day itself:

German intelligence services intercepted a phone call September 11 after the terrorist attacks on the United States in which two followers of Osama bin Laden applauded the deadly assaults, a German intelligence official said.... The official said the phone call did not originate in Germany or any other European nation, but refused to identify the country or region.

_THE WORLD TRADE CENTER BOMBERS WARNED OF MORE STRIKES AGAINST THE WORLD TRADE CENTER[32]

Further destroying the notion that authorities couldn't possibly have foreseen the attacks on the twin towers is the fact that the terrorists who bombed them in 1993 said they would keep trying. In fact, while investigating the bombing of the WTC, authorities found a message on the computer of conspirator Nidal Ayyad: "Next time, it will be very precise."

Days after Ramzi Yousef and his confederates bombed the WTC on February 26, 1993, they sent a letter to the *New York Times*. It read, in part:

We are, the fifth battalion in the LIBERATION ARMY, declare our responsibility for the explosion on the mentioned building. This action was done in response for the American political, economical, and military support to Israel the state of terrorism and to the rest of the dictator countries in the region.

OUR DEMANDS ARE:
1 – Stop all military, economical, and political aid to Israel.
2 – All diplomatic relations with Israel must stop.
3 – Not to interfere with any of the Middle East countries interior affairs.

IF our demands are not met, all of our functional groups in the army will continue to execute our missions against the military and civilian targets in and out the United States. For your own information, our army has more than hundred and fifty suicidal soldiers ready to go ahead....

According to the testimony of two terrorism experts before a Senate committee in 1998:

The conspirators also drafted a second letter, which was later recovered from an erased file on a computer disk seized from Ayyad's office. In this second letter, which the conspirators apparently did not send, [they] proclaimed that the World Trade Center bomb did not do as much damage as had been intended, because their "calculations were not very accurate this time."

"I REMEMBER THAT AFTER THE FIRST WORLD TRADE CENTER BOMBING OSAMA BIN LADEN MADE A STATEMENT THAT ON THE SECOND ATTEMPT THEY WOULD BE SUCCESSFUL."—AVELINO RAZON, WHO WAS MANILA'S CHIEF OF POLICE AT THE TIME

They warned, however, that they would be more precise in the future and *would continue to target the World Trade Center* if their demands were not met.

Obviously, their demands were not met, as the US has continued to support Israel and otherwise keep a heavy hand in Middle Eastern affairs. And as they promised, Muslim terrorists continued to target the US and, specifically, the World Trade Center. Could they have been any clearer about their intentions?

_BIN LADEN SPOKE OF LAUNCHING A SECOND ATTACK ON THE WORLD TRADE CENTER

It wasn't just the 1993 bombers who threatened the World Trade Center, either. Avelino Razon, who was Manila's police chief at the time that Abdul Hakim Murad was arrested in the Philippines, told Agence France-Presse: "I remember that after the first World Trade Center bombing Osama bin Laden made a statement that on the *second attempt* they would be successful."[33]

_OTHER WARNINGS FROM BIN LADEN[34]

According to NBC News: "Bin Laden himself said in June that he was preparing a 'hard hit' against US interests across the globe."

In its supposed indictment of bin Laden—released when the world was demanding some evidence that he was behind the 911 attacks—the British government noted: "In two interviews broadcast on US television in 1997 and 1998 he referred to the terrorists who carried out the earlier attack on the World Trade Center in 1993 as 'role models'."

_WARNINGS FROM BIN LADEN'S "ASSOCIATES"

In its 70-point bill of indictment against bin Laden, the British government admitted blatant signs that were somehow missed: "In August and early September close associates of Bin Laden were warned to return to Afghanistan from other parts of the world by 10 September. Immediately prior to 11 September some known associates of Bin Laden were naming the date for action as on or around 11 September."[35]

_SECURITY AT THE WTC WAS INCREASED IN MID-AUGUST[36]

According to journalists Alexander Cockburn and Jeffrey St. Clair—publishers of the muckraking Washington, DC, newsletter *CounterPunch*—a man who worked at the World Trade Center told them that "security was heightened three weeks ago [before the attacks], including the introduction for the first time of sniffer dogs and the physical search of all trucks prior to their being waved into the entrance from the street."

_THE US SHOULD HAVE BEEN EXPECTING A PRE-EMPTIVE STRIKE[37]

If a nation knows it's about to be attacked, it will often strike first. It turns out that this incredibly obvious piece of military strategy figures heavily into the 911 attacks. As the BBC reported: "Niaz Naik, a former Pakistani Foreign Secretary, was told by senior American officials in mid-July [2001] that military action against Afghanistan would go ahead by the middle of October. Mr Naik said US officials told him of the plan at a UN-sponsored international contact group on Afghanistan which took place in Berlin." This group included Americans, Russians, Iranians, Pakistanis, and a representative of the Northern Alliance opposition in Afghanistan. (At some of the other meetings in the series, members of the Taliban were present.)

The plan was to capture or kill bin Laden and the leader of the Taliban, Mullah Omar, as well as to topple the entire Taliban government. The BBC continues: "Mr Naik was told that Washington would launch its operation from bases in Tajikistan, where American advisers were already in place. He was told that Uzbekistan would also participate in the operation and that 17,000 Russian troops were on standby."

"THERE WERE LOTS OF WARNINGS."
—SECRETARY OF DEFENSE DONALD RUMSFELD

So are we sure that the Taliban knew about this US plan to invade Afghanistan? Absolutely. Naik declared to the *Guardian* of London: "I told the Pakistani government, who informed the Taliban via our foreign office and the Taliban ambassador here."

Naik offered more details during his appearance on a French news program in early November 2001. He said that the US representative at the UN-sponsored talks, Tom Simons, directly threatened Afghanistan and Pakistan: "Simons said, 'Either the Taliban behave as they ought to, or Pakistan convinces them to do so, or we will use another option.' The words Simons used were 'a military operation.'"

A book by two French intelligence analysts makes similar charges. In *Bin Laden: La Verite Interdite* (*Bin Laden: The Forbidden Truth*, published in Paris), they say that the Bush Administration offered the Taliban sweet deals if they would allow oil companies to build a pipeline through Afghanistan, in order to connect the oil-rich countries of Turkmenistan, Uzbekistan, and Kazakhstan to the Indian Ocean. When the Taliban balked at the terms, the US became hostile. The lead author said in an interview: "At one moment during the negotiations, the US representatives told the Taliban, 'Either you accept our offer of a carpet of gold, or we bury you under a carpet of bombs.'" (Much of the information in the book comes from the late

John O'Neill, who quit in disgust as Deputy Director of the FBI in July 2001 because the Bush Administration wasn't letting him pursue Islamic terrorists.)

Furthermore, the *Guardian* independently confirmed the following: "Reliable western military sources say a US contingency plan existed on paper by the end of the summer to attack Afghanistan from the north."

_POWELL AND CHENEY ADMIT A LOT BUT NOT ALL[38]

The revelations that the US had foreknowledge have come out so fast and furiously that Secretary of State Colin Powell was forced to make a halfway admission. Yes, we knew terrorist attacks against American interests were coming, he admitted in early October 2001, but we had absolutely no specifics. No idea that it would be against the US itself.

Vice President Dick Cheney admitted much the same thing during an appearance on *Meet the Press*, saying that they knew a "big operation" was going to occur, but they had absolutely no idea how, when, or where.

An unnamed US official revealed a good bit more: "There was something specific in early August that said to us that he [bin Ladin] was determined in striking on US soil." Still, the official claims that they didn't know exactly what to expect.

The fact that these officials admitted this much is surprising, but it was necessary because signs were undeniable that the US knew something was about to bust loose. As far as not having any idea that the US itself would be the target, many of the warnings discussed in this article show this claim to be ridiculous.

_RUMSFELD ADMITS MORE, THEN PASSES THE BUCK[39]

Secretary of Defense Donald Rumsfeld sat down with *Parade Magazine* for an interview, the raw transcript of which was released by the Department of Defense on October 12, 2001. Here's the key passage:

Q: This is a question that's been asked by many Americans, but especially by the widows of September 11th. How were we so asleep at the switch? How did a war targeting civilians arrive on our homeland with seemingly no warning?

Rumsfeld: There were lots of warnings. The intelligence information that we get, it sometimes runs into the hundreds of alerts or pieces of intelligence a week. One looks at the worldwide, it's thousands. And the task is to sort through it and see what you can find. And as you find things, the law enforcement officials who have the responsibility to deal with that type of thing—the FBI at the federal level, and although it is not, it's an investigative service as opposed to a police force, it's not a federal police force, as you know. But the state and local law enforcement officials have the responsibility for dealing with those kinds of issues.

So the intelligence was there, but according to the Secretary of Defense the attacks were the fault of state and local law enforcement, because they didn't do anything to prevent them.

_WHAT ELSE DID OFFICIALS KNOW?

The *Boston Globe* reports that, based on the investigation of the embassy bombings in 1998, "US officials also were aware that bin Laden had recruited US citizens to join his al Qaeda terrorist group and that many of them received military and intelligence training in Afghanistan, Pakistan and the Sudan. Members of the organization lived in California, Texas and Oregon, among other states."[40]

The idea that authorities had no idea the Pentagon could be a target is laughable, according to information in the *Daily Telegraph*. "For years, staff at the Pentagon joked that they worked at 'Ground Zero', the spot at which an incoming nuclear missile aimed at America's defences would explode. There is even a snack bar of that name in the central courtyard of the five-sided building, America's most obvious military bullseye."[41]

_FLORIDA NATIONAL GUARD ACTIVATED FOUR DAYS BEFORE THE ATTACKS

In what might be a case of ESP, Florida Governor Jeb Bush—who is, of course, the president's brother—called up his state's National Guard on *September 7*, 2001. Executive Order 01-261 repeatedly makes reference to the Guard aiding law enforcement and emergency-management personnel in the event of "civil disturbance." Section 3 expressly tasks the Guard with aiding security at Florida's ports due to the "the potential massive damage to life and property that may result from an act of terrorism at a Florida port, [and] the necessity to protect life and property from such acts of terrorism..."[42] Odd that such an order was signed into effect four days before the terrorist attacks.

_DOMAIN NAMES REVEALED TERROR ATTACKS[43]

From mid-June to mid-July 2000, at least seventeen Internet domain names were registered which indicated where and approximately when the attacks were to occur. Among the Web addresses:

"attackontwintowers.com," "nycterroriststrike.com," "pearlharborin manhattan.com," "terrorattack2001.com," "worldtradetowerattack.com," and "wterroristattack2001.com." Unfortunately, the names were allowed to expire, so tracking the people who bought them may not be easy.

Counterterrorism and security expert Neil Livingstone—author of *America the Vulnerable* and other similar books—was tipped off about the names by someone at a domain name registrar. (In the summer of 2000, around 90 companies were registering domains. To protect his source, Livingstone is refusing to name the individual or the company.) When domains that were registered are allowed by their owners to expire, those names are announced as being available again, and this is apparently how they were first discovered. (Beginning September 11, 2001, some of these domain names have been purchased again, presumably by different people).

Said Livingstone, "It's unbelievable that they [the registration company] would register these domain names, probably without any comment to the FBI. If they did make a comment to the FBI, it's unbelievable that the FBI didn't react to it."

_PEOPLE KNEW BEFOREHAND ABOUT ATTACKS[44]

Reports have been swirling that ordinary people, mostly Arab-Americans in New York City, knew about the attacks before they happened. FBI agents have told the media that they're tracking down numerous people who spoke of the impending attacks in the New York area, thereby confirming that such warnings occurred. A veteran NYPD investigator said that numerous Arab-Americans in New York had heard that the attacks were going to happen. "The officer said the story 'had been out on the street,' and the number of leads turning up was so 'overwhelming' that it was difficult to tell who had heard about the attacks from second-hand sources and who had heard it from someone who may have been a participant," according to the *Journal News* of Westchester, New York.

> ONE WEEK BEFORE THE ATTACKS, A BROOKLYN HIGH-SCHOOL FRESHMAN POINTED OUT A CLASSROOM WINDOW AT THE WTC TOWERS AND SAID TO THE CLASS AND HIS TEACHER: "DO YOU SEE THOSE TWO BUILDINGS? THEY WON'T BE STANDING THERE NEXT WEEK."

A police detective in Brooklyn said that investigations of numerous Middle Easterners who didn't show up for work at the WTC on September 11 are "a serious and major priority." The *Independent* of London reported: "Dozens of members of a mosque in the Bronx told the FBI they had also been given a vague warning to stay out of lower Manhattan."

Three incidents of which we know details involve schoolchildren (which makes sense, since kids are notoriously poor judges of when to keep their lips buttoned). On September 10, 2001, a fifth-grader in a Dallas suburb made a startling declaration to his teacher: "Tomorrow, World War III will begin. It will begin in the United States, and the United States will lose." The boy was absent from school on September 11 and 12.

A school district official "said the boy is multiracial but that she does not believe his ethnicity includes a Middle Eastern background," according to the *Houston Chronicle*. The paper further notes: "Two charities in the neighboring suburb of Richardson have been investigated in the past for possible ties to Palestinian terrorist organizations."

In another incident, this one in Jersey City, a pupil at an unnamed school had warned people to stay away from lower Manhattan on the morning of September 11. Several hijackers lived in Jersey City.

Even more to the point, one week before the attacks, a Brooklyn high-school freshman pointed out a classroom window at the WTC towers and said to the class and his teacher: "Do you see those two buildings? They won't be standing there next week." The boy's family had recently immigrated from Pakistan.

Minutes after the 911 attacks, school officials told the authorities about the student's correct prediction. On September 13, the FBI and NYPD interviewed the boy, his brother, and their father. After the interviews, the father promptly left the country for Pakistan, leaving the rest of his family behind.

_IRAQ'S ACTIONS INDICATED SOMETHING BIG WAS ABOUT TO HAPPEN[45]

Two weeks before the attacks, Saddam Hussein put his military on its highest state of alert, something he hadn't done since the Gulf War a decade earlier. He also hid in his network of bunkers and moved his wives out of their palatial residence in Baghdad.

What makes this so suspicious is that Hussein had no apparent reason for declaring a red alert and going into hiding. A US intelligence official commented: "He was clearly expecting a massive attack and it leads you to wonder why."

Things become clearer when you realize that Hussein "had been providing al-Qaeda, Osama bin Laden's terrorist network, with funding, logistical back-up and advanced weapons training," according to an investigation by the *Daily Telegraph*. The London newspaper further reveals:

The CIA is understood to have evidence that Mohammed Atta, one of the suicide bombers, met an Iraqi intelligence officer earlier this year in Prague.... In the past four months at least three high-ranking Iraqi intelligence officials—among them Hassan Ezba Thalaj, a veteran officer with a reputation for ruthlessness—have visited Pakistan to meet representatives of al-Qaeda. Previous visitors have taken large sums of money with them, including Ahmed al Jafari, a senior Baghdad intelligence officer who took £420,000 [$598,000] 18 months ago. Other funds have been forwarded via banks in Lebanon.

_RUSSIAN MEDIA WARNED OF A HUGE, DESTABILIZING ATTACK ON THE US[46]

During the summer of 2001, Russian media were abuzz with talks of some kind of "attack" against the US that would destabilize and perhaps topple the economy. Russian citizens were urged to convert their dollars to rubles.

On July 12, *Pravda* ran a page-one article headlined: "The Dollar and America Will Fall Down on August 19?" While speaking at a conference focusing on the financial collapse of the US, Dr. Tatyana Koryagina—who works for a division of the Russian Ministry of Economic Development—gave an interview to the newspaper. The interviewer asked her, "All the participants at the hearings stated that America is a huge financial pyramid, which will crash soon. Still, it is hard to understand how this could happen in the first and richest country of the world—without a war, without missile or bomb strikes?" She cryptically replied: "Besides bombs and missiles, there are other kinds of weaponry, much more destructive ones."

Among her other ominous comments:

One must take into account the shadow economy, shadow politics and the religious component, while predicting the development of the present financial situation.

...

The US has been chosen as the object of financial attack because the financial center of the planet is located there. The effect will be maximal. The strike waves of economic crisis will spread over the planet instantly, and will remind us of the blast of a huge nuclear bomb.

...

Serious forces are acting against those who are now preparing the attack on the United States.

On July 17, *Pravda* ran another interview, this time with Dr. Sergei Glazyev, one of Russia's leading economists and the Chairman of the Duma Commission on Economic Politics. The article was entitled "The Dollar and the US Could Fall at Any Moment." Exactly two weeks later, *Pravda* published yet another interview of this type—with Malaysia's ambassador to Russia—titled, "The Dollar and the US Will Fall."

Other Russian papers ran similar stories, and even the Russian-language TV station in New York addressed the situation, assuring Russians in the Big Apple that "the Moscow rumors are ungrounded."

_ANONYMOUS PERSON(S) IN CAYMAN ISLANDS WARNED OF ATTACK[47]

For over a year, authorities in the Cayman Islands were investigating three Afghan men who arrived on the island under strange circumstances. They claimed they boarded a ship in Turkey bound for Canada, but were dropped off in the Caymans, which they initially thought *was* Canada. Authorities say they're sure the trio actually arrived via Cuba using Pakistani passports.

So what's the kicker? As the *Los Angeles Times* reveals: "Two weeks before the hijackings, an anonymous letter sent to a Cayman Islands radio station warned that the three might be involved with Bin Laden in preparing 'a major terrorist act against the US via an airline or airlines.'"

DURING THE SUMMER OF 2001, RUSSIAN MEDIA WERE ABUZZ WITH TALKS OF SOME KIND OF "ATTACK" AGAINST THE US THAT WOULD DESTABILIZE AND PERHAPS TOPPLE THE ECONOMY.

Meanwhile, the *Ottawa Citizen* reports that "a man in the Cayman Islands was said to have contacted American authorities in late August saying he overheard three Afghan men in a bar discussing planned attacks on the US." There's no way to know if this man and the letter-writer are the same person, or whether these three men are the same ones mentioned in the letter, but either way at least one person knew what was going to happen and warned the authorities and the media.

_DAVID SHIPPERS TRIED TO WARN THE FEDERAL GOVERNMENT[48]

David Shippers is the attorney who led the impeachment case against President Clinton. Whether or not you agree with his politics, Shippers is definitely not a fringe figure. He's a heavily connected Washington insider. In interviews since 911, he has told of trying to warn members of Congress and the Attorney General about planned attacks to be carried out by Islamic terrorists. Understandably cagey about his sources, Shippers has said that he learned that the plan involved detonating a suitcase nuclear bomb in lower Manhattan and using hijacked commercial airliners to ram the White House and Capitol building. (Obviously, his sources weren't 100 percent accurate, but they certainly were close.) For months he tried to get John Ashcroft, Speaker of the House Dennis Hastert, the Senate Intelligence Committee, and others to listen. They would initially express interest—sometimes even approaching him—but then he'd never hear from them again.

Shippers is now representing several outraged FBI agents who say they learned about the attacks ahead of time but were forbidden by superiors from doing anything about them. Often, they specialized in Muslim terrorism but were pulled off their beats when they uncovered important information.

_IRANIAN DETAINEE WARNED THE US[49]

In one of the most unusual developments, the German newspaper *Neue Presse* reports that an Iranian man being held in Hanover warned US intelligence officials of an attack that was to take place in America the week of September 10. After pleading with his captors to let him talk to authorities in America, he was allowed to call (at least one of those he called was the Secret Service). However, US officials hung up on him when he said that he was awaiting deportation from Germany. Mere hours before the 911 attacks commenced, the 29-year-old begged to fax a letter to President Bush. He was denied the chance.

Authorities were very interested in him after the fact, though. On September 14, he was interrogated by US officials from the Justice Department and intelligence agencies. Although some German officials attempted to downplay the story by insisting the man didn't know much, the Lower Saxony Justice Ministry confirmed to an Irish news Website that the detainee did indeed warn the US of an impending series of attacks.

_ISRAEL WARNED THE US

According to the *Daily Telegraph* of London:

Israeli intelligence officials say that they warned their counterparts in the United States last month that large-scale terrorist attacks on highly visible targets on the American mainland were imminent.... The *Telegraph* has learnt that two senior experts with Mossad, the Israeli military intelligence service, were sent to Washington in August to alert the CIA and FBI to the existence of a cell of as many of 200 terrorists said to be preparing a big operation.[50]

_RUSSIA WARNED THE US

Agence France-Presse reports:

The Russian intelligence service had warned Washington several times in the past of the possibility of terrorist strikes on US soil, the head of the service, Nikolai Patrushev, said yesterday. "We had clearly warned them," said Mr. Patrushev, who is head of the FSB, the successor organization to the KGB. He added that their US counterparts "did not pay the necessary attention" to their warnings, the Interfax news agency reported.[51]

_GERMAN INTELLIGENCE SAYS THE US KNEW BEFOREHAND OF ATTACKS[52]

According to the highly respected German newspaper *Frankfurter Allgemeine Zeitung*, members of German intelligence confirmed that US, UK, and Israeli intelligence agencies had indeed picked up on the plot by Muslim terrorists to hijack jetliners and crash them into US landmarks. (Israel was targeted, as well.) Using the global snooping system of Echelon, these countries knew at least three months in advance about the 911 attacks.

The German intelligence sources said US intelligence took the threats very seriously, even increasing surveillance of the terrorists. The problem allegedly was that they couldn't agree on a way to prevent the attacks.

"ISRAELI INTELLIGENCE OFFICIALS SAY THAT THEY WARNED THEIR COUNTERPARTS IN THE UNITED STATES LAST MONTH THAT LARGE-SCALE TERRORIST ATTACKS ON HIGHLY VISIBLE TARGETS ON THE AMERICAN MAINLAND WERE IMMINENT."

Israel also took the threats seriously, but unlike the US, they did something about it. The German paper reports: "In the context of the arising fear of airplane hijacks, Israel secretly implemented an X-ray machine—developed by one of Philips' daughter companies—at the Tel Aviv airport, which, in contrast to the conventional systems, analyzes all the chemical elements and is the first airport security system that detects all known explosives, even if they are carried separately or exist sparely." While devices to detect explosives wouldn't have thwarted the terrorists' blade-based hijackings, this measure on Israel's part shows that it was acting on prior knowledge.

_THE PHILIPPINES WARNED THE US

As mentioned earlier in this article, authorities in the Philippines uncovered Project Bojinka, the radical Muslim plot to ram hijacked jets into American landmarks and to blow up eleven or twelve US airliners in two days. They turned over this information to the FBI. It is not known what, if anything, the feds did with it.

> **MEMBERS OF GERMAN INTELLIGENCE CONFIRMED THAT US, UK, AND ISRAELI INTELLIGENCE AGENCIES HAD INDEED PICKED UP ON THE PLOT BY MUSLIM TERRORISTS TO HIJACK JETLINERS AND CRASH THEM INTO US LANDMARKS.**

A *Washington Post* reporter in the Philippines wrote: "Watching the attacks in New York and Washington unfold on television earlier this month, an investigator here gasped, 'It's Bojinka.' He said later: 'We told the Americans everything about Bojinka. Why didn't they pay attention?'"[53]

_EX-OFFICIALS ADMIT KNOWLEDGE OF THE COMING ATTACKS

Rusty Capps, a retired FBI counterterrorism chief: "We've had indications this was coming for some years."[54]

Michael Cherkasky, former New York City prosecutor who worked on the 1993 WTC bombing investigation and the current head of Kroll, Inc., a well-known security firm: "I believe that we had sufficient, specific information to say we were at enormous risk during the year 2000, 2001 of having a very, very serious incident here."[55]

Jerry Bremer, a former State Department terrorism expert and the chair of a national commission on terrorism in 2000: "We all predicted this. We had strategic warning. This is not something the analysts missed."[56]

_THE FINAL PIECE OF THE PUZZLE: CIA DIRECTOR GEORGE TENET KNEW WHAT WAS COMING

The most damning quote of all comes from an on-the-scene bulletin from National Public Radio on the morning of September 11. Congressional correspondent David Welna was reporting from the Capitol building as it was being evacuated:

> **I spoke with Congressman Ike Skelton—a Democrat from Missouri and a member of the Armed Services Committee—who said that just recently the Director of the CIA warned that there could be an attack—an *imminent* attack—on the United States of this nature. So this is not entirely unexpected.**[57]

_CONCLUSION: THE US KNEW

So there you have it. Numerous government reports predicting strikes on US soil. Experts and officials predicting the same thing. Warnings from the State Department and the FAA. The discovery of Project Bojinka. Previous attempts at using hijacked commercial aircraft as weapons of mass destruction. The FBI's prior knowledge of terrorists training at pilot schools in the US. Threats by the 1993 WTC bombers and bin Laden himself to take out the World Trade Center. Members of al Qaeda, including some of the hijackers and bin Laden himself, under surveillance beforehand. Heightened security at the WTC in August. Activation of the Florida National Guard. Domain names that advertised the attacks. Prior knowledge among people on the street. Direct warnings from several countries and individuals. Word from German intelligence that the US knew about the specific plans months in advance. Admissions from ex-officials that this wasn't a surprise. And finally, a Congressman, in the heat of the moment, letting it slip that the Director of the CIA had just warned of "an imminent attack on the United States of this nature."

Case closed.

Endnotes

1. Unsigned. "US Buys Afghan Image Rights." BBC News, 17 Oct 2001. **2.** Unsigned. "The Road to Sept. 11." *Newsweek* 1 Oct 2001. **3.** Dougherty, John. "Recent Report Warns of Bin Laden Threat." WorldNetDaily, 19 Sept 2001; Dougherty, John. "Panel: Attack on US 'Inevitable'." WorldNetDaily, 21 Sept 2001. **4.** Evans, Harold. "We Can't Say They Didn't Warn Us." *Guardian* (London) 2 Oct 2001; Website of the US Commission on National Security/21st Century <www.nssg.gov>. Emphasis added. **5.** Warrick, Joby, and Joe Stephens. "Before Attack, US Expected Different Hit." *Washington Post* 2 Oct 2001. **6.** *Ibid.* **7.** Pipes, Daniel. "Mistakes Made the Catastrophe Possible." *Wall Street Journal* 12 Sept 2001; Pipes, Daniel, and Steven Emerson. "Terrorism on Trial." *Wall Street Journal* 31 May 2001. **8.** Bodansky, Yossef. *Target America: Terrorism in the US Today*. New York: Shapolsky Publishers, 1993. Emphasis added. **9.** Bodansky, Yossef. "Islamic Terrorism in the United States." National Security Caucus Foundation (1996). **10.** Tenet, George. "Remarks As Prepared for Delivery by the Director of Central Intelligence, George J. Tenet, at the Town Hall of Los Angeles, 7 December 2000." Available on the CIA's Website <www.cia.gov>. **11.** Tenet, George. "Statement by Director of Central Intelligence George J. Tenet Before the Senate Select Committee on Intelligence: The Worldwide Threat in 2000: Global Realities of Our National Security, February 2, 2000." Available on the Senate's Website <www.senate.gov>. **12.** Tenet, George. "Statement of the Director of Central Intelligence George J. Tenet As Prepared for Delivery Before the Senate Armed Services Committee Hearing on Current and Projected National Security Threats, 2 February 1999." (Emphasis added.) Available on the CIA's Website. **13.** Unsigned. "Expert: Bin Laden Warned of 'Unprecedented' US Attack." Reuters, 11 Sept 2001, 10:39 AM ET. **14.** Federal Bureau of Investigation. "Fact Sheet: The Charges Against International Terrorist Usama bin Laden." 15 Dec 1999. **15.** Matier, Phillip, and Andrew Ross. "State Department Memo Warned of Terrorist Threat." *San Francisco Chronicle* 14 Sept 2001. Emphasis added. **16.** Unsigned. "US Airlines May Be a Terror Risk Over Next 3 Days." Airjet Airline World News, 23 June 2001. (Emphasis added.) A copy is still posted at the Website of the Honolulu branch of the National Air Traffic Controllers Association <www.hcfhawaii.com/news/terror_risk.htm>. The warning was also posted on 24 June 2001 to the Northwest Airlines Flight Attendants Website. **17.** Matier, Phillip, and Andrew Ross. "Willie Brown Got Low-key Early Warning About Air Travel." *San Francisco Chronicle* 12 Sept 2001. **18.** Doran, James. "Rushdie's Air Ban." *Times* (London) 27 Sept 2001. **19.** Neuffer, Elizabeth. "Feds Knew Bin Laden's Allies Trained as Pilots." *Boston Globe* 15 Sept 2001; Ressa, Maria. "US Warned in 1995 of Plot to Hijack Planes, Attack Buildings." CNN, 18 Sept 2001; Struck, Doug, *et al.* "Borderless Network of Terror." *Washington Post* 23 Sept 2001; unsigned. "Ramzi

Yusef [sic], Architect of First World Trade Center Bombing, Carried Plans for Airliner Suicide Crashes." *World Tribune* 15 Sept 2001; unsigned. "Airline Terror Plan Was Codenamed 'Project Bojinka'." Geostrategy-Direct, date unknown. **20.** An aside: It's quite interesting to note that when speaking of Ramzi's scheme, the media almost never mention his plans to send hijacked commercial planes into targets in the US. Since 911, many mainstream media outlets have discussed Project Bojinka, but they focus only on the assassinations and explosions, deliberately ignoring the aspect of the plan that was actually carried out. A perfect example is this from *Time* magazine: "Investigators discovered plots to assassinate the Pope and President Clinton during visits to the Philippines and to explode a dozen commercial jets over the Pacific." That's it; that's their entire description of Project Bojinka. Bower, Amanda. "Terrorist Hits and Misses: A Chronology of Mayhem." *Time* 12 Nov 2001: 68. **21.** Cullen, Kevin, and Ralph Ranalli. "Flight School Said FBI Trailed Suspect Prior to Hijackings." *Boston Globe* 18 Sept 2001; Drogin, Bob, and Eric Lichtblau. "Search for Suspects Was on for Weeks." *Los Angeles Times* 16 Sept 2001; Fainaru, Steve, and James V. Grimaldi. "FBI Knew Terrorists Were Using Flight Schools." *Washington Post* 23 Sept 2001; Grimaldi, James V. "FBI Had Warning on Man Now Held in Attacks." *Washington Post* 23 Sept 2001; Gugliotta, Guy, and David S. Fallis. "2nd Witness Arrested; 25 Held for Questioning." *Washington Post* 16 Sept 2001: A29; Gullo, Karen. "Investigators Earlier Turned Down Chance to Search Computer of Man Questioned in Terror Attacks." Associated Press, 2 Oct 2001; Isikoff, Michael, and Daniel Klaidman. "Access Denied." Newsweek.com, 1 Oct 2001; Neuffer, Elizabeth. "Feds Knew Bin Laden's Allies Trained as Pilots." *Boston Globe* 15 Sept 2001; Savino, Lenny. "Bin Laden Tipped His Hand." Knight Ridder News Service, 27 Sept 2001; unsigned. "Report: FBI Ignored French Warning on Extremist." Reuters, 13 Sept 2001; unsigned. "FBI 'Ignored Leads'." BBC News, 14 Sept 2001; unsigned. "FBI Tracked Man in Custody 2 Weeks Before Attacks." CNN, 18 Sept 2001; Wehrfritz, George, Catharine Skipp, and John Barry. "Alleged Hijackers May Have Trained at US Bases." *Newsweek* 15 Sept 2001. **22.** Hansen, Chris. "The Lesson of Air France Flight 8969." NBC News, 30 Sept 2001; Neikirk, William, and Christopher Drew. "Small Plane Crashes on White House Lawn, Pilot Dies." *Chicago Tribune* 12 Sept 1994; Sheley, Chuck. "Smokejumper Training Thwarts Hijacking of Pan-Am Clipper 73." *The Smokejumper* (no date); Wald, Matthew L. "Earlier Hijackings Offered Signals That Were Missed." *New York Times* 3 Oct 2001. **23.** Fineman, Mark, and Judy Pasternak. "Suicide Flights and Crop Dusters Considered Threats at '96 Olympics." *Los Angeles Times* 17 Nov 2001. **24.** Unsigned. "Italy: Bush Targeted at G8." *New York Newsday* 19 Sept 2001; unsigned. "Extremists 'Planned Genoa Attack on Bush'." BBC News, 27 Sept 2001. **25.** Wald, Matthew L. "Earlier Hijackings Offered Signals That Were Missed." *New York Times* 3 Oct 2001. **26.** Drogin, Bob, and Eric Lichtblau. "Search for Suspects Was on for Weeks." *Los Angeles Times* 16 Sept 2001; Hosenball, Mark, Michael Isikoff, and Daniel Klaidman. "Hijacker Had Met With bin Laden Agent Connected to Bombing of Destroyer." *Newsweek* 24 Sept 2001; Willman, David, and Alan C. Miller. "'Watch List' Didn't Get to Airline." *Los Angeles Times* 20 Sept 2001. **27.** Guart, Al. "Feds Released 3 Plotters in June." *New York Post* 16 Sept 2001. **28.** Sale, Richard. "Osama bin Laden Planned to Drop Space Needle." United Press International, 3 March 2001. **29.** Stafford, Ned. "CIA Was Shadowing Hijacker While Still in Germany, Magazine Says." News Box, 23 Sept 2001; Rising, David. "Key Suspect Had Been Under German Surveillance." Associated Press, 29 Sept 2001; unsigned. "Immigration Service Denies It Was Lax With Atta." Reuters, 22 Oct 2001. **30.** Borger, Julian. "US Spurned Chances to Kill Bin Laden." *Guardian* (London) 24 Nov 2001; Krauthammer, Charles. "In Defense of Secret Tribunals." *Time* 26 Nov 2001: 104; Lewis, Neil A., and David Johnston. "Jubilant Calls of Sept. 11 Led to FBI Arrests." *New York Times* 28 Oct 2001; Risen, James, and Stephen Engelberg. "Failure to Heed Signs of Change in Terror Goals." *New York Times* 14 Oct 2001; Scarborough, Rowan. "Intercepts Foretold of 'Big Attack'." *Washington Times* 22 Sept 2001. **31.** Fenton, Ben, and John Steele. "Bin Laden Told Mother to Expect 'Big News'." *Daily Telegraph* (London) 2 Oct 2001; Luscher, Bettina. "Bin Laden Supporters Celebrated in Phone Call, Sources Say." CNN 2 Oct 2001. **32.** Neumeister, Larry. "Trade Center Bomber's Threat Foreshadowed September Terrorist Attacks." Associated Press, 30 Sept 2001; Statement by J. Gilmore Childers, Esq., and Henry J. DePippo, Esq., before the Senate Judiciary Committee, Subcommittee on Technology, Terrorism, and Government Information. Hearing on "Foreign Terrorists in America: Five Years After the World Trade Center," 24 Feb 1998. Emphasis added. **33.** Unsigned. "Similar Plot Uncovered in Philippines, Says Police Chief." Agence France-Presse in *Sydney Morning Herald* 13 Sept 2001. Emphasis added. **34.** Hansen, Chris. "Warning Signs." NBC News, 23 Sept 2001; [UK government]. "Responsibility for the Terrorist Atrocities in the United States, 11 September 2001," 4 Oct 2001. **35.** [UK government]. "Responsibility for the Terrorist Atrocities in the United States, 11 September 2001," 4 Oct 2001. **36.** Cockburn, Alexander, and Jeffrey St. Clair. "Sense and Nonsense About Sept. 11." *CounterPunch* Website, 12 Sept 2001. Similarly, security was heightened at an Army base in New Jersey for reasons that weren't apparent. "Our informant says that at the start of July the Arsenal was placed at a very [high] state of alert, with some staff locked in their offices for a period." **37.** Arney, George. "US 'Planned Attack on Taleban'." BBC News, 18 Sept 2001; Godoy, Julian. "US Policy Towards Taliban

Influenced by Oil - Say Authors." Inter Press Service, 15 Nov 2001. Leigh, David. "Attack and Counter-attack." *Guardian* (London) 26 Sept 2001; Steele, Jonathan, Ewen MacAskill, Richard Norton-Taylor, and Ed Harriman. "Threat of US Strikes Passed to Taliban Weeks Before US Attack." *Guardian* (London) 22 Sept 2001. **38.** Leyne, John. "US 'Received Signs of Terror Plan'." BBC News, 3 Oct 2001; Perlez, Jane, and David E. Sanger. "Powell Says U.S. Had Signs, but Not Clear Ones, of a Plot." *New York Times* 3 Oct 2000; unsigned. "CIA Cited Growing Risk of Attack." Associated Press, 4 Oct 2001. **39.** "NEWS TRANSCRIPT from the United States Department of Defense. DoD News Briefing, Secretary of Defense Donald H. Rumsfeld, Friday, Oct. 12, 2001 (Interview with Lyric Wallwork Winik, *Parade Magazine*)." **40.** Neuffer, Elizabeth. "Feds Knew Bin Laden's Allies Trained as Pilots." *Boston Globe* 15 Sept 2001. **41.** Wastell, David, and Philip Jacobson. "Israeli Security Issued Urgent Warning to CIA of Large-scale Terror Attacks." *Daily Telegraph* (London) 16 Aug 2001. **42.** Text of Florida Executive Order 01-261, 7 Sept 2001. Taken from the [Florida] Governor's Office Home Page <www.flgov.com>. **43.** Johnson, Jeff. "Internet Domain Names May Have Warned of Attacks." Cybercast News Service, 19 Sept 2001; Johnson, Jeff. "Investigators Can Access Internet Domain Data." Cybercast News Service, 20 Sept 2001. For the record, the following are all the known suspicious domain names: "attack america.com," "attackonamerica.com," "attackontwintowers.com," "august11horror.com," "august11terror.com" "horrorinamerica.com," "horrorinnewyork.com," "nycterroriststrike.com," "pearlharborinmanhattan.com," "terrorattack2001.com," "towerofhorror.com," "trade towerstrike.com," "worldtradecenter929.com," "worldtradecenterbombs.com," "world tradetowerattack.com," "worldtradetowerstrike.com," "wterroristattack2001.com." Since there are two dates in the names—August 11 and September 29—Livingstone theorizes that this might have been the window for the attacks. **44.** Dougherty, Hugh. "'FBI Tipped off Before Attacks'." *Independent* (London) 13 Oct 2001; Ratcliffe, R.G. "Boy in Dallas Suburb Predicts Start of WW III Day Before Attacks." *Houston Chronicle* 19 Sept 2001; Shapiro, Jeffrey Scott. "Police: Student Spoke of Attacks Before Sept. 11." *The Journal News* (Westchester, New York) 11 Oct 2001. **45.** Berry, Jessica, Philip Sherwell, and David Wastell. "Alert by Saddam Points to Iraq." *Daily Telegraph* (London) 23 Sept 2001. **46.** Nemets, Dr. Alexander. "Expert: Russia Knew in Advance, Encouraged Citizens to Cash Out Dollars." NewsMax, 17 Sept 2001 **47.** Hunter, Janet. "Mossad Warned US of Imminent Attack." *Ottawa Citizen* 17 Sept 2001; Serrano, Richard A., and John-Thor Dahlburg. "Officials Told of 'Major Assault' Plans." *Los Angeles Times* 20 Sept 2001. **48.** Interview of David Shippers by Alex Jones. *Info Wars* (radio program) 10 Oct 2001; Metcalf, Geoff. "Middle East-OKC Connection." WorldNetDaily, 21 Oct 2001. **49.** Unsigned. "Reports of Attempts to Warn US of Impending Attacks." Deutsche Presse-Agentur, 14 Sept 2001; unsigned. "German Police Confirm Iranian Deportee Phoned Warnings. online.ie (Dublin, Ireland), 14 Sept 2001. **50.** Wastell, David, and Philip Jacobson. "Israeli Security Issued Urgent Warning to CIA of Large-scale Terror Attacks." *Daily Telegraph* (London) 16 Sept 2001. **51.** Unsigned. "Russia Gave 'Clear Warning'." Agence France-Presse in *Washington Times* 16 Sept 2001. **52.** Stafford, Ned. "Newspaper: Echelon Gave Authorities Warning of Attacks." *Newsbytes* (*Washington Post*) 13 Sept 2001; unsigned. "Hints for Months." Translated by F.S. *Frankfurter Allgemeine Zeitung* 11 Sept 2001. **53.** Struck, Doug, *et al.* "Borderless Network of Terror." *Washington Post* 23 Sept 2001. **54.** Savino, Lenny. "Bin Laden Tipped His Hand." Knight Ridder News Service, 27 Sept 2001. **55.** Hansen, Chris. "Warning Signs." NBC News, 23 Sept 2001. **56.** Neuffer, Elizabeth. "Feds Knew Bin Laden's Allies Trained as Pilots." *Boston Globe* 15 Sept 2001. **57.** Welna, David. Report on *Morning Edition*. National Public Radio, 11 Sept 2001. I heard this live on the radio and have listened to it again (many times) at the streaming audio archives on NPR's Website <www.npr.org>.

> "WE ALL PREDICTED THIS. WE HAD STRATEGIC WARNING. THIS IS NOT SOMETHING THE ANALYSTS MISSED." —JERRY BREMER, A FORMER STATE DEPARTMENT TERRORISM EXPERT

There was not a word in any of the history texts or history courses I had, either as an under-graduate or a graduate student, about the Colorado Coal Strike of 1913-14. That extraordinary episode came to my attention in two ways, first in a song by Woodie Guthrie called "The Ludlow Massacre," then in a chapter of the book by Samuel Yellen, *American Labor Struggles*, written in 1936. I became fascinated with the event, went through five thick volumes of congressional reports and whatever else I could find, made it the subject of my Masters Essay at Columbia University, and later wrote this essay for my book *The Politics of History* (Beacon Press, 1970).

THE LUDLOW MASSACRE

HOWARD ZINN

In their scholarly history of the labor movement, we find this terse statement by Selig Perlman and Philip Taft: "On April 20, 1914, the Colorado coal strike was brought to the attention of the entire country by the gruesome burning of eleven children and two women in the Ludlow tent colony."

The event they describe became known as the Ludlow Massacre. It was the culminating act of perhaps the most violent struggle between corporate power and laboring men in American history.

I recall it now, but not for its dramatic particulars, which might, in their uniqueness, be seen as a set of events happily submerged in the new welfare state. Rather, I find in it a set of suggestions about the relations between people and government which, stripped of their particularity, are still alive (so that, in place of miners, we might see blacks; in place of unions, we might see student movements or welfare rights organizations). I find, from 1914 to 1969, a continuity of governmental behavior which is easily forgotten if one is distracted by the intricately embroidered veil of words and gestures, or by the specificities of the Colorado countryside: the mining canyons, the strange and unrepeatable sounds, colors, tones, of that time, that place.

I would point to several elements in that continuity, and let the reader judge, from the facts of the Colorado events, from what we know of contemporary America, whether I am concluding too much from too little:

1. The firm connection between entrenched wealth and political power, manifested in the decisions of government, and in the machinery of law and justice.

2. The team play of the federal system, in which crass action by local police on behalf of the rich and powerful is modified—especially after resistance develops—with a more masked but still biased intervention by the national government.

3. The selective control of violence, in which government power is fumbling and incompetent in dealing with corporate and local police violence, sure and efficient in dealing with the violence of protest movements.

4. The somewhat different style of the national government (without difference in substance) in dealing with those outside its bounds who are helpless to resist and impotent as an internal political force—that is, with foreigners (Mexico, 1914; Dominican Republic, 1965). The style there is more like a local police force dealing with the locally powerless.

5. The opiate effect of commissions and investigations.

But let us turn to Colorado, 1913-14.

Formed under the enormous weight of the Rockies, soft coal was found in Southern Colorado not long after the Civil War. Railroads moved south from Denver, north from New Mexico. Settlers, coming down the old Santa Fe trail, converged on the banks of the Purgatory River, just east of the Rockies and about fifteen miles north of the New Mexican border, and built the town of Trinidad. The great Colorado Fuel and Iron Corporation, along with smaller companies, sank shafts into the hillsides, advertised for immigrant labor, and lowered workers into the earth to remove the coal.

THE MINING CAMPS WERE FEUDAL KINGDOMS RUN BY THE COAL CORPORATION, WHICH MADE THE LAWS.

In 1902, Colorado Fuel and Iron was purchased by John D. Rockefeller. Then, in 1911, he turned his interests (about 40 percent of the stock, more than enough to control) over to his son, John D. Rockefeller, Jr., who made major policy decisions from his office at 26 Broadway in New York City.

Two hundred and fifty feet, 300, 400 feet below the surface—in blackness so complete it seemed alive, grotesque—men hacked away at the face of the coal seam with hand picks. Their helpers shoveled the coal into waiting railroad cars, which were drawn through tunnels by mules to the main shaft, and lifted to the surface to the top of the tipple, the coal then showering down through the sorting screens onto flat cars. The average coal seam was about three feet high, so the miner worked on his knees or on his side. The ventilation system depended on the manipulation of tunnel doors by "trapper boys"—often 13- or 14-year-old children being initiated into mining.

At the edge of the mountains, in steep-walled canyons, were the camps where the miners lived, in sagging, wooden huts, with old newspapers nailed to the walls to keep out the cold. Nearby were the mine buildings and the coke ovens. With clouds of soot clogging the air. Behind the huts was a sluggish creek, dirty-yellow, laden with mine slag and camp refuse, alongside which the children played.

The mining camps were feudal kingdoms run by the coal corporation, which made the laws; curfews were imposed, suspicious strangers were not allowed to visit the homes, the company store must be patronized, the company doctor used. The laws were enforced by company-appointed marshals. The teachers and preachers were picked by the company. By 1914, Colorado Fuel and Iron owned 27 mining camps, and all the land, the houses, the saloons, the schools, the churches, the stores. Company superintendents, in charge of the camps, were described once by a corporation employee as "uncouth, ignorant, immoral, and in many instances the most brutal set of men... Blasphemous bullies."[1]

At first the miners were Welshmen and Englishmen, who had gained experience in their home countries. But in the 1880s and 1890s, the new immigration brought Italians, Greeks, Poles, Hungarians. There were many Mexicans and Negroes.[2]

Colorado Fuel and Iron became unmistakably the major political force in Colorado. A letter from C.F. & I. Superintendent Bowers to the secretary of John D. Rockefeller, Jr., written in May 1913, summed up the situation:[3]

> The Colorado Fuel & Iron Company for many years were accused of being the political dictator of southern Colorado, and in fact were a mighty power in the whole state. When I came here it was said that the C.F. & I. Co. voted every man and woman in their employ without regard to their being naturalized or not; and even their mules, it used to be remarked, were registered, if they were fortunate enough to possess names.

Bowers told Rockefeller that the company, in the 1904 election campaign, had contributed $80,605, and that it "became notorious in many sections for their support of the liquor interests. They established saloons everywhere they possibly could." A sheriff elected with company support became a partner in sixteen liquor stores in the mining camps.

Apparently, Bowers' entrance onto this scene did not change the situation. Company officials continued to be appointed as election judges. Company-dominated coroners and judges prevented injured employees from collecting damages. Polling places were often on company property. In Las Animas County, John C. Baldwin, a gambler, bartender, and friend of Colorado Fuel and Iron, was jury foreman in 80 percent of the county cases. During the strike, Governor Ammons was questioned about civil liberties in the state of which he was chief executive, and his interviewer, Rev. Atkinson, reported this exchange:

Rev. Atkinson: Have you no constitutional law and government in Colorado?

Gov. Ammons: Not a bit in those counties where the coal mines are located.

Rev. Atkinson: Do you mean to say that in large sections of your state there is no constitutional liberty?

Gov. Ammons: Absolutely none.

One Colorado official told the House Committee investigating the strike: "It's very seldom you can convict anyone in Huerfano County if he's got any friends. Jeff Farr, the sheriff, selects the jury and they're picked to convict or acquit as the case may be."

"WHAT WOULD THE COAL IN THESE MINES AND IN THESE HILLS BE WORTH UNLESS YOU PUT YOUR STRENGTH AND MUSCLE IN TO BRING THEM?"

In early 1913, the United Mine Workers, which had unsuccessfully led a strike in the southern Colorado coal fields ten years before, began another organizing drive. It asked the mine operators to negotiate. The operators refused and hired the Baldwin-Felts Detective Agency. The governor sent his deputy labor commissioner to Trinidad to investigate what seemed a growing tension. Hundreds of deputies were sworn in by the sheriffs of Las Animas and Huerfano Counties.

On the evening of August 16, 1913, a young United Mine Workers organizer names Gerald Lippiatt arrived in Trinidad by train, walked down the main street through a Saturday night crowd, exchanged angry words with two Baldwin-Felts detectives who had recently been deputized, and was shot to death.

The two detectives, George Belcher and Walter Belk, were released on $10,000 bond, while a coroner's jury was formed. On it were six Trinidad men: the manager of the Wells Fargo Express company, the cashier of the Trinidad National Bank, the president of the Sherman-Cosmer Mercantile Company, the manager of the Columbia Hotel, the proprietor of a chain of mercantile stores, and John C. Baldwin, gambler and saloonkeeper, who acted as foreman.

There were conflicting reports to the jury on who fired first, how many shots were fired, and what was said between Lippiatt and the detectives. The only details on which all witnesses agreed was that Lippiatt walked down the street, encountered Belcher and Belk, exchanged gunfire with Belcher, and was killed. The first man to reach Lippiatt, a miner named William Daselli, said Belk reached for his gun, Belcher pulled his gun and fired, and Lippiatt fell, fired from the ground, wounding Belcher in the thigh, then fell for the last time. When Daselli raised Lippiatt's head, he said, Belk's gun was still trained on him.[4]

The jury's verdict: justifiable homicide.

The pace of union organizing in the mining canyons now quickened. Secret meetings were held in churches, at picnics, in abandoned mine workings hidden in the mountains. A convention was called for mid-September in Trinidad, and delegates were elected at hundreds of meetings.

Meanwhile, the Baldwin-Felts Agency was importing hundreds of men, from the saloons and barrelhouses of Denver, and from points outside the state, to help break the impending strike. In Huerfano County, by September 1, 326 men were deputized by Sheriff Jeff Farr, all armed and paid by the coal companies.

The miners' convention, with 280 delegates, opened in the Great Opera House of Trinidad. For two days, rank-and-file miners registered their complaints: that they were robbed of from 400-800 pounds on each ton of coal, that they were paid in scrip worth 90 cents on the dollar (a violation of Colorado law), that the eight-hour law was not observed, that the law allowing miners to elect checkweighmen of their own choice was completely ignored, that their wages could only be spent in company stores and saloons (where prices were 25-40 percent higher), that they were forced to vote according to the wishes of the mine superintendent, that they were beaten and discharged for voicing complaints, that the armed mine guards conducted a reign of terror which kept the miners in subjection to the company. Their average daily wage was $1.68 for eight hours, $2.10 for ten hours. Casualty rates were twice as high in Colorado as in other mining states.

The high point of the Trinidad convention was the appearance of Mary Jones (the fabled Mother Jones), 80-year-old organizer for the United Mine Workers, just back from a bitterly fought strike in the coalfields of West Virginia. Mother Jones represented a radical view (she had been one of the founders of the Industrial Workers of the World) inside the rather conservative United Mine Workers (which had, for instance, supported Governor Ammons and the Democratic

Party in 1912 against Progressive and Socialist candidates).[5]

Mother Jones' speech deserves to be quoted at length:

The question that arises today in the nation is an industrial oligarchy.... What would the coal in these mines and in these hills be worth unless you put your strength and muscle in to bring them?

I went into the state of West Virginia.... There I saw women that had been beaten to death and a babe of the coming generation was beaten to death and murdered by the Baldwin-Felts thugs in the womb of her mother. That is in America, my friends, and I said, "I will never leave the state until the Baldwin thugs leave too" and I didn't... Three thousand men assembled in Charlestown and we marched up with banners, with demands upon those banners, and we walked into the state house grounds, for they are ours, and we have a right to take possession of them if we want to... I called a committee and I said, "Here, take this document into the governor's office and present it to him. Now don't get on your knees. We have got no kings in America. Stand on both your feet with your head erect," said I, and present that document to the governor, and they said "Will we wait?" and I said, "No, don't wait, and don't say your honor," said I, because very few of those fellows have any honor...

And there was that meeting. I would give the United States Treasury if I had it, boys, if there had been someone there with a pen who grasped the sociology of that meeting—he would have paralyzed the world with it.... Men came from the mountains with toes out of their shoes, with stomachs empty.... Fifteen hundred men came there, the militia was there, the Baldwin thugs came there.... When I was about to close the meeting I said, "Boys, let Mother tell you one thing." And they said, "What, Mother?" And I said, "Liberty is not dead, she is only quietly resting, waiting only for you to call" and that voice of fifteen hundred men rang the air, reached to Heaven, and they said, "Oh God, Mother, call her, call her now!"

Sure we'll get in the bullpen. There is nothing about that. I was in jail. God Almighty, what if you do, you build the jail! I was jailed...and tried in Federal court and the old judge said, "Did you read my injunction?" I said I did. "Did you notice that that injunction told you not to look at the mines and did you look at them?" "Certainly," I said. "Why did you do it?" the judge said. "Because there was a judge bigger than you, and he gave me my eyesight, and I am going to look at whatever I want to."

A lickspittle of the court comes up, and he says, "You must say your Honor, this is the court, His Honor on the bench." Yes, that was His Honor on the bench, the fellow behind the counter with the mustache... You have collected more wealth, created more wealth, than they in a thousand years of the Roman Republic, and yet you have not any...

When I get Colorado, Kansas, and Alabama organized, I will tell God Almighty to take me to my rest. But not before then!

The convention, rebuffed by the company again on requests to negotiate, voted to call a strike for September 23, 1913.

On that day, an epic scene took place in the coal districts of Southern Colorado. Eleven thousand miners, about 90 percent of the workers in the mines, gathered their families and their belongings on carts and mules and on their backs, and marched out of the mining camps to tent colonies set up in the countryside by the union.[6] One observer wrote:

All the tents had not yet arrived and the elements seemed to be in league with the operators. For two days it rained and snowed. There was never a more pitiful sight than the exodus of those miners fortunate enough to get wagons for their household goods. It rained all day Tuesday, and there streamed into Trinidad from every road miners with their wives and kids, crowded up on top of pitifully few household things.

Mother Jones testified later that 28 wagonloads of personal belongings came into the Ludlow tent colony that day, on roads deep in mud, with the horses weary, and mothers carrying tiny babies in their arms. Tents and mattresses were wet, and the children had to sleep on those mattresses that night.

ELEVEN THOUSAND MINERS, ABOUT 90 PERCENT OF THE WORKERS IN THE MINES, GATHERED THEIR FAMILIES AND THEIR BELONGINGS ON CARTS AND MULES AND ON THEIR BACKS, AND MARCHED OUT OF THE MINING CAMPS TO TENT COLONIES SET UP IN THE COUNTRYSIDE BY THE UNION.

The largest of the tent colonies was at Ludlow, a railroad depot eighteen miles north of Trinidad, on a direct line to Walsenburg, at the edge of Colorado Fuel and Iron property. There were 400 tents here, for a thousand people, including 271 children. In the course of the strike, 21 babies were born in this colony. Later a National Guard officer, reporting to the governor, said of the Ludlow colony: "The colony numbered hundreds of people of whom only a few families were Americans. The rest were for the most part Greeks, Montenegrins, Bulgars, Servians, Italians, Mexicans, Tyroleans, Croatians, Austrians, Savoyards, and other aliens from the Southern countries of Europe."[7]

Violence began immediately. The Baldwin-Felts Agency constructed a special auto, steel-armored, with a Gatling gun mounted on top, which became known as the Death Special. It roamed the countryside, and on October 17, attacked the tent colony at Forbes, killing one man, leaving a 10-year-old boy with nine bullets in his leg. Around the same time, two rows of armed guards marched 49 miners to Trinidad, with the Death Special crawling along to the rear, its guns trained on the strikers' backs. When G.E. Jones, a member of the Western Federation of Miners (the militant miners' union which helped form the IWW) tried to photograph the armored car, Albert Felts, manager of the Baldwin-Felts Agency, beat him unconscious with the butt of his pistol. Jones was then arrested for disturbing the peace.

That same month, a steel-clad train manned by 190 guards with machine guns and rifles headed for the Ludlow colony. It was intercepted by a detachment of armed miners, and a battle took place in which one mine guard was killed. The *New York Times* commented, after this first small victory for the union: "The situation is extremely critical tonight. More than 700 armed strikers are reported to be in the field against the mine guards."

By this time there had been at least four battles between strikers and guards, and at least nine men had been killed—mostly strikers. The tent colonies were in a state of siege, with machine guns and high-powered searchlights perched on inaccessible ridges, constantly aimed at the tents.

On October 28, 1913, Governor Ammons declared martial law, issued an order forbidding the import of strikebreakers from outside the state, and ordered General Chase of the Colorado National Guard to move his troops into the strike district. It was one of those "balanced" political moves, in which the concession to one side (the ban on imported strikebreakers) is unenforced, and that to the other side (the reinforcement of the mine guards by government troops) is effectively carried out.

Some of the pressures behind Ammons' calling of the Guard are explained in a letter written by Vice-President Bowers of C.F. & I. to John D. Rockefeller, Jr., in New York:

You will be interested to know that we have been able to secure the cooperation of all the bankers of the city, who have had three or four interviews with our little cowboy governor, agreeing to back the State and lend it all funds necessary to maintain the militia and afford ample protection so our miners could return to work.... Besides the bankers, the chambers of commerce, the real estate exchange, together with a great many of the best business men, have been urging the governor to take steps to drive these vicious agitators out of the state. Another mighty power has been rounded up on behalf of the operators by the getting together of fourteen of the editors of the most important newspapers in the state.

After five weeks of terror organized by the mine operators' private army, the striking miners were ready to believe that the National Guard, representing the government of the United States, had come to restore order. At the Ludlow tent colony, pennies and nickels were collected to buy a large American flag to greet the Guard. A thousand men, women, children, gaunt from lack of food, lined up on the road from the railroad station to the Ludlow colony, dressed in their Sunday best, the children in white, waving little American flags, a hastily assembled band, dressed in faded Greek and Servian army uniforms, playing "The Union Forever." From the station marched the first troop of cavalry, with General Chase himself on a prancing white stallion, then a small detachment of field artillery, then two regiments of infantrymen, in wide-brimmed hats and yellow leggings. The miners and their wives and children shouted greetings and sang until the last troops had disappeared past the colony, down Berwind Canyon.

> THE BALDWIN-FELTS AGENCY CONSTRUCTED A SPECIAL AUTO, STEEL-ARMORED, WITH A GATLING GUN MOUNTED ON TOP, WHICH BECAME KNOWN AS THE DEATH SPECIAL.

But the National Guard turned out to be no different than the Baldwin-Felts men during that cold, hungry winter of 1913-14. In December, a teenager was accosted on the road near the Ludlow colony by Lieutenant Linderfeldt, a stocky, beribboned veteran of the Spanish-American War, and knocked unconscious by the lieutenant's fists. A women's parade in Trinidad in January was attacked by cavalry, and a frightened 16-year-old girl, trying to get away, was kicked in the chest by a man on a rearing white horse—General Chase. The leader of the Ludlow colony, a college-educated Greek man named Lou Tikas, was beaten by Linderfeldt and dragged off to jail.[8]

The National Guard made 172 arrests that winter. A Welsh woman named Mary M. Thomas, mother of two, was held for three weeks in a vermin-ridden cell. One striker, forced to sleep on an icy cement floor, died after 25 days. A 19-year-old-girl, pregnant, was dragged through an alley by National Guardsmen one night until she lost consciousness. One miner's wife, Mrs. Yankinski, was home with four children when militia men broke into her home, robbed her money, and broke her little girl's nose with a kick. In the town of Segundo, a group of drunken Guardsmen forced some children to march about the city for two hours, prodding them with bayonets.

There was violence by the strikers. Strikebreaker Pedro Armijo was murdered near the Aguilar tent colony. A mine clerk named Herbert Smith, scabbing in a Colorado Fuel and Iron mine, was brutally beaten near Trinidad. Strikers fired on the Forbes mining camp, where strike-breakers were living, and were dispersed by an infantry company. Four mine guards were killed at La Veta while escorting a scab. And on November 20, 1913, George Belcher, the killer of Lippiatt, was leaving a Trinidad drugstore, stopped on the corner to light a cigar, and was killed by a single rifle shot by an unseen gunman.[9]

Governor Ammons rescinded his order against out-of-state strikebreakers, and the National Guard began escorting strikebreakers to the mines. A trainload of such men from St. Louis, disembarking in the mine area, were protected by militiamen with unsheathed bayonets. A House committee heard testimony on the violation of federal peonage laws. Salvatore Valentin, a Sicilian, told the committee that he had been brought from Pittsburgh through deception and forced to work in the Delagua mine. One of his fellow strikebreakers, he said, was shot and killed in the mines by an unknown person.[10]

Early in January 1914, Mother Jones came back to Trinidad, "to help my boys," and was immediately deported by the National Guard. Eluding three detectives, she returned, but over a hundred militiamen stormed the Toltec Hotel in Walsenburg and took her prisoner. She was held in prison for 20 days, with two armed sentinels outside her door.

When women paraded in Trinidad to protest her arrest, eighteen were jailed. When General Chase reported later to the governor on the conduct of the National Guard, he wrote: "It is hoped that a just and discriminating public will in the end come to realize the disinterested service of these champions of the state's integrity and honor."

As spring approached in 1914, funds for the Guard began to run out.

The payroll alone was $30,000 a month, and critics pointed to the disproportionate number of officers: 397 officers to 695 privates. The state was heavily in debt to the bankers. As it became unable to pay salaries, the regular enlisted militia dropped out, and their places were taken by mine guards of Colorado Fuel and Iron, now in Guard uniforms, drawing their pay from the company.

ONE STRIKER, FORCED TO SLEEP ON AN ICY CEMENT FLOOR, DIED AFTER 25 DAYS.

In early April 1914, Governor Ammons recalled all but two companies of the National Guard, consisting now mostly of mine guards, in the pay of C. F. & I. and under the command of Major Pat Hamrock, a local saloonkeeper, and Lieutenant Linderfeldt. They were stationed on a rocky ridge overlooking the thousand men, women, and children who lived in the tent colony at Ludlow.

On Monday morning, April 20, two dynamite bombs were exploded in the hills above Ludlow by Major Hamrock's men—a signal for operations to begin. At 9 AM a machine gun began firing into the tents, and then others joined. Women, holding children, ran from tent to tent, seeking shelter, crying out wildly. Some managed to escape into the hills. Others crawled into the dark pits and caves which had been dug under a few of the tents. Miners left the tents to draw off the fire, flung themselves into deep arroyos (gashes left by old creek beds) and fired back. One eyewitness reported later:

The firing of the machine guns was awful. They fired thousands and thousands of shots. There were very few guns in the tent colony. Not over fifty, including shotguns. Women and children were afraid to crawl out of the shallow pits under the tents. Several men were killed trying to get to them. The soldiers and mine guards tried to kill everybody; anything they saw move, even a dog, they shot at.

The old feud between strike leader Tikas and Lieutenant Linderfeldt came to its end that afternoon. Tikas was in the big tent, finding shelter for women and children, helping the wounded, when a telephone, its wires amazingly intact, started ringing. It was Linderfeldt, up on the ridge. He wanted to see Tikas—it was urgent, he said. Tikas refused. The phone rang again and again. Tikas answered, said he would come.

Carrying a white flag, Tikas met Linderfeldt on the hill. The Lieutenant was surrounded by militiamen. The only eyewitness report is from a young engineer visiting Colorado with a friend, who saw the scene from a nearby cliff. They saw the two men talking, then Linderfeldt raised his rifle and brought the stock down with all his strength on Tikas' skull. The rifle broke in two as Tikas fell, face downward. "As he lay there, we saw the militiamen fall back. Then they aimed their rifles and fired into the unconscious man's body. It was the first murder I had ever seen..."

THERE HE FOUND THE MANGLED, CHARRED BODIES OF TWO WOMEN AND ELEVEN CHILDREN, HEAPED TOGETHER IN WHAT HAD BEEN A DESPERATE STRUGGLE TO ESCAPE.

Two other strikers, unarmed and under guard, met their deaths on the hill in a similar manner. The machine guns continued firing into the tents, and five people died in their fire. One of them was Frank Snyder, 10 years old. His father told about it:

Frank was sitting on the floor...and he was in the act of stooping to kiss or caress his sister.... I was standing near the front door of my tent and I heard the impact of the bullet striking the boy's head and the crack...as it exploded inside of his brain.

As the sun fell behind the Black Hills, the firing lessened. Now soldiers moved down the slopes into the shadows alongside the tents, drenched the canvas with coal oil, and set the tents afire. The visiting engineer later described the scene:

We watched from our rock shelter while the militia dragged up their machine guns and poured a murderous fire into the arroyos from a height by Water Tank Hill above the Ludlow depot. Then came the firing of the tents. I am positive that by no possible chance could they have been set ablaze accidentally. The militiamen were thick about the northern corner of the colony where the fire started, and we could see distinctly from our lofty observation place what looked like a blazing torch waved in the midst of the militia a few seconds before the general conflagration swept through the place.

While bullets whistled through the flaming canvas, people fled in panic from their tents and from the caves beneath. A dispatch to the *New York Times* reported some of the results:

A seven-year-old girl dashed from under a blazing tent and heard the scream of bullets about her ears. Insane from fright, she ran into a tent again and fell into the hole with the remainder of her family to die with them. The child is said to have been a daughter of Charles Costa, a union leader at Aguilar, who perished with his wife and another child.... James Fyler, financial secretary of the Trinidad local, died with a bullet in his forehead as he was attempt-

ing to rescue his wife from the flames.... Mrs. Marcelina Pedragon, her skirt ablaze, carried her youngest child from the flames, leaving two others behind.... An unidentified man, driving a horse attached to a light buggy, dashed from the tents waving a white flag, just after the fire started. When ordered to halt he opened fire with a revolver and was killed by a return volley from the militia.

The tents became crackling torches, and for hours the countryside shone in a ghastly light, while men, women, and children roamed through the hills, looking for others in their families. At 8:30 PM the militia "captured" the Ludlow tent colony, now a smoldering pile of ashes.

It was on the following day, April 21, that a telephone linesman, going through the ruins, lifted a twisted iron cot that covered one of the pits dug beneath the tents for shelter. There he found the mangled, charred bodies of two women and eleven children, heaped together in what had been a desperate struggle to escape.

Funerals for the dead were held in Trinidad; according to the Trinidad Red Cross, 26 bodies of strikers had been found at Ludlow. Then the miners turned from the coffins of the dead and took up arms, joined by union miners from a dozen neighboring camps, who left, wives and children behind, and swarmed over the hills, carrying arms and ammunition. From Denver, the day after the discovery of the Ludlow death pit, United Mine Workers' officials issued a "Call to Arms"[11]:

Organize the men in your community in companies of volunteers to protect the workers of Colorado against the murder and cremation of men, women, and children by armed assassins in the employ of coal corporations, serving under the guise of state militiamen.

Gather together for defensive purpose all arms and ammunition legally available...

The state is furnishing no protection to us and we must protect ourselves.... We intend to exercise our lawful right as citizens to defend our homes and our constitutional rights.

Three hundred armed strikers marched from tent colonies in neighboring Fremont County to help. Others came overland inthe dark, carrying guns and ammunition. The press reported a series of encounters between soldiers and strikers in an area of three square miles south of Ludlow, the battlefield isolated by the cutting of telephone and telegraph wires. Four train crews of the Colorado and Southern Railroad refused to take soldiers and ammunition from Trinidad to Ludlow. There was talk of a general strike in Colorado.

Near Aguilar, the Empire mine was besieged, the tipple burned, the mouth of the slope caved in by dynamite explosions. Three mine guards were reported dead there, two mine shafts were in ashes, and the press reported that "the hills in every direction seem suddenly to be alive with men." Two hundred militia and company guards along the tracks at Ludlow were cut off from the rest of the district by "armed bands of strikers whose ranks are swelled constantly by men who swarm over the hills from all directions." At Colorado Springs, 300 union miners quit work to go to the Trinidad district, carrying revolvers, rifles, and shotguns.

The first legal move came from Pueblo, where a federal grand jury returned indictments against eight striking miners on charges of attacking the company post office at Higgins, Colorado.

Governor Ammons reported an attack on Delagua and Hastings by the miners. An attack on Berwind mine was expected momentarily. Now the Trinidad mayor and Chamber of Commerce appealed to President Woodrow Wilson to intervene.

President Wilson was busy at this time with Mexico. Several American sailors from a vessel which was blockading Mexico as an act of pressure against the Huerta regime on April 9, 1914, went ashore at Tampico and were arrested. The American admiral demanded that Mexico apologize, hoist the American flag, and give it a 21-gun salute. Wilson gave Mexico until April 9 to act. Meanwhile, 22,000 men and 52 ships were ready.[12] The Mexican foreign minister responded that Mexico would exchange salutes with the United States, would even salute first, but would not salute unconditionally. The officer who had arrested the American sailors was under arrest, he said, and the Americans had been freed even before investigation. "Mexico had yielded," he said, "as much as her dignity will permit. Mexico trusts to the fairmindedness and spirit of justice of the American people."

On April 20, Wilson asked Congress for the right to use armed force: "There can in what we do be no thought of aggression or selfish aggrandizement. We seek to maintain the dignity and authority of the United States only because we wish always to keep our great influence unimpaired for the uses of liberty, both in the United States, and wherever else it may be employed for the benefit of mankind."

The *New York Times* carried an editorial on the Mexican affair:

Just as when we went to war with Spain there were those who insisted that we should ignore the destruction of the Maine…so there are now those who hold that Huerta is in the right and that he had given us no cause of offense. As to that, we may trust the just mind, the sound judgment, and the peaceful temper of President Wilson. There is not the slightest occasion for popular excitement over the Mexican affair; there is no reason why anybody should get nervous either about the stock market or about his business.

Without waiting for Congress, Wilson ordered American naval forces to act. On April 21, the day of the discovery of the death pit at Ludlow, American ships bombarded Vera Cruz, landed ten boatloads of marines, and occupied the city. Over a hundred Mexicans were killed.

Businessmen had been asking for intervention in Mexico ever since the Mexican Revolution of 1910 created a threat to American investments in Mexican oil, mines, land, and railroad—which totaled a billion dollars by 1913. Now there was enthusiasm for Wilson's move. The *Times* reported[13]:

The five hundred or more business men who attended the luncheon of the Members Council of the Merchants Association of New York, jumped to their feet yesterday when William C. Breed, the toastmaster, called upon those present to express their loyalty to President Wilson "to whatever course he shall determine necessary to restore peace, order and a stable government in the Republic of Mexico."

It took President Wilson several days to turn his attention to Colorado. Meanwhile, the armed revolt of the miners was growing there.

A troop train leaving Denver to carry soldiers to the strike zone ran into trouble. Eighty-two men in Company C mutinied and refused to go to the district. "The men declared they would not engage in the shooting of women and children. They hissed the 350 men who did start and shouted imprecations at them."

Five thousand people demonstrated in Denver, standing in a pouring rain on the lawn in front of the capitol. A resolution was read, asking that Hamrock, Linderfeldt, and other National Guard officers be tried for murder, that the state seize the mines and operate them. Governor Ammons was denounced as a traitor and accessory to the murder, and Colorado citizens were asked to arm themselves for self-protection. The Denver Cigar Makers Union voted to send 500 armed men to Ludlow and Trinidad in the morning, and women of the United Garment Workers Union in Denver announced that 400 of their members had volunteered as nurses to aid the Colorado strikers.

All over the country meetings and demonstrations took place in support of the Colorado miners. Upton Sinclair and others picketed Rockefeller's office at 26 Broadway, in funeral garb. In front of the church where Rockefeller sometimes preached Sunday sermons, a minister was clubbed by police while protesting the massacre. The usually mild Eugene Debs, angered by the Colorado events, wrote:

The time has come for the United Mine Workers and the Western Federation of Miners to levy a special monthly assessment to create a Gunmen Defense Fund. This Fund should be sufficient to provide each member with the latest high power rifles, the same ones used by the corporation gunmen, and 500 rounds of cartridges. In addition to this, every district should purchase and equip and man enough Gatling and machine guns to match the equipment of Rockefeller's private army of assassins. This suggestion is made advisedly, and I hold myself responsible for every word of it.

With the National Guard in Colorado unable to control the marauding miners, with damages amounting to millions of dollars, and over 20 killed since the massacre, pressure grew for President Wilson to restore order with federal troops. The formal request was made by Governor Ammons, but a powerful informal signal was flashed by the New York Times, whose reaction, representing important elements in business and political circles, deserves a moment's attention.

The Times' first account of the Ludlow Massacre was an inaccurate one. Its headline read: "Women and Children Roasted in Pits of Tent Colony as Flames Destroy It. Miners Store of Ammunition and Dynamite Exploded, Scattering Death and Ruin." The Times had been unsympathetic to the miners throughout the strike; now it expressed horror at the killing of women and children. However, it seemed to be most angry that the militia and the authorities had been stupid enough to create a situation on which the strikers might capitalize to their advantage.

Here is the Times editorial following the massacre:

Somebody blundered. Worse than the order that sent the Light Brigade into the jaws of death, worse in its effect than the Black Hole of Calcutta, was the order that trained the machine guns of the state militia of Colorado upon the strikers' camp at Ludlow, burned its tents, and suffocated to death the scores of women and children who had taken refuge in the rifle pits and trenches…. Strike organizers cannot escape full measure of blame for the labor war…. But no situation can justify the acts of a militia that compels women and babes to lie in ditches and cellars twenty-four hours without food or water, exposes them to cannon and rifle fire, and lets them die like trapped animals in the flames of their camp…when a sovereign State employs such horrible means, what may not be expected from the anarchy that ensues?

"THE MEN DECLARED THEY WOULD NOT ENGAGE IN THE SHOOTING OF WOMEN AND CHILDREN. THEY HISSED THE 350 MEN WHO DID START AND SHOUTED IMPRECATIONS AT THEM."

Two days later, when the miners had taken up arms against the militia, the Times ran another editorial:

With the deadliest weapons of civilization in the hands of savage-minded men, there can be no telling to what lengths the war in Colorado will go unless it is quelled by force. The President should turn his attention from Mexico long enough to take stern measures in Colorado.

The indignation at the militia, such as it was, had lasted about a day. The Times had never, in the course of the long, violent series of attacks on the miners, called for federal intervention to stop that. Once the miners took up arms, it became concerned for order. A week after the massacre, another Times editorial criticized two clergymen, Rev. Percy Stickney Grant of Manhattan, and Rev. John Howard Melish of Brooklyn, who had denounced from their pulpits the actions of the National Guard against the strikers. The Times said about the sermons:

These are sympathetic utterances and differ from cold impartiality…. There are those who think that infamy in Colorado consists in the fact that the militia are shooting workers. It may be contended that there is something like infamy in the opposition of workers to society and order. The militia are as impersonal and impartial as the law.

On April 29, Woodrow Wilson sent federal troops into Colorado to bring order. Secretary of War Garrison asked everyone to surrender their arms to federal troops. The commander of the federal forces prohibited the import of strikebreakers from other states, banned picketing, and protected scabs.

For the next seven months, the air was filled with talk of negotiations, peace offers, mediation plans. The governor appointed an investigating commission. The Mines and Mining Committee of the House and the Industrial Relations Commission of the Senate held hearings, while federal troops patrolled the strike area. Testimony for House and Senate added up to over 5,000 pages. The strike petered out, was officially called off in December 1914. The Union had not won recognition. Sixty-six men, women, and children had been killed. Not one militiaman or mine guard had been indicted for a crime.[14] Under the weight of volumes of words, suspended from the tips of bayonets, the miners' resistance was crushed.

How shall we read the story of the Ludlow Massacre? As another "interesting" event of the past? Or as supporting evidence for an analysis of that long present which spans 1914 and 1970. If it is read narrowly, as an incident in the history of the trade union movement and the coal industry, then it is an angry splotch in the past, fading rapidly amidst new events. If it is read as a commentary on a larger question—the relationship of government to corporate power and of both to movements of social protest—then we are dealing with the present. Then we see a set of characteristics which have persisted, not only in American history, but in the history of all nations, although the forms vary. Then we see the complex alternating techniques of brute force and innocent solicitude, and the rain of investigations, words, negotiations, commissions, denunciations—all adding up to inches of progress and the basic retention of power and wealth where it now resides. Of course things have changed; there are now larger portions of material benefits meted out to the underdog; there are now more subtle methods used by both government and business in dealing with resistance[15] and more modern weapons (gas, planes)[16] when other methods fail. And one set of victims exchanged for others of different color, nationality, geography as tolerance runs dry.

The story can be read as a problem in personal responsibility, which leads to a continuing, inane argument about blame. Shall we blame John D. Rockefeller, Jr., who testified after the massacre that he and his company had been fighting to defend the workers' right to work? (A Congressman had asked him: "You'll do that, even if you lose all your money, and have all your employees killed?" And Rockefeller answered: "It's a great principle. It's a national issue.") Or should we blame his managers, or the governor, or the president? Or Lieutenant Linderfeldt?

Or—shall we look beyond blame? In that case, we might see a similarity in behavior among the privileged (and their followers) in all times, all countries: the willingness to kill for a great principle—the word "principle" a euphemism for keeping the fruits of the earth divided according to present rules. Then, we might see that the

killing is not the result of an elitist conspiracy but of a social structure larger than the consciousness of any of its parts. With such a vision, we might conclude that the responsibility belongs to no one in the past, but to us today to figure out—by acts as much as by thought—how to dismantle that structure, while constructing one which does not require as its indispensable workforce a team comprised of executioners and victims.

Endnotes

1. Statement by Rev. Eugene S. Gaddis, Superintendent of the Sociological Department of the Colorado Fuel and Iron Corporation during the strike, to the US Commission on Industrial Relations, 19 May 1915. For descriptions of life in the mining camps see Korson, George. *Coal Dust on the Fiddle*. Folklore, 1965; Coleman, McAlister. *Men and Coal*. Farrar & Rinehart, 1943. **2.** In 1901, out of 7,500 employees of C.F. & I., 500 were Negroes. Spero, Sterling, and Abram Harris. *The Black Worker*. Atheneum, 1968. **3.** West, George P. *Report on the Colorado Strike*. Government Printing Office, 1915: 46. This is the official summary of the report of the Commission on Industrial Relations. **4.** Accounts of the shooting are found in the *United Mine Workers Journal* for 21 August and 28 August 1913. Also in Beshoar, Michael. *Out of the Depths*. Denver: Golden Bell, 1957 (a biography of strike leader John Lawson). **5.** Michael Beshoar wrote: "John Lawson and his miners were naive on the subject of politics. They invariably regarded the Democratic Parry as the champion of the downtrodden, a position that could not have been sustained had they had the experience to draw obvious conclusions from the party's record in the state" (*Out of the Depths*). Beshoar was a grandson of Dr. Michael Beshoar, a physician friendly to the miners in early Colorado history. **6.** President Welborn of C.F. & I. estimated 70 percent of C.F. & I. struck. *Op. cit.*, West. **7.** Boughton, Edward. *Report to the Governor*. Denver, 1914. Boughton headed a military commission asked to report to the governor on the events of April 20, 1914. **8.** These and the other instances of National Guard brutality cited in this essay are part of a 600-page compilation of eyewitness reports by the Colorado State Federation of Labor, which were the basis for a short report, *Militarism in Colorado* (Denver, 1914), by William Brewster of the Yale Law School. **9.** The instances of miners' violence are reported in *The Military Occupation of the Coal Strike Zone of Colorado*, a report to the governor from the adjutant-general's office, 1914. The killing of Belcher was reported in the *International Socialist Review* (Feb 1914). **10.** *New York Times* 11 Feb 1914. Dozens of accusations of peonage appear in House Mines and Mining Committee, *Conditions in the Coal Mines of Colorado*, pp. 749, 1239, 1363, 1374, 1407, and other places in the hearings. **11.** House Mines and Mining Committee. *Conditions in the Coal Mines of Colorado*, Vol. II: Appendix. The call was signed by John Lawson and other U.M.W. officials, and by Ernest Mills, secretary-treasurer of the Western Federation of Miners. **12.** *New York Times* 20 April 1914. The headline read: "Campaign Worked Out by Naval Experts in Recent Months Now Being Carried Out in Detail." **13.** *New York Times* 23 April 1914. By July, Huerta was forced out of office. In November, the US occupation forces withdrew from Vera Cruz. **14.** On the contrary,

NOT ONE MILITIAMAN OR MINE GUARD HAD BEEN INDICTED FOR A CRIME.

John Lawson, the strike leader, was, a year later, tried and convicted of murder. He was accused of murdering John Nimmo, one of the army of deputies paid by the companies. No effort was made to prove Lawson fired the fatal shot; he was held responsible because he led the strike and was at the Ludlow tent colony the day of the battle. The judge, Granby Hillyer, was a former attorney for Colorado Fuel and Iron and had helped prepare cases against the strikers. The jury was chosen by a panel selected by the sheriff of Las Animan County. Lawson's conviction was later overturned. *Op. cit.*, West: 22. **15.** Note the bewildering variety of government agencies and commissions to represent welfare and beneficence; note that Rockefeller, after the Colorado strike, hired Ivy Lee, the nation's leading public relations man, and how public relations has become a vital part of government and business operations; note that the Rockefeller Foundation, new at the time of the strike, stepped up its activities, and that foundations in general multiplied. **16.** I write this shortly after police in Berkeley, California, carried out the first aerial gas attack on a domestic demonstration (May 1969).

MUSHROOM CLOUDS IN PARADISE
A BRIEF HISTORICAL OVERVIEW OF THE PEOPLE OF BIKINI ATOLL
JACK NIEDENTHAL

Bikini Atoll is one of the 29 atolls and five islands that compose the Marshall Islands. These atolls of the Marshalls are scattered over 357,000 square miles of a lonely part of the world located north of the equator in the Pacific Ocean. They help define a geographic area referred to as Micronesia.

Once the Marshalls were discovered by the outside world, first by the Spanish in the 1600s and later by the Germans, they were used primarily as a source for producing copra oil from coconuts. The Bikini islanders maintained no substantial contacts with these early visitors because of Bikini Atoll's remote location in the very dry northern Marshalls.

The fertile atolls in the southern Marshalls were attractive to the traders because they could produce a much larger quantity of copra. This isolation created for the Bikinians a tightly integrated society bound by close extended family association and tradition, where the amount of land you owned was a measure of your wealth.

In the early 1900s, the Japanese began to administer the Marshall Islands. This domination later resulted in a military build-up throughout the islands in anticipation of World War II. Bikini and the rest of these peaceful, low-lying coral atolls in the Marshalls suddenly became strategically important. The Bikini islanders' life of harmony drew to an abrupt close when the Japanese decided to build and maintain a watchtower on their island to guard against an American invasion of the Marshalls. Throughout the conflict, the Bikini station served as an outpost for the Japanese military headquarters in the Marshall Islands, Kwajalein Atoll.

In February 1944, toward the end of the war, the American forces captured Kwajalein Atoll in a gruesome and terrifyingly bloody battle, thereby effectively crushing the Japanese hold on the Marshall Islands. The five Japanese men left on Bikini, while hiding in a covered foxhole, killed themselves with a grenade before the American military forces could capture them.

After the war, in December 1945, President Harry S. Truman issued a directive to Army and Navy officials that joint testing of nuclear weapons would be necessary "to determine the effect of atomic bombs on American warships." Bikini, because of its location away from regular air and sea routes, was chosen to be the new nuclear proving ground for the United States government.

The following February, Commodore Ben H. Wyatt, the military governor of the Marshalls, traveled to Bikini. On a Sunday after church, he assembled the Bikinians to ask if they would be willing to leave their atoll temporarily so that the United States could begin testing atomic bombs "for the good of mankind and to end all world wars." King Juda, then the leader of the Bikinian people, stood up after much confused and sorrowful deliberation among his people, and announced: "We will go believing that everything is in the hands of God."

While the 167 Bikinians were getting ready for their exodus, preparations for the US nuclear testing program advanced rapidly. Some 242 naval ships, 156 aircraft, 25,000 radiation recording devices, and the Navy's 5,400 experimental rats, goats, and pigs soon started arriving for the tests. Over 42,000 US military and civilian personnel were involved in the testing program at Bikini.

> ON A SUNDAY AFTER CHURCH, HE ASSEMBLED THE BIKINIANS TO ASK IF THEY WOULD BE WILLING TO LEAVE THEIR ATOLL TEMPORARILY SO THAT THE UNITED STATES COULD BEGIN TESTING ATOMIC BOMBS "FOR THE GOOD OF MANKIND AND TO END ALL WORLD WARS."

■ ■ ■ ■ ■ ■ ■ ■ ■ ■

The nuclear legacy of the Bikinians began in March 1946 when they were first removed from their islands in preparation for Operation Crossroads. The history of the Bikinian people from that day has been a story of their struggle to understand scientific concepts as they relate to their islands, as well as the day-to-day problems of finding food, raising families, and maintaining their culture amidst the progression of events set in motion by the Cold War that have been for the most part out of their control.

The Bikinians were sent 125 miles eastward across the ocean on a US Navy LST landing craft to Rongerik Atoll. The islands of Rongerik Atoll were uninhabited because, traditionally, the Marshallese people considered them unlivable due to their size (Rongerik is one-sixth the size of Bikini Atoll) and because they had an inadequate water and food supply. There was also a deep-rooted traditional belief that the atoll was inhabited by evil spirits. The administration left the Bikinians food stores sufficient only for several weeks. The islanders soon discovered that the coconut trees and other local food crops produced very few fruits when compared to the yield of the trees on Bikini. As the food supply on Rongerik quickly ran out, the Bikinians suffered from starvation and fish poisoning due to the lack of edible fish in the lagoon. Within two months of their arrival, they started begging US officials to move them back to Bikini.

The two atomic bomb blasts of Operation Crossroads were both about the size of the nuclear bomb dropped on Nagasaki, Japan. Eighteen tons of cinematography equipment and more than half of the world's supply of motion picture film were on hand to record the Able and Baker detonations, as well as the movement of the Bikinians from their atoll.

In July 1946, the Bikinian leader, Juda, traveled with a US government delegation back to Bikini to view the results of the second atom bomb test of Operation Crossroads, code-named Baker. Juda returned to Rongerik and told his people that the island was still intact, that the trees were still there, that Bikini looked the same.

In December 1946 and January 1947, the food shortages worsened on Rongerik; the small population of Bikinians was confronted with near starvation. During the same period of time, the area of Micronesia was designated as a United Nations Strategic Trust Territory to be administered by the United States. It was the only strategic trust ever created by the United Nations. In this agreement, the US committed itself to the United Nations' directive to "promote the economic advancement and self-sufficiency of the inhabitants, and to this end shall...protect the inhabitants against the loss of their lands and resources..." The people of Bikini have long seen the irony in the conduct of the Trust Territory agreement that allowed the bombing of their homeland and that forced them into starvation on Rongerik Atoll.

In May 1947, to make the Bikinians' situation on Rongerik even more serious, a huge fire damaged many of the coconut trees. By July, when a medical officer from the US visited the island, the Bikinian people were found to be suffering severely from malnutrition. A team of US investigators determined in the fall, after a visit to Rongerik, that the island had inadequate supplies of food and water and that the Bikinian people should be moved from Rongerik without delay. The US Navy was harshly criticized in the world press for neglecting the Bikinian people on Rongerik. Harold Ickes, a reporter, stated in his 1947 syndicated column, "Man to Man": "The natives

are actually and literally starving to death."

Immediate preparations were made for the transfer of the Bikinians to Ujelang Atoll in the western Marshalls. In November, a handful of young Bikinian men traveled to Ujelang, and with the help of Navy Seabees, they started to arrange a community area and to construct housing. At the end of the year, however, the US selected Enewetak Atoll as a second nuclear weapons test site. The Navy then decided that it would be easier to move the Enewetak people to Ujelang, despite the fact that the Bikinians had now built all the housing and held high hopes that they would be relocated there.

"THE NATIVES ARE ACTUALLY AND LITERALLY STARVING TO DEATH."

In January 1948, University of Hawaii anthropologist Dr. Leonard Mason traveled to Rongerik at the request of the Trust Territory High Commissioner to report on the status of the Bikinians living there. Horrified at the sight of the withering islanders, Mason immediately requested a medical officer along with food supplies be flown to Rongerik.

That March, after two unpleasant years on Rongerik, the Bikinians were transported to Kwajalein Atoll, where they were housed in tents on a strip of grass beside the massive cement airstrip used by the US military. The Bikinians soon fell into yet another debate among themselves about alternative locations.

It was in June 1948 that the Bikinians chose Kili Island in the southern Marshalls, because the island was not ruled by a paramount king, or *iroij*, and was uninhabited. This choice ultimately doomed their traditional diet and lifestyle, which were both based on lagoon fishing.

That September, two-dozen Bikinian men were chosen from among themselves to accompany eight Seabees to Kili to begin the clearing of land and the construction of a housing area for the rest of the people, who remained on Kwajalein.

In November 1948, after six months on Kwajalein Atoll, the 184 Bikinians set sail once again. This time the destination was Kili Island, their third community relocation in two years.

Starvation also troubled the Bikinians on Kili; this situation led the Trust Territory administration to donate a 40-foot ship to be used for copra transportation between Kili and Jaluit Atoll. Later, in 1951, the boat was washed into the Kili reef by heavy surf and sank while carrying a full-load of copra.

In the following years, rough seas and infrequent visits by the field-trip ships caused food supplies on the island to run critically low many times, once even requiring an airdrop of emergency food rations.

■■■■■■■■■■

While the islanders struggled to set up their new community on Kili, the beautiful atoll of Bikini was in the process of being irradiated. In the northern Marshalls in January 1954, the Air Force and Army men arrived on the Bikinians' former, temporary home of Rongerik Atoll and jointly set up a weather station to monitor conditions in preparation for Operation Castle. This was a series of tests that would include the first air-deliverable, most powerful hydrogen bomb ever detonated by the United States. The US government was operating with the fear that the Russians had already detonated their own hydrogen bomb in 1952. Now decisions concerning the US testing program were being made at the highest levels of the government. The Cold War burned with vigor in the minds of paranoid politicians the world over.

The weather station on Rongerik made regular observations to determine barometric conditions, temperature, and the velocity of the wind up to 100,000 feet above sea level.

As the test date for the Bravo shot grew near, the men at the weather station performed many observations per day. They were checking surface wind direction and barometric conditions hourly and upper-level conditions every two hours.

As the test date neared, late in the month of February, documented proof exists that Joint Task Force-7 knew that the winds were blowing east from Bikini toward Rongerik Atoll and other inhabited islands because of the continuous reports coming in from their weather station.

Indeed, according to a Defense Nuclear Agency report on the Bravo blast, the weather briefing the day before the detonation stated that there would be "no significant fallout...for the populated Marshalls." The briefing at 6:00 PM, however, stated that "the predicted winds were less favorable; nevertheless, the decision to shoot was reaffirmed, but with another review of the winds scheduled for midnight." The midnight briefing "indicated less favorable winds at 10,000 to 25,000-foot levels." Winds at 20,000 feet "were headed for Rongelap to the east," and "it was recognized that both Bikini and Eneman islands would probably be contaminated."[1]

The decision to go forward with the test, knowing that the winds were blowing in the direction of inhabited atolls, was essentially a decision to irradiate the northern Marshall Islands and, moreover, to irradiate the people who were still living on them.

Early in the morning on March 1, 1954, the hydrogen bomb, code-named Bravo, was detonated on the surface of the reef in the northwestern corner of Bikini Atoll. The area was illuminated by a huge and expanding flash of blinding light. A raging fireball of intense heat that measured into the millions of degrees shot skyward at a rate of 300 miles per hour. Within minutes the monstrous cloud, filled with radioactive debris, shot up more than 20 miles and generated winds measuring hundreds of miles per hour. These fiery gusts blasted the surrounding islands and stripped the branches and coconuts from the trees.

Joint Task Force ships, which were stationed about 40 miles east and south of Bikini in positions enabling them to monitor the test, detected the eastward movement of the radioactive cloud from the 15-megaton blast. They recorded a steady increase in radiation levels, which became so high that all men were ordered below decks, and all hatches and watertight doors were sealed.

Millions of tons of sand, coral, plant life, and sea life from Bikini's reef, three islands (Bokonijien, Aerokojlol, and Nam), and the surrounding lagoon waters were sent high into the air by the blast. One and a half hours after the explosion, 23 fishermen aboard a Japanese fishing vessel, the Lucky Dragon, watched in awe as a "gritty white ash" fell on them. The men aboard the ship were oblivious to the fact that the ash was the fallout from a hydrogen bomb test. Shortly after being exposed to the fallout, their skin began to itch, and they experienced nausea and vomiting. One man died.

Meanwhile, on Rongelap Atoll (located about 125 miles east of Bikini), three to four hours after the blast, the same white, snow-like ash fell from the sky onto the 64 people living there and onto the eighteen people residing on Ailinginae Atoll. Bravo was a thousand times more powerful than the Fat Man and Little Boy atomic bombs that were dropped on Nagasaki and Hiroshima during the end of World War II. Its "success" was beyond the wildest dreams of the American scientists who were involved in the detonation—they thought that the blast would carry a payload of only approximately three megatons.

The Rongelapese, not understanding what was happening, watched as two suns rose that morning, observed with amazement as the radioactive dust soon formed a layer two inches deep on their island, turning the drinking water a brackish yellow. Children played in the fallout; mothers watched in horror as night came and their children began to show the physical signs of radiation exposure. The people experienced severe vomiting and diarrhea, their hair fell out, and the island fell into a state of terrified panic. The people had received no explanations or warnings whatsoever from the United

THE DECISION TO GO FORWARD WITH THE TEST, KNOWING THAT THE WINDS WERE BLOWING IN THE DIRECTION OF INHABITED ATOLLS, WAS ESSENTIALLY A DECISION TO IRRADIATE THE NORTHERN MARSHALL ISLANDS AND, MOREOVER, TO IRRADIATE THE PEOPLE WHO WERE STILL LIVING ON THEM.

EVERYTHING YOU KNOW IS WRONG

States government. Two days after the test, the people of Rongelap were finally taken to Kwajalein for medical treatment.

On Bikini Atoll the radiation levels increased dramatically. And, in late March following the Bravo test, the off-limits zones were expanded to include the inhabited atolls of Rongerik, Utirik, Ujelang, and Likiep. It is startling to note that none of these groups of islanders was evacuated prior to this blast or even before the subsequent nuclear weapons tests. In the spring of 1954, Bikar, Ailinginae, Rongelap, and Rongerik were all contaminated by the Yankee and Union weapons tests, which were detonated on Bikini Atoll. They yielded the equivalent of 6.9 and 13.5 megatons of TNT, respectively.

Back on Kili, in January 1955, the Trust Territory ships continued to have problems unloading food in the rough seas around the island, and the people once again suffered from starvation. The following year the food shortage problems grew even worse. Consequently, the United States gave the Bikinians a satellite community located on public land on Jaluit Atoll, 30 miles to the north. Three families moved to Jaluit. During 1957, other families rotated to Jaluit to take over the responsibilities of producing copra for sale.

During this period, the Bikinians signed an agreement with the US government turning over full use rights to Bikini Atoll. According to the agreement, any future claims by the Bikinians based on the use of Bikini by the government of the United States, or on the moving of the Bikinian people from Bikini Atoll to Kili Island, would have to be made against the Bikinian leaders and not against the US government. In return for this agreement, the Bikinians were given full use rights to Kili and several islands in Jaluit Atoll which were Trust Territory public lands. In addition, the agreement included $25,000 in cash and an additional $300,000 trust fund that yielded a semi-annual interest payment of approximately $5,000 (about $15 per person per year). This agreement was made by the Bikinians without the benefit of legal representation.

Typhoon Lola struck Kili late in 1957, causing extensive damage to crops and sinking the Bikinians' supply ship.

Shortly afterwards in 1958, Typhoon Ophelia caused widespread destruction on Jaluit and all the other southern atolls. The Bikinians living on Jaluit moved back to Kili, because the satellite community became uninhabitable due to the typhoon damage. The Bikinians continued to fight the problems associated with inadequate food supplies throughout 1960.

The difficulty of inhabiting Kili is due in part to the small amount of food which can be grown there, but more so because it has no lagoon. Kili differs substantially from Bikini because it is only a single island of one-third of a square mile in land area with no lagoon—compared to the Bikinians' homeland of 23 islands that form a calm lagoon and have a land area of 3.4 square miles. Most of the year Kili is surrounded by 10- to 20-foot waves that deny the islanders the opportunity to fish and sail their canoes. After a short time on Kili—a place that the islanders believe was once an ancient burial ground for kings and therefore overwrought with spiritual influence—they began to refer to it as a "prison" island. Because the island doesn't produce enough local food for the Bikinians to eat, the importation of United States Department of Agriculture rice and canned goods, as well as food bought with their supplemental income, has become an absolute necessity for their survival.

■ ■ ■ ■ ■ ■ ■ ■ ■ ■

Based on data on radiation levels on Bikini Atoll, US government agencies in 1967 began considering the possibility of returning the Bikinian people to their homelands. This scientific optimism stemmed directly from an Atomic Energy Commission (AEC) study that stated, "Well water could be used safely by the natives upon their return to Bikini. It appears that radioactivity in the drinking water may be ignored from a radiological safety standpoint.... The exposures of radiation that would result from the repatriation of the Bikini people do not offer a significant threat to their health and safety."

Accordingly, in June 1968, President Lyndon B. Johnson promised the 540 Bikinians living on Kili and other islands that they would now be able to return to their homeland (the story appeared on the front page of the New York Times). The President also stated, "It is our goal to assist the people of Bikini to build, on these once desolated islands, a new and model community." He then ordered Bikini to be resettled "with all possible dispatch."

In August 1969, an eight-year plan was prepared for the resettlement of Bikini Atoll in order to give the crops planted on the islands a chance to mature. The first section of the plan involved the clearing of the radioactive debris on Bikini Island. This segment of the work was designed by the AEC and the US Department of Defense. Responsibility for the second phase of the reclamation—which included the replanting of the atoll, construction of a housing development, and the relocation of the community—was assumed by the US Trust Territory government.

By late 1969, the first cleanup phase was completed. The AEC, in an effort to assure the islanders that their cleanup efforts were successful, issued a statement: "There's virtually no radiation left and we can find no discernible effect on either plant or animal life."

All that was theoretically left in order for the people to return was for

CHILDREN PLAYED IN THE FALLOUT; MOTHERS WATCHED IN HORROR AS NIGHT CAME AND THEIR CHILDREN BEGAN TO SHOW THE PHYSICAL SIGNS OF RADIATION EXPOSURE.

the atoll to be rehabilitated, but during 1971 this effort proceeded slowly. The second phase of the rehabilitation encountered serious problems because the US government withdrew its military personnel and equipment. It also brought to an end the weekly air service that had been operating between Kwajalein Atoll and Bikini Atoll. The construction and agricultural projects suffered because of the sporadic shipping schedules and the lack of air service.

In late 1972, the planting of the coconut trees was finally completed. During this period it was discovered that as the coconut crabs grew older on Bikini Island, they ate their sloughed-off shells. Those shells contained high levels of radioactivity; hence, the AEC announced that the crabs were still radioactive and could be eaten only in limited numbers.

The conflicting information on the radiological contamination of Bikini supplied by the AEC caused the Bikini

IN MAY 1977, THE LEVEL OF RADIOACTIVE STRONTIUM-90 IN THE WELL WATER ON BIKINI ISLAND WAS FOUND TO EXCEED THE US MAXIMUM ALLOWED LIMITS.

Council to vote not to return to Bikini at the time previously scheduled by American officials. The Council, however, stated that it would not prevent individuals from making independent decisions to return.

Three extended Bikinian families, their desire to return to Bikini being great enough to outweigh the radiological dangers, moved back to Bikini Island and into the newly constructed cement houses. They were accompanied by approximately 50 Marshallese workers who were involved in the construction and maintenance of the buildings.

The population of islanders on Bikini slowly increased over the years until, in June 1975, during regular monitoring of Bikini, radiological tests discovered "higher levels of radioactivity than originally thought." US Department of Interior officials stated that "Bikini appears to be hotter or questionable as to safety," while an additional report pointed out that some water wells on Bikini Island were also too contaminated with radioactivity for drinking. A couple of months later the AEC, on review of the scientists' data, decided that the local foods grown on Bikini Island, i.e., pandanus, breadfruit, and coconut crabs, were also too radioactive for human consumption. Medical tests of urine samples from the 100 people living on Bikini detected the presence of low levels of plutonium-239 and plutonium-240. Robert Conard of Brookhaven Laboratories commented that these readings "are probably not radiologically significant."

In October 1975, after contemplating these new, terrifying, and confusing reports on the radiological condition of their atoll, the Bikinians filed a lawsuit in US federal court, demanding that a complete scientific survey of Bikini and the northern Marshalls be conducted. The lawsuit stated that the US had used highly sophisticated and technical radiation detection equipment at Enewetak Atoll

but had refused to employ it at Bikini. The result of the lawsuit was to convince the US to agree to conduct an aerial radiological survey of the northern Marshalls in December 1975. Unfortunately, more than three years of bureaucratic squabbles between the Departments of State, Interior, and Energy over costs and responsibility for the survey delayed any action on its implementation. The Bikinians, unaware of the severity of the radiological danger, remained on their contaminated islands.

While waiting for the radiological survey to be conducted, further discoveries of these radiological dangers were made. In May 1977, the level of radioactive strontium-90 in the well water on Bikini Island was found to exceed the US maximum allowed limits. A month later a Department of Energy (DOE) study stated, "All living patterns involving Bikini Island exceed Federal [radiation] guidelines for thirty year population doses." Later in the same year, a group of US scientists, while on Bikini, recorded an 11-fold increase in the cesium-137 body burdens of the more than 100 people residing on the island. Alarmed by these numbers, the DOE told the people living on Bikini to eat only one coconut per day and began to ship in food for consumption.

Medical examinations performed by US physicians in April 1978 revealed radiation levels in many of the now 139 people on Bikini to be well above the US maximum permissible level. The very next month, US Interior Department officials described the 75 percent increase in radioactive cesium-137 as "incredible." The Interior Department then announced plans to move the people from Bikini "within 75 to 90 days," and so, in September 1978, Trust Territory officials arrived on Bikini to once again evacuate the people who were living on the atoll. An ironic footnote to the situation is that the long awaited northern Marshalls radiological survey, forced by the 1975 lawsuit brought by the Bikinians against the US government, finally began only after the people were again relocated from Bikini.

■ ■ ■ ■ ■ ■ ■ ■ ■ ■

In the late 1970s, the Bikinians, now living on Kili Island and on Ejit Island in Majuro Atoll, were awarded a $6-million compensation trust fund for the hardships suffered since their relocation. The Bikinians were later given $75 million in trust and in compensation payments under the 1986 Compact of Free Association between the United States and the Republic of the Marshall Islands, and $110 million in 1982 and 1988 through 1992 for the cleanup of Bikini and Eneu islands on Bikini Atoll and for various resettlement activities on Kili Island and Majuro Atoll.

On March 5, 2001, the Nuclear Claims Tribunal of the Marshall Islands handed down a decision on a seven-year-old lawsuit the

Bikinians had brought against the United States for damages done to their islands and their people during the nuclear testing on Bikini. The Tribunal awarded them a total of $563,315,500 (loss of value: $278,000,000, restoration costs: $251,500,000, and suffering and hardship: $33,814,500), which is an amount that was computed by deducting all past compensation awarded by the US government to the people of Bikini.

There is a problem concerning the award. The Nuclear Claims Tribunal was created by the Compact of Free Association of 1986. However, the Tribunal is underfunded and does not have the money to pay the claim. It is now up to the people of Bikini to petition the US Congress for the money to fulfill this award set by the Nuclear Claims Tribunal.

IT IS NOW UP TO THE PEOPLE OF BIKINI TO PETITION THE US CONGRESS FOR THE MONEY TO FULFILL THIS AWARD SET BY THE NUCLEAR CLAIMS TRIBUNAL.

This is expected to take many years, and it is uncertain if the United States will honor the claim. This brings up the major concern of the people of Bikini today: It is clear that Bikini Atoll will not be able to be cleaned to the standards set by the US Environmental Protection Agency without a substantial amount of new funding.

Today, the people of Bikini remain on Kili Island, Ejit Island of Majuro Atoll, and scattered throughout the Marshall Islands and the world as they await the cleanup of Bikini Atoll to begin in earnest.

Endnote

1. Martin and Rowland, Castle Series, 1954, supra note 28, at 22. US Nuclear Tests on Bikini & Enewetak Atolls in the Marshall Islands, U.S. Department of Energy. United States Nuclear Tests: July 1945 through September 1992. Document No. DOE/NV-209 (Rev. 14), December 1994.

SOME LESSONS FROM THE UNDERGROUND HISTORY OF AMERICAN EDUCATION

JOHN TAYLOR GATTO

Editor's note: John Taylor Gatto was the New York State Teacher of the Year in 1991 and has been named New York City Teacher of the Year three times.

_EXTENDING CHILDHOOD

From the beginning, there was purpose behind forced schooling, purpose which had nothing to do with what parents, kids, or communities wanted. Instead, it was forged out of what a highly centralized corporate economy and system of finance bent on internationalizing itself was thought to need; that, and what a strong, centralized political State needed, too. School was looked upon from the first decade of the twentieth century as a branch of industry and a tool of governance. For a considerable time, probably provoked by a climate of official anger and contempt directed against immigrants in the greatest displacement of people known to history, social managers of schooling were remarkably candid about what they were doing. This candor can be heard clearly in a speech Woodrow Wilson made to businessmen before the First World War:

We want one class to have a liberal education. We want another class, a very much larger class of necessity, to forgo the privilege of a liberal education and fit themselves to perform specific difficult manual tasks.

By 1917, the major administrative jobs in American schooling were under control of a group referred to in the press of that day as "the Education Trust." The first meeting of this trust included representatives of Rockefeller, Carnegie, Harvard, Stanford, the University of Chicago, and the National Education Association. The chief end, wrote the British evolutionist Benjamin Kidd in 1918, was to "impose on the young the ideal of subordination."

SCHOOL WAS LOOKED UPON FROM THE FIRST DECADE OF THE TWENTIETH CENTURY AS A BRANCH OF INDUSTRY AND A TOOL OF GOVERNANCE.

At first, the primary target was the tradition of independent livelihoods in America. Unless Yankee entrepreneurialism could be put to death, at least among the common population, the immense capital investments that mass production industry required for equipment weren't conceivably justifiable. Students were to learn to think of themselves as employees competing for the favor of management. Not as Franklin or Edison had once regarded themselves, as self-determined, free agents.

Only by a massive psychological campaign could the menace of overproduction in America be contained. That's what important men and academics called it. The ability of Americans to think as independent producers had to be curtailed. Certain writings of Alexander Inglis carry a hint of schooling's role in this ultimately successful project to curb the tendency of little people to compete with big companies. Overproduction became a controlling metaphor among the managerial classes from 1880 to 1930, and this profoundly affected the development of mass schooling.

I know how difficult it is for most of us who mow our lawns and walk our dogs to comprehend that long-range social engineering even exists, let alone that it began to dominate compulsion schooling nearly a century ago. Yet the 1934 edition of Ellwood P. Cubberley's *Public Education in the United States* is explicit about what happened and why. As Cubberley puts it:

It has come to be desirable that children should not engage in productive labor. On the contrary, all recent thinking…[is] opposed to their doing so. Both the interests of organized labor and the interests of the nation have set against child labor.

The statement occurs in a section of *Public Education* called "A New Lengthening of the Period of Dependence," in which Cubberley explains that "the coming of the factory system" has made extended childhood necessary by depriving children of the training and education that farm and village life once gave. With the breakdown of home and village industries, the passing of chores, and the extinction of the apprenticeship system by large-scale production with its extreme division of labor (and the "all conquering march of machinery"), an army of workers has arisen, said Cubberley, who know nothing.

Furthermore, *modern industry needs such workers*. Sentimentality could not be allowed to stand in the way of progress. According to Cubberley, with "much ridicule from the public press" the old book-subject curriculum was set aside, replaced by a change in purpose and "a new psychology of instruction which came to us from abroad." That last mysterious reference to a new psychology is to practices of dumbed-down schooling common to England, Germany, and France, the three major world coal-powers (other than the US), each of which had already converted its common population into an industrial proletariat long before.

This is the same Ellwood P. Cubberley, it should be noted, who wrote in his Columbia Teachers College dissertation of 1905 that schools were to be factories "in which raw products, children, are to be shaped and formed into finished products...manufactured like nails, and the specifications for manufacturing will come from government and industry."

Arthur Calhoun's 1919 *Social History of the Family* notified the nation's academics what was happening. Calhoun declared that the fondest wish of utopian writers was coming true: The child was passing from its family "into the custody of community experts." He offered a significant forecast, that in time we could expect to see public education "designed to check the mating of the unfit." Three years later, Mayor John F. Hylan of New York said in a public speech that the schools had been seized as an octopus would seize prey, by "an invisible government." He was referring specifically to certain actions of the Rockefeller Foundation and other corporate interests in New York City which preceded the school riots of 1917.

The 1920s were a boom period for forced schooling, as well as for the stock market. In 1928, a well-regarded volume called *A Sociological Philosophy of Education* claimed: "It is the business of teachers to run not merely schools but the world." A year later, the famous creator of educational psychology, Edward Thorndike of Columbia Teachers College, announced: "Academic subjects are of little value." His colleague at Teachers College, William Kirkpatrick, boasted in *Education and the Social Crisis* that the whole tradition of rearing the young was being made over by experts.

_THE GENETICIST'S MANIFESTO

Meanwhile, at the project offices of an important employer of experts, the Rockefeller Foundation, friends were hearing from president Max Mason that a comprehensive national program was underway to allow, in Mason's words, "the control of human behav-

ior." This dazzling ambition was announced on April 11, 1933. Schooling figured prominently in the design.

Rockefeller had been inspired by the work of Eastern European scientist Hermann Müller to invest heavily in genetics. Müller had used X rays to override genetic law, inducing mutations in fruit flies. This seemed to open the door to the scientific control of life itself. Müller preached that planned breeding would bring mankind to paradise faster than God. His proposal received enthusiastic endorsement from the greatest scientists of the day, as well as from powerful economic interests.

Müller would win the Nobel Prize, reduce his proposal to a 1,500-word *Geneticists' Manifesto*, and watch with satisfaction as 22 distinguished American and British biologists of the day signed it. The State must prepare to consciously guide human sexual selection, said Müller. School would have to separate worthwhile breeders from those slated for termination.

Just a few months before this report, an executive director of the National Education Association announced that his organization expected "to accomplish by education what dictators in Europe are seeking to do by compulsion and force." You can't get much clearer than that.

WWII drove the project underground but hardly retarded its momentum. Following cessation of global hostilities, school became a major domestic battleground for the scientific rationalization of social affairs through compulsory indoctrination. Great private corporate foundations led the way.

> AN EXECUTIVE DIRECTOR OF THE NATIONAL EDUCATION ASSOCIATION ANNOUNCED THAT HIS ORGANIZATION EXPECTED "TO ACCOMPLISH BY EDUCATION WHAT DICTATORS IN EUROPE ARE SEEKING TO DO BY COMPULSION AND FORCE."

_PARTICIPATORY DEMOCRACY PUT TO THE SWORD

Thirty-odd years later, between 1967 and 1974, teacher training in the US was covertly revamped through coordinated efforts of a small number of private foundations, select universities, global corporations, think tanks, and government agencies, all coordinated through the US Office of Education and through key state education departments, like those in California, Texas, Michigan, Pennsylvania, and New York.

Important milestones of the transformation were: 1) an extensive government exercise in futurology called *Designing Education for the Future*, 2) the *Behavioral Science Teacher Education Project*, and 3) Benjamin Bloom's multi-volume *Taxonomy of Educational Objectives*, an enormous manual of over 1,000 pages which, in time, impacted every school in America. While other documents exist, these three are appropriate touchstones of the whole, serving to make clear the nature of the project underway.

Take them one by one and savor each: *Designing Education*, produced by the Education Department, redefined the term "education" after the Prussian fashion as "a means to achieve important economic and social goals of a national character." State education agencies would henceforth act as on-site federal enforcers, ensuring the compliance of local schools with central directives. Each state education department was assigned the task of becoming "an agent of change" and was advised to "lose its independent identity as well as its authority" in order to "form a partnership with the federal government."

> **DESIGNING EDUCATION, PRODUCED BY THE EDUCATION DEPARTMENT, REDEFINED THE TERM "EDUCATION" AFTER THE PRUSSIAN FASHION AS "A MEANS TO ACHIEVE IMPORTANT ECONOMIC AND SOCIAL GOALS OF A NATIONAL CHARACTER."**

The second document, the gigantic *Behavioral Science Teacher Education Project*, outlined teaching reforms to be forced on the country after 1967.[1] The document sets out clearly the intentions of its creators—nothing less than "impersonal manipulation" through schooling of a future America in which "few will be able to maintain control over their opinions," an America in which "each individual receives at birth a multi-purpose identification number" which enables employers and other controllers to keep track of underlings and to expose them to direct or subliminal influence when necessary. Readers learned that "chemical experimentation" on minors would be normal procedure in this post-1967 world, a pointed foreshadowing of the massive Ritalin interventions which accompany the practice of forced schooling at present.

The *Behavioral Science Teacher Education Project* identified the future as one "in which a small elite" will control all important matters, one where participatory democracy will largely disappear. Children are made to see, through school experiences, that their classmates are so cruel and irresponsible, so inadequate to the task of self-discipline, and so ignorant that they need to be controlled and regulated for society's good. Under such a logical regime, school terror can only be regarded as good advertising. It is sobering to think of mass schooling as a vast demonstration project of human inadequacy, but that is at least one of its functions.

Postmodern schooling, we are told, is to focus on "pleasure cultivation" and on "other attitudes and skills compatible with a non-work world." Thus the socialization classroom of the twentieth century's beginning—itself a radical departure from schooling for mental and character development—can be seen to have evolved by 1967 into a full-scale laboratory for psychological experimentation.

School conversion was assisted powerfully by a curious phenomenon of the middle to late 1960s, a tremendous rise in school violence and general school chaos which followed a policy declaration (which seems to have occurred nationwide) that the disciplining of children must henceforth mimic the "due process" practice of the court system. Teachers and administrators were suddenly stripped of any effective ability to keep order in schools since the due process apparatus, of necessity a slow, deliberate matter, is completely inadequate to the continual outbreaks of childish mischief all schools experience.

Now, without the time-honored *ad hoc* armory of disciplinary tactics to fall back on, disorder spiraled out of control, passing from the realm of annoyance into more dangerous terrain entirely as word surged through student bodies that teachers' hands were tied. And each outrageous event that reached the attention of the local press served as an advertisement for expert prescriptions. Who had ever seen kids behave this way? Time to surrender community involvement to the management of experts; time also for emergency measures like special education and Ritalin. During this entire period, lasting five to seven years, outside agencies like the Ford Foundation exercised the right to supervise whether "children's rights" were being given due attention, fanning the flames hotter even long after trouble had become virtually unmanageable.

The *Behavioral Science Teacher Education Project*, occurring at the peak of this violence, informed teacher-training colleges that under such circumstances, teachers had to be trained as therapists; they must translate prescriptions of social psychology into "practical action" in the classroom. As curriculum had been redefined, so teaching followed suit.

Third of the new gospel texts was Bloom's *Taxonomy of Educational Objectives*,[2] in his own words, "a tool to classify the ways individuals are to act, think, or feel as the result of some unit of instruction." Using methods of behavioral psychology, children would learn proper thoughts, feelings, and actions, and have improper attitudes they brought from home "remediated."

In all stages of the school experiment, testing was essential to localize the child's mental state on an official rating scale. Bloom's epic spawned important descendant forms: mastery learning, outcomes-based education, and "school to work" government-business collaborations. Each classified individuals for the convenience of social managers and businesses, each offered data useful in controlling the mind and movements of the young, mapping the next adult generation.

_THE DANGAN

In the first decades of the twentieth century, a small group of soon-to-be-famous academics—symbolically led by John Dewey and Edward Thorndike of Columbia Teachers College, Ellwood P. Cubberley of Stanford, G. Stanley Hall, and an ambitious handful of others, energized and financed by major corporate and financial allies like Morgan, Astor, Whitney, Carnegie, and Rockefeller—decided to bend government schooling to the service of business and the political State, as it had been done a century before in Prussia.

Cubberley delicately voiced what was happening this way: "The nature of the national need must determine the character of the education provided." National need, of course, depends upon point of view. The NEA in 1930 sharpened our understanding by specifying in a resolution of its Department of Superintendence that school served as an "effective use of capital" through which our "unprecedented wealth-producing power has been gained." Pronouncements like this mark the degree to which the organs of schooling had been transplanted into the corporate body of the new economy when you look beyond the rhetoric of the left and right.

It's important to keep in mind that no harm was meant by any designers or managers of this great project. It was only the law of nature as they perceived it, working progressively as capitalism itself did for the ultimate good of all. The real force behind school effort came from true believers of many persuasions, linked together mainly by their belief that family and church were retrograde institutions standing in the way of progress. Far beyond the myriad practical details and economic considerations there existed a kind of grail-quest, an idea capable of catching the imagination of dreamers and firing the blood of zealots.

The entire academic community in the US and abroad had been Darwinized and Galtonized by this time, and to this contingent school seemed an instrument for managing evolutionary destiny. In Thorndike's memorable words, conditions for controlled selective breeding had to be set up before the new American industrial proletariat "took things into their own hands."

America was a frustrating petri dish in which to cultivate a managerial revolution, however, because of its historic freedom traditions. But thanks to the patronage of important men and institutions, a group of academics were enabled to visit mainland China to launch a modernization project known as the "New Thought Tide." For two years Dewey himself lived in China, where pedagogical theories were inculcated in the Young Turk elements, then tested on a bewildered population which had recently been stripped of its ancient form of governance. A similar process was embedded in the new Russian state during the 1920s.

While the American public was unaware of this undertaking, some big-city school superintendents were wise to the fact that they were part of a global experiment. Listen to H.B. Wilson, superintendent of the Topeka schools:

The introduction of the American school into the Orient has broken up 40 centuries of conservatism. It has given us a new China, a new Japan, and is working marked progress in Turkey and the Philippines. The schools...are in a position to determine the lines of progress.
—*Motivation of School Work* (1916)

Thoughts like this don't spring full-blown from the heads of men like Dr. Wilson of Topeka. They have to be planted there.

The Western-inspired and Western-financed Chinese revolution, following hard on the heels of the last desperate attempt by China to prevent the British government market in narcotic drugs there, placed that ancient province in a favorable state of anarchy for laboratory tests of mind-alteration technology. Out of this period rose a Chinese universal tracking procedure called the "Dangan," a continuous lifelong personnel file exposing every student's intimate life history from birth through school and onward. The Dangan constituted the ultimate overthrow of privacy. Today, nobody works in China without a Dangan.

By the mid-1960s preliminary work on an American Dangan was underway as information reservoirs attached to the school institution began to store personal information. A new class of expert, like Ralph Tyler of the Carnegie endowments, quietly began to urge collection of personal data from students and its unification in computer code to enhance cross-referencing. Surreptitious data gathering was justified by Tyler as "the moral right of institutions."

_OCCASIONAL LETTER NUMBER ONE

Between 1896 and 1920, a small group of industrialists and financiers, together with their private charitable foundations, subsidized university chairs, university researchers, and school administrators, spending more money on forced schooling than did the government itself. Carnegie and Rockefeller, as late as 1915, were themselves spending more. In this *laissez-faire* fashion a system of modern schooling was constructed without public participation. The motives for this are undoubtedly mixed, but it will be useful for you to hear

IN THORNDIKE'S MEMORABLE WORDS, CONDITIONS FOR CONTROLLED SELECTIVE BREEDING HAD TO BE SET UP BEFORE THE NEW AMERICAN INDUSTRIAL PROLETARIAT "TOOK THINGS INTO THEIR OWN HANDS."

SOME LESSONS FROM THE UNDERGROUND
HISTORY OF AMERICAN EDUCATION
JOHN TAYLOR GATTO

an excerpt from the first mission statement of Rockefeller's General Education Board as it occurred in a document called *Occasional Letter Number One* (1906):

In our dreams...people yield themselves with perfect docility to our molding hands. The present educational conventions [intellectual and character education] fade from our minds, and unhampered by tradition we work our own good will upon a grateful and responsive folk. We shall not try to make these people or any of their children into philosophers or men of learning or men of science. We have not to raise up from among them authors, educators, poets or men of letters. We shall not search for embryo great artists, painters, musicians, nor lawyers, doctors, preachers, politicians, statesmen, of whom we have ample supply. The task we set before ourselves is very simple...we will organize children...and teach them to do in a perfect way the things their fathers and mothers are doing in an imperfect way.

This mission statement will reward multiple rereadings.

_INTELLECTUAL ESPIONAGE

At the start of WWII, millions of men showed up at registration offices to take low-level academic tests before being inducted.[3] The years of maximum mobilization were 1942 to 1944; the fighting force—both those inducted and those turned away—had been mostly schooled in the 1930s. Eighteen million men were tested; 17,280,000 of them were judged to have the minimum competence in reading required to be a soldier—a 96 percent literacy rate. Although this was a 2 percent fall-off from the 98 percent rate among voluntary military applicants ten years before, the dip was so small it didn't worry anybody.

> **"WE SHALL NOT TRY TO MAKE THESE PEOPLE OR ANY OF THEIR CHILDREN INTO PHILOSOPHERS OR MEN OF LEARNING OR MEN OF SCIENCE."**
> **—ROCKEFELLER'S GENERAL EDUCATION BOARD (1906)**

WWII was over in 1945. Six years later another war began in Korea. Several million men were tested for military service, but this time 600,000 were rejected. Literacy in the draft pool had dropped to 81 percent even though all that was needed to classify a soldier as literate was fourth-grade reading proficiency. In the few short years from the beginning of WWII to Korea, a terrifying problem of adult illiteracy had appeared. The Korean War group received most of its schooling in the 1940s; it had more years in school with more professionally trained personnel and more scientifically selected textbooks than the WWII men, yet it could not read, write, count, speak, or think as well as the earlier, less-schooled contingent.

A third American war began in the mid-1960s. By its end in 1973, the number of men found non-inductible by reason of inability to read safety instructions, interpret road signs, decipher orders, and so on—the number found illiterate, in other words—had reached 27 percent of the total pool. Vietnam-era young men had been schooled in the 1950s and the 1960s—much better schooled than either of the two earlier groups—but the 4 percent illiteracy of 1941, which had transmuted into the 19 percent illiteracy of 1952, now had grown into the 27 percent illiteracy of 1970. Not only had the fraction of competent readers dropped to 73 percent, but a substantial chunk of even those were only barely adequate; they could not keep abreast of developments by reading a newspaper; they could not read for pleasure; they could not sustain a thought or an argument; they could not write well enough to manage their own affairs without assistance.

Consider how much more compelling this steady progression of intellectual blindness is when we track it through Army admissions tests rather than college admissions scores and standardized reading tests, which inflate apparent proficiency by frequently changing the way the tests are scored.

Looking back, abundant data exist from states like Connecticut and Massachusetts to show that by 1840 the incidence of complex literacy in the United States was between 93 and 100 percent wherever such a thing mattered. According to the Connecticut census of 1840, only one citizen out of every 579 was illiterate, and you probably don't want to know, not really, what people in those days considered literate; it's too embarrassing. Popular novels of the period give a clue: Cooper's *Last of the Mohicans*, published in 1826, sold so well that a contemporary equivalent would have to move 10 million copies to match it. If you pick up an uncut version, you find yourself in a dense thicket of philosophy, history, culture, manners, politics, geography, astute analysis of human motives and actions, all conveyed in data-rich periodic sentences so formidable that only a determined and well-educated reader can handle it nowadays. Yet in 1818, the US was a small-farm nation without colleges or universities to speak of. Could those simple folk have had more complex minds than our own?

By 1940, the literacy figure for all states stood at 96 percent for whites, 80 percent for blacks. Notice for all the disadvantages blacks labored under, four of five were still literate. Six decades later, at the end of the twentieth century, the National Adult Literacy Survey and the National Assessment of Educational Progress say 40 percent of blacks and 17 percent of whites can't read at all. Put another way, black illiteracy doubled, and white illiteracy quadrupled. Before you think of anything else in regard to these numbers, think of this: We spend three to four times as much real money on schooling as we did 60 years ago, but 60 years ago virtually everyone, black or white, could read.

In their famous bestseller, *The Bell Curve*, prominent social analysts Charles Murray and Richard Herrnstein say that what we're seeing are the results of selective breeding in society. Smart people naturally get together with smart people, dumb people with dumb people. As they have children generation after generation, the differences between the groups get larger and larger. That sounds plausible, and the authors produce impressive mathematics to prove their case, but their documentation shows that they are entirely ignorant of the military data available to challenge their contention. The terrifying drop in literacy between World War II and Korea happened in a decade, and even the brashest survival-of-the-fittest theorist wouldn't argue evolution unfolds that way. *The Bell Curve* writers say black illiteracy (and violence) is genetically programmed, but like many academics they ignore contradictory evidence.

For example, on the matter of violence inscribed in black genes, the inconvenient parallel is to South Africa, where 31 million blacks live, the same count living in the United States. Compare numbers of blacks who died by violence in South Africa in civil war conditions during 1989, 1990, and 1991 with America's peacetime mortality statistics, and you find that far from exceeding the violent death toll in the US, or even matching it, South Africa had proportionately less than one-quarter the violent death rate of American blacks. If more contemporary comparisons are sought, we need only compare the current black literacy rate in the US (56 percent) with the rate in Jamaica (98.5 percent)—a figure considerably higher than the American white literacy rate (83 percent).

If not heredity, what then? Well, one change is indisputable, well-documented, and easy to track. During WWII, American public schools massively converted to non-phonetic ways of teaching reading. They stopped teaching students to look at words as combinations of letters, sounding them out, and instead started using the disastrous whole-word method, which has students memorize the meanings of entire words through sheer repetition (the method used by *Dick and Jane* and Dr. Seuss).

On the matter of violence alone, this would seem to have an impact: According to the Justice Department, 80 percent of the incarcerated violent criminal population is illiterate or nearly so (the rate for all imprisoned criminals is 67 percent). There seems to be a direct connection between the humiliation poor readers experience and the life of angry criminals.[4] As reading ability plummeted in America after WWII, crime soared; so did out-of-wedlock births, which doubled in the 1950s and doubled again in the 1960s when bizarre violence for the first time became commonplace in daily life.

When literacy was first abandoned as a primary goal by schools,

white people were in a better position than black people because they inherited a 300-year-old American tradition of learning to read at home by matching spoken sound with letters; thus, home assistance was able to correct the deficiencies of dumbed-down schools for whites. But black people had been forbidden to learn to read during slavery and as late as 1930 averaged only three to four years of schooling, so they were helpless when teachers suddenly stopped teaching children to read; they had no fallback position. Not helpless because of genetic inferiority but because they had to trust school authorities to a much greater extent than white people.

Back in 1952 the Army quietly began hiring hundreds of psychologists to find out how 600,000 high school graduates had successfully faked illiteracy. Regna Wood sums up the episode this way:

After the psychologists told the officers that the graduates weren't faking, Defense Department administrators knew that something terrible had happened in grade school reading instruction. And they knew it had started in the thirties. Why they remained silent, no one knows. The switch back to reading instruction that worked for everyone should have been made then. But it wasn't.

In 1882, fifth-graders read these authors in their *Appleton School Reader*: William Shakespeare, Henry Thoreau, George Washington, Sir Walter Scott, Mark Twain, Benjamin Franklin, Oliver Wendell Holmes, John Bunyan, Daniel Webster, Samuel Johnson, Lewis Carroll, Thomas Jefferson, Ralph Waldo Emerson, and others like them. In 1995, a student-teacher of fifth-graders in Minneapolis wrote to the local newspaper: "I was told children are not to be expected to spell the following words correctly: back, big, call, came, can, day, did, dog, down, get, good, have, he, home, if, in, is, it, like, little, man, morning, mother, my, night, off, out, over, people, play, ran, said, saw, she, some, soon, their, them, there, time, two, too, up, us, very, water, we, went, where, when, will, would, etc. Is this nuts?"

_WILLIAM TORREY HARRIS

If you have a hard time believing this revolution in the contract ordinary Americans had with their political State was intentionally provoked, it's time to meet William Torrey Harris, US Commissioner of Education from 1889 to 1906. Nobody else who rose out of the ranks of professional pedagogues, other than Cubberley, ever had the influence Harris did. Harris standardized our schools and Germanized them. Listen as he speaks in 1906:

Ninety-nine [students] out of a hundred are automata,

careful to walk in prescribed paths, careful to follow the prescribed custom. This is not an accident but the result of substantial education, which, scientifically defined, is the subsumption of the individual.
—*The Philosophy of Education* (1906)

Listen again to Harris, giant of American schooling, leading scholar of German philosophy in the Western hemisphere, editor/publisher of *The Journal of Speculative Philosophy* which trained a generation of American intellectuals in the ideas of the Prussian thinkers Kant and Hegel, the man who gave America scientifically age-graded classrooms to replace successful mixed-age school practice:

The great purpose of school can be realized better in dark, airless, ugly places…. It is to master the physical self, to transcend the beauty of nature. School should develop the power to withdraw from the external world.
—*The Philosophy of Education* (1906)

Nearly a hundred years ago, this schoolman thought that self-alienation was the secret to successful industrial society. Surely he was right. When you stand at a machine or sit at a computer, you require an ability to withdraw from life, to alienate yourself without a supervisor. How else could that be tolerated unless prepared in advance by simulated Birkenhead drills? School, thought Harris, was sensible preparation for a life of alienation. Can you say he was wrong?

In exactly the years Cubberley of Stanford identified as the launching time for the school institution, Harris reigned supreme as the bull goose educator of America. His was the most influential voice teaching what school was to be in a modern, scientific State. School histories commonly treat Harris as an old-fashioned defender of high academic standards, but this is a grossly inadequate analysis; as a philosophical Hegelian, Harris believed children were property and the State had a compelling interest in disposing of them as it pleased. Some would receive intellectual training, most not. Any distinction that can be made between Harris and later weak-curriculum advocates (those interested in stupefaction for everybody) is far less important than substantial agreement in both camps that parents or local tradition could no longer determine the individual child's future.

Unlike any official schoolman until Conant, Harris had social access to important salons of power in the United States. Over his long career he furnished inspiration to the ongoing obsessions of Andrew Carnegie, the steel man who first nourished the conceit of yoking our entire economy to cradle-to-grave schooling. If you can find copies of *The Empire of Business* (1902) or *Triumphant Democracy* (1886), you will find remarkable congruence between the world Carnegie urged and the one our society has achieved.

Carnegie's "Gospel of Wealth" idea took his peers by storm at the very moment the great school transformation began—the idea that the wealthy owed society a duty to take over everything in the public interest was an uncanny echo of Carnegie's experience as a boy watching the elite establishment of Britain and the teachings of its State religion. It would require perverse blindness not to acknowledge a connection between the Carnegie blueprint, hammered into shape in the Greenwich Village salon of Mrs. Botta after the Civil War, and the explosive developments which restored the Anglican worldview to our schools.

Of course, every upper class in history has specified what can be known. The defining characteristic of class control is that it establishes a grammar and vocabulary for ordinary people, and for subordinate elites, too. If the rest of us uncritically accept certain official concepts such as "globalization," then we have unwittingly committed ourselves to a whole intricate narrative of society's future, too, a narrative which inevitably drags an irresistible curriculum in its wake.

Since Aristotle, thinkers have understood that work is the vital theater of self-knowledge. Schooling in concert with a controlled workplace is the most effective way ever devised to foreclose the development of imagination. But where did these radical doctrines of true belief come from? Who spread them? We get at least part of the answer from the tantalizing clue Walt Whitman left when he said that "only Hegel is fit for America." Hegel was the protean Prussian philosopher capable of shaping Karl Marx on one hand and J.P. Morgan on the other; the man who taught a generation of prominent Americans that history itself could be controlled by the deliberate provoking of crises. Hegel was sold to America in large measure by William Torrey Harris, who made Hegelianism his lifelong project, and forced schooling its principal instrument in its role as a peerless *agent provocateur*.

Harris was inspired by the notion that correctly managed mass schooling would result in a population so dependent on leaders that schism and revolution would be things of the past. If a world-State could be cobbled together by Hegelian tactical manipulation, and such a school plan imposed upon it, history itself would stop. No more wars, no civil disputes, just people waiting around pleasantly like the Eloi in Wells' *The Time Machine*. Waiting for Teacher to tell them what to do. The psychological tool was alienation. The trick was to alienate children from themselves so they couldn't turn inside

"NINETY-NINE [STUDENTS] OUT OF A HUNDRED ARE AUTOMATA, CAREFUL TO WALK IN PRESCRIBED PATHS, CAREFUL TO FOLLOW THE PRESCRIBED CUSTOM. THIS IS NOT AN ACCIDENT BUT THE RESULT OF SUBSTANTIAL EDUCATION, WHICH, SCIENTIFICALLY DEFINED, IS THE SUBSUMPTION OF THE INDIVIDUAL."
—*THE PHILOSOPHY OF EDUCATION* (1906)

for strength, to alienate them from their families, religions, cultures, etc. so no countervailing force could intervene.

Carnegie used his own considerable influence to keep this expatriate New England Hegelian as the US Commissioner of Education for sixteen years, long enough to set the stage for an era of "scientific management" (or "Fordism," as the Soviets called it) in American schooling. Long enough to bring about the rise of the multilayered school bureaucracy. But it would be a huge mistake to regard Harris and other true believers as merely tools of business interest; what they were about was the creation of a modern, living faith to replace the Christian one which had died for them. It was their good fortune to live at precisely the moment when the dreamers of the empire of business (to use emperor Carnegie's label) for an Anglo-American world-State were beginning to consider worldwide schooling as the most direct route to that destination.

Both movements, to centralize the economy and to centralize schooling, were aided immeasurably by the rapid disintegration of old-line Protestant churches and the rise from their pious ashes of the "Social Gospel" ideology, aggressively underwritten by important industrialists, who intertwined churchgoing tightly with standards of business, entertainment, and government. The experience of religion came to mean, in the words of Reverend Earl Hoon, "the best social programs money can buy." A clear statement of the belief that social justice and salvation were to be had through skillful consumption.

Shailer Mathews—dean of Chicago's School of Divinity, editor of *Biblical World*, president of the Federal Council of Churches—wrote his influential *Scientific Management in the Churches* (1912) to convince American Protestants they should sacrifice independence and autonomy and adopt the structure and strategy of corporations:

If this seems to make the Church something of a business establishment, it is precisely what should be the case.

If Americans listened to the corporate message, Mathews told them they would feel anew the spell of Jesus.

In the decade before WWI, a consortium of private foundations drawing on industrial wealth began slowly working toward a long-range goal of lifelong schooling and a thoroughly rationalized global economy and society.

_MR. YOUNG'S HEAD WAS POUNDED TO JELLY

The most surprising thing about the start-up of mass public education in mid-nineteenth-century Massachusetts is how overwhelmingly parents of all classes soon complained about it. Reports of school committees around 1850 show the greatest single theme of discussion was conflict between the state and the general public on this matter. Resistance was led by the old yeoman class—those families accustomed to taking care of themselves and providing meaning for their own lives. The little town of Barnstable on Cape Cod is exemplary. Its school committee lamented, according to Katz's *Irony of Early School Reform*, that "the great defect of our day is the absence of governing or controlling power on the part of parents and the consequent insubordination of children. Our schools are rendered inefficient by the apathy of parents."

> MANY SCHOOLS WERE BURNED TO THE GROUND AND TEACHERS RUN OUT OF TOWN BY ANGRY MOBS. WHEN STUDENTS WERE KEPT AFTER SCHOOL, PARENTS OFTEN BROKE INTO SCHOOL TO FREE THEM.

Years ago I was in possession of an old newspaper account which related the use of militia to march recalcitrant children to school there, but I've been unable to locate it again. Nevertheless, even a cursory look for evidence of State violence in bending public will to accept compulsion schooling will be rewarded: Bruce Curtis' book *Building the Education State 1836-1871* documents the intense aversion to schooling which occurred across North America, in Anglican Canada where leadership was uniform, as well as in the US where leadership was more divided. Many schools were burned to the ground and teachers run out of town by angry mobs. When students were kept after school, parents often broke into school to free them.

At Saltfleet Township in 1859, a teacher was locked in the schoolhouse by students who "threw mud and mire into his face and over his clothes," according to school records—while parents egged them on. At Brantford in 1863, the teacher William Young was assaulted to the point (according to his replacement) that "Mr. Young's head, face and body was, if I understand rightly, pounded literally to jelly." Curtis argues that parents' resistance was motivated by a radical transformation in the intentions of schools—a change from teaching basic literacy to molding social identity.

The first effective American compulsory schooling in the modern era was a reform school movement which Know-Nothing legislatures of the 1850s put into the hopper along with their radical new adoption law. Objects of reformation were announced as follows: respect for authority, self-control, self-discipline. The properly reformed boy "acquires a fixed character," one that can be planned for in advance by authority in keeping with the efficiency needs of business and industry.

Reform meant the total transformation of character, behavior modification, a complete makeover. By 1857, a few years after stranger-adoption was kicked off as a new policy of the State, Boutwell could consider foster parenting (the old designation for adoption) "one of

> ## "I AM SATISFIED OUR GREATEST ERROR IN TEACHING LIES IN BEGINNING WITH THE ALPHABET."
> ### —HORACE MANN, HEAD OF BOSTON'S BOARD OF EDUCATION (C. 1843)

the major strategies for the reform of youth."[5] The first step in the strategy of reform was for the State to become the *de facto* parent of the child. That, according to another Massachusetts educator, Emory Washburn, "presents the State in her true relation of a parent seeking out her erring children."

The 1850s in Massachusetts marked the beginning of a new epoch in schooling. Washburn triumphantly crowed that these years produced the first occasion in history "whereby a State in the character of a common parent has undertaken the high and sacred duty of rescuing and restoring her lost children...by the influence of the school." John Philbrick, Boston school superintendent, said of his growing empire in 1863, "Here is real home!" All schooling, including the reform variety, was to be in imitation of the best "family system of organization"; this squared with the prevalent belief that delinquency was not caused by external conditions—thus letting industrialists and slumlords off the hook—but by deficient homes.

Between 1840 and 1860, male schoolteachers were cleansed from the Massachusetts system and replaced by women. A variety of stratagems was used, including the novel one of paying women slightly more than men in order to bring shame into play in chasing men out of the business. Again the move was part of a well-conceived strategy: "Experience teaches that these boys, many of whom never had a mother's affection...need the softening and refining influence which woman alone can give, and we have, wherever practicable, substituted female officers and teachers for those of the other sex."

A state report noted the frequency with which parents coming to retrieve their own children from reform school were met by news that their children had been given away to others, through the State's *parens patriae* power. "We have felt it to be our duty generally to decline giving them up to their parents and have placed as many of them as we could with farmers and mechanics," reads a portion of Public Document 20 for the state of Massachusetts, written in 1864. To recreate the feelings of parents on hearing this news is beyond my power.

_THE TECHNOLOGY OF SUBJECTION

Administrative utopias are a peculiar kind of dreaming by those in power, driven by an urge to arrange the lives of others, organizing them for production, combat, or detention. The operating principles of administrative utopia are hierarchy, discipline, regimentation, strict order, rational planning, a geometrical environment, a production line, a cellblock, and a form of welfarism. Government schools and some private schools pass such parameters with flying colors.

In one sense, administrative utopias are laboratories for exploring the technology of subjection and as such belong to a precise subdivision of pornographic art: total surveillance and total control of the helpless. The aim and mode of administrative utopia is to bestow order and assistance on an unwilling population. To provide its clothing and food. To schedule it. In a masterpiece of cosmic misjudgment, the phrenologist George Combe wrote to Horace Mann on November 14, 1843:

> **The Prussian and Saxon governments by means of their schools and their just laws and rational public administration are doing a good deal to bring their people into a rational and moral condition. It is pretty obvious to thinking men that a few years more of this cultivation will lead to the development of free institutions in Germany.**

Earlier that year (May 21, 1843), Mann had written to Combe: "I want to find out what are the results, as well as the workings of the famous Prussian system." Just three years earlier, with the election of Marcus Morton as governor of Massachusetts, a serious challenge had been presented to Mann and to his Board of Education, including the air of Prussianism surrounding it and its manufacturer/politician friends. A House committee was directed to look into the new Board of Education and its plan to undertake a teachers college with $10,000 put up by industrialist Edmund Dwight. Four days after its assignment, the majority reported out a bill to kill the board! Discontinue the Normal School experiment, it said, and give Dwight his money back:

> **If then the Board has any actual power, it is a dangerous power, touching directly upon the rights and duties of the Legislature; if it has no power, why continue its existence at an annual expense to the commonwealth?**

But the House committee did more; it warned explicitly that this board, dominated by a Unitarian majority of 7-5 (although Unitarians comprised less than 1 percent of the state), really wanted to install a Prussian system of education in Massachusetts, to put "a monopoly of power in a few hands, contrary in every respect to the true spirit of our democratical institutions." The vote of the House on this was the single greatest victory of Mann's political career, one for which he and his wealthy friends called in every favor they were owed. The result was 245 votes to continue, 182 votes to discontinue, and so the House voted to overturn the recommendations of its own committee. A 32-vote swing might have given us a much different twentieth century than the one we saw.

Although Mann's own letters and diaries are replete with attacks on orthodox religionists as enemies of government schooling, an examination of the positive vote reveals that from the outset the orthodox churches were among Mann's staunchest allies. Mann had general support from Congregational, Presbyterian, and Baptist clergymen. At this early stage they were completely unaware of the doom secular schooling would spell for their denominations. They had been seduced into believing school was a necessary insurance policy to deal with incoming waves of Catholic immigration from Ireland and Germany, the cheap labor army which as early as 1830 had been talked about in business circles and eagerly anticipated as an answer to America's production problems.

The reason Germany, and not England, provided the original model for America's essay into compulsion schooling may be that Mann had a shocking experience in English class snobbery while in Britain, which left him reeling. Boston Common, he wrote, with its rows of mottled sycamore trees, gravel walks, and frog ponds, was downright *embarrassing* compared with any number of stately English private grounds furnished with stag and deer, fine arboretums of botanical specimens from faraway lands, marble floors better than the tabletops at home, portraits, tapestries, giant gold-frame mirrors. The ballroom in the Bullfinch house in Boston would be a butler's pantry in England, he wrote. When Mann visited Stafford House of the Duke of Cumberland, he went into culture shock:

Convicts on treadmills provide the energy to pump water for fountains. I have seen equipages, palaces, and the regalia of royalty side by side with beggary, squalidness, and degradation in which the very features of humanity were almost lost in those of the brute.

For this great distinction between the layered orders of society, Mann held the Anglican Church to blame. "Give me America with all its rawness and want. We have aristocracy enough at home and here I trace its foundations." Shocked from his English experience, Mann virtually willed that Prussian schools would provide him with answers, says his biographer Jonathan Messerli.

Mann arrived in Prussia when its schools were closed for vacation; he toured empty classrooms, spoke with authorities, interviewed vacationing schoolmasters, and read piles of dusty official reports. Yet from this nonexperience he claimed to come away with a strong sense of the professional competence of Prussian teachers! All "admirably qualified and full of animation!" His wife, Mary, of the famous Peabodys, wrote home: "We have not seen a teacher with a book in his hand in all Prussia; no, not one!" This wasn't surprising, for they hardly saw teachers at all.

Equally impressive, he wrote, was the wonderful obedience of children; these German *kinder* had "innate respect for superior years." The German teacher corps? "The finest collection of men I have ever seen—full of intelligence, dignity, benevolence, kindness and bearing...." Never, says Mann, did he witness "an instance of harshness and severity. All is kind, encouraging, animating, sympathizing." On the basis of imagining this miraculous vision of exactly the Prussia he wanted to see, Mann made a special plea for changes in the teaching of reading. He criticized the standard American practice of beginning with the alphabet and moving to syllables, urging his readers to consider the superior merit of teaching entire words from the beginning. "I am satisfied," he said, "our greatest error in teaching lies in beginning with the alphabet."

The heart of Mann's most famous *Report to the Boston School Committee*, the legendary Seventh, rings a familiar theme in American affairs: It seems even then we were falling behind! This time behind the Prussians in education. In order to catch up, it was mandatory to create a professional corps of teachers, just as the Prussians had. And a systematic curriculum just as the Prussians had. Mann fervently implored the board to accept his prescription...*while there was still time*!

That fall, the Association of Masters of the Boston Public Schools published its 150-page rebuttal of Mann's *Report*. It attacked the Normal schools proposal as a propaganda vehicle for Mann's "hot bed theories, in which the projectors have disregarded experience and observation." It belittled his advocacy of phrenology and charged Mann with attempting to excite the prejudices of the ignorant. Its second attack was against the teacher-centered non-book presentations of Prussian classrooms, insisting the psychological result of these was to break student potential "for forming the habit of independent and individual effort." The third attack was against the "word method" in teaching reading, and in defense of the traditional alphabet method. Lastly, it attacked Mann's belief that interest was a better motivator to learning than discipline: "Duty should come first and pleasure should grow out of the discharge of it."

■ ■ ■ ■ ■ ■ ■ ■ ■ ■

Sixty years later—amid a well-coordinated attempt on the part of industrialists and financiers to transfer power over money and interest rates from elected representatives of the American people to a "Federal Reserve" of centralized private banking interests—George Reynolds, president of the American Bankers Association, rose before an audience on September 13, 1909, to declare himself flatly in favor of a central bank modeled after the German Reichsbank. As he spoke, the schools of the United States were being forcibly rebuilt on Prussian lines.

On September 14, 1909, in Boston, the President of the United States, William Howard Taft, instructed the country that it should "take up seriously" the problem of establishing a centralized bank on the German model. As the *Wall Street Journal* put it, an important step in the education of Americans would soon be taken to translate the "realm of theory" into "practical politics," in pedagogy as well as finance.

SOME LESSONS FROM THE UNDERGROUND HISTORY OF AMERICAN EDUCATION
JOHN TAYLOR GATTO

Dramatic, symbolic evidence of what was working deep in the bowels of the school institution surfaced in 1935. At the University of Chicago's experimental high school, the head of the Social Science department, Howard C. Hill, published an inspirational textbook, *The Life and Work of the Citizen*. It is decorated throughout with the *fasces*, symbol of the Fascist movement, an emblem binding government and corporation together as one entity. Mussolini had landed in America.

The *fasces* are strange, hybridized images—one might almost say Americanized. The bundle of sticks wrapped around a two-headed axe, the classic Italian Fascist image, has been decisively altered. Now the sticks are wrapped around a *sword*. They appear on the spine of this high school text, on the decorative page introducing part one, again on a similar page for part two, repeating on part three and part four, as well. There are also fierce, military eagles hovering above those pages.

The strangest decoration of all faces the title page, a weird interlock of hands and wrists which, with only a few slight alterations of its structural members, would be a living swastika.[6] The legend announces it as representing the "united strength" of Law, Order, Science, and the Trades. Where the strength of America had been traditionally located in our First Amendment guarantee of *argument*, now the Prussian connection was shifting the locus of attention in school to *cooperation*, with both working and professional classes sandwiched between the watchful eye of Law and Order. Prussia had entrenched itself deep inside the bowels of American institutional schooling.

"SCHOOL PRODUCES MENTAL PERVERSION AND ABSOLUTE STUPIDITY." —VINCENT YOUMANS, WORLD-FAMOUS AMERICAN PHYSICIAN AND ACADEMIC (1867)

_A CRITICAL APPRAISAL

In the latter half of the nineteenth century, as the new school institution slowly took root after the Civil War in big cities and the defeated South, some of the best minds in the land, people fit by their social rank to comment publicly, spoke out as they watched its first phalanx of graduates take their place in the traditional American world. All of these speakers had been trained themselves in the older, a-systematic, non-institutional schools. At the beginning of another new century, it is eerie to hear what these great-grandfathers of ours had to say about the mass schooling phenomenon as they approached their own fateful new century.

In 1867, world-famous American physician and academic Vincent Youmans lectured the London College of Preceptors about the school institution just coming into being:

School produces mental perversion and absolute stu-

pidity. It produces bodily disease. It produces these things by measures which operate to the prejudice of the growing brain. It is not to be doubted that dullness, indocility, and viciousness are frequently aggravated by the lessons of school.

Thirteen years later, Francis Parkman (of *Oregon Trail* fame) delivered a similar judgment. The year was 1880, at the very moment Wundt was founding his laboratory of scientific psychology in Germany:

Many had hoped that by giving *a partial teaching* to great numbers of persons, a thirst for knowledge might be awakened. Thus far, the results have not equaled expectations. Schools have not borne any fruit on which we have cause to congratulate ourselves.

In 1885, the president of Columbia University said:

The results actually attained under our present system of instruction are neither very flattering nor very encouraging.

In 1895, the president of Harvard said:

Ordinary schooling produces dullness. A young man whose intellectual powers are worth cultivating cannot be willing to cultivate them by pursuing phantoms as the schools now insist upon.

When he said this, compulsion schooling in its first manifestation was approaching its forty-third year of operations in Massachusetts and was running at high efficiency in Cambridge, where Harvard is located.

Then the great metamorphosis to an even more efficient scientific form of pedagogy took place in the early years of the twentieth century. Four years before WWI broke out, a well-known European thinker and schoolman, Paul Geheeb, whom Einstein, Herman Hesse, and Albert Schweitzer all were to claim as a friend, made this commentary on English and German types of forced schooling:

The dissatisfaction with public schools is widely felt. Countless attempts to reform them have failed. People complain about the "overburdening" of schools; educators argue about which parts of curriculum should be cut; but school cannot be reformed with a pair of scissors. *The solution is not to be found in educational institutions.*

In 1930, the yearly Inglis Lecture at Harvard made the same case:

We have absolutely nothing to show for our colossal investment in common schooling after 80 years of trying.

Thirty years passed before John Gardner's *Annual Report to the Carnegie Corporation* in 1960 added this:

Too many young people gain nothing [from school] except the conviction they are misfits.

The record after 1960 is no different. It is hardly unfair to say that the *stupidity* of 1867, the *fruitlessness* of 1880, the *dullness* of 1895, the *cannot be reformed* of 1910, the *absolutely nothing* of 1930, and the *nothing* of 1960 have been continued into the schools of 2000 and beyond. We pay four times more in real dollars than we did in 1930, and thus we buy even more of what mass schooling dollars always bought.

_THE CULT OF FORCED SCHOOLING

The most candid account we have of the changeover from old-style American free-market schooling to the laboratory variety under the close eye of society's managers is a book long out of print. But the author was famous enough in his day that a yearly lecture at Harvard is named after him, so with a bit of effort on your part, and perhaps a kind word to your local librarian, in due time you should be able to find a hair-raising account of the school transformation written by one of the insiders. The book in question bears the soporific title *Principles of Secondary Education*. Published in 1918 near the end of the great school revolution, *Principles* offers a unique account of the project written through the eyes of an important revolutionary. Any lingering doubts you may have about the purposes of government schooling should be put to rest by Alexander Inglis. The principal purpose of the vast enterprise was to place control of the new social and economic machinery out of reach of the mob.[7]

The great social engineers were confronted by the formidable challenge of working their magic in a democracy, the least efficient and most unpredictable of political forms. School was designed to neutralize as much as possible any risk of being blindsided by the democratic will. Nelson W. Aldrich Jr., writing of his grandfather, Senator Aldrich—one of the principal architects of the Federal Reserve System which had come into being while Inglis' cohort built the schools, and whose intent was much the same, to remove economic machinery from public interference—caught the attitude of the builders perfectly in his book *Old Money*. Grandfather, he writes, believed that history, evolution, and a saving grace found their best advocates in him and in men like him, in his family and in families like his, down to the close of time. But the price of his privilege, the senator knew, "was vigilance—vigilance, above all, against the resentment of those who never could emerge." Once in Paris,

Senator Aldrich saw two men "of the middle or lower class," as he described them, drinking absinthe in a cafe. That evening back at his hotel he wrote these words: "As I looked upon their dull wild stupor I wondered what dreams were evolved from the depths of the bitter glass. Multiply that scene and you have the possibility of the wildest revolution or the most terrible outrages."

Alexander Inglis, author of *Principles of Secondary Education*, was of Aldrich's class. He wrote that the new schools were being expressly created to serve a command economy and command society, one in which the controlling coalition would be drawn from important institutional stakeholders in the future. According to Inglis, the first function of schooling is *adjustive*, establishing fixed habits of reaction to authority. This prepares the young to accept whatever management dictates when they are grown.

Second is the *diagnostic* function. School determines each student's "proper" social role, logging it mathematically on cumulative records to justify the next function, *sorting*. Individuals are to be trained only so far as their likely destination in the social machine, not one step beyond.

ACCORDING TO INGLIS, THE FIRST FUNCTION OF SCHOOLING IS *ADJUSTIVE*, ESTABLISHING FIXED HABITS OF REACTION TO AUTHORITY.

Conformity is the fourth function. Kids are to be made alike, not from any passion for egalitarianism, but so future behavior will be predictable, in service to market and political research.

Next is the *hygienic* function. This has nothing to do with individual health, only the health of the "race." This is polite code for saying that school should accelerate Darwinian natural selection by tagging the unfit so clearly that they drop from the reproduction sweepstakes.

And last is the *propaedutic* function, a fancy word meaning that a small fraction of kids will slowly be trained to take over management of the system, guardians of a population deliberately dumbed down and rendered childlike in order that government and economic life can be managed with a minimum of hassle.

And there you have the formula: adjustment, diagnosis, sorting, conformity, racial hygiene, and continuity. This is the man after whom an honor lecture in education at Harvard is named. According to James Bryant Conant—another progressive aristocrat from whom I first learned of Inglis in a perfectly frightening book called *The Child, the Parent, and the State* (1949)—the school transformation had been ordered by "certain industrialists and the innovative who were altering the nature of the industrial process."

President of Harvard from 1933 to 1953, Conant himself is a school name that resonates through the central third of the twentieth century. His book, *The American High School Today* (1959), was one of the important springs that pushed secondary schools to gigantic size in the 1960s and forced consolidation of many small school districts into larger ones. His career began as a poison gas specialist in WWI, a task assigned only to young men whose family lineage could be trusted, with other notable way stations on his path being service in the secret atomic bomb project during WWII and a stint as US High Commissioner for Germany during the military occupation after 1945.

In his book Conant brusquely acknowledges that conversion of old-style American education into Prussian-style schooling was done as a *coup de main*, but his greater motive in 1959 was to speak directly to men and women of his own class who were beginning to believe the new school procedure might be unsuited to human needs, that experience dictated a return to older institutional pluralistic ways. No, Conant fairly shouts, the clock cannot be turned back! "Clearly, the total process is irreversible." Severe consequences would certainly follow the break-up of this carefully contrived behavioral-training machine: "A successful counterrevolution...would require reorientation of a complex social pattern. Only a person bereft of reason would undertake [it]."

**"[WE ARE PRODUCING] MORE AND MORE PEOPLE WHO WILL BE DISSATISFIED BECAUSE THE ARTIFICIALLY PROLONGED TIME OF FORMAL SCHOOLING WILL AROUSE IN THEM HOPES WHICH SOCIETY CANNOT FULFILL."
—ROBERT ULICH, PROMINENT HARVARD PROFESSOR (1961)**

Reading Conant is like overhearing a private conversation not meant for you yet fraught with the greatest personal significance. To Conant, school was a triumph of Anglo/Germanic pragmatism, a pinnacle of the social technocrat's problem-solving art. One task it performed with brilliance was to sharply curtail the American entrepreneurial spirit, a mission undertaken on perfectly sensible grounds, at least from a management perspective. As long as capital investments were at the mercy of millions of self-reliant, resourceful young entrepreneurs running about with a gleam in their eye, who would commit the huge flows of capital needed to continually tool and retool the commercial/industrial/financial machine? As long as the entire population could become producers, young people were loose cannons crashing around a storm-tossed deck, threatening to destroy the corporate ship; confined, however, to employee status, they became suitable ballast upon which a dependable domestic market could be erected.

How to mute competition in the generation of tomorrow? That was the cutting-edge question. In his take-no-prisoners style, acquired mixing poison gas and building atomic bombs, Conant candidly tells us that the answer "was in the process of formulation" as early as the 1890s. By 1905 the nation obeyed this clarion call from coast to coast: "Keep all youth in school full time through grade twelve." All

youth, including those most unwilling to be there and those certain to take vengeance on their jailers.

President Conant was quick to acknowledge that "practical-minded" kids paid a heavy price from enforced confinement. But there it was—nothing could be done. It was a worthy trade-off. I suspect he was being disingenuous. Any mind sophisticated enough to calculate a way to short-circuit entrepreneurial energy, and ideology-driven enough to be willing to do that in service to a corporate takeover of the economy, is shrewd enough also to have foreseen the destructive side effects of having an angry and tough-minded band of prisoners forced against its will to remain in school with the docile. The net result on the intellectual possibilities of class instruction was near total wipe-out.

Did Conant understand the catastrophe he helped cause? I think he did. He, of course, would dispute my judgment that it was a catastrophe. One of his close friends was another highly placed schoolman, Ellwood P. Cubberley, the Stanford education dean. Cubberley had himself written about the blow to serious classwork caused by early experiments in forcing universal school attendance. So it wasn't as if the destruction of academic integrity came as any surprise to insiders. Cubberley's house history of American education refers directly to this episode, although in somewhat elliptical prose. First published in 1919, it was republished in 1934, the year after Conant took office at Harvard. The two men talked and wrote to one another. Both knew the score. Yet for all his candor, it isn't hard to understand Conant's reticence about discussing this procedure. It's one thing to announce that children have to do involuntary duty for the State, quite another to describe the why and how of the matter in explicit detail.

Another prominent Harvard professor, Robert Ulich, wrote in his own book, *Philosophy of Education* (1961): "[We are producing] more and more people who will be dissatisfied because the artificially prolonged time of formal schooling will arouse in them hopes which society cannot fulfill.... These men and women will form the avantgarde of the disgruntled. It is no exaggeration to say [people like these] were responsible for World War II." Although Ulich is parroting Toynbee here, whose *Study of History* was a standard reference of speculative history for decades, the idea that serious intellectual schooling of a universal nature would be a sword pointed at the established order has been common in the West since at least the Tudors, and one openly discussed from 1890 onwards.

Thus I was less surprised than I might have been to open Walter Kotschnig's *Unemployment in the Learned Professions* (1937)—which I purchased from a college graduate down on his luck for 50 cents off a blanket on the street in front of Columbia University—to find myself listening to an argument attributing the rise of Nazism directly to the expansion of German university enrollment after WWI. For Germany, this had been a short-term solution to postwar unemployment, like the G.I. Bill, but according to Kotschnig, the policy created a mob of well-educated people with a chip on their shoulder because there was no work—a situation which led swiftly downhill for the Weimar Republic.

A whole new way to look at schooling from this management perspective emerges, a perspective which is the furthest thing from cynical. Of course there are implications for our contemporary situation. Much of our own 50 to 60 percent post-secondary college enrollment should be seen as a temporary solution to the otherwise awesome reality that two-thirds of all work in the US is now part-time or short-term employment. In a highly centralized corporate workplace becoming ever more so with no end in sight, all jobs are sucked like debris in a tornado into four hierarchical funnels of vast proportions: corporate, governmental, institutional, and professional. Once work is preempted in this monopoly fashion, fear of too many smart people is legitimate, hard to exaggerate. If you let people learn too much, they might kill you. Or so history and Senator Aldrich would have us believe.

Once privy to ideas like those entertained by Inglis, Conant, Ulich, and Kotschnig, most contemporary public school debate becomes nonsense. Without addressing philosophies and policies which sentence the largest part of our people to lives devoid of meaning, we might be better off not discussing school at all.

Endnotes

1. If you ever want to hunt this thing down, it bears the US Office of Education Contract Number OEC-O-9-320424-4042 (B10). **2.** A fuller discussion of Bloom and the other documents mentioned here, plus much more, is available in the writings of Beverly Eakman, a Department of Justice employee, particularly her book *The Cloning of the American Mind* (Huntington House, 1998). **3.** The discussion here is based on Regna Lee Wood's work as printed in Chester Finn and Diane Ravitch's *Network News and Views* (and reprinted many other places). Together with other statistical indictments—from the National Adult Literacy Survey, the *Journal of the American Medical Association*, and a host of other credible sources—it provides chilling evidence of the disastrous turn in reading methodology. But in a larger sense the author urges every reader to trust personal judgment over "numerical" evidence, whatever the source. During the writer's 30-year classroom experience, the decline in student ability to comprehend difficult text was marked, while the ability to extract and parrot "information" in the form of "facts" was much less affected. This is a product of deliberate pedagogy, to what is the burden of my essay. **4.** A particularly clear example of the dynamics hypothesized to cause the correlation can be found in Michael S. Brunner's monograph "Reduced Recidivism and Increased Employment Opportunity Through Research-Based Reading Instruction," United States Department of Justice (June 1992). Brunner's recent book, *Retarding America* (Halcyon House, 1993), written as a Visiting Fellow for the US Department of Justice, is recommended. A growing body of documentation causally ties illiteracy to violent crime. A study by Dennis Hogenson, "Reading Failure and Juvenile Delinquency" (Reading Reform Foundation), attempted to correlate teenage aggression with age, family size, numbers of parents present in home, rural versus urban environment, socioeconomic status, minority group member-

ship, and religious preference. None of these factors produced a significant correlation. But one did. As the author reports: "Only reading failure was found to correlate with aggression in both populations of delinquent boys." An organization of ex-prisoners testified before the Subcommittee on Education of the US Congress that in its opinion illiteracy was an important causative factor in crime, "for the illiterate have very few honest ways of making a living." In 1994 the US Department of Education acknowledged that two-thirds of all incarcerated criminals have poor literacy. **5.** The reader will recall such a strategy was considered for Hester Prynne's child, Pearl, in Hawthorne's *Scarlet Letter*. That Hawthorne, writing at mid-century, chose this as a hinge for his characterization of the fallen woman Hester is surely no coincidence. **6.** Interestingly enough, several versions of this book exist—although no indication that this is so appears on the copyright page. In one of these versions, the familiar totalitarian symbols are much more pronounced than in the other. **7.** A Harvard professor with a Teachers College Ph.D., Inglis descended from a long line of famous Anglicans. One of his ancestors, assistant Rector of Trinity Church when the Revolution began, in 1777 fled the onrushing Republic; another wrote a refutation of Tom Paine's *Common Sense* and was made the first Bishop of Nova Scotia in 1787; and a third, Sir John Inglis, commanded the British forces at Lucknow during the famous siege by the Sepoy mutineers in 1857. Is the Inglis bloodline germane to his work as a school pioneer? You'll have to decide that for yourself.

APPENDIX A: MORE SECRETS AND LIES

RUSS KICK

_ONE NATION, UNDER THE CORPORATION, RULED BY MULTIMILLIONAIRES

The United States is ruled by former high-level executives, many of whom are multimillionaires.[1] The President, Vice President, eleven Cabinet members (out of fourteen), several Cabinet-level members, some White House staff and advisors, and lots of deputy secretaries and department heads have assets totaling into the millions, often the tens of millions. Most of the others have held high positions in big corporations, even though they may not have six- or seven-figure fortunes.

According to a thorough examination by the Center for Public Integrity: "The average net worth of 15 of the top Bush cabinet officials, including the President and Vice President, was between $9.9 and $28.9 million." Totaled, their fortune is $148 million to $434 million. If you average the net worth of the administration's top 100 officials, it comes out to $3.7 to almost $12 million.[2]

Distressingly often, these executives-*cum*-politicians have direct influence over matters that affect the businesses they once ran, directed, consulted for, lobbied for, and/or owned stock in. The Center reports, "Overall, 22 of the top 100 Bush officials had significant holdings in 33 companies that lobbied their departments, agencies or offices."[3] The following is a list of which officials are owned by which corporations. The end of each entry lists the official's assets, as declared on financial disclosure statements filed upon assuming office.[4]

George W. Bush, President. Founder of the Arbusto oil company, which was about to go bust-o when it merged with Spectrum 7. Harken Energy bought Spectrum in 1986 and gave Bush a seat on its board. (Bush sold most of his stock in the company right before it tanked due to a horrible earnings report.) Former co-owner of Texas Rangers baseball team. (By relying on the power of his name and unethical dealings, he made a $14.9 million profit when he sold his share of the team eight years later, while Governor of Texas; that's a 2,800 percent return on his investment of $500,000.) Assets: up to $27 million.[5]

Richard Cheney, Vice President. Former CEO of Halliburton Co. Cheney guided the gigantic oil and chemical firm to the federal banquet table, helping it gobble up $3.8 billion in corporate welfare. And let's not forget that "Halliburton, through its European subsidiaries, sold spare parts to Iraq's oil industry, despite UN sanctions."[6] Cheney also had US diplomats lobby foreign governments and companies for Halliburton.[7] Also a former board member of Procter & Gamble, Union Pacific, and the American Petroleum Institute. Assets: $19.3 - $81.7 million.

> "THE AVERAGE NET WORTH OF 15 OF THE TOP BUSH CABINET OFFICIALS, INCLUDING THE PRESIDENT AND VICE PRESIDENT, WAS BETWEEN $9.9 AND $28.9 MILLION."

John Ashcroft, Attorney General. Ashcroft hasn't served in a corporation, but he has taken generous political donations from Enron, Monsanto, AT&T, Microsoft, Schering-Plough, and others. Despite the fact that he's been a public servant most of his adult life (including a stint teaching business law at Southwest Missouri State University in Springfield, Illinois, which he used to dodge the draft for Vietnam[8]), he has assets worth $1.1 - $3.3 million.

Larry Thompson, Deputy Attorney General. Former partner at the law firm of King & Spalding in Atlanta. Assets: up to $10.5 million.

Donald Rumsfeld, Secretary of Defense. Former CEO of General Instrument Corp. and pharmaceutical giant G.D. Searle & Co. Formerly on the boards of Amylin Pharmaceuticals, Asea Brown Boveri, the Rand Corp., Kellogg, Sears, Allstate, Gilead Sciences, Tribune Company, and Gulfstream Aerospace, plus the advisory board of Salomon Smith Barney. Assets: $61 - $242.5 million.

Paul Wolfowitz, Deputy Secretary of Defense. Former co-chairman at Hughes Electronics. Former consultant for BP-Amoco and Northrop Grumman. Former board member of Hasbro and Dreyfus. Assets: up to $385,000.

Edward C. Aldridge, Jr., Under Secretary of Defense for Acquisition, Technology and Logistics. Founder of the Aerospace Corporation (2000 revenues: $350 million). Assets: up to $3.7 million.

Colin Powell, Secretary of State. Former board member of America Online and Gulfstream Aerospace. Received $100,000 per speech from dozens of corporations. Assets: $19.5 - $68.9 million.

Richard Armitage, Deputy Secretary of State. Founder of Armitage Associates consulting firm; clients have included Boeing, Goldman Sachs, Chase Manhattan, and Halliburton subsidiary Brown & Root. Former board member of Mantech International and Raytheon. Has invested millions of his own money in Pfizer and Chase. Assets: $19.8 - $58.9 million.

Paul O'Neill, Secretary of Treasury. Former CEO of Alcoa (the world's largest aluminum manufacturer) and International Paper Co. Former board member of Eastman Kodak and Lucent Technologies. In an interview with the prestigious *Financial Times*, O'Neill said that corporations should not have to pay taxes.[9] Assets: $62.8 - $103.3 million.

Kenneth Dam, Deputy Secretary of the Treasury. Former corporate vice president at IBM. Former board member of Alcoa. Assets: up to $50 million.

Tommy Thompson, Secretary of Health and Human Services. "The former Wisconsin governor was forced to sell his stock in drugmakers Merck and Abbott Laboratories once he was confirmed as health and human services secretary. But he reportedly kept the $15,000 to $50,000 worth of stock he owns in AOL Time Warner and General Electric, since they weren't considered a conflict of interest.... [P]lans to continue as chairman of Amtrak's board of directors while he serves as HHS secretary."[10] Assets: $1.3 - $3.4 million.

Norman Y. Mineta, Secretary of Transportation: A former vice president at Lockheed Martin Corp., the US's biggest defense contractor. Since 1980, Lockheed (or one of its previous incarnations) donated to Mineta during every election cycle. In 1995, he quit the House of Representatives in mid-term to work for the corporation. Assets: $204,000 - $592,000.

Michael P. Jackson, Deputy Secretary of Transportation. A former vice president at Lockheed Martin. (The appointments of Mineta and Jackson mark the first time the two top positions at the Department of Transportation have been filled by executives from the same corporation. "Lobbying reports analyzed by The Public i show that Lockheed Martin has lobbied the Department of Transportation in every reporting period of the past five years."[11]) Assets: up to $800,000.

Elaine Chao, Secretary of Labor. A former vice president at Bank of America and former board member of Northwest Airlines, Dole Food, Clorox, and Columbia/HCA Health Care. Assets: $2.3 - $5.4 million.

Gale Norton, Secretary of the Interior. "[A]s a lawyer for Brownstein Hyatt & Farber, Norton had represented Delta Petroleum and lobbied for NL Industries, which was defending itself in lawsuits over children's exposure to lead paint."[12] Assets: $207,000 - $680,000.

J. Steven Griles, Deputy Secretary of the Interior. A former vice president at National Environmental Strategies, a firm that lobbies for utility, coal, and oil companies. Former senior vice president at United Company, which is involved in coal, oil, and gas development, as well as gold mining and real estate. Assets: up to $510,000.

Roderick Paige, Secretary of Education. As superintendent of schools in Houston, Texas, he privatized the system, handing out contracts to corporations such as Peoplesoft and Coca-Cola. Assets: $1.1 - $2.9 million.

Spencer Abraham, Secretary of Energy. During his single term as Senator, Abraham was the top receiver of donations from the auto industry, including GM ($89,550), Ford Motor Co. ($70,800), and DaimlerChrysler ($48,850). Assets: $164,000 - $464,000.

Francis S. Blake, Deputy Secretary of Energy. A former vice president at General Electric. Assets: $11.25 - $48 million.

Robert G. Card, Undersecretary of Energy. Until Bush tapped him for the post, he was CEO and president of Kaiser-Hill Co., "a nuclear cleanup contractor that has been fined or penalized more than $725,000 for numerous worker safety, procurement and other violations since 1996." Before that, he was a vice president at CH2M Hill Cos., "a Denver-based engineering, consulting and construction group that was found in the early 1990s to have overbilled the federal government $5 million for inappropriate Superfund expenditures."[13] Assets: up to $7.3 million.

Anne Veneman, Secretary of Agriculture. Formerly with a law firm representing agribusiness giants and biotech corporations. Former board member of Calgene Inc., a subsidiary of Monsanto, the biotech company that gave us genetically engineered crops, patented life-forms, bovine growth hormone, Agent Orange, and DDT. Assets: $680,000 - $2 million.

Donald Evans, Secretary of Commerce. Former chairman and CEO of Tom Brown, a $1.3-billion oil and energy company. Former board member of TMBR/Sharp Drilling, an oil and gas drilling company. Assets: up to $45.1 million.

CONDOLEEZZA RICE, NATIONAL SECURITY ADVISOR. FORMERLY ON THE BOARDS OF CHEVRON, J.P. MORGAN, AND CHARLES SCHWAB. HAS A CHEVRON OIL TANKER NAMED AFTER HER. ASSETS: UP TO $2.2 MILLION.

Samuel W. Bodman, III, Deputy Secretary of Commerce. Former chairman and CEO of Cabot Corporation (2001 revenue: $1.3 billion). Former board member at Security Capital Group. Owns Bay Pond Partners L.P., an investment firm. Assets: up to $164 million.

Mel Martinez, Secretary of Housing and Urban Development. Assets: $1.6 - $4 million.

Anthony Principi, Secretary of Veterans Affairs. Former president of QTC Medical Services, Inc. and Federal Network. Also a former chief operating officer at Lockheed Martin. Assets: $1.5 - $3.4 million.

Christine Whitman, Administrator of the Environmental Protection Agency. Assets: $6.4 - $20.2 million.

Linda Fisher, Deputy Administrator of the Environmental Protection Agency. Former vice president and corporate officer at Monsanto. Assets: up to $8 million.

Karl Rove, Senior Advisor to the President. The Associated Press reports that although he divested himself of his millions in stock upon joining the administration, "Rove will continue to own up to $1.1 million in nearly a dozen mutual funds."[14] Assets: up to $5 million.

Condoleezza Rice, National Security Advisor. Formerly on the boards of Chevron, J.P. Morgan, and Charles Schwab. Has a Chevron oil tanker named after her. Assets: up to $2.2 million.

Nicholas Calio, White House Legislative Affairs Director. Former senior vice president of the National Association of Wholesaler-Distributors. Former corporate lobbyist working for a manufacturer of car exhaust systems and for Arco, which, until bought by BP, was "one of the country's largest oil companies and one with strong ties to the Bush family."[15] (Calio's top deputy, Kirsten Ardleigh Chadwick, is also a former lobbyist who sometimes worked with him.) Assets: $1.4 million - $4.1 million.

Andrew Card, White House Chief of Staff. Former CEO of the American Automobile Manufacturers Association. Former chief lobbyist for General Motors. Assets: $810,000 - $2.1 million

Joseph Hagin, Deputy Chief of Staff. Assets: $1.4 - $5.9 million.

Lawrence Lindsey, Assistant to the President for Economic Policy. Former board member of Enron and General Motors Acceptance Corp. Has consulted for dozens of businesses, including BMW, Citibank, Paine Webber, Banco Sao Paulo, and Hong Kong and Shanghai Bank. Assets: up to $575,000.

Joshua Bolten, Deputy Chief of Staff for Policy. Former executive director of London operations for Goldman Sachs International. Assets: up to $2.6 million.

Clay Johnson, Assistant to the President for Presidential Personnel. Ran divisions of Citicorp and PepsiCo. Assets: up to $7 million.

Mitchell Daniels, Director of the Office of Management and Budget. Former senior vice president of Eli Lilly and Company. Assets: $18 - $75.3 million.

Robert Zoellick, United States Trade Representative. Former adviser to Enron. Assets: $3.3 - $13 million.

Asa Hutchinson, Administrator of the Drug Enforcement Agency. Assets: up to $2.1 million.

Robert Hubbard, Chairman of the Council of Economic Advisors. Former consultant for AT&T, PriceWaterhouseCoopers, and others. Assets: up to $7.2 million.

Harvey Pitt, Commissioner of the Securities and Exchange Commission. As an attorney, represented Lloyd's of London, the New York Stock Exchange, and all of the "Big Five" accounting firms. Has represented clients before the SEC. Coauthor of a law review article that recommended corporations destroy potentially damaging documents.[16] Assets: up to $9.4 million.

Michael K. Powell, Chairman of the Federal Communications Commission. As a member of the law firm O'Melveny & Myers, the son of Colin Powell worked for—and was directly paid by—communications giant GTE, which became Verizon after merging with Bell Atlantic. "FCC spokesman David Fiske told The Public i that, as an FCC commissioner, Powell never recused himself from matters relating to GTE or Verizon, including the merger that was completed in 2000."[17] Assets: up to $50,000 (a suspiciously paltry amount).

John Walters, Director of the Office of National Drug Control Policy. The country's "Drug Czar" owns stock in Eli Lilly and Pfizer, two giant pharmaceutical firms. Assets: up to $560,000.

Donald Powell, Chairman of the Federal Deposit Insurance Corporation. Former chairman and CEO of Tejas Bancshares. Former board member at American Bank of Commerce. Assets: up to $49 million.

John Marburger, Director of the Office of Science and Technology Policy. Assets: up to $2.4 million.

Gordon England, Secretary of the Navy. A former executive vice

> THE COUNTRY'S "DRUG CZAR" OWNS STOCK IN ELI LILLY AND PFIZER, TWO GIANT PHARMACEUTICAL FIRMS.

president of General Dynamics, a defense contractor.

James G. Roche, Secretary of the Air Force. A former vice president of Northrop Grumman, a defense contractor.

Thomas White, Secretary of the Army. Held several high-ranking executive positions with Enron, including vice chairman of Enron Energy Services and chairman and CEO of Enron Operations Corporation; also was a member of Enron's Executive Committee. Assets: $50 - $100 million (mostly in Enron stock, so it's worthless now, unless he sold it before the crash).

Richard Parsons, Co-chair of the Social Security Commission. Current co-chief operating officer of AOL Time Warner. Expected to become CEO of the company in 2002.

William Baxter, Director of the Tennessee Valley Authority. Former CEO of Holston Gases. Assets: up to $25.5 million.

Marc Racicot, Chairman of the Republican Party. A registered lobbyist who is "personally representing the controversial energy firm Enron, the American Forest and Paper Association, Burlington Northern Santa Fe, the National Energy Coordinating Council, the Recording Industry Association of America, and Quintana Minerals," according to research by the Center for Public Integrity. Racicot has declared that he will continue lobbying for corporations while he runs the Republican party, and Bush has given his approval. Though technically not a government official, Racicot meets regularly with the President, VP, Cabinet, and Republican members of the Senate and House.

■ ■ ■ ■ ■ ■ ■ ■ ■ ■

The Enron Administration. As this book goes to press, Enron has recently collapsed, threatening to drag its business partners—the Bush Administration and many other federal and state officials—with it. Since several Congressional investigations and two criminal investigations are currently under way, what we know now is surely nothing compared to what we soon will know. At this point, though, we can look at the officials who we know are part of the Enron team. Bush's chief economic adviser, Lawrence Lindsey, and chief trade negotiator, Robert Zoellick, were advisers to Enron. Vice President Cheney had refused to let Congress' General Accounting Office know which executives met with him during secret energy-policy meetings, but under pressure he finally admitted that Enron's chairman and CEO, Kenneth Lay, met with him or his aides six times. The last time was a mere week before Enron announced it was in deep shit.

Prior to that announcement, Lay put in calls to Treasury Secretary

Paul O'Neill, Commerce Secretary Don Evans, and Federal Reserve Board Chairman Alan Greenspan. The *Financial Times* reports that Enron's president, Greg Whalley, had six to eight phone conversations with Undersecretary of Treasury Peter Fisher, asking him to get the banks off Enron's back. Additionally, "Robert Rubin, Treasury secretary during the Clinton administration and now a top executive of Enron creditor Citigroup, also contacted Mr. Fisher to discuss intervening with credit agencies." In every case, the government officials who were contacted insisted they did absolutely nothing to help Enron.[19]

It's nothing new, though. In 1997, Enron was anxious to get into the Pennsylvania market, so Lay asked Bush, then Governor of Texas, to call Pennsylvania Governor Tom Ridge. Bush did, and the deal was set.[20] (Bush later appointed Ridge as Secretary of Homeland Security.) Enron even greased President Clinton's palm. Clinton helped the company get its $3-billion plant approved in India; days before the deal was finalized, Enron gave $100,000 to the Democrats.[21]

Fourteen top officials own or did own stock in Enron. Senior adviser Karl Rove and Undersecretary of State Charlotte Beers declared the most, falling into the $100,001 - $250,000 category. In the category of $15,001 - $50,000 were Deputy EPA Administrator Linda Fisher, Deputy US Trade Representative Linnet Deily, Undersecretary of Commerce Grant Aldonas, US Trade Representative Robert Zoellick, and Advisor to the President for Communications Margaret Tutweiler. Some, but not all, of them sold their stock before assuming office.[22]

As far as the legalized bribery of donations is concerned, it's a sad story. During Presidential campaign cycles from 1989 to 2001, Enron gave George W. Bush $113,800, Bob Dole $95,650, Al Gore $13,750, and Bill Clinton a meager $11,000. The company and its bigwigs kicked in an astounding $300,000 to the Bush-Cheney Inaugural Fund. During Bush's runs for Governor of Texas, Enron lined his pockets with $146,500. Bush's nickname for his largest benefactor is "Kenny Boy." As far back as 1992, the staid *Investor's Business Daily* noted that "recently, Lay has turned Enron into a corporate bastion for the GOP."[23]

Though Enron favored Republicans, they threw money at officials on both sides of the aisle. The Center for Public Integrity writes: "Twenty-four top executives and board members at Enron Corp. contributed nearly $800,000 to national political parties, President Bush, members of Congress, and others overseeing investigations of the company for possible securities fraud, according to a Center for Public Integrity investigation. In addition, Enron made $1.9 million in soft money contributions during the same 1999-2001 period." Of the current Senate, 71 (of 100) members have received a total of over a half-million dollars of largesse from Enron (41 Republicans,

29 Democrats, and one independent). In the current House, 43 percent of the members (117 Republicans and 71 Democrats) are on the company's dole.

The country's top law enforcement officer, Attorney General John Ashcroft, can't even be involved in the criminal investigation of the company because he sucked so hard from Enron's teat (to the tune of $57,499 for his failed 2000 Senate run, in which he lost to a dead man). Ashcroft recused himself, turning over the investigation to Deputy Attorney General Larry Thompson. Problem is that Thompson was a partner for fifteen years at a law firm that has represented Enron in many matters. Thompson has yet to recuse himself. Texas Attorney General John Cornyn, however, has withdrawn from the investigation, due to—you guessed it—the Enron money in his coffers.

Enron's document-shredding accounting firm, Arthur Andersen, has also given major contributions to government officials. After poring over the paperwork, the sleuths at the Center for Responsive Politics revealed on their Website that Andersen gave almost $146,000 to Bush for his presidential bid, and the head of Andersen's Houston office at the time was a Bush "Pioneer," raising at least $100,000 for the fortunate son. "Since 1989, Andersen has contributed nearly $5 million in soft money, PAC [political action committee] and individual contributions to federal candidates and parties, more than two-thirds to Republicans," the Center reveals. "While Enron's giving was concentrated mainly in big soft money gifts to the national political parties, Andersen's generosity often was targeted directly at members of Congress. For instance, more than half the current members of the House of Representatives were recipients of Andersen cash over the last decade. In the Senate, 94 of the chamber's 100 members reported Andersen contributions since 1989."

_SARA LEE, SERIAL KILLER

During 1998-1999, listeria-contaminated meat products from a Sara Lee factory in Michigan killed fifteen people, triggered six miscarriages, and seriously sickened 101 people. The Inspector General's Office of the US Department of Agriculture (USDA) investigated the matter, and guess what they found: documents, former workers, and a food inspector all indicating that the management of the plant *was aware* that they were shipping poison hot dogs and deli meats months before people began dropping like flies.

In April 1998, three months prior to the outbreak, paperwork reveals that Sara Lee credited a business when it returned turkey contaminated with listeria. A former employee provided a statement that managers knew of the problems. Another former employee said that technicians had been told to stop testing for the deadly bacteria;

instead, they were to test only for *conditions* that might lead to listeria. The report states that lab test results were put into a file that explicitly was kept from the USDA. Thus, Sara Lee was shipping untested meat.

Furthermore, the USDA inspector who worked in the plant at the time said that workers knew about the problem starting in December 1997. Sara Lee didn't recall its 35-million pounds of products until December of the following year.

So what happened to Sara Lee because of this? It pled guilty to *one misdemeanor* and paid a $200,000 fine. It also agreed to make a $3-million grant for the study of food safety. US Attorney Phillip Green said he let Sara Lee off the hook because he didn't think it had deliberately sold deadly food. What about all the evidence in the USDA's report, released ten months before Sara Lee copped a plea? Green claims he never read it.

When a person murders fifteen people, it's called serial killing. When a corporation does it, it's just business as usual. If the person who mailed anthrax after the 911 attacks is caught, perhaps he'll hire Sara Lee's lawyers. After all, his body count is much lower. He killed a mere five people. Based on Sara Lee's "punishment" of $200,000 for fifteen lives, the anthrax-mailer will only have to pay a $66,667 fine.

> IF THE PERSON WHO MAILED ANTHRAX AFTER THE 911 ATTACKS IS CAUGHT, PERHAPS HE'LL HIRE SARA LEE'S LAWYERS.

_MONSANTO: READ AND DESTROY

Washington Post: "[F]or nearly 40 years, while producing the now-banned industrial coolants known as PCBs at a local factory, Monsanto Co. routinely discharged toxic waste into a west Anniston [Alabama] creek and dumped millions of pounds of PCBs into oozing open-pit landfills. And thousands of pages of Monsanto documents—many emblazoned with warnings such as 'CONFIDENTIAL: Read and Destroy'—show that for decades, the corporate giant concealed what it did and what it knew.

"In 1966, Monsanto managers discovered that fish submerged in that creek turned belly-up within 10 seconds, spurting blood and shedding skin as if dunked into boiling water. They told no one. In 1969, they found fish in another creek with 7,500 times the legal PCB levels. They decided 'there is little object in going to expensive extremes in limiting discharges.' In 1975, a company study found that PCBs caused tumors in rats. They ordered its conclusion changed from 'slightly tumorigenic' to 'does not appear to be carcinogenic.'"

The people currently living around the Anniston Monsanto plant have PCB levels ten times higher than those in people living around the notoriously polluted Hudson River. As of the beginning of 2002,

Monsanto had spent $40 million on clean-up and $80 million on legal settlements, with a class-action lawsuit (36,000 plaintiffs) about to begin against its spin-off chemical company, Solutia.

_HABLA ESPAÑOL, TYSON?

Washington Times: "Tyson Foods Inc., the world's largest producer, processor and marketer of poultry products, was indicted yesterday [December 19, 2001] by a federal grand jury on charges of conspiring to smuggle illegal aliens to plants throughout the United States.... According to the indictment handed up in US District Court in Chattanooga, Tenn., Tyson executives and managers conspired to import and transport illegal aliens from the Southwest border to Tyson processing plants throughout the country. Fifteen Tyson plants in nine states were implicated in the conspiracy. The indictment said the firm cultivated a 'corporate culture' in which the hiring of illegal alien workers was 'condoned' in order to meet production goals and cut costs. It said one of the managers told an undercover investigator the firm would pay $200 for each illegal alien delivered."[26]

Washington Post (January 8, 2002): "A former Tyson Foods employee pleaded guilty to conspiracy, admitting that he smuggled illegal immigrants into the United States to work for the poultry giant and provided them with fraudulent identification."[27]

_COCA-KILLAH

On July 20, 2001, the United Steel Workers Union and the International Labor Rights Fund filed a lawsuit in US District court against Coca-Cola, Panamerican Beverages, Inc. (the main bottler of Coke in Latin America), Bebidas y Alimentos (another Coke bottler and distributor), and related parties. Leaders of the union (SINALTRAINAL) at Coke plants in Colombia have been murdered, tortured, and kidnapped. In the suit, the unions allege that employees of Coke were behind at least some of these incidents. Here are some excerpts from that document (Complaint for Equitable Relief and Damages, *SINALTRAINAL, et al. v. The Coca-Cola Company, et al.*):

SINALTRAINAL (hereinafter referred to as the "Union") has been decimated by the intimidation, kidnap, detention, torture and assassination of numerous of its leaders by paramilitary forces working as agents of corporate concerns, including Defendants [i.e., Coca-Cola, *et al.*], in Colombia.

....

The claims in this case arise from Defendants' wrongful actions in connection with their production, bottling and distribution of Coke products in Colombia.

With respect to their business operations in Colombia, the Defendants hired, contracted with or otherwise directed paramilitary security forces that utilized extreme violence and murdered, tortured, unlawfully detained or otherwise silenced trade union leaders of the Union representing workers at Defendants' facilities. The individual Plaintiffs have been subjected to serious human rights abuses, including murder, extrajudicial killing, kidnapping, unlawful detention, and torture...

In April of 1994, paramilitary forces murdered Jose Eleazar Manco David and Luis Enrique Gomez Granado, both of whom were workers at Bebidas y Alimentos and members of SINALTRAINAL.

The paramilitary forces in Carepa then began to intimate [*sic*] other SINALTRAINAL members as well as the local leadership of SINALTRAINAL, telling them, upon threat of physical harm, to resign from the union or to flee Carepa altogether. The management of

> "IN 1966, MONSANTO MANAGERS DISCOVERED THAT FISH SUBMERGED IN THAT CREEK TURNED BELLY-UP WITHIN 10 SECONDS, SPURTING BLOOD AND SHEDDING SKIN AS IF DUNKED INTO BOILING WATER."

Bebidas y Alimentos permitted these paramilitary forces to appear within the plant to deliver this message to Union members and leaders. A number of Union members began leaving town as a result. And, in April of 1995, following more death threats, every member of the executive board of the SINALTRAINAL local representing the Bebidas y Alimentos workers fled Carepa in fear for their lives.

In June of 1995, the SINALTRAINAL local union elected a new executive board to replace the one that had fled. Isidro Gil was elected as a member of this new board as was an individual named Dorlahome Tuborquia. Shortly thereafter, in July of 1995, Bebidas y Alimentos began to hire members of the paramilitaries who had threatened the first Union executive board into fleeing. These members of the paramilitaries were hired both into the sales and production departments.

...

Throughout 1996, SINALTRAINAL members witnessed Bebidas y Alimentos Manager Mosquera socializing with members of the paramilitary forces and providing the paramilitaries with Coke products for their parties.

....

On the night of January 17, 1998, local SINALTRAINAL

Secretary of Cultural Affairs, Rafael Caravajal Peñaranda, an employee of Panamco Colombia, stood outside the Cúcata plant waiting for a ride home. As no ride was forthcoming, he decided to go back into the plant to call for a taxi. For this purpose, Sen. Caravajal entered the plant and was approached by a security guard, Martín Ortega. Caravajal, who exhibited his employee badge, tried to explain to Ortega that he wished to use the phone to call for a taxi and to wait inside the plant until the taxi came. Whereupon, Ortega pulled out a revolver and shot at Caravajal, barely missing him. Carajaval was able to flee the plant without being harmed. This is one of many concrete examples of retaliation suffered by members of SINALTRAINAL at the Coke facility in Cúcata.

....

The local management of Panamco Colombia have openly sided with the paramilitaries in the civil war which is intensely manifested in Barrancabermeja. This management has had meetings with paramilitary leaders and has provided refreshments to paramilitary forces when they have demonstrated against the ongoing peace process between the Colombian government and the ELN, one of the two major guerilla groups in Colombia. Without basis, Panamco Colombia has publicly released communications accusing SINALTRAINAL of being an arm of the guerillas. Such an accusation is incredibly provocative and dangerous in Barrancabermeja which is now wholly controlled by paramilitary forces which are presently assassinating people at a rate of about fifty (50) individuals per month. These paramilitary forces are specifically targeting, among others, human rights workers, and union and peasant leaders.

> "THE ELEVEN VILLAGERS ACCUSE THE OIL GIANT OF PAYING AND DIRECTING INDONESIAN GOVERNMENT SECURITY FORCES WHO COMMITTED ATROCITIES INCLUDING 'MURDER, TORTURE, CRIMES AGAINST HUMANITY, SEXUAL VIOLENCE, AND KIDNAPPING,' IN THE COURSE OF PROTECTING THE LIQUEFIED NATURAL GAS FACILITIES OF THE COMPANY'S JOINT VENTURE WITH INDONESIA'S STATE-OWNED OIL AND GAS COMPANY, PERTAMINA."

Plaintiff Galvis has personally been receiving death threats from paramilitary forces for the past ten years. In particular, the paramilitaries have threatened him and his wife, both in person, over the phone and in writing, that they will kill him if he does not stop his union activities and leave Coca Cola. Some of these threats have appeared in writing on the walls inside the Panamco Colombia plant. For example, in June of 2000, the words, "Get Out Galvis From Coca Cola,

Signed AUC" appeared on the walls of the plant. The AUC is the largest paramilitary force in Colombia. Galvis complained to the regional Panamco Colombia manager about this threat. Other such threats by paramilitary forces have appeared on the plant walls.

_EXXONMOBIL: PUT A TORTURER IN YOUR TANK

"The International Labor Rights Fund sued ExxonMobil Corporation in US District Court for the District of Columbia, yesterday, on behalf of seven men and four women from Aceh, Indonesia. The eleven villagers accuse the oil giant of paying and directing Indonesian government security forces who committed atrocities including 'murder, torture, crimes against humanity, sexual violence, and kidnapping,' in the course of protecting the liquefied natural gas facilities of the company's joint venture with Indonesia's state-owned oil and gas company, Pertamina."[28] The following are excerpts from the lawsuit (Complaint for Equitable Relief of Damages, *John Doe I, et al. v Exxon Mobil Corporation, et al.*):

At all times relevant herein, from the inception of the Arun Project to the present, Defendants [ExxonMobil, *et al.*] and their predecessors in interest have had the ability to control and direct, and have indeed controlled and directed, the activities of the TNI [Indonesia armed forces] units assigned to protect Defendants' interests in the Arun Project. Such control and direction includes conditioning payment on the provision of specific security services, making decisions about where to place bases, strategic mission planning, and making decisions about specific deployment areas.

The Mobil Companies and Defendant PT Arun were no strangers to the atrocities committed by the Indonesian military during the DOM period[29] in Aceh. At the inception of the Arun Project, the Mobil Companies were specifically aware of the Suharto regime's extreme brutality and the public record of TNI's extreme brutality, particularly with respect to ethnic minorities within Indonesia. This knowledge was repeatedly confirmed by ongoing, specific, and publicly reported acts of terror and violence by the TNI, including those assigned specifically to provide "security" for the Arun Project. By November 30, 1999, when Defendant ExxonMobil became the parent company of the Mobil Companies following the merger of

Exxon Corporation with Mobil, there was a clear public record of pervasive and systematic human rights violations perpetrated upon the innocent noncombatant villagers of Aceh by the TNI troops specifically hired to provide "security" for the Arun Project and that had received direct support from the Mobil Companies and Defendant PT Arun. For example, the Mobil Companies provided logistical and material support to the Indonesian troops throughout the DOM period, including:

(a) the construction and/or provision of buildings and supplies for two military barracks located on or next to the Mobil Companies' natural gas extraction facilities and Defendant PT Arun's liquefication plant, commonly referred to as "Post 13" and "Rancong Camp," respectively, and which were used by Indonesian "Kopassus" (special forces) units to interrogate, torture and murder Achenese civilians suspected of engaging in separatist activities;
(b) the provision of heavy equipment such as excavators so that the Indonesian military could dig mass graves to bury their Achenese victims; and
(c) the use of roads constructed by the Mobil Companies and/or their contractors to transport the military's Achenese victims to mass graves located near the Mobil Companies' extraction operations and Defendant PT Arun's adjoining liquefication facilities.

Thus, acting upon the ethnic tensions between the Aceh people and the Indonesian government, the Indonesian military used the pretense of providing "security" for the Arun Project to practice genocide on the people of Aceh, and in furtherance of this program, the troops specifically assigned to protect the Arun Project used the facilities at Rancong Camp and Post 13 to round up, torture and slaughter thousands of ethnic Achenese people.

The Mobil Companies and Defendant PT Arun knew or should have known that their logistical and material support was being used to effectuate the Indonesian military's commission of the human rights atrocities outlined above. Even if the Mobil Companies and Defendant PT Arun were unaware of these atrocities at the time they were committed, they nevertheless learned of them after the fact, yet thereafter continued to use the same troops for "security," and even demanded an increase in the number of troops protecting the Arun Project, thereby acknowledging and ratifying the Indonesian military's conduct.

Throughout the DOM period, the Mobil Companies and

"IF WAGES HAD KEPT PACE WITH RISING PRODUCTIVITY SINCE 1968, THE AVERAGE HOURLY WAGE WOULD HAVE BEEN $24.56 IN 2000, RATHER THAN $13.74."

Defendant PT Arun maintained continuous operations at the Arun Project and profited handsomely therefrom, having made billions of dollars in profits.

Since the collapse of the Suharto regime in 1998, there has been continuous violence in Aceh of the same character as outlined above. While continuing to serve as Defendants' "security" service, the TNI continues to act without restraint, and continues to practice ethnic genocide. As in other Indonesian provinces, including East Timor and Kalimantan, with knowledge and acquiescence of Defendants, the TNI in Aceh escalated the genocide of the people of Aceh following the fall of the Suharto regime. The ongoing slaughter in Aceh is widely acknowledged internationally, and numerous human rights groups and governmental agencies have documented the international human rights violations. Numerous human rights groups, including several based in Aceh with current information on the genocide of the people of Aceh, specifically requested that the Mobil Companies and now, since November 30, 1999, Defendant ExxonMobil, cease its operations in Aceh until it could make arrangements to operate without using the murderous TNI for security. These requests were refused, and Defendant ExxonMobil has instead demanded that the Indonesian military security forces *increase* the number of troops and take all necessary steps to guarantee the security of the Arun Project, without regard for, and with full knowledge of, the human rights impact on the Achenese people who live near the Arun Project. Moreover, the Mobil Companies and, since November 30, 1999, Defendant ExxonMobil, have continued to pay for the TNI's "security services" knowing and expecting that the military units specifically assigned to provide them with such services would continue to take any and all actions, including extreme violence of the character and nature described above, in order to ensure that the Arun Project would continue operating without interruption.

_SHOW US THE MONEY

As the case of Enron demonstrated, a company's profits can look much better on paper than in reality. But Bush's number-one backer isn't the only one playing fast and loose with the accounting ledger. As revealed in a September 2001 report from the Jerome Levy

Forecasting Center—a 50-year-old economic analysis firm—it would appear that most companies engage in heavy exaggeration:

The macroeconomic evidence indicates that corporate operating earnings for the Standard & Poors' 500 have been significantly exaggerated for nearly two decades—by about 10 percent or more early in this period and by over 20 percent in recent years. These figures are conservative—the magnitude of the overstatement may be considerably larger.

The record is replete with accounting practices that fall within the rules (even if just barely) but make it extraordinarily difficult for investors to discern just how well or poorly a company is doing. For many years the investing public has been given a picture of corporate financial performance that is in significant part illusion. Indeed, there are so many questions and issues surrounding the accounting and reporting practices of US corporations that it is difficult to know just how much the public has been misled.[30]

There are two main reasons for this. The first is that corporations are using accounting methods that keep one-time expenses as far from earnings reports as possible. Naturally, these expenses—which include severance payments, selling assets at a loss, costs of restructuring and mergers, etc.—eat into a company's bottom line, but sleight-of-hand accounting methods try to postpone and/or bury the release of this knowledge. The second trick is that stock options—used to pay management and, increasingly, employees—aren't counted as expenses, even when they're exercised. Of course, they are expenses, and they take ways from profits, but corporations pretend they're not. If the S&P 500 companies had legitimately counted options against their earnings in 1999, those earnings would have been 6 percent lower. On top of that, 21 of those companies would've had earnings over 50 percent lower than reported, and seven would've had losses, not profits.

The authors recommend more stringent regulation and enforcement of accounting practices, but they don't hold out much hope, even if this is implemented. The problem, they feel, is simply too deeply rooted in a corporate culture that rewards, and is rewarded for, the appearance of profits rather than actual profits.

_MINIMUM RAGE

Holly Sklar, coauthor of *Raise the Floor: Wages and Policies That Work For All of Us* (Ms. Foundation for Women, 2001), lays out some distressing figures about the minimum wage:

In recent decades, the minimum wage floor has fallen, dragging down average real wages as well. The real value of the minimum wage peaked in 1968 at $7.92 per hour (in 2000 dollars). Since then, worker productivity went up, but wages went down. Productivity grew 74.2 percent between 1968 and 2000, but hourly wages for average workers fell 3 percent, adjusting for inflation. Real wages for minimum wage workers—two-thirds of whom are adults—fell 35 percent.

If wages had kept pace with rising productivity since 1968, the average hourly wage would have been $24.56 in 2000, rather than $13.74. The minimum wage would be $13.80—not $5.15.

Profits also went up, but wages went down. Domestic corporate profits rose 64 percent since 1968, adjusting for inflation. The retail trade industry employs more than half the nation's hourly employees paid at or below minimum wage. Retail profits jumped even higher than profits generally, skyrocketing 158 percent since 1968. The minimum wage would be $13.02 if [it] had kept pace with domestic profits and $20.46 if it had risen with retail profits.

CEO pay went up, but workers' wages went down. In 1980, the average CEO at a major corporation made as much as 97 minimum wage workers. In 2000, they made as much as 1,223 minimum wage workers.[31]

_VATICAN BANK ADDENDUM

After Jonathan Levy had turned in his groundbreaking article on the Vatican Bank for this volume, he relayed more interesting news. According to the *Inside Fraud Bulletin*, in a listing of which global locations launder the most money, Vatican City came in at number ten, ahead of Bermuda and Luxembourg. An estimated $55 billion in filthy lucre passes through the IOR every year. The *Bulletin* also ranked these criminal havens based on the amount of money that ends up there (as opposed to just flowing through and continuing to other destinations). On this scale, Vatican City was number eight, with an estimated $80.5 billion coming to rest there each year.

> OVERALL, VATICAN CITY IS THE EIGHTH MOST ATTRACTIVE SPOT FOR MONEY LAUNDERING.

Overall, Vatican City is the eighth most attractive spot for money laundering, just behind Lichtenstein and Austria, but well ahead of Bermuda, Monaco, Malta, and the Canary Islands.[32]

_CRIME WAVES AROUND THE WORLD

South Africa: Baby-raping. The term "baby-raper" is often applied to pedophiles whose victims are well beyond infancy, but in South Africa the term has taken on a nauseatingly literal meaning. Driven by two beliefs—either that they won't get AIDS from virgins or that they can get rid of HIV by having sex with a virgin—men are sexually assaulting girls who are barely out of the womb.

Six men are charged with gang-raping a 9-month-old in the city of Kimberly. Also in that city, a man allegedly raped his 3-year-old granddaughter. Two men in Free State have been arrested for raping their 14-month-old niece. Reports have surfaced of victims as young as 6 months. Many of the victims receive horrible injuries and/or HIV from the assaults, and some die. The number of reported cases of child sexual abuse in that country has jumped 80 percent, from 37,500 in 1998 to 67,000 in 2000, with the biggest increase among victims under seven years of age.[33]

Brazil: Ritual Murder of Boys. From 1991 to 2001, 21 boys (aged nine to fourteen) from destitute families have been ritualistically killed in São Luis, Brazil. The victims are found naked, usually missing their testicles. Candle wax, black ribbons, chicken blood, and feathers are sometimes in the vicinity of the bodies, and in at least one instance, palm fronds covered the corpse. Many, but not all, of the boys had been raped. Some had all of their blood drained, while others had eyes, organs, or middle fingers removed. Concerned parties, including local children's defense groups, believe the mutilation-killings are the work of a group practicing Macumba, Brazil's version of Voodoo and similar Afro-Cuban religions.

For a decade, the police have shown almost no interest in the crimes and have botched what little effort they've made to investigate. Only a single person has ever gone to jail for one such murder (he served less than a year), and just one other is facing trial for another murder. At long last, with the twentieth killing occurring in 2001, Brazil's Justice Ministry supposedly decided to launch an investigation and provide security in the slums.[34]

United Kingdom: Dognapping. The year 2001 saw a large number of valuable, pedigree dogs stolen from their owners, who would often get a call demanding ransom. A saluki named Phoebe was swiped from Sheryl Steer. After receiving a demand for £2,000 ($2,900), she met with a woman in London to pay the money. "When I arrived," she said, "a woman took the money and called a man on her mobile phone. He turned up two minutes later, handed me the dog and they drove off." Not long after, Steer saw three men abscond with another of her salukis after luring him with sausage. (Luckily, the dog quickly escaped on its own.)

Lurcher Search, a British organization that helps people find their missing dogs, said they received reports of 148 purebreds being snatched from January to November 2001, often with a ransom demand. An official with the Kennel Club has confirmed the phe-

nomenon. Many times, the canines are abused by their abductors. Police often fail to take the crime seriously, but Member of Parliament Malcolm Moss is up in arms: "From the evidence I've seen, it's an organised crime ring which operates with inside knowledge and steals people's pets. The Home Office cannot allow this to go by default and I will be demanding concerted action."[35]

_WEST NILE VIRUS KEEPS ON FLOWIN'

In November 2000, I was reading the raw newswire from Reuters when I happened across a disturbing article.[36] The Centers for Disease Control and Prevention had issued a warning that West Nile Virus was spreading at an alarming rate. "For all we can tell, nothing is going to stop it from spreading throughout the entire US," a CDC scientist told the reporter. I was sure that such an important pronouncement from the country's disease-tracking agency would become big news, but days later a check of major US news Websites (CNN, *New York Times*, etc.) revealed that none of them had picked up the story.

> **FROM 1991 TO 2001, 21 BOYS (AGED NINE TO FOURTEEN) FROM DESTITUTE FAMILIES HAVE BEEN RITUALISTICALLY KILLED IN SÃO LUIS, BRAZIL.**

This lack of media attention didn't upset the virus, though. It's continued on its merry way across the US, infecting 50 known people in 2001, killing five of them. (Up from 21 known infections, including two deaths, the previous year.) WNV has been detected in 27 states, the District of Columbia, and Ontario. It's made it as far north as the Toronto area, as far south as the Florida Keys, and as far west as Iowa. During 2001, human cases were reported in New Jersey, New York, Connecticut, Maryland, Massachusetts, Georgia, Florida, Pennsylvania, and Louisiana. A human case was also reported in the Cayman Islands. The virus was detected in wildlife—usually mosquitoes or wild birds—in just about every state in the Northeast and Southeast (as well as DC), plus several Midwestern states.[37]

For those tuning in late, West Nile is a virus borne by mosquitoes and primarily infecting birds, although it does latch onto humans and other mammals. It had been unknown in North America until the summer of 1999, when it slammed New York City, hospitalizing 62 people and killing seven of them. There is no cure and no vaccine for the illness. Luckily, WNV is still pretty rare and doesn't cause symptoms in most of the people it infects. Only 30 percent get sick with severe flu-like symptoms, and one in 150 becomes seriously ill (encephalitis or meningitis). Of those who are hospitalized, around 10 percent die. One of the myths about WNV is that even those who get sick from it are able to shake it off quickly. However, a little-noticed study by the CDC and the New York City Department of Health revealed that over 60 percent of people who had been hospitalized for WNV were still dealing with lingering health problems (physical and mental incapacities) one year later. The lead scientist noted: "The one big message is that it's not just a transient illness in people who become hospitalized with neurologic complications. For a lot of people—especially elderly patients, but even the younger ones—this severely affects their quality of life for a long time."[38]

THE PLAGUE MAY SEEM LIKE A MEDIEVAL PROBLEM, BUT IT'S STILL ALIVE AND KICKING.

So where in the US does the WNV go from here? Ever westward. Robert McLean, director of the US Geological Survey's National Wildlife Health Center, says that during 2002 the virus will make it at least to Texas and the Rocky Mountains, perhaps to the West Coast. Even if it doesn't get to California in 2002, it's only a matter of time. "The message is this virus is here to stay," says Charles Apperson, an entomologist at North Carolina State University, Raleigh.[39]

This leads us into the issue of pesticide spraying, which is another can of worms. To kill the mosquitoes carrying West Nile, New York City dumped tons of chemical agents on its citizens and wildlife. NYC Mayor Rudolph Giuliani assured everyone that the pesticides were harmless to humans, but the reality was quite different. The first chemical to be sprayed on the populace was Malathion, which the National Institute for Occupational Safety and Health lists as a gastrointestinal or liver toxicant, respiratory toxicant, skin or sense organ toxicant, neurotoxicant, and suspected cardiovascular or blood toxicant. (NIOSH also stresses that Malathion should not come into contact with the skin; it recommends people handling it wear Teflon suits, boots, and gloves.) An international program headed by the World Health Organization has declared that exposure above the occupational limit may result in death. New York artist/activist Robert Lederman got a look at the official bio-agent handbook given to all law enforcement and emergency service agencies in the city. Page 76 notes that the mixture is an "organophosphate insecticide that causes the same biological effects as nerve agents. Malathion itself is relatively non-toxic, but it is quickly metabolized in the body to maloxin, which is the toxic material. This causes effects similar to those caused by nerve agents.... Malathion can be absorbed by ingestion or through the skin."[40]

A 1992 issue of *Epidemiology* contains a study in which children whose mothers were exposed to Malathion spraying during the second trimester of pregnancy had incidents of gastrointestinal disorders 2.5 times the normal rate.[41] A study in *Mutation Research* found that Malathion caused chromosome mutation in human blood cells.[42] The other insecticides being used are just as nasty.

_STILL PLAGUING US

The plague may seem like a Medieval problem, but it's still alive and kicking. Around 300 cases surfaced in the Democratic Republic of Congo in 2001 (no word on how many deaths), and a few people had died of it in Uganda as of October of that year. Mongolia, Zambia, and Brazil also saw at least one case each.[43]

What might be even more surprising is that the plague still exists in the US. Total figures aren't easy to come by, but as of July 1997, ProMED reports: "There have been 390 cases of human plague in the United States since 1947, resulting in 60 deaths. Most of the cases are from Arizona, California, Colorado and New Mexico."[44] Among the incidents in recent years:

• Santa Fe County, New Mexico (June 2001): A 21-year-old man contracted the plague from a flea bite. He recovered. (Several instances of plague in cats and dogs had been reported in that area around that time.)[45]

• Bear Creek Park, Colorado (May 2001): Infected prairie dogs detected.[46]

• Worland area, Wyoming (March 2000): A coyote-trapper became infected with the plague.[47]

• Albuquerque area, New Mexico (January 2000): A 43-year-old woman got plague from handling a mouse. She survived.[48]

• Williamsburg, Colorado (June 1999): A 48-year-old woman contracted pneumonic plague. As of this incident, 45 people had contracted the plague, with nine dying, in Colorado since 1957.[49]

• Red Feather Lakes, Colorado (May 1999): An elderly woman died of pneumonic plague.[50]

• San Diego County, California (July 1998): Two dead squirrels had plague.[51]

• Navajo County, Arizona (August 1998): One non-fatal case of plague, probably bubonic, reported in a human.[52]

• New Mexico (July 17-24, 1998): Three human cases of plague reported.[53]

• US (1996): Five cases of human plague reported, with two deaths (an 18-year-old male in Arizona and a 16-year-old female in Colorado).[54]

• New Mexico (1994): An 8-year-old boy died of the plague.[55]

As you can see, the plague is incredibly rare around the world. In fact, you're much more likely to be killed by lightning in the US than to even *contract* the plague, never mind die from it.[56] Still, it's fascinating to note that even in the twenty-first century, the scourge of the Middle Ages continues to kill people.

_GOOD NEWS ABOUT AIDS IGNORED

In August 2001, the Centers for Disease Control and Prevention released a comprehensive report about HIV/AIDS in the US during 2000. The headlines of subsequent media reports were uniformly pessimistic; the Associated Press' "US AIDS Findings Cause Concern" is a perfect example. Myth-buster Michael Fumento pointed out that the report contained almost completely good news. AIDS peaked in 1993, with 106,000 new cases. The number has fallen every year since, reaching 42,000 in 2000. Sure, no new cases would be fantastic, but until scientists manage to find a vaccine and/or cure, it ain't gonna happen. And even then it's unlikely. If we can't even get rid of the bubonic plague....

> ACCORDING TO THEIR STUDY PUBLISHED IN *LIFE SCIENCES*, IN JUST EIGHT HOURS, 75 PERCENT OF THE RADIATION-RESISTANT BREAST CANCER CELLS IN A TEST TUBE HAD BEEN KILLED.

Now, let's look at some specific demographics from the CDC's report. Despite such slogans as "AIDS is an equal opportunity destroyer," AIDS cases among heterosexuals comprise only 11 percent of the total. The number of new heterosexual AIDS cases is down from 9,750 in 1993 to 6,350 in 2000, despite the fact that the US population had increased by 10 percent during those years (from 256 million to over 280 million). There's no teen epidemic, either. Teenagers comprised less than 1 percent of the new cases in 2000. Childhood AIDS is also way down: from 959 in 1993 to less than 200. Fumento further notes: "Forget all that 'leading cause of death' stuff. AIDS fell off the CDC top 15 list back in 1998. AIDS deaths have declined from a high of over 50,000 in 1995 to about 12,000 per year now. Fewer people died of AIDS last year [2000] than any year since 1985." A look at the report shows that new AIDS cases also have fallen among all the high-risk categories—hemophiliacs, blood-transfusion recipients, intravenous drug users, and gay men.

The one dark spot in the report is that AIDS rates continue to be much higher among minorities: "Blacks have about ten times the AIDS rate of whites, Hispanics four times," Fumento says. In desperately trying to make it seem that everybody—especially the white middle class and heterosexuals—was at equal risk, the AIDS establishment diverted attention from the groups who really were more likely to get it.[57]

_WORMWOOD + IRON = DEAD CANCER CELLS

An extract from wormwood—the bitter herb that gives the outlaw liquor absinthe its kick—has achieved amazing results against cancer cells. Extracted from *Artemesia annua L.*, artemisinin has been used by the Chinese to fight malaria for millennia. It works by destroying the iron-rich malaria parasite. Cancer cells are also drenched in iron, so two researchers from the University of Washington had the idea to attack them with artemisinin. The results weren't good until they hit upon the idea of infusing malignant cells with even more iron, then setting the wormwood compound loose.

According to their study published in *Life Sciences*, in just eight hours, 75 percent of the radiation-resistant breast cancer cells in a test tube had been killed. After another eight hours, almost all of them were dead. In previous studies, 1) artemisinin wiped out all leukemia cells—which are even higher in iron—in eight hours, and 2) a dog that was unable to walk due to advanced bone cancer was prancing around five days after treatment.

Among the other good news: Artemisinin only attacks iron-heavy cancerous cells, leaving alone normal cells; having been used for thousands of years, its safety is well-known; and the cost of the treatment is insanely cheap—$2 per dose. The bad news is that this low cost cuts both ways. Because there's no profit in a natural, non-patentable cure, hospitals and pharmaceutical companies will have no incentive to push it, so you may have to take the initiative.[58]

_FINGERING HEART ATTACKS

If you want to know how likely it is that a particular man or boy will have a heart attack early in adulthood, look at his fingers. If his ring finger is longer than his index finger, he has a typical chance of having a heart attack in later life. In fact, the longer the index finger, the less likely he is to ever have a heart attack. Conversely, if the ring finger is equal to or shorter than the index finger, he runs a high risk of having a heart attack in his thirties or forties. This isn't to say he definitely will have cardiovascular problems, but the odds are much higher and steps should be taken to reduce the risk. Because finger ratios stay constant throughout a person's entire life, this method works equally well for 5-year-olds and 25-year-olds.

Dudes' digits provide the clue because finger length is determined by levels of testosterone, a hormone that protects the heart. The more testosterone a guy has, the longer his ring finger will be compared to his index. These findings were derived from a university study of 151 male heart-attack patients and published in the *British Journal of Cardiology*. Medical studies have also linked finger-length ratios to depression, sporting ability, sexual orientation, and (in women) fertility and breast cancer risk.[59]

_GULF WAR HEALTH PROBLEMS: EVIDENCE

Lou Gehrig's Disease. Toward the end of 2001, the Departments of Defense and Veterans Affairs released the results of a major epidemiological study: Vets who served during the Persian Gulf War are about 30 percent more likely to develop Lou Gehrig's disease than those vets who didn't fight on behalf of the feudal monarchy of Kuwait. The study looked at the health of 700,000 vets who served in Operation Desert Shield/Storm and 1.8 million vets who didn't. Of the Gulf War vets, one in 17,500 had the neurological disease (also known as amyotrophic lateral sclerosis or motor neurone disease). The typical rate—which was found for the non-Gulf vets—is one in 25,000. The *British Medical Journal* also notes: "Motor neurone disease usually affects people in middle age, but the cases among Gulf war veterans have affected a much younger population."[60]

When reporting on this development, most media outlets claimed that this was the first time service in the Gulf had been linked to a physical condition, but this may not be correct. Albert Donnay—"president of MCS Referral & Resources, a nonprofit organization serving civilians and veterans"—corrected the *Washington Post* in a letter:

Many researchers, including the VA's own deputy undersecretary for health and its chief epidemiologist, have published studies documenting that Gulf War veterans are two or more times as likely as nondeployed veterans of the same era to have chronic fatigue syndrome, fibromyalgia or multiple chemical sensitivity. These findings have been replicated by independent researchers and are not refuted by anyone. The VA has initiated research programs into treatments for these disorders, but it discourages their diagnosis, does not track them in its Gulf War registry, offers no information about them to its doctors or veterans and, most important, rejects most compensation claims for them.[61]

Birth Defects. Just months earlier, the Department of Veterans Affairs had released another blockbuster study. It turns out that birth defects are more than twice as common among Gulf War vets as among other vets. The report surveyed 30,000 members of the armed forces, finding that male soldiers from the Gulf War were almost twice as likely to father babies with birth defects, while female soldiers from the Gulf War were almost three times as likely to give birth to children with birth defects.[62]

> **"LACK OF CONFIDENCE IN VACCINE SAFETY MAY NOT BE A MISCONCEPTION, BUT A SCIENTIFICALLY JUSTIFIABLE CONCERN."**

Another result from the study was ignored in news stories: The miscarriage rate for the partners of male Gulf War vets was 62 percent higher than for the partners of male non-Gulf vets. Similarly, female Gulf War vets had a rate of miscarriage 35 percent higher than their non-Gulf peers (technically speaking, this is not considered statistically significant, though the male rate is).[63]

Gulf War Syndrome. Despite these findings, the military continues to deny that there is such a thing as Gulf War Syndrome. However, in May 2000, the health site WebMD reported: "Brain biochemical measurements in a well-studied group of ailing Gulf War veterans show brain-cell damage similar to that seen in the early stages of Parkinson's disease." The June 2000 issue of *Radiology* contains a study from University of Texas Southwestern Medical Center at Dallas, in which magnetic resonance imaging found that 22 sick vets had neurological damage indicating the death of an abnormally high number of brain cells. The government is quick to point out that the findings don't actually establish that something about the Gulf War caused the problems. A Defense Department M.D. summed up the mindset pretty well: "[T]hat is something we are never going to be able to prove or disprove."[64]

_MERCURY IN MAINE

While the dental establishment continues to insist that there's nothing harmful about amalgam fillings which contain half a gram of the highly toxic element mercury, the state of Maine has charged ahead with legislation requiring dentists to fully inform patients about the hazards of fillings with mercury. Specifically, they will have posters and flyers (created by the state's Bureau of Health) listing the pros and cons of mercury fillings and alternatives, such as plastic and porcelain. When these information sources are ready, they'll undoubtedly note mercury's links to autism, infertility, immunodeficiency, and heart problems, plus the fact that amalgam fillings are the main source of mercury in our bodies. Upon signing the bill into law, Governor Angus King said: "Some day we will wonder how we could ever have put such a toxic substance into the human mouth."[65]

_A VACCINE DISSENTER

Not everyone in mainstream medicine toes the line on vaccines. Eric L. Hurwitz, Ph.D.—an assistant professor at the School of Public Health, Department of Epidemiology, at the University of California, Los Angeles—raised some red flags in an article published in the *Los Angeles Times* (and reprinted in the *International Herald Tribune*):

In the United States, vaccine safety has historically taken a back seat to development and rapid deployment. Remarkably, even today, we lack procedures for the systematic collection of valid long-term safety data. Documented cases of abuse of power, unethical

EVERYTHING YOU KNOW IS WRONG

studies and vaccine-induced injury and death may contribute to parents' conceptions.

Evidence of conflicts of interest involving US Food and Drug Administration advisory panel members, the withdrawal of the recently approved vaccine for rotavirus (responsible for severe diarrhea), changes in the hepatitis B vaccine schedule because of possible harm from a mercury-containing preservative and reports from the Institute of Medicine are also likely reasons for concern. The institute concluded that (a) the measles-mumps-rubella and hepatitis B vaccines may cause anaphylaxis, a life-threatening allergic reaction, and (b) the causes of many other adverse outcomes could not be determined because of insufficient data.

Moreover, a recent study suggests that the most widely used current vaccines for whooping cough may be linked with anaphylaxis, while surveillance of the chickenpox vaccine revealed anaphylaxis, encephalopathy (a disorder affecting the brain) and other reactions.
...
Thus, because of how vaccines are tested and marketed, without large, long-term safety studies before widespread public school use, lack of confidence in vaccine safety may not be a misconception, but a scientifically justifiable concern.

In fact, written informed consent may be warranted because there are insufficient data to accurately estimate the risks; current investigatory systems are not designed to assess the risks of rare events or adverse outcomes with long latent periods; and post-marketing surveillance is arguably still research.[66]

_TAKE THE VACCINE CHALLENGE!

Considering all of the garbage that's put into vaccines, wouldn't you love to see someone responsible drink their own tainted creation? That's exactly what the head of an educational charity devoted to natural health is hoping will happen:

The following offer is made to US-licensed medical doctors who routinely administer childhood vaccinations and to pharmaceutical company CEOs worldwide:

Jock Doubleday, president of the California nonprofit corporation Natural Woman, Natural Man, Inc., hereby offers $20,000.00 (US) to the first medical doctor or

pharmaceutical company CEO who publicly drinks a mixture of standard vaccine additive ingredients in the same amount as a six-year-old child is recommended to receive under the year-2000 guidelines of the US Centers for Disease Control and Prevention.

The mixture will not contain viruses or bacteria dead or alive, but will contain standard vaccine additive ingredients in their usual forms and proportions. The mixture will include, but will not be limited to: thimerosal (a mercury derivative), ethylene glycol (antifreeze), phenol (a disinfectant dye), benzethonium chloride (a disinfectant), formaldehyde (a preservative and disinfectant), and aluminum.[67]

Interested parties can contact Doubleday at <jockdoubleday@aol.com>.

_WORLD'S FIRST MAJOR STUDY OF POT, ROUND ONE

Britain's Home Office has launched the world's first major study on the medicinal effects of marijuana. In November 2001, they reported on their pilot study of 23 people with multiple sclerosis and arthritis, and the results are amazing. The *Observer* of London reveals:

Taking the drug—which it is still illegal for doctors to prescribe—has allowed a man previously so crippled with pain that he was impotent to become a father; a woman paralysed by multiple sclerosis to ride a horse for the first time in years; and a man who couldn't sit up in a chair on his own to live without a carer.
...
[The results] suggest that 80 per cent of those taking part have derived more benefit from cannabis than from any other drug, with many describing it as 'miraculous'. The results make it almost inevitable that the Government will bow to public pressure and legalise the cultivation of cannabis for medical purposes by 2002. Scientists now predict that cannabis—first used for medicinal reasons 5,000 years ago—will follow aspirin and penicillin and become a 'wonder drug' prescribed for a wide range of conditions.

"IT APPEARS, AS NEW FACTS EMERGE, THAT THE VAST POWER OF THE STATE WAS USED TO DESTROY HIM."

The physician of a patient taking part in the study said: "The results have exceeded what I dared hope for."[68]

On April 10, 2001, the Government Reform Committee of the US House of Representatives released a report entitled "The Joseph Gersten Case: A Study of the Abuse of Government Power." It reveals in chilling detail how federal, state, and local government and law-enforcement officials ruined the career and life of a Florida politician, Joseph Gersten. It's a damning, and ignored, case study in how the government can indeed be "out to get" someone. The horrifying story was ignored by the media. Two days after the report's release, a search of the Websites for the *New York Times*, *Washington Post*, *Los Angeles Times*, *USA Today*, CNN, and MSNBC showed no articles on this revelatory report. The details are far too complicated to go into here, so let it suffice to show some of the most hair-raising quotations from this Congressional report:

"It appears, as new facts emerge, that the vast power of the state was used to destroy him."

"The principal concern of the Committee is the appearance that government officials were engaged in a headlong rush to destroy Gersten, and that they did so knowing that they were using the sex and drugs allegations as a means to achieve that end."

"It is a matter of some concern that the State Attorney's [i.e., Janet Reno's] Office made great efforts to determine whether Gersten filed a false police report regarding his stolen car, and yet appears to have made no effort to determine why a demonstrably false report was made linking Gersten to a murder. It appears, in hindsight, that the State Attorney's Office was protecting the person responsible for the false murder allegation."

"The State Attorney's Office of the Eleventh Judicial Circuit of Florida appears to be engaged in an ongoing effort to withhold significant information from Congress."

"However, there are so many indications of unfair—and possibly corrupt—practices by state and federal government officials that the Committee believes it important to provide a public explanation of events. Some of the important evidence uncovered by the Committee was kept from the public and, apparently, from key investigators. Indeed, one of the most important matters was deliberately kept from Gersten and his lawyers. Furthermore, it appears that there was even an effort to keep the most significant matter from this Committee."

If you're interested in reading the entire report, it's available in several formats at my Website, alterNewswire <www.alternewswire. com/gersten>.

If you thought the days of Hollywood acting directly as a propaganda machine for the government ended with Warner Bros.' anti-"Jap" WWII cartoons, you haven't been paying attention to the people behind the silver screen: Drug Warriors, Pentagon brass, and intelligence officials. I'm not talking about ways in which ingrained patriotism may make people want to make their country and its institutions look good. Instead, I mean the State using *quid pro quo* to directly influence movies and television to the point of causing scripts to be changed. Meet the almost unknown power players of Hollywood:

The Military.[69] The armed forces help filmmakers by letting them use military vehicles, other hardware, and land, saving the studios millions of dollars in expenses. In return for this service, though, the military often asks for changes to the movie, changes which always make the armed forces look better. With disturbing regularity, the filmmakers—even big-name ones—cave in. Ridley Scott removed a scene from *G.I. Jane* because a Navy commander said it "carries no benefit to the US navy." The producers of *Top Gun* obtained Navy cooperation only after they changed Kelly McGillis' character from an enlisted woman to a civilian (fraternization between officers and enlistees is a no-no). A Marine major complained about *The Jackal* because helicopter pilots didn't have an "integral part in the action—they are effectively taxi drivers," so director Michael Caton-Jones wrote back: "I am certain that we can address the points that you raised...and effect the appropriate changes in the screenplay that you requested." Once the fly-boys were given a better role, the Marines cooperated.

> RIDLEY SCOTT REMOVED A SCENE FROM *G.I. JANE* BECAUSE A NAVY COMMANDER SAID IT "CARRIES NO BENEFIT TO THE US NAVY."

Some filmmakers slobber on themselves in an attempt to appease the military. Dean Devlin, the writer and producer of *Independence Day*, told the Pentagon: "If this doesn't make every boy in the country want to fly a fighter jet, I'll eat this script." A Disney executive reassured the old soldiers, "We firmly believe that with the support of the US military, *Armageddon* will be the biggest film of 1998, while illustrating the expertise, leadership and heroism of the US military."

Among the films that were given military cooperation after passing the acceptability test: *Air Force One*, *A Few Good Men*, *From Here to Eternity*, *The Hunt for Red October*, *Pearl Harbor*, *Apollo 13*, and *Tora Tora! Tora!*. Among those that didn't receive an official stamp of approval and, thus, any military assistance: *Apocalypse Now*, *Catch 22*, *Dr. Strangelove*, *Forrest Gump*, *An Officer and a Gentleman*, *Platoon*, and *Sgt. Bilko*.

As one government memo said: "Military depictions have become more of a 'commercial' for us."

The CIA.[70] As part of its effort to appear more open, the CIA in the mid-1990s began offering "consultation[s] and research assistance," as the *New York Times* terms it, to producers. The spooks have even created a new full-time position: public affairs liaison to Hollywood. "Producers say the CIA will have input on scripts but not script 'approval,'" notes media watchdog Jeff Cohen. At the start of the 2001 TV season, the CIA's first liaison, Chase Brandon, was a consultant to the producers of *The Agency* (CBS) and *Felicity* (ABC). After reviewing the scripts for the former show, he was so delighted that he allowed the pilot episode to be filmed in CIA headquarters at Langley using CIA property as props with CIA employees as extras. (He has refused to help with two recent movies that he says "slander" the CIA: *Spy Game*, with Robert Redford and Brad Pitt, and *The Bourne Identity*, starring Matt Damon.)

Brandon complains, "Year after year, as moviegoers and TV watchers, we've seen our image and our reputation constantly sullied with egregious, ugly misrepresentations of who we are and what we stand for. We've been imbued with these extraordinary Machiavellian conspiratorial capabilities." (In case Mr. Brandon would like a refresher course in Machiavellianism, we refer him to William Blum's heavily-documented *Killing Hope: US Military and CIA Interventions Since World War II* for lessons on the Company's roles in assassination, torture, destabilization, and the overthrow of democratically-elected governments.)

Luckily for Brandon, some producers are now willing to overlook the CIA's indiscretions. "To see our image changing for the outside world makes us feel better about ourselves internally," he told the *Times*. "It's a good morale booster."

The Drug Czar.[71] In early 2000, *Salon* kicked up a lot of dust when it revealed a scam in which the White House Office of National Drug Control Policy (ONDCP) was directly influencing—and even okaying—scripts for TV shows, including *ER*, *Beverly Hills 90210*, *Home Improvement*, and *General Hospital*. What happened was this: Congress passed a plan to spend $1 billion to buy ad time for its anti-drug commercials for the next five years. The catch was that the networks had to sell the ad time for half-price, meaning they would get only $500,000 for a spot that would cost any other advertiser $1 million. The TV execs weren't happy about the reduced rates, so Drug Czar Barry McCaffrey made them a deal they couldn't refuse: The government would relinquish some of its ad time if the networks incorporated anti-drug propaganda into their shows.

Most of the networks sent scripts in advance to the ONDCP, which would then approve the script or ask for changes, which were usually implemented. For example, the ONDCP got the WB Network to change an episode of *Smart Guy*. Two kids taking drugs at a party were changed from cool dudes into losers. *Salon* reveals: "Other drug office-approved shows featured: a career-devastating, pot-induced freakout of angel-dust proportions (*The Wayans Bros.*); blanket drug tests at work (*The Drew Carey Show*) and for a school basketball team (NBC's Saturday morning *Hang Time*); death behind the wheel due to alcohol and pot combined (*Sports Night*); kids caught with marijuana or alcohol pressed to name their supplier (*Cosby* and *Smart Guy*); and a young teen becoming an undercover police drug informant after a minister, during formal counseling, tells his parents he should (*7th Heaven*)."

Salon later learned the ONDCP's influence over content also extended to magazines (including *US News and World Report*, *Family Circle*, and *Seventeen*) and to Channel One, the station that provides news (and commercials) to classrooms across the US. In the latter case, the Drug Czar rejected certain news segments that weren't deemed to have a strong enough anti-drug message.

And all of this was before the White House had a November 2001 meeting with Hollywood bigshots, asking them to toe the post-911 line. According to E! Online: "Viacom chairman Sumner Redstone, Screen Actors Guild president-elect Melissa Gilbert, Viacom entertainment group chairman Jonathan Dolgen, Television Academy chairman Bryce Zabel and reps from both the Writers Guild and Directors Guild all attended."[72] The chiefs of Paramount Pictures, the Walt Disney Company, and the Motion Picture Association of America were there, as well. Much was made in the media of this blatant attempt to turn Hollywood into a propaganda machine, but as we've seen in this section, it's absolutely nothing new.

_PEDO-PRIESTS TO BE TRIED IN SECRET CHURCH TRIBUNALS

In the Catholic Church, the sexual abuse never ends. In August 2001, Church authorities in California agreed to settle a single molestation suit for $5.3 million. In the memorable words of British newswire Ananova, the settlement "also requires that priests sign agreements not to molest children."[73] Father John J. Geoghan is going on trial in Boston; 130 people have claimed the former priest molested them over 34 years, during which time his superiors moved him to different parishes.[74] Toward the end of 2001, John Tolkien—the eldest son of J.R.R. Tolkien (author of *The Lord of the Rings*)—was questioned about allegations he molested boys while he was a priest.[75]

> THE SETTLEMENT "ALSO REQUIRES THAT PRIESTS SIGN AGREEMENTS NOT TO MOLEST CHILDREN."

Faced with this never-ending parade of pedophilia, the Vatican has issued new instructions on how to handle accusations of child molestation by clergy. Whenever abuse of a minor is suspected, local bishops are to inform the Congregation for the Doctrine of the Faith at the Holy See. This body will then decide whether to try the case themselves or let the local diocese handle it. Either way, the accused will be judged by a *secret, closed ecclesiastical tribunal* that will zealously guard against disclosure of its proceedings. Tellingly, the letter announcing these changes—sent to bishops around the world in June 2001—makes absolutely no mention of reporting suspected pedophile-priests to the civil authorities.

It's also interesting to note the extremely quiet way in which this important matter was handled. The Pope drew up a document announcing the creation of new norms in May 2001. It wasn't published until December of that year, when it showed up in *Latin* in *Acta Apostolicae Sedis*, the Vatican's journal of record. In a complete reversal for this type of announcement, there was no press conference or press release. "According to reporter John Thavis of Catholic News Service, which first obtained the new Vatican guidelines and broke the story last month, the way the rules were devised and released 'was unusual even by Vatican standards.'"[76]

_VOTESCAMS, EAST AND WEST

Proving Jonathan Vankin's point that we have no idea who has won almost any election in recent history, the strange goings-on continued at the local level in 2001. San Francisco, California, had an incredibly tight and strange election that year. "As the week wore on, department head Tammy Haygood's estimates of how many ballots remained to be counted changed—over and over and over," notes the *San Francisco Bay Guardian*. "It wasn't clear whether she was covering up information or really didn't have a handle on a key aspect of her job."[77] Although public monitoring of vote-counting is allowed by California law, the government refused to permit such monitoring during the first days of the counting.

At least 20,000 absentee and provisional ballots were stored in odd locations away from city hall. Some were in the Bill Graham Civic Auditorium, while others were kept in a warehouse at the end of a pier (two miles away from city hall). There is evidence that at the former location, a single security guard (with no law enforcement officials) guarded the ballots for two hours on election night. At the pier location, the ballots appear to have been *completely* unguarded all morning on November 7.[78]

Later that month, the Coast Guard found lids from eight ballot boxes floating in the San Francisco Bay. Haygood assured everyone that the tops from the boxes stored at the pier had been washed and left out to dry; the wind then blew them into the drink. Some have been wondering, though, if the rest of the boxes—and the ballots they contained—might be sleeping with the fishes. Supervisor Aaron Peskin said the city should buy "plastic-coated ballots that will float." The activist group Global Exchange is planning Diving For Ballots, in which divers will search the murky depths for lost ballots.[79]

Days after the floating lids were rescued, 240 uncounted votes were found jammed in voting machines.[80] On December 3, city officials announced that they could not account for 400 blank ballots. Had these vanished ballots been misplaced? Had someone stolen them and created 400 votes for a certain candidate? No one knows. At least, no one is telling.[81]

Then there were the flip-flops and haziness surrounding New York City's Democratic primary, which was summed up thusly by the London *Guardian*: "Mark Green, the city's public advocate and an inveterate seeker of public office, beat Fernando Ferrer, who wanted to become the first Hispanic mayor, by 10% for the right to become the Democrats' candidate in the election. Or maybe it was 6%. There again, it could have been 2%. Maybe he did not win at all.

"WE'VE GOT A DICTATORIAL PRESIDENT." —REPUBLICAN CONGRESSMAN DAN BURTON

"About 200,000 votes were counted twice; on the other hand it might have been 40,000. A good 800,000 Democrats turned out; unless it was 764,750; or something in the order of 570,000."[82]

_BUSH IS A DICTATOR, SAYS REPUBLICAN CONGRESSMAN

When a politician from one party bashes a politician from the other main party, it's not even worth mentioning. But when a prominent politician denounces the President and Attorney General, who are members of his own party—now that's news. The incident didn't provoke much notice; a *Boston Globe* article was the only indication that the drubbing took place. The time: mid-December 2001, when even Democrats were afraid to criticize Bush, for fear of upsetting the post-911 spirit of "bipartisanship." The occasion: prior to a House Government Reform Committee hearing on the Boston FBI's handling of a Mob informant, whom they let murder with impunity. "President Bush yesterday invoked executive privilege to block a congressional subpoena exploring abuses in the Boston FBI office," the *Globe* reported. Congress had already been steaming because "the Bush administration has limited access to presidential historical records, refused to give Congress documents about the vice president's energy task force, and unilaterally announced plans for military commissions that would try suspected terrorists in secret."

A Deputy Assistant Attorney General was shaking hands with Congressman Dan Burton, the Republican head of the Reform Committee. Burton lit into him: "You tell the president there's going to be war between the president and this committee. His dad was at a 90 percent approval rating and he lost, and the same thing can happen to him."

Then he delivered the *coup de grâce*: "We've got a dictatorial president and a Justice Department that does not want Congress involved.... Your guy [i.e., Attorney General John Ashcroft] is acting like he's king."[83]

_US FOREIGN POLICY 101

In case you're having trouble keeping track of all the countries the US has bombed since World War II, William Blum has created this handy scorecard:[84]

China 1945-46 • Korea and China 1950-53 • Guatemala 1954 • Indonesia 1958 • Cuba 1959-1961 • Guatemala 1960 • Congo 1964 • Peru 1965 • Laos 1964-73 • Vietnam 1961-73 • Cambodia 1969-70 • Guatemala 1967-69 • Grenada 1983 • Lebanon 1983, 1984 • Libya 1986 • El Salvador 1980s • Nicaragua 1980s • Iran 1987 • Panama 1989 • Iraq 1991-present • Kuwait 1991 • Somalia 1993 • Bosnia 1994, 1995 • Sudan 1998 • Afghanistan 1998 • Yugoslavia 1999 • Afghanistan 2001-present

_KISSINGER LIED ABOUT EAST TIMOR

It's long been suspected that then-Secretary of State Henry Kissinger and President Gerald Ford gave Indonesia the go-ahead to invade the newly-free country of East Timor in December 1975, an act which resulted in the slaughter of 200,000 Timorese (a higher percentage of the population than died during the Nazi Holocaust). Specifically, the two were said to have greenlighted the plan during their trip to Indonesia earlier that December. Kissinger, naturally, has denied such allegations. At a press conference in 1995, he said: "Timor was never discussed with us when we were in Indonesia." He did allow that as he and Ford were literally boarding the plane out of Jakarta, they were told that Indonesia was about to take over East Timor.

But now the National Security Archives has uncovered the smoking gun that proves this is false. The memo of the meeting of Kissinger, Ford, Indonesian President Suharto, and others previously has been released in heavily censored form. It certainly gave the impression that the US approved of the upcoming invasion, but the best "naughty bits" were blacked out. Now we can look at the entire memo, and it is a revelation.

Upset that Timor is holding free elections under a leftist government, Suharto claims he needs to act in order to keep "peace and order" in the region: "These are some of the considerations we are now contemplating. We want your understanding if we deem it necessary to take rapid or drastic action."

To which Ford replies: "We will understand and will not press you on the issue. We understand the problem you have and the intentions you have."

Kissinger, ever the politician, is not concerned about the attack itself but about how it will appear. It would be illegal for Indonesia to use its US-supplied weapons to beat down other countries, but if it could somehow be spun as a self-defense move, that's permissible. Kissinger croaks: "You appreciate that the use of US-made arms could create problems."

Ford interjects: "We could have technical and legal problems. You are familiar, Mr. President, with the problems we had on Cyprus although this situation is different."

Kissinger continues: "It depends on how we construe it; whether it is in self-defense or is a foreign operation. It is important that whatever you do succeeds quickly. We would be able to influence the reaction in America if whatever happens happens after we return. This way there would be less chance of people talking in an unauthorized way. The President will be back on Monday at 2:00 PM Jakarta time. We understand your problem and the need to move quickly but I am only saying that it would be better if it were done after we returned."

Ford: "It would be more authoritative if we can do it in person."

Kissinger: "Whatever you do however, we wil [sic] try to handle in the best way possible."

Ford: "We recognize that you have a time factor. We have merely expressed [sic] our view from our particular point of view."

Kissinger: "If you have made plans we will do our best to keep everyone quiet until the president returns home."

Then Kissinger spills the final bean. As if there were any doubt that they had been talking about an incursion, Kissinger directly asks: "Do you anticipate a long guerrilla war there?"

Suharto replies, "There will probably be a small guerrilla war."[85]

_ISRAEL'S SPY RING IN THE US

While reading news articles about the 1,000+ foreign nationals being "detained" (i.e., arrested and held indefinitely) after the September 11 attacks, I noticed mention of around 60 Israelis among them. My first thought was, "What the hell?" Apparently that question didn't occur to the reporters or editors, because there was no more than a passing mention made of these square pegs amongst hundreds of round holes. The rest of the detainees were Middle Easterners, South Asians, and/or Muslims—they fit the profile of those suspected of carrying out the attacks. But Israelis? Why were they being held in connection with 911?

Now, you'd think that the "liberal media" would jump all over a chance to air some of Israel's dirty laundry, but it was the conserva-

> "EVIDENCE LINKING THESE ISRAELIS TO 9-11 IS CLASSIFIED."

tive Fox News channel that was a voice in the wilderness. In fact, one of Fox's biggest conservatives, Brit Hume, kept the story of the Israeli detainees alive for several days. His show, *Special Report with Brit Hume*, ran a four-part series in mid-December on the revelations. Investigator Carl Cameron reported:

> **Since September 11, more than 60 Israelis have been arrested or detained, either under the new Patriot anti-terrorism law, or for immigration violations. A handful of active Israeli military were among those detained, according to investigators, who say some of the detainees also failed polygraph questions when asked about alleged surveillance activities against and in the United States.**
>
> **There is no indication that the Israelis were involved in the 9-11 attacks, but investigators suspect that the Israelis may have gathered intelligence about the attacks in advance, and not shared it. A highly placed investigator said there are "tie-ins." But when asked for details, he flatly refused to describe them, saying, "Evidence linking these Israelis to 9-11 is classified. I cannot tell you about evidence that has been gathered. It's classified information."**
>
> **Fox News has learned that one group of Israelis, spotted in North Carolina recently, is suspected of keeping an apartment in California to spy on a group of Arabs who the United States is also investigating for links to terrorism. Numerous classified documents obtained by Fox News indicate that even prior to September 11, as many as 140 other Israelis had been detained or arrested in a secretive and sprawling investigation into suspected espionage by Israelis in the United States.**
>
> **Investigators from numerous government agencies are part of a working group that's been compiling evidence since the mid-nineties. These documents detail hundreds of incidents in cities and towns across the country that investigators say "may well be an organized intelligence gathering activity."**
>
> **The first part of the investigation focuses on Israelis who say they are art students from the University of Jerusalem and Bazala Academy. They repeatedly made contact with US government personnel, the report says, by saying they wanted to sell cheap art or handiwork.**
>
> **Documents say they "targeted and penetrated military bases," the DEA, FBI, and dozens of government facilities, and even secret offices and unlisted private homes of law enforcement and intelligence personnel. The majority of those questioned, "stated they served in military intelligence, electronic surveillance intercept and or explosive ordnance units."**

To informed observers, the fact that Israel is spying on the US isn't exactly news. Remember Jonathan Pollard, who confessed to conspiracy to commit espionage on behalf of Israel in 1985? Allies spy on each other all the time; defense intelligence and the US General Accounting Office have even noted in unclassified documents that Israel is the American ally doing the most spying on the US. The big news this time is 1) the size of the spy ring (possibly the largest discovered in the country since WWII) and 2) the fact that investigators believe the Israeli spooks were spying on Islamic terrorists and knew about the plans for 911 but didn't alert American authorities.

On the second night of the series, Cameron revealed the way in which officials think Israel gets some of its info. Six of the detainees work for an Israeli company called Amdocs:

> **Most directory assistance calls, and virtually all call records and billing in the US are done for the phone companies by Amdocs Ltd., an Israeli-based private telecommunications company. Amdocs has contracts with the 25 biggest phone companies in America and more worldwide. The White House and other secure government phone lines are protected, but it is virtually impossible to make a call on normal phones without generating an Amdocs record of it.**

"IN RECENT YEARS, THE FBI AND OTHER GOVERNMENT AGENCIES HAVE INVESTIGATED AMDOCS MORE THAN ONCE."

> **In recent years, the FBI and other government agencies have investigated Amdocs more than once. The firm has repeatedly and adamantly denied any security breaches or wrongdoing. But sources tell Fox News that in 1999, the super secret National Security Agency, headquartered in northern Maryland, issued what's called a top secret sensitive compartmentalized information report, TS/SCI, warning that records of calls in the United States were getting into foreign hands—in Israel, in particular.**

Although Amdocs can't directly listen in on calls, it can tell who is calling whom, where they are, how long they're talking, etc. The National Security Agency is apparently quite concerned that this information can be used—and possibly is being used—to gather intelligence. The fact that 10 percent of the detainees work for this company certainly makes one wonder.

The next night's report focused on another company, Comverse

Infosys, which is a subsidiary of an Israeli telecommunications firm. It just so happens that Comverse manufactures hardware and software that US authorities use to wiretap phones. Because of the 1994 Communications Assistance for Law Enforcement Act (CALEA), the ability to instantly wiretap any phone has been built into the telephone system. No break-ins or physical taps are required. Cameron reports:

Congress insists the equipment it installs is secure. But the complaint about this system is that the wiretap computer programs made by Comverse have, in effect, a back door through which wiretaps themselves can be intercepted by unauthorized parties.

Adding to the suspicions is the fact that in Israel, Comverse works closely with the Israeli government, and under special programs, gets reimbursed for up to 50 percent of its research and development costs by the Israeli Ministry of Industry and Trade. But investigators within the DEA [Drug Enforcement Administration], INS [Immigration and Naturalization Service], and FBI have all told Fox News that to pursue or even suggest Israeli spying through Comverse is considered career suicide.

And sources say that while various FBI inquiries into Comverse have been conducted over the years, they've been halted before the actual equipment has ever been thoroughly tested for leaks. A 1999 FCC [Federal Communications Commission] document indicates several government agencies expressed deep concerns that too many unauthorized non-law enforcement personnel can access the wiretap system. And the FBI's own nondescript office in Chantilly, Virginia, that actually oversees the CALEA wiretapping program is among the most agitated about the threat.

...

A handful of former US law enforcement officials involved in awarding Comverse government contracts over the years now work for the company.

Numerous sources say some of those individuals were asked to leave government service under what knowledgeable sources call "troublesome circumstances" that remain under administrative review within the Justice Department.

In the final report of the series, Cameron revealed the case that probably triggered the probe of Israel's US spy ring:

Los Angeles, 1997: A major local, state and federal drug investigation sours. The suspects: Israeli organized crime with operations in New York, Miami, Las Vegas, Canada, Israel, and Egypt. The allegations: cocaine and ecstasy trafficking, and sophisticated white-collar credit card and computer fraud. The problem: According to classified law enforcement documents obtained by Fox News, the bad guys had the cops' beepers, cell phones, even home phones under surveillance. Some who did get caught admitted to having hundreds of numbers and using them to avoid arrest.

This compromised law enforcement communications between LAPD detectives and other assigned law enforcement officers working various aspects of the case. The organization discovered communications between organized crime intelligence division detectives, the FBI, and the Secret Service.

Shock spread from the DEA to the FBI in Washington, and then the CIA. An investigation of the problem, according to law enforcement documents, concluded: "The organization has apparent extensive access to database systems to identify pertinent personal and biographical information."

"ARGENTINA'S IMPLOSION HAS THE FINGERPRINTS OF THE INTERNATIONAL MONETARY FUND ALL OVER IT."

US authorities are investigating Amdocs to see if it is the source of the data. In this segment, Cameron further says that "most" of the 140 Israelis detained before 911 were found to have intelligence training and to work for Amdocs, Comverse, or other companies in Israel that are involved in such technologies.

The Israeli government, naturally, denies any and all wrongdoing. The story must've put some heat on Fox. Not only did all other mainstream news media refuse to cover this huge story, Fox has done no follow-ups, allowing the story to die.[86] If it weren't for these few reports, we'd have no clue as to why 60 Israelis in the US were rounded up as part of the "war on terror."

_IMF SCREWS ARGENTINA, MEDIA NOTICES

When Argentina's economy melted down toward the end of 2001, it wasn't surprising to see the progressive alternative press blaming the International Monetary Fund. It was very surprising, though, to see bastions of mainstream media—the *New York Times* and its partner paper, the *International Herald Tribune* (a newspaper published with the *Washington Post*)—saying the same thing. Although these "newspapers of record" generally tilt left on social issues, they're economically conservative.

International Herald Tribune: "Argentina's implosion has the fingerprints of the International Monetary Fund all over it.... Argentina will undoubtedly recover, too, after it devalues its currency and defaults on its unpayable foreign debt. But the people will need a government that is willing to break with the IMF and pursue policies which put their own national interests first."[87]

International Herald Tribune and *New York Times*: "Many people may think that Argentina's trouble is just another run-of-the-mill Latin American crisis. But in the eyes of much of the world, Argentina's economic policies had 'made in Washington' stamped all over them.

"The catastrophic failure of those policies is first and foremost a disaster for Argentines, but it is also a disaster for US foreign policy. Here is how the story looks to Latin Americans.

"Argentina, more than any other developing country, bought into the promises of US-$ promoted 'neoliberalism.' (That's 'liberal' as in free markets, not as in Ted Kennedy.)
...
"[W]hen the economy went sour, the International Monetary Fund—which much of the world, with considerable justification, views as a branch of the US Treasury Department—was utterly unhelpful.

"IMF staffers have known for months, perhaps years, that the peso-equals-dollar policy could not be sustained. And the IMF could have offered Argentina guidance on how to escape from its monetary trap, as well as political cover for Argentina's leaders as they did what had to be done.

"Instead, IMF officials—like medieval doctors who insisted on bleeding their patients, and repeated the procedure when the bleeding made them sicker—prescribed austerity and still more austerity, right to the end.

"Now Argentina is in utter chaos."[88]

International Herald Tribune: "In the Argentine case, the IMF encouraged the government to borrow heavily to support the peso. Then, when the worldwide recession of 2001 hit, the IMF reversed itself, saying in effect, 'Now pay.' The result was that hungry Argentines who had not benefited from the profligacy overthrew their elected government. The end is not yet in sight."[89]

New York Times: "Argentina's declaration of a moratorium on repayment of its foreign debt marks the end of a failed economic experiment that has cost the country dearly.

"But it is also a blow to the United States and the International Monetary Fund, which had invested much of their credibility and prestige here, yet proved unwilling to help when things began falling apart.

"'I think this is going to end up being a very costly experience for the United States,' said Walter Molano, chief of research for BCP Securities, a brokerage firm based in Connecticut that focuses on Latin America. 'It was very clearly the Department of the Treasury that pushed Argentina over the edge and allowed it to collapse,' he said, referring to the US government, 'so I think the issue of accountability has to come up.'"[90]

_MINING THE MOON

Brace yourself for the Lunar Gold Rush. At least five companies are in a race to set up mining operations on the Moon, which contains gold, tungsten, platinum, iridium, palladium, and other rare metals that turn Scrooge McDuck's pupils into dollar signs. The biggest obstacle is funding, according to Ian Randal Strock, the head of Artemis Society International, which is involved in the plans. "We're looking at $1.5 billion for that first flight," he said. Another problem is figuring out how to make the process pay, since the costs of lugging metals back from the Moon could amount to more than the material is worth. But with this many entrepreneurs on the case—and with potential payoffs easily in the billions of dollars—rest assured that it will happen in the not-too-distant future. Artemis hopes to have a camera on the Moon by late 2004, and another company (ASR) claims it's on track for a 2006 lunar landing.[91]

_RAINBOW KILLING

The Rainbow Farm in Vandalia, Michigan, is a campground/community created by two men, Grover "Tom" Crosslin and Rolland Rohm. It has been the site of pro-pot and pro-hemp music festivals, and the owners took an activist stance toward freedom and civil liberties. This naturally upset the local authorities, who had been attempting to shut down the place for years. Narcs finally managed to buy drugs at Rainbow Farm, leading to the arrests of Crosslin and Rohm on felony charges. The Cass County prosecutor jumped at the chance to snatch Rohm's 12-year-old son, making him a ward of the State, and to apply for forfeiture (i.e., government seizure) of the Farm.

The men refused to attend a court hearing, and on August 31, 2001, Crosslin set fire to some of the buildings on his property (believing that it was better to destroy them than to let the State steal them). When a news helicopter showed up, the men shot its tail. These were the excuses the authorities needed. In a situation rife with similarities to Waco and Ruby Ridge, 120 armed sheriffs, troopers,

AT LEAST FIVE COMPANIES ARE IN A RACE TO SET UP MINING OPERATIONS ON THE MOON.

National Guardsmen, and federal agents swooped in, accompanied by tanks and helicopters. A stand-off ensued. On September 3, FBI snipers blew off Crosslin's head as he walked with a friend to a neighboring farm for a coffee pot. They claim he had spotted them and raised his rifle at them.

Rohm stayed in the main house. At 6:00 AM the next day—an hour before Rohm had allegedly agreed to surrender—the house started burning. A little while later, Rohm, wearing black face paint, came running out of the house. In a repeat performance, authorities claim he raised his rifle at National Guardsmen in an armored vehicle, so they killed him.

As of November 2001, authorities were still refusing to release the autopsies of the two men, despite Freedom of Information Act requests from their families. There is no known reason why the autopsies cannot be released, so if the authorities are trying to effect the appearance of a cover-up, they're doing an excellent job. A weekly newspaper from the area was able to examine the autopsies. The original autopsy on Rohm—performed by the medical examiner of Cass County—claimed that he was killed by a single shot to the chest. But a second autopsy, this one from a medical examiner in another county, declared that he had been shot *five* times. The new autopsy also indicates an angle for the chest shot that may indicate Rohm was on the ground at the time.

In a move so predictable that no bookie would've taken bets on it, after four months the county prosecutor released his report, declaring that the killings were "justifiable homicide." Other than Crosslin's friend, the only witnesses to the deaths are the authorities themselves. A spokesperson for the men's families said, "There are two unexplained homicides caused by 120 police with snipers, tanks and helicopters."

The Justice Department and the Michigan State Police are each probing the incident. Meanwhile, the county is still attempting to steal the Rainbow Farm through the sham of forfeiture law.[92]

_EXOTIC WEAPONS ON THE OFFICIAL RECORD

Legislation has been introduced in the US Congress that provides official confirmation of the existence or development of many unusual weapons. Going under the prosaic title of the Space Preservation Act of 2001 (H.R. 2977), it calls for the elimination of weapons in space, but the amazing part comes when it lists some of the specific systems to be banned. Here are the relevant portions:

SEC. 3. PERMANENT BAN ON BASING OF WEAPONS IN SPACE.

The President shall—

(1) implement a permanent ban on space-based weapons of the United States and remove from space any existing space-based weapons of the United States; and

(2) immediately order the permanent termination of research and development, testing, manufacturing, production, and deployment of all space-based weapons of the United States and their components.

....

SEC. 7. DEFINITIONS.

In this Act:

(1) The term 'space' means all space extending upward from an altitude greater than 60 kilometers above the surface of the earth and any celestial body in such space.

(2)(A) The terms 'weapon' and 'weapons system' mean a device capable of any of the following:

(i) Damaging or destroying an object (whether in outer space, in the atmosphere, or on earth) by—

(I) firing one or more projectiles to collide with that object;

(II) detonating one or more explosive devices in close proximity to that object;

(III) *directing a source of energy (including molecular or atomic energy, subatomic particle beams, electromagnetic radiation, plasma, or extremely low frequency (ELF) or ultra low frequency (ULF) energy radiation) against that object*; or

(IV) any other unacknowledged or as yet undeveloped means.

(ii) Inflicting death or injury on, or damaging or destroying, a *person* (or the biological life, bodily health, mental health, or physical and economic well-being of a person)—

(I) through the use of any of the means described in clause (i) or subparagraph (B);

(II) *through the use of land-based, sea-based, or space-based systems using radiation, electromagnetic, psychotronic, sonic, laser, or other energies directed at individual persons or targeted populations for the purpose of information war, mood management, or mind control of such persons or populations*; or

(III) by expelling chemical or biological agents

in the vicinity of a person.

(B) Such terms include exotic weapons systems such as—

    (i) electronic, psychotronic, or information weapons;

    (ii) chemtrails;

    (iii) high altitude ultra low frequency weapons systems;

    (iv) plasma, electromagnetic, sonic, or ultrasonic weapons;

    (v) laser weapons systems;

    (vi) strategic, theater, tactical, or extraterrestrial weapons; and

    (vii) chemical, biological, environmental, climate, or tectonic weapons.

(C) The term 'exotic weapons systems' includes *weapons designed to damage space or natural ecosystems (such as the ionosphere and upper atmosphere) or climate, weather, and tectonic systems with the purpose of inducing damage or destruction upon a target population or region on earth or in space.*[93]

At press time, the bill is before two House of Representatives committees (Armed Services, International Relations) and one House subcommittee (Space and Aeronautics Subcommittee of the Committee on Science).

_ARMY AND CIA ADMIT THEY CREATE ANTHRAX

During the anthrax scare after the September 11 attacks, the US Army 'fessed up for the first time about its production of anthrax. In a program that potentially violates international treaties, the Army has been secretly producing weapons-grade anthrax in powdered

"WE'RE LIKELY TO EXPERIENCE MORE RESTRICTIONS ON OUR PERSONAL FREEDOM THAN HAS EVER BEEN THE CASE IN OUR COUNTRY."—SUPREME COURT JUSTICE SANDRA DAY O'CONNOR

form and aerosol form. Scientists at Dugway Proving Ground in Utah had been creating the lethal stuff since 1992 (or earlier), and their strain matched the one sent in letters to the media and officials. (However, the strain is common as anthrax goes, so the Army isn't necessarily the source.)[94]

ABC News reported: "Until the latest anthrax threat, Dugway scientists sent anthrax samples by FedEx to the Army's biodefense center at Fort Detrick, Md., where the bacteria was rendered harmless through radiation before being returned to Dugway for experiments. Those samples were shipped in a wet paste form to minimize the danger of a spill or accident, the Dugway statement said."[95] The Army insists that the various forms of anthrax were developed just to study detection and defensive measures.

But an even bigger revelation was on the way. Two days later—on December 16, 2001—the *Washington Post* reported that the CIA possesses and experiments with weapons-grade anthrax. Government officials said that the FBI—which is conducting the anthrax-letter investigation—didn't even realize that the CIA had anthrax until a few weeks before the article came out. In fact, a lot of officials probably don't know because "the agency was not among 91 labs registered with the federal Centers for Disease Control and Prevention to transfer anthrax specimens." A spokesperson for the CIA confirmed that the spooks possess anthrax, including the Ames strain, but proclaimed that the anthrax used in the letters "absolutely did not" come from the agency.

On the question of whether the CIA buys the anthrax from a lab or produces it in-house, the spokesperson declined to say. He did protest that the agency doesn't "grow, create or produce the Ames strain." This phrasing certainly implies that the CIA makes some strains of anthrax, just not the Ames variety. After all, why wouldn't he have said that the CIA doesn't "grow, create or produce" any strain of anthrax?[96]

While the Army's admission received a lot of press around the world, the CIA's admission was almost completely ignored. Putting aside the mystery of the mailed anthrax's origin, shouldn't we be wondering why the agency charged with foreign intelligence-gathering secretly runs its own biowarfare lab complete with several strains of live anthrax?

_SCARY QUOTES AFTER THE SEPT. 11 ATTACKS

Supreme Court Justice Sandra Day O'Connor: "We're likely to experience more restrictions on our personal freedom than has ever been the case in our country."[97]

Senator Richard Shelby (Republican - Alabama; the top Republican on the Senate Intelligence Committee): "All of us want to see the details of any legislative plan if there's going to be a legislative response, but Congress, I believe, is in the mood to do whatever it takes to win this war against terrorism."[98]

Representative Mary Bono (Republican - California): "The key here is to crack down. I think people are going to have to recognize that some of their conveniences are going to be gone. Whether we are talking about national I.D. cards I don't know, or fingerprinting of everybody, I don't know where we are going to go with security. I'm glad to show my identification where I need to go."[99]

Senator Trent Lott (Republican - Mississippi): "When you are at war, civil liberties are treated differently. We cannot let what happened yesterday happen in the future."[100]

House Minority Leader Richard Gephardt (Democrat - Missouri): "We are going to have to change the balance between freedom and security."[101]

Representative Martin T. Meehan (Democrat - Massachusetts): "I don't think we've done a good enough job in this country utilizing the technology available, like facial recognition technology. We need to make greater investments there.... Given this unspeakable act, Americans will tolerate some restraint on their liberties for the sake of security."[102]

Walter Dellinger (served as acting solicitor general in the Clinton Administration): "With terrorism, our only defense might be infiltration and surveillance, so we're going to have to choose between security and privacy."[103]

Morton H. Halperin (senior fellow at the Council on Foreign Relations in Washington, DC): "The intelligence agencies have a long list of things they want done. They've been waiting for an event to justify them."[104]

Washington Times: "Simply by proclaiming a national emergency on Friday [Sept. 14], President Bush activated some 500 dormant legal provisions, including those allowing him to impose censorship and martial law."[105]

_WHAT CIVILIAN DEATHS?

Even while supporting war, the citizenry of the United States doesn't actually want to see what war is really about. The US press has almost completely ignored the civilian casualties in the Afghanistan war, and the Pentagon is quick to deny almost every report. Articles do appear, but they're sporadic and sparse, requiring good timing in order to catch them. Reports on TV are even fewer and farther between.

Fox News anchor Brit Hume bluntly summed up the media's position on civilian deaths to a *New York Times* reporter: "War is hell; people die. We know we're at war. The fact that some people are dying, is that really news? And is it news to be treated in a semi-straight-faced way? I think not."[106]

Soon after he said that, three US soldiers were killed (by friendly fire) in Kandahar. Hume, Fox News, and the rest of the media found those deaths worthy of reporting.[107] This is a natural, supportable position. Yet it starkly illuminates the hypocrisy: When Americans are killed during war—even soldiers sent to fight and die—it's big news, but when hundreds of innocent bystanders, who happen to be Afghanis, are killed, it's not news.

At least, it's not big news in the US. Civilian deaths manage to regularly make the newspapers in the UK, Australia, Pakistan, India, and elsewhere. Some appeared in American papers, often buried in a larger story. By scouring mainstream foreign and domestic news sources, as well as reports from relief organizations and human rights agencies, Marc W. Herold, Ph.D., of the University of New Hampshire, put together a list of civilian fatalities for the first eight and a half weeks of the bombing. (The total is undoubtedly more if you count people in the remotest parts of Afghanistan, people who didn't die immediately of their wounds, and others.)

In the report "A Dossier on Civilian Victims of United States' Aerial Bombing of Afghanistan: A Comprehensive Accounting,"[108] Herold breaks down the deaths day by day, citing his sources for each. On October 7-8, the first two days of the bombing, 49 to 56 civilians were snuffed. The largest single incident occurred in the Qasba Khan and Bibi Mahru neighborhoods in Kabul. Each was hit by one cruise missile, killing at least twenty people total, according to the *India Express*, *Times of India*, *Chicago Tribune*, *Los Angeles Times*, *Irish Times*, and *Guardian* (London).

> ON NOVEMBER 21, THREE CHILDREN WERE KILLED AS THEY TRIPPED ON UNEXPLODED BOMBLETS FROM CLUSTER BOMBS.

On October 10, ten to fifteen civilians were killed according a lone report by the BBC, citing UN officials. The next day, 160 to 200 people were killed in a village near Jalalabad, cited in articles by Agence France-Presse (a worldwide news agency based in Paris), the *Frontier Post* (Pakistan), *Observer* (London), and *Independent* (London). Three newspapers and Agence France-Presse reported on a 1,000-pound cluster bomb that flattened a hospital and a mosque, killing 100 people on October 21.

On November 5, the *Times of India* and *Pakistan Observer* reported around 90 people killed in ten areas. The worst day was November 15, with over 1,000 people blown up in six incidents reported by the *Sydney Morning Herald*, *Pakistan Observer*, *Hindustan Times*, *Baltimore Herald*, and others. Four days later, an entire refugee family of sixteen was wiped out when a UN building was bombed. On November 21, three children were killed as they tripped on unexploded bomblets from cluster bombs. Doctors Without Borders reported knowing of 80 civilians killed in the first few days of December.

At the start of 2002, the defense editor of the conservative *Times* of London noted that even low estimates of civilian deaths put the figure at 1,000, and the toll "may be considerably higher." In an article titled, "'Precision Weapons' Fail to Prevent Mass Civilian Casualties," he wrote: "American bombers may have caused twice as many civilian deaths in Afghanistan in the past 87 days as Nato did in the 78-day air war against the former Yugoslavia in 1999. Despite an improvement in precision-guided weapons and a determination to avoid 'collateral damage', the number of civilian deaths has been steadily increasing."[109]

_THE LAW THAT NEVER WAS

Most lines of thought which say that US citizens don't have to pay federal income tax seem to rest on malleable interpretations and arcane legal arguments. There's one argument, though, that's powerful, convincing, and fairly simple. Even Michael Louis Minns—the country's top anti-IRS attorney—thinks this theory has a lot going for it. Basically, the problem is that the income tax amendment was not truly passed. Therefore, it is illegitimate and should never have been placed into the Constitution.

The power of the US government to tax its citizens is drawn from the Sixteenth Amendment, which was supposedly passed in 1913. Obviously, amending the Constitution is the most profoundly important legislative action a country can take, so it involves some hard and fast rules. Each house of Congress must pass an amendment by a two-thirds majority. Then three-fourths of the states must pass it. The states must pass the exact amendment sent to them by Congress; there can be absolutely no changes to wording, punctuation, or even capitalization.

Since the US had 48 states at the time, 36 would've had to pass the proposed amendment to put it into effect. In February 1913, Secretary of State Philander Chase Knox announced that the amendment was "in effect." He claimed—and history subsequently has told us—that 38 states passed the amendment establishing a federal income tax. It was a *fait accompli*, and US citizens have been screwed ever since.

But William J. Benson, a criminal investigator for the Illinois Department of Revenue, did something no one had done before—he spent a year traveling to the 48 mainland states and Washington, DC, to examine the original documents pertaining to the passage of the Sixteenth Amendment. What he found was shocking. One of the states that supposedly ratified the amendment is Kentucky. Yet when Benson burrowed into the legislative documents in the basement of Kentucky's capitol building, he found that the state's House of Representatives had passed the amendment, but the state's Senate had not. Also, the governor hadn't signed the measure. Strike one. When Benson dug up the records from Oklahoma, he saw that the state's Congress had passed a version with different wording that gave the amendment another meaning. Strike two. When he looked at the text of the amendment that California had passed, it left out the key words "any" and "or" (it also changed some capitalization and punctuation). Strike three. Which means we're now down to 35 states, which is less than two-thirds. At this point, the amendment is invalid.

But Benson didn't stop there. He kept going and found that not one single state actually passed the amendment. Tennessee and Wyoming are recorded by history as having ratified it, but the original documents show that they didn't. Some states require that the governor or another official sign a Constitutional amendment passed by the state legislature, but in six of these states (including Kentucky), the necessary official did not sign. Many of the other states had other procedural errors in the ratification process. On top of that, twenty-two states (almost half) changed the wording. Others changed spelling, capitalization, and/or punctuation. All in all, every state had at least two invalidating circumstances, and some even had six.

As further proof, at the National Archives and Records Administration, Benson unearthed a report written in 1913 by a State Department attorney who examined all the state legislation relating to the Sixteenth Amendment that had been sent to Washington, DC. He declared that almost every one of them differed from the amendment that the US Congress had sent to the states (and, thus, the amendment in the Constitution as it now stands).

Benson has published his work in two massive volumes containing reproductions of all the original documents, which he has had certified. *The Law That Never Was* is heresy of the highest order, but it's convincing, well-documented heresy.[110]

Endnotes

1. Most of the information in this section comes from the Websites of the Center for Public Integrity <www.publicintegrity.org>; its investigative arm, the Public i <www.public-i.org>; and the Center for Responsive Politics <www.opensecrets.org>. Particularly useful is the Public i's online database of the financial disclosures and corporate ties of the top 100 members of the Bush Administration <www.public-i.org/cgi-bin/whoswhosearch.asp>. I can't recommend this resource highly enough. Other info comes from financial disclosure forms filed with the Office of Government Ethics, as reported by the *Wall Street Journal*, the Associated Press, the *Daily Telegraph* (London), and elsewhere; PoliticsandElections.com (Website created and directed by Kathleen Thompson Hill and Gerald Hill, coauthors of *The Facts on File Dictionary of American Politics* and several other books on politics and law); and official biographies of officials provided at government Websites. **2.** Wetherell, Derrick. "Snapshot of Professional and Economic Interests Reveals Close Ties Between Government, Business." Public i (Center for Public Integrity) 14 Jan 2002. **3.** *Ibid*. **4.** Assets are

> TENNESSEE AND WYOMING ARE RECORDED BY HISTORY AS HAVING RATIFIED IT [THE SIXTEENTH AMENDMENT], BUT THE ORIGINAL DOCUMENTS SHOW THAT THEY DIDN'T.

expressed either as a range or as "up to" a certain amount because officials don't have to list the exact worth of their assets. Rather, they use ranges (for example, Defense Secretary Rumsfeld's stock in GE falls into the $100,001 - $250,000 category). Keep in mind that some of these officials may have divested at least some of their fortunes, particularly the stock holdings, upon assuming office. Then again, they may not have. **5.** Ivins, Molly. *Shrub: The Short but Happy Political Life of George W. Bush*. New York: Random House, 2000; Lewis, Charles, and the Center for Public Integrity. *The Buying of the President* 2000. New York: Avon Books, 2000; Romano, Lois, and George Lardner, Jr. "Bush Earned Profit, Rangers Deal Insiders Say." *Washington Post* 31 July 1999. **6.** Royce, Knut, and Nathaniel Heller. "Cheney Led Halliburton to Feast at Federal Trough." Public i (Center for Public Integrity) 2 Aug 2000. **7.** Pfleger, Katherine. "US Embassies Assisted Cheney Firm." Associated Press, 26 Oct 2000. **8.** Robinson,

EVERYTHING YOU KNOW IS WRONG

Walter V. "In Ashcroft's Past, a Vietnam Deferment." *Boston Globe*, 16 Jan 2001: "But when Ashcroft faced induction into the Army in 1967, at the height of the Vietnam War, he sought an occupational deferment from his local draft board on the grounds that his civilian job was critical. The Springfield, Mo., board approved the deferment. The critical job for the new 25-year-old law school graduate? Teaching business law to undergraduate business students at Southwest Missouri State University in Springfield. Ashcroft's teaching position was arranged by an SMSU business professor who was an active member of the Assemblies of God church where Ashcroft's father was pastor and an influential figure in the community. That professor, Vencil Bixler, said last week that Ashcroft knew he would not escape the draft without the teaching job and the deferment it afforded him. In an interview, Bixler said Ashcroft was offered the teaching job three months before he graduated from law school at the University of Chicago. At the time of his graduation, Ashcroft had already passed a pre-induction physical and would have been quickly drafted, but for the offer by SMSU and the decision by his hometown draft board.... Under Selective Service guidelines in force in 1967, Ashcroft's position was not deemed critical to the economy, according to documents examined by the *Globe*." **9.** Interview by Amity Shlaes. *Financial Times* 19 May 2001. As referenced by Norman Solomon's "MediaBeat" column, *Newsday* (New York), and *In These Times* magazine. **10.** Tommy G. Thompson page on the Center for Responsive Politics Website. **11.** Mayrack, Brenda R. "Unprecedented: Top Two at DOT From Same Company." Public i (Center for Public Integrity) 23 March 2001. **12.** Gale Norton page at the Center for Responsive Politics Website. **13.** Ballenger, Josey. "Nominee for Energy's No. 3 Headed Company Faulted on Worker Safety." Public i (Center for Public Integrity) 25 April 2001. **14.** Sobieraj, Sandra. "Disclosure Forms Show Both Bush, Cheney With Millions in Assets." Associated Press, 2 June 2001. **15.** Heller, Nathaniel, and Asif Ismail. "Bush's Carbon Dioxide Flip-Flop Came Through Staffer Who Had Lobbied for Car-Exhaust Firm." Public i (Center for Public Integrity) 30 March 2001. **16.** Mokhiber, Russell, and Robert Weissman. "When In Doubt, Shred It." Syndicated column, 12 Jan 2002. **17.** Heller, Nathaniel. "New FCC Chairman Had Big Telephone Player as a Major Client." Public i (Center for Public Integrity) 13 Feb 2001. **18.** Lewis, Charles. "New GOP Chairman Marc Racicot Mixes Politics and Profits." Public i (Center for Public Integrity) 20 Dec 2001. **19.** Gordon, Marcy. "Enron Asked Treasury for Credit Extension." Associated Press, 11 Jan 2002; Spiegel, Peter. "White House to be Quizzed Over Enron Role." *Financial Times* 13 Jan 2002; unsigned. "Enron's Lay Called

"THAT PROFESSOR, VENCIL BIXLER, SAID LAST WEEK THAT ASHCROFT KNEW HE WOULD NOT ESCAPE THE DRAFT WITHOUT THE TEACHING JOB AND THE DEFERMENT IT AFFORDED HIM."

Greenspan in October." Reuters, 11 Jan 2002. **20.** Vulliamy, Ed. "Price of Power." *Observer* (London) 13 Jan 2002. **21.** Weisskopf, Michael. "That Invisible Mack Sure Can Leave His Mark." *Time* 1 Sept 1997. **22.** For the complete list, see Wetherell, Derrick. "Fourteen Top Bush Officials Owned Stock in Enron." Public i (Center for Public Integrity) 11 Jan 2002. **23.** The Center for Public Integrity Website. *Investor's Daily* quote and "Danny Boy" from: Scheer, Robert. "Bush to Lay: What Was Your Name Again?" *The Nation* Website, 15 Jan 2002. **24.** Dixon, Jennifer. "Workers: Bil Mar Knew Meat Was Bad." *Detroit Free Press* 30 Aug 2001. Also see the multi-part report: Young, Alison, Jeff Taylor, and Janet L. Fix. "A Killer in Our Food." *Detroit Free Press*, 1999 <www.freep.com/outbreak/>. **25.** Grunwald, Michael. "Monsanto Hid Decades of Pollution: PCBs Drenched Ala. Town, But No One Was Ever Told." *Washington Post* 1 Jan 2002. **26.** Seper, Jerry. "Tyson Foods Indicted in Smuggling." *Washington Times* 20 Dec 2001. **27.** Unsigned. "News in Brief." *Washington Post* 8 Jan 2002. **28.** "Exxon Mobil Sued in US Court for Human Rights Abuses in Indonesia." Press release from the International Labor Rights Fund. **29.** The International Labor Rights Fund explains: "In 1989, then-president Suharto declared Aceh [a province in Indonesia] a 'military operational area,' known by the Indonesian acronym DOM, and sent in 30,000 troops to occupy the province and defeat the growing separatist movement. As in East Timor, the Indonesian military slaughtered, tortured, maimed, raped, and 'disappeared' thousands of villagers. The DOM period ended only when General Suharto was ousted in mid-1998. During the months following Suharto's departure, a national human rights commission investigated the military's operations in Aceh and unearthed numerous human rights abuses, including mass graves containing the bodies of Acehnese villagers." **30.** Cadette, Walter M., David A. Levy, and Srinivas Thiruvadanthai. "Two Decades of Overstated Corporate Earnings: The Surprisingly Large Exaggeration of Aggregate Profits." Levy Institute Forecasting Center, Sept 2001. Available at <www.levyforecast.org>. **31.** Sklar, Holly. "Minimum Wage: It Just Doesn't Add Up." Knight Ridder/Tribune News Service, 29 Aug 2001. **32.** John Walker Crime Trends Analysis. "Modeling Global Money Laundering Flows: Some Findings." John Walker Crime Trends Analysis Website; Walker, John. "Asset Stealth." *Inside Fraud Bulletin* (Sept/Oct 2001); unsigned. "Gangster's Paradise Across the Atlantic." *Daily Telegraph* (London) 19 Nov 2001. **33.** Flanagan, Jane. "South African Men Rape Babies as 'Cure' for Aids." *Daily Telegraph* (London) 11 Nov 2001; McGreal, Chris. "Aids Myth Drives South African Baby-rape Crisis." *Guardian* (London) 3 Nov 2001. **34.** Faiola, Anthony. "'Witchcraft' Murders Cast a Gruesome Spell." *Washington Post* 18 Nov 2001; McGirk, Jan, and Natasha Parkway. "Black Magic Rites Blamed for Deaths of 20 Brazilian Boys." *Independent* (London) 16 Oct 2001. **35.** Mays, Nick, and Jenny Jarvie. "Pedigree Dogs Stolen for Ransom by Gang." *Daily Telegraph* (London) 25 Nov 2001. **36.** Patten-Hitt, Emma. "Report: West Nile Virus Will Spread Throughout US." Reuters, 24 Nov 2000. **37.** Unsigned. "West Nile Virus Surveillance 2001: New World Update." ProMED-mail, 12 Dec 2001; unsigned. "West Nile Virus Surveillance: USA 2000 Final Report." 23 April 2001. ProMED-mail is a program of the International Society for Infectious Diseases. **38.** Mozes, Alan. "West Nile Patients May Have Lingering Problems." Reuters 12 Nov 2001. **39.** Manning, Anita. "West Nile Virus Could Reach Rockies This Year." *USA Today* 8 Jan 2002. **40.** Lederman, Robert. "Guiliani Flip-Flops on West Nile Spraying." Robert Lederman Website, 4 May 2001; "Government Lists." No Spray Coalition Website <www.nospray.org>. "NIOSH Pocket Guide to Chemical Hazards—Malathion." **41.** Thomas, D.C., *et. al.* "Reproductive Outcomes in Relation to Malathion Spraying in the San Francisco Bay Area, 1981-1982." *Epidemiology* 3.1: 32-9 (Jan 1992). **42.** Balaji M, and K. Sasikala. "Cytogenetic Effect of Malathion in in Vitro Culture of Human Peripheral Blood." *Mutation Research* 301: 13-7 (1993). **43.** Various alerts from ProMED-mail, a program of the International Society for Infectious Diseases. **44.** Unsigned. "Plague, Human - USA 1996." ProMED-mail, 16 July 1997. **45.** Unsigned. "Plague - USA (New Mexico)." ProMED-mail, 30 June 2001. Referencing the *Albuquerque Journal*. **46.** Unsigned. "Plague, Prairie Dog, Other Rodents - USA (Colorado)." ProMED-mail, 24 May 2001. Referencing *Denver Post*. **47.** Unsigned. "Plague, Bubonic, Human - USA (Wyoming)." ProMED-mail, 23 March 2000. Referencing an Associated Press article. **48.** Unsigned. "Plague, Bubonic, Human - USA (New Mexico)." ProMED-mail, 27 Jan 2000. **49.** Unsigned. "Plague, Human - USA (Colorado) (02)." ProMED-mail, 7 June 1999. Referencing articles from the *Durango Herald* and the *Denver Post*. **50.** *Ibid.* **51.** Unsigned. "Plague, Wild Rodents, Warning - USA (California)." ProMED-mail, 5 July 1998. **52.** Unsigned. "Plague, Human - USA (Arizona)." ProMED-mail, 2 Oct 1998. **53.** Unsigned. "Plague, Human - USA (Colorado, New Mexico)." ProMED-mail, 24 July 1998. **54.** Unsigned. "Plague, Human - USA 1996." ProMED-mail, 16 July 1997. **55.** Unsigned. "Plague, Bubonic, Human - USA (New Mexico)." ProMED-mail, 27 Jan 2000. **56.** Lightning kills an average of 82 people annually in the US: Centers for Disease Control and Prevention. "Lightning-Associated Deaths: United States, 1980-1995." *Morbidity and Mortality Weekly Report* 47.19 (22 May 1998) 391-4. **57.** Centers for Disease Control and Prevention. "HIV/AIDS Surveillance Report, 2000" 12.2; Fumento, Michael. "The Band Plays on: Good News on AIDS—Why the Silence?" *American Spectator* (Sept/Oct 2001). Population data was taken from US Census Bureau Website <www.census.gov>. **58.** Singh, Narendra P., and Henry Lai. "Selective Toxicity of Dihydroartemisinin and Holotransferrin Toward Human Breast Cancer Cells." *Life Sciences* 70.1 (Nov 2001): 49-56; unsigned. "Chinese Folk Remedy Fights Cancer." MSNBC, 4 Dec 2001. **59.** Hagan, Pat, and Lorraine Fraser. "Is Your Son at Risk of Heart Disease? Look at His Hands." *Daily Telegraph* (London), 21 Oct 2001; unsigned. "Finger Length Heart Attack Clue." BBC News, 22 Oct 2001. **60.** Charatan, Fred. "US Links Motor Neurone Disease With Gulf War Service." *British Medical Journal*, 324: 65 (12 Jan 2002); Williams, Rudi. "DoD, VA Study Finds Lou Gehrig's Disease in Gulf War Vets." American Forces Press Service, 21 Dec 2001. Note: Almost every media report said that the study found Gulf vets were "almost twice as likely" as non-Gulf vets to have Lou Gehrig's disease. As a quick look at the numbers will tell you, this is absolutely untrue, unless you think a 30 percent increase is the same as an almost 100 percent increase. **61.** Donnay, Albert. "Gulf War and Illness" (letter). *Washington Post* 30 Dec 2001. **62.** Unsigned. "Gulf War Children's 'Defect Risk'." BBC News, 3 Oct 2001. **63.** Kang H., *et al.* "Pregnancy Outcomes Among US Gulf War Veterans: A Population-based Survey of 30,000 Veterans." *Annals of Epidemiology* 11.7 (Oct 2001): 504-11. **64.** Boyles, Salynn. "Brain Scans Show Physical Evidence of Gulf War Syndrome but the Cause Is Still in Question, Government Official Says." WebMD Medical News, 25 May 2000. **65.** Quinn, Francis X. "Crusade Against Mercury Fillings Renewed." Associated Press in *Bangor Daily News* (Maine) 27 Aug 2001; unsigned. "Maine Mandates Dentists Disclose Mercury Amalgam Toxicity." *Dental Truth* 30 Aug 2001. **66.** Hurwitz, Eric L. "Parents Should Know Both the Benefits and Risks of Vaccinations." *Los Angeles Times* 30 Jan 2001. (Also reprinted in the *International Herald Tribune*.) **67.** Doubleday, Jock. "$20,000 Offer." Natural Woman, Natural Man, Inc. Website <www.gentlebirth.org/nwnm.org>, 29 Jan 2001. **68.** Browne, Anthony. "Cannabis a Medical Miracle—It's Official." *Observer* (London) 4 Nov 2001. **69.** Campbell, Duncan. "Top Gun Versus Sergeant Bilko? No Contest, Says the Pentagon." *Guardian* (London) 29 Aug 2001; Robb, David. "Hollywood Goes to War." *Brill's Content* (Aug 2001). **70.** Bernstein, Paul. "Hardest-working Actor of the Season: the C.I.A." *New York Times* 2 Sept 2001; Cohen, Jeff. "The CIA Goes Primetime on CBS." *Newsday* (New York) 4 Sept 2001. **71.** Forbes, Daniel. "Prime Time Propaganda." *Salon* 13 Jan 2000; Forbes, Daniel. "The Drug War Gravy Train." *Salon* 31 March 2000; Forbes, Daniel. "Reading, Writing and Propaganda." *Salon* 8 Aug 2001. **72.** Armstrong, Mark. "Hollywood, White House Talk Terrorism." E! Online, 12 Nov 2001. **73.** Unsigned. "Catholic Church

Settles £3.7 Million Molestation Case." Ananova (UK), 21 Aug 2001. **74.** Rezendes, Michael. "Church Allowed Abuse by Priest for Years." *Boston Globe* 6 Jan 2002. **75.** Unsigned. "Tolkien's Eldest Son in Sexual Abuse Inquiry." Ananova (UK), 6 Jan 2002. **76.** Pullella, Philip. "Vatican Issues New Rules on Pedophile Priests." Reuters, 9 Jan 2002; Thavis, John. "Papal Letter Announces New Norms for Clergy Sex Abuse Cases." Catholic News Service, 9 Jan 2002. Quote from: Lattin, Don. "Vatican Inquiries into Pedophilia to be Kept Secret." *San Francisco Chronicle* 9 June 2002. **77.** Unsigned. "Elections Debacle?" *San Francisco Bay Guardian* 14 Nov 2001. **78.** *Ibid.* **79.** Brakinsky, Rachel. "Ballots Found, Ballots Lost." *San Francisco Bay Guardian*, no date; Quinn, Andrew. "San Francisco Shocked Amid Ballot Scandal." Reuters, 29 Nov 2001. **80.** Unsigned. "San Francisco Finds Ballots in Machines." *New York Times* 30 Nov 2001; *op cit.*, Brakinsky and Quinn. **81.** *Op cit.*, Brakinsky. **82.** Ellison, Michael. "New Yorkers Vote for Deja Vu." *Guardian* (London) 18 Oct 2001. **83.** Johnson, Glen. "Bush Halts Inquiry of FBI and Stirs Up a Firestorm." *Boston Globe* 14 Dec 2001. **84.** For further details on most of these campaigns, check out Blum's books *Killing Hope: US Military and CIA Interventions Since World War II* (Common Courage Press, 1995) and *Rogue State: A Guide to the World's Only Superpower* (Common Courage Press, 2000). **85.** Burr, William, and Michael L. Evans. "East Timor Revisited" (National Security Archive Electronic Briefing Book No. 62). National Security Archives, 6 Dec 2001. <www.gwu.edu/~nsarchiv/NSAEBB/NSAEBB62/>. Especially: "Ford-Suharto Meeting" (memo). December 1975. <www.gwu.edu/~nsarchiv/NSAEBB/NSAEBB62/doc4.pdf>. **86.** Some observers note with consternation that these four reports quickly disappeared from the Fox News Website, but there's nothing nefarious about that. *All reports from Special Report with Brit Hume are taken off the site within one week.* **87.** Weisbrot, Mark. "How the IMF Messed Up Argentina." *International Herald Tribune* 26 Dec 2001. **88.** Krugman, Paul. "Argentina's Crisis Is a US Failure." *International Herald Tribune* 1 Jan 2002; Krugman, Paul. "Crying With Argentina." *New York Times* 1 Jan 2002. Although these two columns are essentially the same, the *Tribune* version—in its headline and text—is more blunt about assigning blame to the IMF and the US. I have excerpted the *Tribune* version. **89.** Levine, Robert A. "Economic Puritanism Is Bad for Argentina, Too." *International Herald Tribune* 31 Dec 2001. **90.** Rohter, Larry. "A Fiscal Crisis, Paid in Credibility." *New York Times* 25 Dec 2001. **91.** Smith, Jeremy. "Moon Mining: Want to Invest in the Final Frontier?" Reuters, 24 Nov 2001. **92.** Helfman, Ivan. "Westland Lawyer Questions Deadly SWET [Michigan Southwest Enforcement Team] Raid." *Westland Eagle* (Michigan) 18 Oct 2001; Jackson, Adam. "Rainbow Farm Fallout." *South Bend Tribune* (Indiana) 1 Nov 2001; Jackson, Adam. "Officials Taken to Task For Not Releasing Documents." *South Bend Tribune* (Indiana) 2 Nov 2001; Lowery, Ashley. "FBI, Michigan State Police Probe Stalemate Deaths." *South Bend Tribune* (Indiana) 6 Sept 2001; unsigned. "Prosecutor Says Authorities Acted Properly in Fatal Standoff at Michigan Campground." Associated Press, 8 Jan 2002; Wishnia, Stephen. "Weed Waco." High Times Website, 29 Sept 2001. **93.** Short title: "Space Preservation Act of 2001." Full title: "To preserve the cooperative, peaceful uses of space for the benefit of all humankind by permanently prohibiting the basing of weapons in space by the United States, and to require the President to take action to adopt and implement a world treaty banning space-based weapons." Bill number H.R. 2977. Introduced into the US House of Representatives on October 2, 2001 by Rep. Dennis J. Kucinich (Democrat - Ohio). Emphasis added. In January 2002, Rep. Kucinich introduced a new, extremely watered-down version of this bill, titled "Space Preservation Act of 2002." This new version eliminates all specific references to "exotic weapons," chemtrails, psychotronics, plasma beams, tectonic weapons, weather manipulation, mood control, mind control, and the like. The emasculated version would ban only "space-based weapons" that fire projectiles, detonate explosive devices, or direct sources of energy (the latter being a veiled reference to lasers, ultrasonics, ELF radiation, and some other weapon systems that are no longer mentioned by name). **94.** Campbell, Duncan. "FBI Uncovers US Military Production of Anthrax Powder." *Guardian* (London) 14 Dec 2001; unsigned. "Government Anthrax." ABCNews.com, 13 Dec 2001. **95.** *Op cit.*, ABCNews.com. **96.** Weiss, Rick, and Susan Schmidt. "Capitol Hill Anthrax Matches Army's Stocks." *Washington Post* 16 Dec 2001. **97.** Greenhouse, Linda. "O'Connor Foresees Limits on Freedom." *New York Times* 29 Sept 2001. **98.** Associated Press, 18 Sept 2001. **99.** Spillman, Benjamin. "Bono Urges Constituents to be Ready for Sacrifices." *The Desert Sun* (Palm Springs, CA) 16 Sept 2001. **100.** Toner, Robin. "Some Foresee a Sea Change in Attitudes on Freedoms." *New York Times* 15 Sept 2001. **101.** Cabbage, Michael. "Price of Security Will Likely be Paid in Loss of Freedom." *Orlando Sentinel* 16 Sept 2001. **102.** *Op cit.*, Toner. **103.** *Op cit.*, Toner. **104.** Associated Press, 16 Sept 2001. **105.** *Washington Times*, 18 Sept 2001. **106.** Quoted in Campbell, Duncan. "Where No News Is Good News." *Guardian* (London), 5 Dec 2001. **107.** Still, lost in the mix was the fact that five Afghan anti-Taliban fighters were also killed in the incident. **108.** Herold, Marc W., Ph.D. "A Dossier on Civilian Victims of United States' Aerial Bombing of Afghanistan: A Comprehensive Accounting." Cursor, Dec 2001. <www.cursor.org/stories/civilian_deaths.htm>. **109.** Evans, Michael. "'Precision Weapons' Fail to Prevent Mass Civilian Casualties." *Times* (London), 2 Jan 2002. **110.** Available from Constitutional Research Associates, PO Box 550, South Holland IL 60473. $50 for either volume; $90 for both. <www.thelawthaneverwas.com>.

THIS NEW VERSION ELIMINATES ALL SPECIFIC REFERENCES TO "EXOTIC WEAPONS," CHEMTRAILS, PSYCHOTRONICS, PLASMA BEAMS, TECTONIC WEAPONS, WEATHER MANIPULATION, MOOD CONTROL, MIND CONTROL, AND THE LIKE.

APPENDIX B: MORE READING
RUSS KICK

Taken for a Ride: Detroit's Big Three and the Politics of Pollution, by Jack Doyle

The earnest people on the commercials tell us that the big auto companies are doing everything possible to reduce pollution by making their cars as clean and fuel-efficient as possible. Corporate investigator Jack Doyle tells us the *real* story, putting sugar in the gas tank of the auto industry with *Taken for a Ride*. He shows us—through corporate and government documents, Congressional hearings, industry literature, etc.—that the Big Three (Ford, General Motors, and Chrysler, now DaimlerChrysler) actually have done everything possible to derail clean air legislation, sandbag innovations that would reduce car emissions, and thwart public transportation. Throughout the 1950s, the automakers denied that exhaust from their cars was causing pollution. When they finally admitted that car emissions were a problem, they started the song and dance about drastically cutting pollutants. Reading these claims from 40+ years ago up to today is startling, since they sound the same, practically word for word.

Perhaps one of the most shocking portions of the book deals with attempts to create cars with steam-powered engines. Wedded to the internal combustion engine, the auto industry claimed that steam-driven cars were impractical, yet inventors outside the industry developed prototypes that burned extremely cleanly and had all the power of their gas-drinking cousins. The inventors even took members of Congress for a spin in them during hearings on the matter. This was all the way back in the late 1960s. If only this line had been pursued, the world would be a very different place now.

Quote: " '93 was the first model year we ever built a model certified to '73 standards."—Sam Leonard, General Motors. [p 81]

Quote: "By December 1972, sensing that he was on his way out, [vice president of GM's North American division John] DeLorean wrote a nineteen-page single-spaced memo to his boss and former supporter Thomas Murphy, which recounted, in DeLorean's view, GM's failings and poor record on safety and pollution control. One small portion of that memo read '...In no instance, to my knowledge, has GM ever sold a car that was substantially more pollution-free than the law demanded—even when we had the technology. As a matter of fact, because the California laws were tougher, we sold 'cleaner' cars there and 'dirtier' cars throughout the rest of the nation.'" [p 95]

Quote: "In fact, when the automakers discovered that consumer sentiment was more pro-EV [electric vehicle] in 1995, they and the oil companies redoubled their PR efforts and mounted an orchestrated 'grassroots' campaign to turn public opinion around to help repeal the ZEV [zero emission vehicle] mandate." [p 319]

Four Walls Eight Windows • 2000 • 563 pp • softcover • $22 • ISBN 1-56858-147-5

> "AS A MATTER OF FACT, BECAUSE THE CALIFORNIA LAWS WERE TOUGHER, WE SOLD 'CLEANER' CARS THERE AND 'DIRTIER' CARS THROUGHOUT THE REST OF THE NATION.'"
> —JOHN DELOREAN

The Water Manifesto: Arguments for a World Water Contract, by Riccardo Petrella

Most of us who can turn on a faucet in our homes probably take water for granted, yet 1.4 billion people don't have access to clean drinking water, and the UN estimates that 15 million people die from thirst/dehydration every year. Food shortages tend to grab the headlines, but water shortages have been getting notice in the alternative press. As far as I know, *The Water Manifesto* is the first book entirely devoted to the subject.

The author offers a detailed look at how this situation came to be. Many factors are involved, and one of the biggest is the mindset—promoted by the World Bank, IMF, governments, and corporations—that water is a valuable commodity that needs to be privatized so businesses can make money off of its scarcity. Another factor is wasteful use of H_2O by governmental and corporate entities (agribusiness being a prime culprit), in addition to increasing pollution of water. Politics figures into the picture, too, with various countries trying to control *agua* supplies, to the detriment of other countries in the region and even their own populations. To remedy the situation, the author proposes the World Water Contract. Its philosophical basis is "the recognition of water as a vital common global heritage." Its application, which is complex, is laid out in detail. It involves global charters and conventions, national laws and constitutions, NGOs, community movements, corporations, and other parties acting together. Good luck with that.

Quote: "In the world today, there are some fifty local wars between states. This does not mean that artillery and missiles are actually being fired at this moment in fifty different places. It means that, in some fifty parts of the world, neighbouring states are at war with each other for reasons that include water (the river Jordan and the River Senegal regions), or that the guns have fallen quiet but the conflict remains unresolved (the states through which the Tigris and Euphrates pass), or that water is the cause of serious political and economic differences (e.g., the Nile Basin, the Ganges)." [p 41]

Quote: "The private Swiss bank Pictet announced the launch in January 2000 of a unit trust geared to the stock market values of eighty water companies (between $50 billion and $100 billion). This is the first time in financial history that such a public fund has been exclusively devoted to water securities. The companies comprising its reference portfolio were chosen by Pictet because of their high profitability and great hopes for their long-term appreciation. If this initiative proves convincing, we shall see the birth of a global water market dominated by the logic of finance. Companies will be driven to keep raising their return on investment, lest they see capital desert them for more profitable enterprises." [p 71]

Zed Books • 2001 • 140 pp • softcover • £9.99, $17.50 • ISBN 1-85649-906-5

The Fed: The Inside Story of How the World's Most Powerful Financial Institution Drives the Markets, by Martin Mayer

Written by a high-profile financial journalist who knows the movers and shakers in the Federal Reserve System, *The Fed* contains some early history of the US's central bank, but it focuses more on the relatively recent past—the 1970s, 1980s, and especially the 1990s. Martin Mayer explains how the Fed still manages to maintain such control over the economy when 1) short-term interest rates (which it sets) are much less important than long-term rates and 2) "[o]nly one-fifth of the nation's commercial and industrial financing now comes from the banks." This is in no way presented as a conspiratorial book, but when you read about the power, secrecy, and groupthink of the Federal Reserve, it's impossible not to become chilled.

Quote: "It is understood that the staff works for the chairman.... Still, in the old days, unanimity of view had not been demanded at the Fed.... Now, in part because the press magnifies every statement that might be construed as off the page from which the chairman

reads, every speech is vetted. 'This is a great job,' said Janet Yellen before resigning as a governor of the Fed to be chair of President Clinton's Council of Economic Advisors, 'if you like to travel around the country and read speeches written by the staff.'"

The Free Press • 2001 • 355 pp • hardcover • $27.50 • ISBN 0-684-84740-X

Nickel and Dimed: On (Not) Getting by in America, by Barbara Ehrenreich

In this unexpected bestseller, lefty writer Barbara Ehrenreich volunteered for wageslavery to see how millions of people (an estimated near-30 percent of the workforce) can make it on minimum wage. Short answer: They can't. Medium answer: After doing time as a waitress, a hotel maid, a Wal-Mart "associate," and three similar jobs, she couldn't make ends meet, the main killer being rent. Only by working an extra part-time job, a seven-day week, or an eleven-hour-per-day job could she have eked out a minimal living. Long answer: Read this witty book (which is obviously aimed at the middle and upper classes—who are primarily unaware of the situation—not the people who have to live this shit every day).

Quote: "My first task is to find a place to live. I figure that if I can earn $7 an hour—which, from the want ads, seems doable—I can afford to spend $500 on rent or maybe, with severe economies, $600 and still have $400 or $500 left over for food and gas. In the Key West [Florida] area, this pretty much confines me to flophouses and trailer homes—like the one, a pleasing fifteen-minute drive from town, that has no air conditioning, no screens, no fans, no television, and, by way of diversion, only the challenge of evading the landlord's Doberman pinscher. The big problem with this place, though, is the rent, which at $675 a month is well beyond my reach. All right, Key West is expensive. But so is New York City, or the Bay Area, or Jackson, Wyoming, or Telluride, or Boston, or any other place where tourists and the wealthy compete for living space with the people who clean their toilets and fry their hash browns. Still, it is a shock to realize that 'trailer trash' has become, for me, a demographic category to aspire to." [p 12]

Metropolitan Books (Henry Holt and Co.) • 2001 • 221 pp • softcover • $13 • ISBN 0-805063897

Rats in the Grain: The Dirty Tricks and Trials of Archer Daniels Midland, by James B. Lieber

A detailed exposé of the price-fixing, bribery, corporate espionage, and other shenanigans at Archer Daniels Midland—maker of food (especially grains), vitamins, pesticides, ethanol, and much more—that led to the biggest corporate crime trial of the 1990s. The Fortune 50 corporation was fined $100 million, and, astonishingly, two high-level executives went to the slammer (the whistleblower himself got a much longer sentence, though). James Lieber also examines past misdeeds that "The Supermarket to the World" got away with because of its extensive political connections.

Quote: "[ADM chairman and CEO Dwayne] Andreas' role in Watergate came up again in 1996, when a deposition transcript from President Nixon's secretary, the late Rosemary Woods, was released. In it, she recalled during a 1972 visit to the White House, Andreas left an envelope containing $100,000 in cash." [p 89]

Four Walls Eight Windows • 2000 • 436 pp • softcover • $16.95 • ISBN 1-56858-218-8

Fast Food Nation: The Dark Side of the American Meal, by Eric Schlosser

In this sleeper hit, investigative reporter Eric Schlosser peels back the bun and looks at the gross meat of the fast food industry—teenage wageslaves, injured meatpackers, clogged arteries, obesity, cruelty to animals, contaminated food, flavor additives, lobbying, unfair labor practices, marketing in public schools, and global conquest (there's a McDonald's one-third of a mile from the Dachau concentration camp).

Quote: "The most common workplace injuries at fast food restaurants are slips, falls, strains, and burns. The fast food industry's expansion, however, coincided with a rising incidence of workplace violence in the United States. Roughly four or five fast food workers are now murdered on the job every month, usually during the course of a robbery. Although most fast food robberies end without bloodshed, the level of violent crime in the industry is surprisingly high. In 1998, more restaurant workers were murdered on the job in the United States than police officers.... The restaurant industry has continued to fight not only guidelines on workplace violence, but any enforcement of OSHA regulations [concerning workplace violence]." [p 83]

HarperCollins • 2001 • 384 pp • softcover • $13.95 • ISBN 0060938455

Cigarettes: Anatomy of an Industry From Seed to Smoke, by Tara Parker-Pope

Wall Street Journal reporter Tara Parker-Pope's witty little book unrolls every aspect of the $300-billion-per-year ciggy industry—the history of smoking, the growing of tobacco, the making of cigarettes, the financial costs and benefits of the industry (the US government collects $15.5 billion every year in tobacco taxes, and twelve percent of the Chinese government's annual revenue comes from its monopoly on cigarette *sales*, never mind the taxes), the big five tobacco corporations, targeting poor countries, targeting children, sneaky marketing and advertising, dangers to tobacco workers,

nicotine addiction, litigation, public health, "safe" cigarettes, anti-smoking crusades, and more. Although it's not intended as an exposé, just telling the truth about the tobacco industry means that it's an eye-opener.

Quote: "It costs surprisingly little to create that slender white stick of shredded tobacco leaves—just 18 cents a pack, including leaf, labor, packaging, and transportation. Throw in overhead costs, such as the manufacturing plant and equipment, as well as advertising and promotional discounts and even litigation expenses (including billions of dollars in recent industry settlements in the United States) and cigarette makers still enjoy underlying profit margins of 40 to 50 percent. The cigarette business is more than twice as profitable as other large-scale consumer products businesses, which post underlying profits of ranging from 15 to 20 percent." [p 26]

The New Press • 2001 • 198 pp • small hardcover • $24.95 • ISBN 1-56584-503-X

_THE HIGH AND MIGHTY

The Trial of Henry Kissinger, by Christopher Hitchens

He exudes power and authority. He was National Security Advisor from 1969 to 1976 and Secretary of State from 1973 to 1976. He is directly responsible for the deaths of hundreds of thousands, perhaps millions, of people. At last, someone is calling Henry Kissinger on his record of barbarity. Bad-boy essayist and commentator Christopher Hitchens has assembled all the known evidence for Kissinger's war crimes and other violations of law (and human decency), distilling it into a book that can be read in a couple of sittings. To do so, he draws on declassified government documents, the writings of those involved (including Nixon and Kissinger himself), and new interviews.

In 1968, as a consultant to the State Department, Kissinger played the pivotal role in sabotaging the Vietnam peace talks so that Democrats couldn't claim to be the ones who ended the war. This led directly to Nixon's election and Kissinger's immediate appointment as National Security Advisor. In 1972, when Kissinger "negotiated" peace (and won the Nobel Prize for it), both sides agreed to the same terms they had been ready to accept four years prior. The blood of every American, Vietnamese, and other person who died in that conflict after 1968 is on Kissinger's hands.

Further chapters look at Kissinger's role in the slaughter of civilians in Vietnam, as well as the secret wars on Cambodia and Laos; his support of Pakistan's genocide in Bangladesh (he thanked Pakistan's leader, General Yahya Khan, for his "delicacy and tact" while the General was overseeing the butchering of 500,000 to 3 million civilians); his orchestration of the kidnap and assassination of General René Schneider of Chile, which was intended to destabilize the country and thwart a democratic election; his "collusion [in the Cyprus matter] in an assassination attempt on a foreign head of state, in a fascist military coup, in a serious violation of American law (the Foreign Assistance Act, which prohibits the use of military aid and *materiel* for non-defensive purposes), in two invasions which flouted international law, and in the murder and dispossession of many thousands of noncombatant civilians"; his advance knowledge of (and perhaps a more active role in) a plot to kidnap and probably kill a dissident Greek journalist in Washington, DC; and his thumbs-up for Indonesia to invade East Timor and slaughter hundreds of thousands of civilians (a charge which has subsequently been proven beyond all doubt by the release of an official memo; see "Kissinger Lied About East Timor" in Appendix A).

Hitchens closes with a look at the various legal mechanisms which might be used to bring Kissinger to trial for violations of international law, including war crimes. The most promising avenue seems to be the rising trend of "third-party" nations trying cases involving violations of international law when the plaintiff and defendant are from other countries. Indeed, since Hitch's book has been published— and possibly because of it—the heat has been turned up on Kissinger. Chile wants to question him about an American journalist who disappeared during that country's 1973 coup (in which Kissinger naturally had a hand). While Kissinger was in Paris in May 2001, a judge summoned him to answer questions about French citizens who had been "disappeared" in Chile. He immediately left the country. Perhaps one day justice will be served.

THE BLOOD OF EVERY AMERICAN, VIETNAMESE, AND OTHER PERSON WHO DIED IN THAT CONFLICT AFTER 1968 IS ON KISSINGER'S HANDS.

Quote: "The concept of 'deniability' was not as well understood in Washington in 1970 as it has since become. But it is clear that Henry Kissinger wanted two things simultaneously. He wanted the removal of General Schneider, by any means and employing any proxy. (No instruction from Washington to leave Schneider unharmed was ever given; deadly weapons were sent by diplomatic pouch, and men of violence were carefully selected to receive them.) And he wanted to be out of the picture in case such an attempt might fail, or be uncovered. These are the normal motives of anyone who solicits or suborns murder." [p 66]

Quote: "In most of his writings about himself (and, one presumes, in most of his presentations to his clients) Kissinger projects a strong impression of a man at home in the world and on top of his brief. But there are a number of occasions when it suits him to pose as a sort of Candide: naive, and ill-prepared for and easily unhorsed by events. No doubt this pose cost him something in point of self-esteem. It is a pose, furthermore, which he often adopts at precisely the time when the record shows him to be knowledgeable, and

when knowledge and foreknowledge would also confront him with charges of responsibility or complicity." [p 77]

Verso • 2001 • 162 pp • small hardcover • $22 • ISBN 1-85984-631-9

"Feeling Your Pain": The Explosion and Abuse of Government in the Clinton-Gore Years, by James Bovard

President Bush and Attorney General Ashcroft are doing their best to turn the US into a literal police state, using the 911 attacks as a great excuse (they were already trashing freedoms before September 11, however), but we shouldn't forget that their predecessors likewise treated the Constitution as a non-entity. James Bovard, one of the keenest and most unforgiving watchdogs of our rights, has written what is likely to be the definitive cataloging of the fascist tendencies of Clinton, Gore, Reno, and Company. He stays away from such well-trod areas as Whitewater, Chinagate, and Tailgate, instead revealing: "Many of the worst abuses of the Clinton administration never appeared on the media's radar screen. Instead, they were buried in Inspector General reports, General Accounting Office studies, or the proceedings of court cases followed by few."

Some chapters look at violations of civil liberties championed by (and increased by) Clinton: no-knock drug raids, "zero tolerance" idiocy that expels students for chewing breath mints, the dramatic expansion of law enforcement's power to search, seize, and surveil, naked hostility toward the Second Amendment, the Clipper Chip proposal to give the feds a back door into your telephone, the murders at Waco and Ruby Ridge, and the IRS's unchecked power to destroy lives. Bovard examines the fabrication of evidence at the FBI's crime lab, saturation bombing of Kosovo (and the resulting civilian casualties), Attorney General Reno's failure to appoint independent counsels to investigate a number of obvious crimes, the official hatchet job on Olympic park guard Richard Jewell, and the family members of high-ranking officials who were busted for drugs but got off scot-free when the rest of us would've gone straight to jail. Still other chapters look at the boondoggles of various federal agencies and programs—such as AmeriCorps, the Department of Housing and Urban Development, and the Federal Emergency Management Agency— while others look at the travesties wrought by often extreme application of affirmative action, trade barriers, environmental laws, farming regulations, and the Americans with Disabilities Act.

Bovard makes it clear that the Clinton Administration didn't invent abuse of power (in fact, many of its egregious policies were continuations of those started by Reagan and Bush Sr.), but it certainly did more than its part in escalating such abuses, as part of an ever-heightening trend being carried on by Bush Jr.

Quote: "From concocting new prerogatives to confiscate private property, to championing FBI agents' right to shoot innocent Americans, to bankrolling the militarization of local police forces, the Clinton administration stretched the power of government on all fronts. From the soaring number of wiretaps, to converting cell phones into homing devices for law enforcement, to turning bankers into spies against their customers, free speech and privacy were undermined again and again. From dictating how many pairs of Chinese silk panties Americans could buy, to President Clinton's heroic efforts to require trigger locks for all handguns in crack houses, no aspect of Americans' lives was too arcane for federal intervention." [p 2]

Quote: "The Clinton administration also argued, curiously, that seizing someone's property is less intrusive than searching their vehicle. The administration's brief asserted that 'the standard of reasonableness' that governs 'seizure of property that affects the owner's possessory interest' should be more lenient than the standard that governs a search 'which intrudes upon expectations of privacy.'" [p 141]

Quote: "Since taking office in January 1993, President Clinton has declared a 'major disaster' some place in the nation on average every week. Clinton has doled out more than $50 billion in disaster relief—far more than any previous president." [p 67]

Quote: "Clinton's perennial message was that people should trust political action far more than the voluntary efforts of individuals to improve their own lives. Clinton sought to continually remind people of the greatness of the State and the helplessness of the citizen." [p 342]

St. Martin's Press • 2000 • 426 pp • softcover • $16.95 • ISBN 0-31224052X

How to Survive the IRS: My Battles Against Goliath, by Michael Louis Minns

Defense attorney Michael Louis Minns is regarded as one of the best tax-case lawyers in the US. He has defended scores of clients from the IRS—almost all of them successfully. In his rare position as a "veteran of courtroom wars against the IRS," he has witnessed the tax agency in all its unbridled horror—incompetent, arrogant, vindictive, bullying, cruel, untruthful, and outright violent. *How to Survive the IRS* details ten of Minns' most important and terrifying cases, including "an IRS raid on a day care center where children were held hostage for money; a two-year-old who got to see her mom and grandma sprayed by lethal combat mace because IRS agents were trying to collect money; and a false-evidence scam to indict a businessman the IRS knew was innocent[;... and] another man who saw commercials the IRS ran telling people who had not filed, 'Come in and file and get amnesty.' This man came in, filed, and got indicted." It acts as a bill of indictment against the agency, while offering tips

on how each US citizen can best cope with the Federal Mafia. The last two sections of the book are the most directly practical, distilling Minns' hard-won advice into "One Hundred Tax Secrets" and "Not Quite Everything You Ever Wanted to Know About Write-offs, Deductions, Shelters, Trusts, Offshore Banking, Perpetual Travelers, Personal Privacy and the Future of Taxes."

Quote: "IRS agents lie, commit crimes, and destroy families.... You are getting the stories directly from the trial lawyer who handled them. None are secondhand. I've *seen with my own eyes* the blood, the privacy invasions (like seventy-year-old Mrs. Buford's pictures in her pajamas taken through an IRS pervert's spy lens), the cruel brutality, the injustices, and *heard with my own ears* the bald-face lies of IRS agents under oath. I've seen dreams, families, and retirement plans pulverized into dust while sadistic IRS agents laughed about it." [p xx]

> **"IRS AGENTS LIE, COMMIT CRIMES, AND DESTROY FAMILIES."**

Quote: "Today, many IRS agents are non-citizens who haven't yet mastered the fundamentals of English. Horror stories abound about collection agents who have trouble with basic math and fifth-grade grammar fundamentals." [p xiv]

Quote: "To say that the Proctor case was a gross miscarriage of justice would be an understatement akin to saying that the Grand Canyon was a hole in the ground. The IRS agent intruded on the attorney-client privilege, illegally withheld evidence to protect his snitch, and then deliberately ruined the Proctors' glass business by notifying their customers of alleged criminal improprieties. He did it simply because he had the power to do it." [p 284]

Quote: "You have the right to record any interview you give [to IRS agents]. In some states you can't do so without notifying the other party.... You have the right to remain silent if you are being criminally investigated or have a reasonable fear of criminal investigation.... It is common practice for the IRS to ask for more money than you owe and then bargain down unless you just agree to the inflated amount, which is also common, or just default, which is also common.... You do not have to go personally to an audit of your taxes.... IRS agents have posed as priests and lawyers.... The penalties for not filing are far worse than the penalties for not paying." [286-92]

Barricade Books • 2001 • 332 pp • hardcover • $29.95 • ISBN 1-56980-170-3

_TRUE TRUE CRIME

The Gates of Janus: Serial Killing and Its Analysis, by the "Moors Murderer" Ian Brady

Writings about serial killers are a dime a dozen. Writings *by* serial killers are considerably rarer, but there are a few out there. Writings about serial killers by a serial killer—well, there's only one of those:

The Gates of Janus. The author is Ian Brady, aka the Moors Murderer, who is known to have killed, tortured, and raped two teenagers, two twelve-year-olds, and a ten-year-old. Publishing a work by him is guaranteed to unleash furious debate and howls of protest. Indeed, the publication of this book in Britain—Brady's home country—was blocked by a court, though the decision was soon reversed. Defenders, such as the prolific criminologist and true-crime writer Colin Wilson (who penned the introduction and convinced Brady to write the book in the first place), stress that we can learn a lot about the criminal mind through such a book, especially since Brady spends most of it discussing the motives of eleven serial killers, some of whom he knew personally. (Well, technically ten serial killers; Brady believes Henry Lee Lucas committed just two murders.) The shorter part of the book is a meditation on the nature of crime, murder, serial murder, morality, and ethics.

Brady says next to nothing about his own crimes. At one point he writes: "For instance, I regard personal disloyalty as the worst crime of all, and have killed some guilty of it without a qualm." Since his known victims were children and teenagers snatched at random, this would indicate more murders. Or, it could be argued, it indicates he's lying in order to boost his body count. This unique and troubling tome is filled with such conundrums. In the end, it just may be more of a cipher than a book of answers.

Quote: "The fact is, many criminals know more about morality and ethics, via the process of opposition, than the conforming masses do from acceptance. I would even predicate that it is the criminal's astute understanding that the morality and ethics of the powerful is purely cosmetic, that persuades him to emulate their amoral plasticity....

"People are not so remorseful or ashamed of their criminal thoughts; they are more afraid of criminal thoughts being ascribed to them by others. To compensate, they rationalise their timidity or indolence as an indication of moral character, and their vociferous clamour for harsher punishment of criminals is mob retribution against a will to power they covertly envy. This envy is exacerbated by the media's colourful, exciting stories about criminals riotously enjoying every forbidden pleasure the 'decent citizen' can only dream about. Good and evil might therefore be presented simply as a matter of what we think we can get away with without sacrificing reputation." [p 36]

Quote: "A large, powerfully built man with an affable extrovert air, he [John Wayne Gacy] took an active part in local Democratic politics, raised funds for charity, and dressed himself as Pogo the Clown to entertain children in hospitals.

"There is no reason to suppose his charitable activities were not genuinely altruistic. Crime is no more a full-time profession than any other, and serial killers are no exception to the rule. I will raise this point again in future pages re: another prolific serial killer, Dean Corll, to further illustrate that criminals do have a spectrum of other natural talents and genuine interests outside of their law-breaking activities. The sensationalist media and law enforcement agencies, for political and social manipulation, would have the public believe otherwise, usually inferring that the innocent enthusiasms of the criminal were in fact spurious in some way." [p 119]

Feral House • 2001 • 311 pp • hardcover • $24.95 • ISBN 0-922915-73-3

Holy Homicide: An Encyclopedia of Those Who Go With Their God....and Kill!, by Michael Newton

Michael Newton is a one-man encyclopedia of crime knowledge, particularly in the area of murder and other violent acts. In *Holy Homicide*, he present a valuable reference work covering those who kill in the name of a god or gods. With 66 detailed entries, Newton hits the most important cases, since covering every case of divinely-inspired murder would be impossible. Some of the incidents involve individuals, while others look at murders that have taken place within the context of specific religious organizations and movements, including Aum Shinrikyo, the Christian Identity movement, the International Society for Krishna Consciousness, the Ku Klux Klan, the Nation of Islam, the People's Temple (Jim Jones), the Temple of Love (Yaweh ben Yaweh), etc. A few entries look at broad topics like biblical bloodshed, capital punishment, gay-bashing, and terrorism. One of the most valuable sections offers an annotated chronology of wars and conquests that were "fueled by religious hatred." It's a long list.

Quote from "Mormonism": "Modern Mormons avoid discussion of the [Mormon] Reformation whenever possible, dismissing a 'handful' of violent incidents as the work of individual fanatics, executed without official sanctions, but the truth is rather different. In fact, the Prophet's own remarks not only justified, but *demanded* execution of 'sinners,' albeit for their own good, and his call for Mormons to 'love' their neighbors by spilling their blood was published in the official LDS *Journal of Discourses* on the very day Young's Reformation was announced. One documented victim was Rosmo Anderson, condemned in 1857 for the 'crime' of adultery. Danite assassin John Lee—himself convicted and ultimately executed for mass murder—described how Anderson was seized by church elders in Cedar City, allowed to pray beside his open grave, before they cut his throat and held his body up to let the blood spill out....

"So busy were the Danite murder squads, in those days, that subsequent expansion of Salt Lake City provided no end of embarrassment for the church, construction crews constantly turning up skeletons from shallow graves in vacant lots. The 'Avenging Angels' were so flagrant and brutal, that their notoriety reached all the way to London, where Sir Arthur Conan Doyle used them as villains in his first recorded case of Sherlock Holmes..." [pp 177-8] Note: Danites were a secret group of Mormon "enforcers" who unquestioningly obeyed the leaders of the church.

EVERYTHING YOU KNOW IS WRONG

Loompanics Unlimited • 1998 • 284 pp • softcover • $16.95 • ISBN 1-55950-164-2

Black Collar Crimes: An Encyclopedia of False Prophets and Unholy Orders, by Michael Newton

In the companion volume to *Holy Homicide* (above), prolific crime chronicler Michael Newton expands his subject area, examining 250 individual clergy (and a few churches) who have committed all kinds of crimes—murder, assault, rape, child molestation, embezzlement, kidnapping, sedition, drunk driving, solicitation of prostitutes, etc., etc.

Quote: "A voyeur with an eye for the ladies, Rev. Jeffrey Horton of Oakland, Michigan, installed hidden video cameras in the Liberty Christian Center bathrooms, at his home, and in the home of a parishioner, so that he could watch various women using the toilets." [p 149]

Quote: "Kevin Connolly, 34-year-old ex-pastor of the MacArthur Park Lutheran Church in Tarrant County, Texas, was arrested in February 1997 on charges of molesting a 10-year-old girl. He was held in lieu of $50,000 bail, on one count of indecency with a child by sexual conduct. In custody, Connolly confessed to a court-appointed therapist that he had fondled between 20 and 50 other children, while exposing himself to many more. Connolly had already resigned his pulpit, in the spring of 1996, after exposing himself to a church member's child, but no criminal charges were filed in that case. According to one police spokesman, Sgt. Fred Pendergraf, Connolly's favorite trick was to pull up beside school buses, in his car, then expose himself and masturbate before a captive audience." [p 107]

Quote: "A Roman Catholic priest in Clearfield, Pennsylvania, 35-year-old Francis Bolek joined Rev. Bernard Kaczmarzyk in a six-year scam that swindled close to a million dollars from gullible contributors, ostensibly to purchase a shrine from the Pittsburgh diocese. In fact, as Bolek later admitted to authorities, he spent $340,000 of the ill-gotten cash on vacations to Hawaii and New Zealand, a winter home in Florida, plus entertainment, clothing, and gold jewelry." [p 5]

Loompanics Unlimited • 1998 • 265 pp • softcover • $18.95 • ISBN 1-55950-185-5

The Shadow Over Santa Susana: Black Magic, Mind Control and the "Manson Family" Mythos, by Adam Gorightly

A worthy addition to the Manson corpus, the encyclopedic *The Shadow Over Santa Susana* stands out in two respects. First, it offers a huge amount of info on Charles Manson and his followers, including a valuable appendix that catalogs every known Family member and his or her fate. Second, the book brings together some of the stranger strands in the whole affair, including mind control, Satanism, the Process Church, intelligence connections, drug gangs, Sirhan Sirhan (he and Manson were cell-neighbors in prison), and the theory that Manson was used as a patsy to discredit the counterculture.

Quote: "The concept of embracing Death became another 'power tool' Manson used to instill his will. One of his favorite games was to hand a knife to someone, and suggest that they kill him. When they refused—as, of course, they always did—Charlie would then say that he now had the right to kill them. Such tactics insured that his followers would always remain on edge, in the process becoming super-aware of everything around them, much like the coyotes of the desert that Charlie so greatly admired. Charlie had a word for this state of heightened awareness: *Coyotenoia*. It all revolved around fear. Fear—in the canon of Charlie's teachings—was the source of all awareness." [p 144]

iUniverse.com and the Konformist Kollective • 2001 • 582 pp • softcover • illus • $28.95 • ISBN 0-595-19936-4

Death in Paradise: An Illustrated History of the Los Angeles County Department of the Coroner, by Tony Richard and Brad Schreiber

By examining the Coroner's Office in L.A., *Death in Paradise* covers a large number of forgotten, bizarre, and unsolved crimes. Highlights (or, perhaps, lowlights) include the Chinese Massacre of 1871; Barbara La Marr, the first star to O.D. on narcotics; the unsolved Black Dahlia murder and a similar, less-known killing that took place almost a month later; the "strange circumstances" surrounding the alleged suicide of Superman George Reeves; the *L.A. Times* columnist whose head was shattered by a tear gas canister fired by a sheriff's deputy; Donald "Cinque" DeFreeze of the Symbionese Liberation Army; Richard "Nightstalker" Ramirez; Marilyn Monroe; the Manson murders; Karen Carpenter, who didn't die of bulimia, but of deteriorated heart muscle caused by the syrup she had used to induce vomiting; and Dr. Thomas Noguchi, "coroner to the stars." The text isn't too detailed, but the big draw is the heavy use of images, with loads of rare and unreleased photos of murder scenes and key documents. One caveat: Made with the cooperation of the L.A. Coroner's Office, this is something of an "official" book, so don't expect any dirt about the office itself.

Quote: "Did DeFreeze meet his end from a police bullet or his own? The coroner's team applied an electron microscope to glean trace metals from the death-inflicting bullet hole. In a report from the Forensic Science Center, while the conclusion did not categorically credit the police, the following phrase does lead to an answer: 'Note that in the decedent's GSW [gunshot wound] we found little evidence of primer residue. This observation...suggests that the lethal bullet was not discharged at contact distance.'" [pp 142-3]

Four Walls Eight Windows • 1998 • 192 pp • oversized softcover • heavily illustrated • $18 • ISBN 1-56858-205-6

Actual Innocence: Five Days to Execution, and Other Dispatches From the Wrongly Convicted, by Barry Scheck, Peter Neufeld, and Jim Dwyer

If you want to read a book that will shake your faith in the legal system, make sure it's *Actual Innocence*. In 1992, attorneys and professors Barry Scheck and Peter Neufeld started the Innocence Project at the Benjamin N. Cardozo School of Law <www.innocenceproject.org>. Using DNA evidence, they prove conclusively that some people in prison—even those on death row—did not commit the crimes of which they've been found guilty. As of the beginning of 2002, they had secured the release of 101 innocent people from the US gulag system.

In this book, they discuss ten of their cases, and it makes for infuriating reading. A woman is raped and catches only a fleeting glimpse of her attacker's profile as he climbs out a window. She later sees a neighbor, Walter Snyder, across the street and is positive he's the rapist. The police detective who interviews Snyder swears the man confessed repeatedly to the crime, yet there is no recording, not even any notes, of this interview. In court, the prosecutor displays Snyder's shorts inside out to make them appear solid red, because that's what the woman said her attacker was wearing. Yet when presented the right way, the shorts are red with white trim and lettering. Snyder is convicted and sentenced to 45 years in prison. Seven years later, a DNA test on the evidence proved that Snyder could not have been the rapist. But even then, it was an uphill battle. The state of Virginia gives people found guilty 21 days to prove their innocence. After that, no state court can grant a motion for release, even with incontrovertible evidence of innocence. Snyder appealed to the governor to free him, but the governor was afraid of appearing soft on crime. Only after the media in Richmond started covering the story did the governor free an innocent man.

The other cases are at least as noxious. They're rife with mistaken eyewitnesses, prosecutors who just want someone's head on a platter, incompetent defense attorneys, uncaring judges, jailhouse snitches who lie, bad laws, dishonest law enforcement, and crime lab workers who outright fabricate the results of tests that are used to send people to the execution chamber. In the midst of all this chicanery, the authors also explain—using real-world cases—why evidence such as eyewitness testimony, alleged confessions, and hair matching are unreliable. Besides their ten cases, they relate many other gross miscarriages of justice, such as the man who was sentenced to death based on a dog that sniffed the evidence five days after the crime, and the detective who destroyed his notes and recordings regarding a rape investigation before the appeals case (a "harmless error," the appellate court ruled).

Quote: "Some six thousand people have been sent to death row since 1976. As of this writing, eighty of them have been cleared through a variety of means, including DNA tests. 'Some people think that an error rate of one percent is acceptable for the death penalty,' notes Kevin Doyle, the capital defender for the state of New York. 'But if you went to the FAA and asked them to approve an airplane, and you said, oh, by the way, on every one hundredth landing, it causes or almost causes fatalities, people would say you were nuts.'" [p xvii]

> AS OF THE BEGINNING OF 2002, THEY HAD SECURED THE RELEASE OF 101 INNOCENT PEOPLE FROM THE US GULAG SYSTEM.

Quote: "A semen stain the size of a dime saved Kirk Bloodsworth; he owes his life to the depravity of a murderer. Suppose the killer of Dawn Hamilton had 'merely' murdered her, and not added sexual assault to his crime; there would have been no semen on Dawn's panties to find, no sperm cells barcoded with the murderer's DNA and not Kirk Noble Bloodsworth's. But for that, the state of Maryland, under authority granted it by the US Supreme Court, would have murdered an innocent man." [p 221]

Quote: "Beyond the vista of the wrongly convicted looms another phenomenon, barely noticed but of vast importance. Today, DNA tests are used before trial. Of the first eighteen thousand results at the FBI and other crime laboratories, at least five thousand prime suspects were excluded *before* their cases were tried. Overall, more than 25 percent of the prime suspects could not be implicated because many, if not most, were innocent. For this unseen legion of innocent suspects, only the genetic tests halted their forced march from wrongly accused to wrongly convicted. How many other innocent people, charged with crimes that involve no biological evidence, were chained and led at gunpoint into prison? Thousands, these tests suggest, far more than the most jaded jurists or cynical scholars ever envisioned." [p xv]

Doubleday • 2000 • 306 pp • hardcover • $24.95 • ISBN 0-385-49341-X

Police Unbound: Corruption, Abuse, and Heroism by the Boys in Blue, by Anthony V. Bouza

Retired after 36 years in law enforcement, Anthony V. Bouza was the commander of the Bronx police force and the chief of police in Minneapolis. Like retired police chief Joseph D. McNamara (see "When Cops Become the Gangsters"), Bouza is talking with unprecedented frankness about the profession he still loves. He has great respect for cops in general, many of whom go beyond the call of duty to help people and save lives. But he's also disturbed by the corruption in the ranks, plus the awkward position the police are put in. Specifically, he says that the mission that cops have been given is to keep the underclass at bay. This belief on its own isn't highly unusual, but hearing it from a toughened, pro-law enforcement ex-cop is downright revolutionary.

Like McNamara, Bouza also directly admits the existence of a code of silence among the police. Of course, everybody knows that this "blue wall of silence" exists, yet no cop has ever admitted it. To this day, officers will swear in court that there is no such code, yet we now have two ex-police chiefs who are publicly testifying to its reality. Bouza concurs with McNamara that this code of silence implicates all cops in the dirty doings of a minority of their comrades.

Bouza offers a sweeping look at policing, including merciless criticism of (as well as suggestions for improving) all that is wrong with law enforcement. He dives right into such hot-button topics as the War on Drugs, race, enforcing moral values, police spying, entrapment, the insanity defense, brutality, fudging crime statistics, the Amadou Diallo killing, corruption, internal politics, sweeps and round-ups, the media, police unions, guns, and capital punishment. *Police Unbound* is one of the most amazingly honest and insightful examinations of law enforcement we are ever likely to see from an insider.

Quote: "There is a clear, yet subliminal, message being transmitted that the cops, if they are to remain on the payroll, had better obey. The overclass—mostly white, well-off, educated, suburban, and voting—wants the underclass—frequently minority, homeless, jobless, uneducated, and excluded—controlled and, preferably, kept out of sight. Property rights are more sacred than human lives. And some lives are more precious than others." [p 13]

Quote: "It is kind of remarkable how cops take a callow youth and transform him into a compliant member of the cult.... Acculturation invariably starts with a slogan that rarely varies by a syllable, 'Forget about the bullshit they taught you at the academy, kid; this is the real world.'" [p 17]

Quote: "The Mafia never enforced its code of blood-sworn omerta with the ferocity, efficacy, and enthusiasm the police bring to the Blue Code of Silence." [p 18]

> "THE MAFIA NEVER ENFORCED ITS CODE OF BLOOD-SWORN OMERTA WITH THE FEROCITY, EFFICACY, AND ENTHUSIASM THE POLICE BRING TO THE BLUE CODE OF SILENCE."

Quote: "The reason seemingly sociopathic cops aren't filtered out is that too many are made, not born. It is the institution that not only shapes them but that affords tempting opportunities to pursue submerged predilections for violence and worse." [p 29]

Quote: "The idea of police as crime preventers is rubbish. By the time the cop appears the criminal has been formed and the crime has been committed." [p 40]

Quote: "Unquestionably, racism is endemic in the ranks." [p 62]

Quote: "I had, over the years, not only occasionally benefited from the protective cover-ups of my superiors, but participated in things that made me deeply ashamed and which, this not being the confessional, I have no interest in revealing the details of, even as I am compelled to acknowledge their existence." [p 113]

Quote: "I've always known that cops do beautiful things and policing is a line of work in which ennobling behavior is both likely and relatively common. No one could bear witness to these daily triumphs of courage over fear without deep feelings of admiration for its practitioners." [p 213]

Prometheus Books • 2001 • 303 pp • hardcover • $25 • ISBN 1-57392-877-1

_MIND AND BODY

Botanical Influences on Illness: A Sourcebook of Clinical Research (second edition), by Melvyn R. Werback, M.D., and Michael T. Murray, N.D.

I keep hearing the refrain, mainly from people who like to call themselves "skeptics," that there is not one bit of medical evidence supporting natural, alternative medical therapies. This is absolutely and unequivocally wrong. Anyone who says it is either 1) lying or 2) doesn't know his or her ass from a hole in the ground. In *You Are Being Lie To*, I reviewed *Alternative Medicine: What Works* by Adriane Fugh-Berman, M.D., which presented lots of evidence in a popular style for a general audience. Afterward, I cast around for a book with even more such information. I wanted lots of detail. It took a while, but I finally bumped into *Botanical Influences on Illness*, in which a doctor of medicine—who is also a professor at the UCLA medical school—and a doctor of nutrition present hundreds (probably well over a thousand) medical studies on natural substances and therapies. These studies come from a huge number of medical journals, including *Lancet*, *Pharmacopsychiatry*, *British Medical Journal*, *Cancer*, *AIDS*, *Journal of the Canadian Medical Association*, *European Journal of Surgical Oncology*, a bunch of German-language journals, and many others.

The book is organized by disease/disorder (e.g., cataract, depression, herpes, kidney stones, multiple sclerosis, pain, PMS, rheumatoid arthritis, and many others). The bulk of it gives the results of studies—ones that achieved significant results, as well as those that didn't—and is definitely written for professionals. Don't expect anything but hardcore statistics and results in 90 percent of the book. Some of its many findings follow:

Taking bilberry extract resulted in a statistically significant improvement in night vision, compared to a placebo, in 50 people. In 46 patients with myopia syndrome, bilberry and vitamin E prevented deterioration in all but one patient over a period of two years. Numerous double-blind studies have shown that ginger is significantly better at relieving nausea and vomiting than a placebo. In fact, it's been shown as effective as metoclopramide (Reglan), a prescription drug often used to fight nausea. Several double-blind studies demonstrated that licorice extract heals a statistically significant number of patients with ulcers, compared to placebo. It's been shown to be only slightly less effective than several prescription drugs used for the same purpose.

Garlic whups up on infections, killing large numbers of *Bacillus*, salmonella, staph, and strep bacteria in vitro. In a study of 34 people with athlete's foot (a fungal infection), 27 were *completely* cured after one week of applying ajoene cream (derived from garlic). The additional seven patients were completely cured by the end of the second week. An experimental double-blind crossover study on people with normal blood pressure found that garlic significantly decreased BP, compared to placebo. A meta-analysis of eight trials showed that garlic reduced BP by an average of 11 mm Hg systolic and 5 mm Hg diastolic (e.g., blood pressure of 120/90 would've gone down to 109/85).

> **SEVERAL DOUBLE-BLIND STUDIES DEMONSTRATED THAT LICORICE EXTRACT HEALS A STATISTICALLY SIGNIFICANT NUMBER OF PATIENTS WITH ULCERS, COMPARED TO PLACEBO.**

Several natural substances have done well in tests on cancer. In one study of women with breast cancer who were undergoing chemotherapy, half the patients were given a preparation of mistletoe, while half were given a placebo. After the fourth round of chemo, those getting mistletoe had three times as many white blood cells as the control group (3,000 count vs. 1,000 count). The *Journal of the National Cancer Institute* reported that polyphenals from green tea induced cell death in carcinoma cells in vitro. An extract of green algae showed a "pronounced antitumor effect" in mice. Coumarin, found in several plants used as folk remedies for cancer, prevented the recurrence of melanoma in a significant number of patients, compared to placebo.

Extract of the herb known as black cohosh has achieved amazing results in relieving the symptoms of menopause. In a double-blind study in Germany, the average number of hot flashes for each patient dropped from five per day to less than one per day for the women taking cohosh, but only to 3.5 for those receiving estrogen. Also, while estrogen and placebo didn't do anything for vaginal lining, the cohosh produced "a dramatic increase in the number of superficial cells." In an open study involving 629 patients, cohosh produced "clear improvement of menopausal symptoms in over 80%" of the patients. It completely eliminated heart palpitations and

ringing in the ears for over 54 percent of the patients, and lessened those problems in an additional 35.2 percent and 38.1 percent (respectively), for a success rate of over 90 percent each.

Quote: "The chemistry, pharmacology and clinical applications of Echinacea has [*sic*] been the subject of over 350 scientific studies. Echinacea possesses a broad-spectrum of effects on the immune system as a result of its content of a broad range of active components affecting different aspects of immune function... Numerous clinical studies have confirmed Echinacea's immune enhancing actions. Various Echinacea extracts or products have shown results in general infectious conditions, influenza, colds, upper respiratory tract infections, urogenital infections, and other infectious conditions." [p 381]

Quote: "Ginkgo biloba extract (GBE) may be the most important plant-derived medicine available. It offers significant benefit to many elderly people with impaired blood flow to the brain or cerebral insufficiency.... GBE has been extensively studied and appears to work primarily by increasing blood flow to the brain, resulting in an increase in oxygen and glucose utilization. However, this explanation is quite simplistic as GBE exerts profound, widespread tissue effects including membrane stabilizing, antioxidant and free radical scavenging effects... GBE has been confirmed by more than 50 double-blind studies to be effective against cerebral, as well as peripheral arterial, insufficiency. GBE may offer significant protective action against the development of Alzheimer's disease, hearing loss, and strokes." [p 23]

Third Line Press • 2000 • 622 pp • oversized, library-quality hardcover • $59.95[1] • ISBN 1-891710-00-1

Nutritional Influences on Mental Illness: A Sourcebook of Clinical Research (second edition), by Melvyn R. Werbach, M.D.
In this companion to *Botanical Influences on Illness* (above), Dr. Melvyn Werbach takes much the same approach: He scours medical journals worldwide and relays the results of hundreds of trials, experiments, meta-analyses, observational studies, etc. involving the effects of nutrients. There are three main differences, though. This time 1) the focus is on various problems defined as mental illness (alcoholism, ADHD, depression, eating disorders, obsessive compulsive disorder, schizophrenia, etc.); 2) no herbs are covered (only vitamins, minerals, amino acids, etc.); and 3) besides examining nutrients that have a positive effect, Werbach also looks at the evidence that some substances contribute to the disorders, whether through shortage, overabundance, or presence at any level. For example, a 1994 double-blind study in the *Journal of Pediatrics* found that an artificial coloring, yellow dye #5, increased behavior disorders in 19 of 23 hyperactive kids but only in two of 20 non-hyper kids.

After being injected with glucose (a sugar), a group of bulimic women experienced a surge in their urge to binge. Non-bulimics in the same study who were injected with glucose experienced *less* desire to eat sweets. Also, five minutes after getting the sugar shot, the bulimics experienced a jump in their levels of depression, fatigue, etc., while bulimics injected with a placebo solution did not.

In another double-blind study, L-Tryptophan was given to 24 manic patients for a week. During this time, "there was a clinically and statistically significant reduction in manic symptom scores." During the second week, half the patients were switched to a placebo, while the others kept taking Trypto. Only the placebo patients showed an increase in their manic scores.

Twenty-six juvenile delinquents were divided into two groups—one received a vitamin and mineral supplement, while the other got a placebo. After thirteen weeks, five of the kids receiving nutrients, but only one on placebo, showed a huge difference in their IQ scores—an average increase of *20* points. All of the five in the test group who improved had started out with below normal concentrations of nutrients in their blood.

Quote: "In a study of 24 pairs of male siblings aged 8-18 with one of each pair delinquent and violent, hair from the violent boys, but not the normal boys, was high in calcium compared to previous norms[.]" [p 9]

Quote: "Depressed pts. [patients] were found to have 4.5 times as many antibody reactions to 21 foods and 12 inhalants as normal controls.... 100% of the depressives were allergic to egg white, the most frequently positive single allergen. Results suggest that removing egg white, milk and cereal grains from the diet would be an inexpensive way to initiate treatment for depressives." [p 271]

Third Line Press • 1999 • 459 pp • oversized, library-quality hardcover • $59.95² • ISBN 0-9618550-8-8

Plague Time: The New Germ Theory of Disease, by Paul W. Ewald

When we think of infectious diseases, we tend to think of the flu, malaria, Ebola—acute, quick-impacting conditions that you either recover from or die from fairly quickly. On the other hand, we typically believe that cancer and diseases of the heart are caused by conditions such as bad diet, pollutants, and stress. But according to Amherst College biologist Paul W. Ewald, we should be looking for the germs that cause these chronic, often terminal ailments and many others.

While this seems far-fetched at first, Ewald notes that we already

recognize a whole set of chronic, germ-caused conditions—sexually-transmitted diseases. STDs are caused by viruses, bacteria, and other beasties, yet, left untreated, they'll infect a person for a lifetime, sometimes cutting that lifetime short. These are long, lingering diseases, not the quick, punch-in-the-gut type we normally associate with germs (although some STDs, such as herpes, do have acute phases).

Even more important, science has already officially recognized that germs cause disorders long thought to result from other causes (although this fact hasn't made it to public consciousness yet). Ulcers are now known to be the result of a bacterium (*Heliobacter pylori*), not excess stomach acid caused by stress (although this will aggravate the hell out of an ulcer). Adult T-cell leukemia is usually caused by a retrovirus (HTLV) from breast milk (sometimes it is transmitted sexually). Chlamydia can cause infertility and, less well known, even arthritis.

Venturing much deeper into territory currently being charted, Ewald examines the persuasive evidence that breast cancer, Alzheimer's, schizophrenia, bipolar disorder (manic-depression), heart disease, atherosclerosis, sickle cell anemia, and other diseases and disorders are in reality caused by microorganisms. He also looks at why the infectious causation theory of chronic diseases has met so much resistance, and how this resistance is fading. He believes we're at the verge of a paradigm shift in medicine.

Quote: "During the first three decades of the germ theory, about 1880 to 1910, the scope of acute infectious diseases was quickly resolved. Chronic diseases that were the most easily linked to their acute beginnings were broadly accepted during this period as different manifestations of the specific infectious processes. During the first half of the twentieth century, medical researchers confirmed that infections caused various chronic diseases that appeared as delayed consequences of acute diseases with entirely different symptoms.... After about half a century of observation, experimentation, and debate about rheumatic fever, it was finally accepted during the 1940s as a delayed, often chronic manifestation of previous infection with Streptococcus pyogenes, the primary agent of strep throat. By the middle of the twentieth century medical science was poised to move into an even more cryptic realm of the spectrum of infectious disease—those chronic diseases that were caused by infections that did not generate obvious acute phases. Then medical science dropped the ball." [pp 49-50]

Quote: "Consider breast cancer. Infectious causation has been virtually ignored by most experts on breast cancer despite the infectious causation of mammary tumors that is the rule rather than the exception among other mammals. Two research groups have recently found evidence of retroviruses in [human] breast tumors but not in surrounding healthy tissue." [p 105]

Quote: "I go on to mention the less widely recognized damage from venereal diseases, such as T-cell leukemia, paralysis, infertility due to oviduct scarring, ectopic pregnancies, cervical cancer, liver cancer, Kaposi's sarcoma, and pelvic inflammatory disease. I also mention the high probability that there are many more chronic diseases that may be caused by sexually transmitted pathogens but for which there is presently insufficient information to label them sexually transmitted diseases. In this category are endometriosis, miscarriages, chromosomal damage of fetuses, low sperm counts, and penile cancer." [pp 206-7]

Anchor Books • 2000 • 282 pp • softcover • $13 • ISBN 0-385721846

The Antidepressant Fact Book: What Your Doctor Won't Tell You About Prozac, Zoloft, Paxil, Celexa and Luvox, by Peter R. Breggin, M.D.

Dr. Peter Breggin has been writing about the dark side of psychiatric drugs for quite a while, and in this book he synthesizes and condenses his vast knowledge into a relatively short look at all that is wrong with antidepressants. Two things give Breggin a perspective you're not likely to find elsewhere. First, he's been practicing psychiatry for over 30 years, so he has street-level knowledge of the effects of psychiatric drugs. Second, he has been an expert witness in many trials involving antidepressants, and this has given him unprecedented access to internal documents from the drug companies. By combining his professional experience and unique access to information with publicly available (but generally ignored) data—FDA reports, medical studies in peer-reviewed journals, and even drug warning labels—he offers a frightening look at some popular drugs (with US sales in the billions of dollars annually).

The focus is mainly on the selective serotonin reuptake inhibitor (SSRI) class of antidepressants (which includes Prozac, Paxil,[3] and Zoloft), with some coverage of other fairly new drugs such as Wellbutrin (aka Zyban) and Remeron. Breggin looks at the damage to the brain and body caused by antidepressants, their stimulant effects, and their ties to suicide, violence, criminal behavior, and the worsening of depression. Other chapters look at the dangers to children, withdrawal effects, the skullduggery of drug firms (including fixing a trial), overcoming depression with non-drug methods, and other forms of brain-damaging psychiatry (lobotomies and electroshock). One of many very telling chapters reveals that clinical trials show 1) the SSRIs are only as effective or less effective than older types of antidepressants and 2) the SSRIs perform only moderately better than placebos. If you want one book that concisely lays out the case against antidepressants, this is the one you need.

Quote: "The German label for Prozac warns that patients should be given tranquilizers early in their treatment to counteract stimulation and to prevent suicide." There is no such warning on the US label. [p 56]

Quote: "In Great Britain, an editorial in the world's most prestigious medical journal, Lancet, warned that SSRIs were associated with 'the promotion of suicidal thoughts and behavior,' and more recently the British regulatory agency put a suicide warning on the label of Prozac." [p 80]

Quote: "Eli Lilly and Co.'s own internal review found that the suicide attempt rate was indeed much higher for patients taking Prozac than for patients receiving the sugar pill or Elavil [an older, non-SSRI antidepressant]. In fact, [the] suicide attempt rate was six times higher on Prozac than on placebo or Elavil.... When the company later defended itself before an FDA committee investigating Prozac and suicide, Eli Lilly and Co. continued to withhold the existence of its own damning study. I came upon the study while reviewing materials for discovery purposes as the medical and scientific expert in the initial series of lawsuits against the drug company." [pp 84-5]

"THE GERMAN LABEL FOR PROZAC WARNS THAT PATIENTS SHOULD BE GIVEN TRANQUILIZERS EARLY IN THEIR TREATMENT TO COUNTERACT STIMULATION AND TO PREVENT SUICIDE."

Quote: "As I went through the cartons of material tracking the development of the label [for Prozac], I found a photocopy of the label as it was edited on the day that Prozac was finally approved for marketing. At the last minute, a high-ranking FDA official edited the entire label and drew a line through items he personally deemed unnecessary. Without explaining why he was deleting something as important as 'depression' as a common adverse effect, he simply drew a line through it." [p 90] This, despite the fact that Eli Lilly's own researchers had found worsening of depression to be one of the most common side effects of Prozac.

Quote: "Mania in response to Luvox occurred in a whopping 4 percent of depressed youngsters (ages eight-seventeen) during the FDA trials, whereas it never occurred in the control group of similar young patients who were administered placebo." [p 50]

Quote: "I found estimates by drug advocates that Prozac had been tested on 10,000 people before it was approved. I then went to a great deal of trouble to count the total number of patients who finished the controlled clinical trials for the FDA approval of Prozac. The total turned out to be 286 patients—a far cry from the thousands that most people imagine." [p 148]

Perseus Publishing • 2001 • 228 pp • softcover • $13 • ISBN 0-7382-0451-X

Still Doing It: Women and Men Over 60 Write About Their Sexuality, edited by Joani Blank

One of the many, many myths about sex is that old people don't engage in it and aren't even interested. Various studies have found this to be untrue. A survey from the American Association of Retired Persons found that over 25 percent of Americans over 75 have sex at least once a week. Two-thirds of people over 60 told pollsters for the *Minneapolis Star Tribune* that their sex lives are at least as good, even better, compared to when they were in their forties. Pioneering sex educator Joani Blank now provides further proof with *Still Doing It*, a collection of 34 essays in which people over 60 talk about getting it on in the golden years. The contributors are male, female, and transgendered, gay, straight, and bi; a few are in their 80s and 90s. Most aren't professional writers, so you shouldn't read the book for its literary qualities. Instead, read it for the insights and inspiration (not to mention the sex tips) that it provides.

Quote from "Senior Games" by Tony Aiello: "We sometimes take advantage of society's prejudice that people over sixty just don't do it anymore by playing a game in a public setting, usually at a restaurant. No one is aware that we two old and gray codgers are engaged in sexual play, and to the others in the room it looks as if we're having our ordinary, boring senior conversation. Meanwhile, I am masturbating her to climax.

"She is nude beneath her clothes—no underwear of any kind. Shortly after we arrive at the restaurant, she goes to the ladies room and inserts a vibrating egg into her pussy and returns to our table. I'm handed the remote control under the table so that I can control the frequency, intensity and duration of the vibrations without anyone seeing or being aware of what I'm doing (at least I hope they're not).... Eventually she gets to a point where just a slight amount of vibration on her clit will do the job and it's up to me to decide when that happens." [pp 37-8]

> **"NO ONE IS AWARE THAT WE TWO OLD AND GRAY CODGERS ARE ENGAGED IN SEXUAL PLAY."**

Quote from "Getting Better All the Time" by Andrea Anderson: "This summer I will be celebrating my seventy-fifth birthday. My partner is seventeen years younger than I, which has presented no problems. Viagra is not for us in the foreseeable future!" [p 102]

Quote from "Clean Old Man" by Steve McDonald: "What is this idea that you have to stop having sex when you reach a certain age? It can be even more fun when your arthritis acts up. Wow, it took us two hours to get all of our clothes off! Or, we had to do it twice when we couldn't get out of the tub....

"When I die I will be cremated and my ashes will be put on top of [my deceased partner] George's in a California military cemetery. Although it might shock people, I sometimes say, 'I will be on top of George, even in death.'" [pp 157-8]

Down There Press • 2000 • 209 pp • softcover • $12.50 • ISBN 0-940208-27-X

The Seven Myths of Gun Control: Reclaiming the Truth About Guns, Crime, and the Second Amendment, by Richard Poe

In an easily readable style, conservative journalist and editor Richard Poe dismantles seven of the biggest myths about guns and crime. He spends the most time on one of the biggest fallacies, that access to guns increases violent crime. We know this is false in several ways, one of which being that the nation that has the highest rate of gun ownership (including handguns and machine guns)—Switzerland—has an extraordinarily low crime rate. Another piece of evidence is the fact that, after Australia essentially banned guns in 1996, the amount of violent crime in that country shot up, since criminals no longer had to worry that their victims might be packing heat. An analysis of crime statistics from around the US shows "that violent crime dropped by 4 percent for each 1 percent increase in gun ownership." States that start allowing concealed carrying of guns witness a 10 percent drop in the murder rate, on average.

Poe also takes on the idea that the Second Amendment only applies to members of formal, government-created militias, such as the National Guard, not to ordinary citizens. This belief is absurd on its face: Why in the world would the Founders have wasted an amendment in the Bill of Rights to say that members of the armed forces are allowed to be armed? When in the history of the world has a nation's army not been allowed to have weapons? Every other amendment in the Bill applies to the rights of each individual citizen, yet this one doesn't? Looking at the writings of the Founders as they discussed and debated the Second Amendment makes it clear that the right to bear arms applies to the general citizenry. Poe also notes that the Harvard professor Laurence Tribe—widely considered that greatest living scholar on the US Constitution—fully supports the notion that the Second Amendment gives everyone the right to own guns.

In other chapters, Poe makes mincemeat of the myths that pulling a gun on a criminal is more dangerous to the person pulling the gun, that guns pose a special threat to children, that "the Second Amendment is an obsolete relic of the frontier era," that gun users should be licensed, and that "reasonable gun-control measures are no threat to law-abiding gun owners." Poe doesn't break any new ground in *Seven Myths*, but the book serves its purpose well by presenting convincing, easy-to-digest (though meandering) arguments for the right to bear arms.

Quote: "Criminals in America are keenly aware that about half of all homes contain firearms. Consequently, they treat occupied houses with respect. Hot burglaries—in which the criminal enters while people are home—account for only 13 percent of all burglaries. But in countries with strict gun control, such as England and Canada, criminals know that their victims are unarmed. They enter houses at will, without worrying whether anyone is home. The hot burglary rate in those countries is nearly 50 percent." [p 87]

Quote: "[N]o matter how many officers you hire, there are built-in limits to what the police can and will do for you. Police have no legal or constitutional obligation to guard or protect you from harm. Their only obligation is to enforce the law—which generally means to arrest criminals after they have committed a crime. The right of police to stand by and do nothing while citizens are attacked and even killed has been upheld many times in court." [p 155]

Quote: "As recently as 1959, the belief that armed citizens provided the ultimate check against tyranny was so widely accepted in America that even a liberal Democrat such as then-Senator Hubert Humphrey could say, without fear of criticism, 'The right of citizens to bear arms is just one more guarantee against arbitrary government, one more safeguard against the tyranny which now appears remote in America, but which historically has proved to be always possible.'" [p 163]

Forum (Prima Publishing) • 2001 • 298 pp • hardcover • $23.95 • ISBN 0-7615-2558-0

_NOT ON THE NIGHTLY NEWS

Extreme Islam: Anti-American Propaganda of Muslim Fundamentalism, edited by Adam Parfrey
While the US was snoozing, fundamentalist Islam has been calling in no uncertain terms for the destruction of all enemies (which pretty much means anybody who isn't a Muslim fundamentalist). It's hard to believe that even after the 911 attacks, it's politically incorrect to say anything bad about any aspect of Islam. Adam Parfrey—the force behind Feral House, one of the very few truly untamed publishers—has found a way around this: He simply lets radical Islam speak for itself. Using primary documents, such as essays, *fatwas*, interviews, political cartoons, and poems—many of which have never before appeared in English and haven't been seen by Western eyes—he shows us what this violent movement is really saying.

Inside this unprecedented collection you'll find a paean to martyrs, writings by Muslim Brotherhood founder Hassan al-Banna Shaheed (executed by Egypt for his militancy), a diatribe from Anwar Sadat's anti-Western book *Story of Arab Unity* (1957), an interview with the founder of Hamas, "You Have Made Me Your Human Bomb," "Killing Infidels in Chechnya: A Foreign Mujahid's Diary," a speech by Ayatollah Khomeini, and excerpts from a *Jihad* manual on torture and making poisons.

To be fair, Parfrey includes texts that make intelligent points about Israel's brutal treatment of Palestinians. Likewise, there are articles from Muslims who are radical but not necessarily part of the *Jihad*-oriented fundamentalist movement: Saddam Hussein, Moammar Kadaffi, the Nation of Islam, *et al*. Some of the most revealing material comes from fundamentalist Jewish and Christian movements who are anxious to see the destruction of the mosque on the Temple Mount in Jerusalem (this is supposed to partially trigger the Apocalypse). Proving that this is a multifaceted collection, there are also articles that shed light on the hidden history of Israel (especially its founding) and the strange ties between extreme Islam and Nazism.

Among the other entries in this textbook for fundamentalist Islam 101:

• A (too) brief excerpt from *The Neglected Duty*, written by the mouthpiece of Jama At al-Jihad (Society of Struggle), the group that assassinated Anwar Sadat. This book directly inspired Osama bin Laden, who cribbed portions of it for his own writings.

• Osama Bin Laden's infamous 1998 *fatwa*, in which he urges all Muslims to "kill the Americans and their allies—civilians and military..."

• A transcript of an interview with Mullah Omar Mohammad, leader of the Taliban, conducted by the government-funded radio station Voice of America. Due to pressure from high-ranking US officials, the interview was never broadcast.

• A transcript of the bizarre press conference in which Hon. Louis Farrakhan, head of the Nation of Islam, talked about being taken aboard a UFO. ("I was told to relax and a beam of light came from the Wheel and I was carried up on this beam of light into the Wheel.")

• Eight pages of illustrations reproduced in color. Images include anti-US graffiti in Tehran, postage stamps celebrating the Intifada, and a painting of a hand strangling a red, white, and blue snake.

Quote in the Hamas weekly Al-Risala: "Oh Anthrax, despite your wretchedness, you have sown horror in the heart of the lady of arrogance, of tyranny, of boastfulness! Your gentle touch has made the US's life rough and pointless...." [p 133]

Quote: "[According to Mishkat, Volume Three:] Every man who enters paradise shall be given 72 houris; no matter at what age he died, when he is admitted into paradise, he will become a 30-year-old, and shall not age any further." [p 17] The physical description of the comely, virginal houris ("a most beautiful woman with a transparent body") makes for interesting reading.

Quote from "I Am With Terrorism":
"I am with terrorism
if it is able to free a people
from tyrants and tyranny
if it is able to save man from the cruelty of man
to return lemon, olive tree, and bird to the South of Lebanon
and the smile back to Golan"
[p 162]

"OH'ANTHRAX, DESPITE YOUR WRETCHEDNESS, YOU HAVE SOWN HORROR IN THE HEART OF THE LADY OF ARROGANCE, OF TYRANNY, OF BOASTFULNESS!"

Quote from "Jihad, Mankind's Only Hope" by Abdul Malik: "In the aftermath of the attacks on the World Trade Center, George Bush declared, 'Islam is peace.' The concept of jihad came under scrutiny and a number of apologists were wheeled out to tell the West what they wanted to hear. One of these media darlings, who was given '100% security clearance' by the FBI and now advises the White House, declared: 'The Prophet said the greatest jihad is the struggle of a man against his own evil influences.' ... In fact, the Shari'ah meaning of jihad is to exert one's utmost effort in fighting the disbelievers for the sake of Allah (SWT), directly by fighting in the battlefield or indirectly by helping this struggle by monetary means, scholarly verdicts, and encouraging people to participate in the jihad." [pp 226-7]

Feral House • 2002 • 321 pp • softcover • illustrated • $16 • ISBN 0-922915-78-4

A People Betrayed: The Role of the West in Rwanda's Genocide, by L.R. Melvern

From April through July 1994, genocide occurred in the African nation of Rwanda. Extremist Hutus massacred a million Tutsis and moderate Hutus, a rate five times that of the Nazis. Not only were people shot and blown up, many were hacked to death with machetes and axes. No one was spared—not pregnant women, not newborn babies. A member of Doctors Without Borders told of rescuing an eleven-year-old boy and his nine-year-old sister from a gang of Hutus, who were laughing at them and spitting on them. By that time, both children had already been raped, and their father's severed penis had been stuffed into the girl's mouth.

Investigative journalist Linda Melvern, formerly a reporter with the *Sunday Times* of London, spent years figuring out what happened, interviewing hundreds of people, prying official documents loose from the authorities' hands. She found that many countries turned a blind eye to the genocide, while others actively abetted it. The Clinton Administration has claimed it didn't know what was happening until it was too late. As the documents prove, the US knew almost from the beginning. James Woods, who was then Deputy Assistant Secretary of Defense, admitted that the US knew by the second week that genocide was being perpetrated.

Leaked minutes from the Security Council of the UN—the organization set up specifically to prevent genocide—demonstrate how that august body sat on its hands. The UN brigadier-general in charge of the peacekeeping forces in Rwanda had immediately drawn up a plan to airlift troops into the capital city of Kigali, but America fought the plan, causing no action to be taken during May. Boutros Boutros-Ghali, then Secretary-General of the UN, told US Ambassador Madeline Albright about what was happening in Rwanda, but she told him the US wasn't going to do anything because that would put America in an awkward position. Despite the excuse that no troops were available, at least six African countries volunteered military forces to restore order in Rwanda, but the UN—following instructions from its richest members—refused to fund them.

Melvern digs up further proof that Rwanda prepared for the slaughter by buying millions of dollars' worth of weapons with money from the World Bank, and that the Bank knew this; that France, China, Egypt, and South Africa armed the mass murderers; that France helped evacuate Hutu extremists after the genocide had begun; and that two years before the killing commenced, Belgium's ambassador to Rwanda warned of a secret plot to wipe out the Tutsi and moderate Hutu.

As with the Nazi Holocaust, the US and the UK (among other countries) try to play the "we didn't know" card, and once again we see that it isn't true. This book has the proof.

Quote: "The stories of betrayal, of insensate cruelty, of human suffering, are reminiscent of stories of Treblinka or Babi Yar. But, unlike the Holocaust, far from trying to conceal what was happening, the killing took place in broad daylight. The incitement to genocide was broadcast via a radio station and the people were psychologically prepared for months, and were ordered and coerced to carry out the extermination. In Rwanda, the perpetrators and organizers of genocide were secure in the knowledge that outside interference would be at a minimum." [p 4]

Quote: "My force was standing knee-deep in mutilated bodies, surrounded by the guttural moans of dying people, looking into the eyes of children bleeding to death with their wounds burning in the sun and being invaded by maggots and flies. I found myself walking through villages where the only sign of life was a goat, or a chicken, or song-bird, as all the people were dead, their bodies being eaten by voracious packs of wild dogs." [pp 174-5]

Quote: "The Rwandan genocide should be the defining scandal of the presidency of Bill Clinton. Rwanda had been an issue requiring leadership and responsibility, as Senator Paul Simon had reminded Clinton in his letter of 13 May 1994. But the administration took the easy option and failed to push the moral boundaries; there were no votes to be gained advocating help for another collapsed African state. Africa was less important since the end of the Cold War. The recent example of Somalia had shown the risks of intervention. For three months the Clinton administration played down the crisis and tried to impede effective intervention by UN forces. The secretary of state, Warren Christopher, avoided the issue altogether." [p 229]

Zed Books • 2000 • 277 pp • softcover • £16.95, $19.95 • ISBN 1-85649-831-X

Why Our Drug Laws Have Failed and What We Can Do About It: A Judicial Indictment of the War on Drugs, by Judge James P. Gray

It appears that James P. Gray—a judge of the Superior Court in Orange County, California, and a former federal prosecutor in L.A.—is the first Leader Against the Drug War to write an entire book on the subject. In part one of this well-reasoned, impassioned but not emotional book, Gray lays out each of the ways the Drug War has failed, often causing more harm than good. From foreign and domestic corruption, to the destruction of the Constitution, to the health threats to drug users, he covers most of the bases. The second main part of the book is a special treat, because it isn't often that a drug-law reformer looks in detail at each of the options. They're often lumped together under the nebulous term "legalization," but Gray parses the approaches of drug education, rehabilitation programs, drug maintenance programs, drug substitution programs, needle exchanges, complete legalization, decriminalization, regulated distribution, and others. He takes the time to examine the pros and cons of each one, looking at its likely real-world effects (including those times and places when these policies have been implemented in the real world). Into the mix, Gray adds thoughts from over 40 other US judges and justices who are fed up with current drug policy; around half of them had never previously gone on the record with their disillusionment.

Having clearly laid out the problems and the possible solutions, Gray devotes some space to the concrete steps we can take to make changes: writing letters to the editor, calling radio shows, organizing public forums, communicating with Congressional representatives, and so on. A highly useful appendix assembles the findings of government-commissioned studies of drug law—spanning from 1894 to 1999, and coming from the US, UK, Australia, and India—and the funny thing is that every one of them concludes that "prohibition [is] personally and socially destructive."

Quote: "I am so convinced of the rightness and the benefits of the course I am proposing that I will end this discussion with a guarantee. If we abandon our failed drug policy and implement the programs I have outlined here, crime in the United States will be reduced by a minimum of 35 percent. I am not talking about straight drug crime, which will also be substantially reduced. The crime reduction will include burglaries, robberies and homicides, purse-snatchings, automobile thefts and check offenses, prostitution, shoplifting, money laundering, and both public and private corruption. And this minimum 35 percent reduction in crime will be realized within as little as one year after the reforms take effect. Public safety and health will increase; taxes will be reduced." [p 246]

Temple University Press • 2001 • 272 pp • softcover • $19.95 • ISBN 1-56639-860-6

Final Report on the Bombing of the Alfred P. Murrah Federal Building, April 19, 1995, by the Oklahoma Bombing Investigation Committee

At last, we have the definitive book on the Oklahoma City bombing. Layer by layer, piece by piece, this humongous books dismantles the Official Version of Events until it collapses like the house of cards that it is. Written by the Oklahoma Bombing Investigation Committee, it is the brainchild of former Oklahoma State Congressman Charles Key. From 1986 to 1998, Key served as a respected, well-liked member of the state's House of Representatives. But when he refused to stop digging for the truth about the act of terrorism that occurred in his backyard, he suddenly couldn't get re-elected and was facing every roadblock imaginable. He formed the Investigation Committee to look for answers, and this meticulously detailed, heavily illustrated book is the end result.

> "IF WE ABANDON OUR FAILED DRUG POLICY AND IMPLEMENT THE PROGRAMS I HAVE OUTLINED HERE, CRIME IN THE UNITED STATES WILL BE REDUCED BY A MINIMUM OF 35 PERCENT."

Using eyewitness reports (including sworn affidavits), government documents, buried media reports, expert opinions, scientific evidence, and other solid material, the authors shed light on every aspect of the crime: all the unknown people who were seen with Timothy McVeigh before, during, and after the bombing; reports of other bombs inside the federal building; the explosives experts who concur that a truck bomb could never cause that amount of damage; the pattern of damage to the building, which indicated interior explosives; the government's prior knowledge of the bombing; the Middle Eastern and white supremacist connections to the bombing; and numerous government improprieties. (For example, during trial the authorities called almost none of the many witnesses who had seen McVeigh with other people—often a dark, olive-skinned man. Another example: The FBI refuses to release video surveillance tapes and satellite photos of the area. Also, the records show that several trial witnesses radically changed their testimony from depositions and earlier testimony, yet they were never charged with perjury. Want more? How about the three credible eyewitnesses who say that agents from the Bureau of Alcohol, Tobacco and Firearms told them, in the minutes after the bombing, that they (the ATF) were told not to come into work on April 19. Then we have the fact that the FBI lifted 1,034 fingerprints and 87 palm prints related to the case, but they only checked them against fourteen suspects, including McVeigh, Terry Nichols, and Nichols' two-year-old daughter; they never ran them through their own extensive fingerprint database to check for matches with other criminals nationwide.) Unfortunately, a brief review such as this one can barely scratch the surface of what's revealed in this 560-page tome. Most highly recommended.

Quote: "In a television interview shortly after the bombing, Gov. Frank Keating, a former FBI agent and 'number two at Justice' (and therefore, previously over the ATF, the Secret Service and the US Marshal's Office) said, 'The reports I have is [*sic*] that one device was deactivated and, apparently, there's another device; and, obviously, whatever did the damage to the Murrah Building was a tremendous, very sophisticated explosive device.'" [p 178] Furthermore, on-the-scene reports from CNN and a local TV station, Oklahoma Highway Patrol dispatch logs, a memo from the Department of Defense's Atlantic Command, and numerous eyewitnesses also confirm additional explosives inside the building.

Quote: "Only moments before the explosion(s), bombing victim Daina Bradley was inside the Murrah Building on the first floor at the Social Security Office with her mother, her two children, and her sister. Bradley was there to change her son's social security card. She looked out the window and saw a Ryder truck parked by the front door. As she watched, two men got out of the truck. The man on the driver's side immediately walked across the street. She described him as a white male. The second man got out of the truck on the passenger's side, went to the rear of the truck, then back toward the front, 'and proceeded to walk very fast forward in front of the truck.... He went back on the sidewalk and left.'

....

"She described the passenger in the truck as being '...an olive-complexion man with short hair, curly, clean cut. He had on a blue Starter jacket, blue jeans, and tennis shoes and a white hat with purple flames.'... When she was shown a sketch of John Doe #2, she identified him as the man she had seen on the passenger's side of the truck." [p 167] Bear in mind that the authorities now say that John Doe #2 never existed, that he was a false alarm.

Quote: "Randall A. Yount, working as a park ranger for the Oklahoma Tourism and Recreation Department, felt the explosion from his house in Bethany, Oklahoma, a suburb west of Oklahoma City. He immediately turned on the television and heard news of the bombing and the need for emergency assistance; so he put on his uniform and went downtown, arriving at 9:23 a.m. An Oklahoma Highway Patrol officer saw him walking in the downtown area and offered to give him a ride to the bombing area. The trooper dropped him at the Southwestern Bell

Building where the Highway Patrol was setting up a command post in the parking lot. Yount was subsequently partnered with a trooper to help at the Murrah Building. While in the telephone company parking lot, Yount saw a marked Oklahoma Bomb Squad white truck with a trailer behind it. Sitting in the truck was an acquaintance of his named Terry. Terry told him, 'Yeah we've been down here since early this morning looking. We got word that there was going to be a bomb, and we thought it was going to be [in] the courthouse. We went over everything and couldn't find anything.'" [p 276]

Quote: "The Government case had a piece missing: Where was the bomb mixed? So, to bolster their case, they decided that the bomb must have been mixed at Geary Lake, outside of Junction City, Kansas. The lake is partially visible from US Highway 77, so the FBI set up a roadblock to stop residents in the area to see if anyone had seen a Ryder truck at the lake on Tuesday, 18 April 1995, the day before the bombing. What they heard was that there were over 20 sightings of a Ryder truck at the lake the week before the 18th. Some of the witnesses reported seeing several individuals around the Ryder truck, as well as other vehicles, such as a dark blue pickup. So what did the prosecution do with this information? They chose to ignore it. Instead, they called one witness, Gary Kitchener, who had not seen a Ryder truck at the lake." [p 351]

Quote: "FEMA [the Federal Emergency Management Agency] sent a Building Performance Assessment Team (BPAT) to Oklahoma City 09-13 May 1995 to investigate the damage caused to the Murrah Building. The team was composed of American Society of Civil Engineers and Government engineers. In their investigation, they were not allowed to physically inspect the structure or the crater. As stated in their official report: 'Physical inspection of the structure was limited to visual observations from a distance of approximately 200 feet.'

....

"The Government imploded the Murrah Building on 23 May 1995, 33 days after the bombing. General Benton K. Partin had asked that the demolition be delayed until explosives experts could examine the building. The request was denied and the demolition proceeded on schedule." [p 352]

Oklahoma Bombing Investigation Committee • 2001 • 560 pp • oversized softcover • heavily illus • $29.95 • ISBN 0-9710513-0-5

Body of Secrets: Anatomy of the Ultra-Secret National Security Agency, by James Bamford
Despite the fact that the National Security Agency is the biggest and most powerful intelligence operation in the US and the world (and the largest employer in the state of Maryland), this is only the second book about it. The first one, *The Puzzle Palace*, also by James

"PEOPLE WOULD BE FRAMED FOR BOMBINGS THEY DID NOT COMMIT; PLANES WOULD BE HIJACKED."

Bamford, has become a touchstone for all investigators of cloak and dagger activity. In this sequel, Bamford reveals what the NSA has been up to in the nineteen years since his first book, and he fills in the gaps in the pre-1982 knowledge.

Besides detailing the intricacies of the agency's structure and day-to-day operations, Bamford sheds much-needed light on the NSA's role during the Vietnam war, the Joint Chiefs of Staff's plot to commission terrorist acts and blame them on Cuba, Israel's purposeful attack on the USS *Liberty* (34 Americans killed), losses of cryptographic equipment, the investigation of JFK's death, attempts to control the press, spying on American citizens, the agency's classification fetish ("the NSA classifies somewhere between 50 million and 100 million documents a year"), the process by which people become employees, the agency's computer systems, and much, much more. An absolute must-have for the truly informed.

Quote: "According to secret and long-hidden documents obtained for *Body of Secrets*, the Joint Chiefs of Staff drew up and approved plans for what may be the most corrupt plan ever created by the US government. In the name of anticommunism, they proposed launching a secret and bloody war of terrorism against their own country in order to trick the American public into supporting an ill-conceived war they intended to launch against Cuba.

"Codenamed Operation Northwoods, the plan, which had the written approval of the Chairman and every member of the Joint Chiefs of Staff, called for innocent people to be shot on American streets; for boats carrying refugees fleeing Cuba to be sunk on the high seas; for a wave of violent terrorism to be launched in Washington, DC, Miami, and elsewhere. People would be framed for bombings they did not commit; planes would be hijacked. Using phony evidence, all of it would be blamed on Castro, thus giving [Joint Chiefs Chairman Lyman] Lemnitzer and his cabal the excuse, as well as the public and international backing, they needed to launch their war." [p 82]

Quote: "Although it is not found on any map, Crypto City, if incorporated, would be one of the largest municipalities in the state of Maryland. Each working day more than 32,000 specially cleared people—civilian, military, and contractors—travel over its thirty-two miles of roads, which are named in honor of past NSA notables. They park in one of the 17,000 spaces that cover 325 acres and enter one of fifty buildings whose combined floor space totals more than seven million square feet. In terms of growth, Crypto City is one of the most vibrant metropolises in the country.... Crypto City's budget, long a closely held secret, has been revealed in a closed door meeting in the City's Engineering and Technology Building. Addressing a group of technology employees in September 1999, Deputy Director for Services Terry Thompson said, 'Were we a corporate company based on our four-billion-dollar budget and the number of employees that we have, we kind of bench ourselves against Hewlett-Packard.'" [p 481]

Doubleday • 2001 • 721 pp • hardcover • $29.95 • ISBN 0-385-49907-8

_HIDDEN HISTORY

Gentle Swastika: Reclaiming the Innocence, by ManWoman
It's hard to imagine a symbol with more of an emotional charge. Just a glimpse of its bent arms triggers visions of concentration camps, blitzkriegs, stiff-arm salutes, and midnight visits from the Gestapo. The Nazis have completely ruined the swastika. You see, this symbol—which blends a cross and a spiral—has existed since prehistory and has been used by almost every culture on earth, always with *positive* connotations (with the one big exception noted above). A Canadian artist who has changed his name to ManWoman has made it his life's mission to restore this universal symbol of light, life, and good luck to its original illustrious stature. To that end, he has published a richly illustrated book that offers a crushing amount of proof that the swastika is a good symbol.

In it, we're treated to photographs (and a few illustrations) of the swastika as it appeared in the cultures of the ancient Mayans, Aztecs, Incans, Greeks, Romans, Vikings, Egyptians, Goths, Hittites, Essenes, Native Americans, and Bronze Age Europeans. It shows up in Christian churches, Islamic mosques, Hindu temples, the Dalai Lama's throne, and, yes, even in Jewish synagogues. It plays a role in other belief systems, as well, including Jainism, Shintoism, Theosophy, Freemasonry, and the Raelian movement. Rudyard Kipling used it as his personal symbol, and it appears on the first page of the early editions of his books. In 1916, the British put out a War Savings Stamp emblazoned with the swastika. A year later, Russia added it to their 250-ruble note. It shows up in a painting by Goya. There are even towns named Swastika in New York State and Ontario, Canada (this book contains numerous photos of ManWoman's visit to the latter burg).

The Swastikas, women's hockey team in Edmonton, Alberta, 1916.

Photo courtesy of ManWoman

EVERYTHING YOU KNOW IS WRONG

"COCA-COLA MADE A WATCH FOB IN THE SHAPE OF A SWASTIKA; A CAR (THE KRIT) MADE IN DETROIT FROM 1906 TO 1916 HAD A SWASTIKA HOOD ORNAMENT"

Blowing the lid off of a stunning case of cultural amnesia, the author shows how widespread the swastika was in North America up to the 1930s. Coca-Cola made a watch fob in the shape of a swastika; a car (the Krit) made in Detroit from 1906 to 1916 had a swastika hood ornament; the Boy Scouts had a badge called the White Swastika. Los Angeles was home to the Swastika Surfboard Company in the 1920s, and two Canadian female hockey teams were called the Swastikas in the early twentieth century. One of the book's most memorable images is of a teenage Jackie Bouvier (later Kennedy-Onassis) wearing a Native American costume with a swastika on the front. During the 1800s and into the 1900s, the swastika was considered a good-luck sign, and we see it adorning children's books, poker chips, postcards, silverware, cigar bands, horse saddles, Tru-Flite golf clubs, and streetlamps in Los Angeles. Numerous buildings—hotels in New Mexico and British Columbia, Exposition Monument in Seattle, a post office in Pennsylvania (not to mention the Louvre in Paris)—have swastikas designed into the walls and floors, as evidenced by photographs.

Looking beyond the West, we find swastikas embedded in artifacts from Africa, China, Japan, Tibet, India, and elsewhere. The elephant-headed Hindu deity Ganesha is often surrounded by swastikas. In fact, an explanatory sign in a Hindu temple claims that all Aryan scripts—including Sanskrit, Chinese, Greek, etc.—are believed to have originated from the swastika.

The book ends with non-Nazi swastika tattoos, including the over *200* that adorn ManWoman's body, all part of his quest to return this symbol to its ancient, universal meaning.

Quote: "For thousands of years almost every race, every tribe, every religion on earth has revered the Swastika, using it in a variety of shapes and styles, associating it with the hammer of Thor, the footprints of Buddha, the emblem of Shiva, Apollo, Jupiter, and even Jesus Christ. Scholars agree that for the first three hundred years of the infant Christian religion the Swastika was the only form of cross used in the catacombs and early churches; the crucifix-style cross was not used until later when Christianity became the official Roman church." [p 21]

St. Mary's Basilica in Phoenix, Arizona.

Quote: "A mosaic floor of the era of King Herod uncovered at the Jewish Quarter of the Old City in Jerusalem displays many Swastikas. Fractions of stone reliefs bearing Swastikas, part of a wall and gates built by Herod, were excavated at the Southern Wall in Jerusalem. The Swastika was found as a floor decoration in King Herod's summer palace when it was excavated. I've been told it is also marked on the Wailing Wall." [pp 28-9]

Quote: "One of the most exciting proofs of this continent-wide attitude to the Swastika is the Girls' Club founded in 1903 by *Ladies' Home Journal Magazine*, which credited to their club the enormous popularity of the Swastika in America. The membership consisted of a network of young ladies earning money by selling subscriptions. They referred to themselves as Swastika Girls. They had a diamond-studded Swastika pin, Swastika stationery, and a silver thimble bearing the 'mystic' Swastika which hardworking members could earn. The gold pin was advertised as 'What Every Girl Wants—Her Own Swastika.'" [p 46]

The Boy Scouts' Badge of Thanks (no longer used)

Quote: "Hitler did not invent the Swastika. He stole it from the ancients!" [p 24]

Quote: "There are many theories about the symbolic meaning of this mystic cross—that it represents fire, the sun, the source, creativity, fertility, the sex act, the moon, the cardinal points, the sacred four, many deities, divine power, light, lightning, eternity, etc., almost everything of importance in life as we know it! This is why it is such an important sign. It is the most sacred and historically respected symbol." [p 106]

Flyfoot Press • 2001 • 115 pp • oversized softcover • profusely illustrated • $19.95 • ISBN 0-9688716-0-7 • <www.gentleswastika.com>

Magic: The Untold Story of US Intelligence and the Evacuation of Japanese Residents From the West Coast During WWII, by David D. Lowman

Very often, history is not politically correct. Take, for example, the US government's placement of people of Japanese descent into internment camps during World War II. The received wisdom is that this act was motivated purely by racist paranoia. We are assured that no Japanese people in America were engaged in spying or other treasonous acts on behalf of the Empire of Japan. This is incorrect.

Late in 1940, US intelligence broke Japan's top-level diplomatic code, "MAGIC," allowing the government to read all communications at will. This book reproduces scores of these translated cables, so we can see exactly what FDR knew when he ordered the detentions. It turns out that Japanese officials in America were busy recruiting Japanese people—including US citizens, even second-generation citizens—into their "intelligence web." Thousands of them were involved, principally on the West Coast. (Furthermore, some Japanese-American organizations raised money for their mother country's war fund and pledged to commit acts of sabotage in the US.)

Confirmation of this comes from other sources besides the cables themselves. In March 1941, the FBI broke into the Japanese consulate in Los Angeles and found documents on spies in the US who had provided maps, locations, and other data relating to military installations, defense factories, power stations, dams, etc. When a high-ranking Japanese spymaster was arrested, his documents listed many Japanese-Americans who were spying on the US.

So does this mean that the internment of Japanese-Americans was justified? That's still up to each individual to decide, but at least we now have the facts before us.

Quote from a cable from Los Angeles to Tokyo (May 9, 1941): "We have already established contacts with absolutely reliable Japanese in the San Pedro and San Diego area, who will keep a close watch on all shipments of airplanes and other war materials, and report the amounts and destinations of such shipments. The same steps have been taken with regard to traffic across the US-Mexico border.

"We shall maintain connections with our second generations who are at present in the (U.S.) Army, to keep us informed of various developments in the Army. We also have connections with our second generations working in airplane plants for intelligence purposes." [p 147]

> WHEN A HIGH-RANKING JAPANESE SPYMASTER WAS ARRESTED, HIS DOCUMENTS LISTED MANY JAPANESE-AMERICANS WHO WERE SPYING ON THE US.

Quote from a cable from Seattle to Tokyo (May 11, 1941): "We are using foreign company employees, as well as employees in our own companies here, for the collection of intelligences having to do with economics along the lines of the construction of ships, the number of airplanes produced and their various types, the production of copper, zinc, and aluminum, the yield of tin for cans, and lumber....

"For the future we have made arrangements to collect intelligences from second generation Japanese draftees on matters dealing with the troops, as well as troop speech and behavior." [p 148]

Athena Press • 2000 • 393 pp • softcover • illus • $29.95 • ISBN 0-9602736-1-1

Jihad in the West: Muslim Conquests from the 7th to the 21st Centuries, by Paul Fregosi

Interestingly, I was planning to review this book well before the September 11 attacks. By uncovering forgotten and suppressed history, it perfectly fits the theme of the Disinformation Guides. Due to death threats and some political correctness, Islam hasn't been subjected to the same harsh examination that Christianity has received for over 100 years. Everyone knows about the Christian Crusades, Inquisition, and witch hunts, but Islam's bloody, millennium-long conquest of Europe and other parts of the world has been consigned to the dustbin of history. Howard Bloom tells me that a colleague of his wrote a history of the conquests on assignment for a publisher who then backed out on their agreement. Similarly, Paul Fregosi's publisher suddenly dropped *Jihad in the West* like a hot potato. Luckily, Prometheus Books—a humanist-freethought outfit that is the only publisher with the guts to regularly put out books critical of Islam—was there to rescue this important work.

While the Crusades lasted less than 200 years and were confined almost completely to the Holy Land, the *Jihad* has lasted 1,300 years, involving the invasions of Europe, Africa, Asia, and the Middle East. Fregosi's book sticks almost exclusively to the European realms, covering Italy, France, Spain, parts of Russia, and elsewhere. The *Jihad* began in the early 600s and more or less petered out by the middle of the 1800s. It flared up during World War I, when Turkey led a holy war against Russia, Britain, France, and any other country that messed with its ally, Germany. It also resurged in the Balkans during WWII. Most controversially, the author believes that the Muslim terrorist attacks of the 1980s and 1990s are a part of the newly revived *Jihad* (this book was published three years before the 911 attacks). It's too bad that Fregosi chose to dis Islam so much, since this opens him up to the now-overused charge of "Islamophobia," allowing defenders of the faith to dismiss this unique, epic history of conquest in the name of religion.

Quote: "The Crusaders wanted to establish themselves in the Holy Land, formerly Christian. Islam's motives, through the Jihad, were far grander. The Muslims wanted to take and occupy Europe and, hopefully, to Islamize it. A large part of Europe was taken, occupied for centuries, sometimes devastated, and some of it was Islamized. Spain, Portugal, France, Italy, Sicily, Austria, Bosnia, Serbia, Croatia, Hungary, Romania, Wallachia, Albania, Moldavia, Bulgaria, Greece, Armenia, Georgia, Poland, Ukraine, and eastern and southern Russia were all Jihad battlefields where Islam conquered or was conquered. Many of those lands were occupied by the Muslims, in some cases by Arabs and Moors, and others by the Ottoman Turks, usually for hundreds of years: Spain 800 years, Portugal 600 years, Greece 500 years, Sicily 300 years, Serbia 400 years, Bulgaria 500 years, Romania 400 years, and Hungary 150 years. Hungary, particularly, was ruined, plundered, and ravaged and took 200 years to recover from Muslim occupation." [pp 23-4]

EVERYONE KNOWS ABOUT THE CHRISTIAN CRUSADES, INQUISITION, AND WITCH HUNTS, BUT ISLAM'S BLOODY, MILLENNIUM-LONG CONQUEST OF EUROPE AND OTHER PARTS OF THE WORLD HAS BEEN CONSIGNED TO THE DUSTBIN OF HISTORY.

Quote: "The Jihad originates in the Koranic teaching and was practiced by Muhammed in his lifetime against Jewish and pagan tribes in the Arabian peninsula, and soon after his death against the Persians and against the Christian peoples of the Byzantine empire, Syria, and Palestine. Hundreds of years later it terrified Europe. 'From the fury of the Mahommedan, spare us, O Lord' was a prayer heard for centuries in all the churches of central and southern Europe." [p 22]

Quote: "Three thousand of their own were killed in the battle [of Zalaca in Spain in 1086], the Muslim victors said afterward, but the Christian casualties were far heavier. The Muslims stopped counting the numbers of enemy dead after reaching the figure of 24,000. They then began to cut the heads off the corpses and piled them up to make a sort of minaret for the muezzins who, standing on the piles of headless cadavers, sang the praises of Allah and called the faithful to prayer." [pp 159-60]

Prometheus Books • 1998 • 442 pp • hardcover • $34 • ISBN 1-57392-247-1

Islam's Black Slaves: The Other Black Diaspora, by Ronald Segal

The final book in this Muslim trilogy (*Extreme Islam* and *Jihad in the West*) is another one that I was planning to review before Islam became a topic of dinner-table conversation. In much the same way that the Christian Crusades are remembered and the longer Muslim *Jihad* is forgotten, the Atlantic slave trade (carried out by Europeans and Americans with the help of Africans) is remembered while the longer Islamic slave trade is forgotten. Written by the author of the highly acclaimed book *The Black Diaspora*, *Islam's Black Slaves* is one of the few books in existence that sheds light on this other slave trade, which began around 650 A.D. and has yet to completely end.

The African slaves taken by Muslims ended up in Persia, the Ottoman Empire, Zanzibar, Egypt, China, India, Spain, and elsewhere, where they were used as concubines, laborers, soldiers, etc. Approximately two-thirds of the slaves were female. Many of the men and boys were turned into eunuchs by the severing of not just their testicles but their penises, as well. For its first 1,250 years, the Islamic slave trade is thought to have trafficked 11.5 million to 13.7 million individuals from central and southern Africa. A further estimated 300,000 were traded during the first half of the 1900s. Saudi Arabia imported black slaves into the 1980s, and many other countries, including Lebanon, probably did. Currently, the Islamic states of Mauritania and Sudan are the only two countries where slavery is supported. The former nation is home to around 100,000 slaves, while the latter has tens of thousands.

Ronald Segal traces the history and practice of this trade: the slave traders, the slaves, and those who bought them; the treatment of the slaves and their fate; the religious implications; the eventual pressure from the British and French against the Islamic trade; and the relationship of the Black Muslim movement in the US to Islamic slavery. (Because this book focuses exclusively on black slaves, it ignores the many Europeans and Americans who were kidnapped and sold by Islamic slavetraders in Morocco and Algeria. For information on these other slaves, see *White Slaves, African Masters*, edited by Paul Michel Baepler (University of Chicago Press, 1999).)

Quote: "Among the most notorious of the Afro-Arab traders was Tippu Tip, who had by the late 1860s established himself west of Lake Tanganyika. When H.M. Stanley reached, in 1883, what would come to be called Stanley Falls, he encountered the consequences of the raiders: 'Every three or four miles we came in view of the black traces of the destroyers. The scarred stakes, poles of once populous settlements, scorched banana groves, and prostrate palms, all betokened ruthless ruin.'

"Added to the multitude of slaves who died during the raiding were those who perished in the journey to the coast. The missionary A.J. Swann, on his way to Lake Tanganyika, encountered Tippu Tip's caravan, with slaves who had already journeyed 1,000 miles from the Upper Congo and had an additional 250 miles to go. They were chained by the neck in long files, some of them in six-foot forks, and with many of the women bearing babies on their backs. They were in a filthy condition, and many of them were scarred by the cuts of the hide whip....

"Routes favored by slave traders could be easily identified by the skeletons that were visible at intervals alongside the track. The Reverend Horace Waller, for a long time Lay Superintendent of the Universities Mission to Central Africa, estimated that 'four or five lives were lost for every slave delivered safe at Zanzibar.'" [pp 159-60]

Farrar, Straus and Giroux • 2001 • 276 pp • softcover • $14 • ISBN 0-374527970

_GRAB BAG

Dissenting Electorate: Those Who Refuse to Vote and the Legitimacy of Their Opposition, edited by Carl Watner with Wendy McElroy

People who choose not to vote are often derided as lazy, apathetic, and apolitical. While there may be a few folks who don't cast a ballot out of sheer sloth, lots of people have convincing reasons. The most eloquent explanations and defenses of those reasons have been collected in *Dissenting Electorate*.

Across these 25 pieces, spanning from 1845 to 2001, some themes present themselves. Perhaps most often, politics and government are seen as worthless, even harmful, systems that exist solely to exercise power over people. By voting, you play the game, you support the very system that imprisons you. By not voting, you commit a revolutionary act by refusing to be a part of the machine. You are withdrawing your consent to be governed by an inherently corrupt system. Another typical reason is that all politicians are greedy, power-hungry crooks, so it doesn't matter who wins. In a choice between two self-serving liars, refusing to decide makes clear your contempt for this non-choice.

Other reasons for not voting include rejection of the principle that a majority of people should get to decide things for everybody; voting limits peoples' participation in government; the Constitution is not a valid contract that binds the people of the United States; and government officials pretend that the fact that a lot of people voted for them is a "mandate." The only reason for non-voting that I didn't see spelled out is that elections are filled with fraud and technical problems; there's absolutely no guarantee that the winners actually received the most votes.

One of the most fascinating aspects of the book is the historical statistics on non-voting in the US. In every presidential election since 1920 (when universal suffrage was in place), non-voters have outnumbered those who voted for the winning candidates, often by a large margin (in fact, the ratio was close to or more than 2:1 in six of those elections, including the ones in 1920, 1924, and 1948). Earlier elections were worse. In the first presidential contest for which we have records of the popular vote (1824), a total of 352,062 votes were cast, though the census of 1820 showed the population to be 9,638,453. Even when factoring out those who couldn't vote (all females, male children, and slaves), this is still a strikingly low turn-out, well under 20 percent of eligible voters.

Quote from "On Underwriting an Evil" by Frank Chodorov: "At first it was sheer instinct that dissuaded me from casting my ballot. I listened to the performance promises of the various candidates and the more I listened the more confused I became. They seemed to me to be so contradictory, so vague, so devoid of principle, that I could not bring myself in favor of one or the other. Particularly was I impressed by the candidates' evaluations of one another. Neither one had a good word to say of his opponent, and each was of the opinion that the other fellow was not the kind of man to whom the affairs of state could be safely entrusted. Now, I reasoned, these fellows were politicians, and as such should be better acquainted with their respective qualifications for office than I could be; it was their business to know such things. Therefore, I had to believe candidate A when he said that candidate B was untrustworthy, as I had to believe candidate B when he said the same of candidate A. In the

circumstances, how could I vote for either? Judging by their respective evaluations of each other's qualifications, I was bound to make the wrong decision whichever way I voted." [p 26]

Quote from "Abstain From Beans" by Robert LeFevre: "When we express a preference politically, we do so precisely because we intend to bind others to our will. Political voting is the legal method we have adopted and extolled for obtaining monopolies of power. Political voting is nothing more than the assumption that might makes right. There is a presumption that any decision wanted by the majority of those expressing a preference must be desirable, and the inference even goes so far as to presume that anyone who differs from the majority view is wrong or possibly immoral." [p 35]

Quote from "An Argument in Defense of the Invisible Hand" by John Pugsley: "History does not support the hypothesis that electoral politics might lead to a freer society. There is no case of which I am aware where electoral politics has reduced the size and scope of government in a fundamental or lasting sense." [p 97]

BY VOTING, YOU PLAY THE GAME, YOU SUPPORT THE VERY SYSTEM THAT IMPRISONS YOU.

Quote from "End of the Mandate" by Gregory Bresiger: "They say that people who don't vote can't complain about the outcome. But they also say that if your candidate didn't win, you can't complain because that's being a sore loser. You also can't complain if the guy you voted for does something you don't like. Hey, you voted for him, didn't you? You can't win. The game is rigged." [p 113]

McFarland & Company • 2001 • 135 pp • softcover • $29.95 • ISBN 0-7864-0874-X

gasstationthoughts and the daily journal of wheeler antabanez, by Matt Kent

I usually wouldn't include a work of fiction here, but a work of fiction usually doesn't cause the arrest of its author. At the time, Matt Kent was 23 years old. He had assumed the pen name of Wheeler Antabanez; or maybe Wheeler had assumed him. The lines get kind of blurry, as when Kent refers to Antabanez as "my best friend and alter ego.... [B]y the end of the book, there was no separation between the two of us." Antabanez is an angry young man whose writings bear a remarkable resemblance to the raw, incendiary postings and diaries of Eric Harris and Dylan Klebold (the two known gunmen at the Columbine massacre), except that Antabanez/Kent is more literate.

After putting "gasstationthoughts"—a collection of his stream-of-consciousness journals—on his Website, people asked Kent for more, so he began posting "the daily journal of wheeler antabanez" on February 1, 2000. On April 19 (the day before the one-year anniversary of Columbine), Kent was arrested at his apartment. The charge: making terroristic threats on his Website. During his first court date, the prosecutor said Kent was a menace to society and recommended committing him to an insane asylum. The judge didn't agree but did have the young writer submit to a psychiatric examination. Long story short, six months later a grand jury refused to indict him. Now we get to read what all the fuss was about.

Quote from "gasstationthoughts": "matt kent will never do anything worthwhile. he is but a host. do not mistake matt kent for a caterpillar who will one day become a butterfly. when wheeler antabanez is fully matured, matt kent will die. at the time of this essay or manifesto, if you will, matt kent is losing more and more control. he is sure to be dead within a year's time. why bother to live anyway? there is no use for matt kent. matt kent is just as useless as all the creatures that surround him." [p 63]

Quotes from "the daily journal of wheeler antabanez":

"**March 6, 2000**

bloomfield ave
machine gun in every window
confetti in the air
victory
all of you are fanatics
in the making"
[p 117]

"**March 18, 2000**

all my emotions have died
the only thing i have left inside me is confidence
soon the whole world will be at my mercy
things can only get worse from here"
[p 127]

"**April 12, 2000**

i feel good
i think my plan just might work
8 more days to columbine"
[p 152]

Barricade Books • 2001 • 160 pp • softcover • $14.95 • ISBN 1-56980-199-1

The Skeptical Environmentalist: Measuring the Real State of the World, by Bjorn Lomborg
What *The Satanic Bible* is to Christians, *The Skeptical Environmentalist* is to environmentalists: pure anathema, a sustained assault on their beliefs. Statistician Bjorn Lomborg contends that, by using the same reports and statistics that environmentalists use, we can see that the planet is not on the brink of destruction. Depending on what he's looking at (life expectancy, population, forests, pollution, biodiversity, cancer, global warming, etc.), his conclusions fall into one of three categories: the situation is getting better, not worse; the situation is holding steady, not getting worse; the situation is getting somewhat worse, but not nearly as bad as we've been told.

Naturally, this book shouldn't be accepted as the final word, but neither should it be dismissed out of hand, as some would prefer. Lomborg makes many powerful points. Balance them out by reading some critiques of the book (such as those at <www.anti-lomborg.com>). Then balance those out by reading Lomborg's impressive responses to his most prominent critics at <www.lomborg.com>.

Quote: "We are not running out of energy or natural resources. There will be more and more food per head of the world's population. Fewer and fewer people are starving. In 1900 we lived for an average of 30 years; today we live for 67. According to the UN we have reduced poverty more in the last 50 years than we did in the preceding 500, and it has been reduced in practically every country.

"Global warming, though its size and future projections are rather unrealistically pessimistic, is almost certainly taking place, but the typical cure of early and radical fossil fuel cutbacks is way worse than the original affliction, and moreover its total impact will not pose a devastating problem for our future. Nor will we lose 25-50 percent of all species in our lifetime—in fact we are losing probably 0.7 percent. Acid rain does not kill the forests, and the air and water around us are becoming less and less polluted. Mankind's lot has improved in terms of practically every measurable indicator." [p 4]

"MANKIND'S LOT HAS IMPROVED IN TERMS OF PRACTICALLY EVERY MEASURABLE INDICATOR."

Quote: "In 1992 a group of Danish scientists, led by Professor Niels Skakkebaek of Copenhagen University Hospital, published a report which showed that the number of sperm cells in men's semen had fallen from 113 to 66 million per milliliter from 1938 to 1990... [T]he primary question remains as to whether it really is correct that the sperm count has halved over the last 50 years. The 1992 article has led to numerous critical responses and new studies which have shown both deterioration and stable sperm counts. Sperm counts in Paris have fallen, while in Toulouse the count remained stable. Sperm counts in Scotland have fallen, whereas those in Finland remained constant or increased slightly. Studies in Belgium and parts of London showed a fall in the count, whereas those in the US, in New York, Los Angeles, Minnesota as well as Seattle were constant. *Our Stolen Future* only mentions the surveys which showed a fall in the sperm count." [pp 238-9]

Cambridge University Press • 2001 • 536 pp • softcover • illus • $28 • ISBN 0-521-01068-3

Food Not Bombs (revised edition), by C.T. Butler and Keith McHenry

The food industry in the US throws out approximately 46 billion pounds of food per year, and an awful lot of it is still perfectly edible. It's been estimated that only 4 billion pounds of food would be needed to end hunger in America. In 1980, a group of activists started Food Not Bombs in Cambridge, Massachusetts, to collect food that would otherwise be wasted and give it free of charge to the homeless and hungry. The idea has spread like wildfire, and now over 250 communities have a Food Not Bombs volunteer collective feeding people for free. In this book, two of the people who began the Cambridge group explain how to start and run Food Not Bombs in your area. They cover all the nitty-gritty: scoring the wasted food from grocery stores, restaurants, co-ops, etc., preparing it (33 pages of recipes and instructions), and setting up tables in public places to distribute it. You'll want to pay attention to the part about handling the local government and police, who often don't take kindly to this sort of thing (the San Francisco group has dealt with hundreds of arrests and dozens of beatings). You'll also get a heavy dose of philosophy, politics, and inspiring stories from 20 years of feeding and protesting.

Quote: "It is the Food Not Bombs position that we have a right to give away free food anytime, anywhere, without any permission from the state." [p 22]

See Sharp Press • 2000 • 122 pp • softcover • illus • $8.95 • ISBN 1-884365-21-3

Why Bother?: Getting a Life in a Locked-down Land, by Sam Smith

Sam Smith is the founder, publisher, and editor of *The Progressive Review*, "since 1964 Washington's most unofficial source" (he also contributed to *You Are Being Lied To*). After almost four decades of activism, reporting, and other forms of rabble-rousing, Smith offers personal reflections in *Why Bother?* Hard to describe—part manifesto, part meditation, a little bit of memoir, quite a few facts and quotes, and a lot of hard-won insight—*Why Bother?* isn't a step-by-step activist's manual. Smith offers little-known facts, hopeful stories, and provocative ideas about the wasteland of the post-post-modern world and what we can do to give our lives and our society some meaning. He doesn't pretend to offer easy answers, just lots of food for thought. It's a soothing tonic for alienated people who still want to contribute something to a world that doesn't seem to offer much hope.

Quote: "Sometime around the middle of the 1980s I suddenly noticed that the truth was no longer setting people free; it was only making them drowsy. This realization first came in the midst of a meeting held to discuss a worthy investigative journalism project.

We had considered every aspect of the proposal save one and now, unbidened, a heretical question wiggled into my mind, never to leave: did the truth being sought really matter anymore?" [p 7]

> "SOMETIME AROUND THE MIDDLE OF THE 1980s I SUDDENLY NOTICED THAT THE TRUTH WAS NO LONGER SETTING PEOPLE FREE; IT WAS ONLY MAKING THEM DROWSY."

Quote: "Neither is America stuck with rigid economic models that have caused so much individual and aggregate pain. There are all sorts of mixed economies. There are big consumer cooperatives like Land O'Lakes butter and the United Services Automobile Association that have thrived happily amongst conventional capitalists. The town of Green Bay, Wisconsin, holds its professional football team in community ownership. As a result, it's one of the few professional sports teams in America that we know won't be moving to someplace else. There are various forms of local currency, including 'time dollars' with which people earn time credits that can be redeemed in services." [p 48]

Quote: "We can, as those in charge would like, continue to define ourselves primarily by neatly described identities—either natural or acquired. We can remain interminably and ineffectually absorbed and angry about the particulars of infinite special injustices. Or we can ask what is it that makes out society seem so unfair to so many who are so different? If the young Hispanic in Watts and the militia member in Montana and the mother of six in Dorchester share unintended miseries, might these miseries share common origins? Can we find universal stories in particular pain? If we can, it is a beginning of true change." [p 139]

Feral House • 2001 • 151 pp • softcover • $12.95 • ISBN 0-922915-72-5

Endnotes

1. This book might be too expensive for many individuals to buy, especially if they're interested in only one disease or disorder. To get around this, the publisher has an online database from which you can purchase information *a la carte* from over 90 selections (from restless leg syndrome, soft tissue injury, and autism to hypertension, lupus, and AIDS). These individual chapters are continuously updated and contain much more information than their corresponding chapters in the book. Prices range from $2.50 to $12. Go to <www.third-line.com> and select "Nutritional Influences on Illness Online Database." **2.** See note #1. **3.** As *Everything You Know Is Wrong* goes to press, the FDA has announced that GlaxoSmithKline has finally changed the warning label for its antidepressant, Paxil. The company now tacitly admits that the drug causes dependence in a disturbingly high percentage of people. At long last, Glaxo warns that stopping its previously "non habit-forming" pill can cause "dizziness, sensory disturbances (e.g., paresthesias such as electric shock sensations), agitation, anxiety, nausea, and sweating." The new label then notes: "Similar events have been reported for other selective serotonin reuptake inhibitors." Glaxo now recommends that people who quit the drug gradually taper off with smaller and smaller doses. Even then, however, clinical trials show that 2.0 percent of patients experience paresthesia, 2.3 percent experience "abnormal dreams," and 7.1 percent (one out of every fourteen people) experience dizziness.

APPENDIX C: PUBLISHER INFORMATION

_BOOKS EXCERPTED IN *EVERYTHING YOU KNOW IS WRONG*

"The Ludlow Massacre" was originally published in *The Politics of History*, now out of print, and is currently in *The Zinn Reader* by Howard Zinn (Seven Stories Press, 1997). Price: $19.95. Seven Stories Press • 140 Watts Street / New York NY 10013 • <www.sevenstories.com> • <info@sevenstories.com>

"'Call It Off!'" is comprised of excerpts from *This Is Not An Assault* by David T. Hardy with Rex Kimball. Price: $19.54 (softcover). Xlibris • 1-888-795-4274 • <orders@xlibris.com> • <www.xlibris.com/bookstore>

"Fission Stories" is comprised of excerpts from *Fission Stories* by David Lochbaum. It is available only from the author. Price: $10 (cash, check, or money order). David Lochbaum • 20820 Aspenwood Lane • Montgomery Village MD 20886.

"Mushroom Clouds in Paradise" is the introduction to *For the Good of Mankind: A History of the People of Bikini and Their Islands* (second edition) by Jack Niedenthal (Bravo Publishers, 2001). US & Canada: $16 (incl. shipping); elsewhere: $24 (incl. shipping). Jack Niedenthal, Trust Liaison for the People of Bikini • PO Box 1096 / Majuro MH 96960 • <www.bikiniatoll.com/Bikinioffers.html> • <bikini@ntamar.com>

"Some Lessons From the Underground History of American Education" is comprised of excerpts from *The Underground History of American Education* (The Odysseus Group, 2001). Price: $30 plus $4 (continental US). The Odysseus Group Order Form / Suite 3W 295 East 8th Street / New York City NY 10009 • <www.johntaylorgatto.com> • <info@johntaylorgatto.com>

_BOOKS REVIEWED IN *EVERYTHING YOU KNOW IS WRONG*

Note: Minimal contact information is given for major, corporate publishers and their subsidiaries, as their books are widely available in bookstores. Also, toll-free numbers are only for orders.

Anchor Books • <www.anchorbooks.com>

Athena Press • 1743 North Oak Lane / Provo UT 84604 • <www.athenapressinc.com> • <feedback@athenapressinc.com>

Barricade Books • 185 Bridge Plaza North, Suite 308-A / Fort Lee NJ 07024 • 201-944-7600 • <www.barricadebooks.com> • <customerservice@barricadebooks.com>

Cambridge University Press • Customer Service Department / Cambridge University Press / 110 Midland Avenue / Port Chester NY 10573 • 1-800-872-7423 • <www.cup.org>

Doubleday • <www.doubleday.com>

Down There Press • 938 Howard Street, Suite 101 / San Francisco CA 94103 • 1-800-289-8423 • <www.goodvibes.com/dtp/dtp.html> • <downtherepress@excite.com>

Farrar, Straus and Giroux • 19 Union Square West / New York NY 10003 • 1-888-330-8477 • <www.fsgbooks.com> • <sales@fsgee.com>

Feral House • PO Box 13067 / Los Angeles CA 90013 • <www.feralhouse.com> • <info@feralhouse.com>

Flyfoot Press • ManWoman / 221-11th Ave. South / Cranbrook, BC / Canada V1C 2P6 • <www.gentleswastika.com> • <manwoman@cyberlink.bc.ca>

Four Walls Eight Windows • 39 West 14th Street #503 / New York NY 10011 • 1-800-788-3123 • <www.4w8w.com> • <orders@4w8w.com>

The Free Press • <www.thefreepress.com>

HarperCollins • <www.harpercollins.com>

Henry Holt and Co. • <www.henryholt.com> • <customerservice@vhpsva.com>

iUniverse.com • <www.iuniverse.com>

Konformist Kollective <www.konformist.com> • For info on ordering *The Shadow Over Santa Susana*: <www.mansonmythos.com> • <gorightly@hotmail.com>

Loompanics Unlimited • PO Box 1197 / Port Townsend WA 98368 • 1-800-380-2230 • <www.loompanics.com>

McFarland & Company • PO Box 611 / Jefferson NC 28640 • 1-800-253-2187 • <www.mcfarlandpub.com> • <info@mcfarlandpub.com>

The New Press • 450 West 41st Street, 6th Floor / New York NY 10036 • 1-800-233-4830 • <www.thenewpress.com>

Oklahoma Bombing Investigation Committee • PO Box 75697 / Oklahoma City OK 73147 • 1-800-334-5597 • <www.bombing.tv> • <report@bombing.tv>

Perseus Publishing • Perseus Books Group / Customer Service Department / 5500 Central Avenue / Boulder CO 80301 • 1-800-386-5656 • <www.perseuspublishing.com> • <info@perseuspublishing.com>

Prima Publishing • <www.primapublishing.com>

Prometheus Books • 59 John Glenn Drive / Amherst NY 14228-2197 • 1-800-421-0351 • <www.prometheusbooks.com> • <marketing@prometheusbooks.com>

See Sharp Press • PO Box 1731 / Tucson AZ 85702 • 1-800-243-0138 • <www.seesharppress.com> • <seesharp@earthlink.net>

St. Martin's Press • <www.stmartins.com>

Temple University Press • c/o Chicago Distribution Center / 11030 South Langley Avenue / Chicago IL 60628 • 1-800-621-2736 • <www.temple.edu/tempress>

Third Line Press • 4751 Viviana Drive, Suite 500 / Tarzana CA 91356 • 1-800-916-0076 • <www.third-line.com> • <tlp@third-line.com>

Verso • WW Norton/National Book Company / 800 Keystone Industrial Park / Scranton PA 18512 • 1-800-233-4830 • <www.versobooks.com> • <versoinc@aol.com>

Zed Books • 7 Cynthia Street / London N1 9JF / UK • <www.zedbooks.demon.co.uk> • <general@zedbooks.demon.co.uk> • Zed is distributed in the US through St. Martin's Press

CONTRIBUTORS

Dominick T. Armentano is professor emeritus in economics at the University of Hartford (Connecticut). He is the author of numerous articles and op-eds on taxes and regulatory policy, some of which have appeared in *National Review*, the *Cato Journal*, *The Antitrust Bulletin*, the *New York Times*, the *Financial Times*, and the *Wall Street Journal*. He has presented over 100 talks to academic and business audiences in the US and abroad. Between 1978 and 1985, he was a regular commentator on *BYLINE*, a nationally syndicated public affairs radio program. His books include *The Myths of Antitrust* (Arlington House, 1972), *Antitrust & Monopoly* (John Wiley, 1982 and Independent Institute, 1998), and *Antitrust: The Case for Repeal* (Mises Institute, 1999). He currently resides with his wife and cat in Vero Beach, Florida.

Sandra Bisin is a TV and print journalist living in Paris.

Howard Bloom is author of *The Lucifer Principle: A Scientific Expedition into the Forces of History* (Atlantic Monthly Press, 1997; now in its fourteenth printing) and *Global Brain: The Evolution of Mass Mind From the Big Bang to the 21st Century* (John Wiley & Sons, 2000). Bloom is a visiting scholar at New York University, founder of the International Paleopsychology Project, a founding board member of the Epic of Evolution Society, an advisory board member of Youthactivism.org, and a member of the New York Academy of Sciences, the American Psychological Society, the Human Behavior and Evolution Society, and the American Academy of Political Science. Bloom has lived in the Middle East and has written extensively about geopolitics. His stories have appeared in the *Washington Post*, the *Village Voice*, *Cosmopolitan*, *Omni*, and the Knight Ridder Financial Service. His Website is located at <www.howardbloom.net>.

William Blum left the State Department in 1967, abandoning his aspiration of becoming a Foreign Service Officer, because of his opposition to what the United States was doing in Vietnam. In 1969, he wrote and published an exposé of the CIA that revealed the names and addresses of more than 200 employees of the Agency. Blum has been a freelance journalist in the United States, Europe, and South America. In 1999, he received a Project Censored award for "exemplary journalism" for his article on how, in the 1980s, the United States gave Iraq the material to develop chemical and biological warfare capability. He is the author of *Killing Hope: US Military and CIA Interventions Since World War II* (Common Courage Press, 1995) and *Rogue State: A Guide to the World's Only Superpower* (Common Courage Press, 2000). Portions of the books can be read at <members.aol.com/superogue/homepage.htm>.

Known as the "conscience of psychiatry," **Peter Breggin, M.D.**, is the International Director of the Center for the Study of Psychiatry and Psychology and the author of dozens of scientific reports and books, including *Talking Back to Prozac* (with Ginger Ross Breggin; St. Martin's Press, 1994), *Your Drug May Be Your Problem* (Perseus Publishing, 1999), *Talking Back to Ritalin* (second edition; Perseus Publishing, 2001), and *The Antidepressant Fact Book* (Perseus Publishing, 2001). His background includes Harvard College, a teaching fellowship at Harvard Medical School, and two years at the National Institute of Mental Health. He has been in private practice in psychiatry for over 30 years and has appeared as an expert witness in numerous trials. He and his wife, Ginger Ross Breggin, have a Website at <www.breggin.com>.

Alex Burns is editor of Disinformation <www.disinfo.com>, the Internet's leading alternative news and subcultures portal. Formerly a contributing editor with *21.C*, Burns' antipodean journalism has appeared in Playboy.com's Digital Culture, *Desktop*, *Marketing*, and *REVelation* magazines. He conducts research for the National Values Center, Inc. <www.spiraldynamics.com> and the Integral Institute <www.integralage.org>.

Rory Carroll is a reporter for the *Guardian* (London) and the *Observer* (London).

Philip Cook is the author of *Abused Men: The Hidden Side of Domestic Violence* (Praeger Publishing, 1997). His presentation and book have received high praise: "I highly recommend him as a speaker and the research he has done for your organization."—James J. Londis Ph.D., Director of Ethics and Values Integration, Kettering Medical Center. "Explains the many aspects of domestic violence and a wealth of material that could be helpful to professionals."—Abigail Van Buren ("Dear Abby"). "The engaging style of a journalist provides an in-depth discussion of a topic that he acknowledges is controversial, and emotionally laden."—*Journal of Marriage and the Family*. Cook is available for seminars and workshops. His Website is <www.abusedmen.com>. He has appeared on numerous national television shows and more than 50 radio talk-shows. He has been published in *The Journal of Human Behavior in the Social Environment*, as well as in many magazines and newspapers.

Camelia Fard is an Iranian journalist living in New York.

John Taylor Gatto did undergraduate work at Cornell, the University of Pittsburgh, and Columbia, then served in the US Army medical corps at Fort Knox, Kentucky, and Fort Sam Houston, Texas. Following army service, he did graduate work at the City University of New York, Hunter College, Yeshiva, the University of California, and Cornell. He climaxed his teaching career as New York State Teacher of the Year after being named New York City Teacher of the Year on three occasions. He announced his departure from teaching on the op-ed page of the *Wall Street Journal* in 1991 while still New York State Teacher of the Year, claiming that he was no longer willing to hurt children. Later that year he was the subject of a show at Carnegie Hall called "An Evening With John Taylor Gatto," which launched a career of public speaking in the area of school reform, which has taken Gatto over 1.5 million miles in all 50 states and seven foreign countries. In 1992, he was named Secretary of Education in the Libertarian Party Shadow Cabinet, and he has been included in *Who's Who in America* from 1996 onward. His books include *Dumbing Us Down: The Hidden Curriculum of Compulsory Schooling* (New Society Publishers, 1992), *The Exhausted School* (Oxford Village Press/The Odysseus Group, 1993), *A Different Kind of Teacher* (Berkeley Hills Books, 2000), and *The Underground History of American Education* (2001), the special author's pre-publication edition of which is for sale at his Website <www.johntaylorgatto.com>. He is currently at work on a documentary film about the nature of modern schooling entitled *The Fourth Purpose*, with his friend and former student, Roland Legiardi-Laura.

Annie Laurie Gaylor, with her mother Anne Gaylor, cofounded the Freedom From Religion Foundation in 1976. Annie Laurie graduated from the University of Wisconsin-Madison Journalism School in 1980, then founded the *Feminist Connection*, a Midwest-based monthly newspaper which she edited and published for four years. She has edited *Freethought Today*, the newspaper of the Freedom From Religion Foundation, since 1985. She is author of *Woe to the Women: The Bible Tells Me So* (FFRF, 1981), *Betrayal of Trust: Clergy Abuse of Children* (FFRF, 1988), and editor of the anthology *Women Without Superstition: No Gods - No Masters—The Collected Writings of Women Freethinkers of the 19th & 20th Centuries* (FFRF, 1997). She is married to Dan Barker and lives in Madison, Wisconsin, with their daughter, Sabrina. The Foundation is a national association of freethinkers (atheists, agnostics) working to protect the constitutional principle of the separation of church and state (FFRF, PO Box 750, Madison WI 53701) <www.ffrf.org>.

Peter Gorman is the former editor-in-chief and current senior editor at *High Times* magazine, where his beat for the past fifteen years has been the hard news of the War on Drugs, from medical marijuana to forfeiture and mandatory minimum sentencing. In addition to his work with *High Times*, Gorman has spent a considerable amount of the past 20 years in South America, primarily Peru's Amazon. In that region he has worked as a collector of indigenous artifacts for the American Museum of Natural History and plant medicines for Shaman Pharmaceuticals; his work on these subjects has been published in most major magazines worldwide. The politics of Latin America and Peru in particular have long been one of Gorman's primary interests. From his perch behind the bar of the Cold Beer Blues Bar, a restaurant he owns in Iquitos, Peru, Gorman regularly interacts with Drug Enforcement Administration agents and Special Forces soldiers, river smugglers, expatriates, local politicians, and other assorted ne'er-do-wells, giving him a firsthand glimpse into the workings of the politics there.

Lucy Gwin is author of *Going Overboard* (Viking Press, 1982), a memoir of her year as the solitary female deckhand in the Louisiana offshore oilfields, and editor of *Mouth* magazine <www.mouthmag.com>. Her bulletins from the freak front have appeared in both the mainstream and the disability-rights press. She lives in Topeka, Kansas, of all places, where she fends off aggressive Christians and wishes a tornado would take her over the rainbow or anyway back East. She doesn't use email. Forget about it.

David T. Hardy is a former US Department of the Interior headquarters staff attorney, now in private practice in Tucson, Arizona. From 1995 to 2001, he engaged in a series of Freedom of Information Act lawsuits seeking information regarding the Waco tragedy, and he recently authored a book, *This Is Not an Assault: Penetrating the Web of Official Lies Regarding the Incident at Waco* (Xlibris, 2001). Further documentation is available at <www.hardylaw.net/waco.html>.

Noreena Hertz has been called "one of the world's leading young thinkers" (*Observer* of London), "one of the 35 women under 35 to watch" (*Management Today*), and "Best of Young British" (*New Statesman*). She has written op-ed pieces in the *New Statesman*, the *Observer* (London), the *Guardian* (London), the *Washington Post* and the *Financial Times*, has been profiled in hundreds of international publications and media, and is a regular commentator on various networks, including CNN and the BBC. Hertz has a Ph.D. from Cambridge University, an M.B.A. from Wharton, and a B.A. from University College London. She is currently Associate Director of the Center for International Business and Management at Cambridge University. Her bestselling book, *The Silent Takeover: Global Capitalism and the Death of Democracy* (William Heinemann, 2000), has been translated into French, German, Italian, Spanish, Dutch, and Korean. The American edition of her book is published by Free Press.

Arianna Huffington is a nationally syndicated columnist and author of eight books, including *The Female Woman* (Random House, 1973), *The Fourth Instinct* (Simon & Schuster, 1994), *Maria Callas* (Simon & Schuster, 1981), *Picasso: Creator and Destroyer* (Simon & Schuster, 1988), and *Greetings From the Lincoln Bedroom* (Crown, 1998). Her most recent book, *How To Overthrow the Government* (Regan Books, 2000), is a rabble-rousing look at the corruption of our political system and the urgent need for reform. During the 2000 presidential campaign, Huffington was the driving force behind the Shadow Conventions, a pair of alternative gatherings that ran parallel to the Republican and Democratic party conventions. Designed to alter the tone and nature of our national political conversation, the Shadow Conventions featured appearances by a broad range of speakers, including Sen. John McCain, Sen. Russ Feingold, Rev. Jesse Jackson, Tim Robbins, Bill Maher, and Gore Vidal. The result was described by one journalist as "a media-savvy mix of civics and satire." Arianna Huffington lives in Los Angeles with her two daughters. (*Editor's note: Huffington's official Website is at <www.ariannaonline.com>.*)

Dr. K. Jamanadas: "I am a surgeon by profession, being F.R.C.S. (1964) from Edinburgh, UK. I am now 69 years old and retired from practice for the last fifteen years or so. I am also a graduate in ancient Indian history, culture, and archaeology from Nagpur University and was a member of the Board of Studies in History at Nagpur University for two terms of three years each. I am an active worker in the Ambedkarite movement. My research work, *Tirupati Balaji Was a Buddhist Shrine*, published in 1991, received international exposure. The book was translated into Hindi in 1998 and is in its second edition. My other book, *Decline and Fall of Buddhism: A Tragedy in Ancient India* (2000), is published by the Dalit Forum. One of my long research articles, "Rise and Fall of Buddhist Nuns," dealing with the theory that present-day devdasis are degraded Buddhist nuns, was published in the international magazine *World Fellowship of Buddhist Review* (January 2000). Many of my articles are published in *Dalit Voice*, and all of my writings are available on <www.ambedkar.org> and <www.dalitstan.org>."

Lindsay Jenkins spent nearly ten years as a senior civil servant in the British Ministry of Defence. She then worked in the City of London for both British and American investment banks, including Morgan Stanley. Her first major book, a history of the parties who created the European Union and why they did, *Britain Held Hostage: The Coming Euro-Dictatorship* (Orange State Press, 1998), with a foreword by Fredrick Forsyth, is now in its second edition. Her second book, *The Last Days of Britain: The Final Betrayal* (Orange State Press), was published in 2001 with a foreword by the former British Chancellor of the Exchequer Lord Lamont of Lerwick. It illustrates how much independence Britain has already lost and how quickly Britain is becoming just another province in the new European superstate, which is challenging the US for world hegemony. She lives in both the UK and US.

Russ Kick is the editor of *Everything You Know Is Wrong* and *You Are Being Lied To* (Disinformation Books, 2001). He has also written two guides to nonmainstream ideas, facts, and literature: *Outposts* (1995) was called "the *Whole Earth Catalog* of alternative thought" by Reuters, and *Psychotropedia* (1999) was hailed as an "encyclopaedia of forbidden thought, the underground, and extremism" (*Guardian* of London), "a fabulous 'must-own' for freethinkers" (*Mayfair*), and "an indispensable guide to every type of publication that exists on the fringe of mainstream culture" (*Bizarre*). He also edited a taboo-shattering collection of erotica, *Hot Off the Net* (1999), and is a regular contributor to the *Village Voice*, *Gauntlet* (the only magazine devoted to free-speech issues), and Disinformation. *Details* magazine once called him "a happily maladjusted and radically tolerant Renaissance man." Check out his Website <www.alternewswire.com> for more hidden information.

Working primarily as a photojournalist, **Gabe Kirchheimer** was the first to write a series of articles on the US mad cow crisis in a national magazine, *High Times*. His groundbreaking story, "Mad Cows Recycled by Demented Humans," in January 1998, was followed by "Mad Cows and Englishmen" and "How Now Mad Cow," which detailed hazardous cannibalism within the meat industry. Kirchheimer has authored numerous articles on food safety, and his photographs have been published in the *New York Times Magazine*, *Time*, *Newsweek*, *US News and World Report*, the *Los Angeles Times*, *Rolling Stone*, *Forbes*, *Wired*, *Maxim*, *Psychology Today*, *Colors*, the *Independent Sunday Review* (London), the *Times* (London), *Il Venerdi di Repubblica*, *Panorama*, *Le Monde*, *Die Zeit*, *Science Illustrated*, and elsewhere. A vegan for the past 20 years, Kirchheimer believes that "the plight of the Earth demands positive solutions and the media has a primary responsibility to go beyond token reportage."

Born in Montreal in 1970, **Naomi Klein** is an award-winning journalist and author of the international bestselling book *No Logo: Taking Aim at the Brand Bullies* (Picador, 1999), which has been translated into eighteen languages. The *New York Times* called *No Logo* a movement bible. The *Guardian* (London) short-listed it for their First Book Award in 2000. In April 2001, *No Logo* won the Canadian National Business Book Award, and in August 2001 it was awarded the Le Prix Médiations in France. Klein's articles have appeared in numerous publications, including *The Nation*, the *New Statesman* and the *New York Times*. She writes an internationally syndicated column for the *Globe and Mail* (Toronto). She is a frequent media commentator and has guest-lectured at Harvard, Yale, and New York University. In December 2001, Klein was named as one of *Ms. Magazine*'s Women of the Year.

Lucy Komisar is a freelance journalist on international affairs who, since 1997, has written on the offshore bank and corporate secrecy system for publications that range from *The Nation* to the *Wall Street Journal*. Over several decades, she has reported from Europe, Latin America, Asia, and Africa, with a special focus on democratization, human rights, and security issues. Her articles have appeared in the

New York Times, Washington Post, Christian Science Monitor, Los Angeles Times, Chicago Tribune, Boston Globe, The Progressive, and other publications in the US and abroad. She is the author of books on Corazon Aquino, the US public welfare system, and feminism. She is a past John Simon Guggenheim fellow and John D. and Catherine T. MacArthur Foundation grantee. She is a member of the Council on Foreign Relations.

Paul Krassner calls himself an investigative satirist. The FBI labeled him "a raving, unconfined nut." "The FBI was right," said George Carlin. "This man is dangerous—and funny; and necessary." Krassner published *The Realist* from 1958 to 2001. Mission statement: "Irreverence is our only sacred cow." His style of personal journalism constantly blurred the line between observer and participant. He interviewed a doctor who performed abortions when illegal, then ran an underground abortion referral service; covered the antiwar movement, then cofounded the Yippies with Abbie Hoffman and Jerry Rubin; published material on the psychedelic revolution, then took LSD with Tim Leary, Ram Dass, and Ken Kesey. *People* magazine referred to Krassner as "father of the underground press," but he immediately demanded a paternity test. He is the only person in the world ever to win awards from both *Playboy* and the Feminist Party Media Workshop. In November 2001, at the fourteenth annual Cannabis Cup in Amsterdam, he was inducted into the Counterculture Hall of Fame. His latest book is *Murder at the Conspiracy Convention and Other American Absurdities* (forthcoming).

Kalle Lasn is the editor/publisher of *Adbusters* magazine <www.adbusters.org> and author of *Culture Jam: The Uncooling of America* (William Morrow, 1999).

Helen Jefferson Lenskyj, Ph.D. is a professor in the Department of Sociology and Equity Studies in Education at the University of Toronto's Ontario Institute for Studies in Education. She received her Ph.D. from the University of Toronto. She is the author of several books, including *Out of Bounds: Women, Sport and Sexuality* (Womens Press, 1987), *Inside the Olympic Industry: Power, Politics, and Activism* (State University of New York, 2000), and *The Best Olympics Ever: Social Impacts of Sydney 2000* (State University of New York, 2002).

Jonathan Levy is a California attorney who is lead co-counsel in a class-action lawsuit against the Vatican Bank and Franciscan Order filed in 1999 on behalf of Serb, Jewish, and Ukrainian Holocaust survivors seeking restitution of Nazi gold. Levy also represents the Kronzer Foundation, a nonprofit religious organization that fights corruption within the Roman Catholic Church. For more information see <www.vaticanbankclaims.com>.

David Lochbaum worked as a nuclear engineer in the US nuclear power industry for over seventeen years. He joined the staff of the Union of Concerned Scientists <www.ucsusa.org> in 1996 as their

Nuclear Safety Engineer. His contributions to this book reflect his personal views.

Mike Males has a Ph.D. in social ecology from the University of California, Irvine, and teaches sociology at UC Santa Cruz. His books include *Framing Youth: Ten Myths About the Next Generation* and *The Scapegoat Generation* (both Common Courage Press). He is a senior researcher for the Justice Policy Institute, with papers published in *The Lancet*, the *American Journal of Public Health*, and Scribner's *Violence in America: An Encyclopedia*, among others. Email: <mmales@earthlink.net>.Website: <home.earthlink.net/ ~mmales>.

Nick Mamatas has written on politics, digital culture, fringe thought, and philosophy for the *Village Voice*, *In These Times*, *Artbyte*, *Silicon Alley Reporter*, Disinformation, and other magazines and Websites. He cowrote the first English edition of *Kwangju Diary* (Center for Pacific Rim Studies, 1999), an account of an urban insurrection against South Korea's 1980 military coup, and the introduction to *Fortunate Son: George W. Bush and the Making of an American President* (Soft Skull Press, 2000). His fiction has appeared in *Strange Horizons*, *Talebones*, and *Speculon*. His first novella, *Northern Gothic*, was published by Soft Skull Press in late 2001 and was called "undeniably brilliant, unrelentingly violent, unredeeming in its hopelessness" by Janet Berliner. Visit his stupid Website here: <www.kynn.com/wwnkd>.

Wendy McElroy is the author of *XXX: A Woman's Right to Pornography* (St. Martin's Press, 1995), *Sexual Correctness: The Gender-Feminist Attack on Women* (McFarland, 1996), *The Reasonable Woman: A Guide to Intellectual Survival* (Prometheus Books, 1998), and *Queen Silver: The Godless Girl* (Prometheus Books, 2000). Her most recent book is entitled *Individualist Feminism of the Nineteenth Century* (McFarland, 2001). She has recently edited a new anthology, *Women and Liberty*, to be released by Ivan R. Dee, publisher. McElroy is the editor of *Freedom, Feminism and the State* (1st ed., Cato, 1983; 2nd ed., Holmes & Meier, 1991), which provides an historical overview of individualist feminism in America. She is a contributing editor to *Ideas on Liberty* (formerly *The Freeman*), *The New Libertarian*, *Free Inquiry*, and *Liberty* magazines. She has written and edited audio cassettes for Knowledge Products. You can visit her Websites at <www.ifeminists .com> and <www.wendymcelroy.com>.

Joseph D. McNamara is a research fellow at the Hoover Institution. His law enforcement career spans a 35-year period, beginning in Harlem as a beat patrolman for the New York Police Department. In 1976, McNamara was appointed police chief for the city of San Jose, California, where he remained until his retirement in 1991. During his tenure, San Jose (the third largest city in California and the eleventh largest in the US) became the safest city in the country, despite having the least police staffing per capita. McNamara has been a criminal justice fellow at Harvard Law School, and he obtained a doctorate in public administration at Harvard. He is the author of four bestselling detective novels—including his latest, *Code 211 Blue* (Fawcett, 1996)—and a respected crime prevention text, *Safe and Sane*. He has been a consultant for the US Justice Department, the State Department, the FBI, and some of the nation's largest corporations. He has published articles in the *Washington Post*, *New York Times*, *Los Angeles Times*, *Wall Street Journal*, *Harper's*, and elsewhere, and has appeared on *60 Minutes*, *48 Hours*, *Nightline*, *Larry King Live*, and elsewhere.

Cletus Nelson is an LA-based freelance journalist who specializes in extreme culture and conspiracy. His work has appeared in *EYE*, *Panik*, *Signum*, *CounterPunch*, *Generations*, and several other publications.

Jack Niedenthal. Title: Trust Liaison for the People of Bikini (hired by the Bikinians). Having lived, studied, and worked in the Marshall Islands from 1981 until the present, Niedenthal speaks fluent Marshallese. His wife, Regina, is a Bikini islander. They have four children. His first six years in the Marshalls were all spent in the isolated jungles of the outer islands. He was a Peace Corps volunteer on Namu Atoll (1981-84), then contracted to work with the Bikini Council on Kili Island (1984-late 1986) teaching English to the adults, teaching in the elementary school, and working with the Kili/Bikini/Ejit Local Government Council. He currently works as the Trust Liaison for their local government (1987 to present). Duties include the management and coordination of the funds allocated by the United States government to compensate the Bikinians for their suffering and to facilitate the radiological cleanup of Bikini Atoll. He has published a number of articles and photos about the people of Bikini in *World View* magazine, *The Health Physics Journal*, the *San Francisco Chronicle*, and others, and is the author of the book *For the Good of Mankind: A History of the People of Bikini and Their Islands* (2nd ed., Bravo Publishers, 2001). His film credits include work on *Radio Bikini*, produced by Robert Stone (nominated for an Academy Award in 1988); *Nuclear Exiles*, produced by the *National Geographic Explorer* series (nominated for an Emmy Award in 1988); *Bikini: Forbidden Paradise*, produced by Bill Livingston for ABC's *World of Discovery* (nominated for an Emmy Award in 1994); *The Bikini Atoll*, produced by the A&E Channel in 1996; and *Live From a Shark Cage with Al Giddings* by the Discovery Channel in 1999. The government of the Marshall Islands awarded him an honorary Marshallese citizenship in December 2000.

Greg Palast, columnist with the *Observer* newspaper of London and reporter with BBC Television's *Newsnight*, is author of *Burning Down the House: The Incendiary Writings of an Investigative Journalist*. At <www.gregpalast.com> you can read and subscribe to Palast's columns and view his report for the BBC, "Theft of the Presidency." Read Joe Conason's story about the attack on Palast's investigations: "Exporting Corporate Control: A Gold Company With Ties to the Bush Family Tries to Muzzle a Muckraking Journalist" and the update by CBS News, "Barrick Gold Against Investigative

Journalist." The full, uncut version of the controversial article ("Bush Family Finances: Best Democracy Money Can Buy") remains online at <www.onlinejournal.com>.

Preston Peet is a musician, actor, and full-time writer/activist living in NYC's Lower East Side. His work has appeared in the national magazine *Media Bypass*; in the book *09-11, 8:48 AM: Documenting America's Greatest Tragedy*, edited by BlueEar.com; online at Disinformation and <www.drugwar.com>; and in the first book from Disinformation, *You Are Being Lied To*. Preston is a regular news contributor to *High Times* magazine and Website, and writes a monthly column in NYC's best punk rock newspaper, the *New York Waste*. His first book, *Something in the Way*, a misadventure story about street-bound junkies, still needs a publisher. Having spent his younger years traveling extensively, he's now settled into a domestic life with his longtime companion and love Vanessa and their six cats, sharing an apartment with a view of the lower Manhattan skyline. Preston can be contacted at <ptpeet@nyc.rr.com> or <ppeet@hightimes.com>. End the War on Drugs *now*.

Diane Starr Petryk-Bloom, winner of six journalism awards, has worked at newspapers in New Zealand, Florida, Savannah, Michigan, and upstate New York. She's also a professional photographer and photojournalist, often shooting the pictures that illustrate her stories.

James Ridgeway is the Washington correspondent of the *Village Voice*. He is the author of sixteen books, including *Red Light* (powerHouse Books, 1996), an inside look at the sex industry, and *Blood in the Face* (Thunder's Mouth Press, 1990), the story of the new white, far-right political movement. He also is a producer and director of the documentary films *Blood in the Face* (with Kevin Rafferty and Anne Bohelmn) and *Feed* (with Kevin Rafferty), which tells the story of the 1992 New Hampshire presidential primary.

Brad Shellady was Henry Lee Lucas' chief case investigator from 1988 to Lucas' death in March 2001. Shellady has investigated hundreds of Lucas' confessions and has been given access to tens of thousands of documents concerning all facets of the case. He was an integral member of the defense team and on a number of occasions has testified in state and federal court concerning this matter.

Oliver Shykles is an undergraduate student reading humanities at the University of Brighton in the United Kingdom. He is president of the Philosophy Society and the Politics Society, a researcher, and an investigative journalist.

Robert Sterling is the editor of the Konformist <www.konformist.com>, the top underground Internet conspiracy magazine of the world. In 2001, he won a Project Censored Award for his work on the site. He is the author of "Uncle Ronnie's Sex Slaves" in *Apocalypse Culture II* and is a contributing editor at Disinformation. He is easily bribed.

Thomas Szasz, A.B., M.D., D.Sc. (Hon.), L.H.D. (Hon.), is professor of psychiatry emeritus at the State University of New York Upstate Medical University in Syracuse, New York. He is the author of 25 books, among them the classic *The Myth of Mental Illness* (1961) and, most recently, *Pharmacracy: Medicine and Politics in America* (Praeger, 2001) and *Liberation by Oppression: A Comparative Study of Slavery and Psychiatry* (Transaction Publishers). Szasz is widely recognized as the world's foremost critic of psychiatric coercions and excuses. He has received many awards for his defense of individual liberty and responsibility threatened by the Therapeutic State, a modern form of totalitarianism masquerading as medicine. A frequent and popular lecturer, he has addressed professional and lay groups, and has appeared on radio and television, in North, Central, and South America, as well as in Australia, Europe, Japan, and South Africa. His books have been translated into every major language. For more information about Szasz's work, see <www.szasz.com>.

Tristan Taormino is the author of *Pucker Up: A Hands-on Guide to Ecstatic Sex* (Regan Books, 2001) and *The Ultimate Guide to Anal Sex for Women* (Cleis Press, 1997), which won a 1998 Firecracker Award. She is director, producer, and star of two erotic instructional videos based on her book: *Tristan Taormino's Ultimate Guide to Anal Sex for Women 1* and 2, which are distributed by Evil Angel Video. The first video won two AVN Awards (the Oscars of the porn world) and an X-Rated Critics Organization Award. She is editor of *On Our Backs*, a columnist for the *Village Voice*, and sex-advice columnist for *Taboo* magazine. She is also series editor of *Best Lesbian Erotica* (Cleis Press), for which she has edited eight volumes. She has been featured in over 100 publications, including the *New York Times*, *Playboy*, *Penthouse*, *Entertainment Weekly*, *Details*, *New York Magazine*, *Out Magazine*, and *Spin*. She has appeared on the Discovery Channel, MTV, HBO's *Real Sex*, the *Howard Stern Show*, and *Loveline*. She teaches sex workshops and lectures on sex nationwide, and you can find her in cyberspace at her official Website <www.puckerup.com>.

Douglas Valentine is the author of three books. *The Hotel Tacloban* (1984) is a widely praised account of his father's experiences as a POW in the Second World War. *The Phoenix Program* (1990) is called "the definitive account" by Professor Alfred McCoy, and is ranked by *CounterPunch* as one of the top 100 nonfiction books of the twentieth century. *TDY* (2000) is a based-on-fact story set in 1967, about an Air Force photojournalist's involvement in a military mission that uncovers the truth about CIA drug smuggling in Southeast Asia. Valentine's books are now available through iUniverse.com. For more information about Valentine, his books and articles, and his forthcoming book, *The Strength of the Wolf: The Federal Bureau of Narcotics 1930-1968*, please visit his Website: <www.douglasvalentine.com>.

In what can only be described as an irrational leap of faith, **Jonathan Vankin** has voted in every major election since 1980. However, candidates he has voted for rarely if ever won, which may be the result of a conspiracy. Or it may just be him. He has written or cowritten seven books, including *The 70 Greatest Conspiracies of All Time* (Citadel Press, 1998) and *The Big Book of the '70s* (Paradox Press, 2000). His serial graphic novel *Tokyo!* will be published starting July 2002 by DC/Vertigo Comics. He lives in LA with his beautiful wife, Deb, who writes about arts and culture for the *LA Weekly*, and his lovely cats, Fenway and Merlin, who torture small lizards and sleep a lot. Visit Vankin at <www.jonathanvankin.com>.

Mickey Z. (Michael Zezima) is the author of *Saving Private Power: The Hidden History of "The Good War"* (Soft Skull Press, 2000) and is a contributor to *You Are Being Lied To*. His work has appeared in hundreds of publications and is available online at Disinformation, <www.onlinejournal.com>,<www.corpse.org>, <www.dsazine.com>, <www.thundersandwich.com>, <www.enoughfanzine.com>, <www.znet .org>, <www.konformist.com>, <www.apr.org>, <www.mrbellersneigborhood .com>, <www.sailnet.com>, <www.alternewswire.com>, and several other Websites. He lives in New York City and teaches writing at LaGuardia Community College and in the Writer's Voice program of the West Side YMCA. Both he and his wife, Michele, are vegans. Mickey Z. can be reached at <mzx2@earthlink.net>.

Howard Zinn grew up in New York City of working-class parents, was a shipyard worker at the age of eighteen, a bombardier in the Air Force at 21 (European theater, World War II), and went to New York University and Columbia under the G.I. Bill of Rights, receiving his Ph.D. in history and political science from Columbia in 1958. His doctoral dissertation, *LaGuardia in Congress*, was a Beveridge Prize publication of the American Historical Association. His first teaching job was at Spelman college in Atlanta, Georgia, a black women's college, where he taught for seven years. After that he taught at Boston University, becoming a professor emeritus in 1988. He has written over a dozen books, his best known being *A People's History of the United States* (1980), which has sold over 700,000 copies. His most recent books are *You Can't Be Neutral on a Moving Train* (a memoir; 1995), *The Zinn Reader* (1997), and *The Future of History* (1999). He has been active in various social movements for civil rights and against war.

ARTICLE HISTORIES

"The Accidental Operative" by Camelia Fard and James Ridgeway originally appeared in the *Village Voice*.

"The Antitrust and Monopoly Myth" by Dominick T. Armentano was written especially for this volume.

"Battle Boring" by Naomi Klein was originally published in the *Globe and Mail* (Toronto).

"The Bombing of PanAm Flight 103: Case Not Closed" by William Blum was written especially for this volume.

"Bovine Bioterrorism and the Perfect Pathogen" by Gabe Kirchheimer is a combination of previously published articles and new material created especially for this volume.

"Burn the Olive Tree, Sell the Lexus" by Greg Palast and Oliver Shykles was written especially for this volume.

"'Call It Off!': New Revelations About Waco" by David Hardy is a collection of material from *This Is Not an Assault: Penetrating the Web of Official Lies Regarding the Incident at Waco* (Xlibris, 2001). It appears in its current form for the first time in this volume.

"A Canticle for Osama Bin Laden" by Alex Burns originally appeared on Disinformation <www.disinfo.com>.

"Charlie Manson's Image" by Paul Krassner originally appeared in *High Times*. It was given a new ending by its author especially for this volume.

"Dirty Money and Global Banking Secrecy" by Lucy Komisar is made up of articles that originally appeared in *The Nation* and elsewhere. It appears in its current form for the first time in this volume.

"Drug Companies: Sell Hard, Sell Fast...and Count the Bodies Later" by Arianna Huffington was originally published as a syndicated column. It has been updated by the author for inclusion in the volume.

"The European Union Unmasked" by Lindsay Jenkins was written especially for this volume.

"Fear of a Vegan Planet" by Mickey Z. was written especially for this volume.

"Fission Stories: Nuclear Power's Secrets" by David Lochbaum is a collection of material from Lochbaum's self-published book of the same name.

"Free Lauriane" by James Ridgeway and Sandra Bisin originally appeared in the *Village Voice*. It has been expanded especially for this volume.

"Globalization for the Good of All" by Noreena Hertz is based on a speech given in Belgium, October 30, 2001. It appears for the first time in this volume.

"Henry: Fabrication of a Serial Killer" by Brad Shellady was written especially for this volume.

"How to Rid the World of Good" by Nick Mamatas was written especially for this volume.

"Leaders Against the Drug War" by Russ Kick first appeared in the *Village Voice*. It has been expanded especially for this volume.

"The Ludlow Massacre" by Howard Zinn originally appeared in *The Politics of History* (Beacon Press, 1970).

"Mental Illness: Psychiatry's Phlogiston" by Thomas Szasz, M.D., originally appeared in the *Journal of Medical Ethics*.

"The Monster of Florence" by Rory Carroll originally appeared as two articles in the *Guardian* (London) and the *Observer* (London).

"Mushroom Clouds in Paradise" by Jack Niedenthal is an excerpt from *For the Good of Mankind: A History of the People of Bikini and Their Islands* (2nd ed.,

Bravo Publishers, 2001).

"Myths About Youth" by Mike Males is a combination of previously published articles and new material created especially for this volume.

"Olympic Industry Mythology" by Helen Jefferson Lenskyj was written especially for this volume.

"Pornography" by Wendy McElroy was written especially for this volume.

"Postcards From the Planet of the Freaks" by Lucy Gwin was written especially for this volume.

"Prostitution" by Wendy McElroy was written especially for this volume.

"Psychiatric Drugging of Children for Behavioral Control" by Peter Breggin, M.D., originally appeared in the newsletter of the International Center for the Study of Psychiatry and Psychology.

"Scenes From a Secret War" by Peter Gorman is comprised of three articles originally published on the Narco News Website <www.narconews.com>. It has been assembled and updated by the author especially for this volume.

"The Senator's Ashes" by Douglas Valentine originally appeared in the *CounterPunch* newsletter. It has been updated by the author for inclusion in this volume.

"September 11, 2001: No Surprise" by Russ Kick originally appeared in Loompanics Main Catalog 2002. It has been expanded especially for this volume.

"Some Lessons From The Underground History of American Education" by John Taylor Gatto is comprised of material from *The Underground History of American Education* (pre-publication edition, 2001). It appears in its current form for the first time in this volume.

"Toxic TV Syndrome" by Kalle Lasn was originally published in *Adbusters*.

"Treatment or Jail: Is This Really a Choice?" by Preston Peet was written especially for this volume.

"Two's Too Tough" by Tristan Taormino originally appeared in the *Village Voice*.

"Untouchables in the Twenty-first Century" by Dr. K Jamanadas was written especially for this volume.

"The Vatican Bank" by Jonathan Levy was written especially for this volume.

"Viva Kadaffi!" by Robert Sterling was written especially for this volume.

"Votescam 2000" by Jonathan Vankin originally appeared in the *New York Press*. It was expanded by the author especially for this volume.

"Watchdog Nation" by Cletus Nelson was written especially for this volume.

"When Cops Become the Gangsters" by Joseph D. McNamara originally appeared in the *Los Angeles Times*.

"The Whole Truth About Domestic Violence" by Philip Cook was written especially for this volume.

"Why Women Need Freedom From Religion" by Annie Laurie Gaylor is a greatly expanded version of a "nontract" published by the Freedom From Religion Foundation.

"Will This Be the Chinese Century?" by Howard Bloom and Diane Starr Petryk-Bloom was written especially for this volume.

"Witnesses to a Massacre: Other Participants in Columbine" by Russ Kick was written especially for this volume.